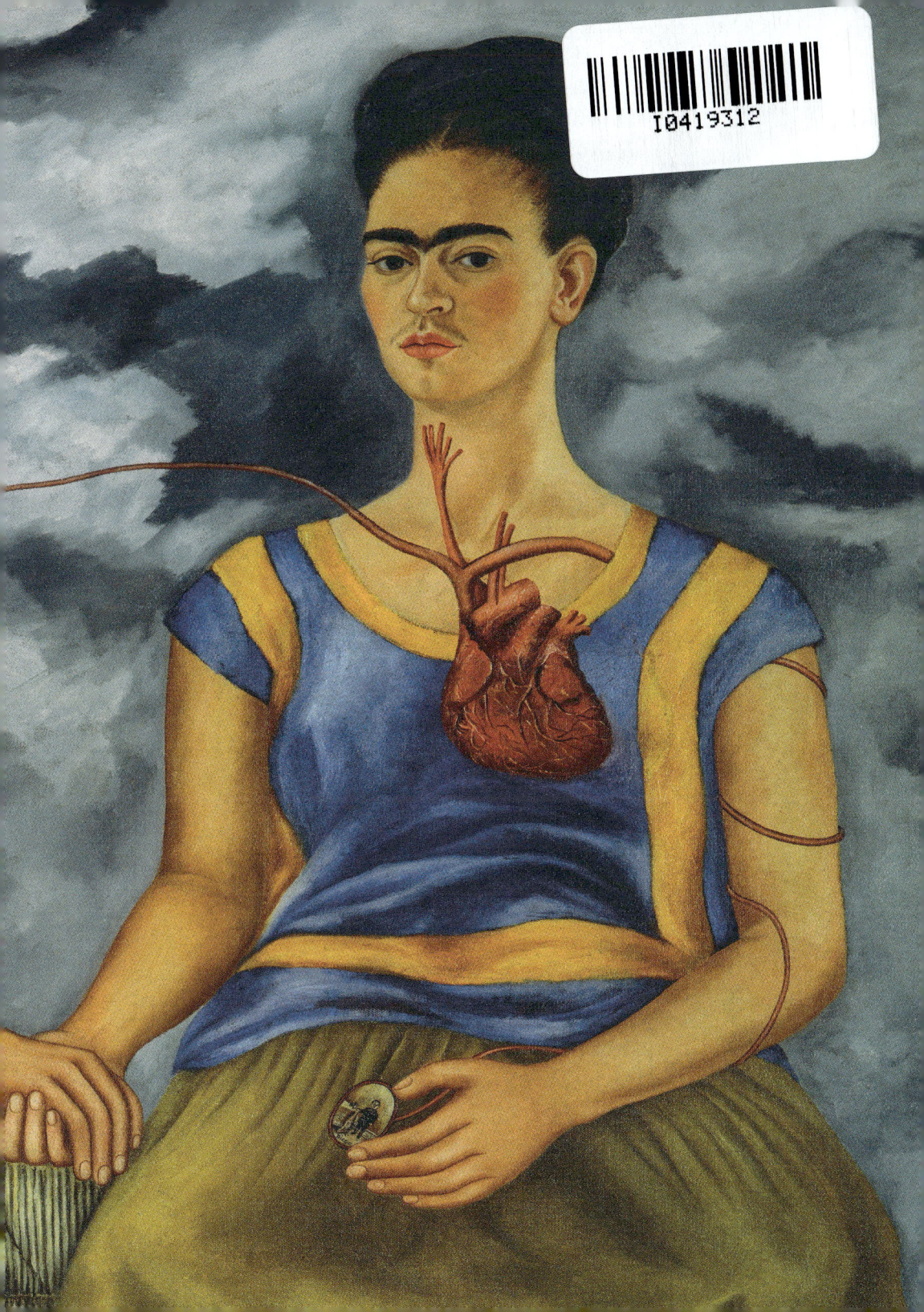

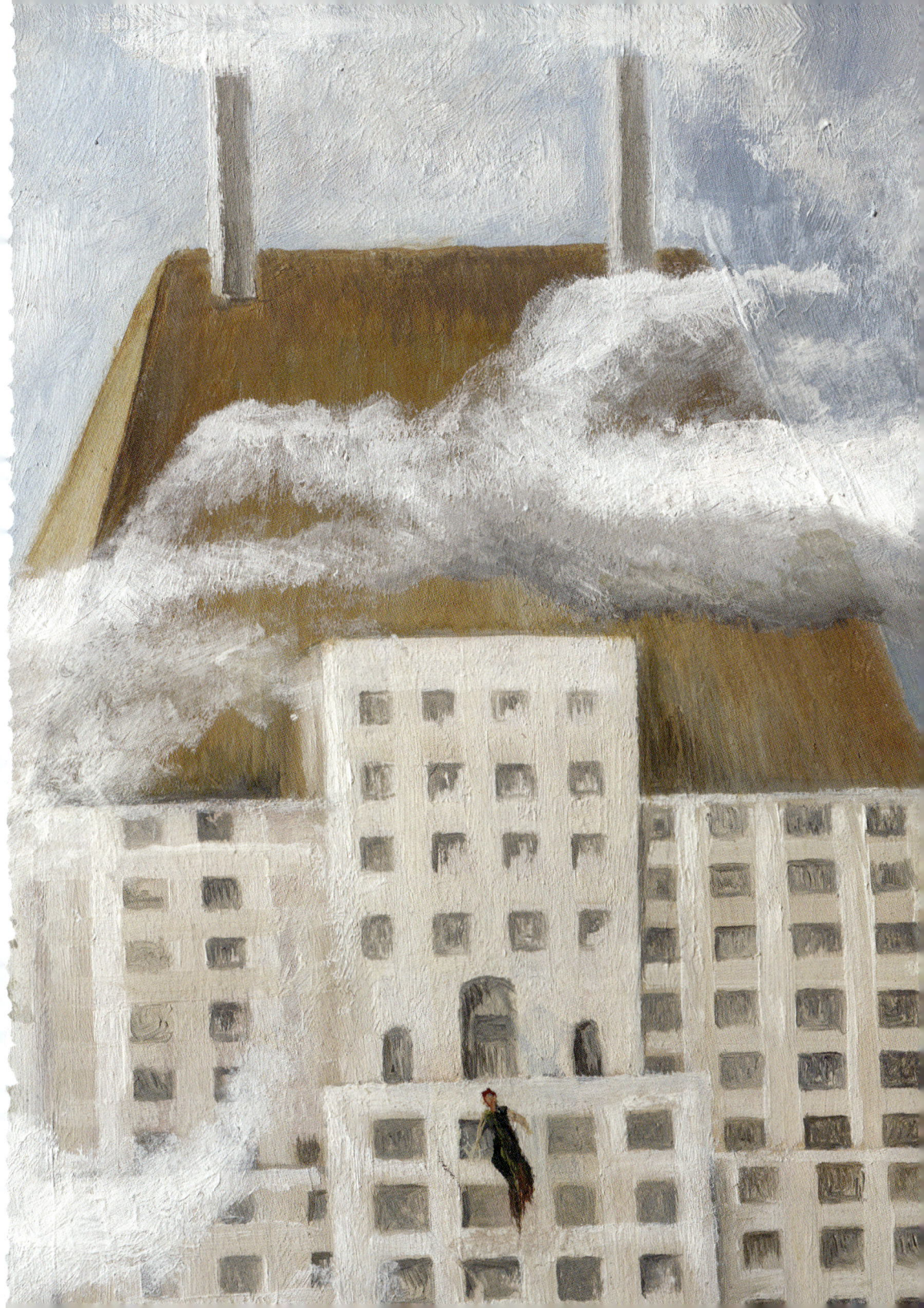

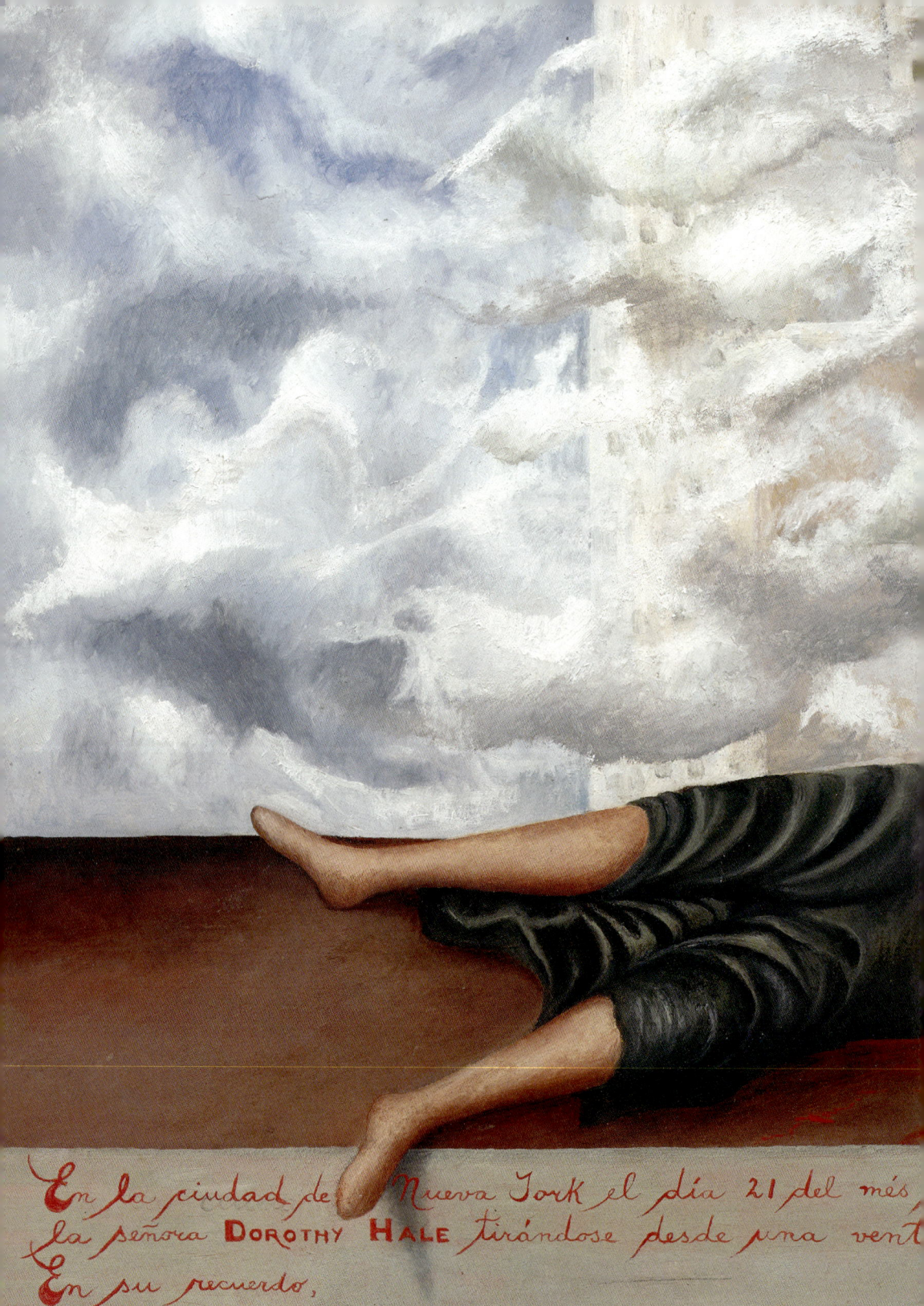

En la ciudad de Nueva York el día 21 del més,
la señora DOROTHY HALE tirándose desde una vent
En su recuerdo,

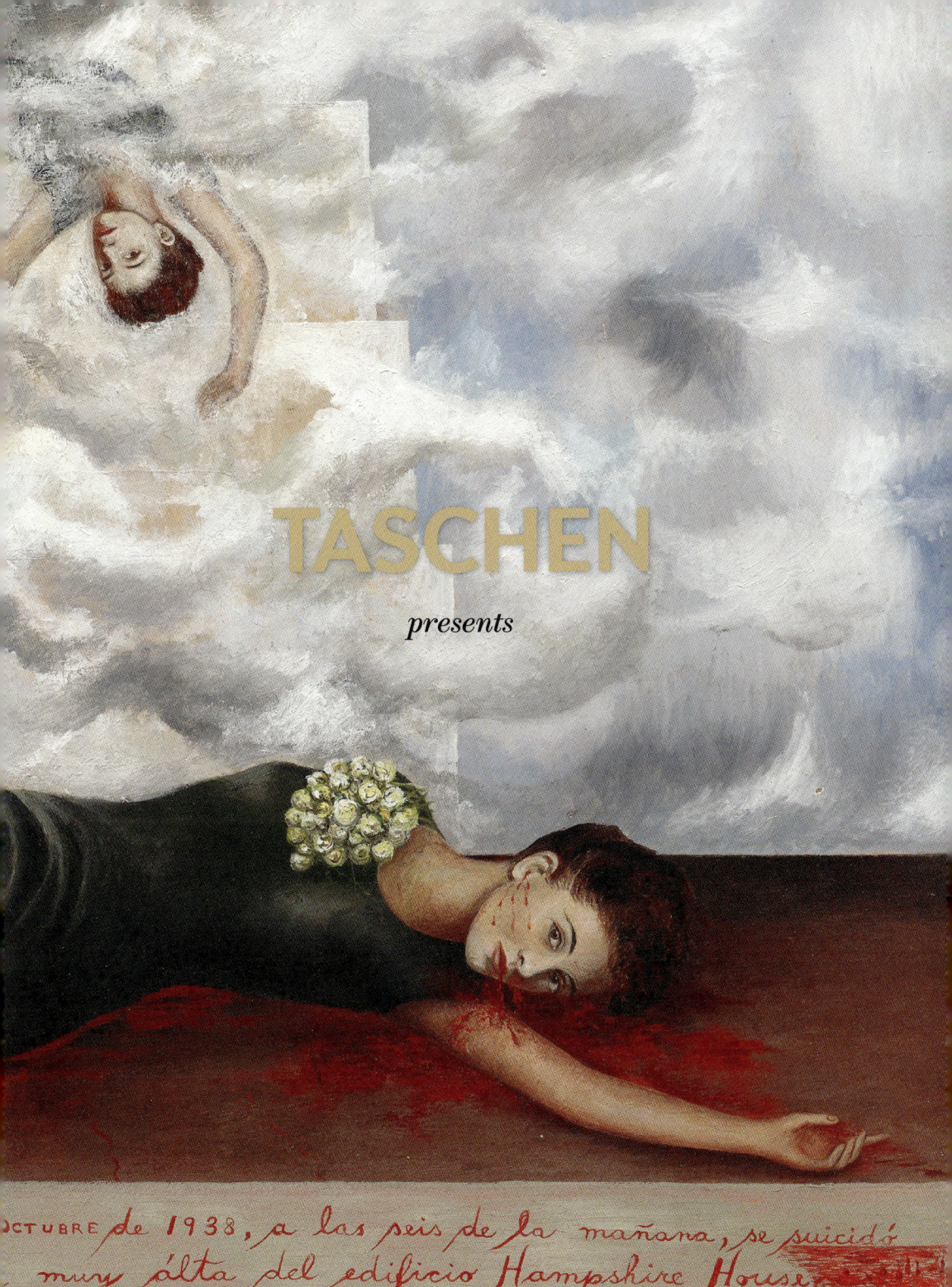

TASCHEN

presents

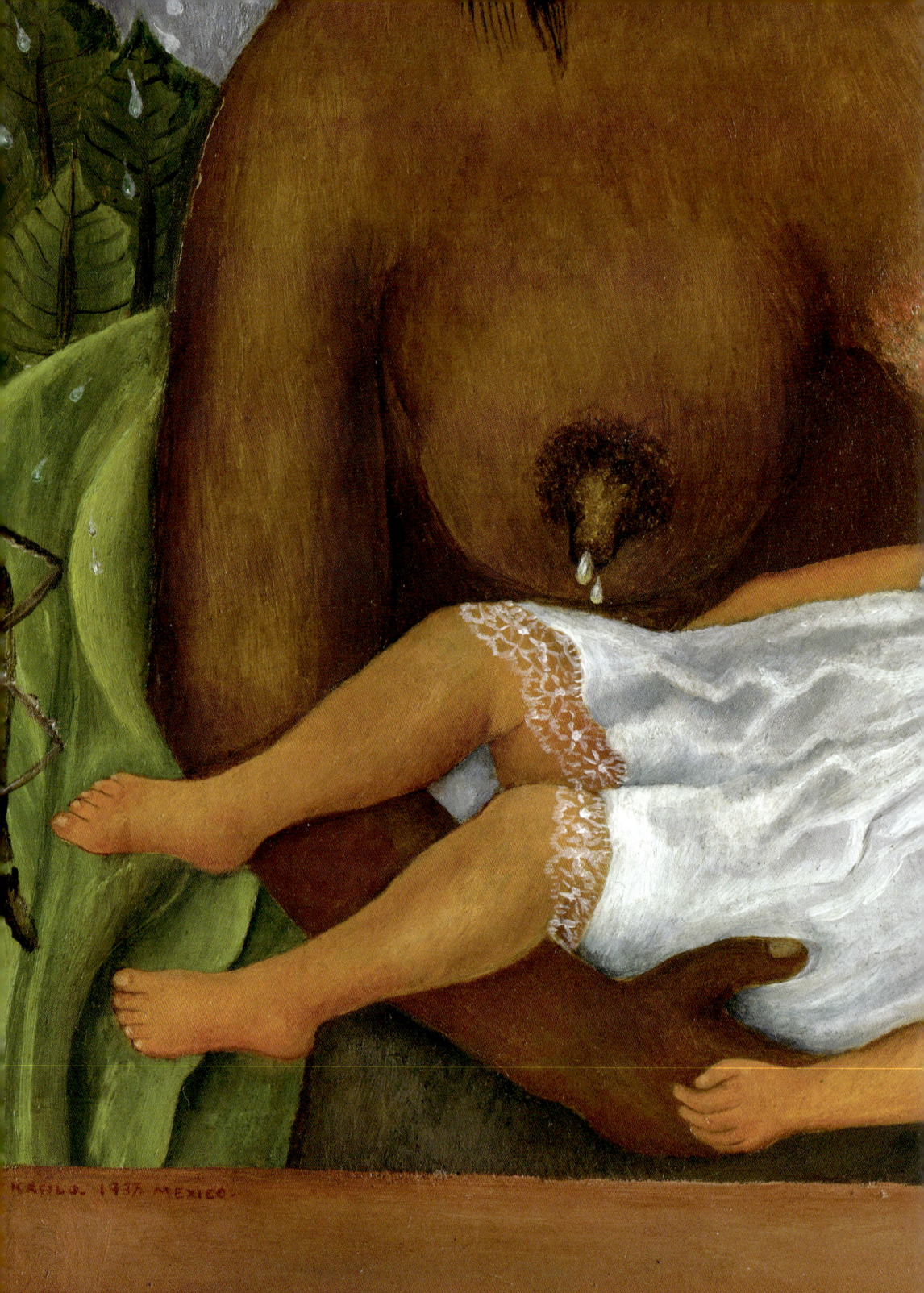

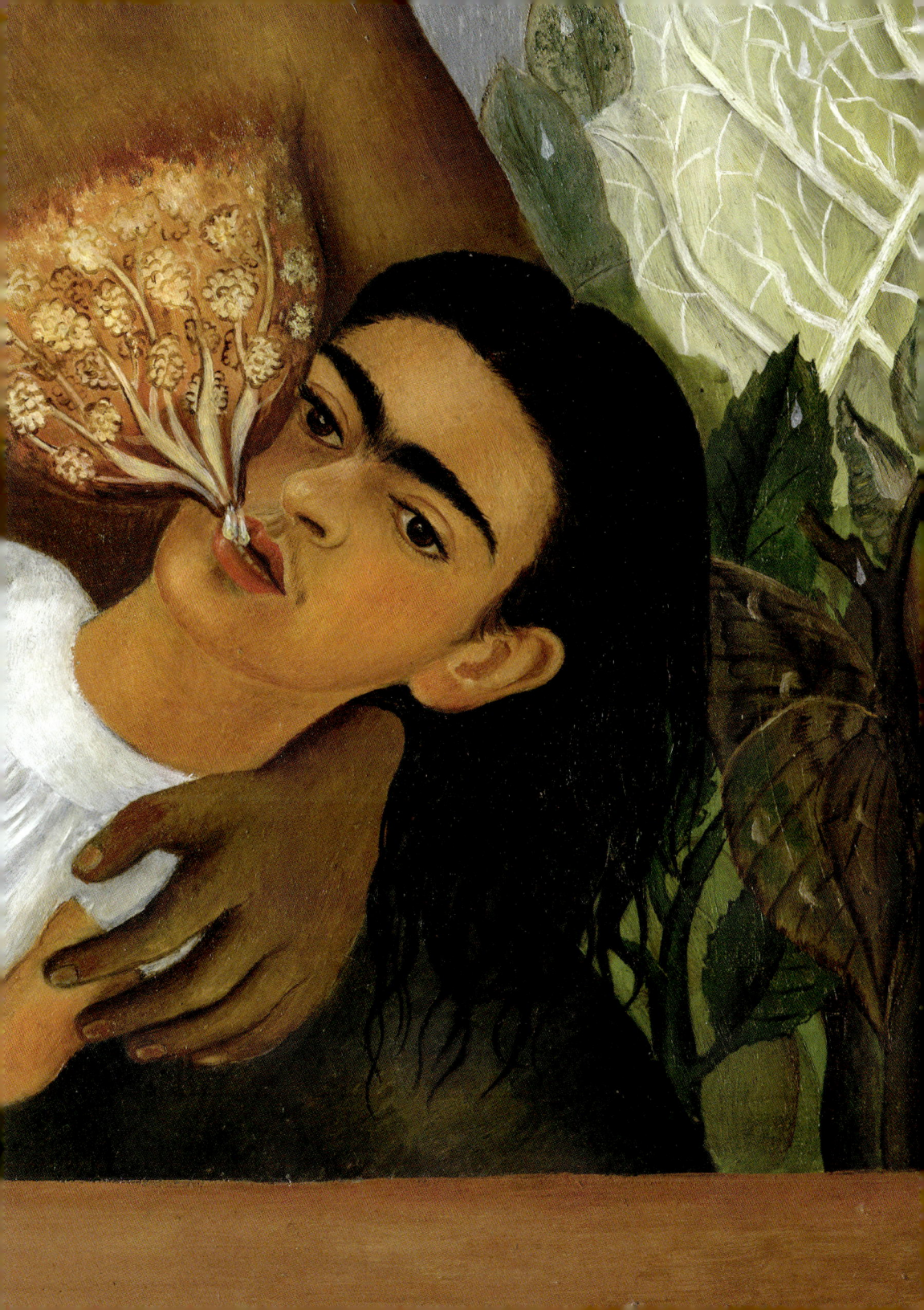

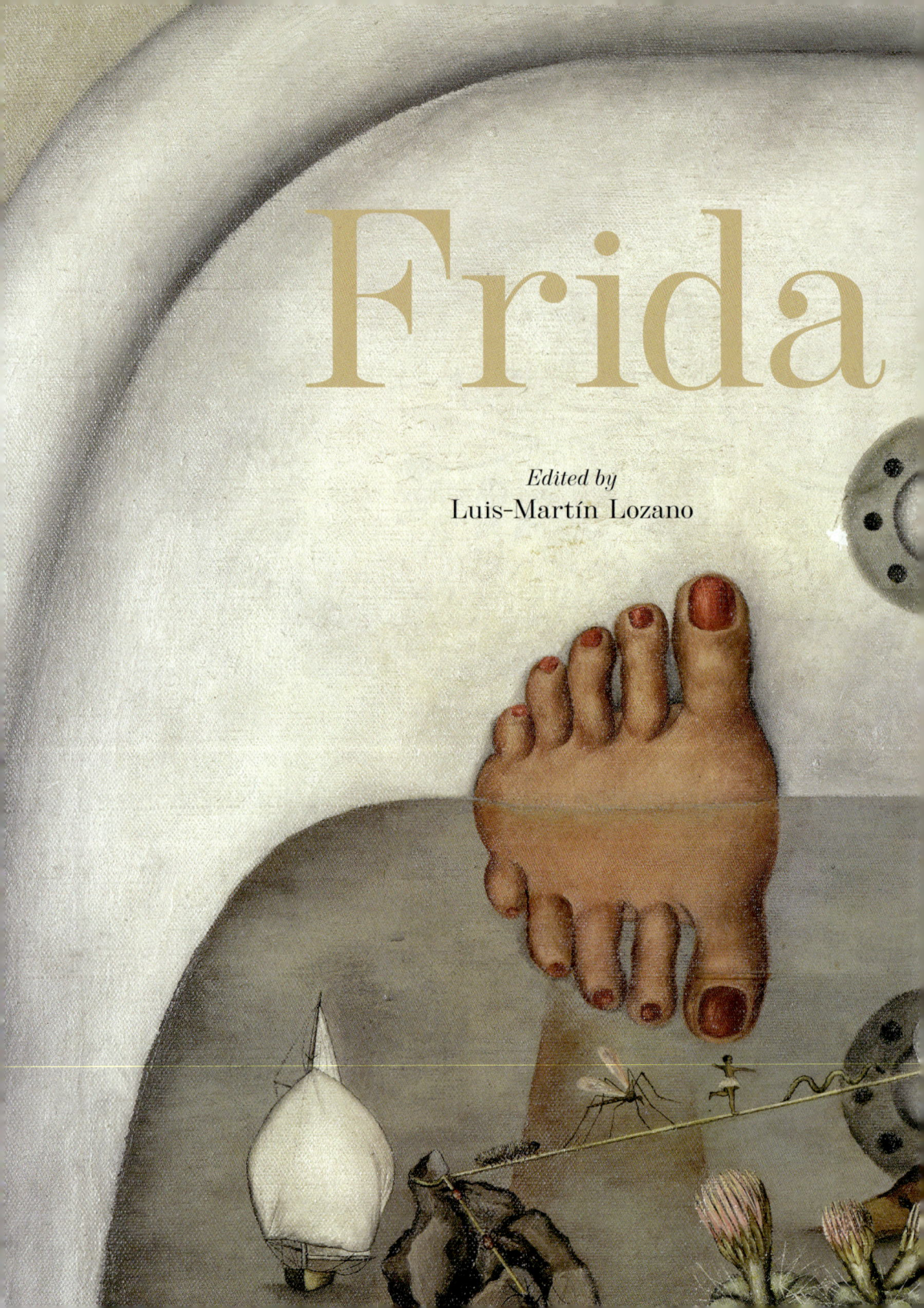

Frida

Edited by
Luis-Martín Lozano

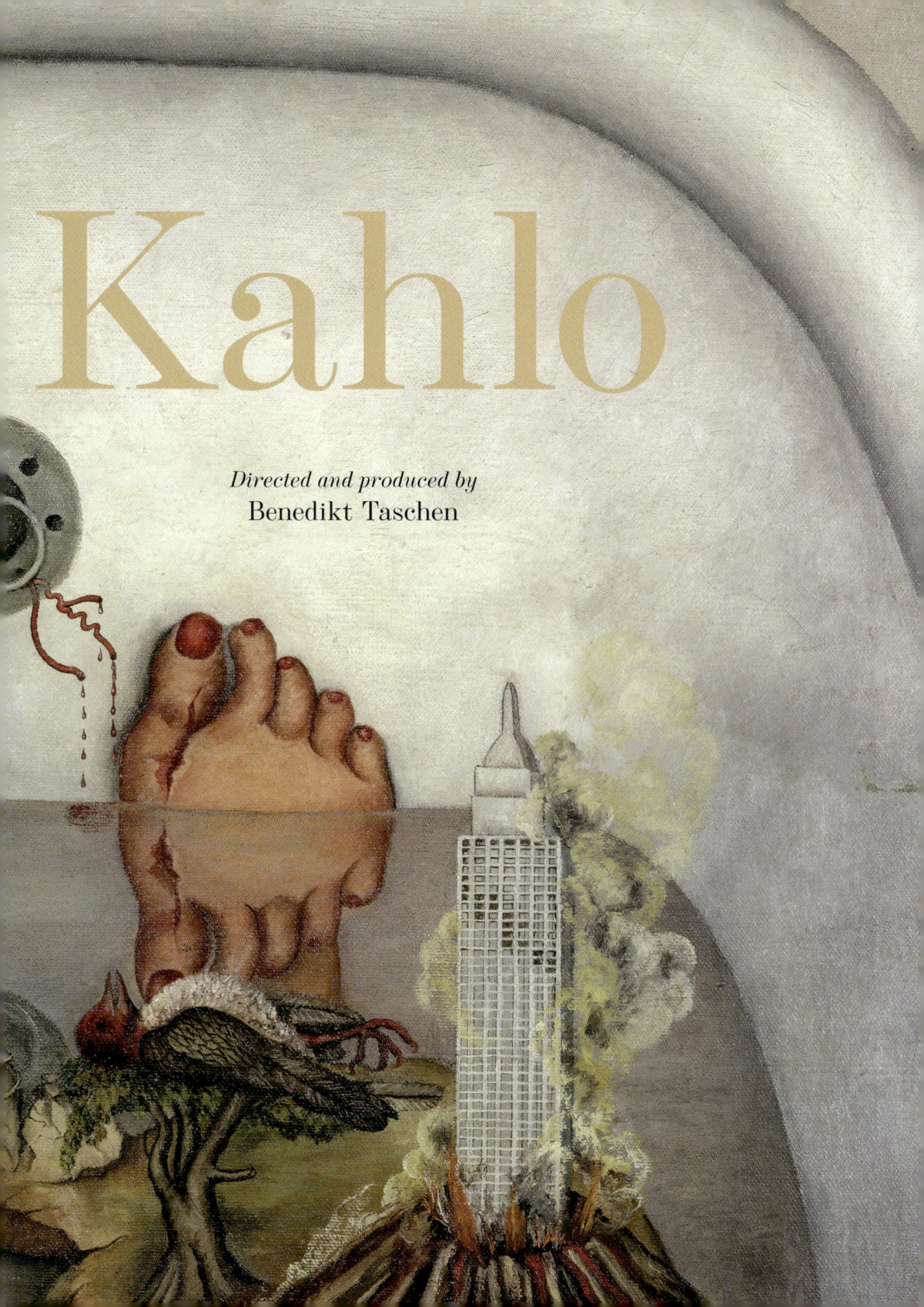

Kahlo

Directed and produced by
Benedikt Taschen

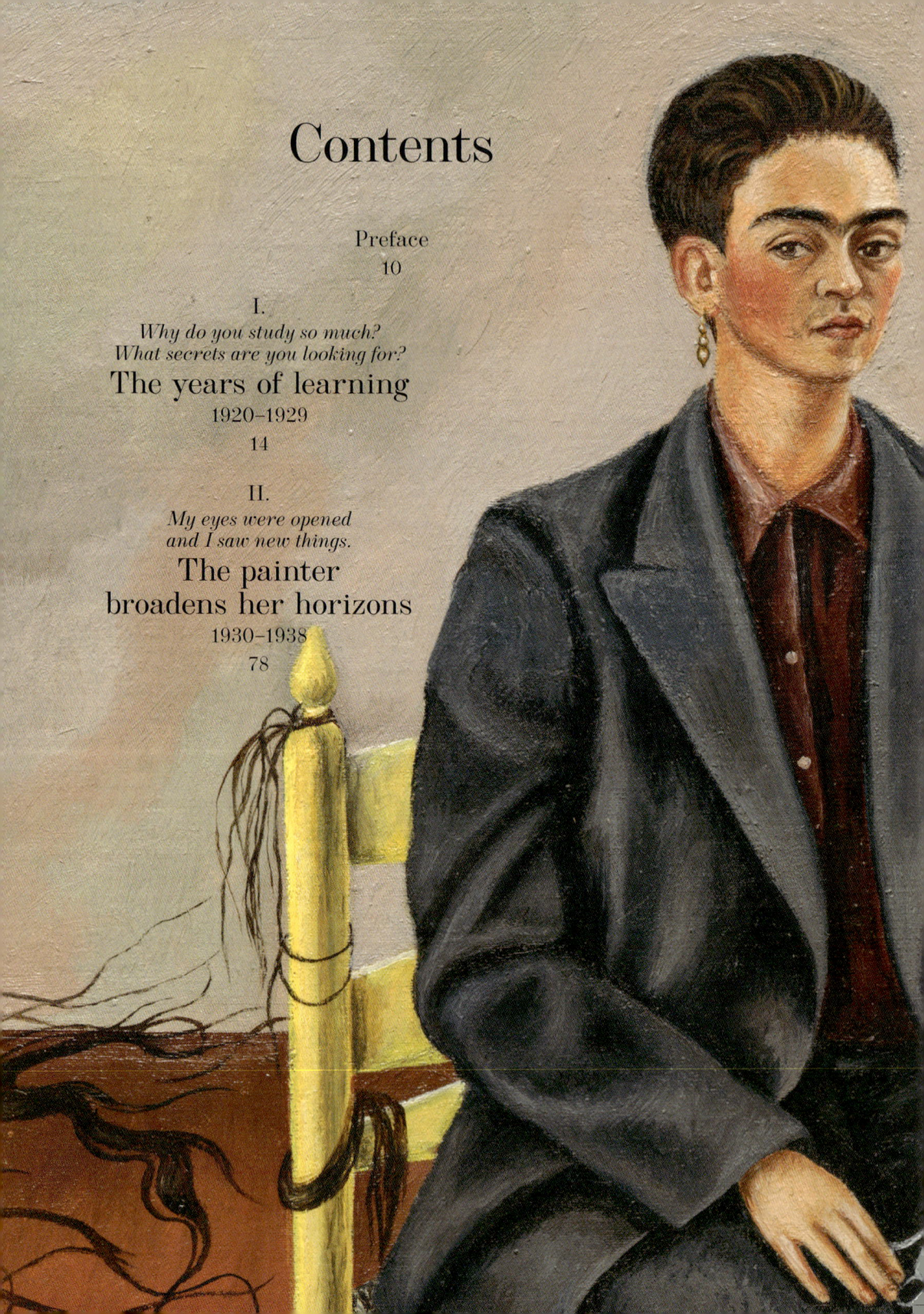

Contents

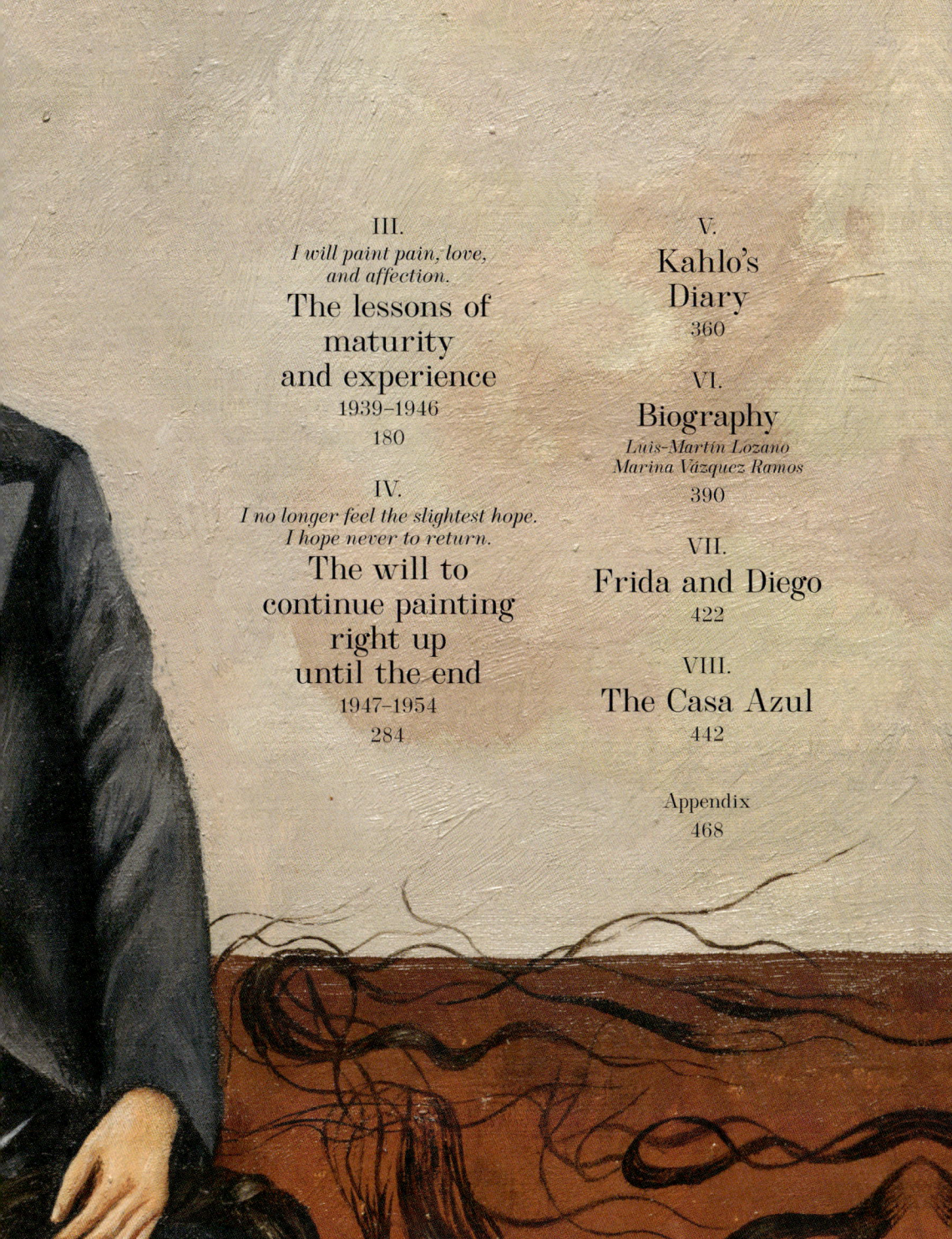

Preface

In the last 50 years there has been an astonishing revival of interest in the work of the Mexican painter Frida Kahlo (1907–1954). The number of books and articles that have appeared about her life story, her house, her recipes, and even the way she dressed has continued to increase, yet in comparison there has been rather less analysis of her paintings.

When Kahlo died, she was at the height of her creative ability, and her paintings had been exhibited in New York, Paris, and Mexico City. Her work was becoming a part of the art-historical writing on Mexican modern art, and celebrated authors, critics, and historians had taken an interest in her paintings, including Margarita Nelken in 1935, André Breton in 1938, and Elena Garro in 1941, an interest that also extended to American collectors such as MacKinley Helm. She featured in Laurence Schmeckebier's pioneering book *Modern Mexican Art*, published in 1939, and in 1943 Henry McBride reviewed the exhibition organized at Peggy Guggenheim's Art of this Century gallery in New York, which included one of Kahlo's drawings. The art critic Antonio Rodríguez had been writing about her since 1944, and from 1951 onward his fellow critics Luis Cardoza y Aragón, Raúl Flores Guerrero, and Ceferino Palencia also began to follow her work. In 1952, Justino Fernández included her in his first great survey of Mexican modern and contemporary art, and in the following year Raquel Tibol, a pioneer in the study of Kahlo's work, wrote her first piece about her as a journalist in Santiago de Chile.

Following Kahlo's death, Diego Rivera took on the task of maintaining her legacy by establishing a museum in her name, which was opened to the public in 1958. Her work was also included in a number of important international exhibitions held in the years after the war which showcased Mexico's contributions to 20th-century culture. Within Mexico, Kahlo's painting has always been highly regarded in the annals of modern art, and in 1977 the major "Exposicion Nacional de Homenaje" was organized in celebration of her work at the Palacio de Bellas Artes in Mexico City. However, it has really been since the 1980s that exhibitions of her paintings have become more frequent, and in places as far afield as Finland, Australia, and South Korea. Kahlo's works in the Museo Dolores Olmedo and the Jacques and Natasha Gelman collection have traveled around the world, while paintings such as *The Broken Column* (p. 257) and *Self-portrait (Diego on My Mind)* (p. 251) are true icons of Mexican art, with Kahlo as the country's ultimate ambassador.

In addition, a number of specific factors have also influenced the revival of interest in Kahlo's work around the world. One of these is the feminist movement in the United States which, since the 1970s, has made Kahlo a torchbearer for freedom and

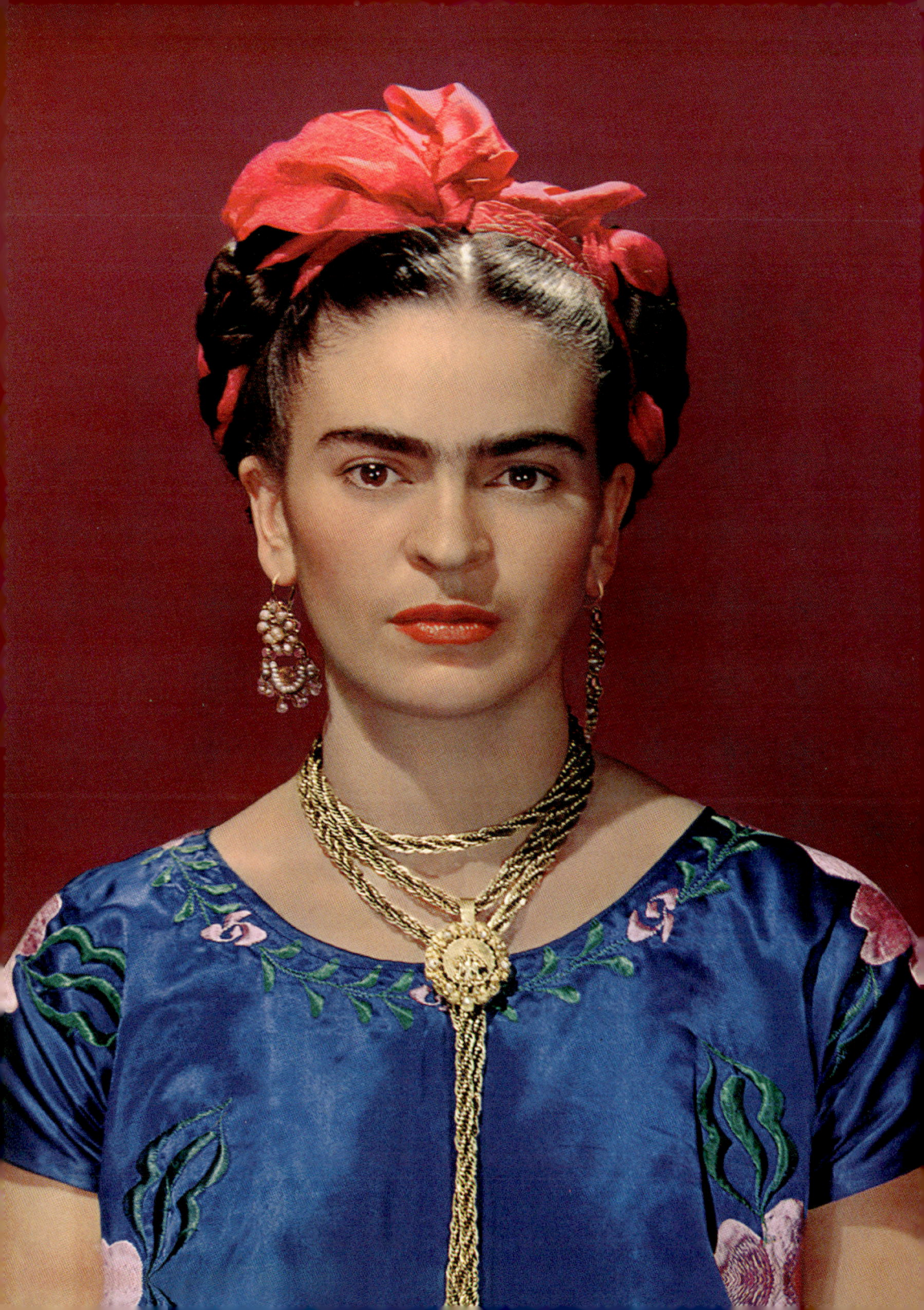

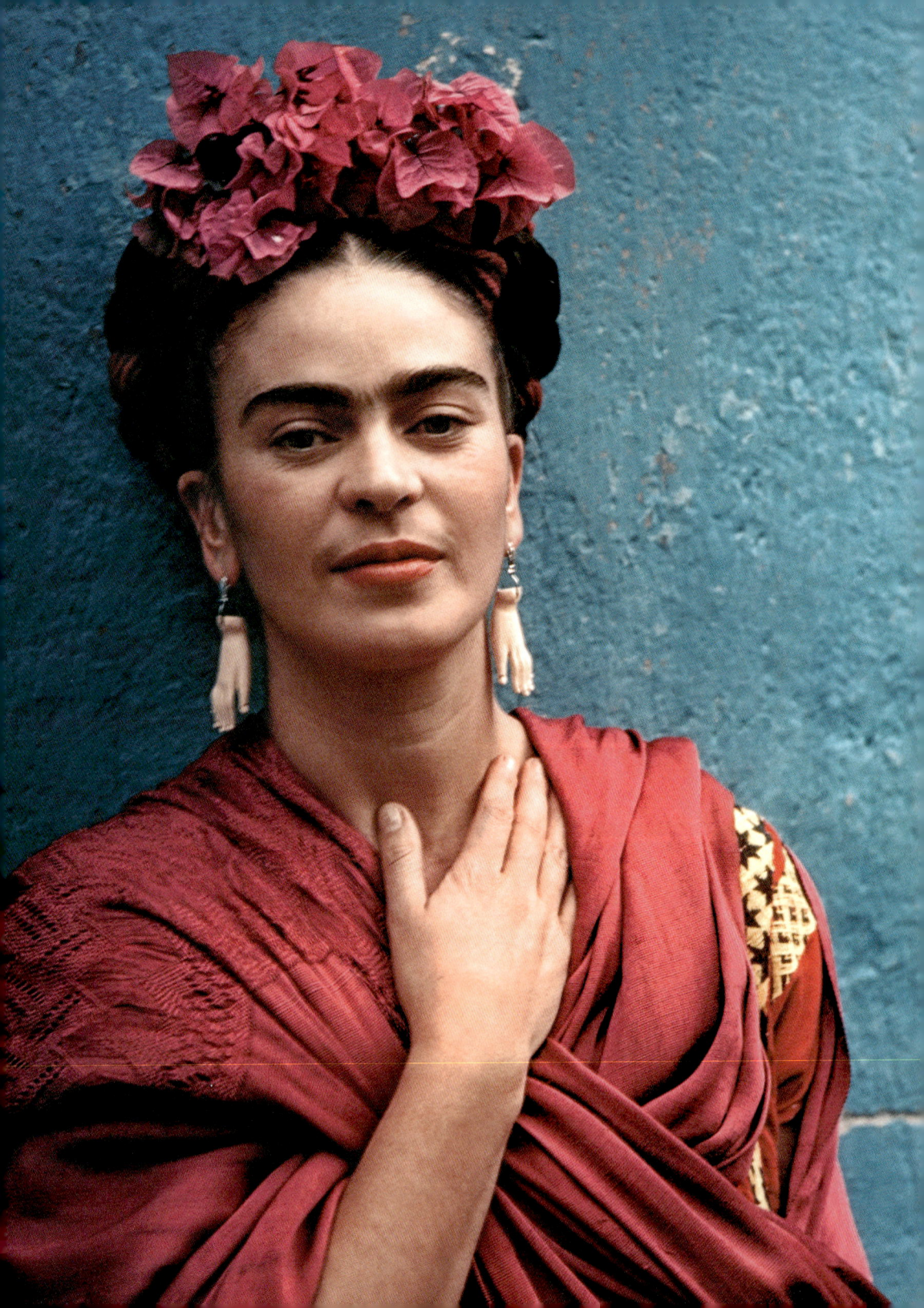

women's choice, in particular with regard to sexuality, reproduction, and equal opportunities. At around this time too Kahlo's painting started to become a subject for interdisciplinary study in sociology and psychology, and for new ways of considering art history. Meanwhile, the first auctions of Latin American art in New York in 1979 transformed Mexican art into a mainstay of the new vogue in collecting, which in turn raised the profile of Kahlo's work among international collectors and resulted in increased demand for her paintings. Art collecting has in fact played a decisive role in Kahlo becoming more well known, and while the majority of her works are in the collections of various museums, not only in Mexico but also in the United States, private collectors have been very generous in continuing to lend their works for different exhibitions.

The book consists of an essay divided into four chapters that roughly correspond to the four decades and four phases of Kahlo's artistic career. The discussion in each of these chapters involves a selection of Kahlo's paintings and some of her drawings, together with various photographs and works by other artists with whom she had a number of influences, interpretations, and conceptual references in common.

The book also includes a concise biographical section with photos. At the editors' suggestion there are excerpts from Kahlo's diary; a pictorial survey of the house where she lived, the Casa Azul; and a series of photographs of Kahlo and Rivera, preceded by an essay she wrote about him.

We would like to extend our thanks to the many collectors and institutions whose artworks are included in this book, and to the Banco de México for copyright permission to reproduce Kahlo's paintings, letters, and drawings. In particular, we would like to acknowledge the commitment and invaluable support provided by Mary-Anne Martin and her important gallery in New York, Mary-Anne Martin Fine Art, and also the assistance provided by Christie's and Sotheby's auction houses, which has been essential in producing this book. Our special thanks go to Spencer Throckmorton for giving us complete access to his superb collection of photography, and we are equally grateful to Vicente Wolf and Mimi Muray for the use of photographs from their unique collections as well.

This book would never have been possible without the initiative and determination of Benedikt Taschen, who for years has cherished the idea of publishing a properly presented volume that would show Kahlo's work in all its complexity and seductive fascination. I would like to express my appreciation for the dedicated and tireless work of the entire TASCHEN editorial team.

Luis-Martín Lozano

I.

Why do you study so much?
What secrets are you looking for?

The years
of learning

1920–1929

"*I first met Frida when we were at the Escuela Nacional Preparatoria together, when we were both very young. What really struck me about her was not just how animated she was about everything but what an exceptional mind she had, and even at that age she already seemed to have the intelligence of a woman who was 30 years old.*"

— ADELINA ZENDEJAS, *c.* 1982

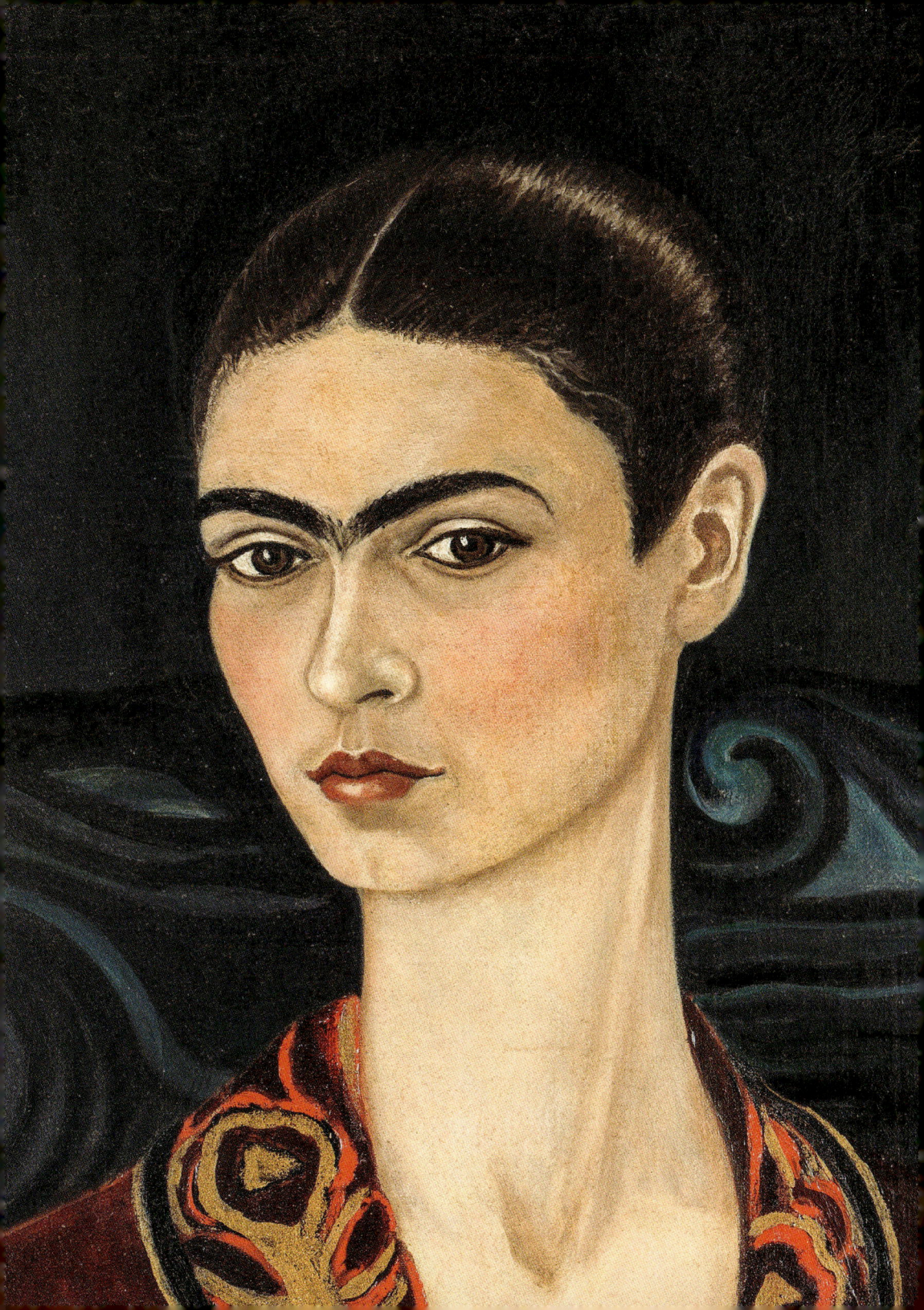

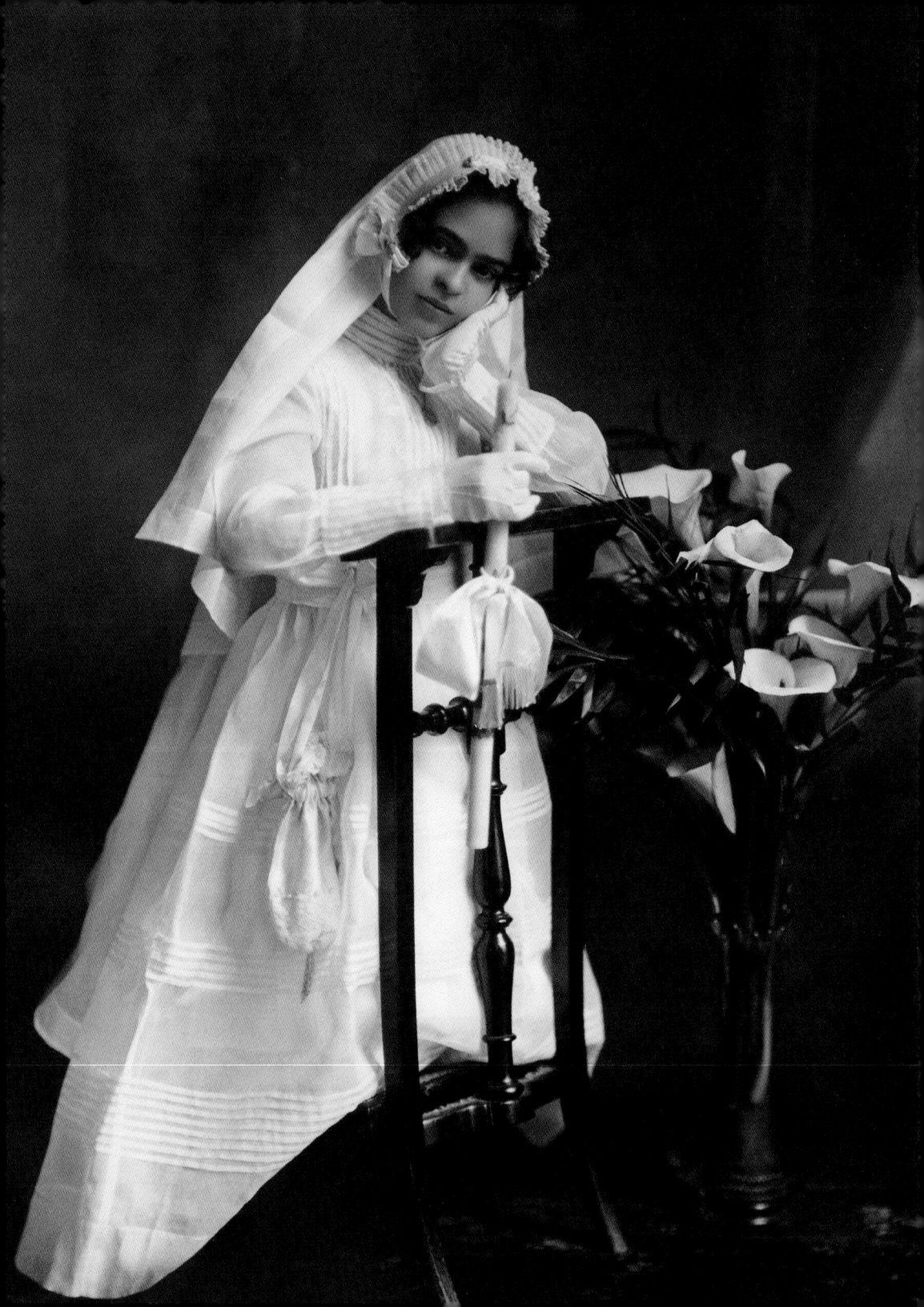

Few artists of the 20th century have had their personal and private lives as closely examined as the Mexican painter Frida Kahlo (1907–1954). Her work has created intense interest concerning even the most minute details of her life story, turning her in the process into a cult figure with a somewhat fanatical following.[1] Today her work might seem to be very much in keeping with the way society in the 21st century has become obsessed with individuality and the consumption, and rapid turnover of images, and with such a voracious materialism that it even threatens the future of the planet and all the species that inhabit it. By way of contrast, this book seeks to go back to the source, and is intended to be a monograph about Kahlo in which each and every one of her authenticated paintings is described in detail – including those that were destroyed or lost.

Kahlo's artistic career was marked by a series of upheavals that were intimately connected to events in her personal life, and these, combined with certain exceptional opportunities that enabled her to develop, make it impossible for her to be compared with any other Mexican artist of her time. Several different factors contributed to her profile as an artist and have helped to sustain an ever-growing interest in Kahlo since her death in 1954, among the general public and specialists alike. In spite of the fact that her career as an artist was relatively short and her output amounts to little more than 150 paintings (together with several drawings that have only come to light in recent years and have not yet been studied in full), her aesthetic and conceptual ideas continue to inspire enormous fascination across the world.

The first chapter of this introduction focuses on Kahlo's early development as an artist, on her initial sense that she wanted to become a painter and her earliest experiences of art in Mexico. Three main sources have been used for this first phase of her artistic career, chief among which is of course, and most importantly, her own work. Beyond this there are the written sources that have gathered together much of the factual information about Kahlo as it is known today, the series of interviews she had in 1953 with Raquel Tibol (1923–2015), which became the basis for Tibol's book as it was eventually published in 1977, and the archival and testimonial research carried out in the 1970s by Hayden Herrera (born 1940) for her doctoral thesis which later became a bestseller when it was published, as Kahlo's biography, in 1983. Lastly, two other works have been

Page 15
Self-portrait (in a Velvet Dress) (detail), September 1926
(see ill. p. 53)

Guillermo Kahlo, **Frida Kahlo at her first Communion**, *c.* 1920
Gelatin silver print, 20.8 x 16.1 cm (8¼ x 6⅜ in.)
Mexico City, Isolda P. Kahlo Archive

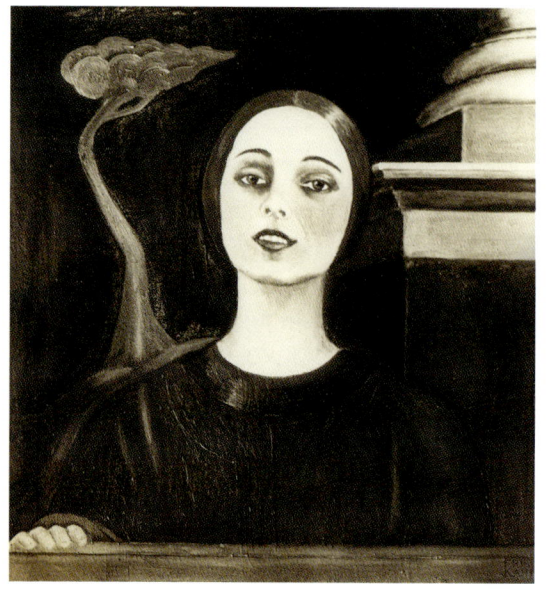

invaluable sources for additional research, namely the catalogue raisonné published in 1988 by Prignitz-Poda, Grimberg, and Kettenmann, which was the first work to collect all of Kahlo's paintings as they were known at the time, albeit without including a critical description for each entry; and Herrera's monograph, published in 1991, which discussed almost all of Kahlo's pictorial output as it was known up until that date.[2]

In 1953, Kahlo's husband Diego Rivera (1886–1957) traveled to South America to take part in the Congreso Continental de la Cultura (Continental Conference of Culture) being held in Santiago de Chile. While he was there he met Tibol, a young fiction writer from Argentina who was living in Chile at the time and trying her hand at journalism.[3] Tibol interviewed Rivera for the culture section of the Buenos Aires newspaper *La Prensa* and he was the first to speak to her about the "mutilated beauty" of Kahlo's paintings: "… the tragedy in Frida's work is not its dominant theme […] the darkness of her pain is only the velvety background for the marvelous light that pours out from her biological strength, her exquisitely refined sensitivity, magnificent intelligence, and her invincible compulsion to fight for life."[4] I am inclined to think that it was Rivera, given his awareness of the fragile state of Kahlo's health, who realized the need to put something in writing about her artistic career. It is possible that he saw an opportunity for someone in Tibol's position to take on the task of collecting information to publish a biography of Kahlo, and with that aim in mind he invited Tibol to go to Mexico, where he arranged for her to stay in Kahlo's house in Coyoacán.[5] Tibol admitted that she "was going there to be her nurse. Although I already had my little heart set on being a journalist, it didn't bother me."[6]

However, despite what Rivera was hoping for with the situation and Tibol's initial enthusiasm, it quickly became apparent that it was going to be difficult since Kahlo was suffering periods of pain and distress as a result of all her operations, and her health was not at all good.[7] As Tibol wrote: "[…] I arrived on May 25, 1953 […] I was supposed to stay with Frida and by living with her I would then be available to look after her, as she had sunk into a deep and uncontrollable state of depression [...] Cristina Kahlo, who helped her sister as much as she could, approved of this idea as it offered her some respite from her vigil which she had otherwise not been able to leave unless someone took her place. [Rivera] had given me no forewarning about the heavy atmosphere surrounding her in her unwell condition, for which it would have been better if I had been prepared in some way, with a kind of spiritual passport so that I could move about more freely in that strange environment into which my presence had intruded without any prior warning for either me as the visitor or my hostess [...] I suggested to Frida that she dictate the story of her life to me, she agreed enthusiastically, and we soon made a start [...] that poor wounded deer, so badly wounded, our plan soon floundered in the face of her continued suffering. When it became clear that the difficulty of the situation and the strained energies inside that house in Coyoacán clashed with any efforts on my part to try and collect information, I decided to move out."[8]

Following the amputation of part of her leg, Kahlo never recovered the mental fortitude to be able to continue with anything, and after several months of living together in such difficult circumstances, Tibol left.[9] Even so, the valuable information she was able to gather from her interviews served as the beginning of a biography as told by Kahlo herself, which was published on March 7, 1954 with the title "Fragmentos para una vida de Frida Kahlo" (Fragments toward a Life of Frida Kahlo) in *México en la cultura*, a supplement of the newspaper *Novedades*. The amount of information Kahlo provided for Tibol shows that she did want to tell her story and leave a record of her life, and to share her observations and memories. Kahlo's words are the main source for what is known about her parents, her childhood, and her youth, and the first two books published by Tibol about her are largely based on that information: *Frida Kahlo. Crónica, testimonios y aproximaciones* (1977) and *Frida. Una vida abierta* (1983). They were also a key source for Herrera's biography, *Frida. A Biography of Frida Kahlo* (1983). While this information provided directly by Kahlo herself was clearly presented in these first books about her, which were essentially biographical, subsequent publications about Kahlo's relationships and her family life have been plagued with imaginative conjectures and mistaken interpretations (for example, a supposed antagonism between her parents, which has no basis at all in fact), the sole purpose of which is to fuel false ideas that distort not only the reality of Kahlo's relationships with her family, but also the subject matter of some of her paintings. In truth, she had an exceptionally good relationship with her father, and was, it seems, the daughter to whom

Portrait of Ruth Stallsmith, June 1927
Oil on canvas, dimensions unknown. Whereabouts unknown
Photograph by Guillermo Kahlo

he felt closest. The two of them shared a taste for the arts and had a professional interest in photography. But Kahlo also adored her mother and had strong emotional ties with her sisters, including her half-sisters, who were the children of her father's first marriage to María Cardeña Espino.[10] Moreover, the fact that she grew up in a loving family later had a profound effect on her adult life and on her painting too, but above all, its influence was felt in the quality of the human relationships she tried to establish, and in her constant need to feel loved by those around her.[11]

Kahlo's father was German and had emigrated to Mexico during the period known as the Porfiriato (1876–1911), when political stability and centralized institutions gave rise to economic growth and in turn attracted foreign investment, which contributed to the modernization of the country. Carl Wilhelm Kahlo was born in Pforzheim in 1871, and came to Mexico in 1890 when he was 18 years old (p. 394). He had a well-educated upbringing in a family of jewelers and manufacturers of precision measuring instruments.[12] In Mexico he adopted the Spanish form of his first name, Guillermo, and became an official photographer during the Porfiriato; this enabled him to provide financial security for his family, but when the Mexican Revolution broke out in 1910 his business and income were severely affected. The discipline and rigor Guillermo brought to his work as a photographer had a significant influence on his daughter who first learned in his studio how to bring photographs to life by retouching them with painstakingly detailed brushstrokes and thus add delicate touches of color to the portraits. She also learned about composition from working with her father's photographs, and about how light and shadow behaved.[13] Kahlo's first painted portraits, from 1926 and 1927, were inevitably marked by the classic style of photographic portraiture that prevailed in the early 20th century. They also seem to have been painted from photographs, rather than using live models. This is especially noticeable in her *Portrait of Ruth Stallsmith* (p. 18), which Kahlo painted between January and June 1927.

This portrait, whose whereabouts are currently unknown, bears a resemblance to the photographs of actresses from silent movies that were published in magazines at the time, such as Ludmila Babková, which may perhaps explain why it has also been referred to as "Ludmila."[14] It is now known that this portrait was painted from a photograph taken by Edward Weston (1886–1958), one of the most innovative American photographers of the 20th century, which also helps to explain the modern aesthetic of Kahlo's paintings since two distinct types of photography converge in them: the personal portrait,

Guillermo Kahlo, **Frida at 12 years old**, June 15, 1919
Gelatin silver print, 19 x 13.4 cm (7½ x 5¼ in.)
Mexico City, Coyoacán, Museo Frida Kahlo

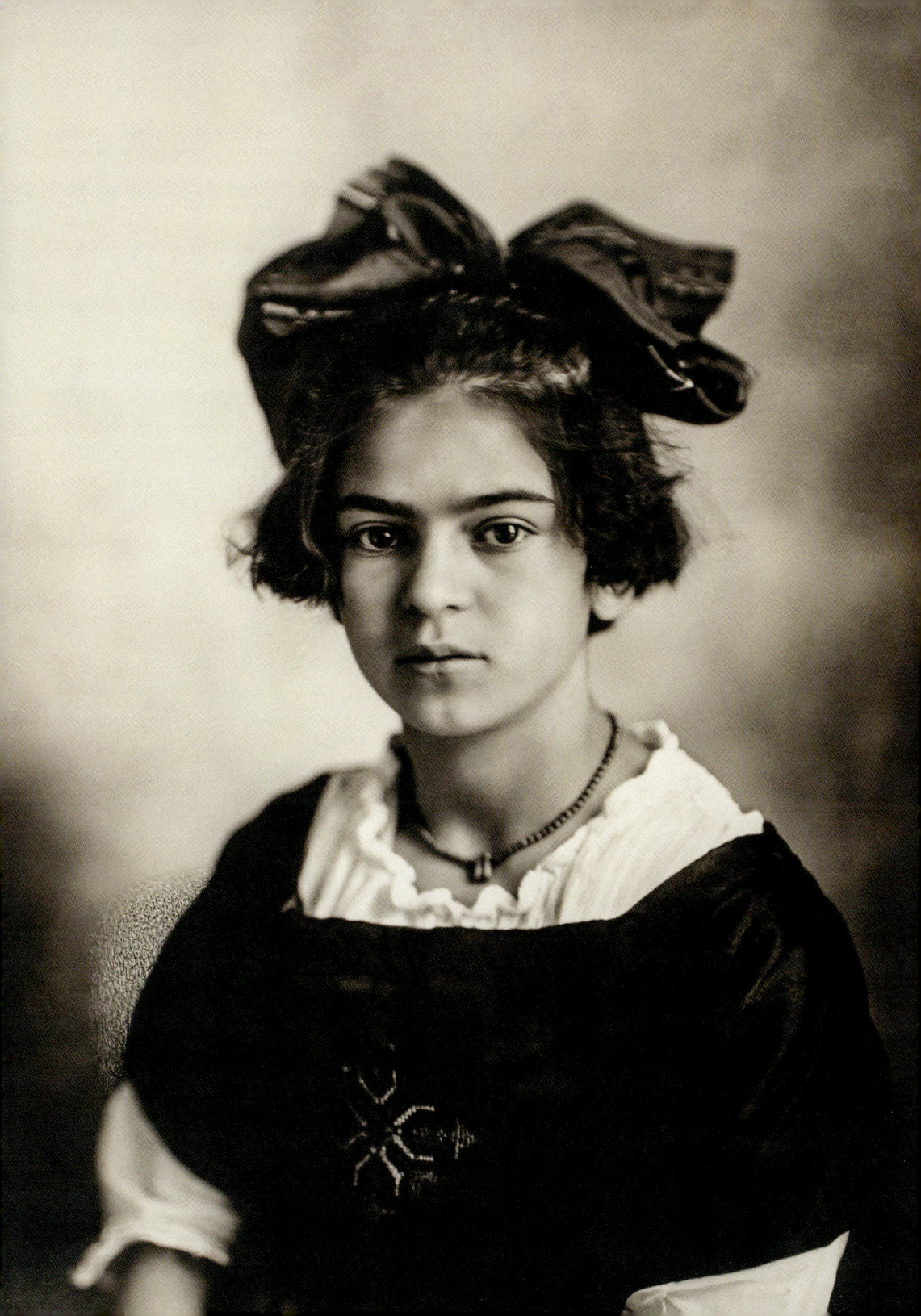

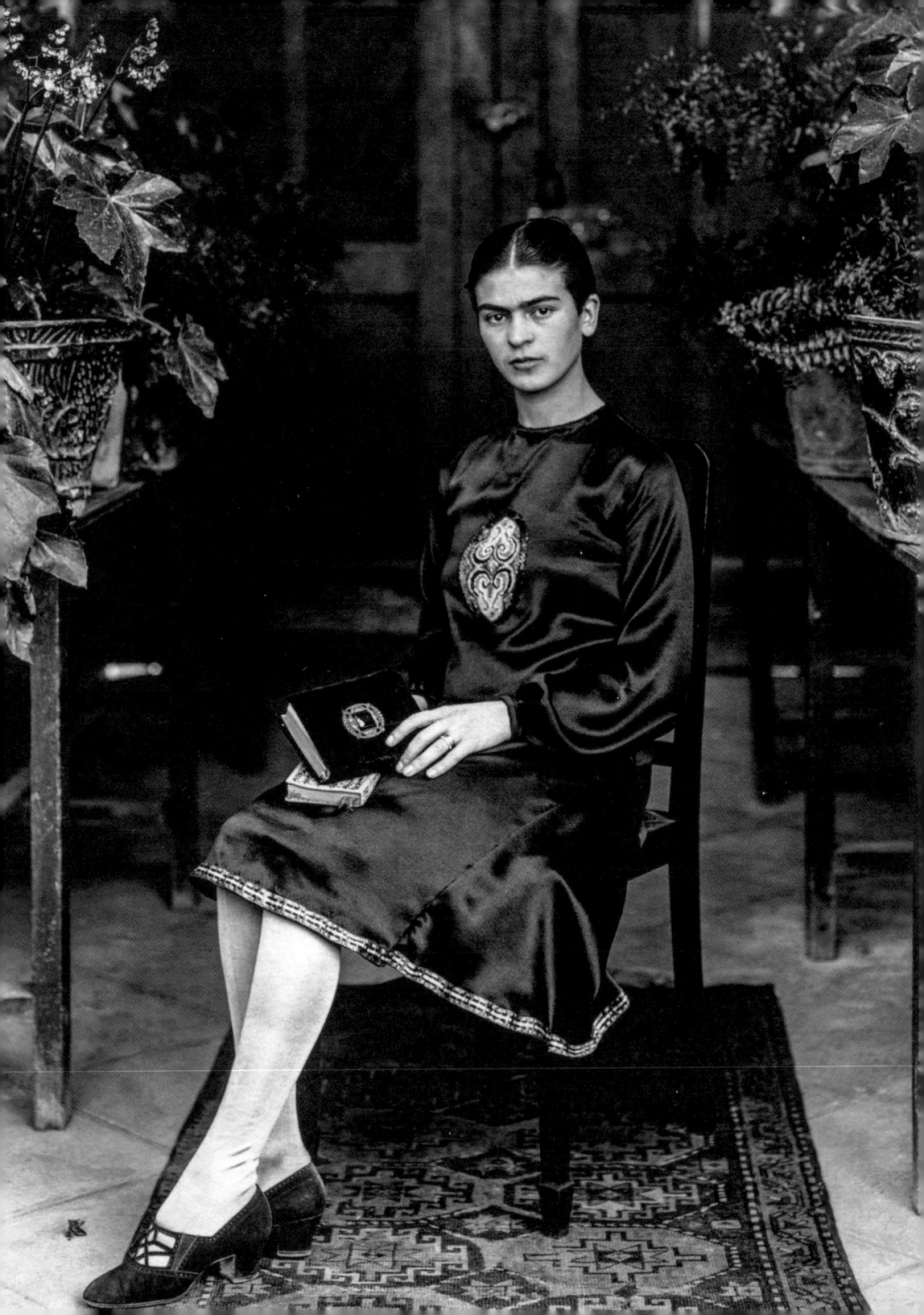

taken in a studio or similar private space, and the commercial portrait, as associated with the film industry. It can thus be seen that Kahlo's early experience with photography and of working with her father helped guide her decision to become an artist, while at the same time enabling her to understand the various innovative ideas that were being introduced in photography by those in the avant-garde, in particular by Weston (whom years later she met in San Francisco through Rivera) and Tina Modotti (1896–1942). As it happens, a number of photographs signed by Kahlo and dated to 1929 were recently found in the archives of the Museo Frida Kahlo in which the influence of Weston and Modotti is obvious, as too Anita Brenner's book *Idols behind Altars*, which was published in 1929 as well.[15]

As well as being a noted photographer in Mexico, Guillermo was also an amateur painter who liked modernist art of the *fin de siècle*, both European and Mexican.[16] Judging from the books he owned, it is clear that he admired the great masters of the German Renaissance, such as Albrecht Dürer (1471–1528), Lucas Cranach the Elder (1472–1553), and Hans Holbein the Younger (c. 1497–1543), along with more modern painters such as Adolph Menzel (1815–1905), Franz von Stuck (1863–1928), and Max Liebermann (1847–1935), and that he was familiar with the work of the Mexican artists Germán Gedovius (1867–1937) and Ángel Zárraga (1886–1946). He also collected magazines from the *belle époque*, including *El mundo*, *Semanario ilustrado*, and *El arte y la ciencia*, which enabled him to keep up to date with new ideas in painting, music, and the fine arts. Guillermo Kahlo liked painting landscapes outdoors but also still lifes and floral compositions, in the style of the Mexican painter Alfredo Ramos Martínez (1871–1946). This was a genre little regarded at the time, but was the subject matter Kahlo used for her first paintings, perhaps even before her accident in September 1925.

A very early pictorial work of hers was painted on a tray, a simple Mexican craft item, and shows just such a bunch of flowers with poppies (p. 49). This painting, which is still owned by Kahlo's family, gives an insight into her technical and aesthetic beginnings. It reveals that she was self-taught as an artist and how close in style her work is here with her father's paintings. A small bunch of flowers is depicted, with a certain sentimentality and a beginner's pictorial technique, although the composition is very well worked out within the circular format that was the usual shape of such Mexican trays.[17] It is noteworthy that Kahlo chose to use an everyday object with a decorative border and then paint a modernist composition in the center of it, since this would seem to present an opposition that

Guillermo Kahlo, **Frida Kahlo at 18 years old** (detail), February 7, 1926
Gelatin silver print, 11.4 x 9.8 cm (4½ x 3⅞ in.)
Mexico City, Isolda P. Kahlo Archive

interested her from her very earliest pictorial works, namely the integration of Western art forms with folk traditions in Mexican art that had typically been seen as marginal, and the corresponding dialogue between these two influences. In the 1920s, folk art was just starting to be rediscovered in Mexico by painters such as Roberto Montenegro (1885–1968) and Jorge Enciso (1879–1969), and above all Adolfo Best Maugard (1891–1964), whose research later resulted in him devising an innovative manual, the *Método de dibujo* (Drawing Method), that was adopted in elementary schools and a number of art and vocational colleges.[18]

Beyond her family, Kahlo was exposed to the dynamic cultural conditions of Mexico during the 1920s. In the period that followed the revolution and the bloody civil war of 1911–1917, a climate of national reconstruction and institutional consolidation was ushered in. The former Secretaría de Instrucción Pública y Bellas Artes (Ministry of Public Education and Fine Arts), which in its modern form had been established in 1905 during the Porfiriato, was abolished in 1917 with the ratification of the new Constitution, although the bill to replace it with a new Secretaría de Educación Pública (Ministry of Public Education) was not passed by the government of General Álvaro Obregón (1880–1928) until October 1921. In 1920, José Vasconcelos (1882–1959), who at the time was rector of the Universidad Nacional Autónoma de México (National Autonomous University of Mexico), was appointed to head the new ministry which also included a fine arts department, that in turn served as a platform for developing various strategies to promote and stimulate the arts in Mexico, as a direct adjunct to general education. This was the situation when Kahlo began her high-school studies at the Escuela Nacional Preparatoria (National Preparatory School) in 1922. Before this she had attended the Escuela Normal Primaria (Normal Primary School), as was expected for daughters of middle-class Mexican families.[19] In 1920 and 1921 she took classes in anatomy, physiology, and biology and got excellent grades. She also studied writing, English, and drawing, and so from a very early age it can be seen how her interest in studying medicine took shape but also what would prove to be her actual calling as an artist.

The years Kahlo spent at the Escuela Nacional Preparatoria were critical for her intellectual development which began to take shape when she was only 15. While she was there, she also came to understand that she was part of a generation that was destined to change Mexico since she and her peers firmly believed that the sacrifices of the Mexican Revolution, the first social revolution of the 20th century, were essential in order to lead the country toward a new order of justice and modernity. While she was at this school as well, Kahlo joined a group of restless students known as Los Cachuchas (the Peaked Caps), and through being in contact with them she became an avid reader and began to develop a keen interest in what was happening in the world of visual arts.[20]

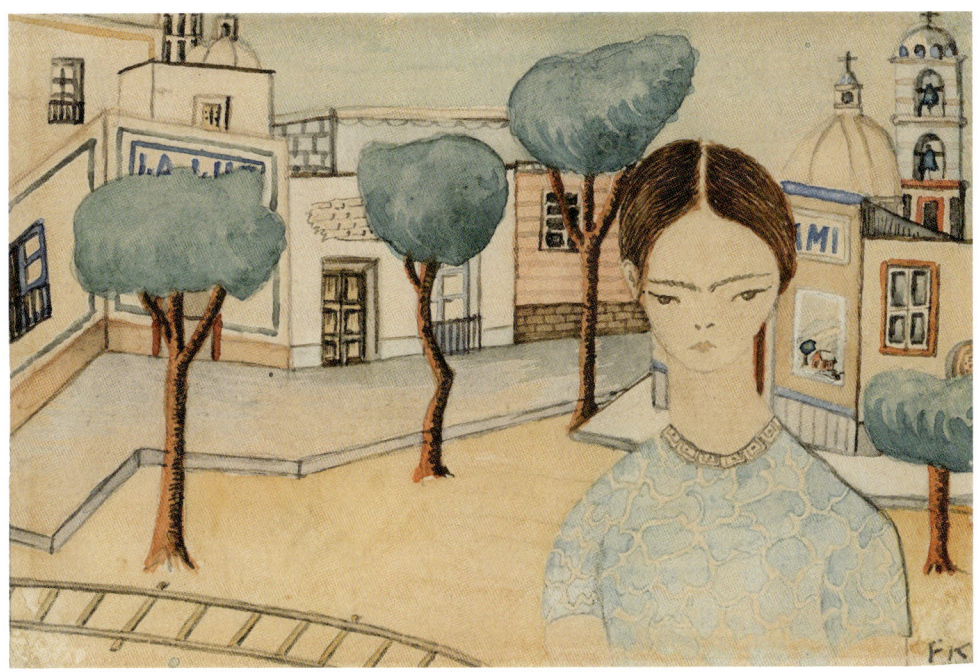

Frida in Coyoacán, *c.* 1927
Watercolor on paper, 16 x 21 cm (6¼ x 8¼ in.). Mexico, State Government
of Tlaxcala, Instituto Tlaxcalteca de la Cultura, Museo de Arte de Tlaxcala

One of the most influential methods for teaching art that was tried out at this time
was the so-called Escuela de Pintura al Aire Libre (Open-air School of Painting), which
was established in Santa Anita, Iztapalapa, in 1913 by Ramos Martínez. Initially the
school depended on the Academia Nacional de Bellas Artes (National Academy of Fine
Arts, formerly the Academia de San Carlos), but in the 1920s it was further developed
and its scope broadened as a result of the cultural policy set up by Vasconcelos when
he took charge of the Ministry of Public Education. In 1921, one of these schools was
opened in the Chimalistac neighborhood of San Ángel, and then a few months later it
was moved to Coyoacán, only three blocks from Kahlo's home within the former hacienda of San Pedro Mártir. Once the school became established in Coyoacán it attracted
a number of young painters who had already studied at the academy and who now
wanted to understand the new ideas being introduced by Ramos Martínez, including
Ramón Alva de la Canal (1892–1985), Fernando Leal (1896–1964), and Gabriel Fernández
Ledesma (1900–1983), who were all peers of Kahlo's and later her professional colleagues

in the 1930s and 1940s.[21] It is very unlikely that Kahlo as a young artist herself would not have visited this experimental school and seen the students painting outdoors, in emulation of the painters of the French Barbizon school so admired by Ramos Martínez. This idea gains further support from some of the paintings Kahlo made around 1928 (p. 65; Lozano 2021, cat. 16) which reveal a certain influence from the primitivism and Mexican indigenism that were endorsed by the school and, even more so, championed by the works of its founder (p. 34).

Ever since she was very young, from the age of about six or eight, Kahlo loved to draw, and some of these drawings were kept by her family. They are not the drawings of a child prodigy, but compositions done with very simple lines, and mostly landscapes, which she drew perhaps when she and her father went on outings together so that he could paint outdoors.[22] Her liking for drawing continued to grow during the two years she spent as a student at the Escuela Normal Primaria, and more so while she was at the Escuela Nacional Preparatoria, where she was able to take classes in "constructive drawing," "observational drawing," and "free drawing."[23] Around 1925, Kahlo began learning printmaking at the studio of Fernando Fernández, where part of her training involved copying the etchings of the Swedish artist Anders Zorn (1860–1920), who by chance was also one of her father's favorite artists. This copy work awakened in her an aptitude for drawing that up until then had not been fully revealed, since instead of simply making faithful reproductions of Zorn's etchings, Kahlo gave them an expressive presence through her use of light which added a sense of drama to the images and lifted them from being mere copies.[24] While the works she was copying continued to conform to the taste for European painting that Kahlo shared with her father, the drawing style she was beginning to explore at this time would later lead her down the new paths being established by modern painting in Mexico.

Kahlo's own beginnings as a professional painter coincide with one of the most fruitful periods in the development of modern art in Mexico. During the 1920s, several new stylistic trends took hold, in painting, sculpture, printmaking, and also photography.[25] The young Kahlo did not stand on the sidelines amid all this artistic excitement, which even at this date was rightly being referred to by critics and writers, both at home and abroad, as the Mexican Renaissance.[26] The Ministry of Public Education's Department of Fine Arts put its support behind a number of different strategies, including reviving Ramos Martínez's Open-air Schools of Painting and encouraging the use of Best Maugard's drawing manual. The main aim for Vasconcelos was to channel these experimental teaching methods in such a way that they would assist in the democratization of culture by providing access for hundreds of children and young people, in a country that had been devastated by the revolution, to a balanced education that included art as a way to understand their immediate reality. Children in the Ramos Martínez schools were allowed to paint their landscapes with a freedom to interpret colors and a perception of light and handling of spatial perspective that was utterly removed from the academic rules that had dominated the formal teaching of art in Mexico since the 18th century. Meanwhile, Best Maugard's drawing method was intended to provide students with a tool to develop new visual forms based on observing their environment. The general approach required students to reinterpret the way their reality was constructed, by looking afresh at the landscape around them together with their traditions and the beauty implicit in everyday objects. This would then be recodified through a new language of drawing based on seven signs, designed by Best Maugard himself, using lines and points on a plane. It was a new way of learning to see reality, and was intended to stimulate students' imagination.[27] Best Maugard based his methodology on his belief that he had found a common pattern in the artistic forms created by different cultures around the world, in particular within the heritage of Mexico's pre-Hispanic past and its legacy of folk art.

The ideas of Ramos Martínez and Best Maugard underlie some of the visual techniques Kahlo used between 1925 and 1927. A group of drawings and watercolors that she gave to the poet Miguel N. Lira (1905–1961) and which are now in the Museo de Arte de Tlaxcala (pp. 25, 39), along with other similar works in private collections, confirm the close attention Kahlo was paying even in these early works to the whole panorama of art in Mexico, as she absorbed new and more modern visual ideas compared with those she had learned at home and in her first years of school. In these small watercolors she has depicted various parts of Coyoacán, with its parks and churches and scenes of everyday life, presented with all the spontaneity that characterized the works of students in the Open-air Schools of Painting. In one of them, which includes what may be Kahlo's first self-portrait, the lines and structures used in Best Maugard's method (p. 25) are clearly visible. A number of other painters from this generation also made use of this method, including Rufino Tamayo (1899–1991), Agustín Lazo (1896–1971), and Julio Castellanos (1905–1947), as well as Manuel Rodríguez Lozano (1896–1971), who later headed the Pro-Mexican Art Movement. Among his better-known followers was Abraham Ángel (1895–1924), whose painting *The Little Mule* from 1923 was unmistakably the compositional model Kahlo used for her watercolor with the self-portrait, although she painted her own interpretation of Ángel's Coyoacán street view, as inspired by Best Maugard's methodology.[28]

When looking back over the first decade of Kahlo's artistic activity one of the most interesting aspects to bear in mind is that she was a self-taught painter who set about exploring, with total freedom, the different aesthetic possibilities that emerged in the

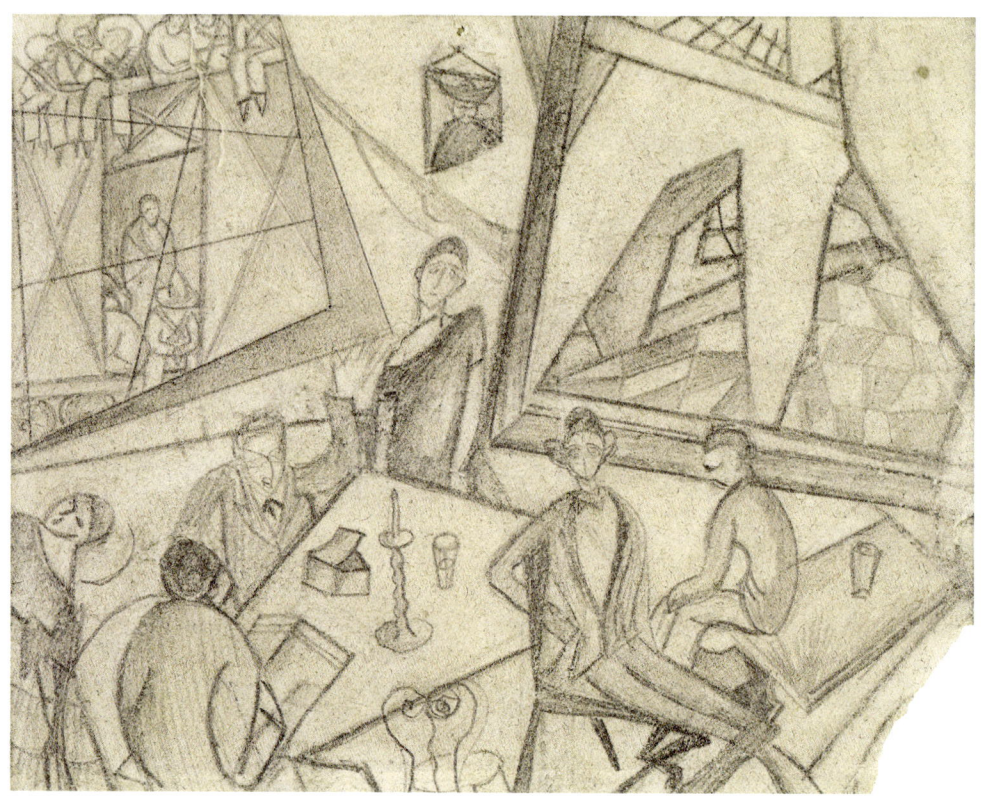

Sketch for *Pancho Villa and Adelita*, *c.* 1927
Graphite pencil on paper, 18 x 21 cm (7⅛ x 8¼ in.)
Private collection, courtesy Christie's, New York

strikingly rich and varied cultural context of Mexico in the years following the revolution. She had no desire simply to comply with the academic canon imposed by the Escuela Nacional de Bellas Artes, but instead attached great importance to drawing and likewise appreciated the painting of European masters. Her lack of academic training made it easier to engage with what was being taught by Ramos Martínez and with Rodríguez Lozano's ideas, and without having to give precedence to one aesthetic over another. At the same time, she was able to make use of photography in its most traditional form to paint her portraits, as her father had taught her to do, yet without being unaware of the modern, avant-garde vision being developed by photographers such as Weston and Modotti. She was also able to keep up with reviews of modern art by reading magazines such as *Forma* and also read about German painters, including Dürer, Cranach, and

Matthias Grünewald (1470–1528), in books in her father's library. For Kahlo, there was no sense of incompatibility when it came to art, and she thrived on both the traditional and the avant-garde. However, this vigorous process by which her creative potential became known to her and then established was suddenly disrupted by the horrific accident she suffered in 1925.

While Kahlo went to school in Mexico City, she was still living at home in Coyoacán with her parents. For her journey home each day she took the bus (pp. 70/71) from the raucous Zócalo in the center of the city to the Churubusco station, and from there walked along the tree-lined streets of the peaceful Del Carmen neighborhood that ran beside the former hacienda of San Pedro Mártir. In 1953, Kahlo recounted to Tibol all the details of that awful event:

"When I was young the buses were completely rickety. They had just been introduced in the city, and were a big success; the streetcars were running empty. I got on the bus with Alejandro Gómez Arias [her boyfriend at the time]. I sat on the end of the seat, next to the rail, with Alejandro beside me. Moments later, the bus collided with a streetcar on the Xochimilco line. It crushed the bus right into the street corner. The crash itself was strange, there was no violent shock, it all happened slowly and in silence, and everyone got knocked about. Me much more than anyone else. I remember it exactly as it happened on September 17, 1925, the day after the holiday on the 16th. I was 15 years old [she was in fact 18, since she was born in 1907], but I looked much younger, even younger than Cristi [her younger sister], although I'm 11 months older than her […]. I was a clever girl but not very practical, despite the freedom I'd acquired. Maybe that's why I didn't fully grasp the situation, or really understand how I had been injured. The first thing I thought of was a pretty-colored cup and ball toy I had bought that day and was carrying with me. I tried to find it, not imagining there'd be anything major that would have happened after the collision. It's a lie what they tell you about a crash like that, that it makes you cry. I had no tears. The crash made us all lurch forward and the handrail went right through me like a bullfighter's sword. A man saw how badly I was bleeding, and picked me up and carried me over to a pool table where I lay until the Red Cross came to get me […] As soon as I saw my mother, I said: I haven't died, and in any case, I have something to live for. That thing is painting."[29]

After a month in hospital, Kahlo was released but was confined to her bed, and since she could not move she began to paint on an easel that her family had adapted for her. Painting helped her to recover more quickly, but at the same time it strengthened her calling to become an artist. Three months later, Kahlo was able to walk again and was eager to resume the plans she had for her life, although she was not able to continue as a student at the Escuela Nacional Preparatoria because her recovery had taken so long.

In September 1926, one year after her accident, she finished painting her first self-portrait in oil, a present for her boyfriend Gómez Arias (p. 63). The extraordinary skill in terms of draftsmanship makes it difficult to believe that it was her first portrait. The composition does not reflect any of the new artistic ideas with which she had come into contact but takes the form of an entirely traditional image. Painting had started to become something serious for Kahlo, and, perhaps for the first time, she wondered whether it could become what she did for a living. She also continued to develop intellectually, and wrote several times to Gómez Arias while he was away on an extended trip to Europe. As well as telling him about her convalescence and the pain she still had, she wrote enthusiastically about the European paintings he was discovering on his travels: "Alex, my love […] you have no idea how delighted I am that you have actually seen the wonderful portrait of Eleonor of Toledo, and all the other things you've told me about […]." She then continued right away by recommending painters whose works the inexperienced Gómez Arias should try and see, "everything by Lucas Cranach and Dürer, and above all, Bronzino" (p. 52).[30]

Kahlo's extensive knowledge of European painting should come as no surprise, given that after her father had introduced her to the works of the great masters she then read as much as she could about Paolo Uccello's use of perspective, the brushwork of Velázquez, and Pieter Bruegel the Elder's masterful compositions; she was also very fond of the mystical proportions in El Greco's works, the exquisite draperies painted by Van Dyck, and the masterful portraits by Holbein and Titian. In short, she found that she was now immersed in an aesthetic world that offered a refuge for her newfound creativity. Ultimately, art and

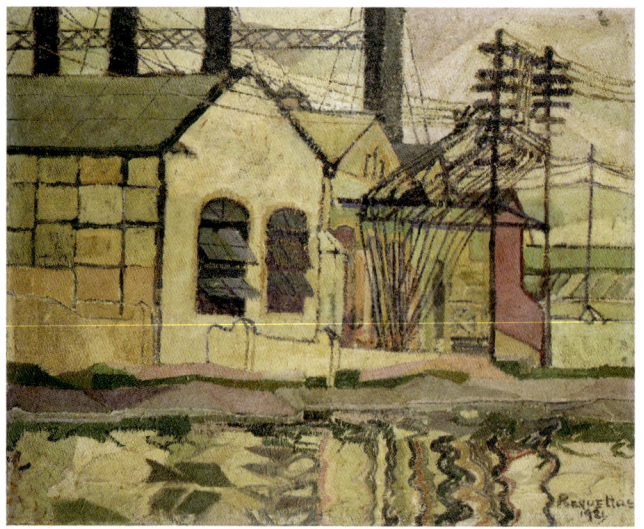

books were a source of relief from her discomfort, but also from the pain caused by Gómez Arias leaving her behind.[31]

This may also have been the reason why *Self-portrait (in a Velvet Dress)* was so packed full of symbolism and educated references to art history, and why Kahlo's likeness in this painting is not the result of studying herself in a mirror but is based on a

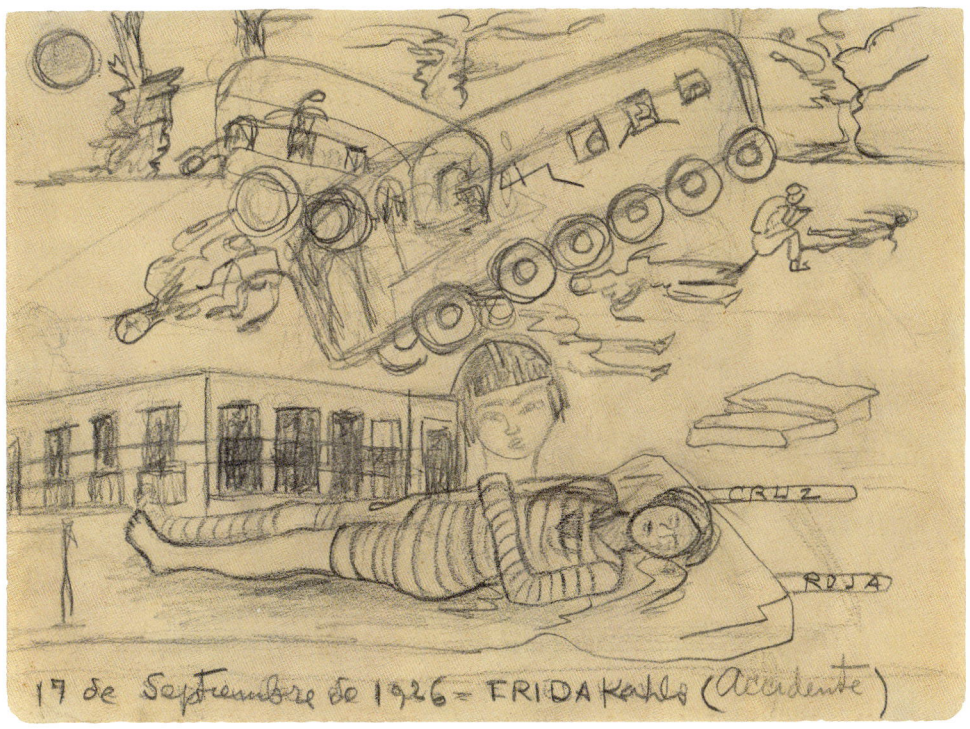

photograph taken by her father on February 7, 1926, in which she appears in profile and the features, including her hairstyle, are the same (p. 22).[32] In the self-portrait, however, she turned her attention away from the strict naturalism of photography, freeing her imagination so that it could explore the aesthetic ideal of the portraits by the great masters of European painting she so admired. Her clothing is both whimsical and elegant, giving her a courtly presence as if in a portrait from the Cinquecento.

At the same time, she has depicted herself with a proud manner similar to that of Eleonora de' Medici in the portrait painted around 1580 by Sofonisba Anguissola (c. 1535–1625), court painter to Philip II of Spain, in which the young woman is shown

Fermín Revueltas, **La Indianilla Substation**, 1921
Oil on canvas, 100 x 120 cm (39½ x 47¼ in.)
Mexico City, SURA Asset Management collection

The Accident, September 17, 1926
Graphite pencil on paper, 20 x 27 cm (7⅞ x 10⅝ in.)
Mexico City, private collection

at marriageable age, as indicated by her red dress. She was the granddaughter of Eleonor of Toledo, whose portrait was painted by Agnolo di Cosimo de Mariano, il Bronzino (1503–1572), which Kahlo greatly admired (p. 52). Eleonora appears distant and aloof although her gaze still makes contact with the viewer, in the same way as Kahlo's does, as she gazes fixedly out at her beloved Gómez Arias, hoping that he will think of her each time he sees the painting. Equally, however, there is the hope that he would sense her reproach for having abandoned her, while at the same time perceiving the depth of passion she was capable of showing him. Kahlo faces the one she loves pleading for his affection, as can be seen too in the letters she sent him over the course of two years and which he did not always answer. But this vulnerable love on Kahlo's part would never again be shown in such a way to the viewers of her paintings. From now on her image would always be a cryptic invention, "a woman in charge of her own destiny, an artist searching for the secrets of painting, a painter with the desire to transcend through art, and through the art of painting herself."[33]

This sophisticated relationship with art history continued in the portraits Kahlo painted subsequently for her friends and family. She was very concerned by the medical expenses her parents had incurred, and after finishing her self-portrait for Gómez Arias she considered the possibility of taking commissions for her painting, and it is even possible that people had begun to pose for her at this stage. In 1927 she completed four more portraits. The first two were of her friends Jesús Ríos y Valles and Ruth Stallsmith (p. 18), but Kahlo threw the first of these into a bonfire because she didn't like the way it had turned out, so there is no knowing what this portrait looked like. The whereabouts of the other portrait are currently unknown, although its existence was recorded in a photograph taken by Guillermo Kahlo, in which it is evident that the face was painted from a photograph by Edward Weston.[34]

Elena Boder, 1925
Gelatin silver print, 6 x 3.5 cm (2⅜ x 1⅜ in.)
Mexico City, Hemeroteca Nacional,
Universidad Nacional Autónoma de México

In April, Kahlo completed her *Portrait of Alicia Galant* (p. 54), who came from a family of German origin and was her neighbor in Coyoacán. The Kahlo sisters were well known in the Del Carmen neighborhood and were devoutly Catholic. They attended the various different religious services in the church of San Juan Bautista, and were acquainted with the wealthiest and most conservative families. As Kahlo's childhood friend Isabel Campos recalled, there were four daughters in the Galant family, "all of them lovely," Esperanza, Marque, Anita, and Alicia, who was the prettiest, "so lovely that she looked like a doll." They sometimes ran into each other at the entrance to the Cuauhtémoc movie theater, and Kahlo in her envy would say to her friends: "Look at that lot! They think they're shit hot!"[35] Even so, she not only decided to paint Alicia's portrait, but also did justice to her fashion-model beauty. Kahlo depicted her against a background at night with a stylized landscape similar to that in her self-portrait from 1926 and which evoked a sense of *fin de siècle* modernism. Both works bear a resemblance to the mannerist portraits of Roberto Montenegro, a noted painter of Mexican symbolism (p. 55). Alicia is wearing an elegant velvet dress in an art déco style, as elaborate in its design as the one Kahlo herself wore in the aforementioned photograph her father took of her that she used as the source for her self-portrait. It is possible that both dresses were made by Kahlo's mother, Matilde Calderón, who had a reputation for being an excellent seamstress and took pleasure in dressing her daughters for every occasion.[36] The somewhat artificial pose and refined gestures are reminiscent of the anatomical distortions and affectations that characterize Bronzino's mannerist portraits. With such a nod to art history it seems that Kahlo wanted to stress how serious she was about her new profession, and she must have been very pleased with the result, so much so that she wrote on the back: "My first work of art, Frida Kahlo, 1927."

The fourth of the portraits Kahlo painted that year was of Miguel N. Lira, as commissioned by the poet himself (p. 61), the two of them having first met in 1920 when Kahlo was at the Escuela Normal Primaria. In 1922 they were at the Escuela Nacional Preparatoria together, where Lira became Kahlo's mentor, and then her friend for many years. They also both joined Los Cachuchas (the Peaked Caps), a group with an anarchist bent that included Gómez Arias, José Gómez Robleda, Manuel González Ramírez, Carmen Jaime, Agustín Lira, Jesús Ríos y Valles, and Alfonso Villa.[37] Lira's appreciation of the poetry of Manuel Maples Arce (1898–1981) led him to join the Stridentist group, which had been founded by Maples Arce, and to sign their manifesto *¡Viva el mole de guajolote!* (Here's to turkey with mole sauce!) as published by the group in Puebla on January 1, 1923.

Stridentism was the first political avant-garde movement in Mexico to call for a radical renewal in literature and the arts in the years following the revolution. Its members

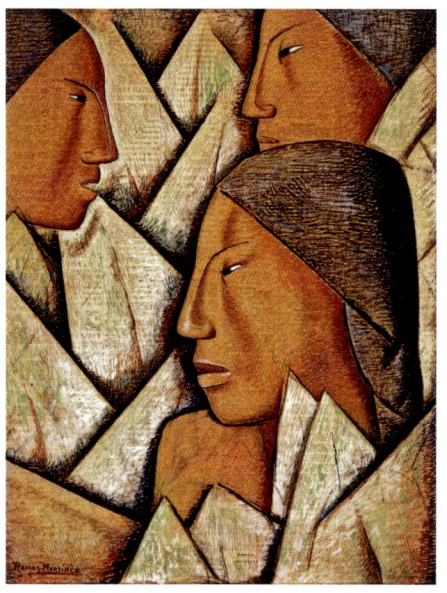

demanded that artists turn their back on tradition and decorative nationalism, including the Best Maugard method, and instead look toward the revitalizing modernity of their own present.[38] Mexico's transformation into a modern country led them to celebrate cities, industry, and technology, while at the same time demanding complete change in state policies and the teaching of the arts.[39] The Cachuchas group at the Escuela Nacional Preparatoria was clearly fertile ground for these Dadaist demands, and the young students who had joined it, Kahlo included, duly adopted an anarchist stance at this time. In 1927, she and Lira were experimenting with a Stridentist aesthetic through drawings, paintings, and watercolors, some of which can be seen in her portrait of Lira painted in the same year. At his request Kahlo portrayed him using the Cubist language of Rivera's portrait of Ramón Gómez de la Serna, from 1915 (p. 60), for, as Tibol noted, "To say that something was in the style of Gómez de la Serna meant that it was avant-garde, and the avant-garde in Mexico at that time was Stridentism."[40]

Meeting in cafés has long been associated with intellectuals and artists, and in Mexico this tradition can be traced back to the emergence of modernism at the end of the 19th century. The Stridentists tended to congregate with Maples Arce at the Café de Nadie, and the Cachuchas group followed suit at the so-called Chinese cafés. Kahlo made one of them the subject of a drawing she did between 1926 and 1927, and which is considered a preparatory study for *Pancho Villa and Adelita* (pp. 28, 59), an oil painting that was never completed.[41] The drawing is especially interesting because it shows how much Kahlo and

Alfredo Ramos Martínez, **Primitive Mixtecs**, *c.* 1929
Tempera on newsprint, 56.7 x 42.2 cm (22⅜ x 16⅝ in.)
Private collection, courtesy Louis Stern Fine Arts, West Hollywood

Peter A. Juley & Son, **Frida Kahlo**, *c.* 1930
Gelatin silver print, 25.4 x 20.3 cm (10 x 8 in.)
Washington, D.C., Smithsonian American Art Museum,
Archives and Special Collections, collection Peter A. Juley & Son

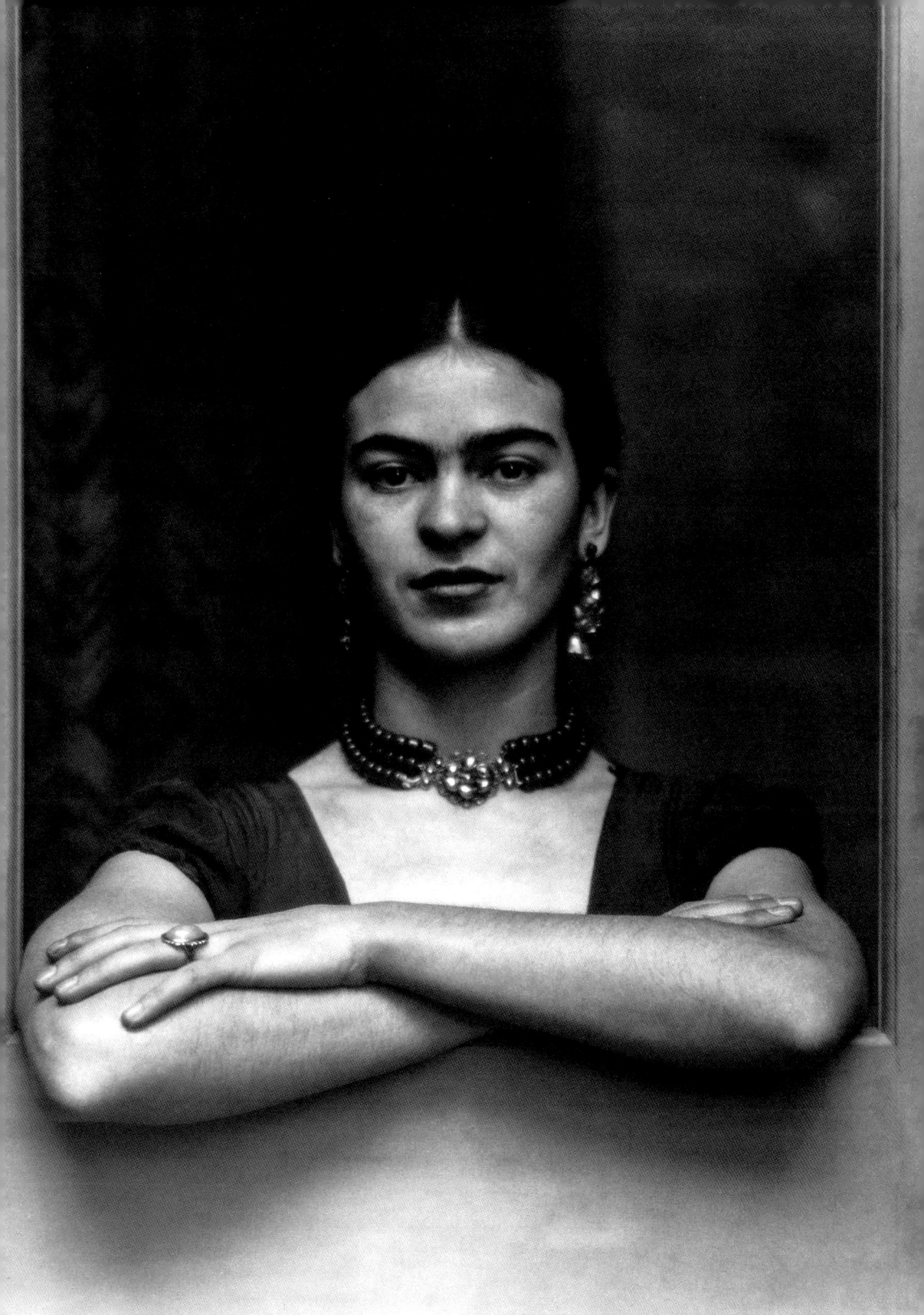

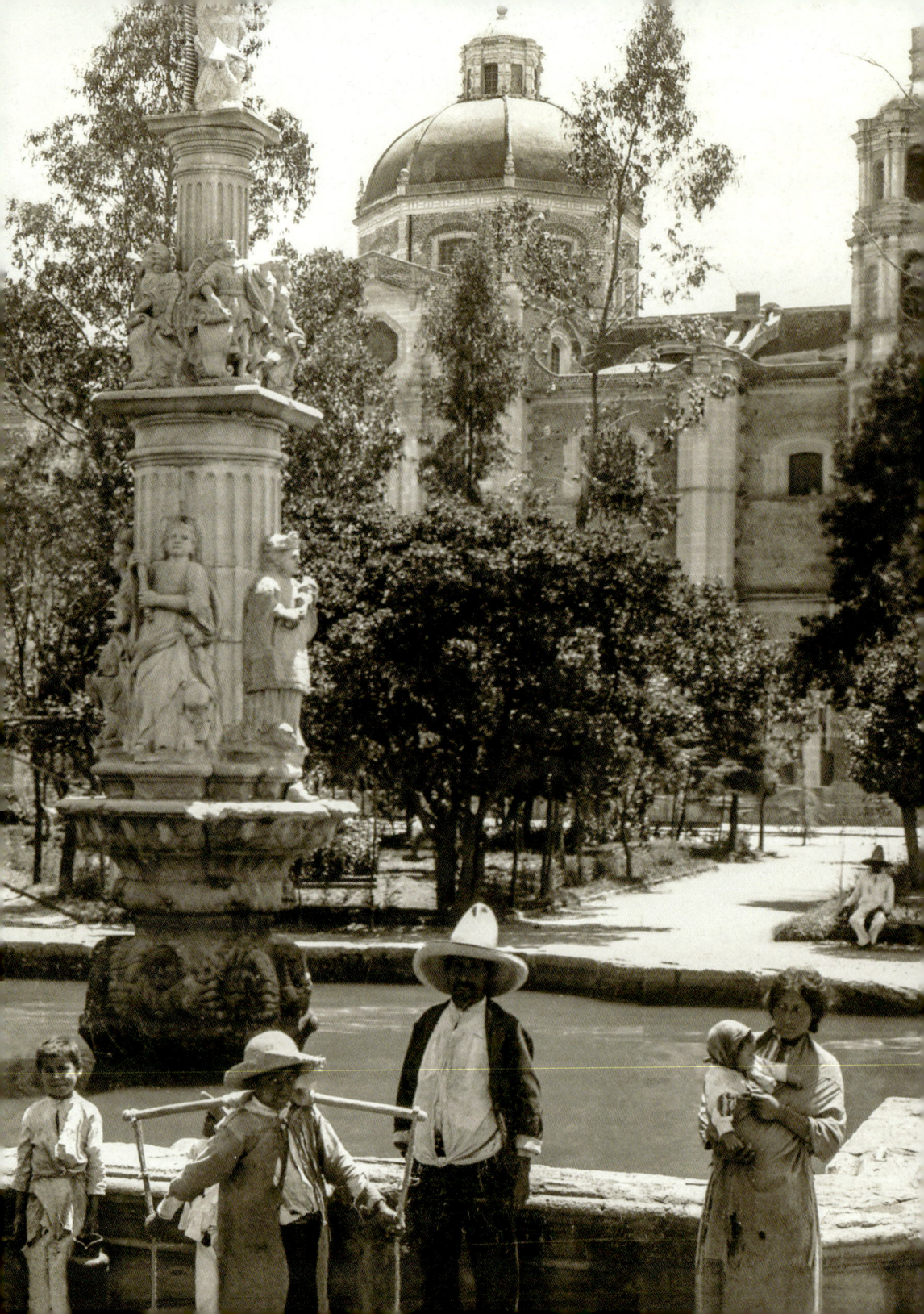

the Cachuchas in general had absorbed the Stridentists' avant-garde ideas. There is an unusual sense of modernity in the drawing, even for Mexico in the 1920s, while the bold diagonal lines are surprising and at the same time reminiscent of some of the Stridentist work done by Ramón Alva de la Canal (p. 58). The directional lines, which intersect and terminate in sharp angles, generate a sense of movement that converges on the central figure of a woman, Kahlo herself, while the other pictorial elements and the five other figures, seated around a table and all of them members of Los Cachuchas, revolve around her. Apart from its artistic interest, the drawing is of great value in the way that it helps to fill in the blanks in the unfinished painting *Pancho Villa and Adelita*. The young intellectuals are shown debating which of two aesthetic paths they should follow: whether to be the youthful face of the various different artistic trends that had emerged under the aegis of the Revolution of 1910 (the Muralist Movement, the Open-air Painting Schools, the Pro-Mexican Art Movement, and Best Maugard's Drawing Method) or to side with the radical arguments of the Stridentists and become the generation of change that would lead Mexico into a new era of justice and modernity.

Mexico was not the only place though where discussions were under way about renewing the formal languages of the avant-garde movements that had been active in the years before the First World War. Similar debates were taking place in Europe as well, particularly in Germany in the Weimar Republic (1918–1933), where, following the avant-garde frenzy of Expressionism, a new period had begun in which Germany's great artistic tradition of the 16th century and the artists of German Romanticism were being reassessed. By 1925 the search for new aesthetic directions had coalesced in the so-called New Objectivity movement (Neue Sachlichkeit), a name coined by the German historian and critic Gustav Hartlaub (1884–1963) for the exhibition he organized in Mannheim in 1925 where he brought together works by a number of artists including Otto Dix (1891–1969) (p. 62), George Grosz (1893–1959), Rudolf Schlichter (1890–1955), Georg Scholz (1890–1945), and, especially, Christian Schad (1894–1982) (p. 56). These artists all called for a new realism and a reinterpretation of the conventions adhered to by Renaissance masters, in order to reclaim some of their qualities for themselves, such as realistic representation and high levels of pictorial mastery.[42]

The most conservative faction among these modern artists, who were seen as the exponents of "magical realism" to use the name applied to them by the historian and critic Franz Roh (1890–1965), looked to Italy for inspiration for their painting. Hartlaub's and Roh's ideas were debated in Mexico throughout the 1920s and particularly after Roh's book

Plaza and church of Santo Domingo in Mexico City, *c.* 1920

Nach-Expressionismus, Magischer Realismus: Probleme der neuesten europäischen Malerei (1925; *Post-Expressionism, Magical Realism: Problems of the New European Painting*) was translated into Spanish and published in Madrid in 1927 by Revista de Occidente. This small book was circulated in Mexico among Stridentist writers and artists, and Kahlo's friendship with Lira made it easier for her to gain access to the writings of both these German authors. In this way, the great pictorial tradition of art in Germany, which Kahlo had known about and admired since childhood thanks to her father, made its own impact in the artistic debate in Mexico at this time. These same old German masters were also the very figures the artists of the New Objectivity movement had used as the historical foundation for their own desire to represent the reality of their time, in an objective manner and removed from any suggestion of Expressionist subjectivity, yet while maintaining their celebration of urban life and their immediate everyday surroundings. The objectivity in their engagement with the instability and chaos of modern life, and the high regard in which they held the artists of the German and Italian Renaissance, in other words, the balance between modern figurative art and tradition, came together in the idea of a "return to order" advocated by the followers of New Objectivity.[43] Painting was not to reject the importance of representing the reality of its time, but this was to be done with extreme skill and veracity.

In Mexico, arguments between those who supported the Open-air Painting Schools and those who opposed them had become radically polarized. For Ramos Martínez, the solution was clear: what was required was to embrace the cultural reality of a modern Mexico, born out of the Revolution, but to do so with formal authenticity and without political rhetoric. Kahlo and other Mexican painters at the time, including María Izquierdo (1902–1955), Fernando Leal, and Gabriel Fernández Ledesma, defended the Ramos Martínez schools, which in their view had brought great creative potential to the arts in Mexico. To Kahlo the choice was clearer than for many others since she understood the importance of developing a modern Mexican approach to painting, at a national level, yet at the same time she did not believe that the European tradition in which it had been created should be abandoned.

Roh's book and the ideas put forward by Hartlaub's New Objectivity offer an explanation, at least in part, for the straightforwardly modern quality of a number of the portraits Kahlo painted between 1927 and 1929, for example, the portrait of Agustín M. Olmedo (p. 57) and that of Alejandro Gómez Arias (p. 63). The works in which Kahlo fully embraced the ideas of New Objectivity were, in this author's view, *Portrait of Cristina, My Sister* (p. 68) and *Two Women (Portrait of Salvadora and Herminia)* (p. 65). Both these works were signed and dated 1928, which is to say at the height of the discussions for and against Ramos Martínez's ideas mentioned earlier, and both were painted in the garden of

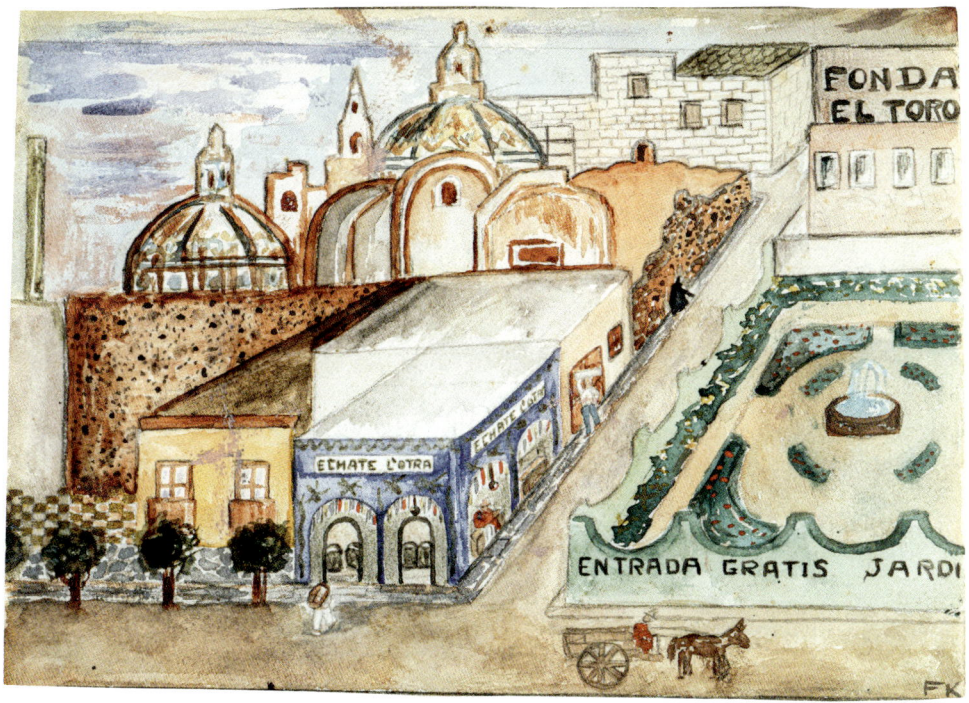

Échate la otra (Have Another One), 1925
Watercolor and pencil on paper, 18 x 24.5 cm (7⅛ x 9⅝ in.). Mexico, State Government
of Tlaxcala, Instituto Tlaxcalteca de la Cultura, Museo de Arte de Tlaxcala

her parents' home in Coyoacán. It is apparent in these works how exceptionally well Kahlo has developed in terms of her technical abilities, and in place of the earlier distortions she had borrowed from Italian mannerism there is now a realistic style of representation, with accomplished drawing skills and restraint in the composition. The stylistic artifice of the previous works has been left behind and instead the modernity of her time has been captured with remarkable visual clarity. The manner of painting Kahlo used in the portrait of her sister Cristina bears a close similarity to the portraits painted by Christian Schad between 1925 and 1926 (p. 69). In the same way as Kahlo, Schad admired Bronzino's mannerist portraits (p. 52), as is evident in his own portraits from the 1920s. Cristina is shown posing in an idyllic landscape with metaphysical associations, in which the leaves of a grapefruit tree *(Citrus paradisi)* are encroaching on one side, an allusion, therefore, to the Tree of Knowledge, of truth and life, from that lost Biblical paradise, which turns Cristina into an Eve for the modern world.[44]

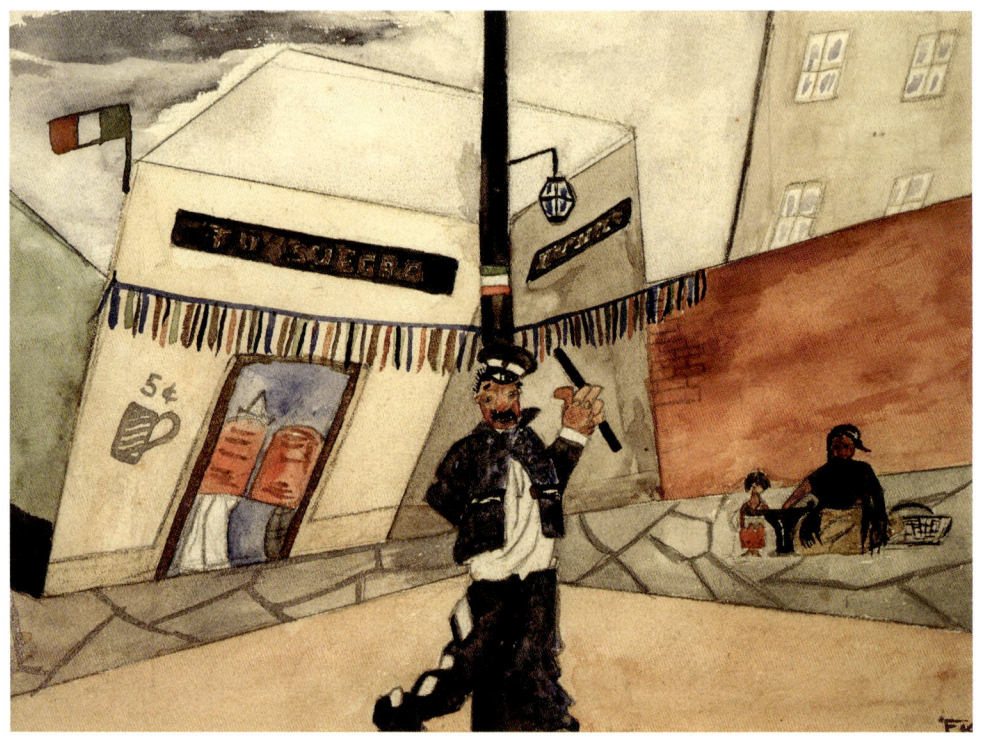

Saloon "Tu Suegra", July 18, 1927
Watercolor and pencil on paper, 18.5 x 24.6 cm (7¼ x 9⅔ in.)
Private collection

Marriage of Diego Rivera to Frieda Kahlo, August 23, 1929
Newspaper *La Prensa*. Mexico City, Fototeca,
Hemeroteca y Biblioteca Mario Vázquez Raña,
Archivo y Fundación de la Organización Editorial Mexicana

PORTESGIL

Hará Respetar el Voto Popular

INFORMACION EN PAGINA TRES

TIRO DE AYER:
47,183
EJEMPLARES

LA PRENSA
Diario Ilustrado de la Mañana

Registrada como artículo de segunda clase en México, D. F., el 6 de septiembre de 1928.

FALTAN **7** días para Suscribirse

TOMO I. NUM. 358 — MEXICO, D. F., VIERNES 23 DE AGOSTO DE 1929. — 24 Páginas Cinco Centavos

DAMA VICTIMA DE EXTRAÑA AVENTURA

INFORMACION EN PAGINA TRES

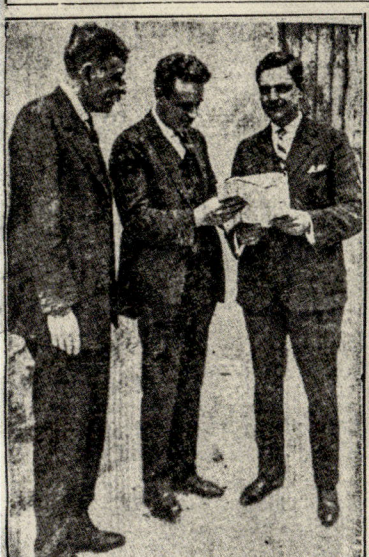

AMPARADO.—La justicia federal amparó ayer a J. Miguel Félix Cuevas, quien había sido condenado por el jurado popular a sufrir dieciséis años de prisión, por haber dado muerte a su esposa y a su suegro, y haber herido a su cuñado. El licenciado Víctor Velázquez, que defiende a Cuevas, se presentó ayer en Belén para comunicar a éste la resolución, dictada en vista de haber sido juzgado dos veces por el mismo delito, estando esto estrictamente en la Constitución. No se sabe si el procesado saldrá desde luego a la calle, o si tendrá que esperar el fallo de la Suprema Corte. Información en página 22.

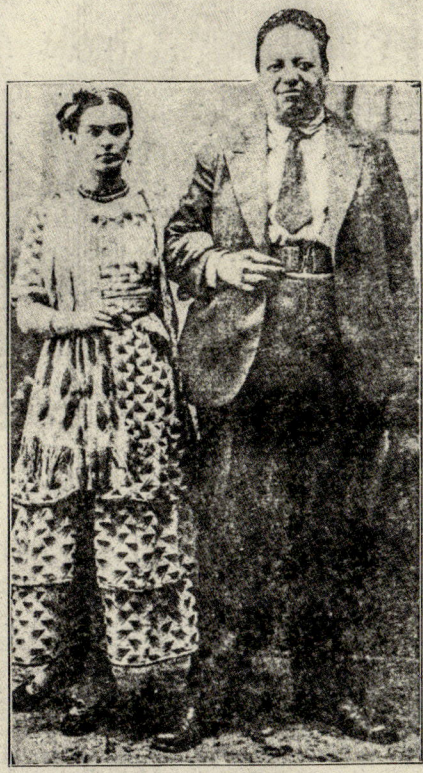

SE CASO DIEGO RIVERA.—El miércoles último, en la vecina población de Coyoacán, contrajo matrimonio el discutido pintor Diego Rivera con la señorita Frieda Kahlo, una de sus discípulas. La novia vistió, como puede verse, sencillísimas ropas de calle, y el pintor Rivera de americana y sin chaleco. El enlace no tuvo pompa alguna; se celebró en un ambiente cordialísimo y con toda modestia, sin ostentación y sin aparatosas ceremonias. Los novios fueron muy felicitados, después de su enlace, por algunos íntimos.

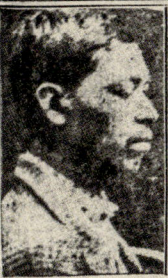

ENCAPILLADO.—Erasmo Vilchis, de quien se asegura que será entregado hoy al Departamento Central para ser encapillado, antes de ser ejecutado. Información en página 23.

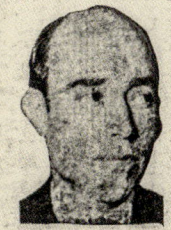

EN EL CONGRESO.—Licenciado Federido Medrano, quien resultó ayer electo Presidente de la Cámara de Diputados, para el mes de septiembre. Información en página 3.

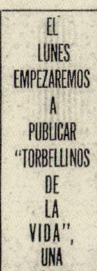

EL LUNES EMPEZAREMOS A PUBLICAR "TORBELLINOS DE LA VIDA", UNA NOVELA SENSACIONAL

Meanwhile, in the same way as Raphael painted his lover Margherita Luti in the famous portrait known as *La Fornarina* with her naked torso set against a dense background of myrtle bushes (where they symbolize faithfulness but are also associated with the fertility of the goddess Aphrodite), Kahlo used a background of leaves from a grapefruit tree with two ripe fruits and butterflies, symbols of change and transformation, for her portrait of Salvadora and Herminia, the two maids at her parents' house.[45] Kahlo was employing a visual and sensory approach that stemmed from a classical tradition and which was very different from what was known in Mexico, a kind of Neoplatonic innovation in the way the composition was presented in which the subject's portrait was inserted into a landscape filled with significance and meaning, just as Leonardo da Vinci had done (p. 64). In this way Kahlo was able to reconcile the realistic representation of her immediate surroundings, as New Objectivity demanded, with the moralizing aspect of Renaissance painting. However, the immediate formal reference for *Two Women (Portrait of Salvadora and Herminia)* was to be found in Mexico, in the paintings by Ramos Martínez from the late 1920s, which his students at the Open-air Painting Schools considered the epitome of modern Mexican art (p. 34).

By 1929, Kahlo had found her own style, which conformed to her concept of what modern painting should be in terms of its content while at the same time staying true to her own sensibility. From this point on, she found new inspiration in other sources, including the classic style of photographic portraiture from the early years of the century, a source also used by Tamayo and Izquierdo. In 1929, she began to paint a new portrait of a young woman (p. 76), who must have been someone she felt close to, someone she had a special affection for. She used the same setting that appeared in her own picture, entitled *Self-portrait (Time Flies)* (p. 75), which was painted around the same time and heralded an open modernity. An airplane and an alarm clock can be understood as metaphors for the dawn of new ideas about art in the post-revolution period; these iconographic elements reference the Stridentism of the painters and poets associated with this movement.

In each case the figure of a woman is shown half-length, positioned in front of a window with heavy drapes that are tied back on both sides by a thick cord so that the wrought-iron railing of a balcony is revealed, a visual device that had previously been explored by others artists, such as Tamayo. The similarity of the two paintings in terms of their composition suggests that Kahlo wanted them to be connected, and in doing so that she would be associated with the unidentified woman in the second painting, which, in the absence

Víctor M. Reyes, **Wedding portrait of Frida Kahlo and Diego Rivera** (detail), 1929
Hand-colored gelatin silver print, 18 x 12.6 cm (7⅛ x 5 in.)
Boston, Museum of Fine Arts, anonymous gift, inv. 2016.112

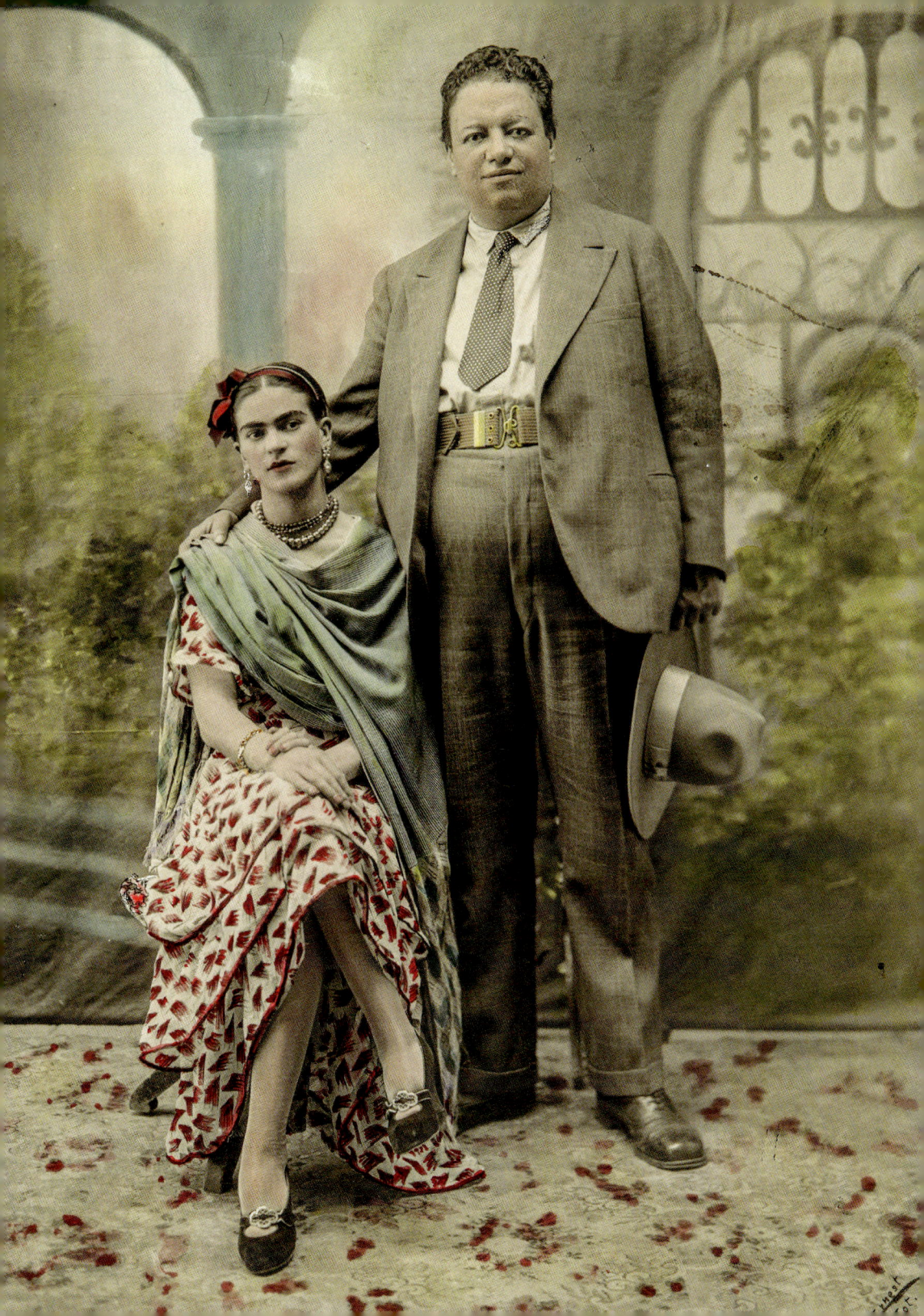

of any name in the long speech scroll above her head, is entitled *Portrait of a Lady in White* (p. 76). But who was this tight-lipped young woman that Kahlo decided to depict, dressed so elegantly in the fashion of the 1920s? In my view it could be Elena Boder, a classmate of Kahlo's at the Escuela Nacional Preparatoria, given the resemblance to a photograph of Boder taken in 1925 which I discovered recently in my research for this introductory essay in the archives of the Universidad Nacional Autónoma de México (p. 32). Boder was a Russian immigrant who had been born in Odessa in the Ukraine but had fled the Bolshevik Revolution, traveling first to Japan before reaching Mexico in around 1919. After studying medicine, she emigrated permanently to the United States in 1932, where she became a respected neurosurgeon. Many years later she met Kahlo again, who dedicated one of her final still lifes to her (p. 341).

In 1927, Kahlo began to spend time with Rivera and also joined the Communist Party.[46] After the two of them were married in 1929, the unconventional couple became a magnet for the press, who referred to the event as the union of the "elephant" and the "dove" (p. 41). This was certainly something more than a simple physical metaphor since it evoked an image of Rivera as being like a wise pachyderm, with a long road already traveled and two marriages behind him, while Kahlo was just beginning to "take flight," having left her youthful idyll, with her boyfriend Gómez Arias, in the past. She must have realized quite quickly that Rivera was attracting all the attention, that he was literally front-page news, and that if she did not find her own personality as an artist she would be regarded as nothing more than the artist's wife, "Madame Rivera," as she was referred to in the newspapers in San Francisco.

It was not just her youth that separated her from Rivera and his vast experience as a painter, but more significantly the fact that the two of them had diametrically opposed views on the function of painting. Rivera firmly believed that murals could serve as a tool for social change in his time, and that the artist's role was to be an active agent in effecting that change. For Kahlo, however, since she had become involved with Rivera painting had become the best means of knowing herself, as a kind of exercise in introspection. Moreover, this shift in her perspective was rapidly becoming established all the while she stood by her "beloved husband." In the end, the collision between the two opposite types did not take place in relation to their feelings for each other, but their sense of aesthetics.

Kahlo continued to try and add to her knowledge by absorbing everything she could about other painters that attracted her attention, whether seen in books or magazines, or from stylistic references she read in poetry or art criticism. It all contributed to the process in which she had immersed herself, to construct the inexhaustible source of her own artistic inspiration: herself. By the time she painted her second self-portrait in oil three

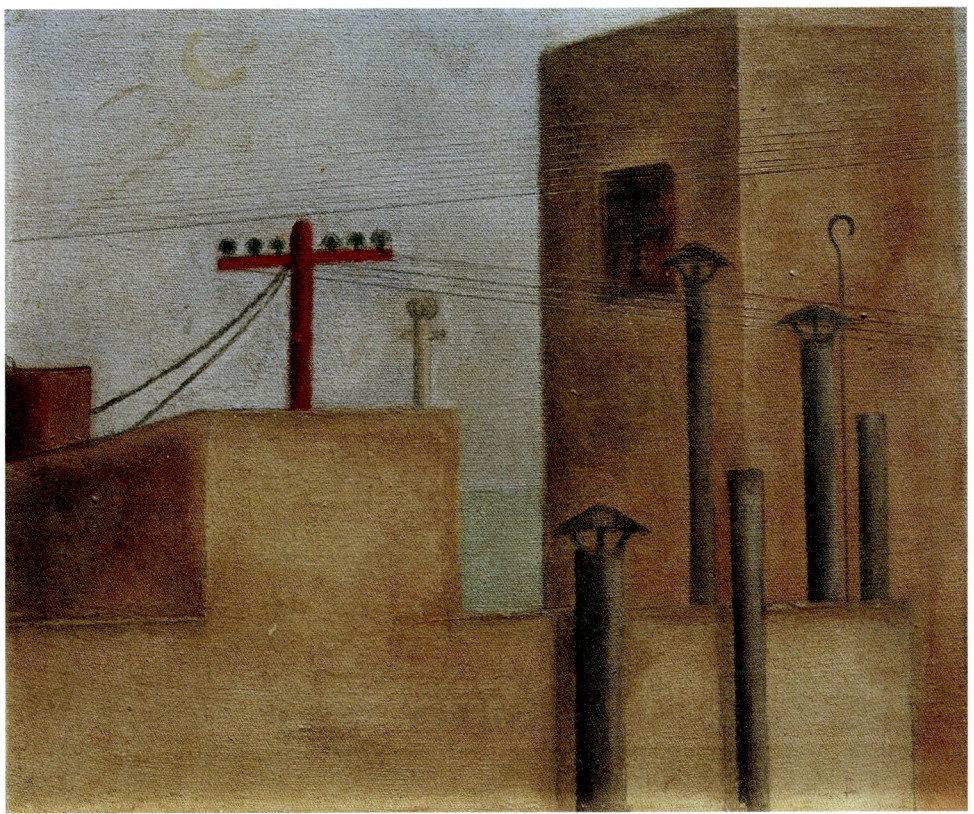

years later in 1929, the previously mentioned *Self-portrait (Time Flies)* (p. 75), Kahlo was a "firmly rooted" woman, to paraphrase the title of the noucentist novel *La ben plantada* by Eugeni d'Ors (1881–1954), which she had read and reread only two years previously while she was convalescing after the bus accident.[47] Kahlo seems to have identified with Teresa, the literary protagonist d'Ors presented as the personification of all the virtues of a Mediterranean people and their classical roots, and in her second self-portrait she depicted herself in the image of a young Mexican woman with intellectual aspirations and a road of her own to travel, next to, but not subordinate to Rivera. It is

Urban Landscape, *c.* 1925–1931
Oil on canvas, 34.4 x 40.2 cm (13½ x 15⅞ in.)
Mexico City, Secretaría de Cultura, Instituto Nacional
de Bellas Artes y Literatura, Museo Nacional de Arte

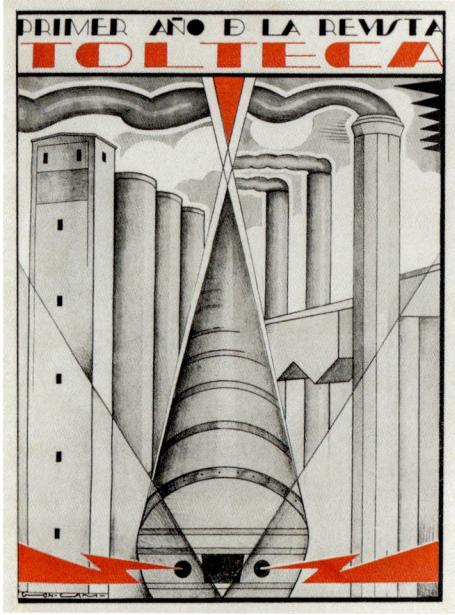

thus a self-portrait with which Kahlo ended the first phase of her life as a woman and as an artist, the phase that ran from her adolescence and the early dreams of youth up to her marriage and her development into an established artist.

Before leaving Mexico to go and live in San Francisco, where Rivera had been asked to paint a mural at the Art Institute, Kahlo made another painting which was unlike the rest of her works and has been largely neglected over the years. *Urban Landscape* (p. 45) remained with the Kahlo Calderón family until it was sold to a collector, and depicts a small view of Mexico City in the 1920s with concrete buildings, utility pole, telegraph cables, and chimneys, as if Kahlo wanted to make a study of a modern utopia.[48] The pictorial elements in part recall the Stridentopolis referred to in the manifestos and writings of the Stridentist group, or the urban imagery in Maples Arce's Bolshevik poems that appear in *Urbe* (1924): "Oh city, filled with the tension of your cables and industry, alive with the sound of wings and engines."[49] These were the lyrical visions that influenced painters such as Fermín Revueltas (1901–1935) (p. 30), Fernando Leal, and Jean Charlot (1898–1979), and which were introduced by Lira to Kahlo and the other Cachuchas.[50]

Mexico's transformation into a modern country was a matter of interest to countless artists with all sorts of different visual and conceptual strategies, ranging from those who sought refuge from change in idyllic landscape scenes showing country folk living in harmony with nature (as encouraged to some extent by Ramos Martínez's Open-air Painting Schools) to those who wanted to document Mexico's gradual transformation from a rural society into a country of large industrialized cities, a kind of paradise that was being transformed, on a daily basis, by the unstoppable advance of the modern world.[51]

The visual purity of *Urban Landscape* establishes a distance between this work by Kahlo and both the color palette of the Pro-Mexican Art Movement and the interpretive

Jorge González Camarena, **Cover of *Tolteca***, no. 1, June 1928
Mexico City, private collection

freedom of the Open-air Painting Schools, and instead brings it closer to the urban paintings of Rodríguez Lozano, who painted similar industrial landscapes with geometric volumes in around 1925, somewhat in the style of Le Corbusier's paintings from the 1920s. Kahlo's image was created by means of volumetric blocks and a limited range of colors, which cause it to resemble some of the metaphysical spaces painted by Giorgio Morandi (1890–1964). Her aim was not to depict a faithful representation of something that actually existed, but of what was possible within her imagination. The idea was thus avant-garde, although the painted result itself was still in the process of taking shape, as was the case in Kahlo's Stridentist paintings from 1927. There may also have been another reason for the constructivism in *Urban Landscape*, which opens up the possibility that it was in fact painted in the early 1930s. In 1931, Associated Portland Cement Manufacturers launched a national competition in Mexico through their local affiliate, La Tolteca, inviting painters, draftsmen, and photographers to submit works that reflected the modern qualities of their newly built factory in Mexico City (p. 46). The jury consisted of Mariano Moctezuma, director of the School of Engineering, the architect Manuel Ortiz Monasterio, and Rivera.[52] Kahlo was not eligible to take part because her husband was on the jury, but it could be that the competition and subject matter inspired her to explore a similar celebration of concrete as a building material.

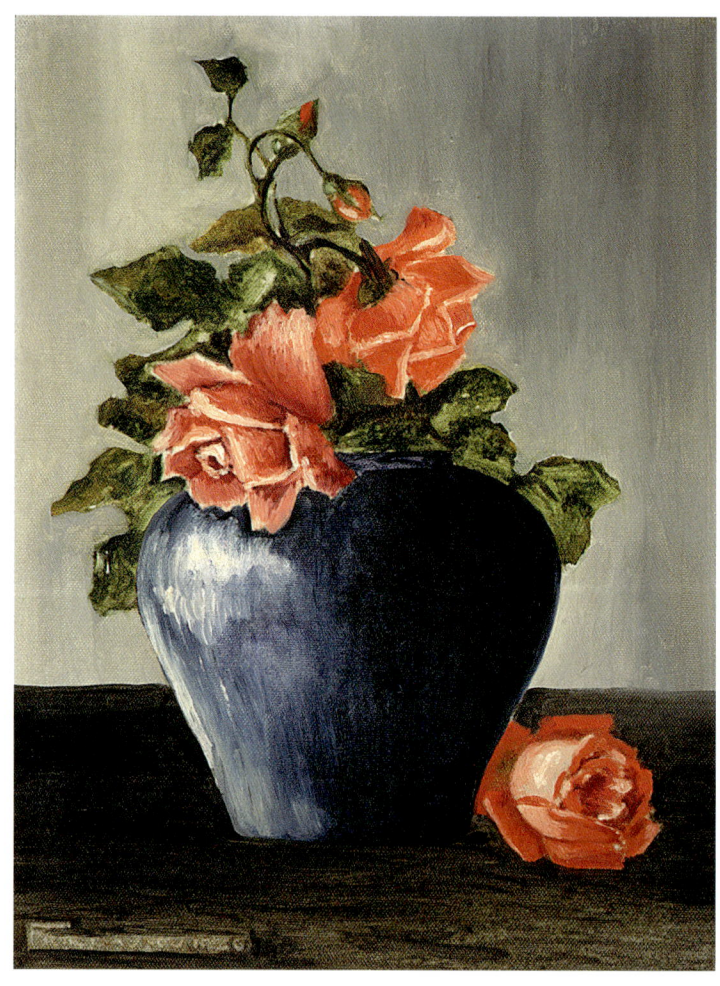

Still Life (with Roses), *c.* 1925
Oil on canvas, mounted on wood, 41.3 x 30.5 cm (16¼ x 12 in.)
Private collection, courtesy Sotheby's, New York

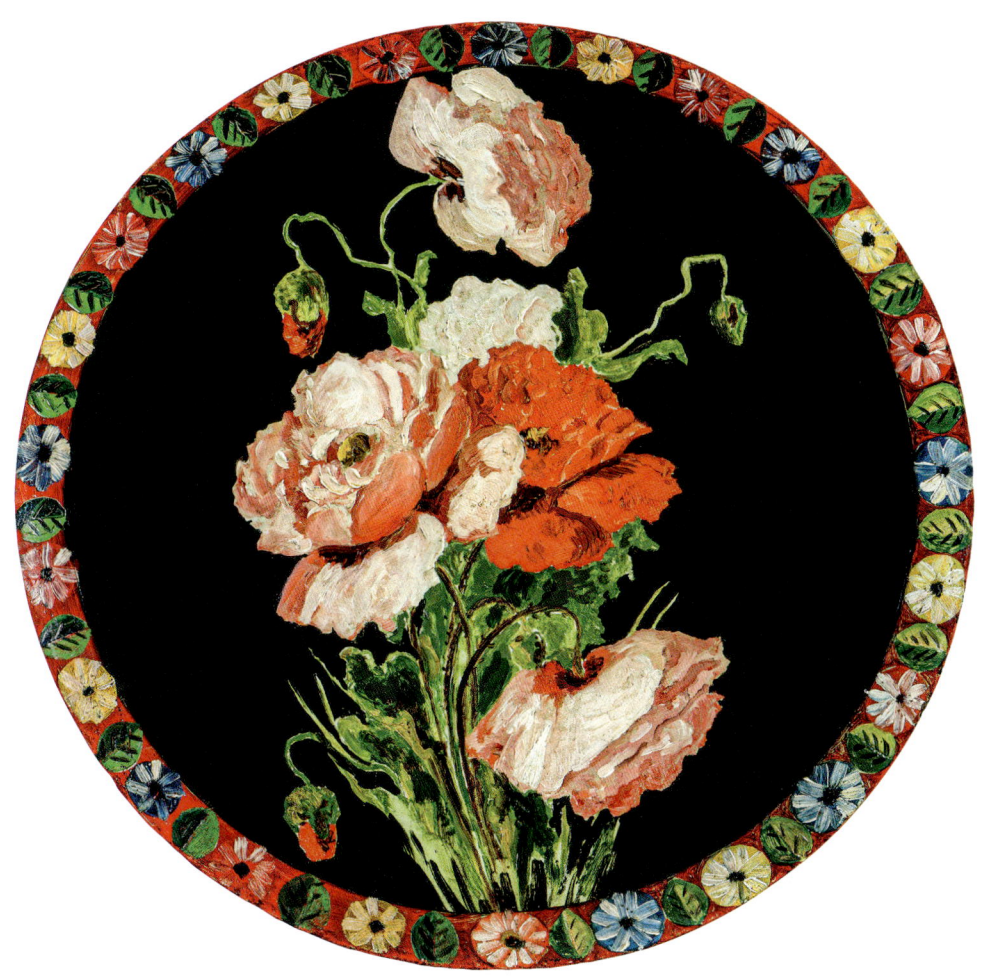

Tray with Poppies, *c.* 1924
Oil on wood, diameter 40.5 cm (16 in.)
Mexico City, Isolda P. Kahlo collection

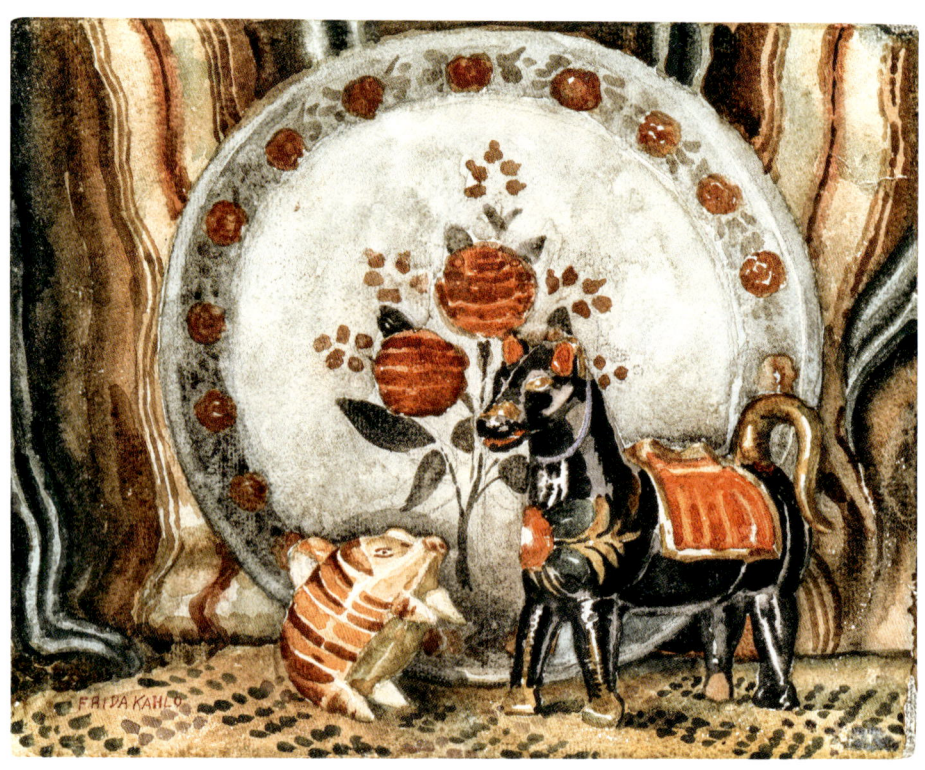

Horse and Little Pig, *c.* 1928
Watercolor on paper, 27.9 x 34.3 cm (11 x 13½ in.)
Private collection, courtesy Sotheby's, New York

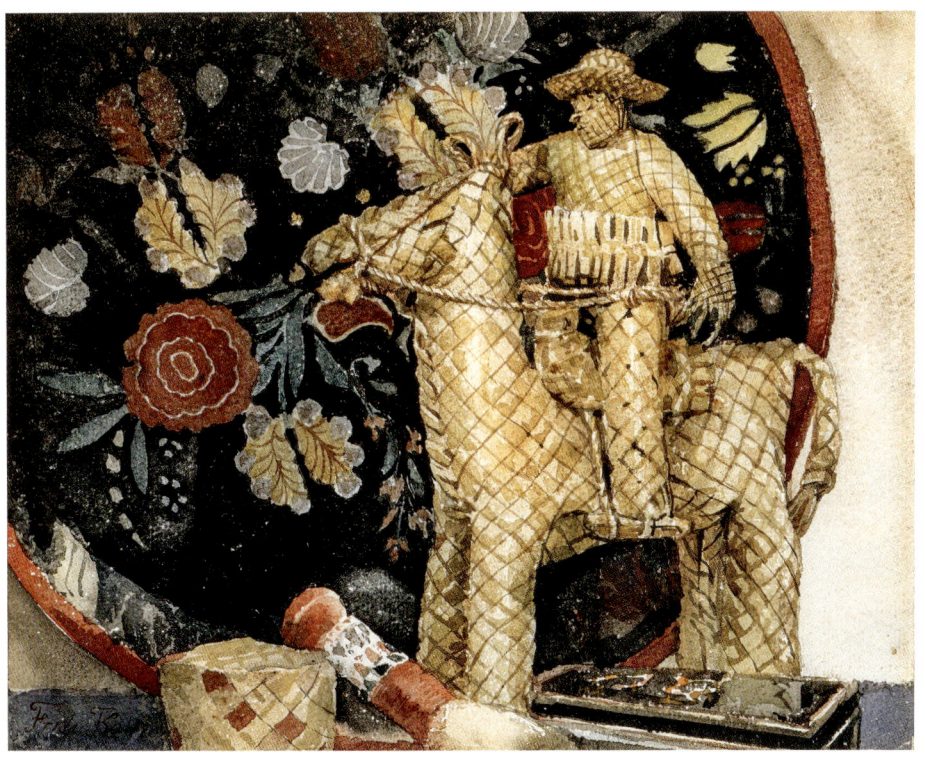

Little Mexican Horse, *c.* 1928
Watercolor on paper, 27 x 33 cm (10⅝ x 13 in.)
Mexico, private collection

Agnolo Bronzino,
Eleonor of Toledo and Her Son Giovanni, 1545
Oil on poplar panel, 115 x 96 cm (45⅜ x 37⅞ in.)
Florence, Gallerie degli Uffizi

Self-portrait (in a Velvet Dress), September 1926
Oil on canvas, 79.9 x 59.9 cm (31⅛ x 23⅜ in.)
Mexico City, private collection

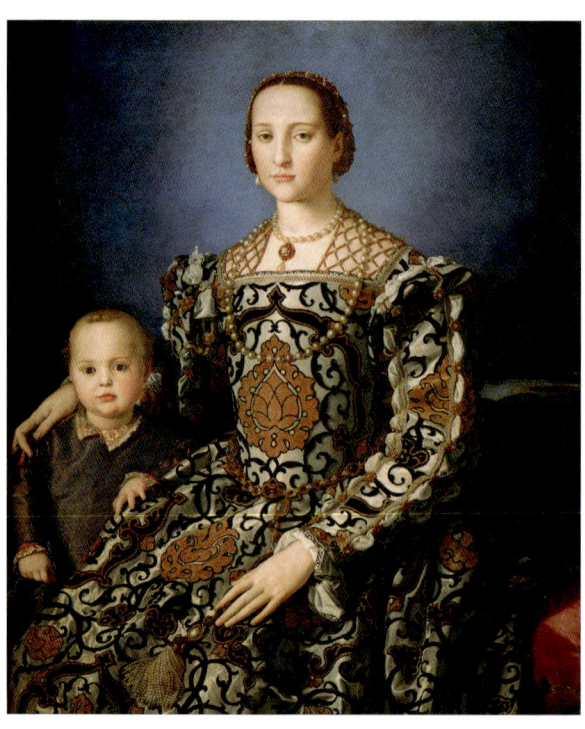

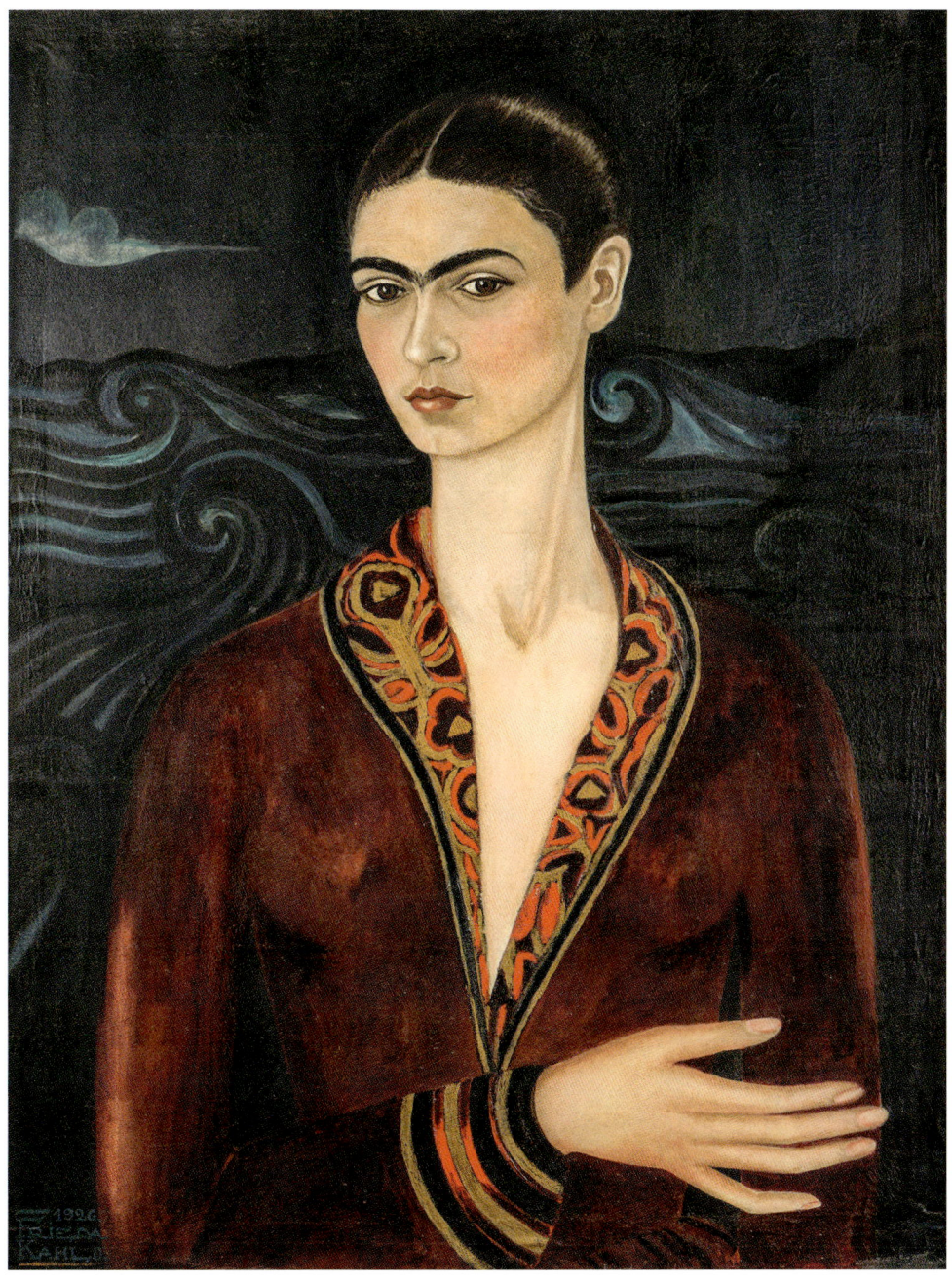

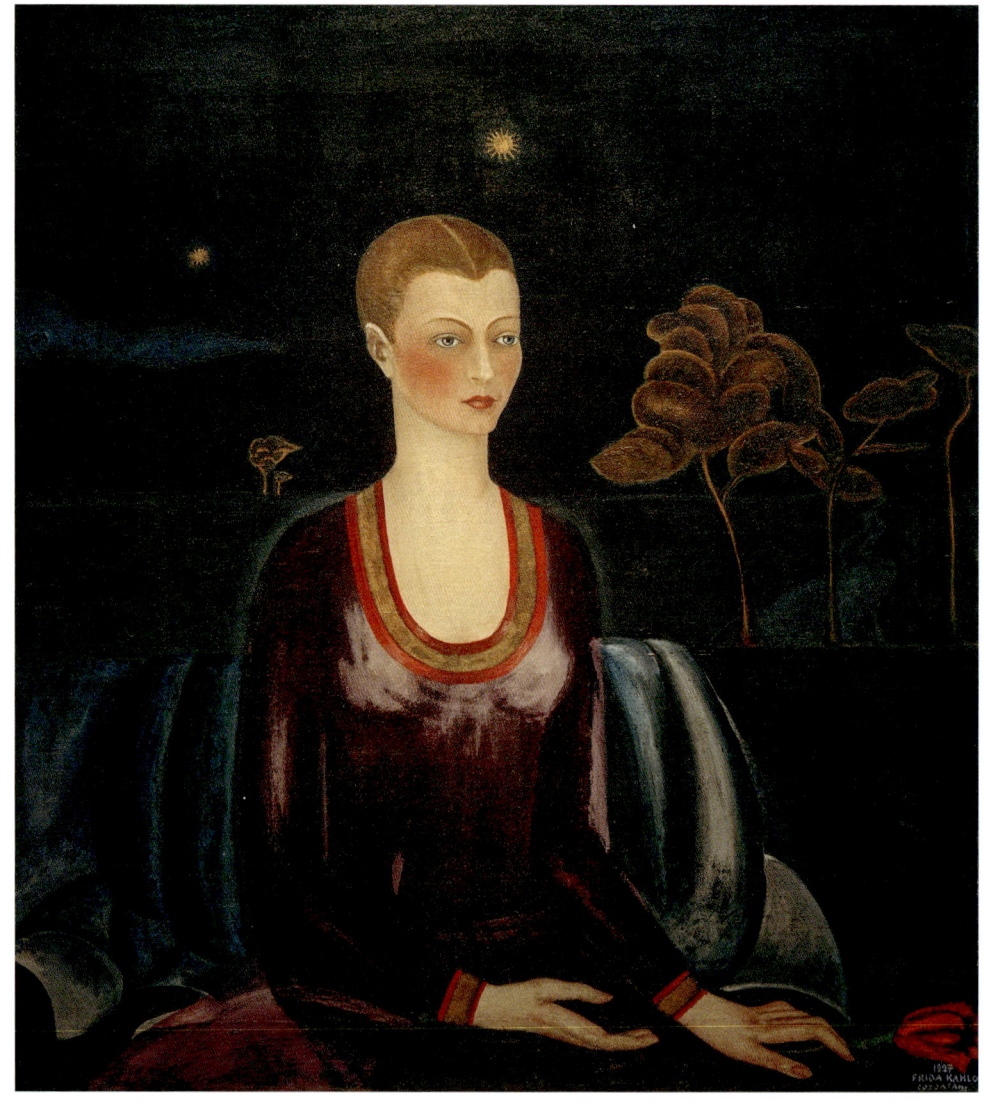

Portrait of Alicia Galant, April 1927
Oil on canvas, 107 x 93.5 cm (42⅛ x 36¾ in.)
Mexico City, Xochimilco, Museo Dolores Olmedo

Roberto Montenegro,
Portrait of Xavier Villaurrutia y González, *c.* 1925
Oil on canvas, 69.9 x 54.9 cm (27½ x 21⅝ in.)
Private collection, courtesy Christie's, New York

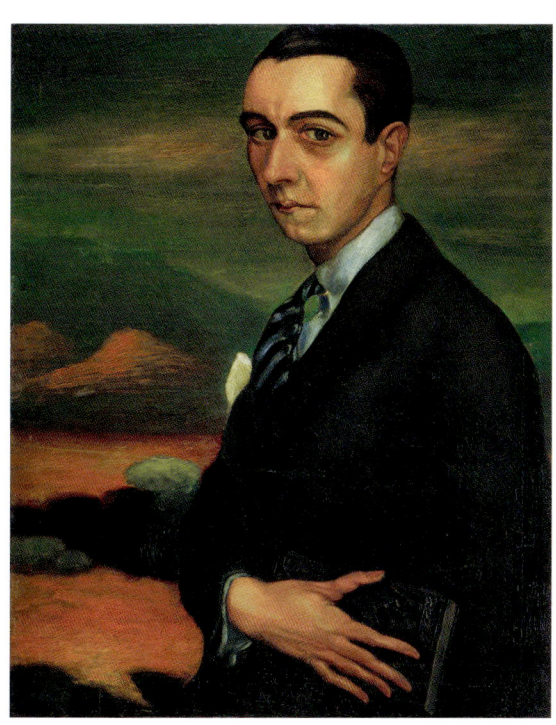

Christian Schad, **Portrait of the Writer Ludwig Bäumer**, 1927
Oil on wood, 61 x 50 cm (24 x 19¾ in.). Berlin, Berlinische Galerie,
Landesmuseum für Moderne Kunst, Photographie und Architektur

Portrait of Agustín M. Olmedo, *c.* 1927
Oil on canvas, 79 x 59 cm (31⅛ x 23¼ in.)
Mexico City, Coyoacán, Museo Frida Kahlo

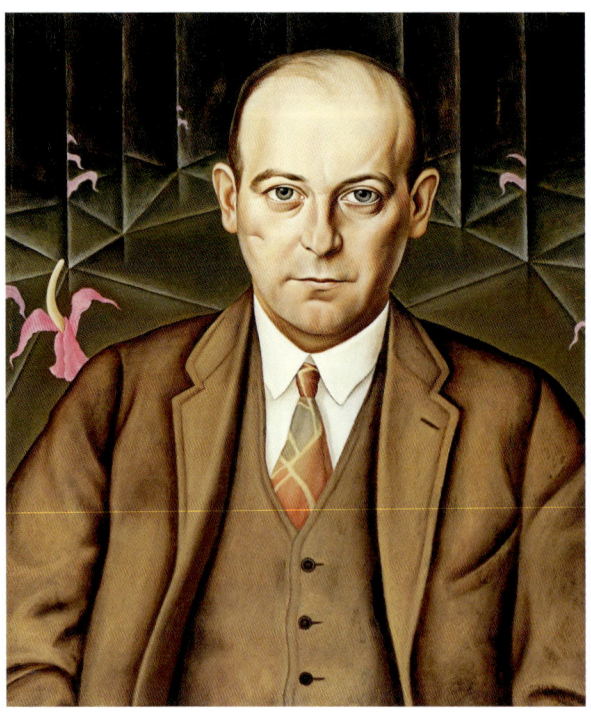

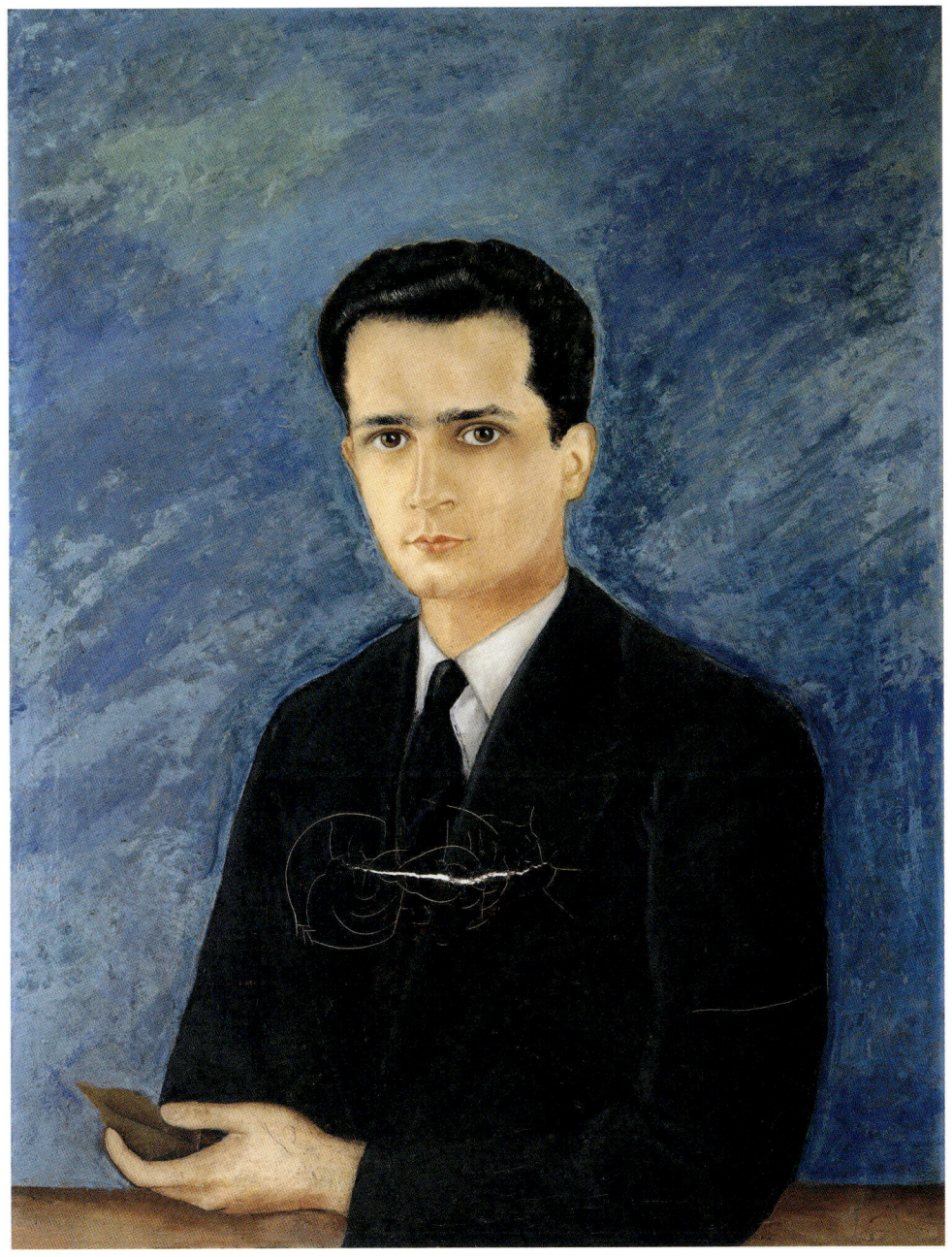

Ramón Alva de la Canal, **The Café de Nadie** (second version), *c.* 1930
Oil and collage on canvas, 46 x 32 cm (18⅛ x 12⅝ in.)
Mexico City, Secretaría de Cultura, Instituto Nacional de Bellas Artes y Literatura,
Museo Nacional de Arte, gift of the Maples Arce Vermeersch family, 1992

Pancho Villa and Adelita (unfinished), *c.* 1927
Oil on canvas, 65 x 45 cm (25⅝ x 17¾ in.)
Mexico, State Government of Tlaxcala, Instituto Tlaxcalteca
de la Cultura, Museo de Arte de Tlaxcala

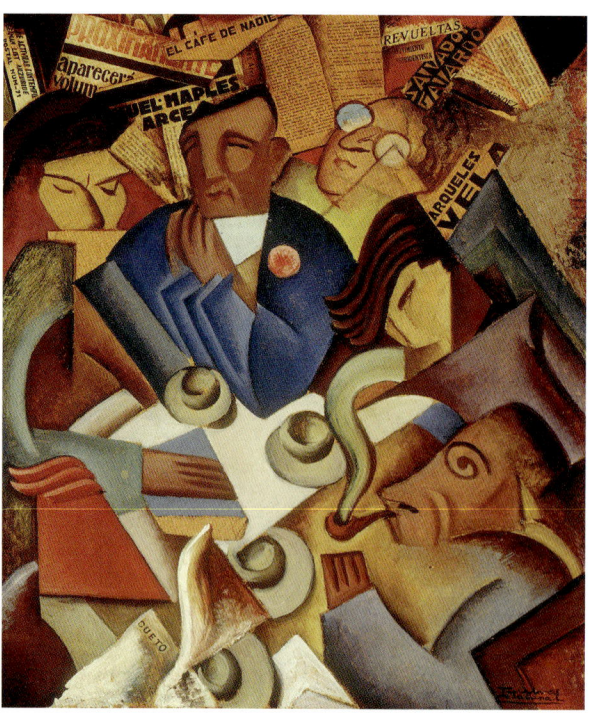

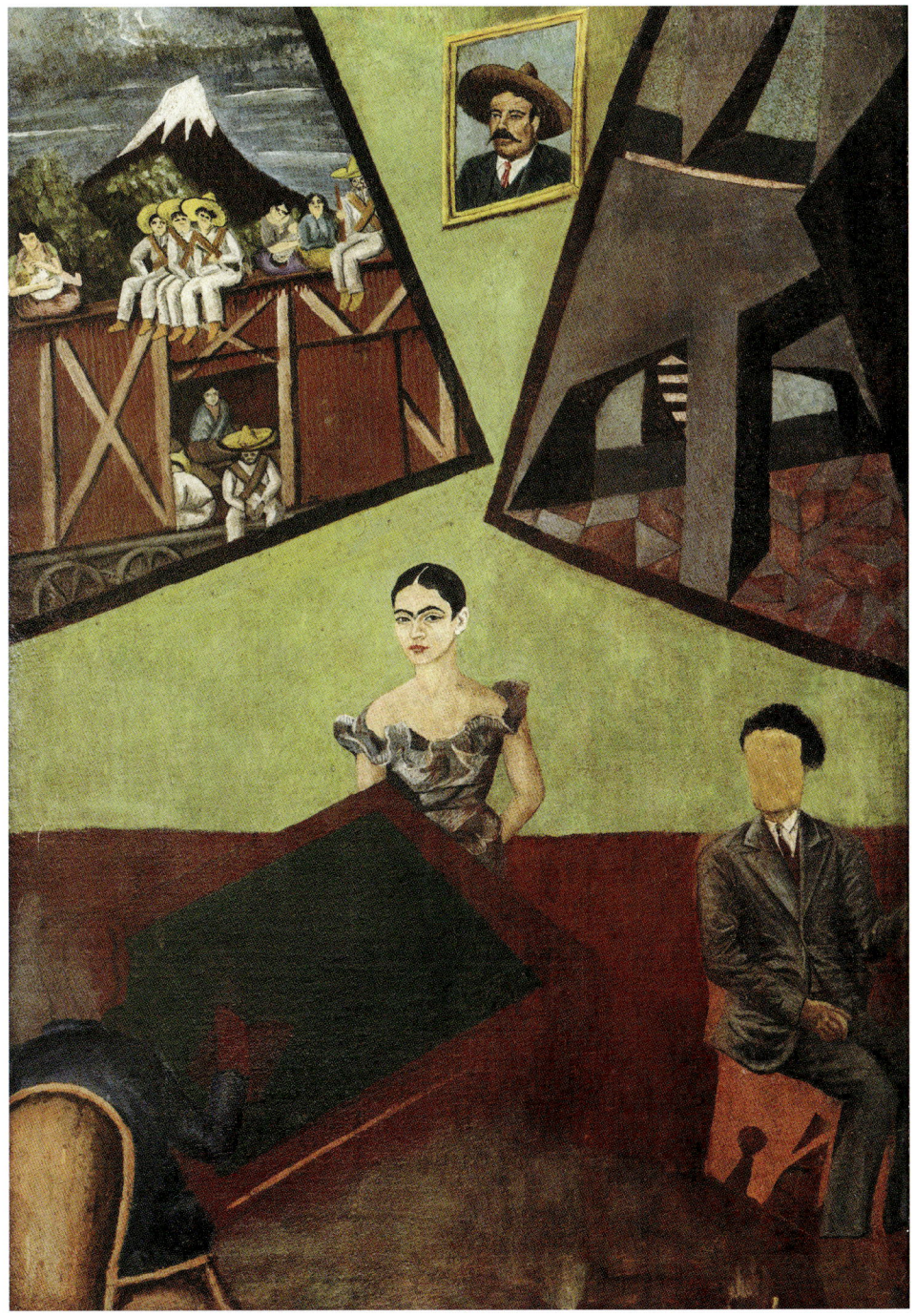

Diego Rivera, **Portrait of Ramón Gómez de la Serna**, 1915
Oil on canvas, 110.5 x 90.5 cm (43½ x 35⅝ in.)
Museo de Arte Latinoamericano de Buenos Aires,
Fundación Costantini, gift of Eduardo F. Costantini, 2001

Portrait of Miguel N. Lira, 1927
Oil on canvas, 99.2 x 67.5 cm (39 x 26⅝ in.)
Mexico, State Government of Tlaxcala, Instituto Tlaxcalteca
de la Cultura, Museo de Arte de Tlaxcala

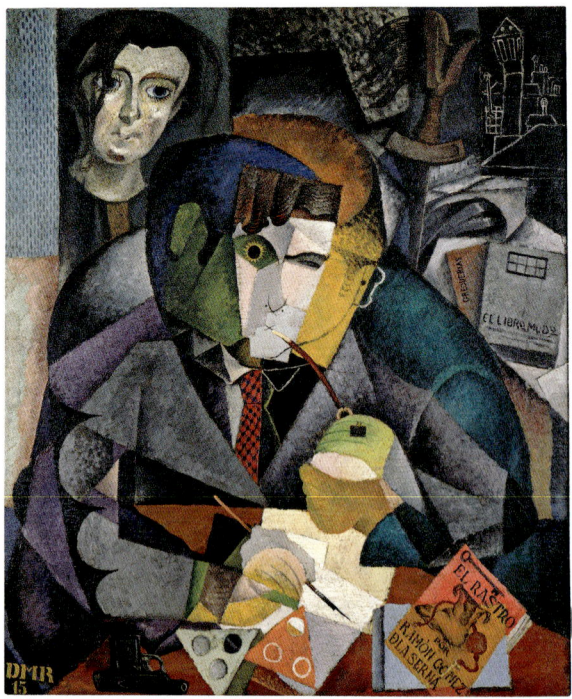

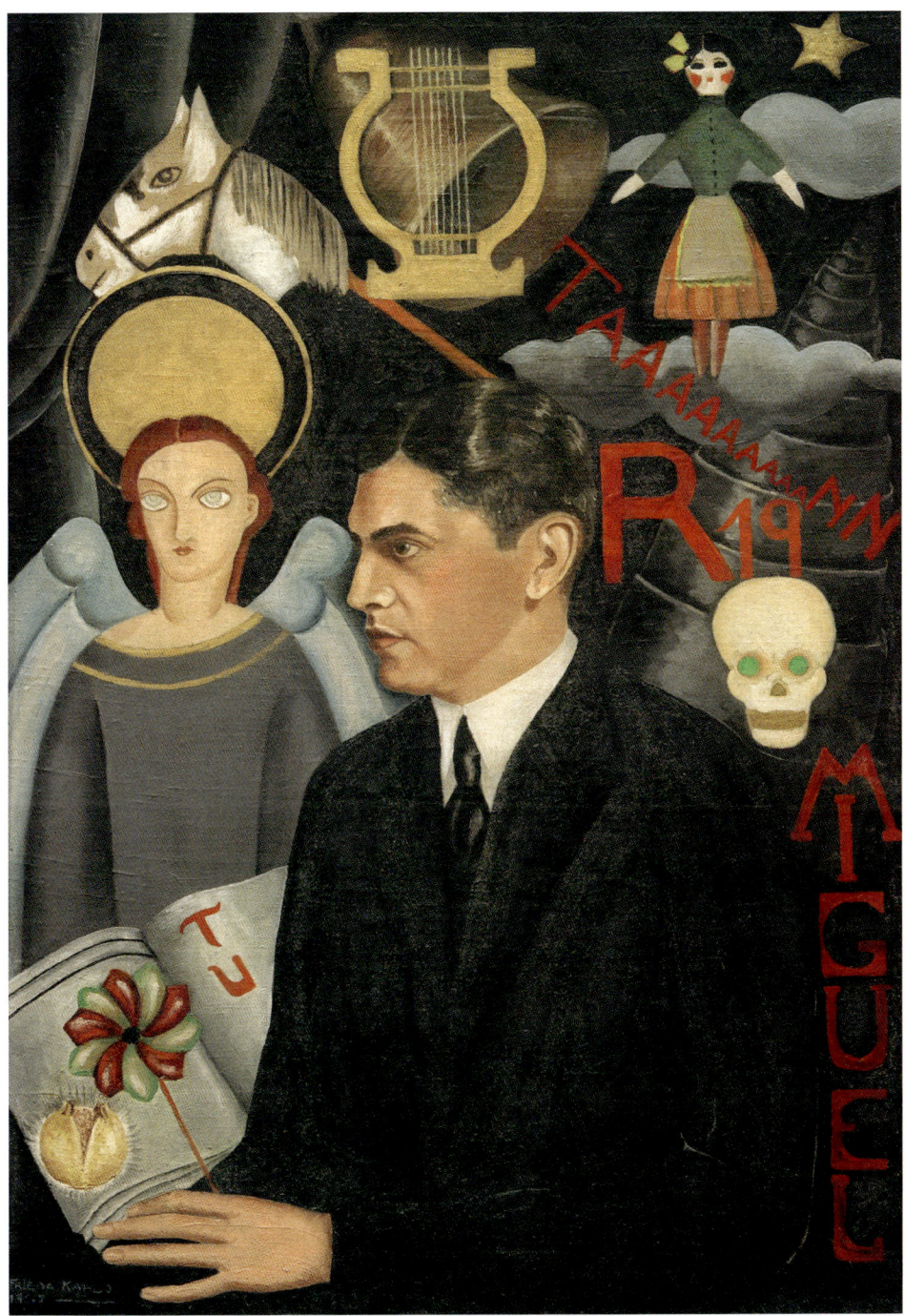

Otto Dix, **Portrait of the Lawyer Dr. Hugo Simons**, 1925
Oil and tempera on plywood, 100.3 x 70.3 cm (39½ x 27⅝ in.)
Montreal, Museum of Fine Arts

Portrait of Alejandro Gómez Arias, 1928
Oil on board, 61.5 x 41 cm (24¼ x 16⅛ in.)
Inscribed t. r.: ALEX / CON CARIÑO PINTE TU /
RETRATO QUE ES EL DE / MI CAMARADA DE /
SIEMPRE / FRIDA KAHLO. 1952 / 30 AÑOS DESPUES.
(Alex / with love I painted your / portrait showing you /
my old comrade / forever / Frida Kahlo. 1952 / 30 years later.)
Mexico City, private collection

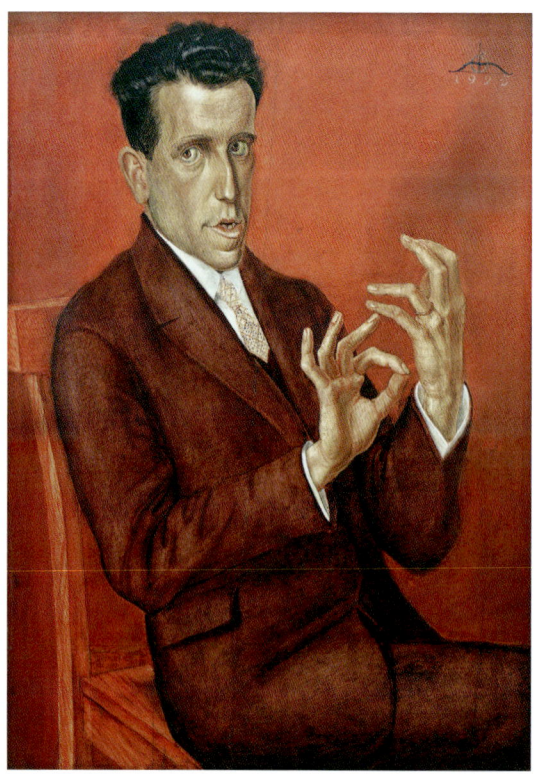

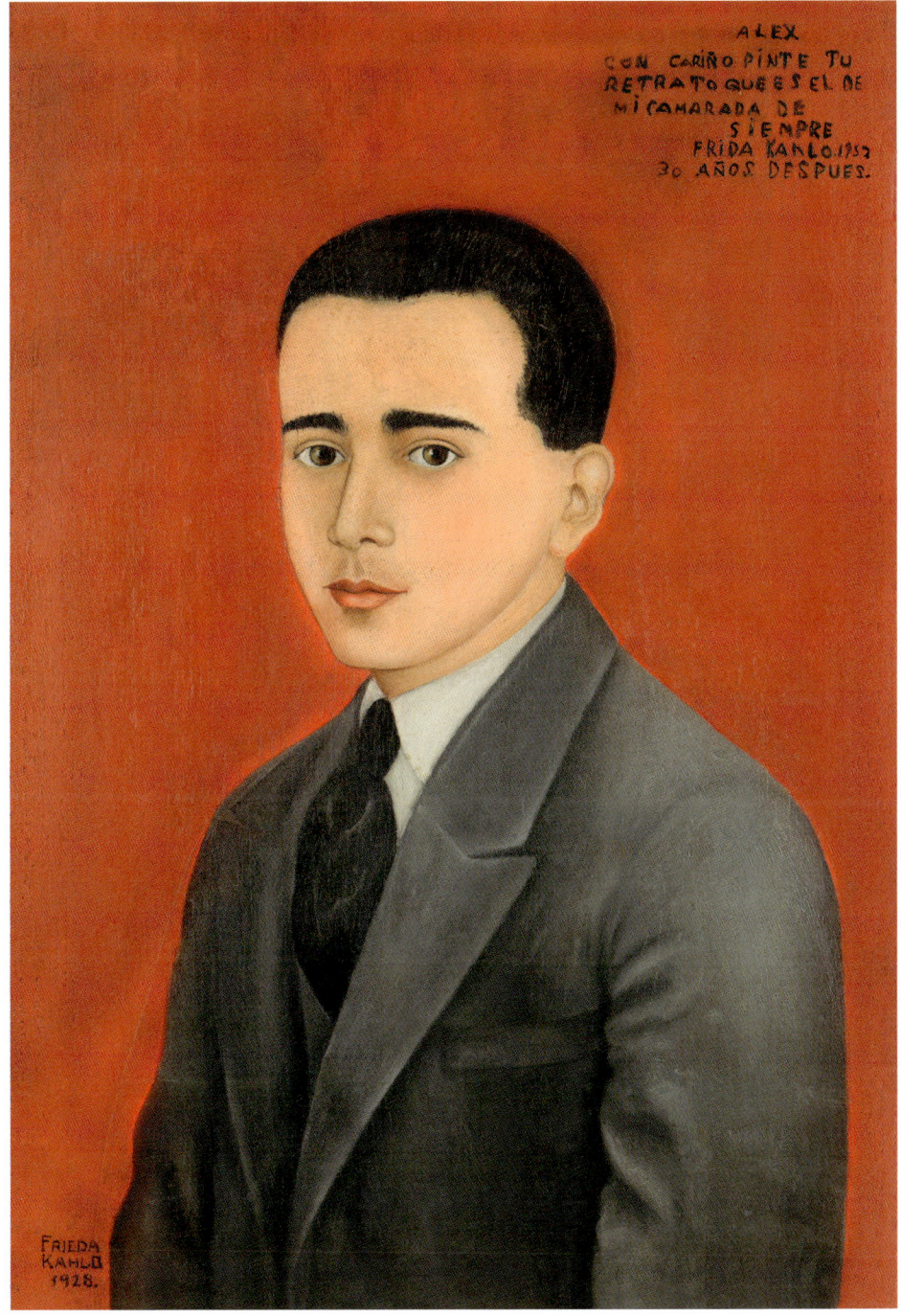

Leonardo da Vinci, **Ginevra de' Benci**, *c.* 1474–1478
Oil on wooden panel, 38.1 x 37 cm (15 x 14⅝ in.)
Washington, D.C., National Gallery of Art, Ailsa Mellon Bruce Fund

Two Women (Portrait of Salvadora and Herminia), 1928
Oil on canvas, 69.5 x 53.3 cm (27⅜ x 21 in.)
Boston, Museum of Fine Arts, Charles H. Bayley Picture and Paintings Fund, William
Francis Warden Fund, Sophie M. Friedman Fund, Ernest Wadsworth Longfellow Fund,
Tompkins Collection – Arthur Gordon Tompkins Fund, gift of Jessie H. Wilkinson –
Jessie H. Wilkinson Fund, and Robert M. Rosenberg Family Fund, 2015

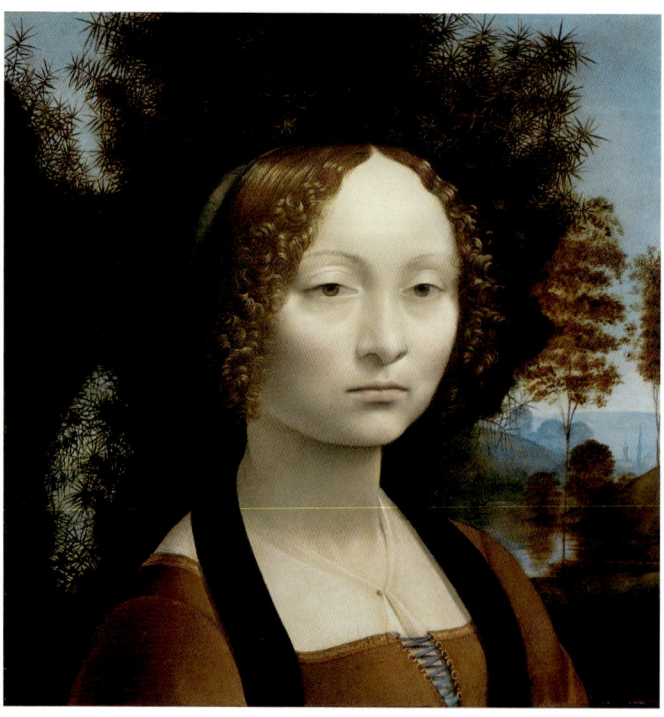

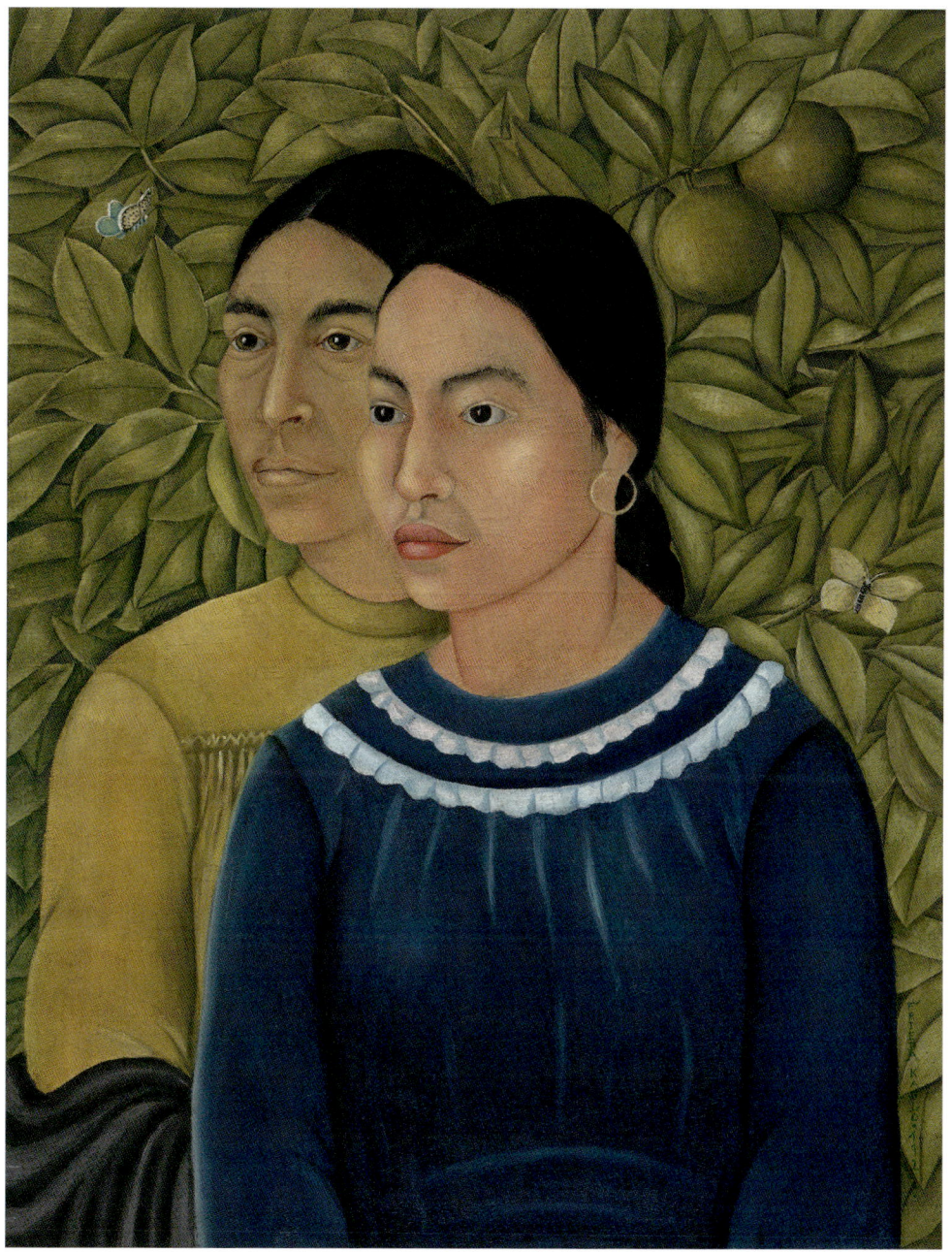

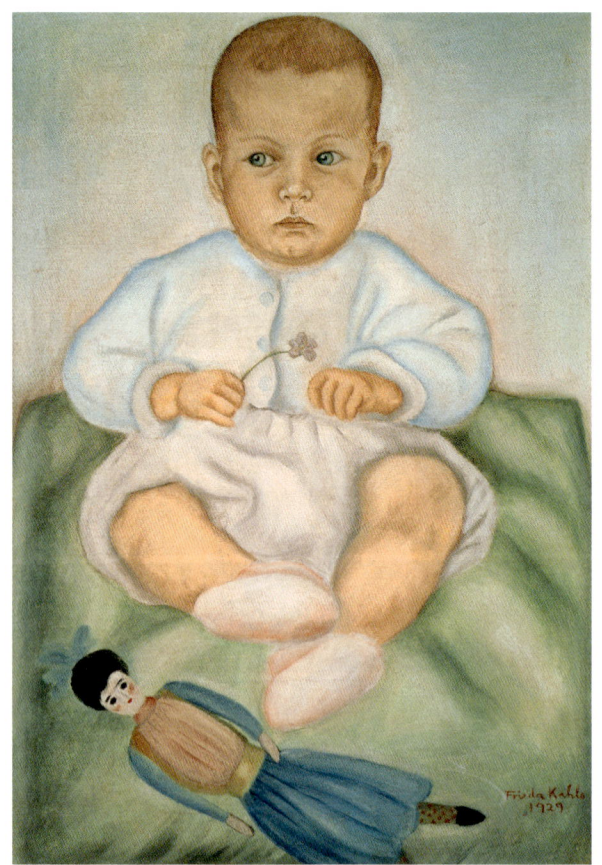

Baby Girl in Diapers, 1929
Oil on canvas, 65.5 x 44 cm (25¾ x 17⅜ in.)
Mexico City, SURA Asset Management collection

Sitting Girl with Duck, December 1928
Oil on canvas, 100.3 x 40.3 cm (39½ x 15⅞ in.)
Private collection, courtesy Sotheby's, New York

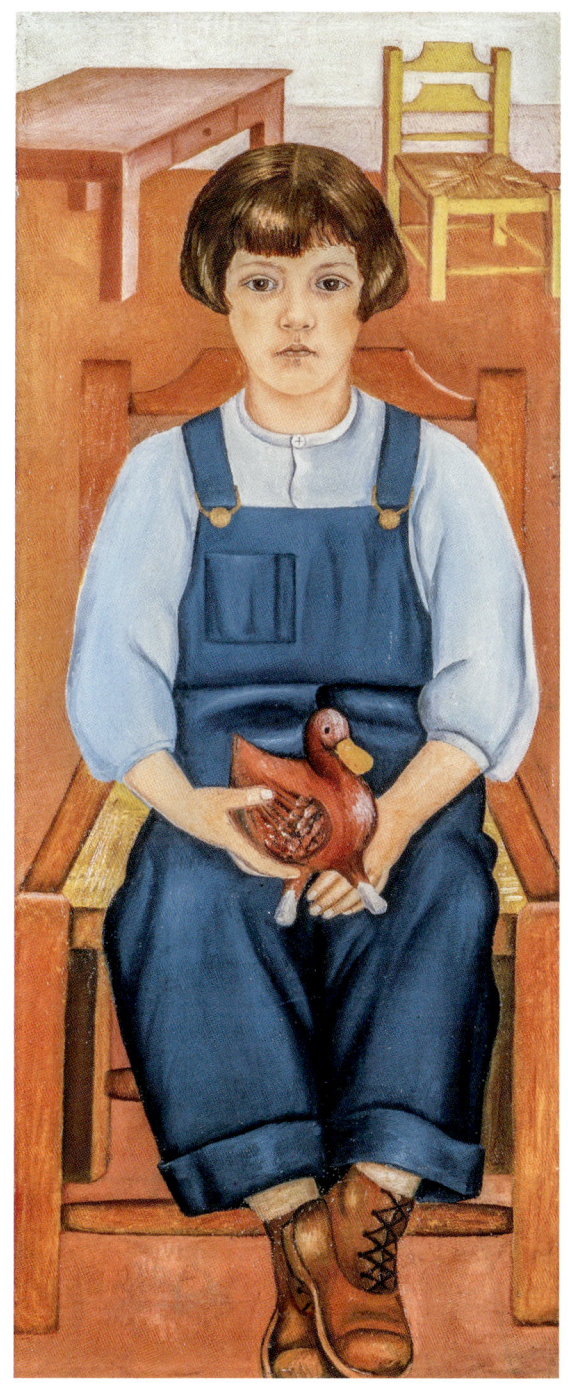

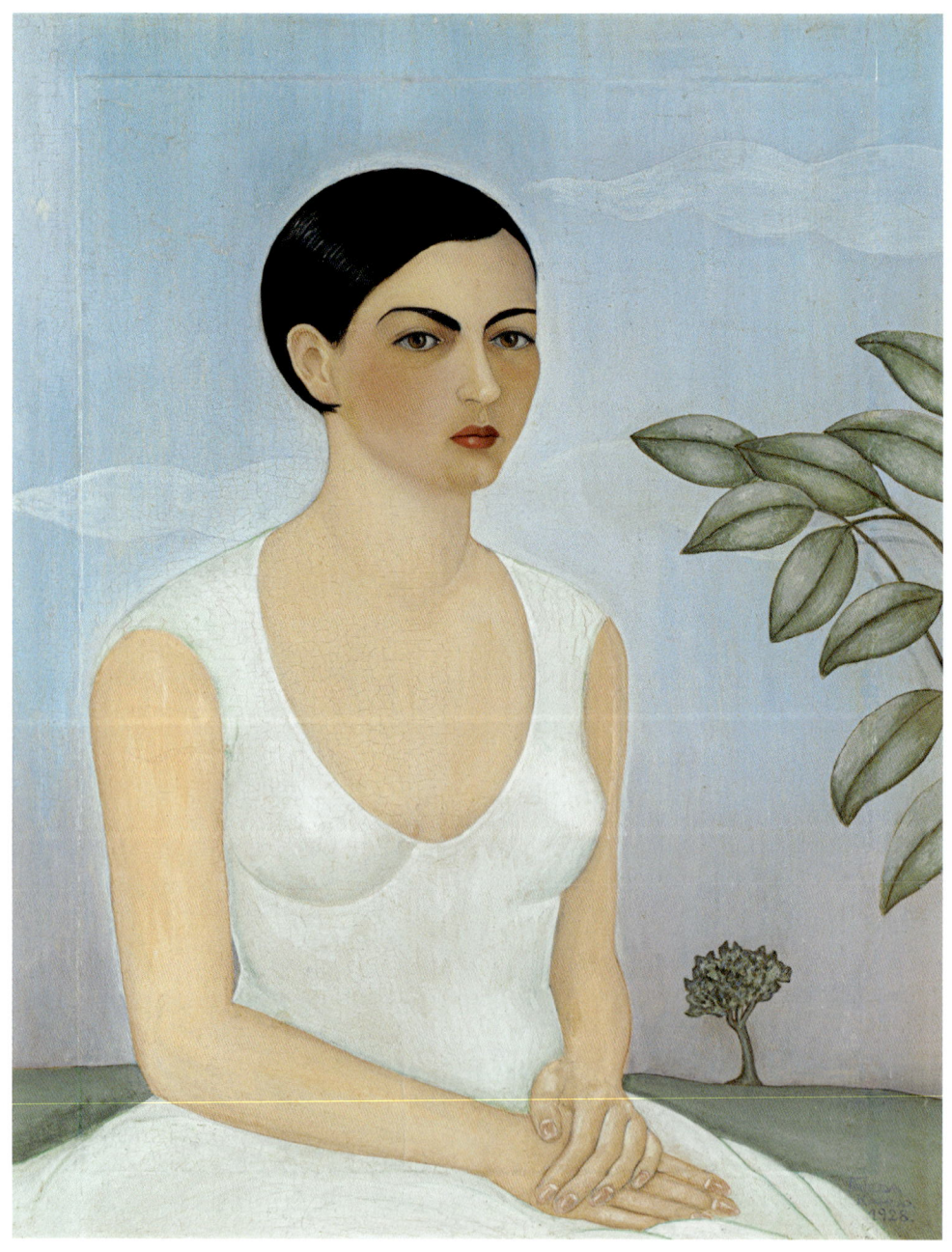

Portrait of Cristina, My Sister, 1928
Oil on board, 99 x 81.5 cm (39 x 32⅛ in.)
Private collection, courtesy Sotheby's, New York

Christian Schad,
Portrait of an English Woman (Lilian Kennard), 1926
Oil on canvas, 57.5 x 47 cm (22⅝ x 18½ in.)
Private collection

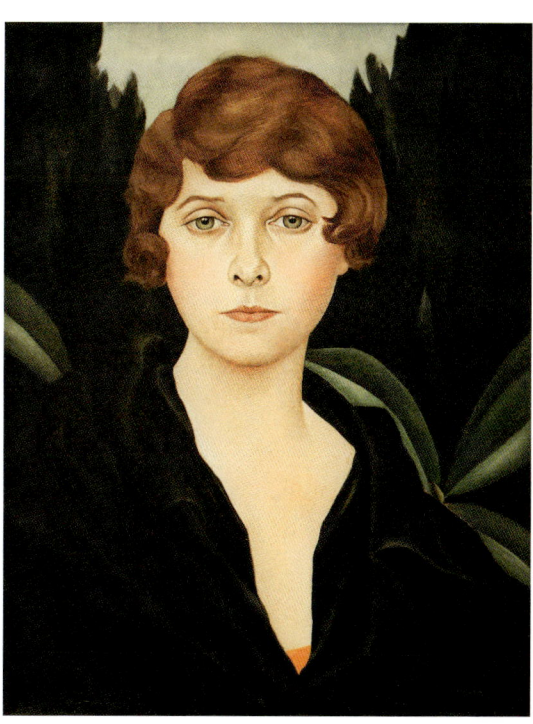

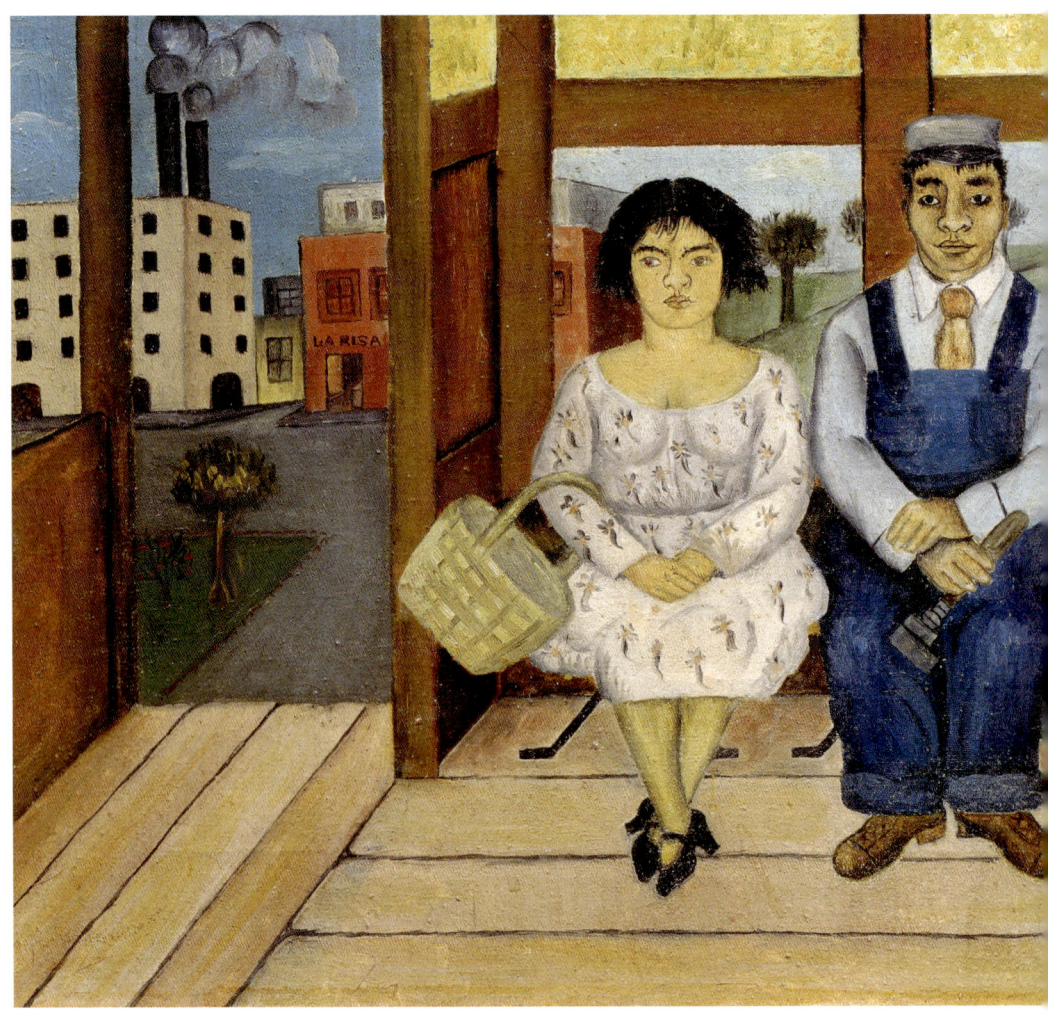

The Bus, 1929
Oil on canvas, 25.8 x 55.5 cm (10⅛ x 21⅞ in.)
Mexico City, Xochimilco, Museo Dolores Olmedo

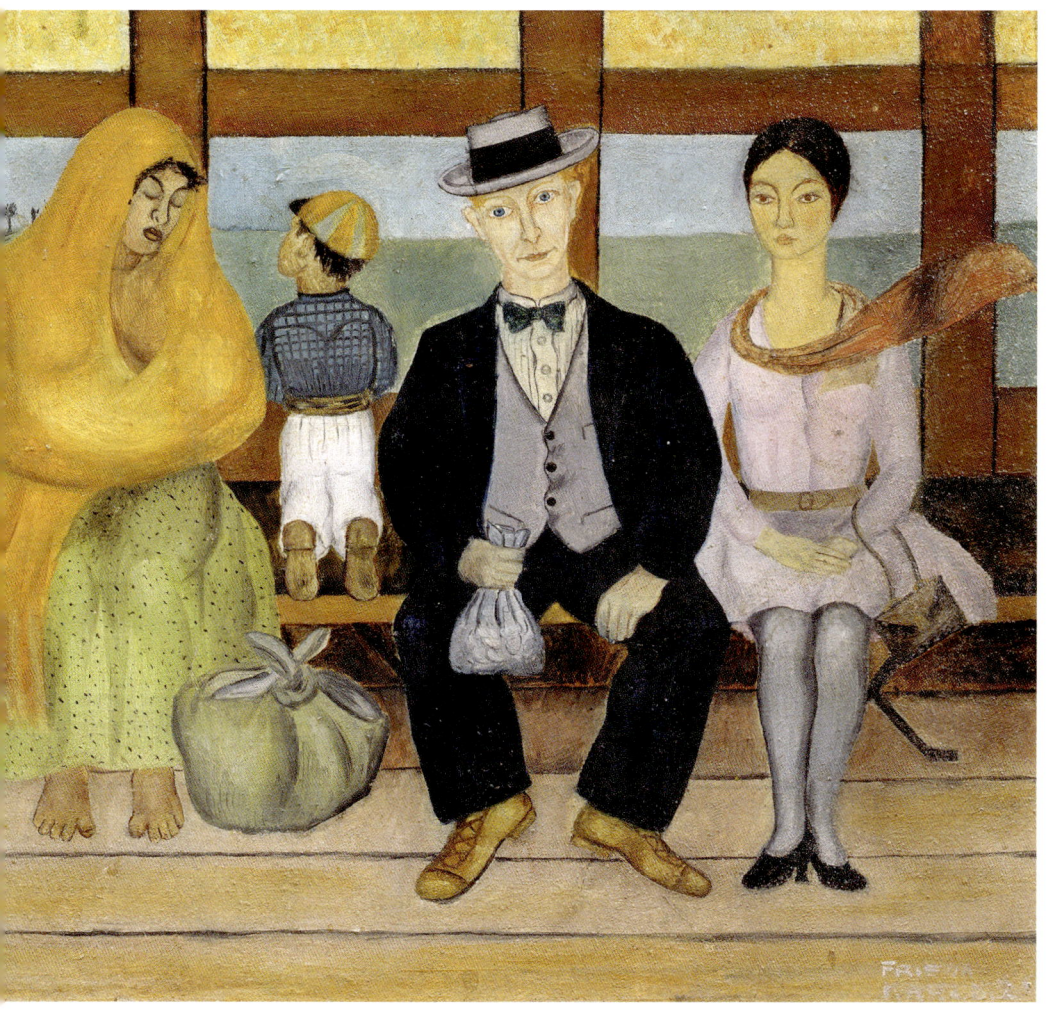

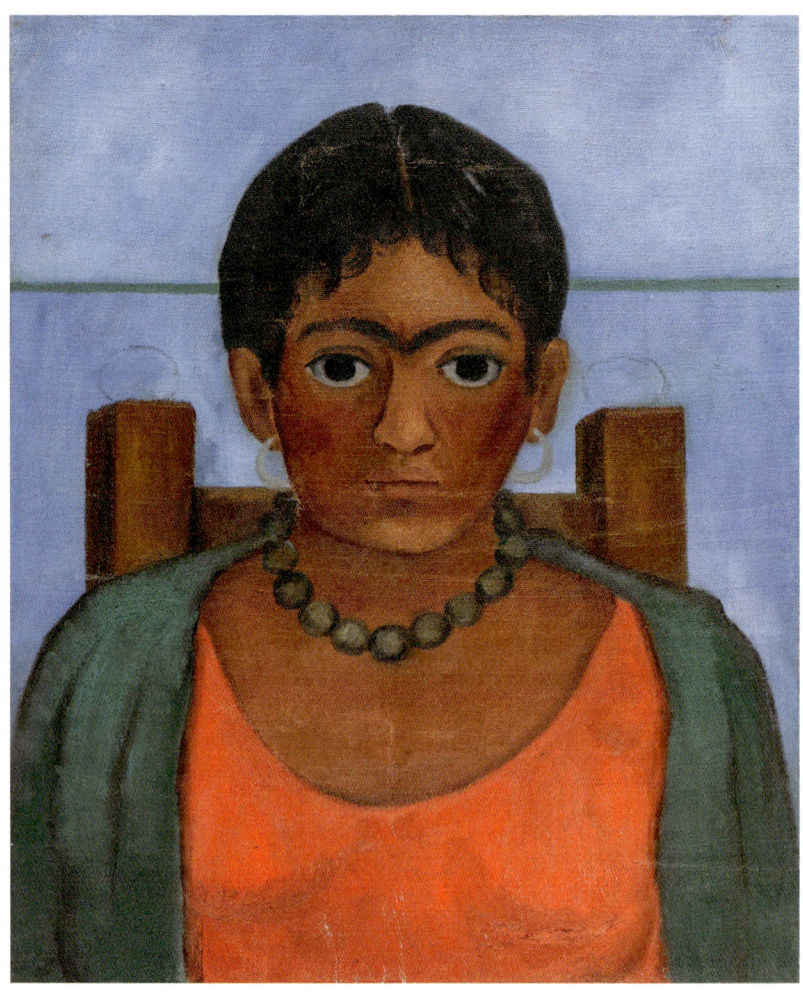

Portrait of a Girl Wearing a Necklace, *c.* 1929
Oil on canvas, 57 x 46 cm (22½ x 18⅛ in.)
Brussels, private collection, courtesy Sotheby's, New York

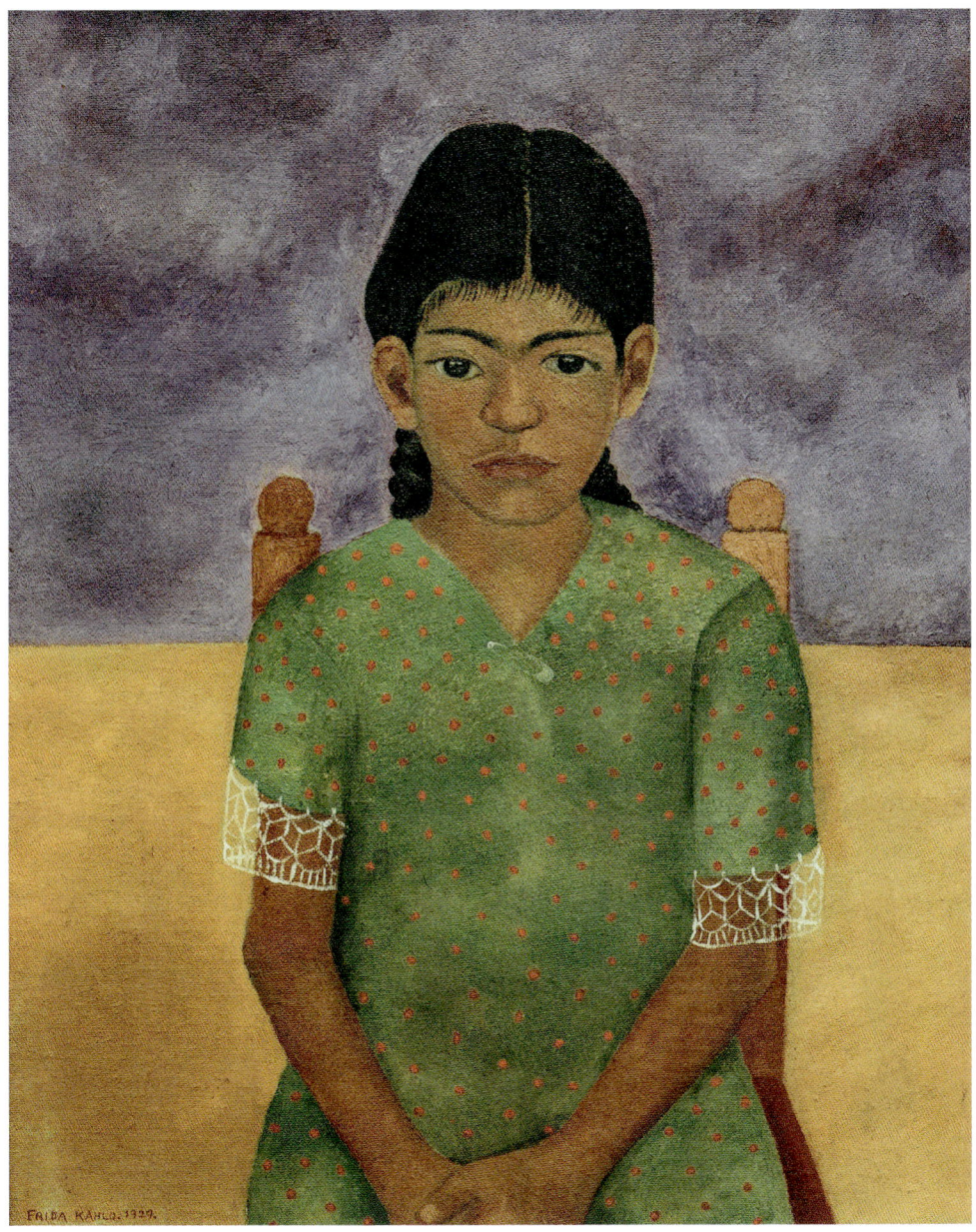

The Girl Virginia, 1929
Oil on masonite, 78 x 61 cm (30¾ x 24 in.)
Mexico City, Xochimilco, Museo Dolores Olmedo

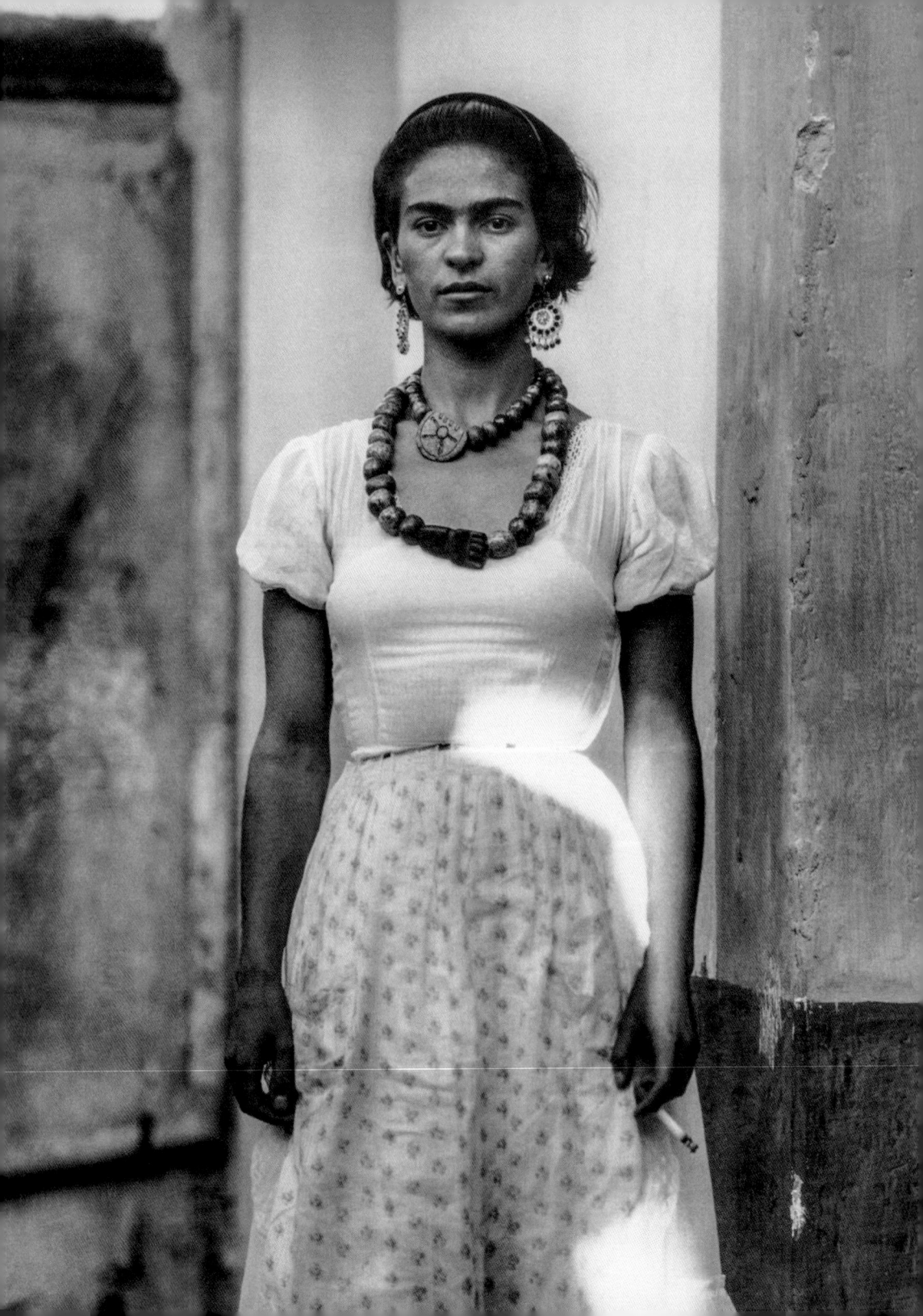

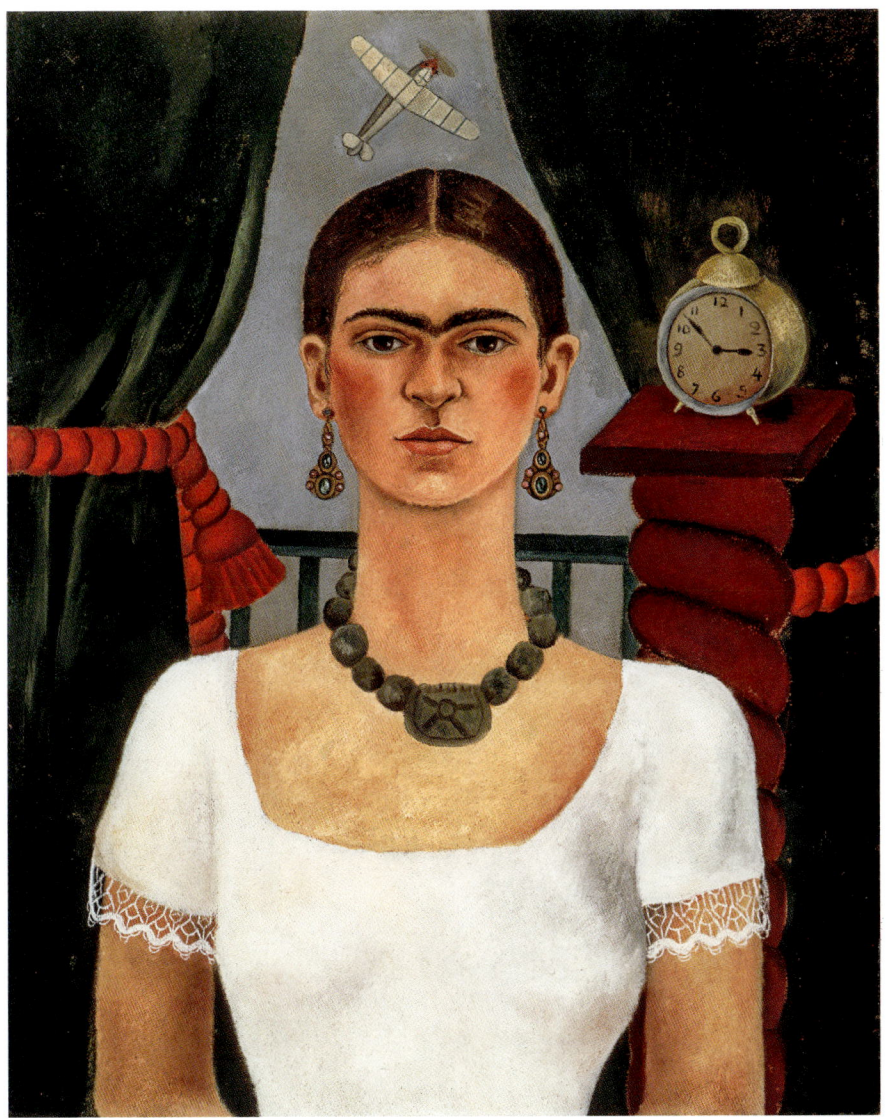

Guillermo Davila, **Frida Kahlo** (detail), 1929
Gelatin silver print, 15.2 x 10.1 cm (6 x 4 in.). New York, collection of Spencer Throckmorton

Self-portrait (Time Flies), *c.* 1929
Oil on masonite, 77.5 x 61 cm (30½ x 24 in.)
California, private collection, courtesy Sotheby's, New York

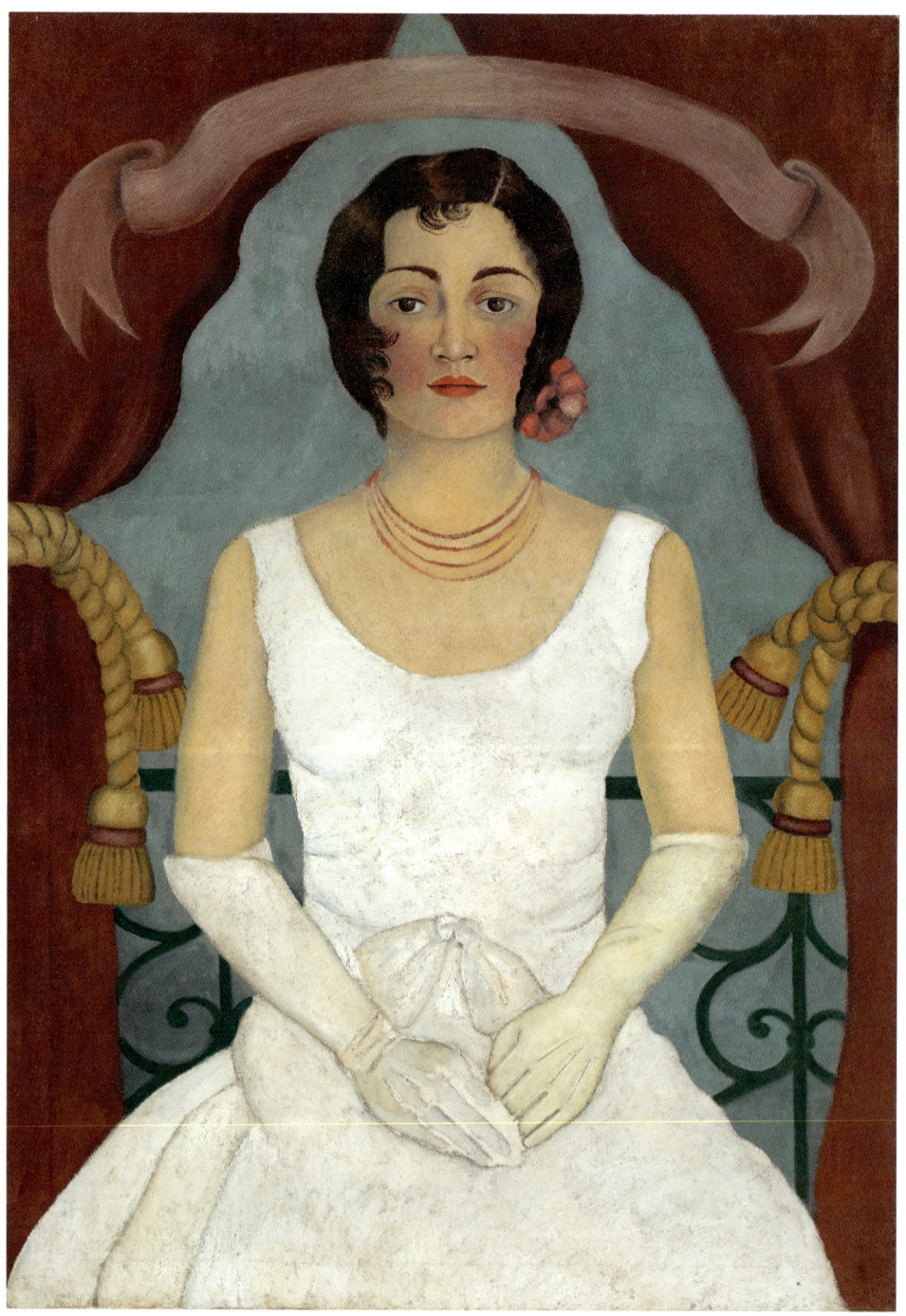

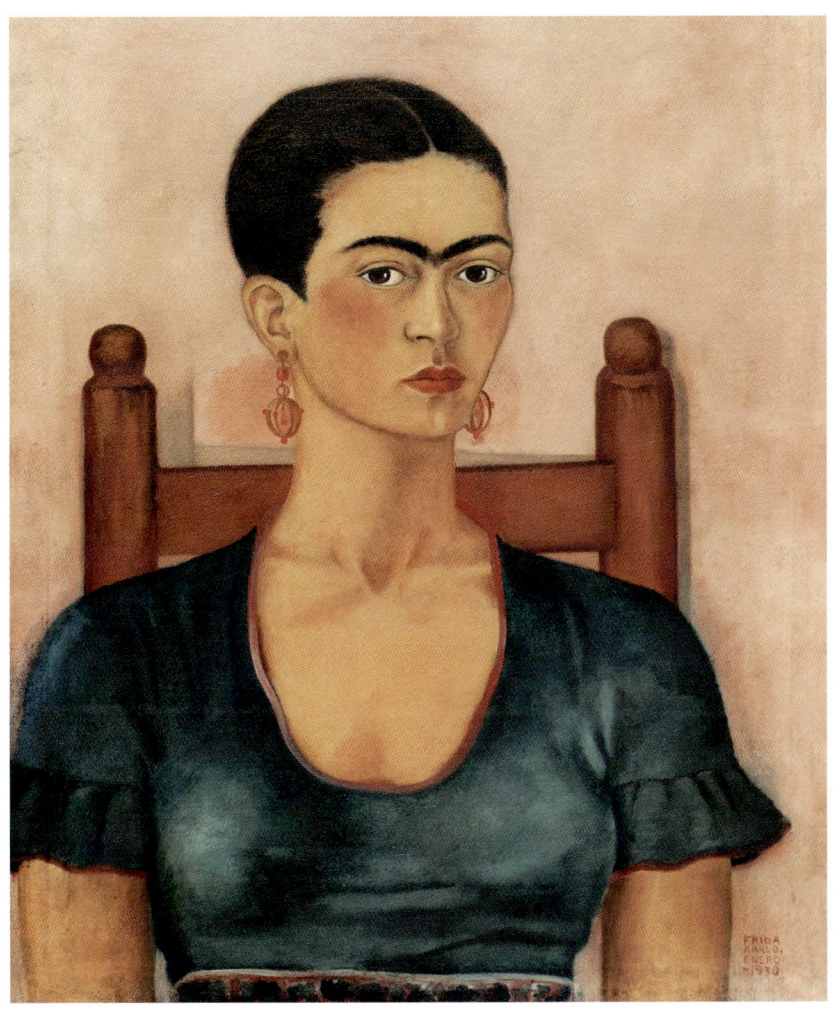

Portrait of a Lady in White (unfinished), *c.* 1929
Oil on canvas, 118.1 x 81.3 cm (46½ x 32 in.)
United States, private collection, courtesy Christie's, New York

Self-portrait, January 1930
Oil on canvas, 65 x 55 cm (25⅝ x 21⅝ in.)
United States, private collection

II.

My eyes were opened and
I saw new things.

The painter broadens her horizons

1930–1938

"*In 1939, Frida sailed for Paris and conquered it.*
[...] Kandinsky was so moved by Frida's paintings that,
right in front of everyone else in the room where
the exhibition was being presented, he lifted her up
in his arms and kissed her on the cheeks [...] Even
Picasso, the most difficult and critical of all, sang
Frida's praises as an artist and as a person."

— DIEGO RIVERA, *c.* 1945

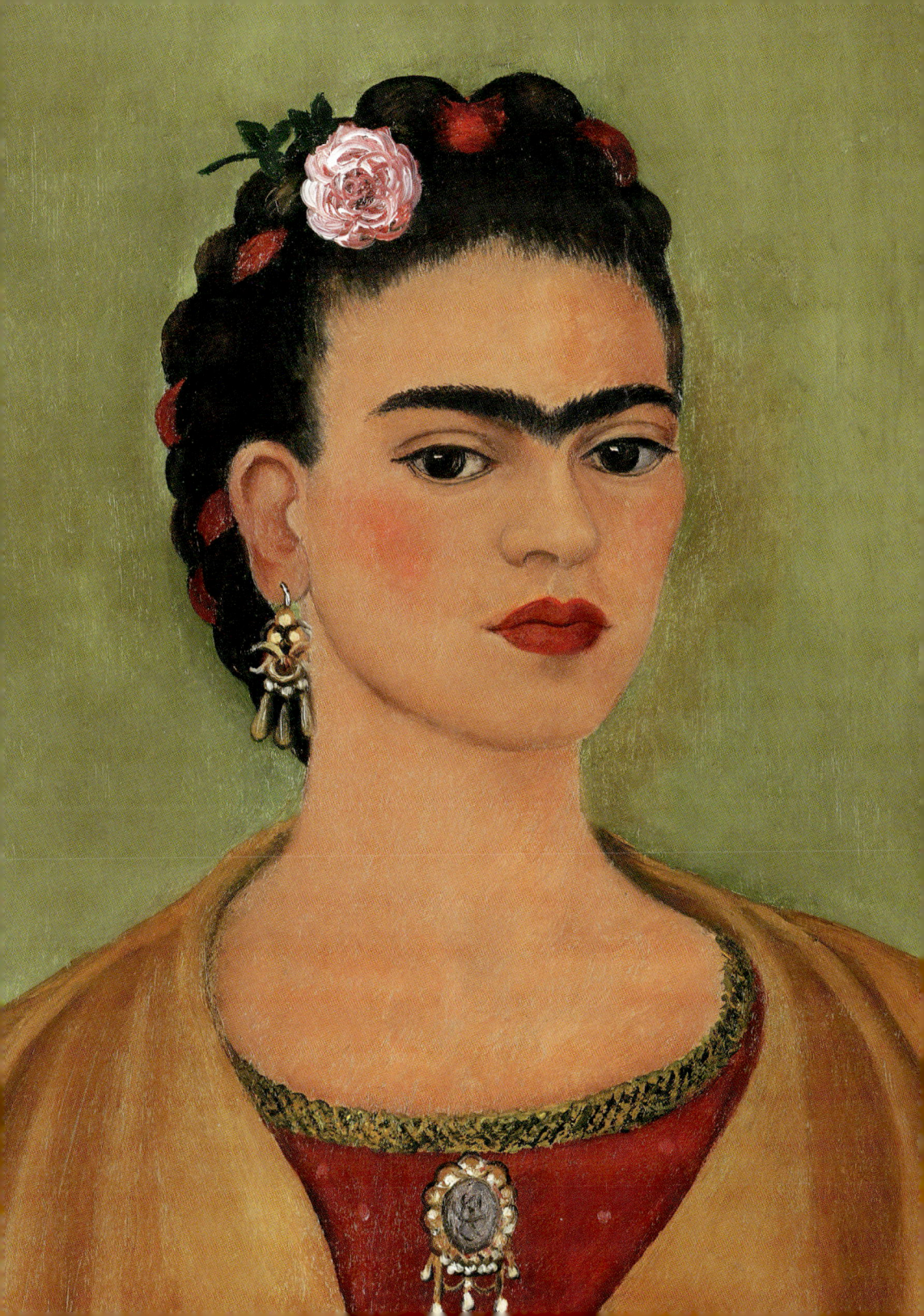

The 1930s were of fundamental importance for Frida Kahlo's intellectual development and for the way in which her personality as an artist became established. During the time she was living in the United States, from 1931 to 1933, she was exposed to several new aesthetic and conceptual ideas and also found recognition among the public for her artistic talent.

After her marriage to Rivera on August 22, 1929, Kahlo's life took a dramatic turn. She went from being the young girl from Coyoacán who wanted to go on and study medicine, and who was a friend of Los Cachuchas, to being the wife of the most acclaimed mural painter in Mexico, which immediately catapulted her into the midst of the cultural activities and political life in which her husband was involved. After the wedding, Rivera was at last able to accept the invitation he had received to paint a mural in San Francisco, which he had been putting off since 1926 because of other work commitments. The experience of traveling and living abroad must have made a deep impression on Kahlo, and indeed this is well attested in the letters she wrote to her family and friends. The perception she had of what her future life as an artist might be like was influenced by several different factors, although there can be no doubt that she was struck by the great respect that important artistic institutions showed for Rivera's work, and also the keen interest declared by his patrons for developing his art in the United States.[1]

In San Francisco, the first city they traveled to and where they arrived in November 1930, Kahlo felt welcomed by a community of lively and dedicated artists (p. 81). As a result, she decided to become a recognized figure herself on Montgomery Street, around which the artists' quarter was based at the time, and a serious painter in her own right. She was also able to take part in the "Sixth Annual Exhibition of the San Francisco Society of Women Artists," held in November and December 1931, where she showed one painting.[2] In San Francisco too, Kahlo felt the freedom to explore traditional 19th-century Mexican painting and folk art, without fear of being judged as merely a decorative painter or as one of Rivera's followers, and in fact she settled so well into this new and artistically stimulating environment that by February 1931 she had managed to complete at least six paintings, including *Portrait of Eva Frederick* (p. 103), *Portrait of Jean Wight* (p. 99), and *Portrait*

Page 79
Self-portrait Dedicated to Leon Trotsky (Between the Curtains) (detail),
November 1937 *(see ill. p. 175)*

Ralph Stackpole with Frida Kahlo and Diego Rivera, 1931
Gelatin silver print, 20 x 25 cm (7⅞ x 9⅞ in.)
Washington, D.C., Smithsonian Institution, Archives of American Art,
Emmy Lou Packard Papers, 1900–1990

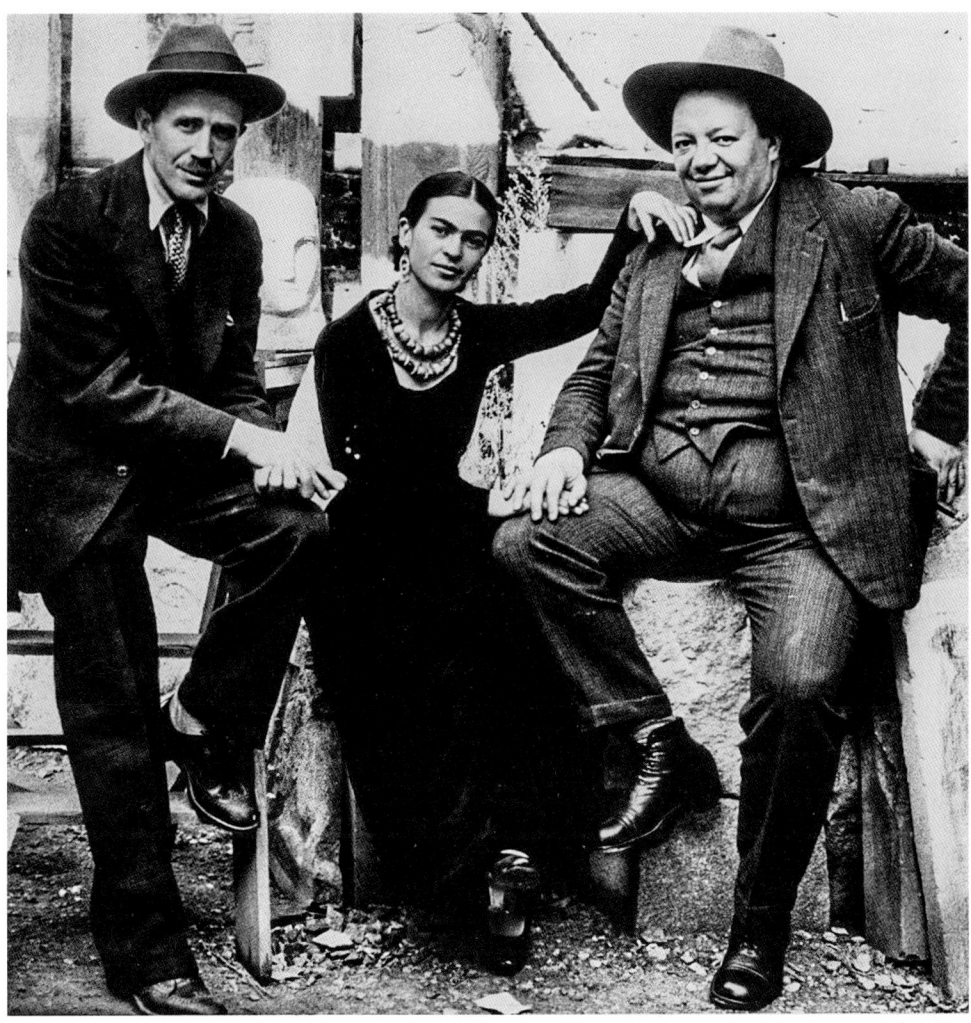

of Dr. Leo Eloesser (p. 107). The last two of these clearly show how the time Kahlo spent painting in San Francisco helped her to establish her technique with regard to the aesthetics of New Objectivity, which she had begun experimenting with while she was still in Mexico (pp. 106, 107). Her use of this style can also be seen in the portrait she drew of Cristina Hastings (1901–1955), the wife of Viscount Hastings (1901–1990), both of whom were, together with the sculptor Clifford Wight (*c.* 1900–1960) and his wife, the beautiful model Jean Abbott-Wight (1906–1955), part of the group of friends Kahlo and Rivera saw almost every day.

Kahlo's extended stay in California was also long enough for her to reevaluate what it was she wanted to do as a painter. She was aware that she had not had the academic training Rivera had received, but on the other hand she was fortunate to have had a different kind of education with her father, whose interest in art extended to teaching her to appreciate the benefits of studying the works of the great masters. While in the United States she also worked to improve the technical quality of her drawings and paintings, as well as looking for new methods and ideas to explore. After San Francisco she and Rivera returned to Mexico for a few months, and then in November 1931 they moved to New York for a major retrospective of his work at the Museum of Modern Art. From there they traveled on to Detroit, where Rivera painted murals at the Detroit Institute of Arts (p. 85), after which they went back to New York City where Rivera had been commissioned to paint a mural at the Rockefeller Center.

They arrived in Detroit on April 21, 1932, and here again Kahlo was able to spend more time on her painting so that what had up until this point been an amateur pastime

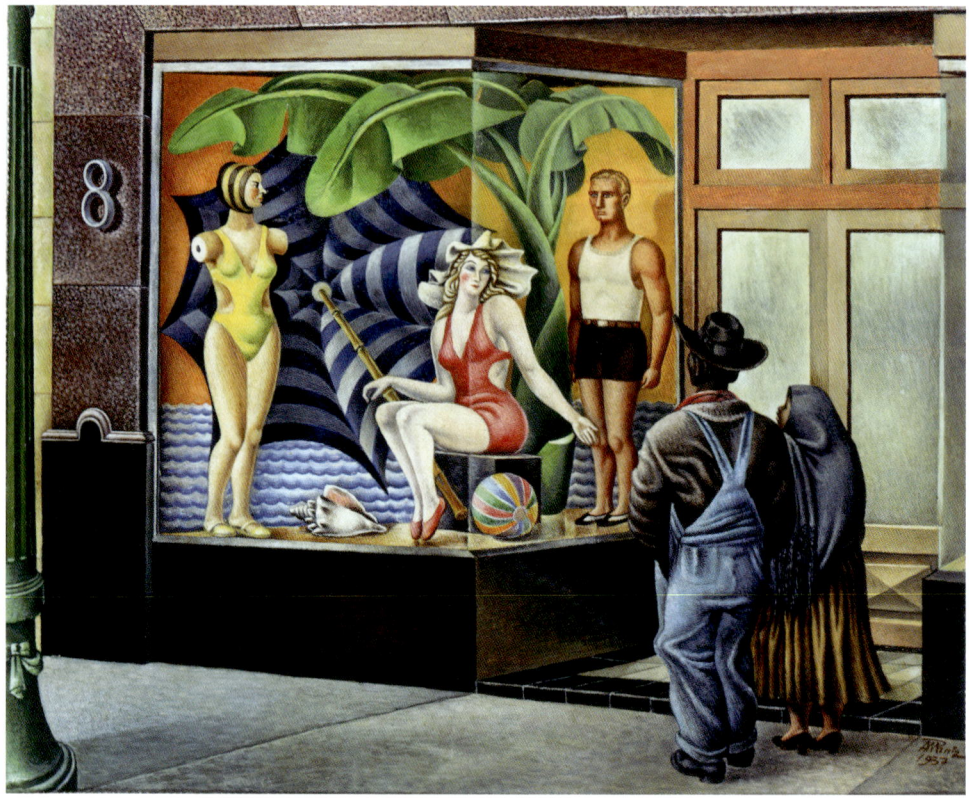

now became something she approached with greater discipline and rigor. Being naturally alert to developments in modern painting, a subject that was being much discussed in Mexico at the time, Kahlo sought to broaden her artistic horizons by studying the various works she saw in the exhibitions, museums, and private collections she visited. There was also Rivera's constant presence, and the fact that he always encouraged her to find her own path and to paint the experiences she knew from life. Thus it was that when by chance she happened upon a number of items laid out in the window of an ordinary neighborhood store in Detroit to celebrate the 4th of July, she decided at Rivera's suggestion to make this the subject of a small oil painting, *Window Display in a Street of Detroit* (p. 105).[3] It should be noted, however, that despite the date when Kahlo arrived in Detroit, the painting is dated to 1931. A number of similar discrepancies in dates have been identified in other works of hers, which tends to suggest that this was not done by accident but on purpose. In some cases Kahlo dated her paintings when she had completed them, but in others she wanted to record the date when they were begun, or again where and when they were finished.

In the case of *Window Display in a Street of Detroit*, it may be that the idea for the painting came to her in 1931, while she was still in New York.[4] The composition itself is filled with the same magical realism and metaphysical references that can be found in the writings of Franz Roh, which Kahlo had been reading since her formative years in Mexico. It is quite possible that this window display reminded her, and perhaps not without a pang of nostalgia, of the shops in downtown Mexico City, with their windows decorated with brightly colored pieces of paper, ribbons, and posters and offering all manner of merchandise piled up at random after being brought in from near and far. Such an urban scene was of course nothing new for Mexican art from this time, and in fact the Detroit shop window may also have brought back memories for Kahlo of similar photographs taken by Manuel Álvarez Bravo (1902–2002) (p. 104), or again some of the paintings by Rufino Tamayo or Antonio Ruiz, known as El Corcito (1892–1964; p. 82). In any case, in this small oil painting, seemingly so detached from anything to do with Mexico, the arrangement of elements nevertheless offers an understanding of the intellectual process Kahlo was experimenting with in her work.

Throughout the time she was living in the United States Kahlo wrote several letters to her friends and family that reveal what she felt about her experience of living there. In a number of these letters she was openly critical about some of the wealthy Americans

Antonio Ruiz, "El Corcito," **Summer**, 1937
Oil on wood, 28.5 x 35 cm (11¼ x 13¾ in.)
Mexico City, Museo de la Secretaría de Hacienda y Crédito Público

involved in the art world, yet even so, it is important to note that Kahlo also experienced situations that enriched her artistic and intellectual understanding. At the same time she was well aware of the enormous advantages that were available which might help an artist to develop, given the opportunities to work for large institutions or gain the support of wealthy patrons. In fact, the way she viewed the United States as an artist was rather more discerning than might be suggested by some of her casual opinions about the "gringos" and their behavior.

In this way Kahlo was given the opportunity to consider and take stock of her intellectual progress during the time she spent abroad. She began work on a small painting, *Self-portrait (on the Border between Mexico and the United States)* (pp. 110/111), which she painted as a gift for William R. Valentiner (1880–1958), then director of the Detroit Institute of Arts, whom she had got to know as a friend while visiting the museum's collection with him. In this self-portrait, Kahlo depicted herself positioned between two different world views that represent Mexico and the United States, and the painting would seem to be her uneasy if inquisitive response to what she had been hearing about the "technocratic movement" or technocracy being discussed in Detroit at the time. Through the painting though, she was setting out for her viewers the dilemma in which she found herself personally, not on a border between two nations but between two ways of seeing the world.

Kahlo's work was now becoming better known, and also noted in the intellectual and artistic groups in which she and Rivera were involved. However, it was not until 1938 that Kahlo had her first solo exhibition, when she presented between 25 and 30 paintings at the prestigious Julien Levy Gallery in New York. Most of them had been painted specifically for the show, but a few had been started years before and were then reworked or completed, as was the case with *Burbank – American Fruit Maker* (p. 109) and also *My Dress Was There Hanging (New York)* (pp. 130/131), which shows an imaginary urban space, albeit held together by realistic representations of various city landmarks, chosen as the setting for Kahlo's biting critique of American capitalist society and its supposed level of social development. Hayden Herrera has identified some of the landmarks that appear in the painting, and also noted the short text on the back where Kahlo has written that it was painted while she was in New York at the time Rivera was working on the mural for the Rockefeller Center.[5]

However, Kahlo also had other, aesthetic reasons for exploring political themes. While in the two previous paintings, *Window Display in a Street of Detroit* and *Self-portrait (on the Border between Mexico and the United States),* she had used metaphors to convey her particular view of the relationship between art and politics, she now had a powerful incentive to put them to practical use. The public art championed by her husband had been

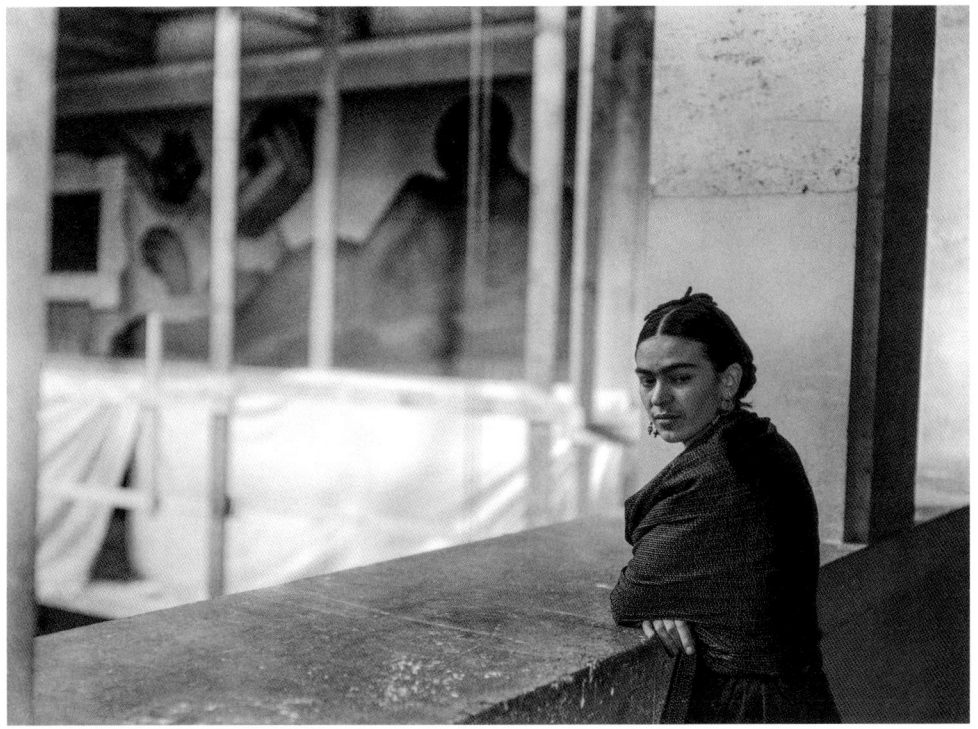

W. J. Stettler, **Frida Kahlo on the courtyard balcony of the Detroit Institute of Arts**, 1932
Gelatin silver print, 18 x 22.5 cm (7⅛ x 8⅞ in.)
Detroit Institute of Arts

censored in the mural he had been painting for the Rockefeller Center for daring to suggest a different future course for the American working class other than capitalism, and for not having respected the ideological interests of his patrons. The cost to Rivera, and therefore Kahlo as well, was to be ostracized by one of the most powerful families in the United States, with the result that overnight he became an outcast and doors were now closed to any possible future mural commissions in the country. As an artist, Kahlo decided not to remain silent about what had happened. Her response was to protest, and in doing so she turned to the rhetoric of belligerent avant-garde groups such as the Dadaists (p. 134), whose objectives were focused specifically on denouncing the *status quo* of bourgeois society and mocking the hypocrisy of its establishment practices, with which the structures of the art world obediently complied. She was thus turning again to avant-garde models as a source of stylistic methods and innovation that coincided with her own concerns about the content and mission of art.

The process of adapting the avant-garde to Kahlo's own artistic purposes did not happen all at once, and Rivera himself recalled seeing that "sometimes she kept on painting, with no sense of order about what she was doing and producing works only at great intervals, which are Surrealist in a personal way, but not academically. They are strange paintings, introspective, fantastical, enchanting, and extremely individual."[6] In the collection of the Museo Frida Kahlo in Coyoacán there is a canvas with roughly sketched-out beginnings that Rivera described as "the outlines of a composition about New York" and which he dated 1933 (p. 136). The sketch shows a view of the Statue of Liberty, and the dimensions of the canvas suggest that it was a very ambitious project compared with the typically more modest sizes Kahlo had been working with in the United States. The composition was clearly an early design for a political painting she was planning, motivated by her experiences in the United States and her realization of the terrible consequences of the Great Depression.

Kahlo's intellectual development was, however, not matched by recognition of her status as an artist. Between 1925 and 1934, she studied and examined, with great speed, several art movements both in Mexico and within the context of the serious theoretical and political discussions taking place on the great international stage in the United States. Yet while this period was certainly fruitful for Kahlo intellectually, she did not have many

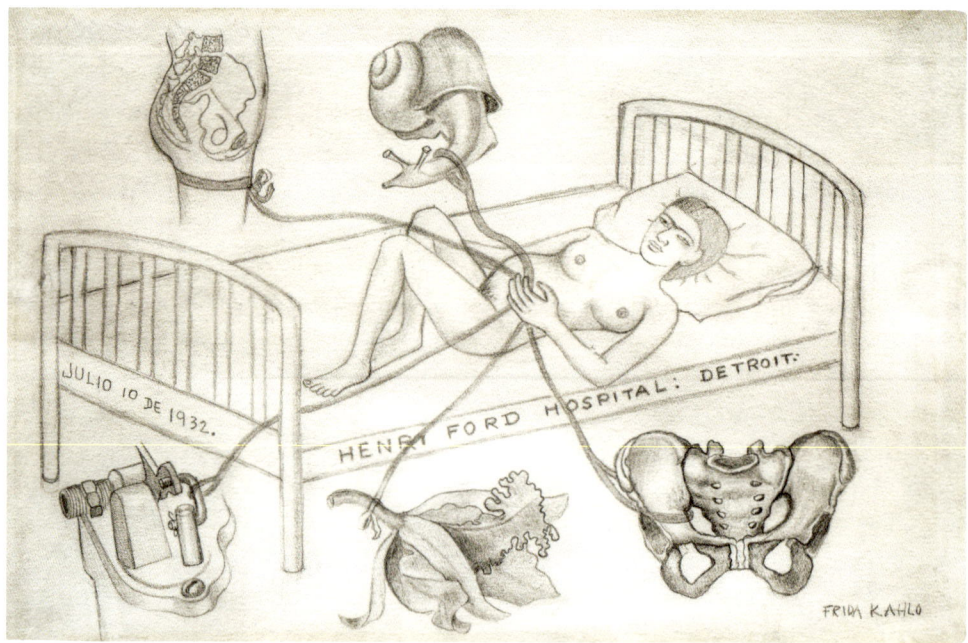

opportunities to exhibit her work. As already noted, this did not in fact happen until the end of the decade, with the exhibition in New York.

On December 20, 1933, Kahlo and Rivera returned to Mexico, and each went back to their own work as artists. Kahlo concentrated once again on her vernacular and traditional painting, although by this time her marriage was beginning to deteriorate as a result of Rivera's affair with Cristina (1908–1964), her younger sister and the one she loved the most. The pain she felt from this betrayal affected her deeply, and the hurt, which took many years to heal, was reflected in the imagery of a number of unsettling paintings she made in the years that followed, such as *Passionately in Love*, better known as *A Few Small Nips*, which was begun in around 1935 (pp. 156/157). The generally accepted view in arthistorical writing about this painting has maintained that Kahlo took her subject matter from a newspaper article about a woman who was murdered by her lover, who stabbed her to death when he discovered that she had been unfaithful (p. 154 t.). However, such an account reveals only half of the truth, and does not consider the personal impulse that led Kahlo to make use of the murder as a metaphor, nor even less the possible formal models she may have been able to examine in order to depict this macabre subject. To that end, two possible references may be noted, the first of which is the German painter George Grosz, who had emigrated to the United States shortly before Hitler's rise to power. Since 1918 Grosz had produced a series of drawings, watercolors, and oil paintings exploring the theme of sexual violence against women.[7] It is not unreasonable to assume that Kahlo may have seen a few of these works, especially since some of Grosz's art had been exhibited at the Weyhe Gallery in New York in 1931, the same gallery that was acting as Rivera's dealer for paintings and drawings of his from the previous decade. Moreover, Kahlo must also have got to know Grosz personally since he and Rivera had met in New York, when Rivera was working on the mural at Rockefeller Center, and again later in 1933 when he was painting the murals at the New Workers School.

The second possible source to bear in mind is that Kahlo may also have known the graphic work of Otto Dix and Rudolf Schlichter, who in the 1920s had both been especially interested in crimes of passion and the more sensationalist type of newspaper reports. In fact, there is an undeniable similarity in terms of composition between *A Few Small Nips* and the etching *Sex Murder*, from Dix's series of etchings *Tod und Auferstehung* (Death and Resurrection) from 1922 (p. 154 b.). These artists were also, according to Franz Roh, bursting with Expressionism, cynicism, and brutality, and

Sketch for *Henry Ford Hospital*, July 10, 1932
Graphite pencil on paper, 14 x 21 cm (5½ x 8¼ in.)
Private collection, courtesy Mary-Anne Martin/Fine Art, New York

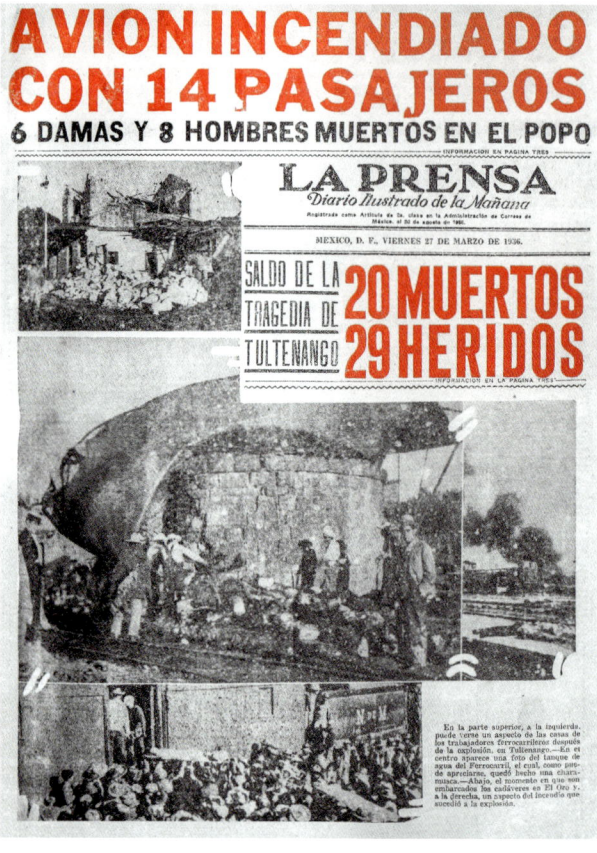

were representatives of the so-called magical realist trend in European painting that Kahlo had first read about in 1927.

A Few Small Nips was not the only painting of Kahlo's though that was inspired by a real-life event reported in the newspapers in Mexico City. In her first exhibition, at the Julien Levy Gallery in New York in 1938, a few of the paintings that were included had been sold shortly before-hand, among them four oil paintings which the actor Edward G. Robinson (1893–1973) had bought directly from Kahlo when he was visiting Mexico City. These purchases were very important since they enabled Kahlo not only to attend her own solo exhibition in New York, but also the show held in Paris the following year. Moreover, the money meant that she was able to travel for the good of her own career, and not just as an accessory to her husband's projects.[8]

One of the paintings Robinson bought was *The Airplane Crash* (Lozano 2021, cat. 48), in which Kahlo again took her subject matter from journalists' reports of a dramatic real-life event (p. 88). The scene allowed her to make two very powerful statements on the transience of life and the fact that we can never know when death may arrive, but beyond that the painting is a metaphorical representation of the critical point in her life in which

Avión incendiado con 14 pasajeros (Plane Consumed by Fire with Loss of 14 Crew and Passengers), March 27, 1936
Newspaper *La Prensa*. Mexico City, Fototeca, Hemeroteca y Biblioteca Mario Vázquez Raña, Archivo y Fundación de la Organización Editorial Mexicana

she found herself, with her dreams of beginning to be able to make decisions that would benefit her own future as an artist left destroyed and shattered by her husband's adulterous relationship with her sister.

Notwithstanding everything that has been written about Rivera's infidelities, it should also be remembered that he was always her greatest supporter, and sought all manner of opportunities for her to develop as an artist. As Raquel Tibol noted, "Frida and Diego understood and admired each other. They were like two forces, each nurturing the other, and made a love pact with conditions that only they could have imagined or would be able to put into practice."[9]

Kahlo's career advanced in giant leaps from the moment she began her relationship with Rivera, who always encouraged her to use her own reality as the subject matter for her paintings. She started to do so from 1931 and continued throughout the years they were living in the United States. In this way she discovered her creative potential, her technical ability, and her own views on the questions of aesthetics and ideology that she and Rivera found were being discussed in San Francisco, Detroit, and New York. For Kahlo, her creative experience abroad even helped to strengthen her sense of her own identity as a Mexican. Since the early 1920s she had been aware of the arguments about art taking place in Mexico between the advocates of nationalism on the one hand, whose aim was to consolidate the country's national identity in the years following the revolution, and on the other hand the painters and intellectuals who felt that modernism should not be subordinate to ideological rhetoric. It was an ongoing discussion, and its influence reached as far as the international political and artistic groups in which Rivera was involved, which included his detractors and also those who admired the ideological range of his art.

As such, Kahlo had to be very careful to ensure that the subject matter of her paintings did not brand her as part of a movement about Mexican cultural identity, especially since she had always had a strong interest in learning about and experimenting with avant-garde techniques and the great tradition of European art. At the same time, she understood that art produced outside of the European canon could make its own aesthetic contribution to the conceptualization of modern art. This was a point on which she and Rivera, along with a number of other Mexican artists of the 1930s, strongly agreed. Kahlo also recognized that there was still an active cultural heritage within the established codes of practice of the visual arts, and that it was the task of modern art to reassess the aesthetics of that tradition and, as she saw it, give it shape through the living contribution of Mexican art.

Both Rivera and Kahlo were involved in discussions of this sort not only in Mexico but also when they were abroad, and their friendships with art critics and historians such

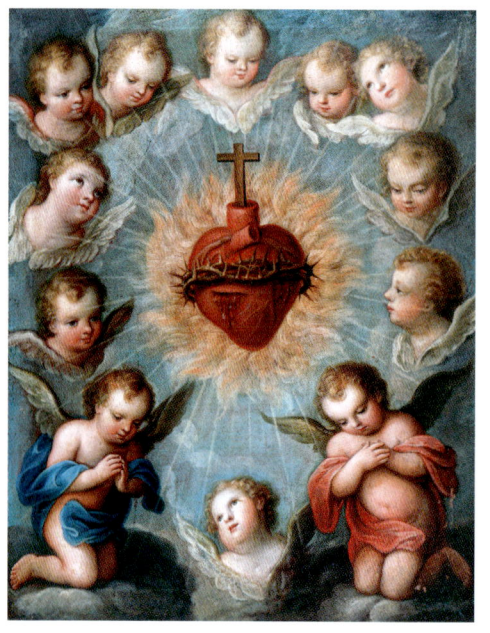

as Paul Westheim (1886–1963), Walter Pach (1883–1958), Holger Cahill (1887–1960), and Meyer Schapiro (1904–1996) in turn played a decisive role in helping Mexican art become recognized at an international level, and for it to become part of more general cosmopolitan debates on various conceptual problems in modern art. For example, between May and July 1933, Kahlo was able to see the exhibition "American Sources of Modern Art" at the Museum of Modern Art in New York, which the curator Holger Cahill had assembled to show various cultural artifacts from the Americas in a new light and to demonstrate how they were related aesthetically and conceptually with examples of modern art. Kahlo was thus able to see sculptural pieces and carvings, ceramics, gold, and silver from the Olmec, Huastec, Mexica, Zapotec, and Maya cultures of Mexico, Guatemala, Honduras, Ecuador, and Costa Rica, and also from the Inca, Nazca, and Chimú cultures of Peru; she was then able to observe these objects in conjunction with works by Jean Charlot, William Zorach (1889–1966), Carlos Mérida (1891–1984), David Alfaro Siqueiros (1896–1974), and Max Weber (1881–1961), among a number of other modern artists. This made it clear that the relevance of pre-Columbian art was not limited to its being a subject for debate in postrevolutionary Mexico but that it was a fundamental source which had been inherited by artists from all of these different countries and was thereby a legitimate part of their identity which they could turn to, even if they were not Mexican.

This conceptual argument began to appear with greater emphasis in Kahlo's work from the late 1930s in such important paintings as *My Nurse and I* (pp. 120/121), *The*

José de Páez, **Allegory of the Sacred Heart of Jesus**, 1775
Oil on canvas, 63 x 48.1 cm (24¾ x 19 in.)
Mexico City, Museo Soumaya, Fundación Carlos Slim

Nickolas Muray, **Frida**, Coyoacán, 1938
Carbon pigment print, 34.9 x 24.1 cm (13¾ x 9½ in.)
New York, collection of Spencer Throckmorton/Nickolas Muray Photo Archives

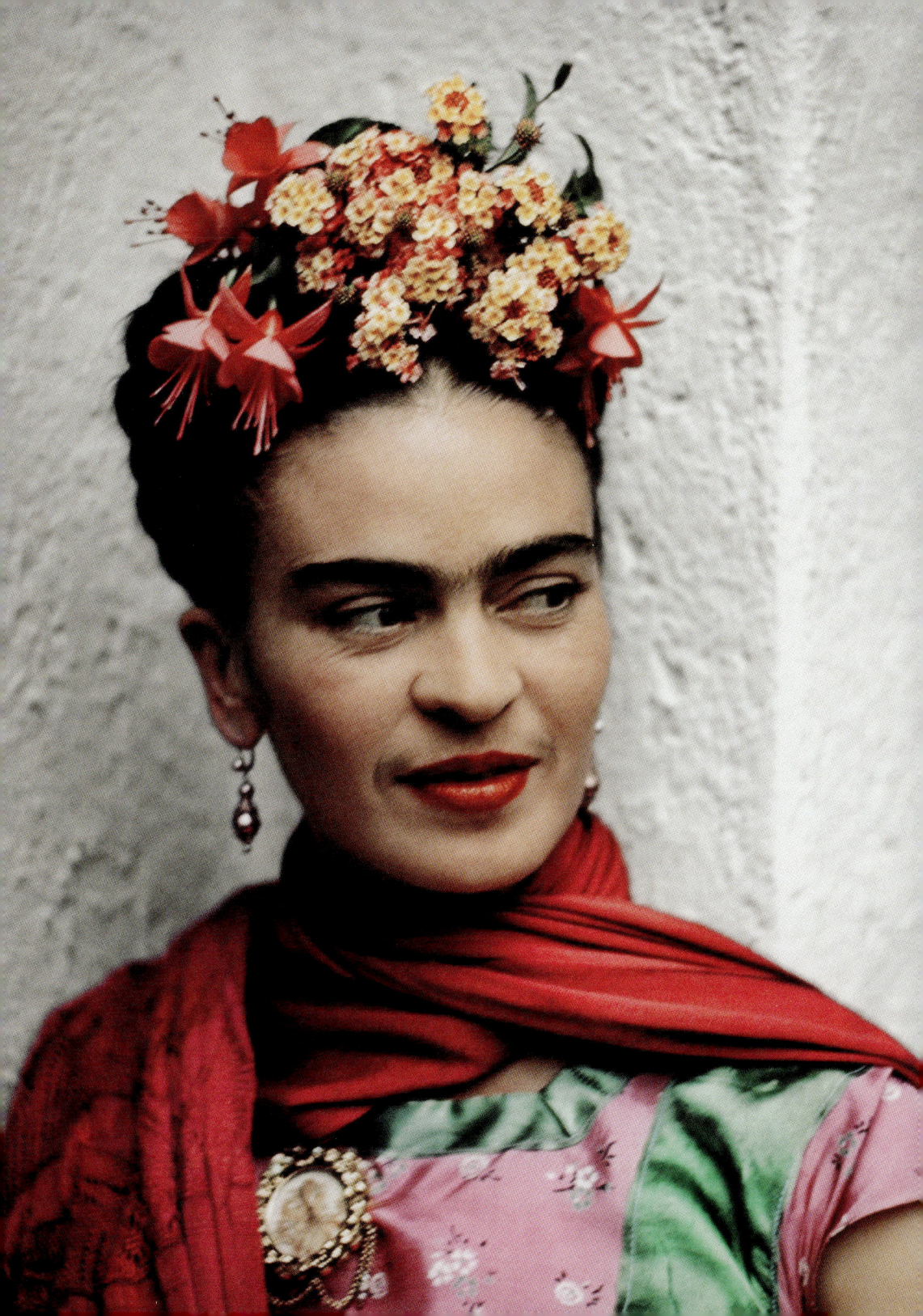

Square Is Theirs (pp. 158/159), and *Survivor* (p. 262). Around 1937, Kahlo began to develop ideas for a painting that would be rooted in the traditions of folk art while allowing her to construct an informed narrative about Mexican identity in the context of modern art. This was the basis for conceiving the deathbed portrait of a child in the style of the so-called "*angelitos muertos*" (dead little angels) (p. 93) that were characteristic of Mexican popular tradition and which still retained a measure of imagery from the colonial period right into the 20th century. In the painting, the young Dimas is shown dressed as a little St. Joseph, crowned in readiness for being admitted to the kingdom of heaven on account of his innocence and lack of sin. This was the specific message Kahlo wanted to emphasize when she titled the painting *Dressed Up for Paradise (The Deceased Dimas Rosas at Three Years of Age)* (p. 160) when it was included in her first solo exhibition at the Julien Levy Gallery in New York.

The still lifes Kahlo painted in the 1930s were also tied to the Mexican pictorial tradition of the 19th century, including *Tunas (Still Life with Prickly Pear Fruit)* (pp. 166/167) and *Food from the Earth* (p. 164). Kahlo collected traditional Mexican still lifes, and these are today in the Museo Frida Kahlo in Coyoacán.[10] Furthermore, and as noted in the previous chapter, her first known paintings were themselves small still lifes painted in the early 1920s, such as *Tray with Poppies* (p. 49) and *Still Life (with Roses)* (p. 48). Kahlo's still lifes owe a significant debt to her family upbringing, although this has largely been overlooked in the art-historical writing about her. While her father was a photographer by profession, he was also an amateur painter, mainly of floral compositions. Guillermo Kahlo passed his love of plants and flowers on to some of his daughters, and taught them about their symbolism and meanings. This detail has escaped the attention of even scholars who have made a study of Kahlo's still lifes, yet it was through her family that she learned to love flowers and got to know their meanings, names, and what they were used for, both socially and personally. From her mother, Matilde Calderón, she acquired a taste for putting fresh flowers in her hair, as is shown in the dozens of photographs of her mother in which she appears in exactly this way. Consequently, flowers and fruits became for Kahlo extensions of her personal thoughts and understanding, and in this way she learned to endow objects with a soul. Rocks, toys, insects, monkeys, and parrots, in short, everything that appeared in her still lifes, had both symbolic meaning as well as representing the physical interaction they had with her and with the viewers of her paintings.

In *Still Life with Prickly Pear Fruit*, for example, the fruits have a very specific set of religious associations that almost amount to a hagiography. Unlike other still lifes Kahlo painted between 1937 and 1938 (pp. 162/163 and p. 164), the fruits in this painting are placed on a plate, trimmed and ready for eating. There is a kind of religious symbolism in

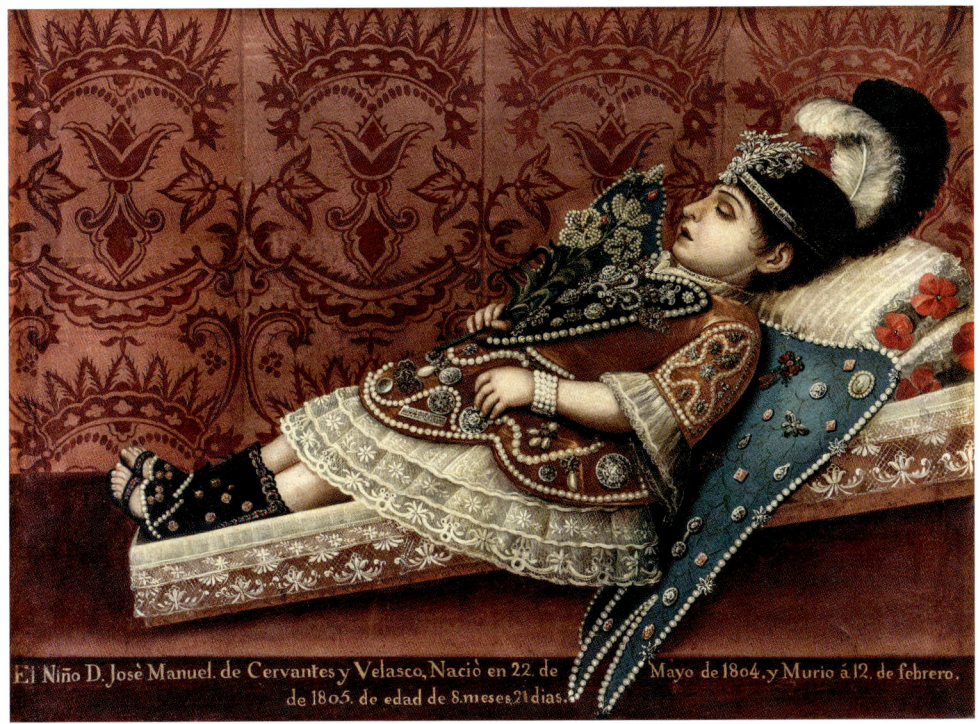

El Niño D. José Manuel. de Cervantes y Velasco, Nació en 22. de · Mayo de 1804. y Murió á 12. de febrero. de 1805. de edad de 8. meses 21 dias.

Anonymous Spanish colonial artist
Deathbed Portrait of the Boy José Manuel Cervantes y Velasco, Mexico, 1805
Oil on canvas, 62 x 83 cm (24⅜ x 32⅝ in.)
Mexico City, private collection, courtesy Sotheby's, Mexico

these bleeding fruits, as if they were martyrs about to be killed, and it is not difficult to see a metaphysical and supernatural aspect to them which perhaps alludes to religious allegories of the Heart of Jesus in the 18th-century paintings of New Spain (p. 90). In my opinion, however, these three fruits on a white plate were carefully chosen by Kahlo to convey a specific meaning, and are a clear reference to the different ages or stages in the development of a human being, whereby the redder the fruit, the more succulent it is, while at the other end of the scale, the very green fruit is not sweet at all. Could this symbolic reading apply to Kahlo's own history? It is quite possible.

Kahlo's painting had clearly evolved from the small world that was all she knew in the 1920s, even if at this early date too she was always open to innovation, to a point where she could now choose the subjects that best suited her desire to communicate her emotional state by means of her art.

In early 1937 Kahlo was in Tampico, a port city on the Gulf of Mexico in the north-eastern state of Tamaulipas, to meet the political exile Leon Trotsky (1879–1940) who had been expelled from Norway and was being pursued by Stalin's (1878–1953) agents. Rivera had interceded with the president of Mexico, Lázaro Cárdenas (1897–1970), on Trotsky's behalf to secure asylum for him. Kahlo's friendly welcome must have been a great relief for the revolutionary and former leader of the Red Army and his wife, Natalia Sedova (1882–1962). They immediately boarded a train for Mexico City, and then moved into Kahlo's family home in Coyoacán which she and Rivera had prepared as their residence during their new phase of life in exile. Rivera had been expelled from the Communist Party in 1929, and slowly gravitated toward Trotskyism and the Fourth International, while also openly showing his sympathy for Communist factions in the United States and support-ing them financially. In the eyes of the international left, it seemed that he was the man who had saved Trotsky and who continued to show his deep ideological commitment as a revolutionary artist. For his part, Trotsky had a particular interest in meeting internation-ally recognized artists and theorists, such as Rivera and the Surrealist writer André Breton, in order to urge the global community to defend creative autonomy, which he viewed as an essential requirement for turning art into a revolutionary force in the service of social progress. When the three of them met a few months later, it was thus part of a much-anticipated ideological agenda.

Once Trotsky and Sedova had settled in Coyoacán, they immediately began to work on setting up a truth commission (known as the Dewey Commission after its chair, the American philosopher John Dewey (1859–1952) to investigate the charges made against Trotsky in the Moscow Trials, where he was accused of having betrayed the October Revolution. Within this bigger picture of art and politics, Kahlo also had her own crea-tive agenda. At this time, she was occupied with making the cultural reality of Mexico an essential component in her painting. Her intellectual development through art led her to examine various different modes of identity and to validate the role of popular culture, but without falling into merely picturesque representations of Mexican identity, or banal decorative exercises on the same themes. She also wanted to avoid making her concerns into a dogmatic social platform, or any kind of simplistic observation that was lost in the past, as a sort of late flowering of nationalist romanticism. On the contrary, she saw the perpetuation of Mexican culture as taking place through the living manifestations of tradi-tion. For example, she liked to find ideas in newspapers such as *La Prensa* (p. 154), where the situations she was looking for were those that eluded any simple rational explanation in events from daily life, and which, against all logic, were equivalent to the Surrealist idea of objective chance, which she had been experimenting with in Detroit and New York in the early 1930s through the techniques of automatic drawing and the exquisite corpse.

As the work of the commission got under way, Kahlo maintained a respectful distance although her admiration for Trotsky grew as she learned of the reasons for him being persecuted and why his sons were later murdered. Between the sessions of the commission and the fact of their meeting on a daily basis, an attraction began to develop between the two of them. There has been much speculation about whether the subsequent affair held the same intensity for Kahlo as it seems to have had for Trotsky, but by all accounts, in July 1937 she decided to put an end to their relationship. Four months

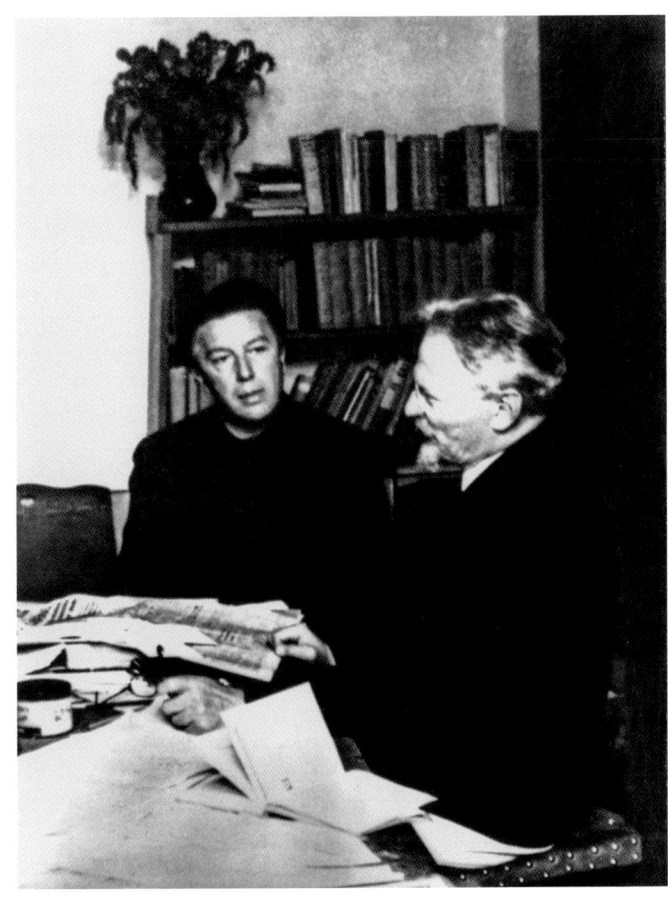

after they had broken up, however, Kahlo gave him one of her most beautiful self-portraits for his birthday, on which she wrote: "For Leon Trotsky, with great affection, I dedicate this painting on November 7, 1937. Frida Kahlo. In San Angel. Mexico" (p. 175). It is an extraordinary example of her own awareness of her Mexican identity, presented with the conviction of the time in which she lived and depicting herself both as an artist and as an intelligent woman. However, Kahlo's real purpose in presenting this portrait was actually to attract the attention of André Breton (1896–1966), the writer, aesthete, and undisputed leader of the international Surrealist movement, to the visual techniques she had been experimenting with since 1932, and which had resulted from the Surrealist drawings she

André Breton and Leon Trotsky in Mexico City, 1938

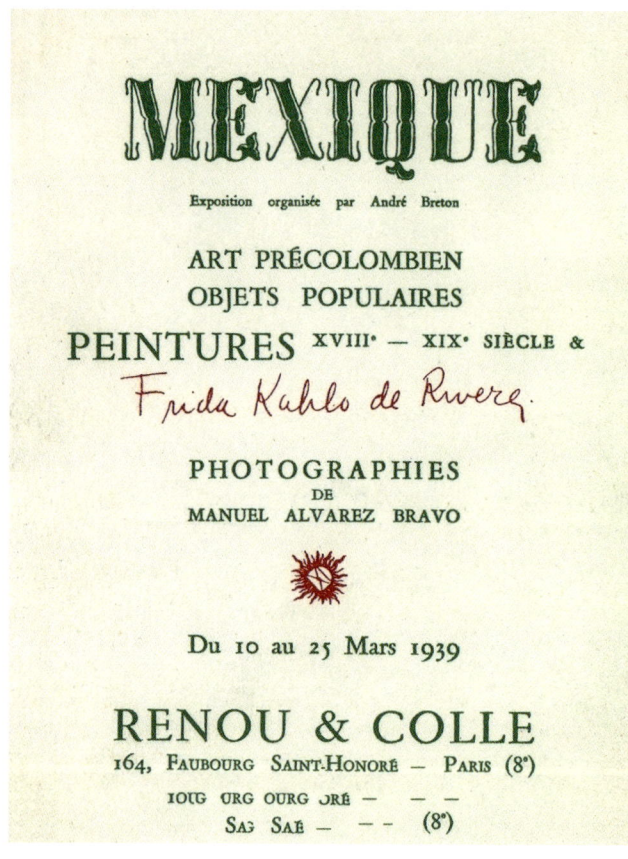

MEXIQUE

Exposition organisée par André Breton

ART PRÉCOLOMBIEN
OBJETS POPULAIRES

PEINTURES XVIIIᵉ — XIXᵉ SIÈCLE &
Frida Kahlo de Rivera.

PHOTOGRAPHIES
DE
MANUEL ALVAREZ BRAVO

Du 10 au 25 Mars 1939

RENOU & COLLE
164, FAUBOURG SAINT-HONORÉ — PARIS (8ᵉ)

had seen at the Julien Levy Gallery and from her own use of objective chance in her drawings.

On April 18, 1938, Breton and his wife, the painter Jacqueline Lamba (1910–1993), arrived at the port of Veracruz where they were met by Rivera, who brought them to Mexico City where they then stayed at his house in the Altavista neighborhood. Breton had been asked by the French Ministry of Foreign Affairs to give a series of lectures on art and literature in order to promote French culture in Mexico, but he also took advantage of his visit to arrange to meet Trotsky (p. 95). Aside from the ideological matters he had to discuss with Trotsky and also Rivera, Breton was amazed by everything he saw in Mexico, and was equally impressed by the great nobility of its indigenous people. He even praised Rivera's painting, with all its political commitment.[11] It can thus be understood that when Breton saw the paintings Kahlo was preparing for her first solo show at the Julien Levy Gallery later that year, he believed he had discovered an innately Surrealist painter living and working in Mexico, and that it was for that reason he wrote the preface for the leaflet published to accompany the exhibition in New York: "Such was my surprise and joy to discover, once I had arrived in Mexico, that her work in her most recent paintings had flourished in a state of pure Surrealism, even though it had been conceived with no prior knowledge of the ideas that underpinned my own activities and those of my friends."[12]

The first of Kahlo's paintings that Breton saw was in fact the *Self-portrait Dedicated to Leon Trotsky* mentioned earlier, which was hanging on one of the walls in Kahlo's house, the Casa Azul in Coyoacán (p. 175). He was captivated by this "fairy-tale princess, with magic spells at her fingertips, an apparition in the quetzal bird's flash of light, which scatters opals among the rocks as it flies away."[13] He believed he had found in Kahlo's work the exegesis of the Surrealist movement, and the following year, in 1939, her work was admired in Paris by Picasso, Duchamp, Kandinsky, Tanguy, and several other Surrealist artists. *Self-portrait Dedicated to Leon Trotsky* had served its purpose.

When Kahlo and Rivera settled in Detroit, she began to paint small compositions on metal, the same surface that was typically used in the painting of traditional Mexican ex-votos, which testified to the miraculous intercession of a saint or the Virgin Mary in securing a favorable outcome to certain dramatic incidents in the life of the believer, whose prayers were believed to have brought about this intervention. The practice still continues today in churches and shrines throughout Mexico, and having originally been introduced in the colonial period it has since been modified to suit the needs of the 21st century where it remains important in certain levels of society. Both Kahlo and Rivera were keenly interested in Mexican ex-votos and collected them, as can be seen from the walls of the Museo Frida Kahlo in Coyoacán. It is hardly surprising then that, whether by her own decision or following Rivera's suggestion, Kahlo herself decided to take up this tradition of Mexican painting in 1931.[14]

Looking back on her work from the 1930s, it becomes clear how Kahlo was, in effect, using ex-votos as a starting point for dealing with the way her life might develop in the United States. As such, it is evident how the ex-voto format became a sophisticated and significant resource for her to adapt.[15] At first, she seems to have chosen events from her own life that she wanted to highlight, as if trying to present herself as the main character in a narrative that would unfold in successive episodes, beginning with her ancestors, birth, and early education with wet nurses or nursemaids. But suddenly, this carefully told biography is disrupted by unexpected turns of events, such as the question of her identity while she was living abroad, the loss of an unborn child, her exile from a country for which she could no longer feel sympathy, and, finally, the betrayal by her sister and her husband. These unanticipated accidents in life thus altered the storyline of what her paintings had been intended to present.

In the first of these compositions inspired by ex-votos, the narrative is specific and concise, and its resolution involves a supernatural element. So, in *My Grandparents, My*

Invitation to the "Mexique" exhibition, March 10–25, 1939
Printed card, 16.2 x 12.3 cm (6⅜ x 4⅞ in.)
Collection Tracts Dada et Surréalistes – Frida Kahlo – Surr 1939 9015
Archigny, Association Atelier André Breton

Parents, and I (My Family) (pp. 118/119), beneath the family tree a human egg is shown being fertilized by sperm; in *Birth* (pp. 116/117), Kahlo is shown emerging covered in blood from between her mother's legs; and in *My Nurse and I* (pp. 120/121), the nurse is an indigenous woman wearing a pre-Columbian mask of an ancient Olmec jaguar deity with a downturned mouth (p. 120). However, as Kahlo became more proficient in her technique (which at times could be quite obsessive in the devotional detail she applied to her brushstrokes) narrative clarity, cohesion, and the synthesis of different elements were replaced by ambiguity, confusion, and absence of logic, which enabled her to explore further into the unknown. For example, the mismatched symbols that surround the bed in *Henry Ford Hospital (The Lost Desire)* make Kahlo's miscarriage less comprehensible, and therefore more painful (pp. 112/113). In *Self-portrait (on the Border between Mexico and the United States)* (pp. 110/111), meanwhile, past and present, day and night, the ground and what lies beneath it are all mingled together irrationally, while in *A Few Small Nips* (pp. 156/157) the viewer is left to identify both the victim and the murderer in this toxic relationship run through with betrayals and infidelities.

For Kahlo, 1938 was a prolific year for her creativity in which she managed to produce enough work to fulfill the requirements for her first solo exhibition in New York. Her use of ex-votos as a model had evolved into a new and more refined visual strategy that was closer to the intellectual and expressive content she sought for her painting, and which was otherwise unknown in modern art. It was never the primitive archaism of ex-votos that captured her attention, but rather the powerful ability these images had for being able to communicate with their viewers, regardless of the fact that the subject matter was essentially supernatural and thus could not be explained on rational grounds. This, of course, is entirely understood since their ultimate purpose is to celebrate the divine intervention that resolves the problems of believers. Kahlo saw that this particular quality, which was unlike anything else in the history of art, could be a very effective means for constructing more complex narratives from her own experience, but which the viewer could only understand directly if the image was as unexpected as it was disturbing. To give a few examples: Kahlo controlling time and the forces of the universe while standing between the two nations in *Self-portrait (on the Border between Mexico and the United States)* (pp. 110/111); Kahlo lying

Portrait of Jean Wight, January 1931
Oil on canvas, 63.5 x 46 cm (25 x 18⅛ in.); inscribed on the speech scroll:
Retrato de Mrs. Jean Wight / pintado en Enero de 1931, en la ciudad /
de San Francisco Cal. por Frieda Kahlo. (Portrait of Mrs. Jean Wight /
painted in January 1931, in the city / of San Francisco Cal. by Frieda Kahlo.)
San Francisco, Berggruen collection

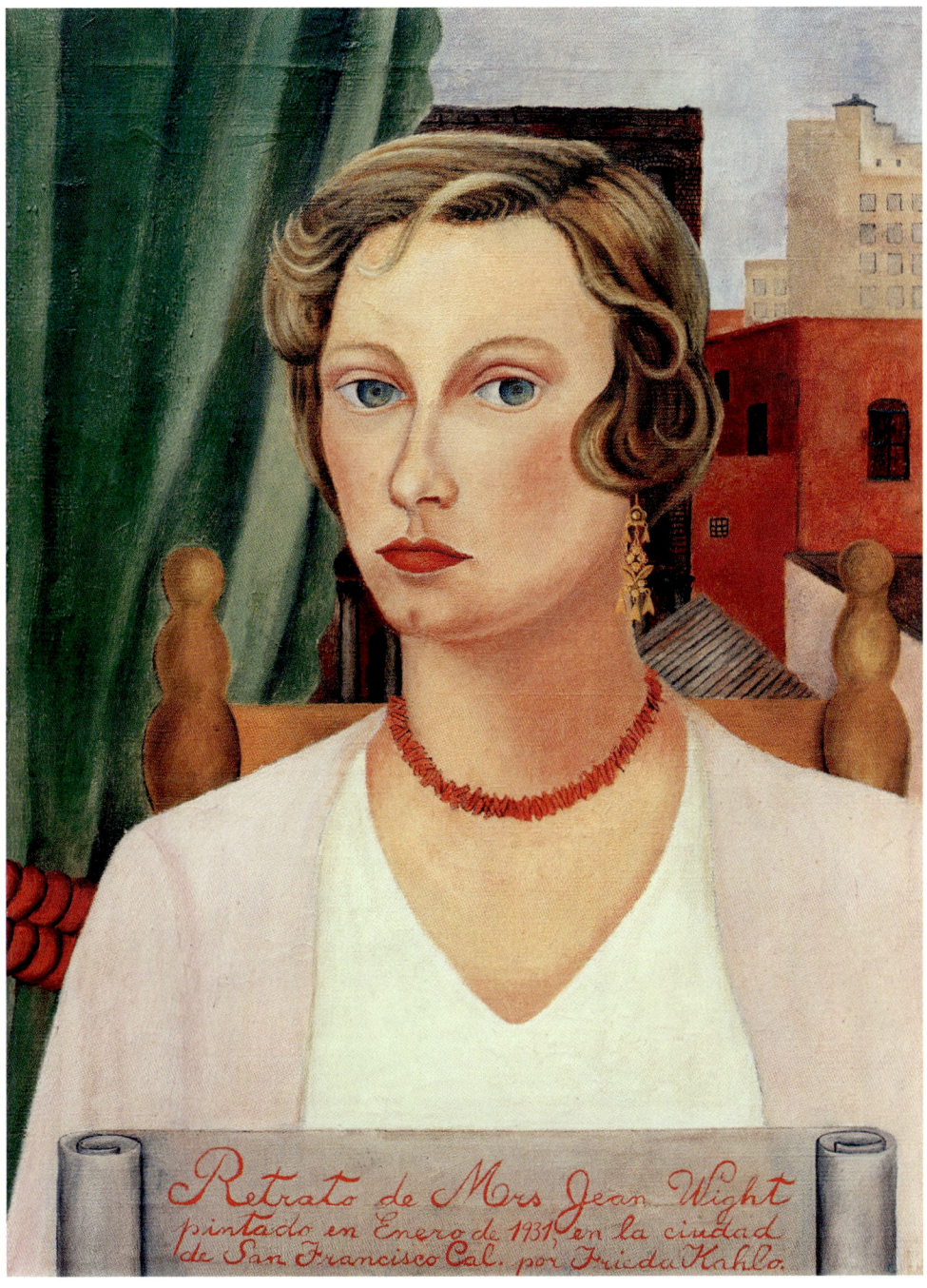

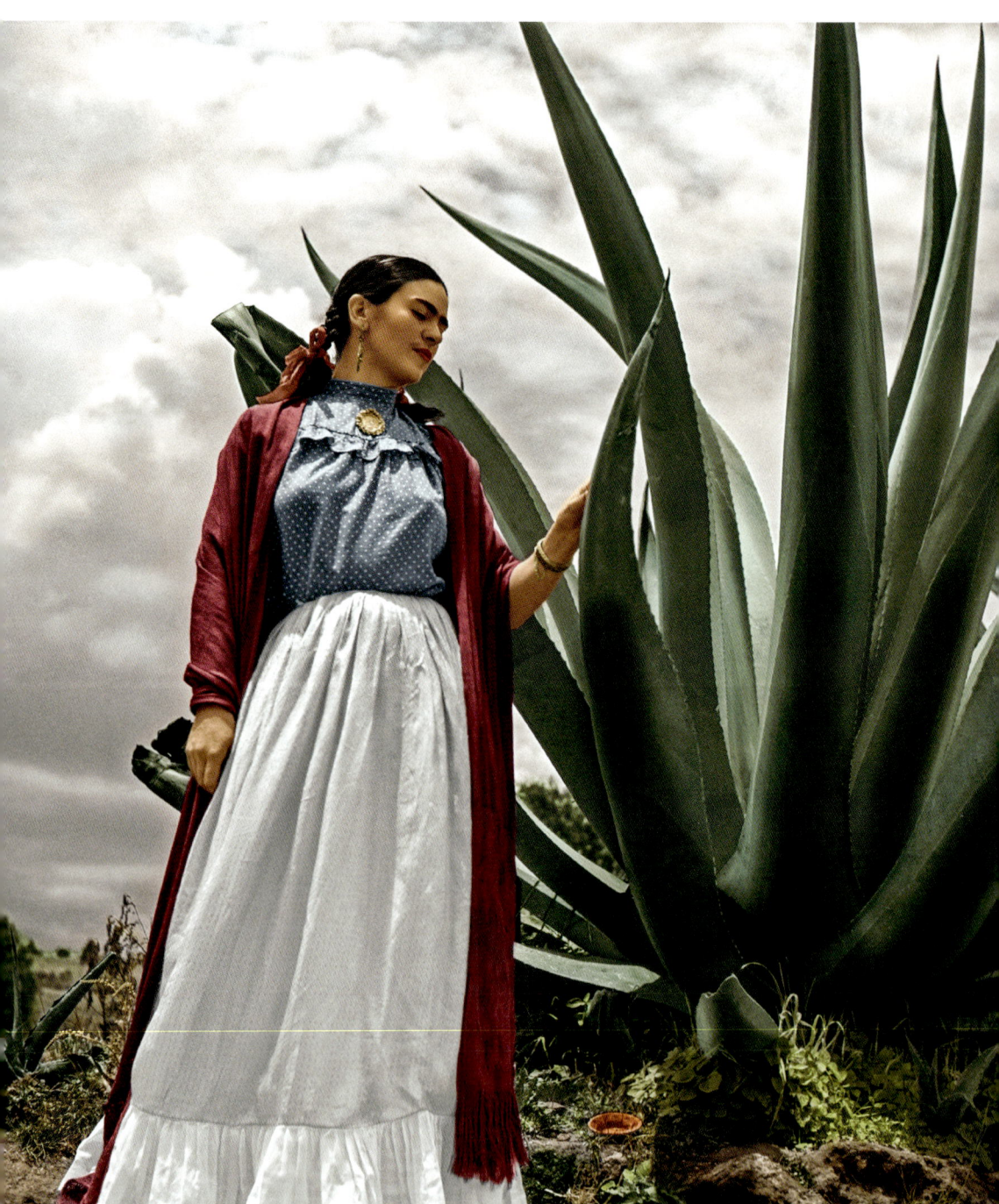

bleeding on a bed after a miscarriage in *Henry Ford Hospital* (pp. 112/113); emerging dead and covered in blood from between her mother's legs as she is born in *Birth* (pp. 116/117); a simple dress of hers hanging limply on its own from a line in New York City in *My Dress Was There Hanging* (pp. 130/131); and lastly, Kahlo's love, stabbed to death in *A Few Small Nips* (pp. 156/157).

Once Kahlo had discovered the potential that Mexican ex-votos offered in terms of communicating a message she must have realized that she had found the right formula for expressing her own conflicts and dilemmas by letting go of the rational logic normally associated with painting in its traditional, conservative form. As such, when Kahlo's work is discussed in terms of its relationship with ex-votos, what is meant is not the format, the surface, or the style, but the way she incorporated divine and nonlogical aspects into her work, although these in turn were gradually set aside as she began to experiment with the techniques of free association and objective chance that were characteristic of Surrealism. It is thus easy to see how Kahlo's work provoked such a sense of fascination in Breton, in relation to both his way of thinking and his theoretical ideas, who saw in it a revitalizing energy and a new direction for Surrealism, whereby the mythical nature and vital force that he took to be inherent in cultures which had developed outside the Western canon would supply the essential element for creativity. For that reason Breton believed that Kahlo's paintings could not be considered separately from their association with Mexico, and all its folk expressions, funeral rites, festivals, drama, and tragedy. In his view, this all constituted an inexhaustible source for the international avant-garde which, on the eve of the Second World War, was a creative foothold for art.

The painting referred to as *The Heart* (p. 177) in the list of works published by the Julien Levy Gallery in 1938 is actually a self-portrait by Kahlo, and is also known as *Memory.* Both of these titles identify in equal measure the two main themes Kahlo wanted to examine, namely the affairs of the heart and the bitter traces of memory. These were also the two facets of Kahlo's personal life that became a constant in her work as an artist as she developed. In this painting, however, she chose not to treat them as isolated chapters in her biography and thus avoided falling into the pattern of a linear narrative. *Memory* is, in fact, a rearrangement in the face of how events actually unfolded, and at the same time a rationalization of feelings and of the dilemma of how to deal with what cannot be foreseen. The image is neither logical nor plausible, but serves as the perfect metaphor: because the pain in Kahlo's heart is so great it has had to leave her body, thus changing her destiny and the world around her; this then is the essence of what she learned from Mexican

Antoinette Frissell Bacon, "Toni Frissell," **Frida Kahlo** (detail), 1937

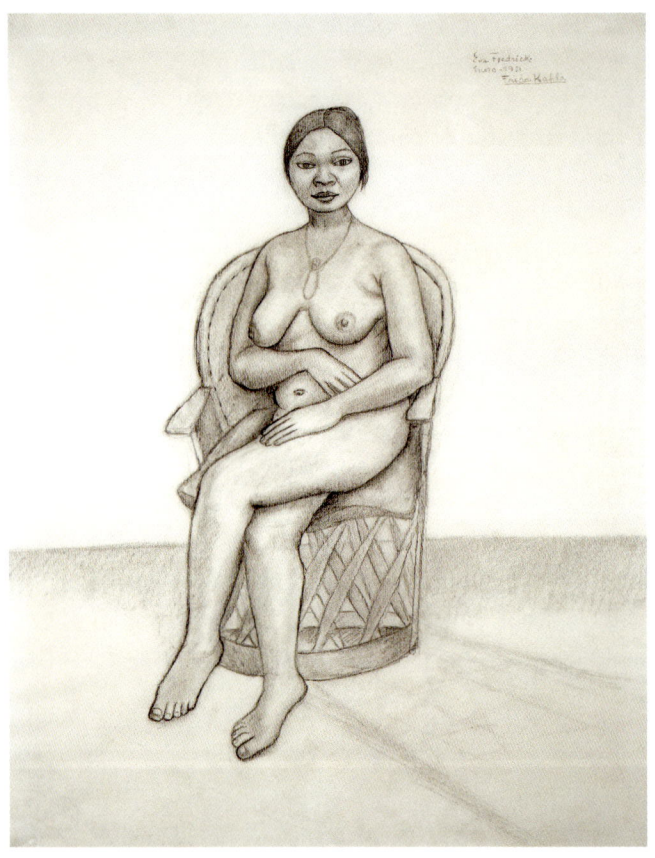

ex-votos. Although the painting does not include the block of text to explain the image that would usually appear on an ex-voto, the scene was evidently motivated by Rivera's betrayal when he was unfaithful to Kahlo with her sister Cristina.[16]

Once the exhibition in New York had ended, Kahlo returned to Mexico to spend Christmas with Rivera. She went back to New York later on since she was concerned because Breton had still not confirmed where the "Mexique" exhibition was to be held in Paris (p. 96).[17] At last, following a series of organizational mistakes and oversights, the exhibition opened at the gallery of Pierre Colle and Maurice Renou, which enjoyed a certain prestige among the Surrealists. The show brought together pieces of pre-Columbian art, folk art, and vernacular paintings from the 18th and 19th centuries, as well as Kahlo's paintings and a collection of photographs by Manuel Álvarez Bravo. Breton introduced Kahlo to Pierre Colle, who in turn introduced her to Michel Petitjean, who was in

Nude of Eva Fredrick *[sic]*, January 1931
Graphite pencil on paper, 61.5 x 48.5 cm (24¼ x 19⅛ in.)
Mexico City, Xochimilco, Museo Dolores Olmedo

Portrait of Eva Frederick, 1931
Oil on canvas, 63 x 46 cm (24¾ x 18⅛ in); inscribed t.: Retrato de
Eva Frederick, nacida / en Nueva York, pintado por Frida Kahlo.
(Portrait of Eva Frederick, born in New York, painted by Frida Kahlo.)
Mexico City, Xochimilco, Museo Dolores Olmedo

charge of overseeing the exhibition at the gallery.[18] Kahlo had earlier arrived at the port of Le Havre on January 21, 1939, where she was met by Jacqueline Lamba and her friend, the photographer Dora Maar, who at the time was Picasso's lover. Kahlo and Maar became friends during the train journey to Saint Lazare station. In Paris, Kahlo first stayed with Breton and Lamba in their apartment at 42, Rue Fontaine, but when she found she was not comfortable there she moved to the Hotel Regina at 2, Place des Pyramides, near to the Louvre and the Renou & Colle Gallery, which was at 164, Rue du Faubourg Saint-Honoré, in the 8th arrondissement.

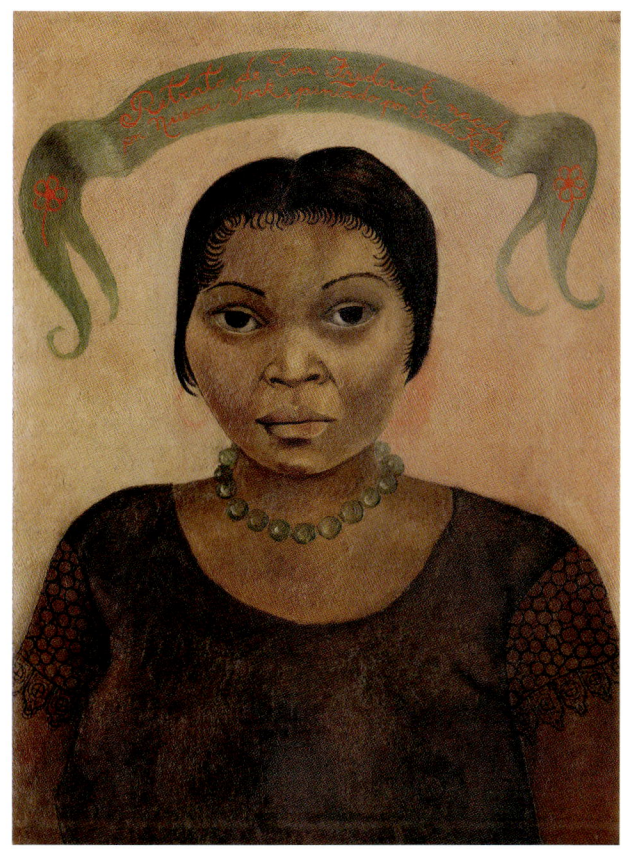

In conclusion, in 1939 once she was back in Mexico again, Kahlo was finally able to reap the rewards of an artistic career that had begun almost 15 years earlier. As will be seen in the next chapter, the 1940s were to be the period of Kahlo's greatest intellectual maturity, as well as the time when opportunities to exhibit her paintings began to increase, and with that, her work would finally begin to gain acceptance with critics.

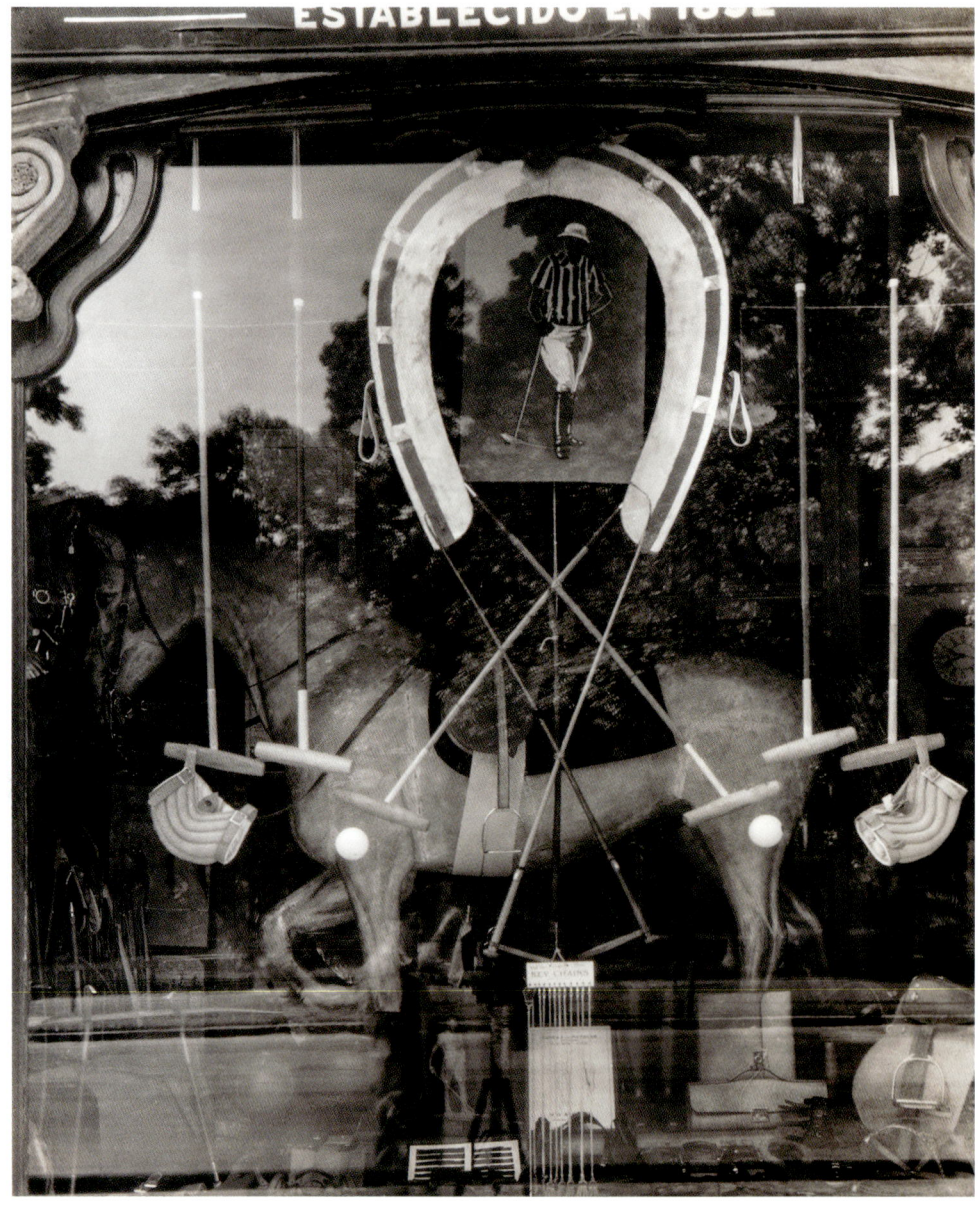

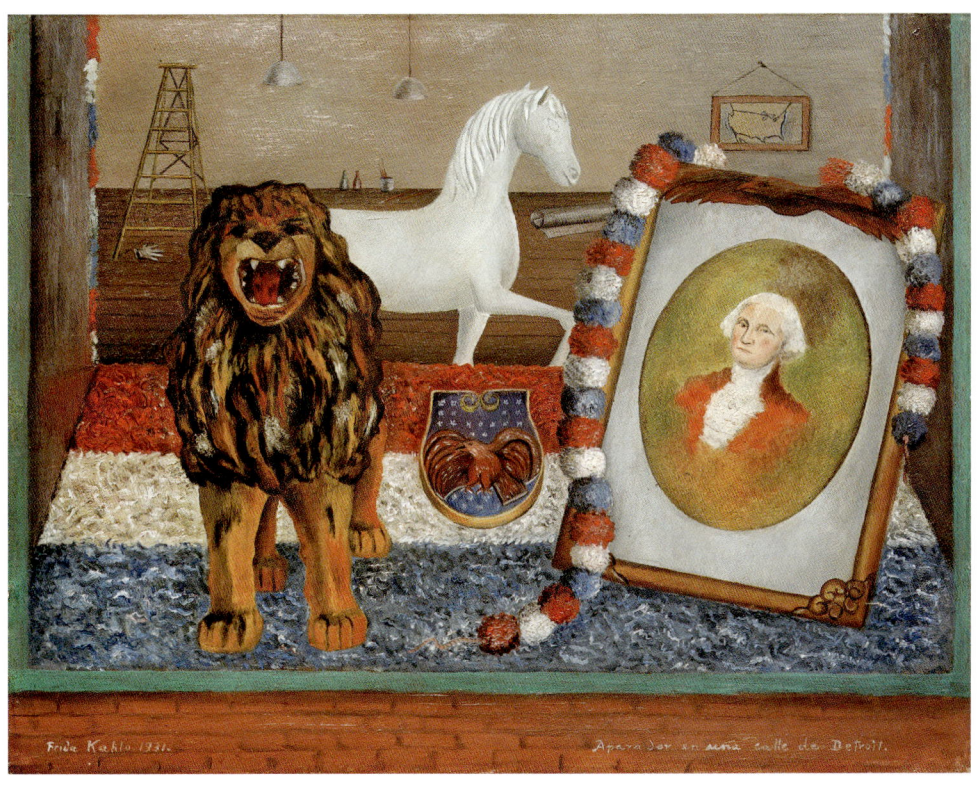

Manuel Álvarez Bravo, **Horse in shop window**, *c.* 1930
Gelatin silver print, 31.7 x 24.8 cm (12½ x 9¾ in.)
Mexico City, Manuel Álvarez Bravo Archive

Window Display in a Street of Detroit, 1931/32
Oil on metal, 30.3 x 38.2 cm (11⅞ x 15 in.)
Fiorella and Francisco Pérez Díaz collection,
courtesy Gary Nader Fine Arts, Miami

Otto Dix, **The Businessman Max Roesberg**, Dresden, 1922
Oil on canvas, 94.3 x 63.8 cm (37⅛ x 25⅛ in.)
New York, The Metropolitan Museum of Art, Purchase,
gift of Lila Acheson Wallace, 1992

Portrait of Dr. Leo Eloesser, 1931
Oil on masonite, 85.1 x 59.7 cm (33½ x 23½ in.)
San Francisco, Zuckerberg San Francisco General Hospital and
Trauma Center, University of California School of Medicine

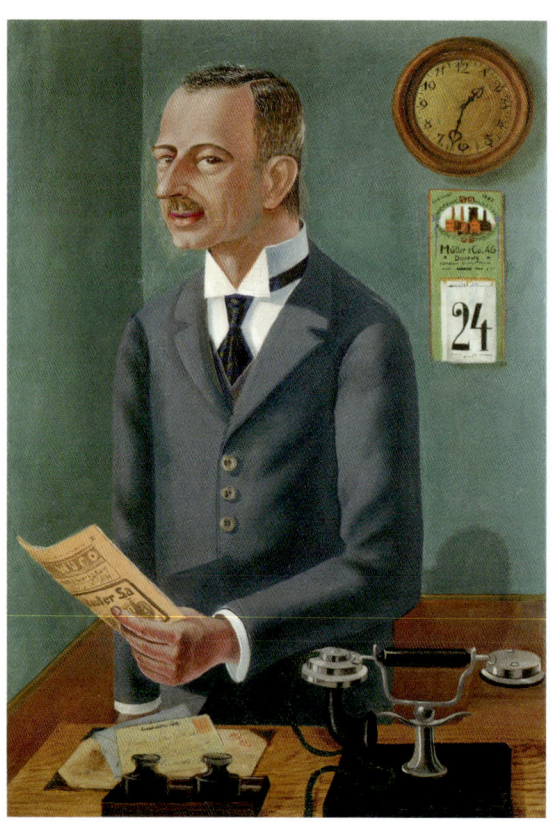

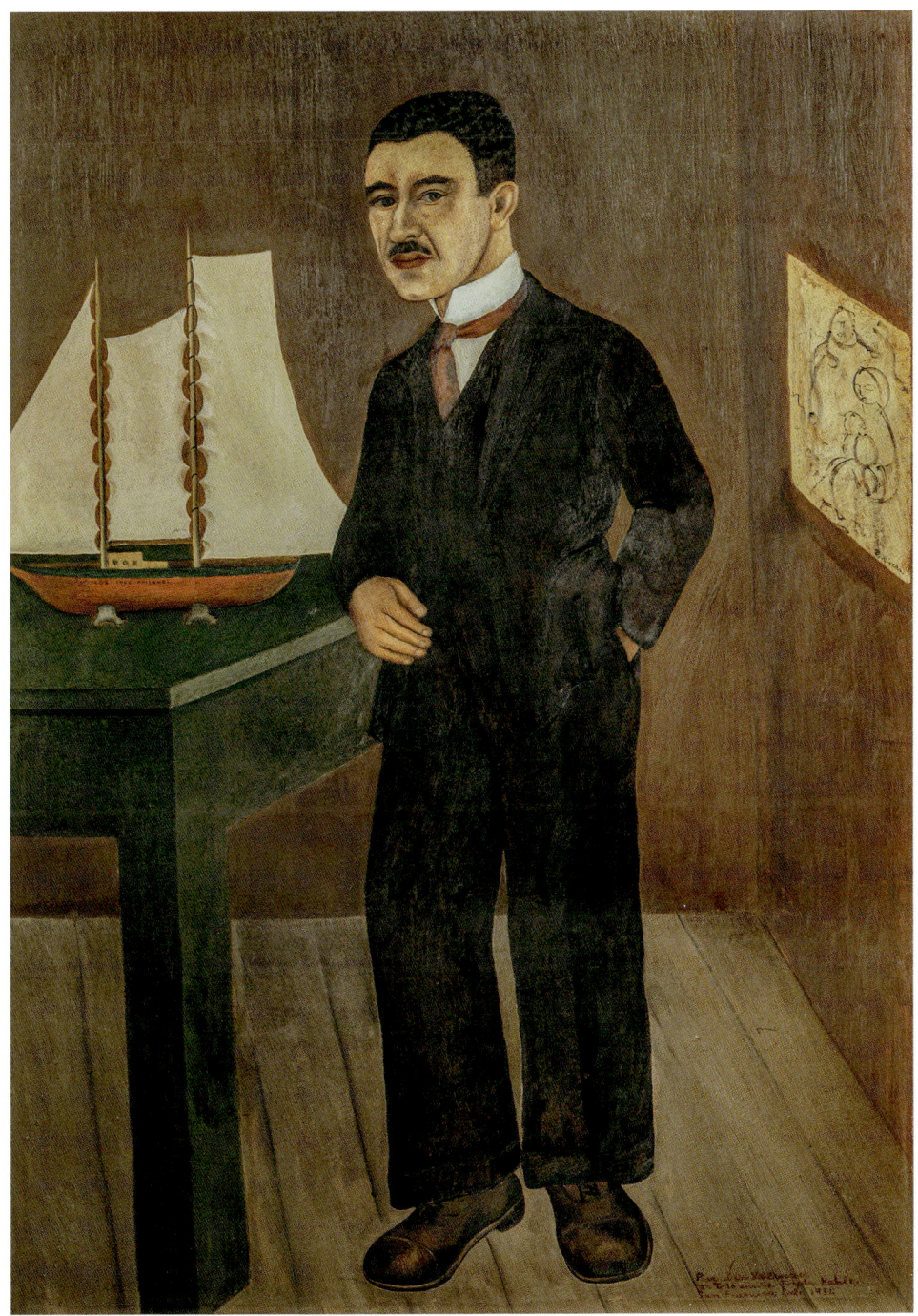

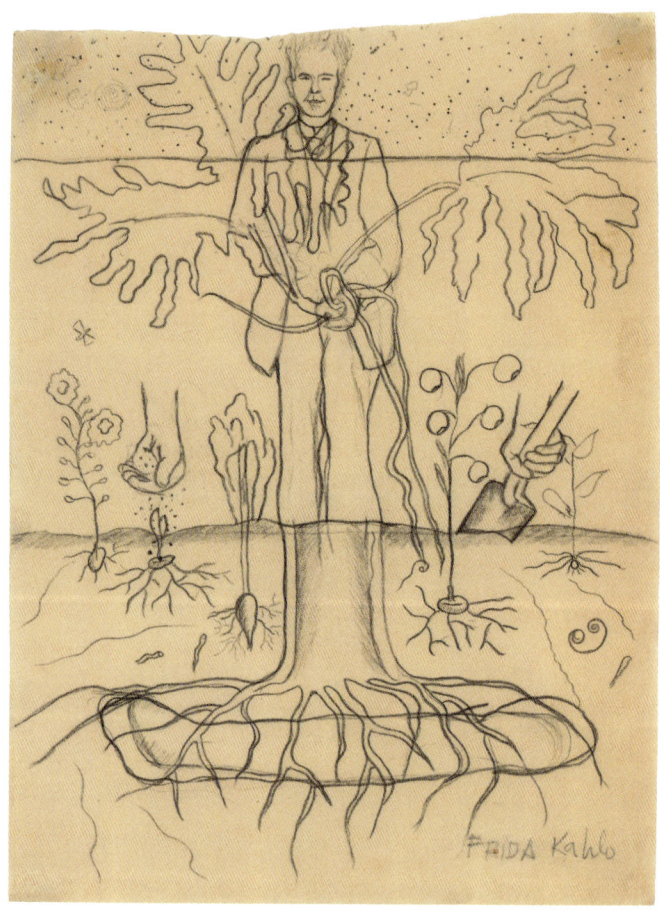

Sketch for *Portrait of Luther Burbank*, *c.* 1931
Graphite pencil on paper, 29 x 21 cm (11⅜ x 8¼ in.)
Mexico City, private collection

Portrait of Luther Burbank (Burbank – American Fruit Maker), 1931
Oil on masonite, 86.5 x 61.7 cm (34 x 24¼ in.)
Mexico City, Xochimilco, Museo Dolores Olmedo

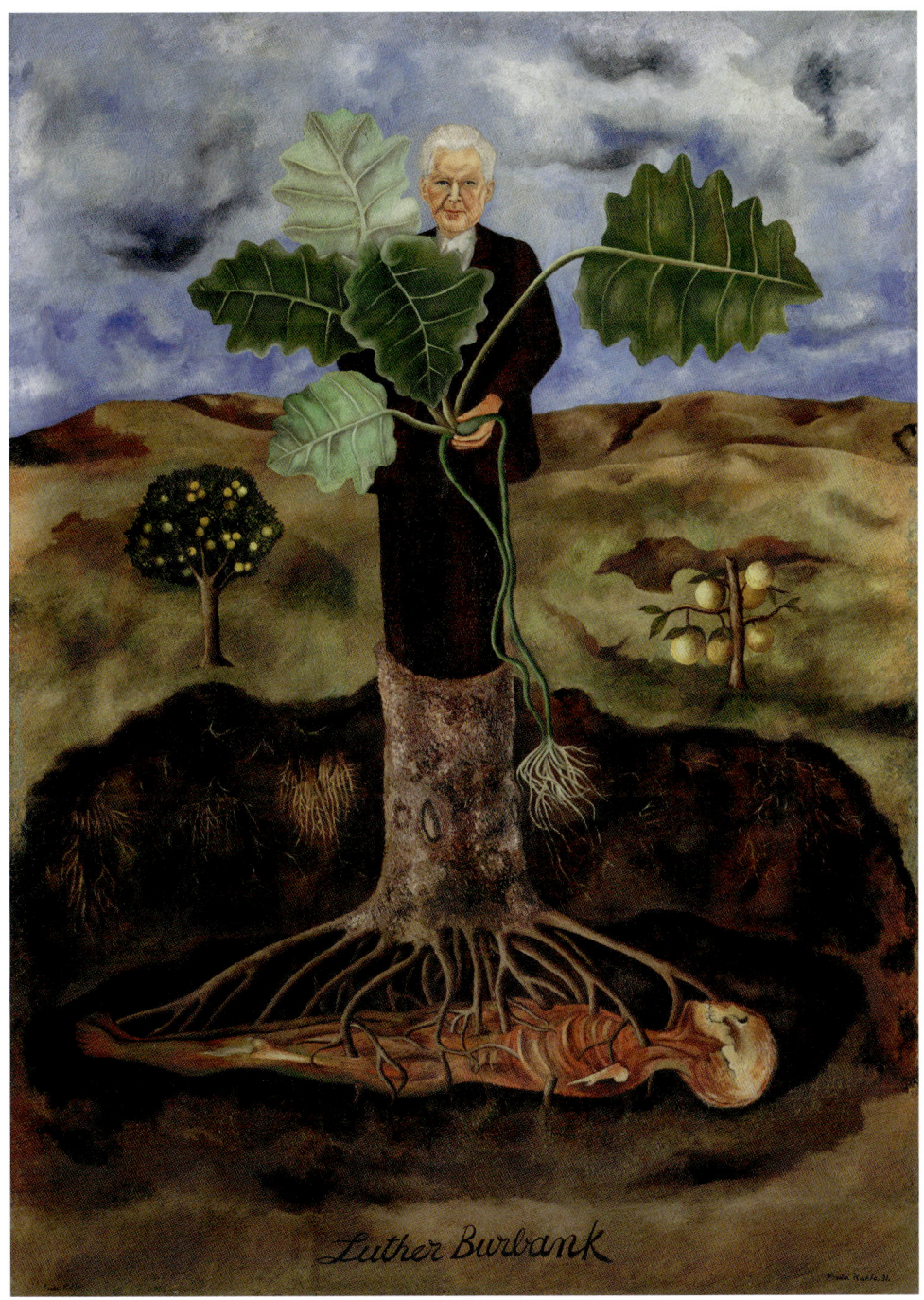

**Self-portrait (on the Border between Mexico
and the United States)**, 1931/32
Oil on zinc, 31.8 x 34.9 cm (12½ x 13¾ in.)
New York, Modern Art International Foundation,
courtesy Manuel and María Reyero

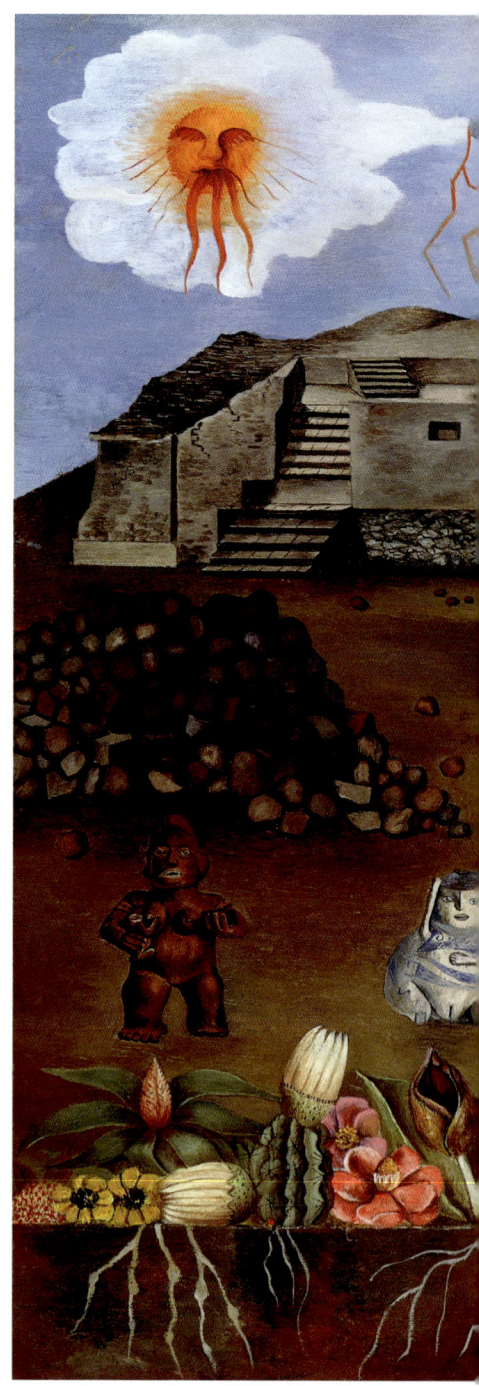

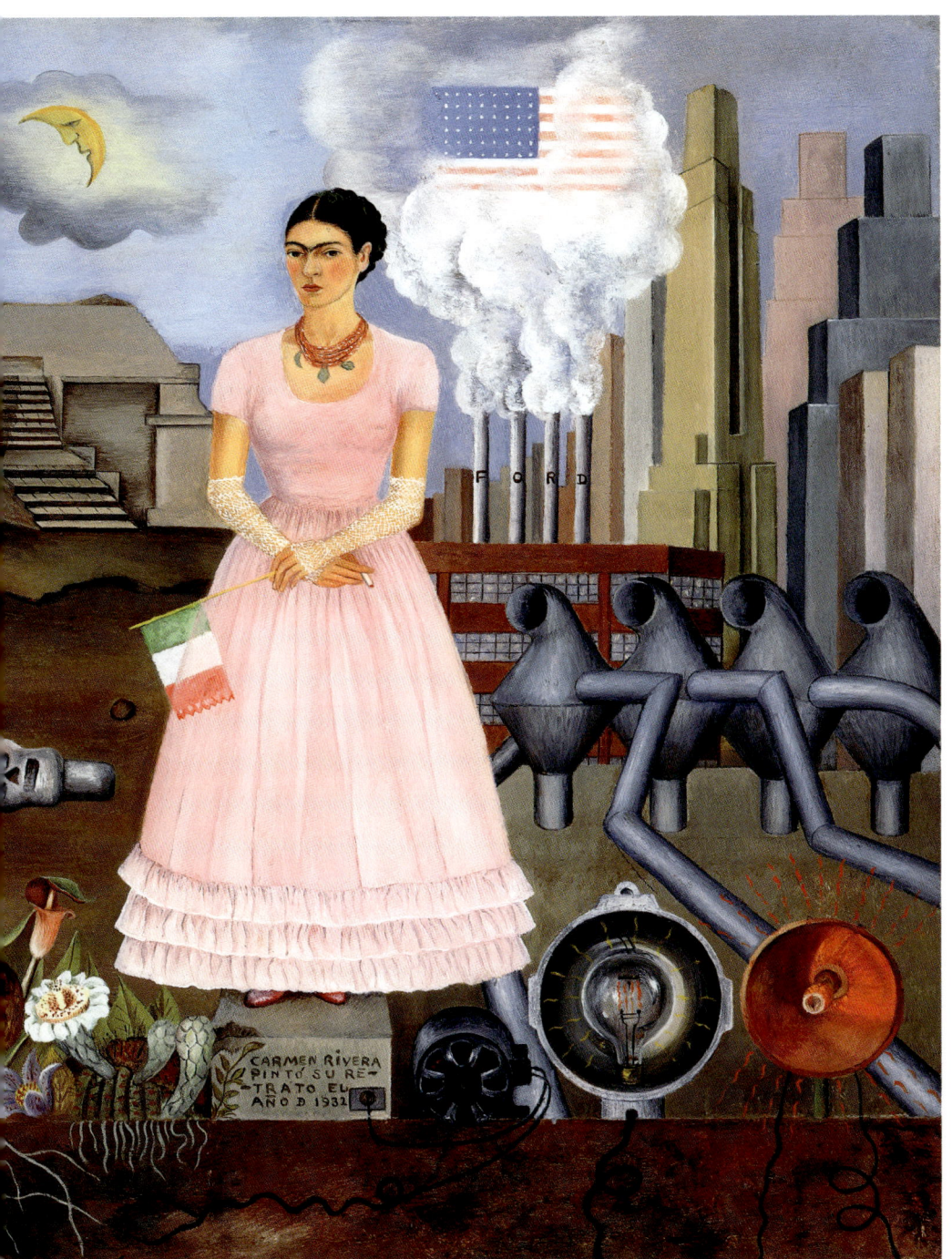

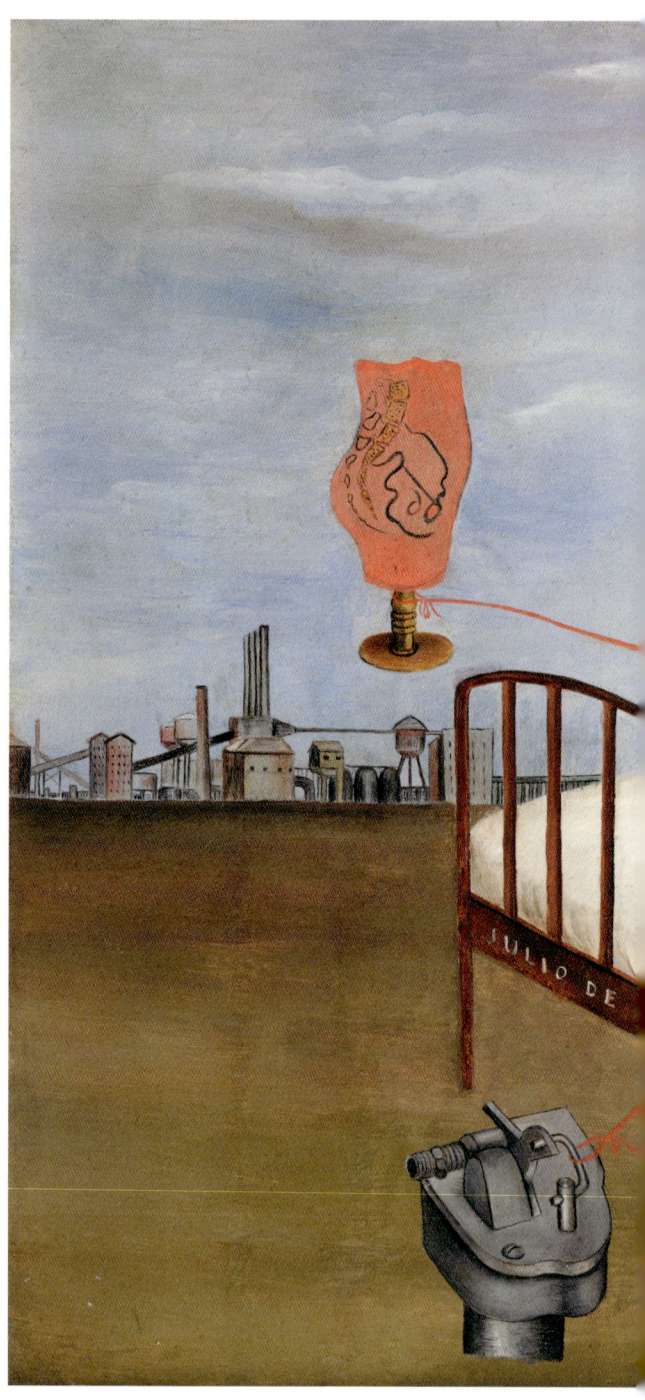

**Henry Ford Hospital
(The Lost Desire)**, July 1932
Oil on metal, 30.5 x 38 cm (12 x 15 in.)
Mexico City, Xochimilco,
Museo Dolores Olmedo

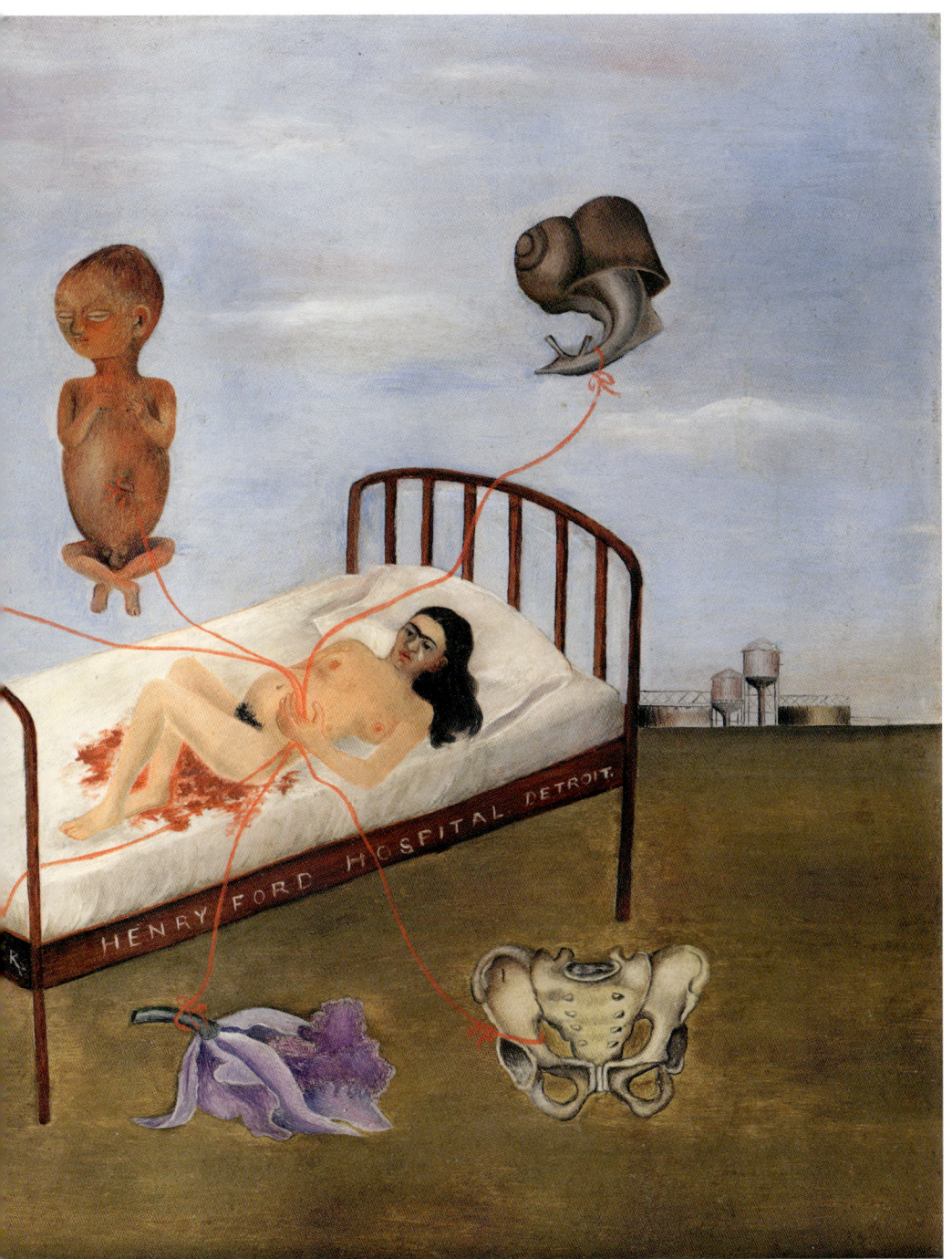

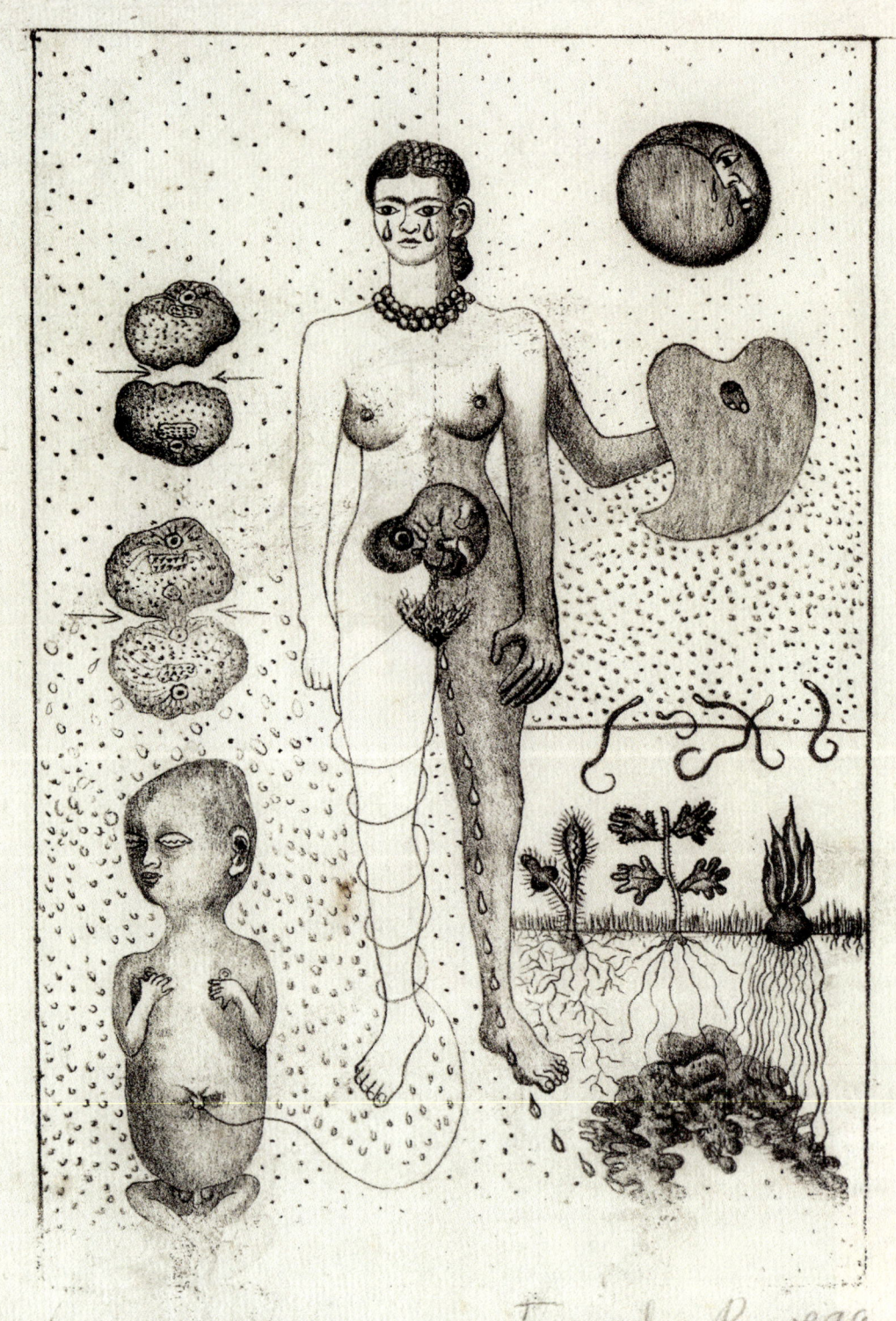

Frieda Rivera

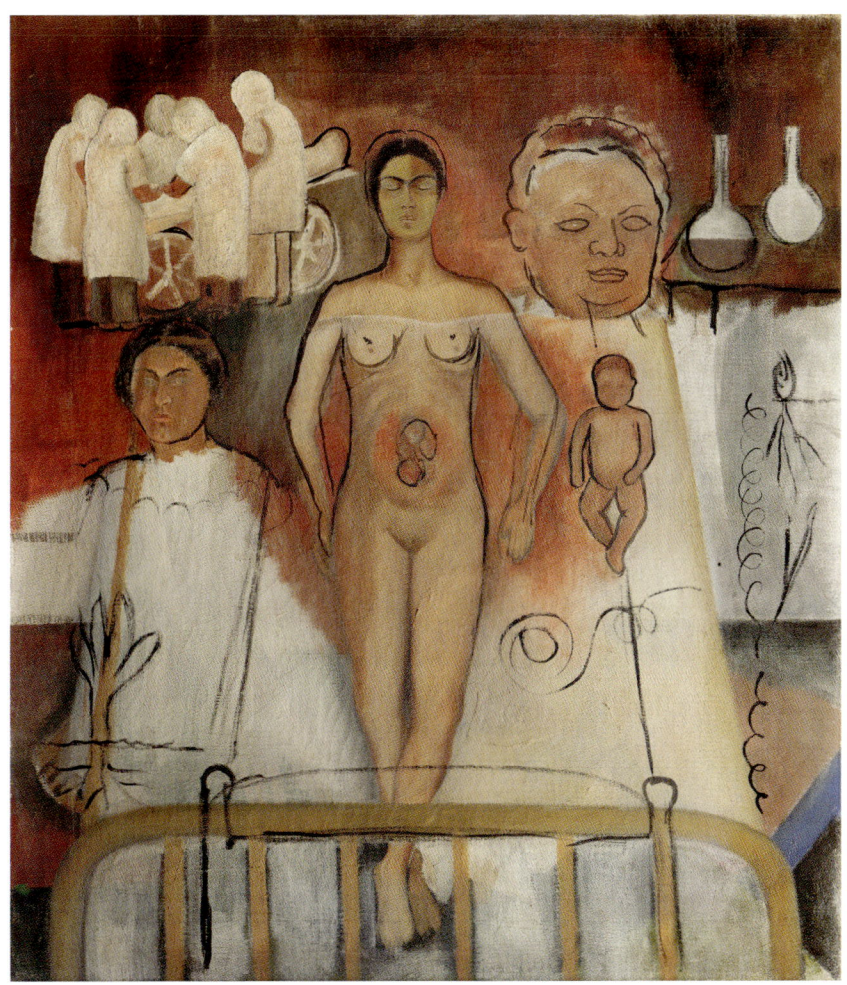

The Miscarriage (Frida and the Miscarriage), Detroit, August 1932
Lithograph (second proof), 31.7 x 24 cm (12½ x 9½ in.)
Mexico City, Xochimilco, Museo Dolores Olmedo

Frida and the Caesarean (unfinished), 1929–1931
Oil on canvas, 73 x 62 cm (28¾ x 24⅜ in.)
Mexico City, Coyoacán, Museo Frida Kahlo

Birth, 1932
Oil on copper, 30.5 x 35 cm (12 x 13¾ in.)
Private collection of Madonna

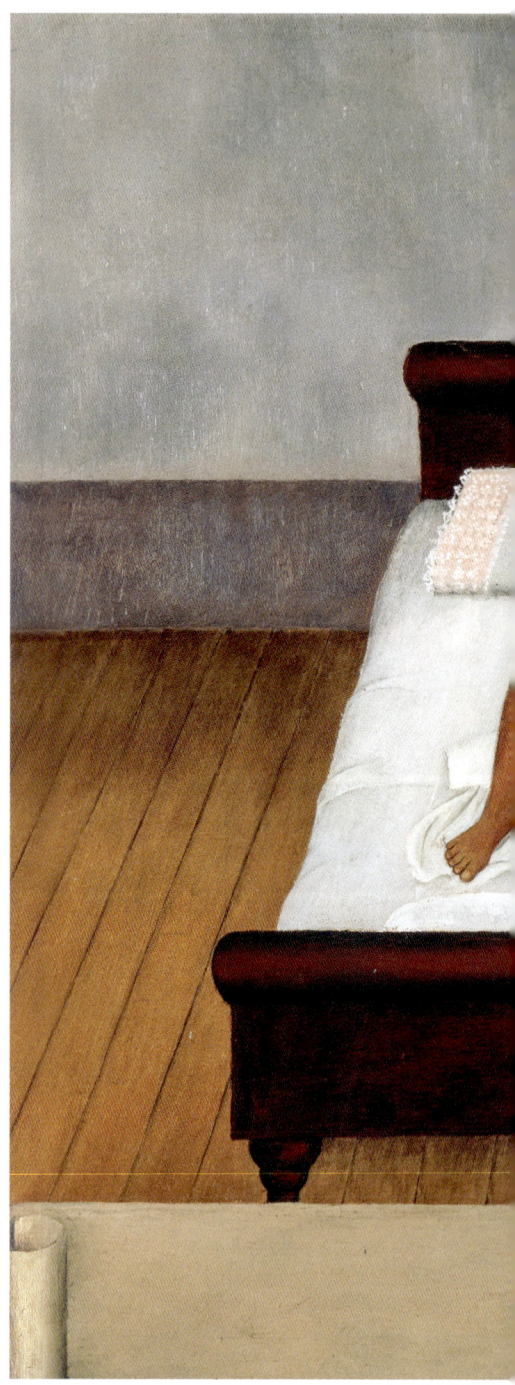

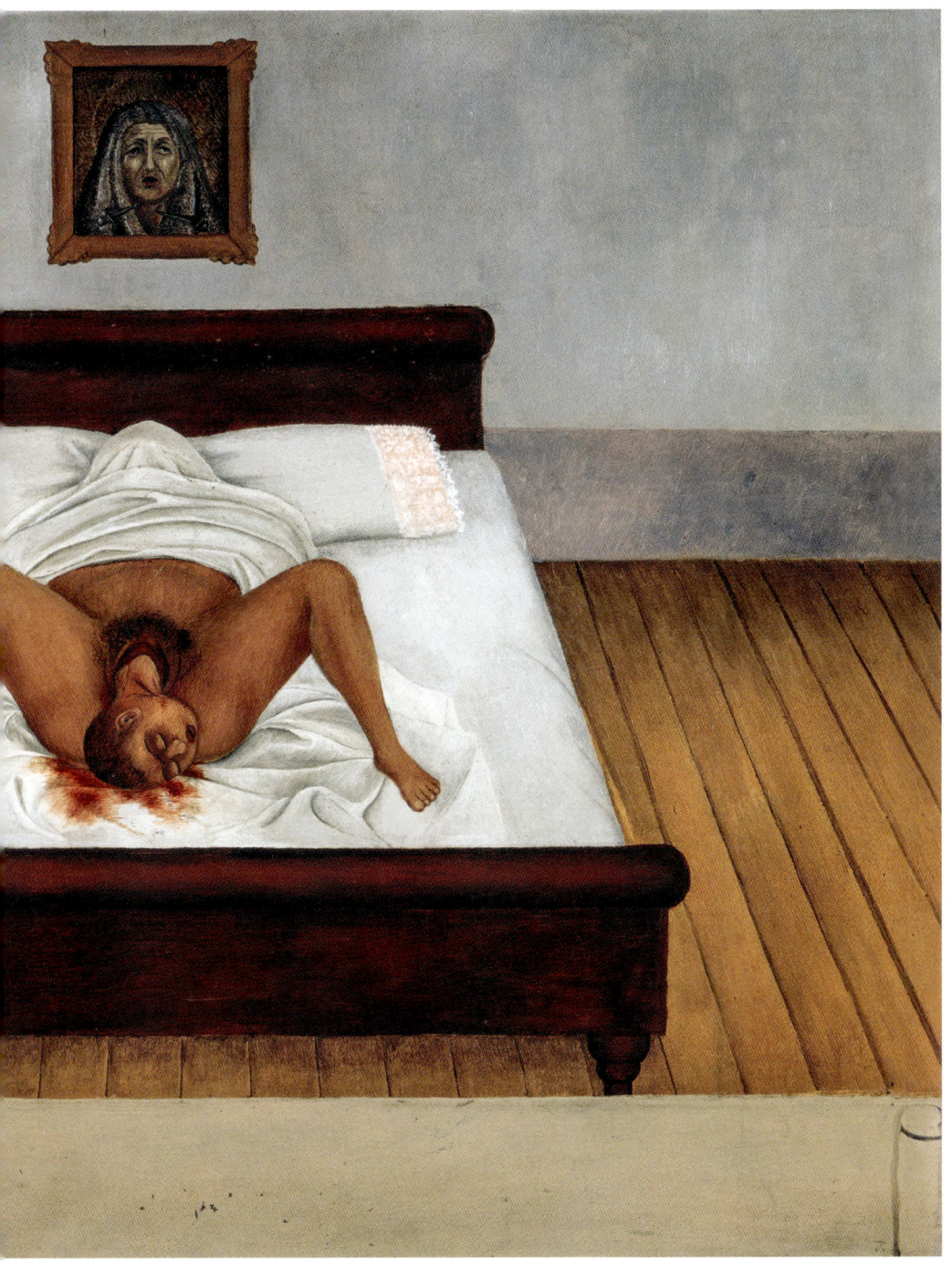

My Grandparents, My Parents, and I
(My Family), 1936
Oil and tempera on zinc, 30.7 x 34.5 cm (12⅛ x 13⅝ in.)
New York, Museum of Modern Art, gift of Allan Roos,
M. D. and B. Mathieu Roos, inv. 102.1976

Bottom center: Frida; *center*: her mother Matilde
Calderón and father Guillermo Kahlo;
top left: her maternal grandparents, Antonio
Calderón and Isabel González y González;
top right: her paternal grandparents,
Rosine Marie Henriette Kaufmann and
Johann Heinrich Jakob Kahlo

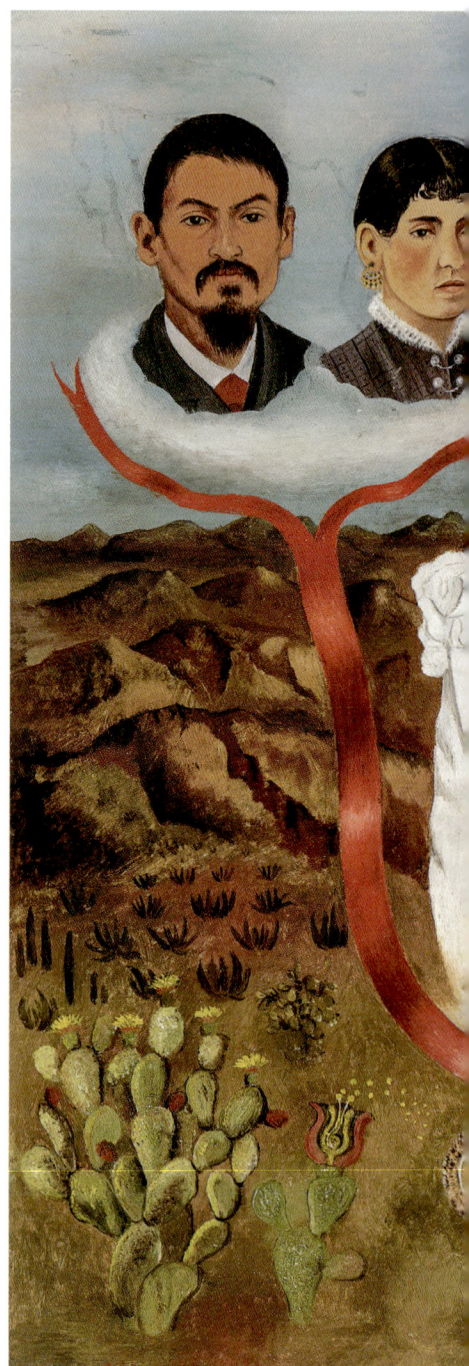

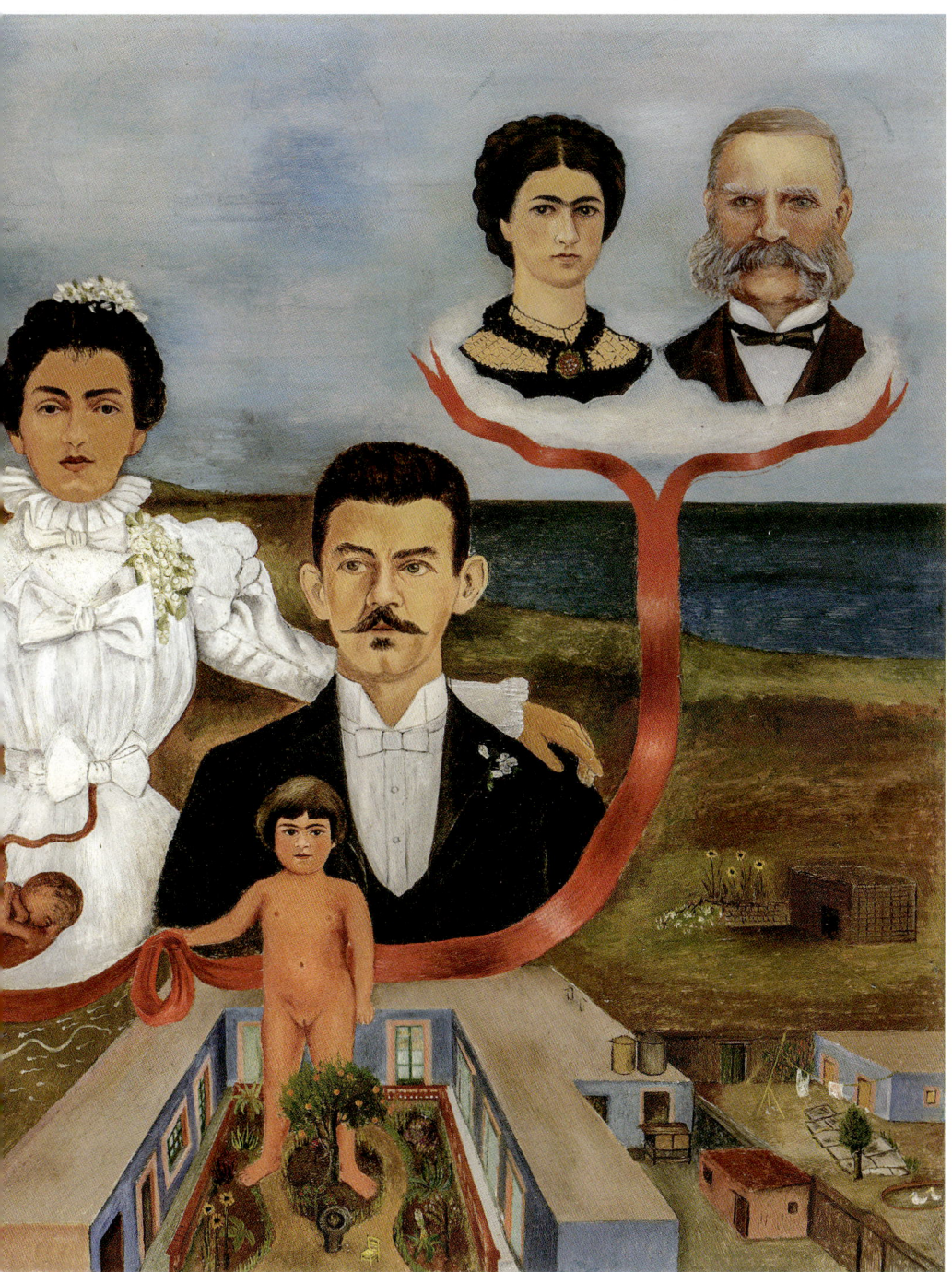

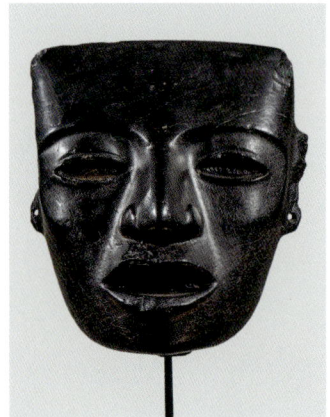

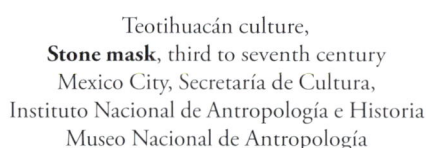

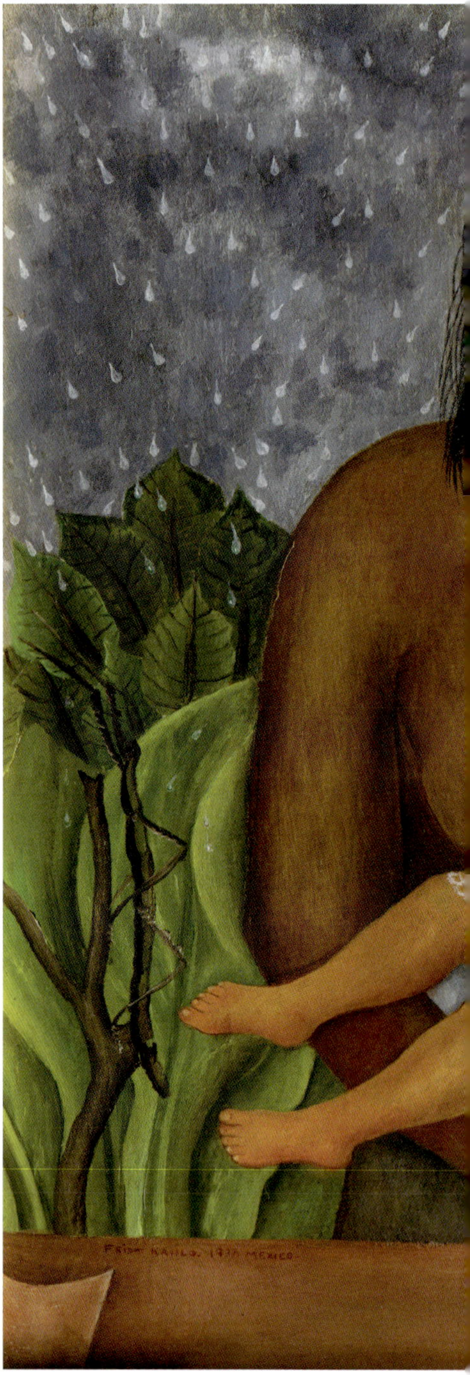

Teotihuacán culture,
Stone mask, third to seventh century
Mexico City, Secretaría de Cultura,
Instituto Nacional de Antropología e Historia
Museo Nacional de Antropología

My Nurse and I, 1937
Oil on metal, 30.5 x 34.7 cm (12 x 13⅝ in.)
Mexico City, Xochimilco, Museo Dolores Olmedo
(detail pp. 4/5)

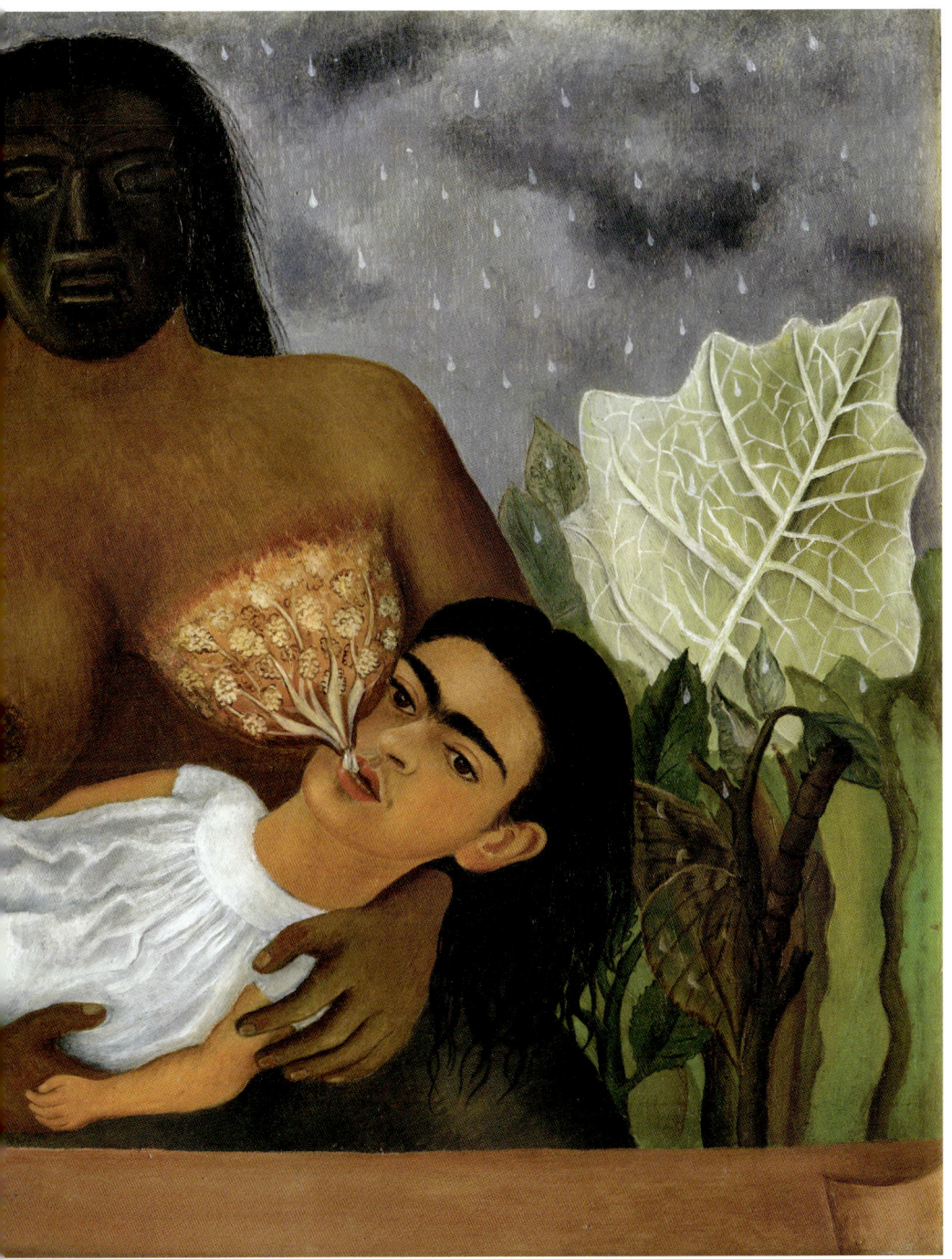

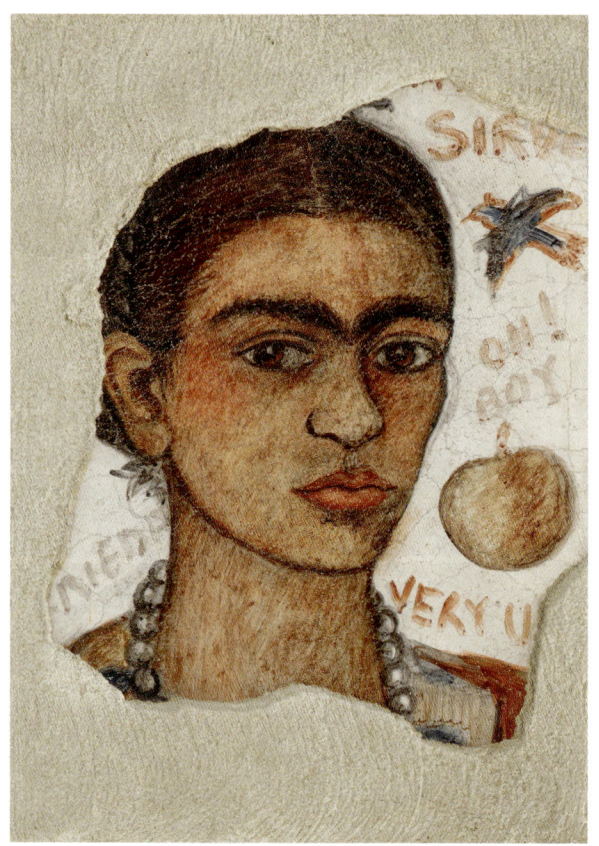

Self-portrait (Very Ugly) (unfinished), *c.* 1933
Fresco on panel, 27.3 x 22.2 cm (10¾ x 8¾ in.)
Inscription: [...] RIEDA [...] SIR[...] / OH! / BOY / VERY U[...]
United States, private collection, courtesy Christie's, New York

Me and My Doll, 1937
Oil on metal, 40 x 31 cm (15¾ x 12¼ in.)
Mexico, The Jacques and Natasha Gelman Collection
of 20th-century Mexican Art/The Vergel Foundation

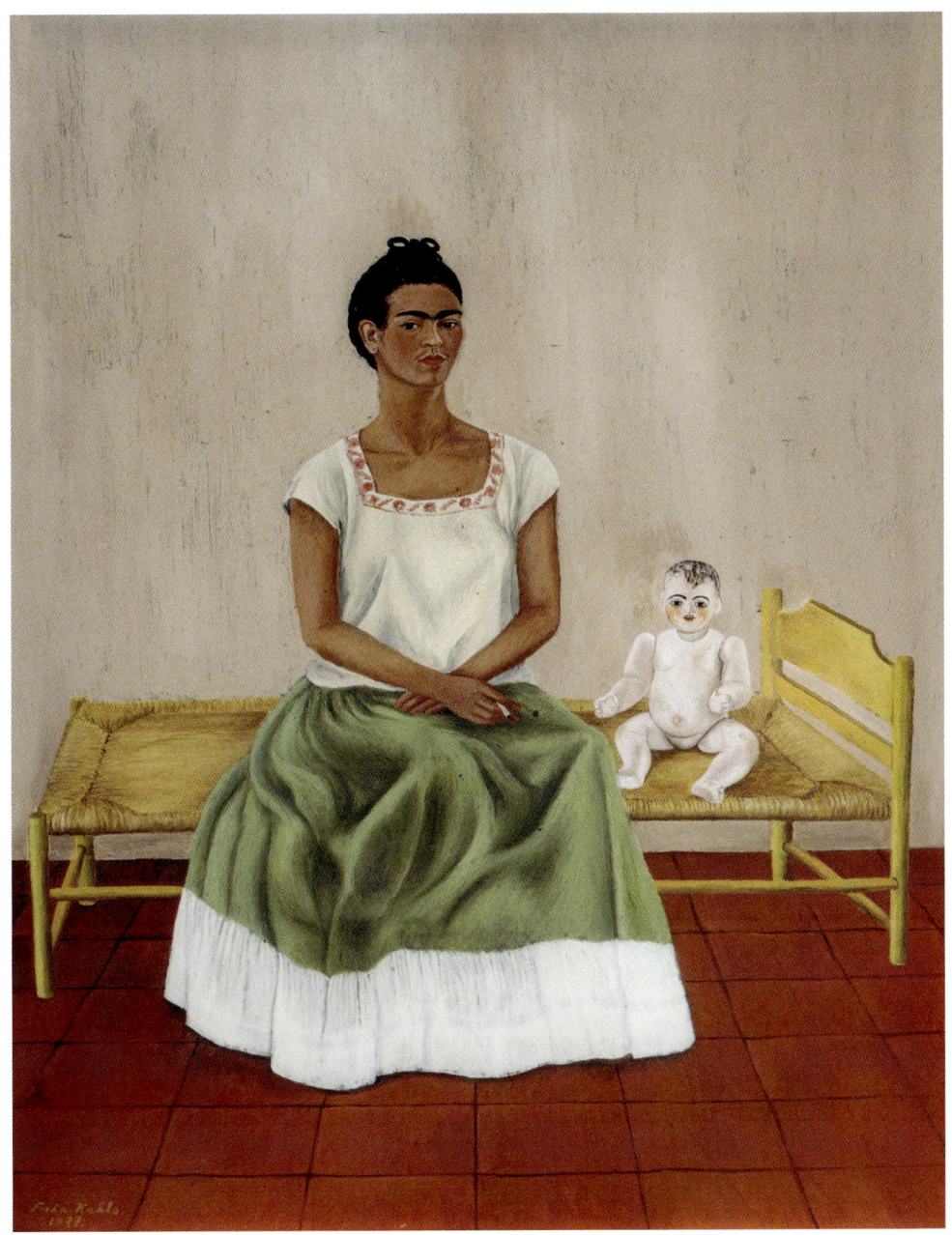

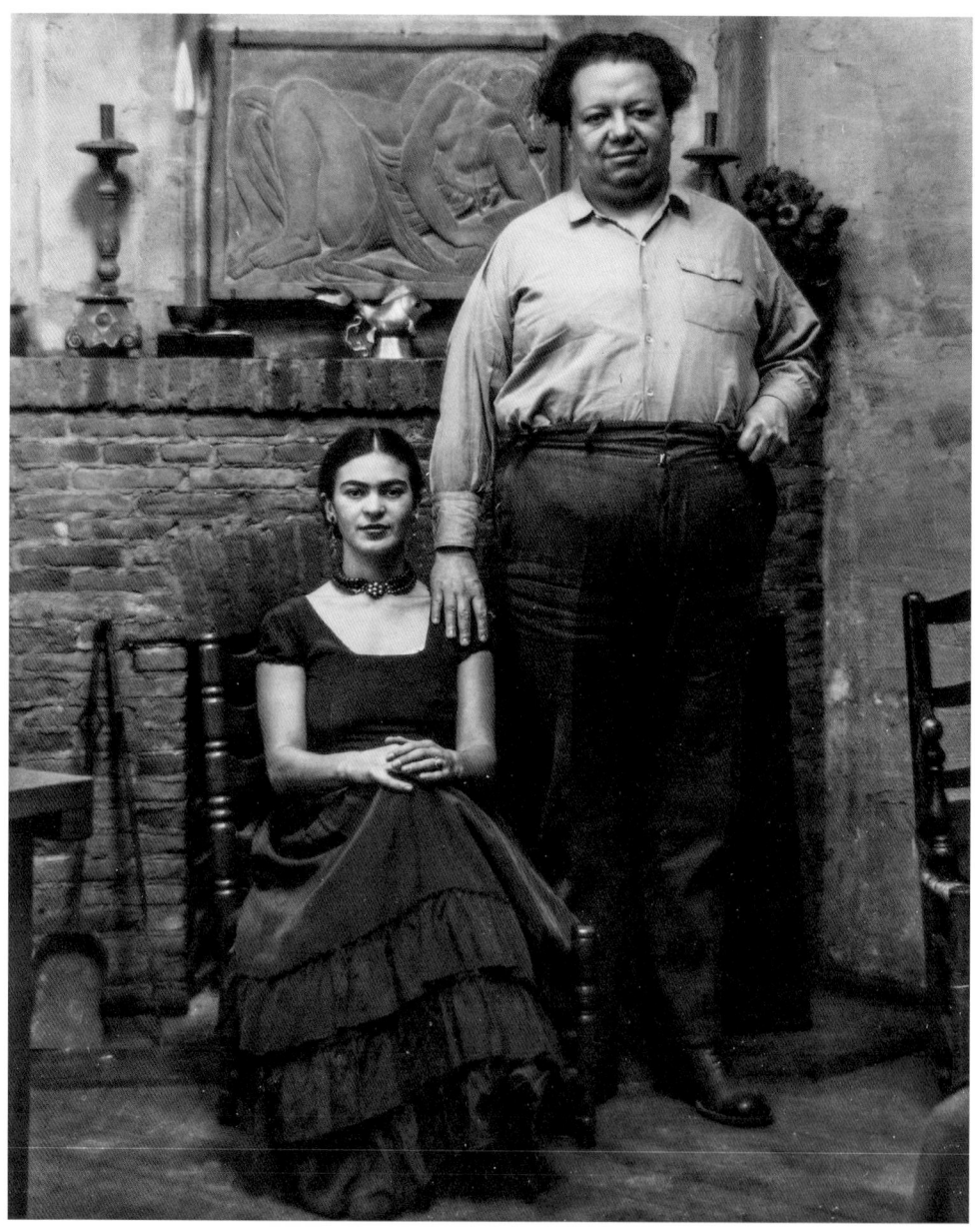

Paul Juley / Peter A. Juley,
Diego Rivera and Frida Kahlo, San Francisco, 1931
Gelatin silver print, 24.8 x 19.7 cm (9¾ x 7¾ in.). Detroit Institute of Arts

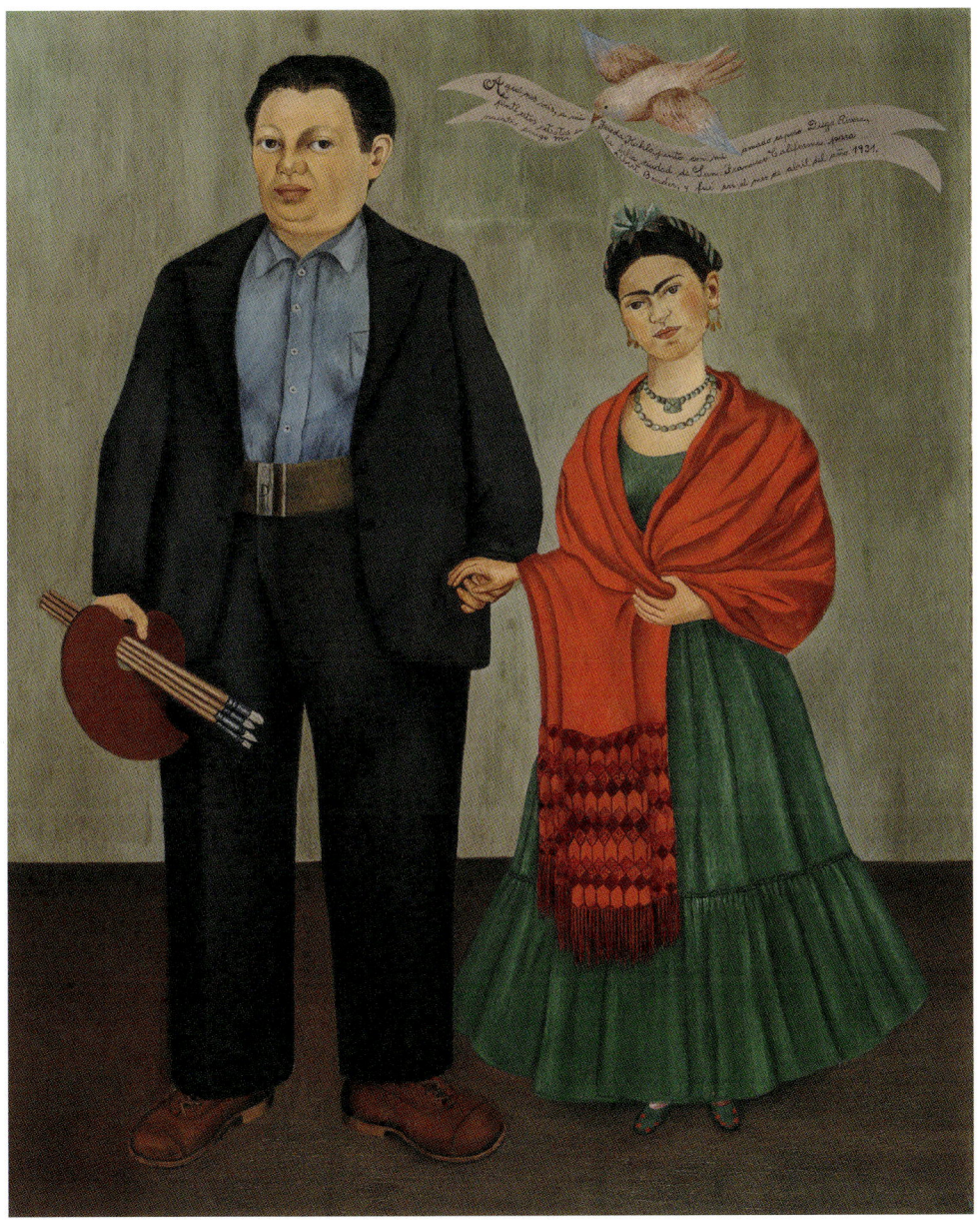

Frieda and Diego Rivera, April 1931
Oil on canvas, 100 x 78.7 cm (39⅜ x 31 in.). San Francisco Museum of
Modern Art, Albert M. Bender Collection, gift of Albert M. Bender

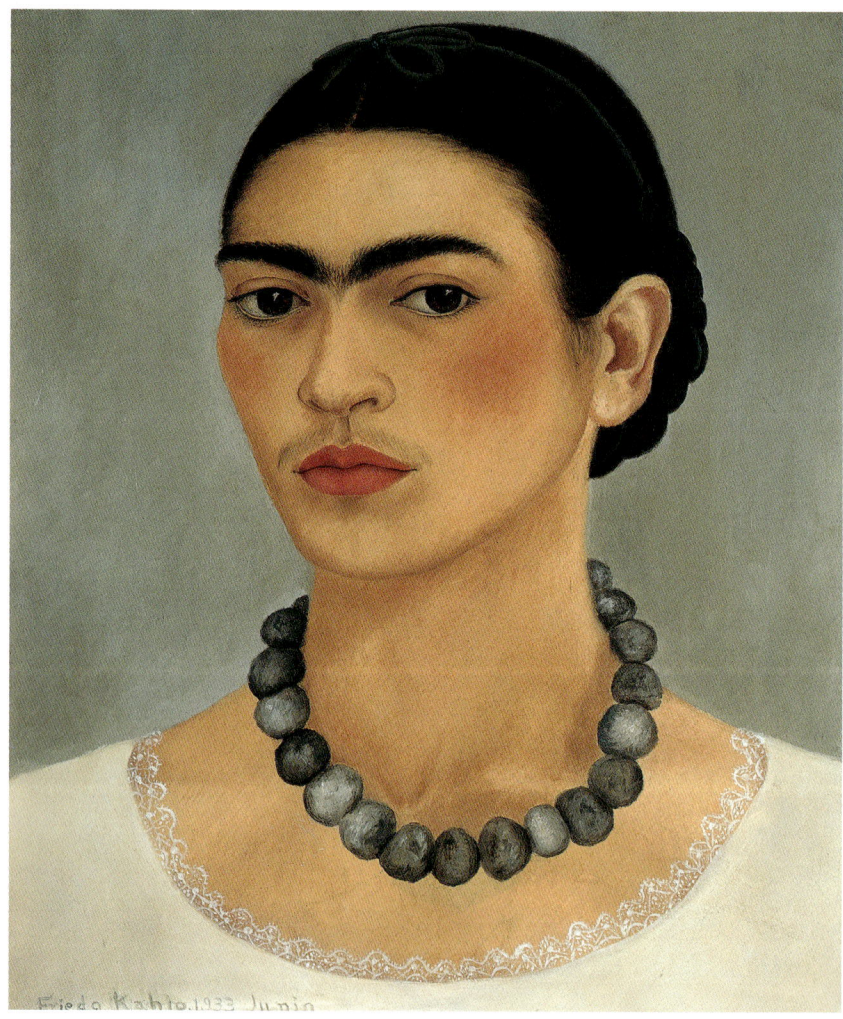

Self-portrait (with Necklace), June 1933
Oil on metal, 34.5 x 29.5 cm (13⅝ x 11⅝ in.). Mexico, The Jacques and Natasha Gelman
Collection of 20th-century Mexican Art/The Vergel Foundation

Lucienne Bloch, **Frida Kahlo in the Barbizon Plaza Hotel**, New York, April 8, 1933
Gelatin silver print, 16.3 x 11.2 cm (6⅜ x 4⅜ in.)
New York, collection of Spencer Throckmorton

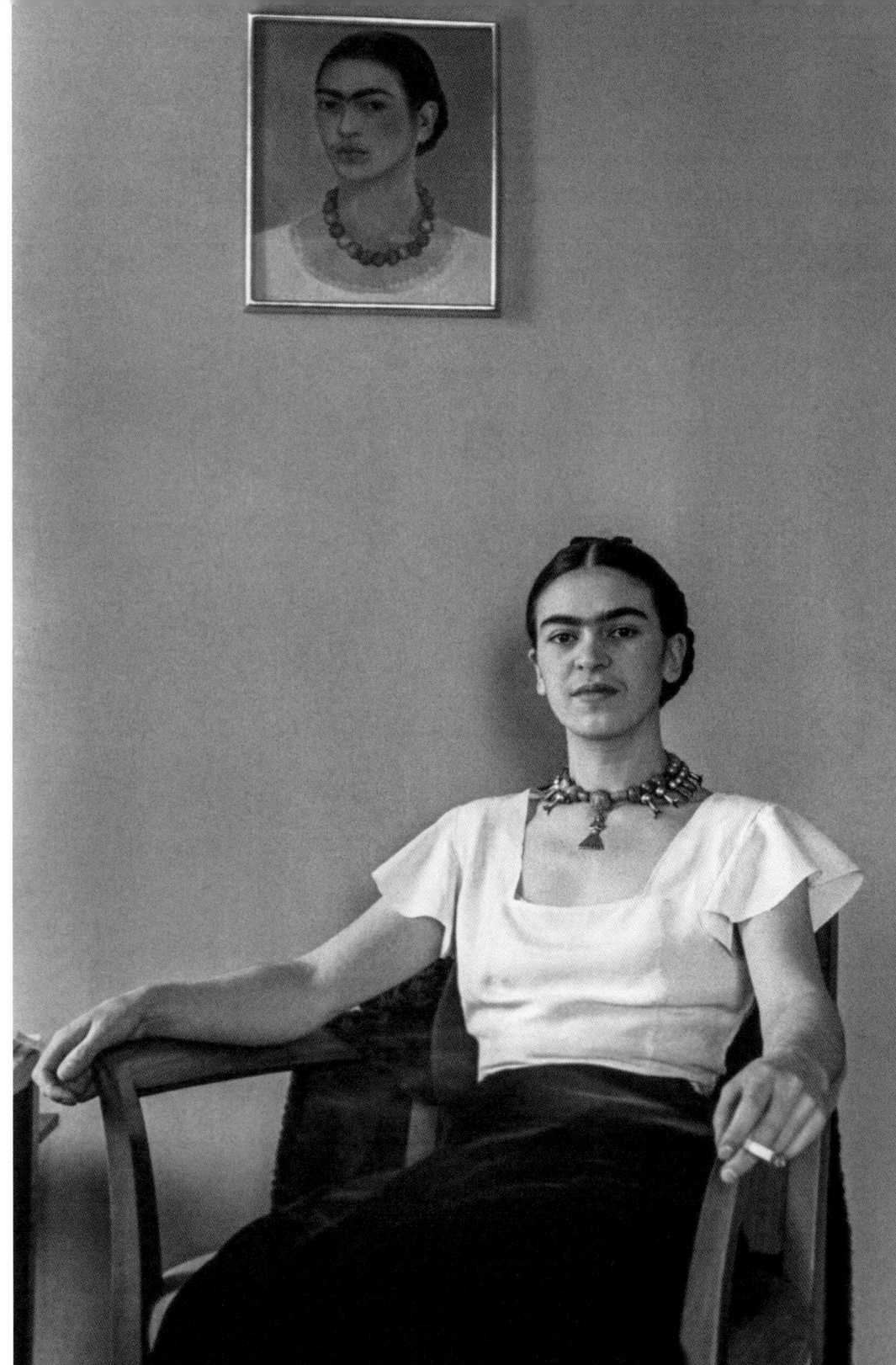

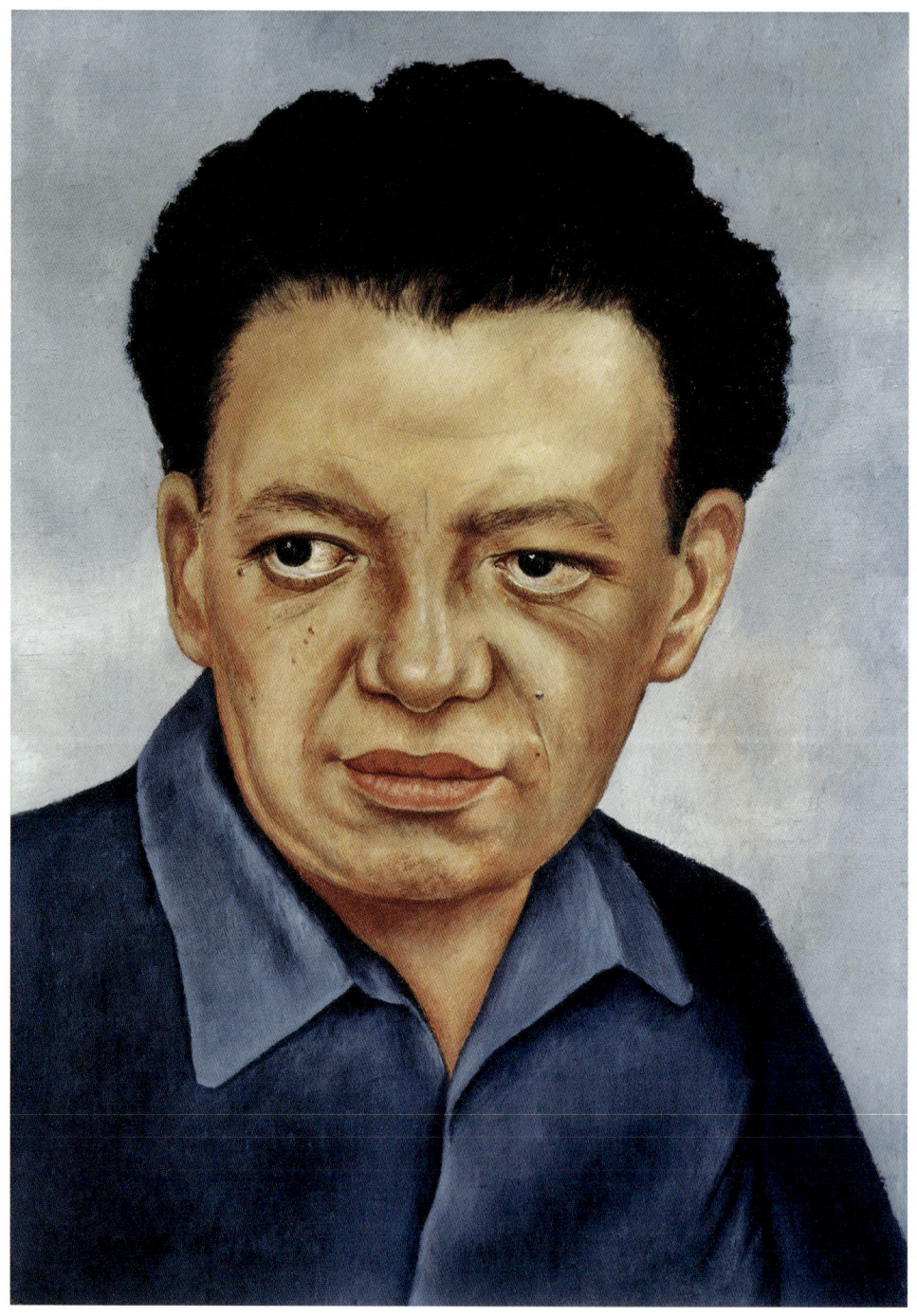

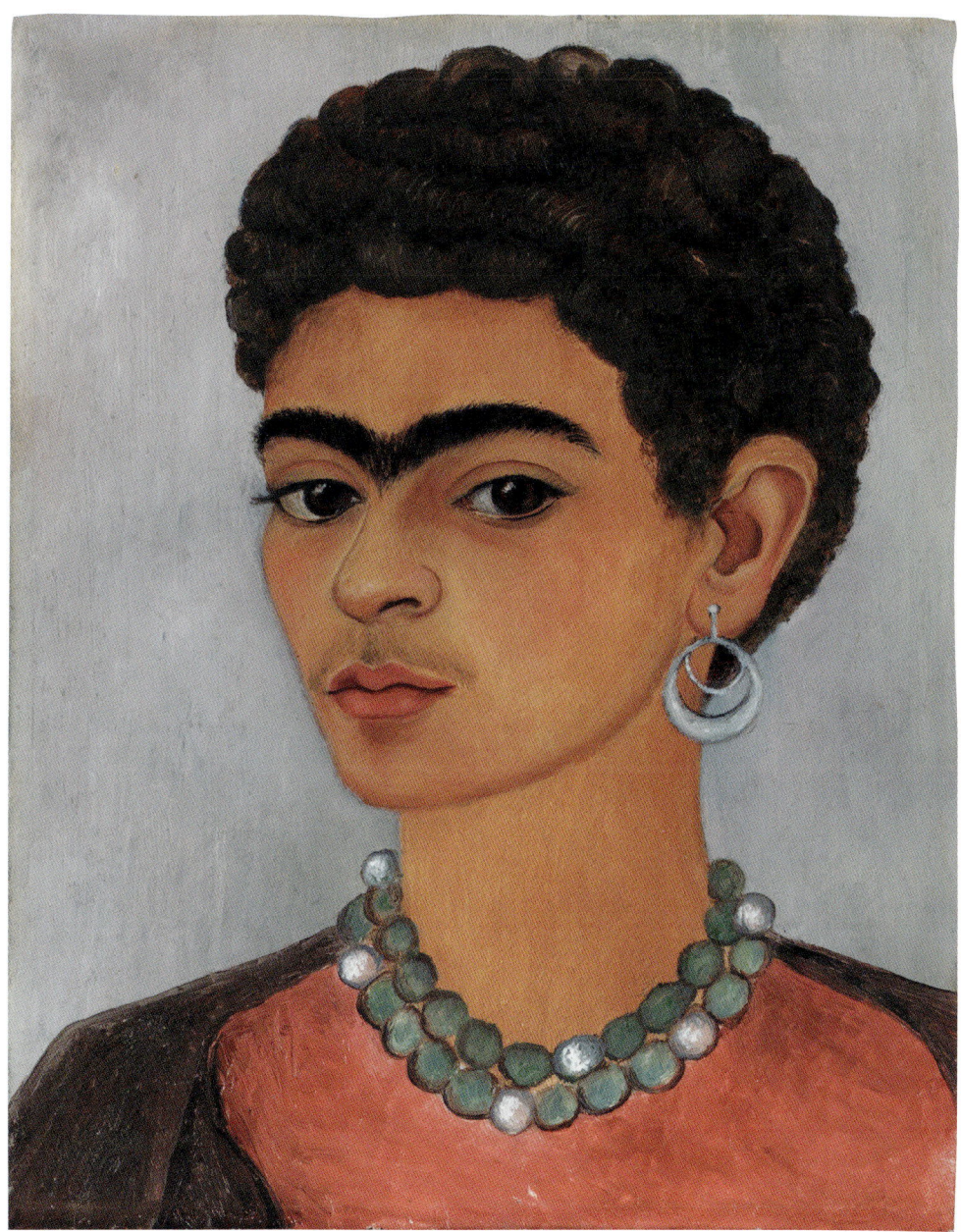

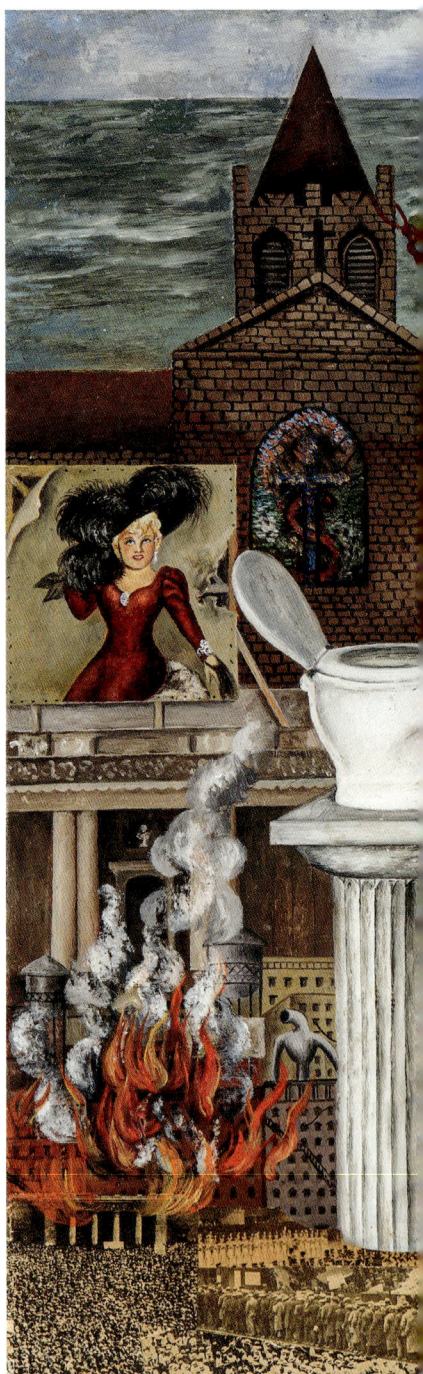

Page 128
Portrait of Diego Rivera, 1937
Oil on masonite, 53 x 39 cm (20⅞ x 15⅜ in.)
Mexico, The Jacques and Natasha Gelman Collection
of 20th-century Mexican Art/The Vergel Foundation

Page 129
Self-portrait (with Curly Hair), *c.* 1935
Oil on tinplate, 18.3 x 14.6 cm (7¼ x 5¾ in.)
Private collection, courtesy Christie's, New York

My Dress Was There Hanging (New York), 1933–1938
Oil and collage on masonite, 46 x 55 cm (18⅛ x 21⅝ in.)
Monterrey, FEMSA collection
(details pp. 132/133, 135)

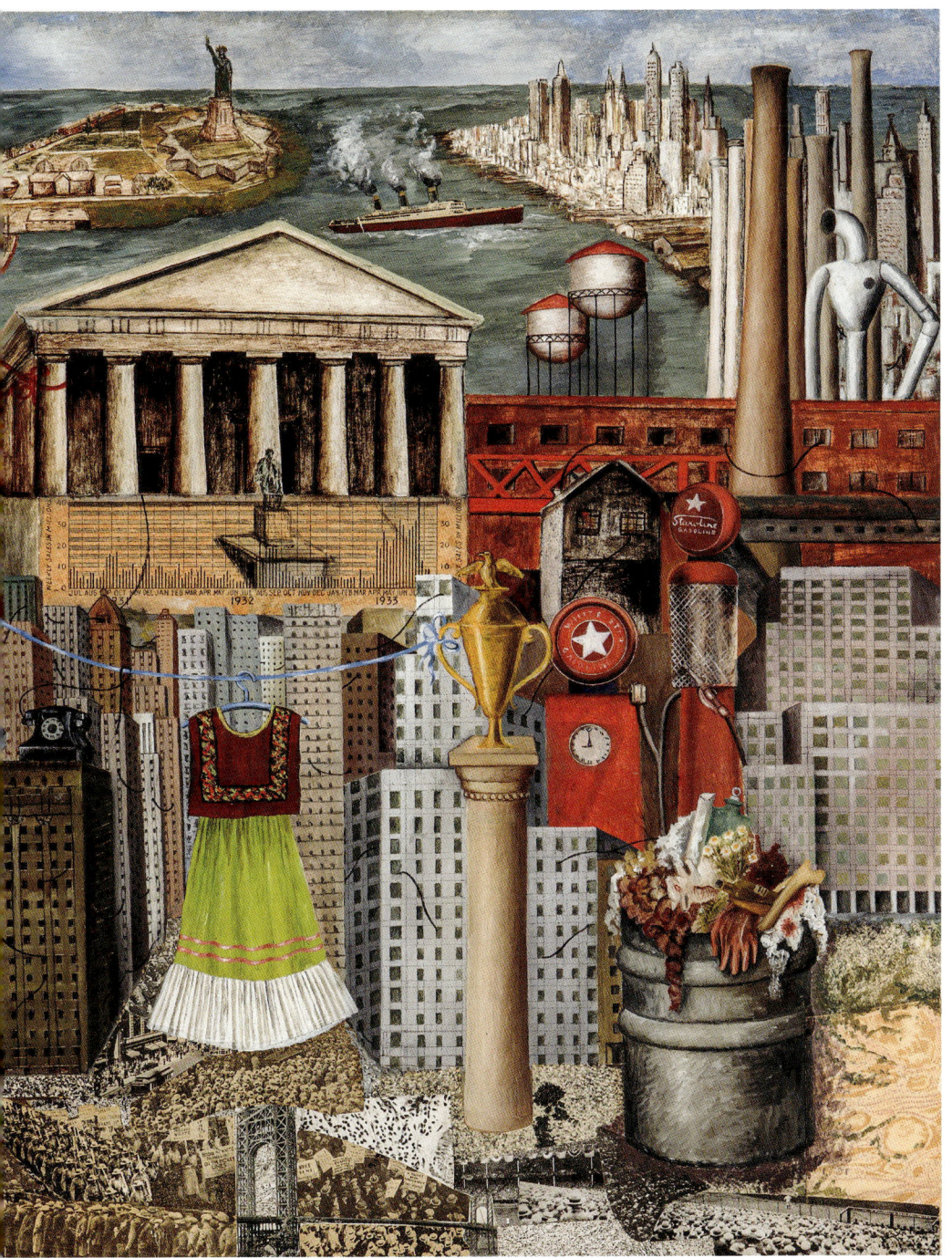

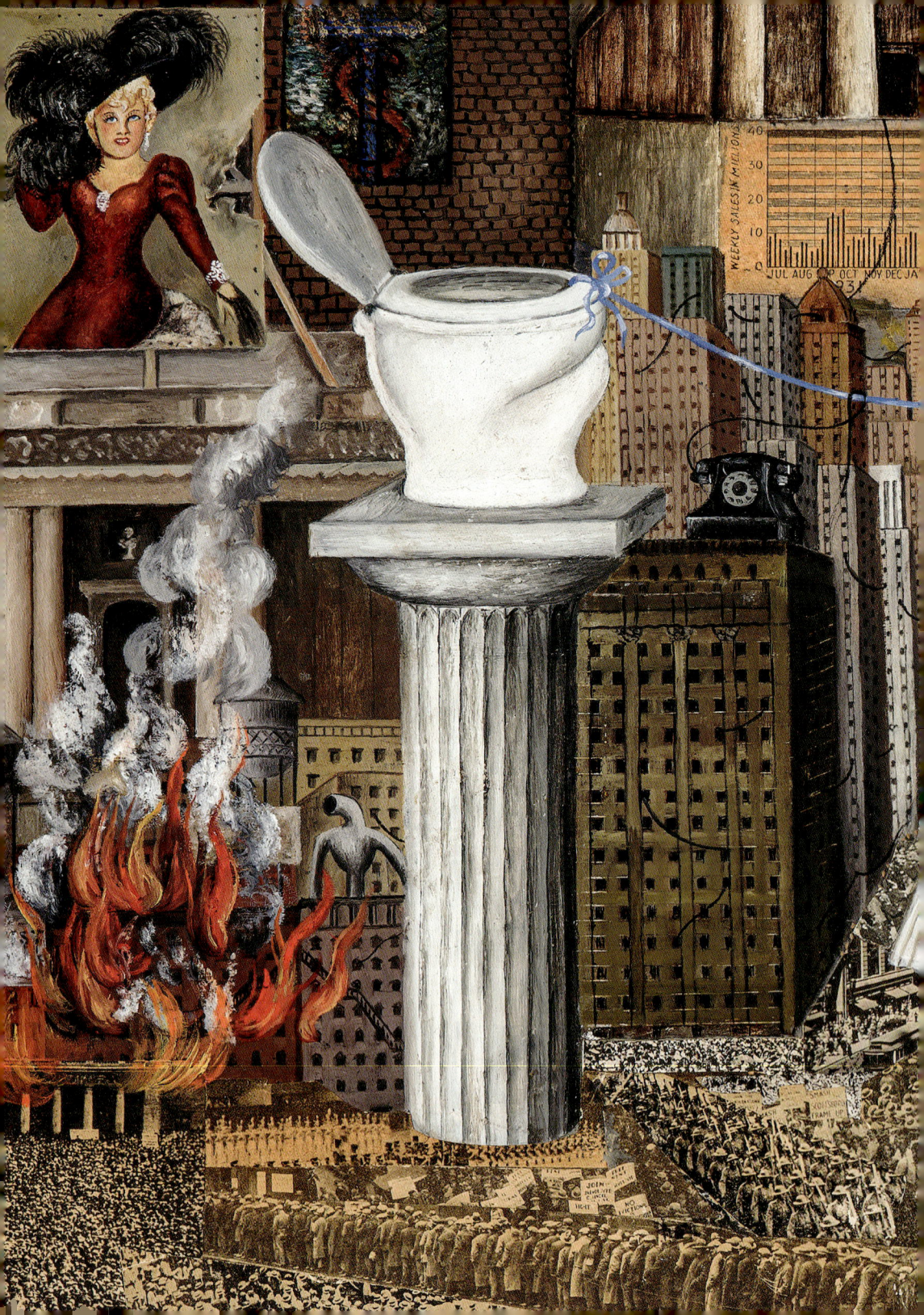

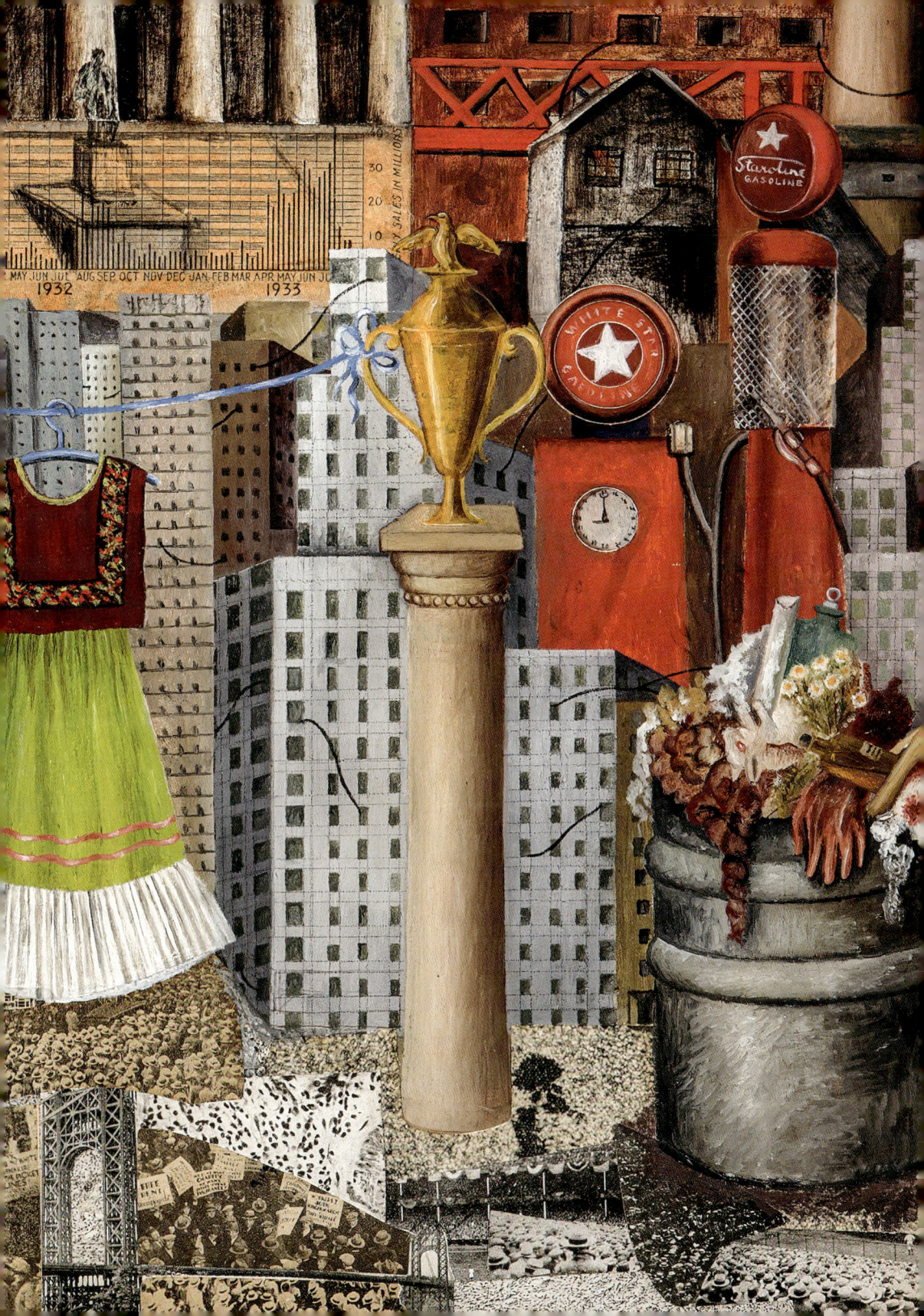

Staroline
GASOLINE

WHITE STAR
GASOLINE

Hannah Höch, **Cut with the Kitchen Knife Dada through
the Last Weimar Beer-belly Cultural Epoch in Germany**, 1919
Photomontage and collage with watercolor, 114 x 90 cm (45 x 35½ in.)
Berlin, Staatliche Museen zu Berlin, Nationalgalerie

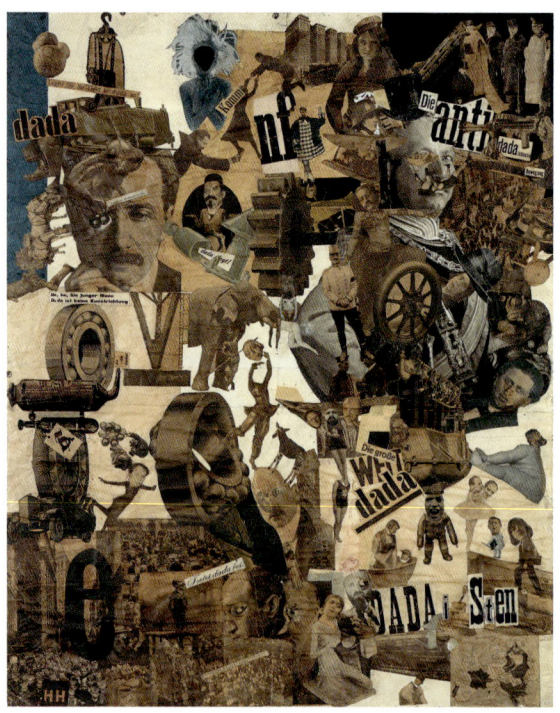

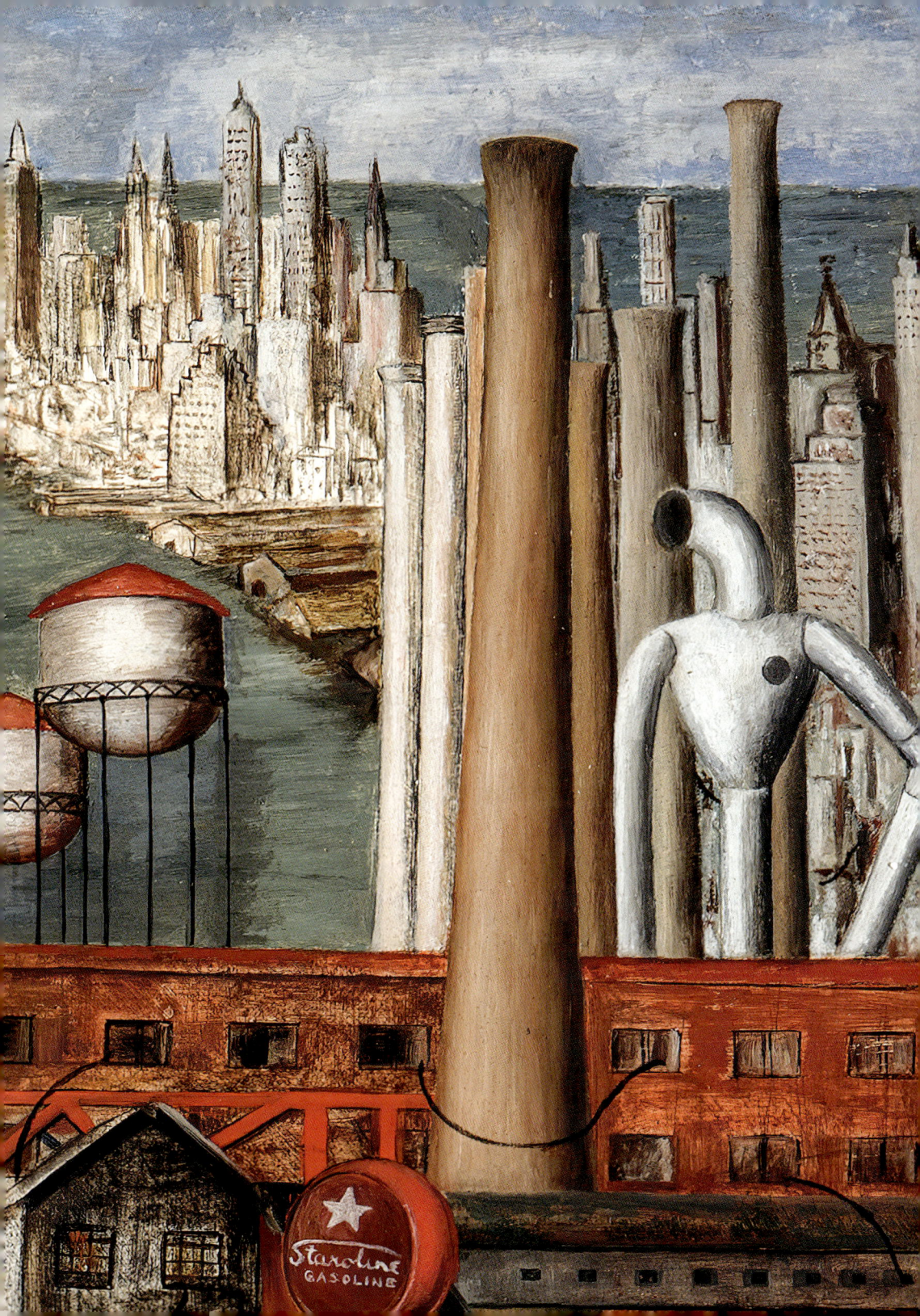

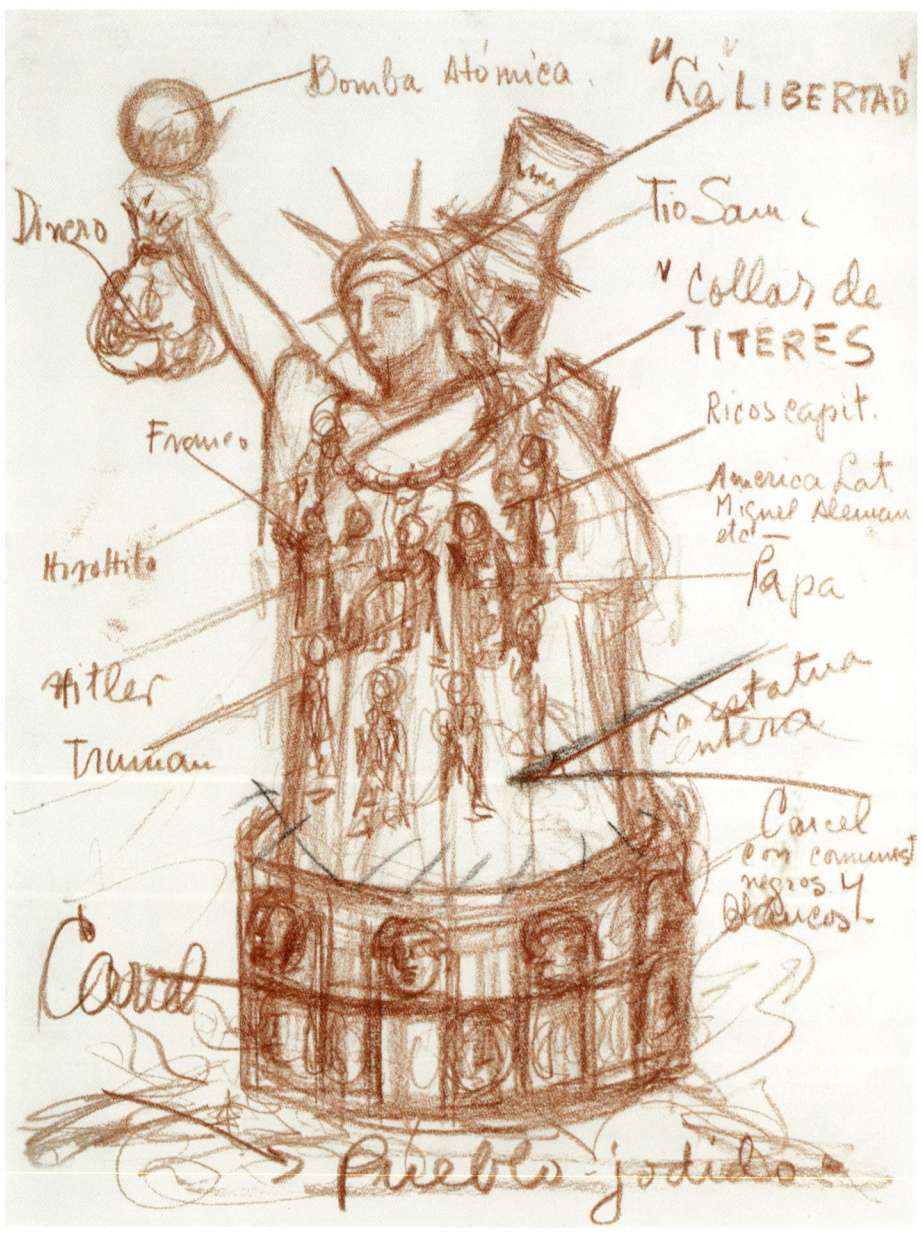

Liberty, 1949
Sepia Conté crayon and charcoal on paper, 28.9 x 21.6 cm (11⅜ x 8½ in.)
Mexico, The Jacques and Natasha Gelman Collection
of 20th-century Mexican Art/The Vergel Foundation

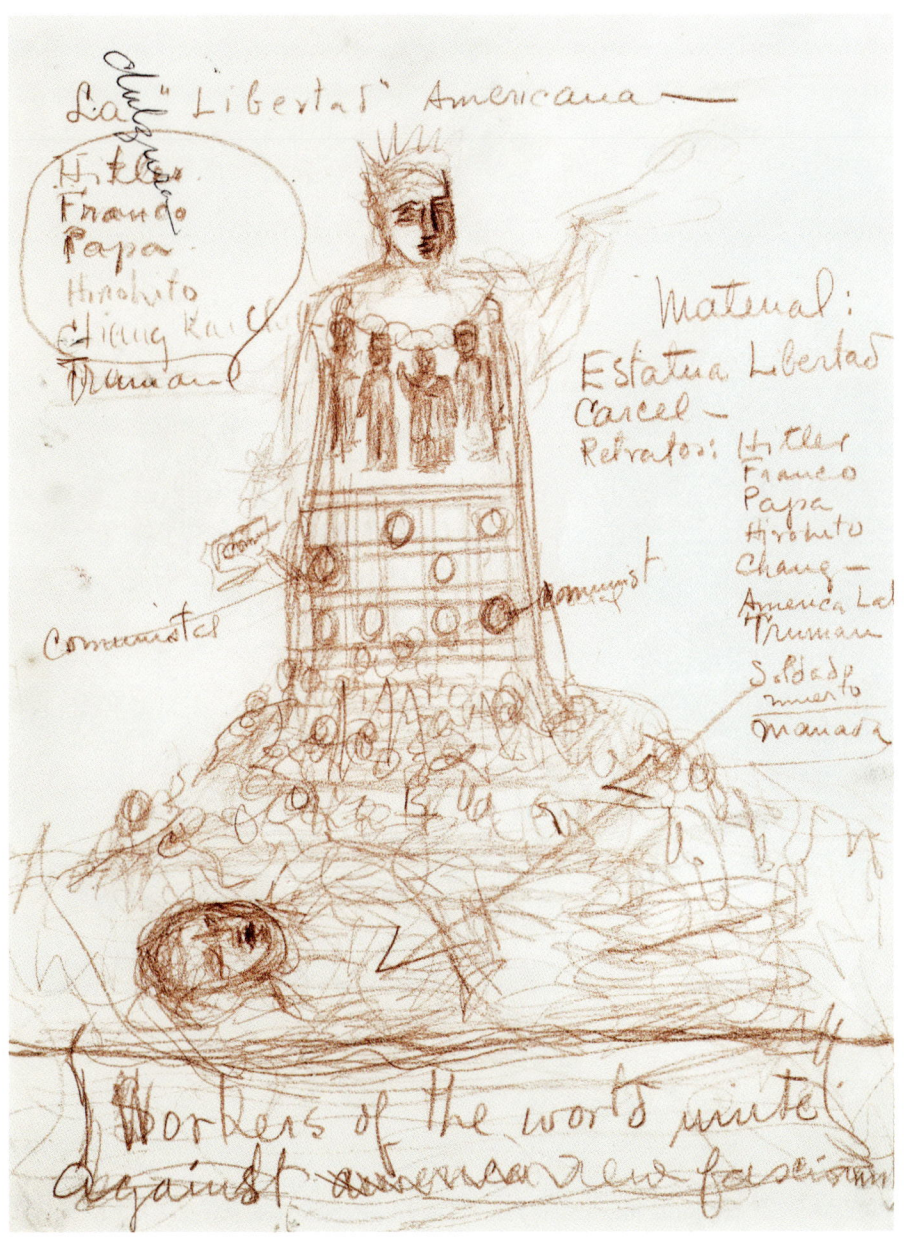

American Liberty, undated
Conté crayon and ink on paper, 28.9 x 21.6 cm (11⅜ x 8½ in.)
Mexico, The Jacques and Natasha Gelman Collection
of 20th-century Mexican Art/The Vergel Foundation

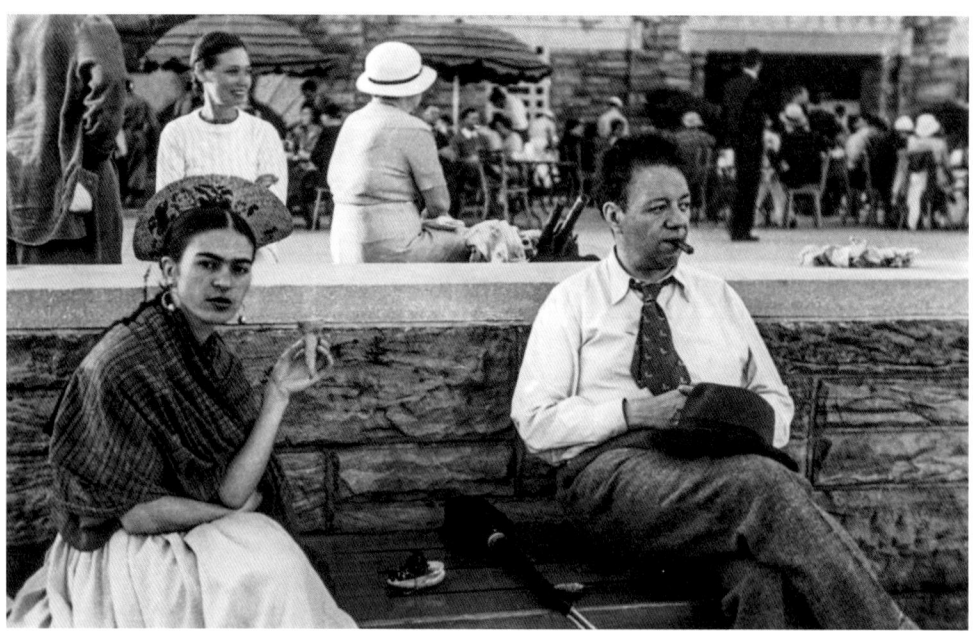

Lucienne Bloch, **Frida Kahlo and Diego Rivera at
Jones Beach State Park, Long Island**, New York, 1933
Gelatin silver print, 7.6 x 10.2 cm (3 x 4 in.)
New York, collection of Spencer Throckmorton

View of Central Park (From the Barbizon Plaza Hotel), 1932
Watercolor and graphite pencil on paper, 26.7 x 20.3 cm (10½ x 8 in.)
Private collection

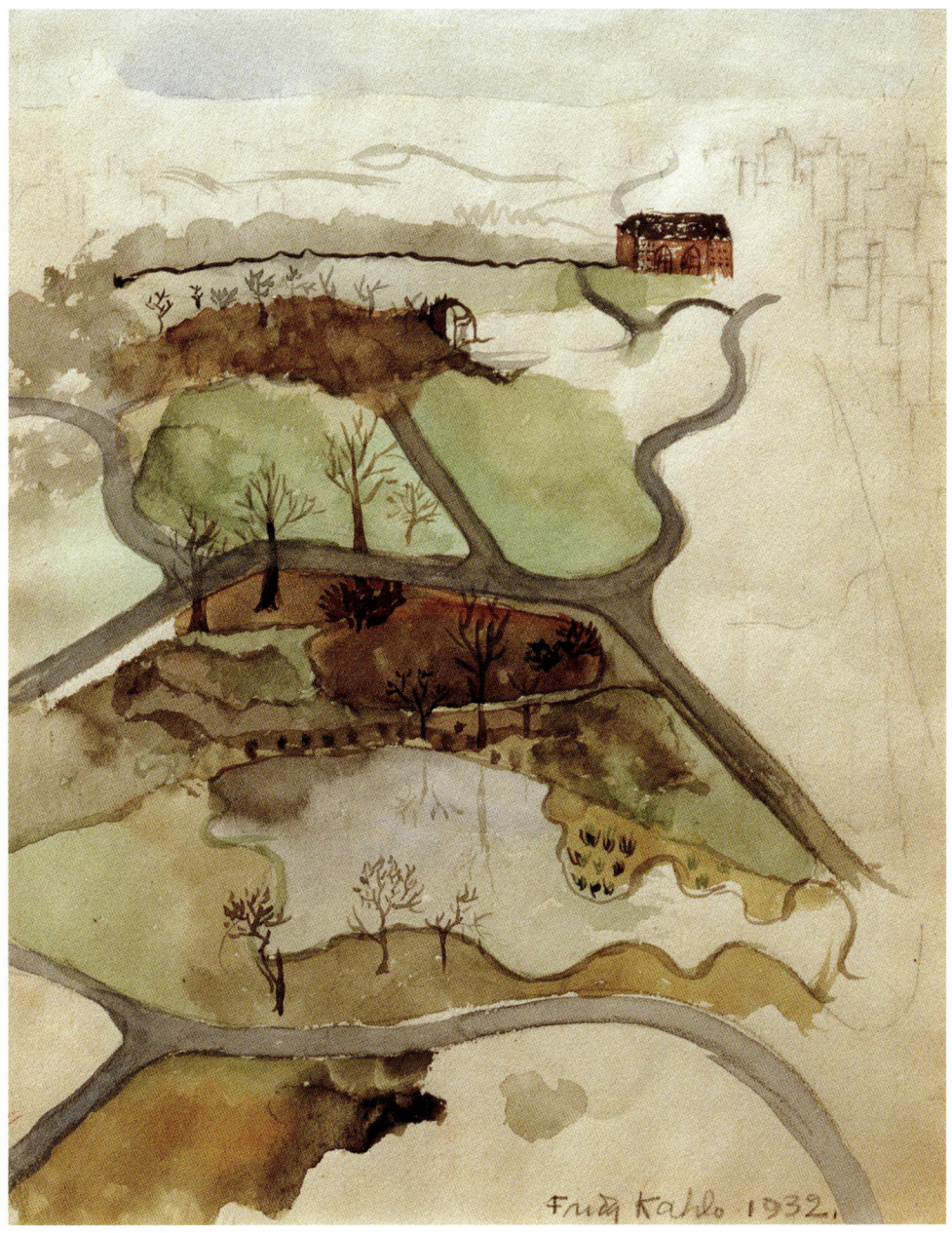

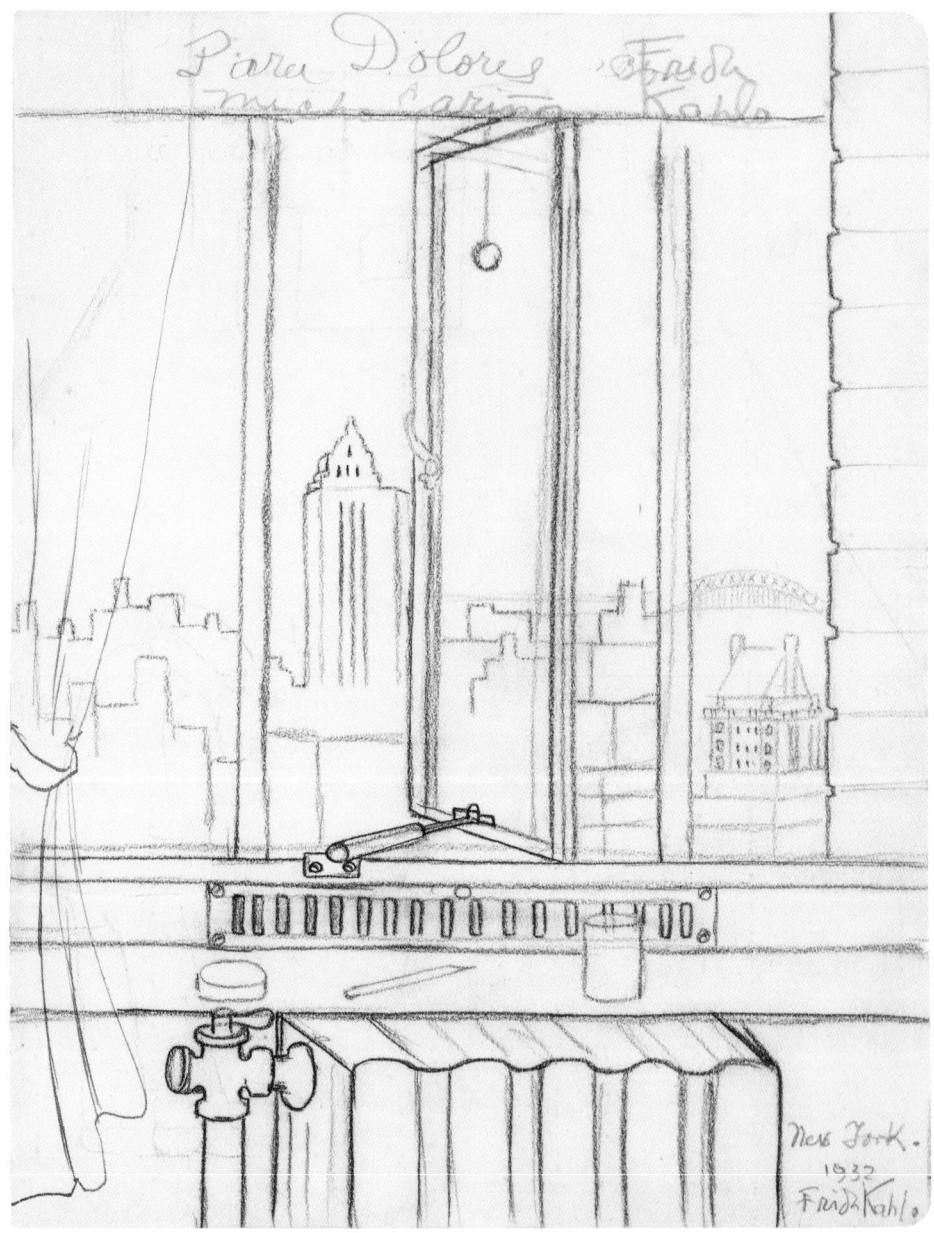

View of New York (dedicated to Dolores Del Río), 1932
Conté crayon, graphite pencil, and ink on paper,
27 x 20 cm (10⅝ x 7⅞ in.)
Private collection, courtesy Arvil gallery, Mexico City

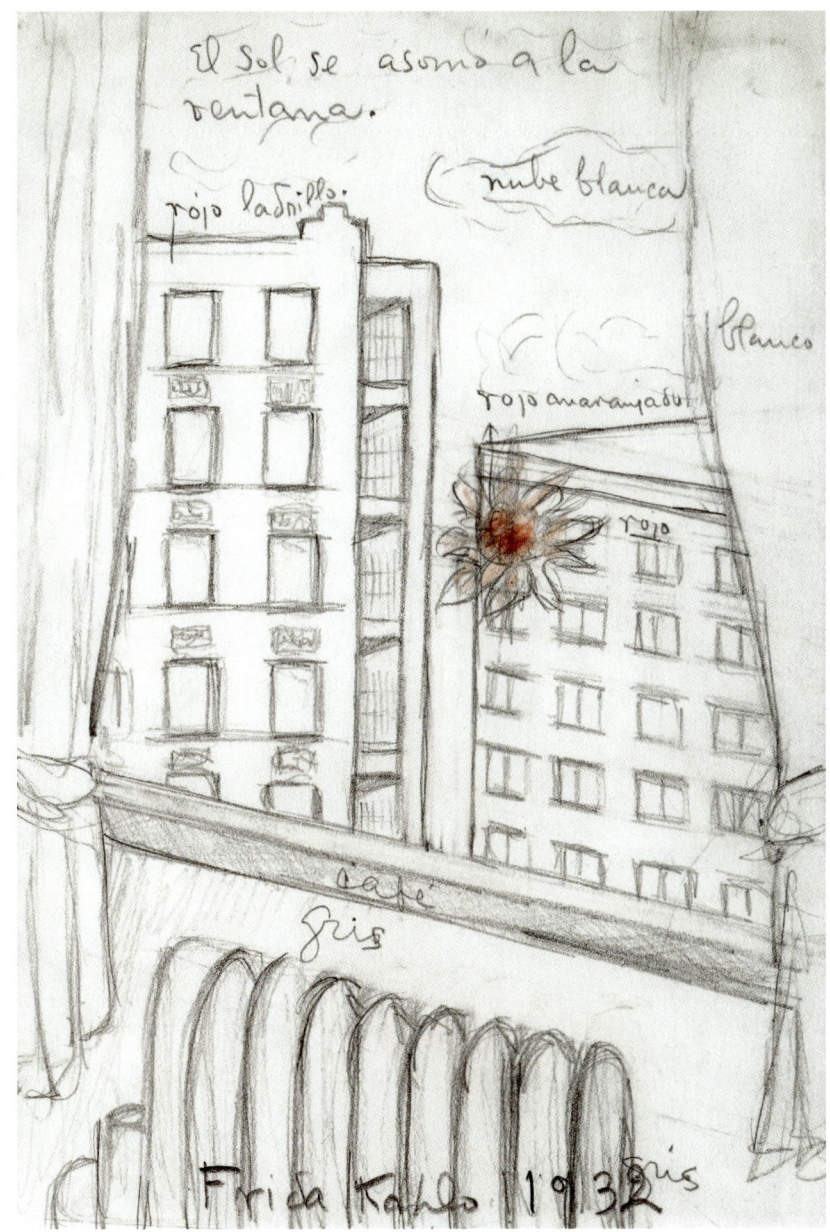

"The Sun Appears at the Window", 1932
Conté crayon, graphite pencil, and watercolor on paper, 27 x 18 cm (10⅝ x 7⅛ in.)
Mexico, The Jacques and Natasha Gelman Collection
of 20th-century Mexican Art/The Vergel Foundation

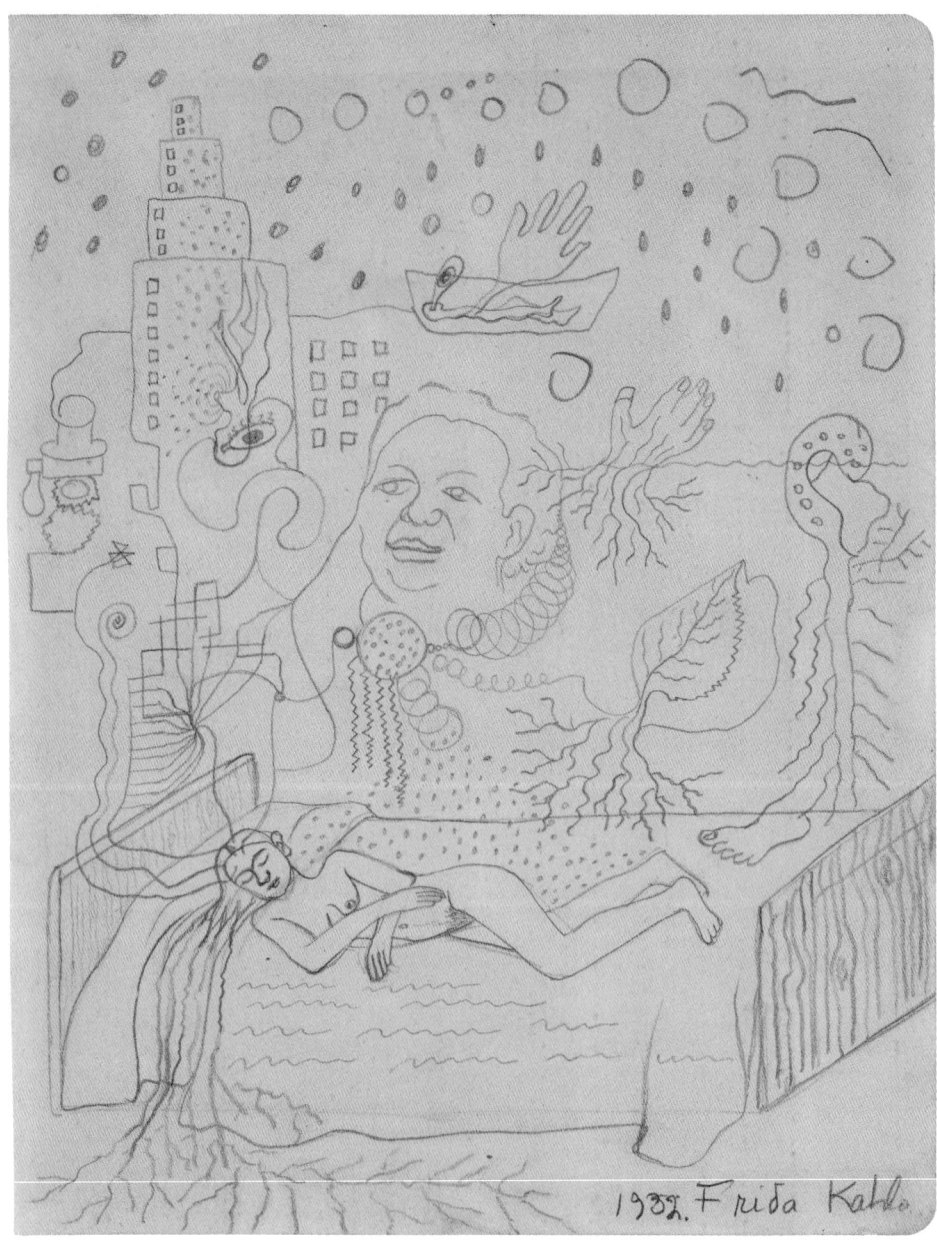

The Dream, 1932
Graphite pencil on paper, 27 x 20 cm (10⅝ x 7⅞ in.). Mexico City, Secretaría de Cultura,
Instituto Nacional de Bellas Artes y Literatura, Museo de Arte Moderno

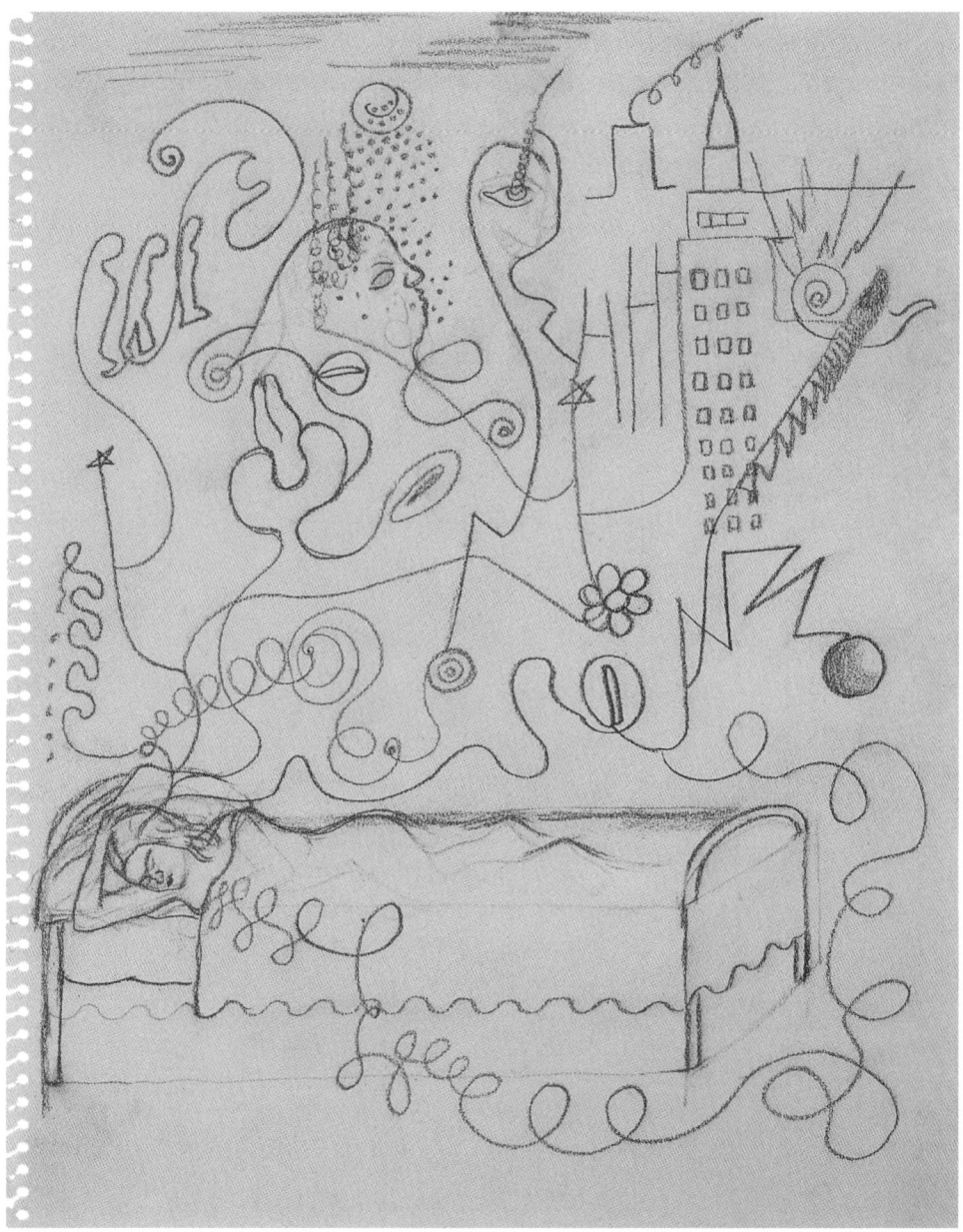

Dream (The Dream II), *c.* 1932
Conté crayon on paper, 27 x 20.9 cm (10⅝ x 8¼ in.)
Mexico City, Coyoacán, Museo Frida Kahlo

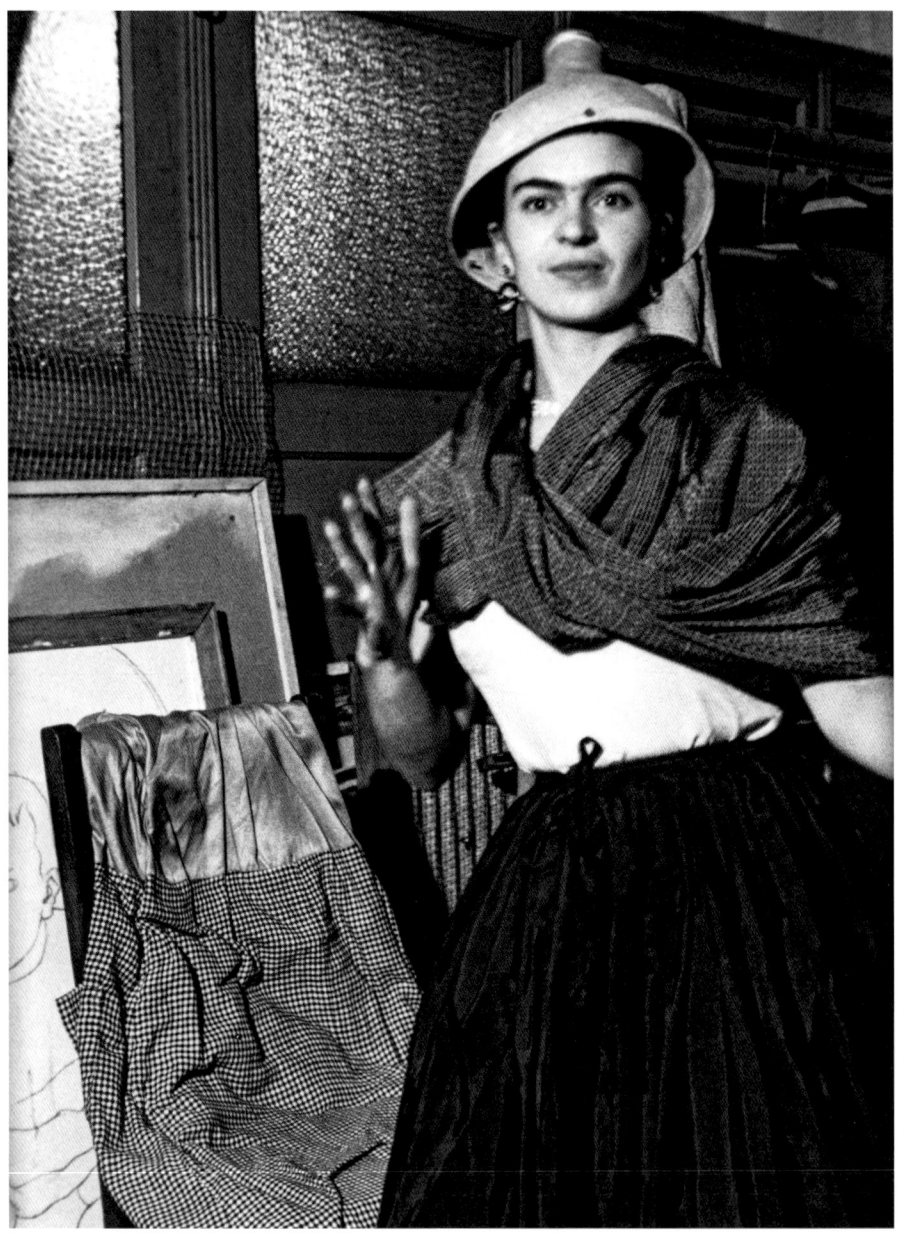

Lucienne Bloch, **Frida Kahlo at the New Workers School**, New York, 1933
Gelatin silver print, 25.4 x 15.2 cm (10 x 6 in.)
New York, collection of Spencer Throckmorton

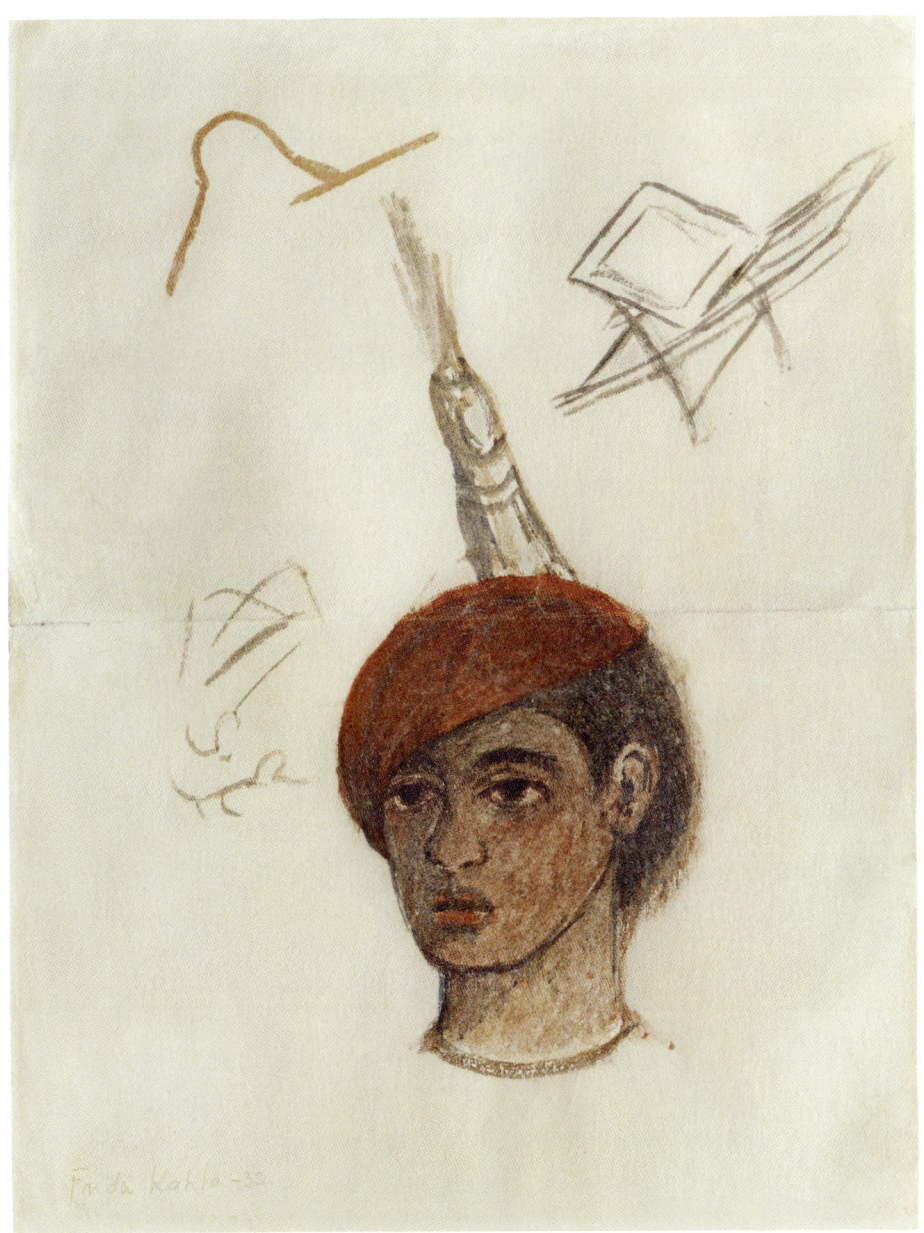

Self-portrait with Beret (Head with Red Cap), *c.* 1932
Watercolor, pastel, and graphite pencil on paper, 30 x 22 cm (11¾ x 8⅝ in.)
Mexico City, Xochimilco, Museo Dolores Olmedo

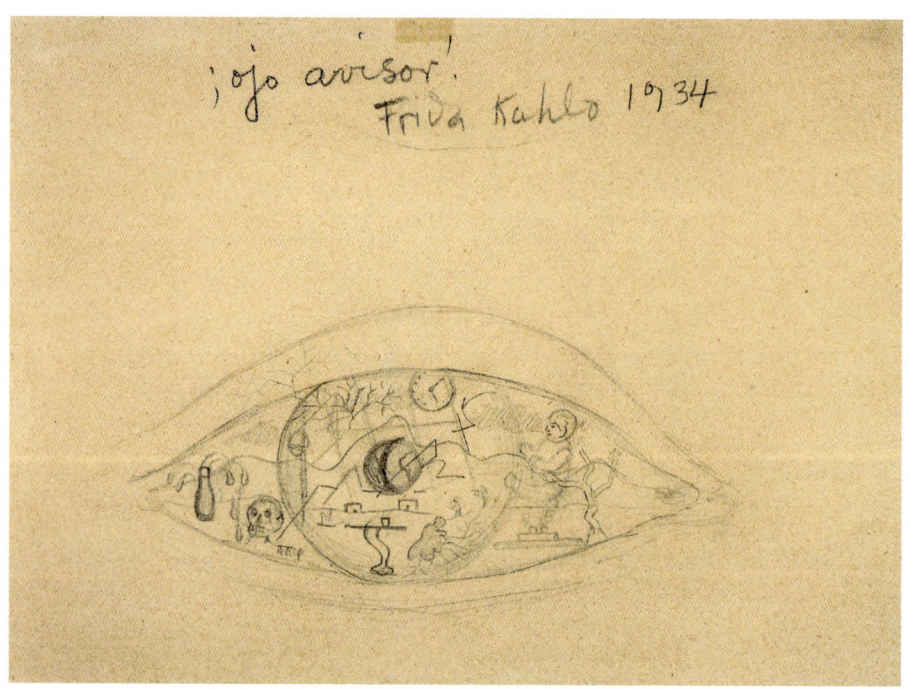

Watchful Eye!, 1934
Graphite pencil on paper, 20.6 x 30.2 cm (8⅛ x 11⅞ in.)
Mexico City, Secretaría de Cultura, Instituto Nacional
de Bellas Artes y Literatura, Museo de Arte Moderno

Self-portrait, July 9, 1932
Graphite pencil on paper, 20.5 x 13.5 cm (8⅛ x 5¼ in.)
Mexico City, private collection

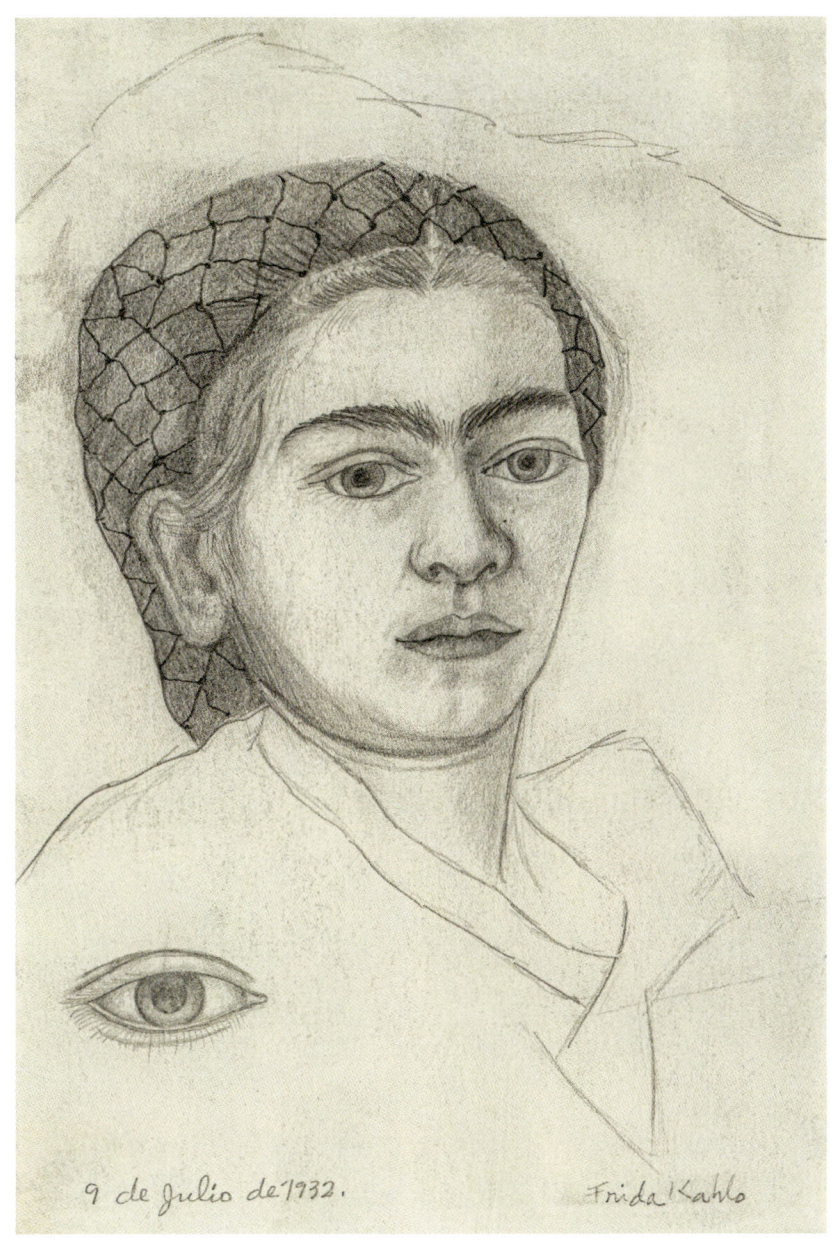

9 de Julio de 1932.   Frida Kahlo

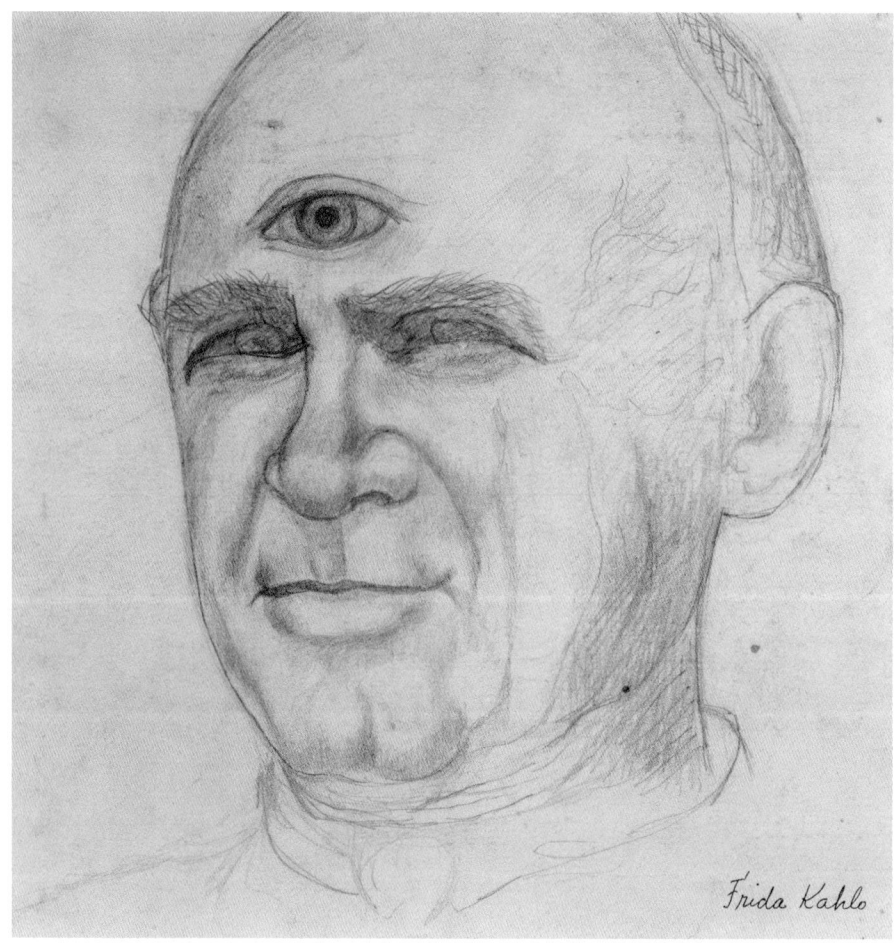

Portrait of Arcady Boytler, *c.* 1946
Graphite pencil on paper, 22.3 x 21.7 cm (8¾ x 8½ in.)
Mexico, The Jacques and Natasha Gelman Collection
of 20th-century Mexican Art/The Vergel Foundation
(recto of page 149)

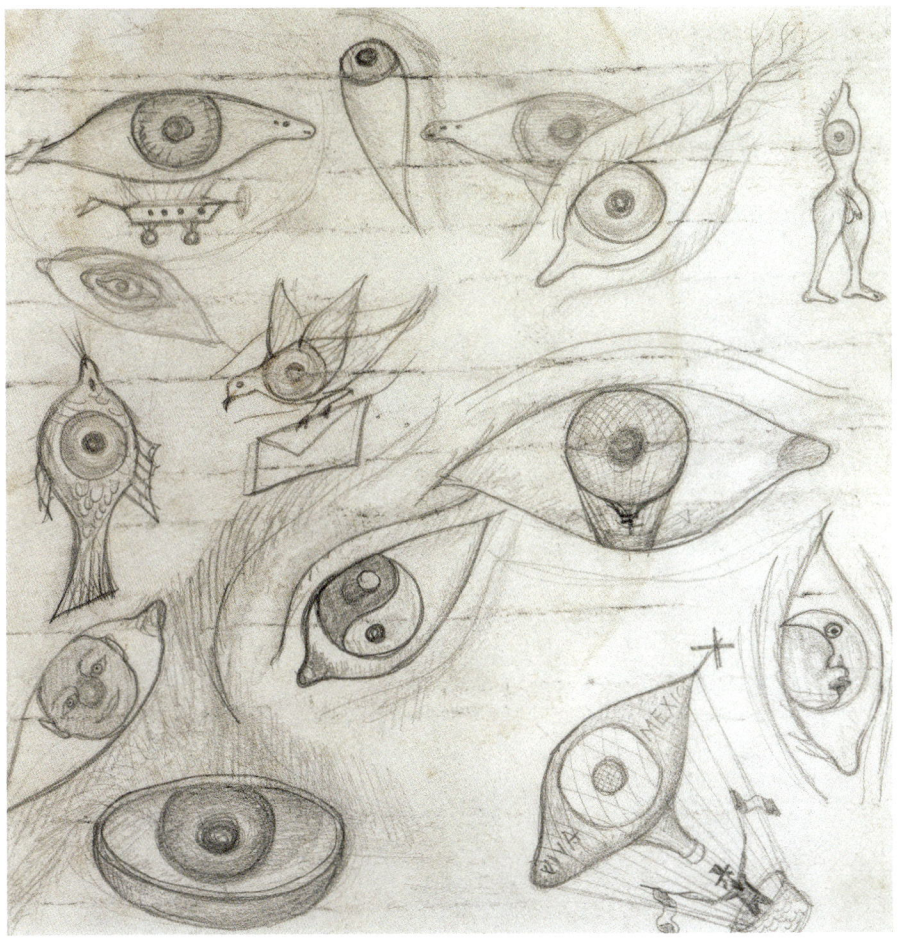

Drawing of Eyes (Viva México), *c.* 1946
Graphite pencil on paper, 22.3 x 21.7 cm (8¾ x 8½ in.)
Mexico, The Jacques and Natasha Gelman Collection
of 20th-century Mexican Art/The Vergel Foundation
(verso of page 148)

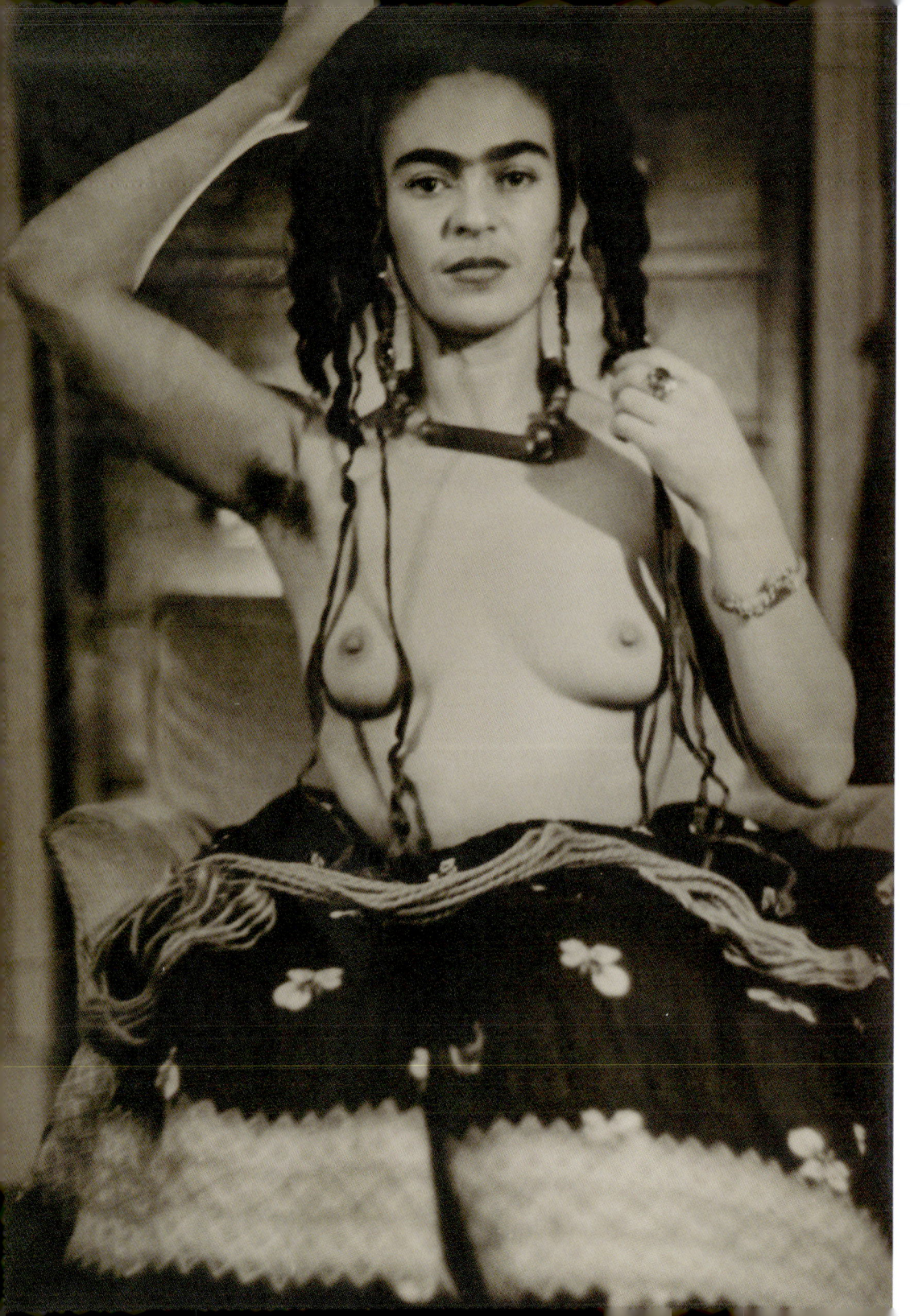

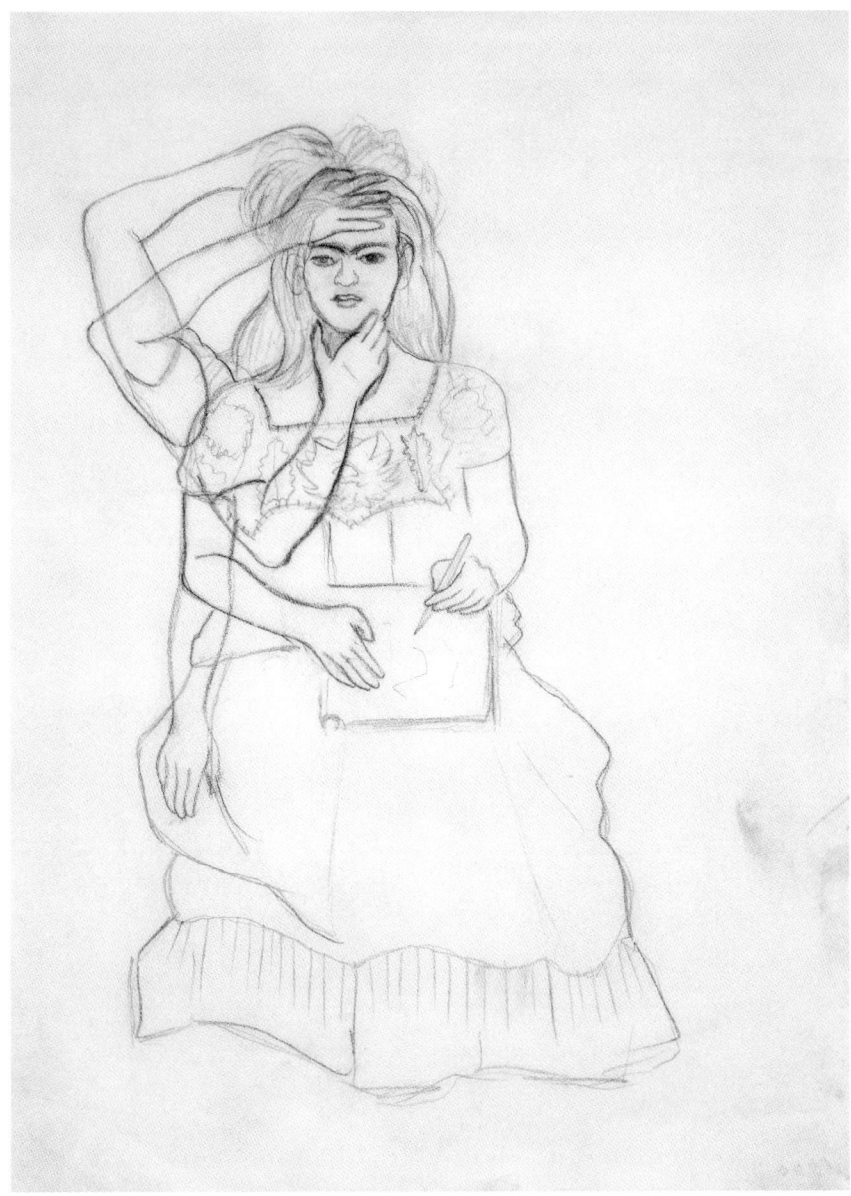

Julien Levy, **Frida Kahlo** (detail), 1938
Gelatin silver print, 17 x 16 cm (6¾ x 6¼ in.). Philadelphia Museum of Art,
The Lynne and Harold Honickman Gift of the Julien Levy Collection, 2001

Self-portrait while Drawing, *c.* 1937. Graphite pencil and colored pencil
on paper, 29.7 x 21 cm (11¾ x 8¼ in.). United States, private collection

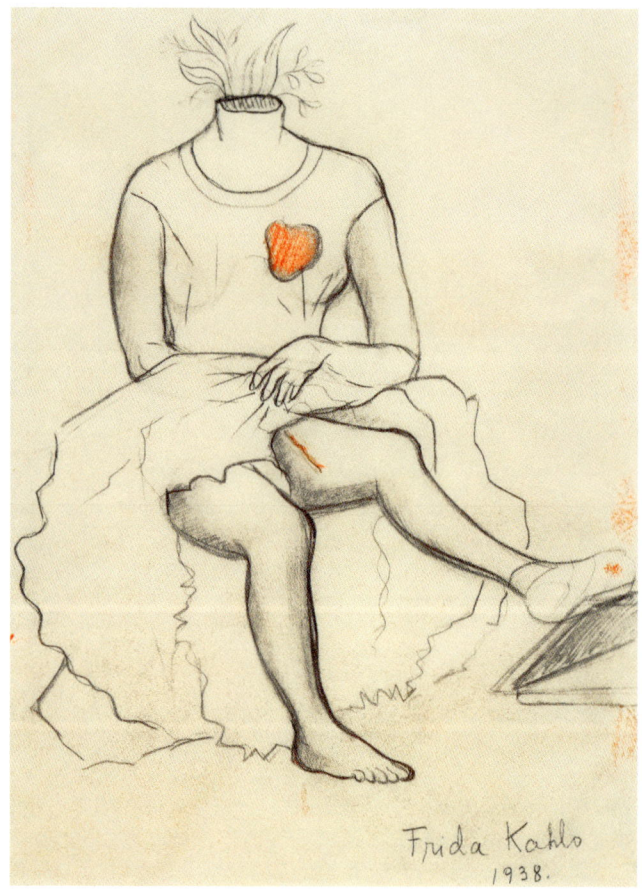

Showing the Scar. Study for *Remembrance of an Open Wound*, 1938
Graphite pencil and colored pencil on paper, 28.6 x 19.7 cm (11¼ x 7¾ in.)
New York, private collection

Self-portrait (Seated with Bandaged Foot), 1931
Graphite pencil and colored pencils on paper, 30 x 21 cm (11¾ x 8¼ in.)
Inscribed b. r.: Tere te quiero tanto que aunque quisiera darte más – [no] puedo sino
este dibujo. Frida (Tere I love you so much that even though I would like to give you more –
I [cannot] give anything but this drawing. Frida). Mexico City, private collection

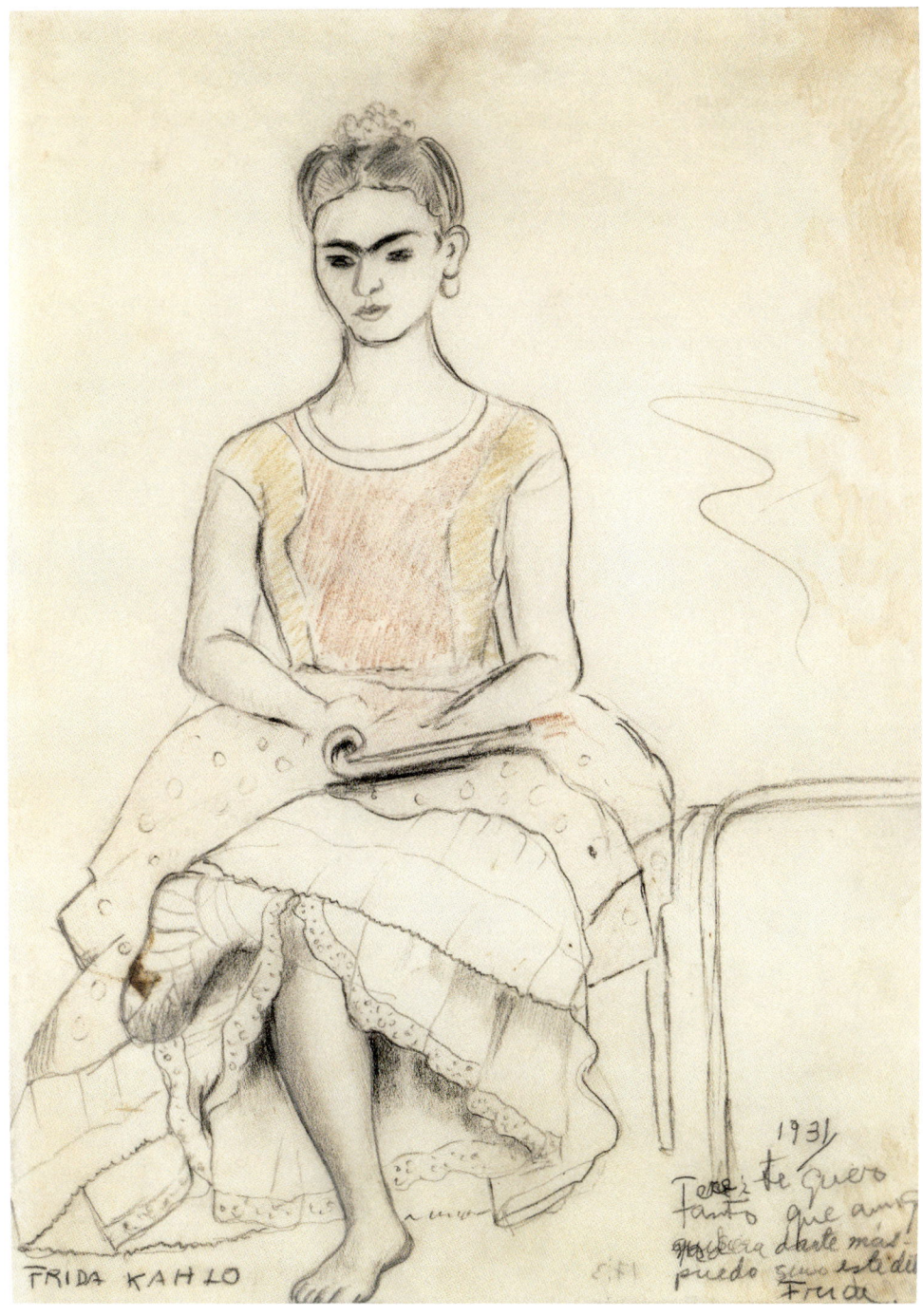

FRIDA KAHLO

1931

Tere: te quero
tanto que amo
...darte más!
puedo...esté...
Frida.

Espeluznante crimen en Coyoacán
(Horrific Crime in Coyoacán), March 28, 1936
Newspaper *La Prensa*. Mexico City, Fototeca,
Hemeroteca y Biblioteca Mario Vázquez Raña,
Archivo y Fundación de la Organización
Editorial Mexicana

Otto Dix, **Sex Murder**, 1922
Etching, 27.5 x 34.6 cm (10⅞ x 13⅝ in.)
Vaduz, Otto Dix Foundation

Wallace Marly, **Frida Kahlo in front of**
A Few Small Nips (Passionately in Love)
of 1938, with its frame unpainted, *c.* 1944

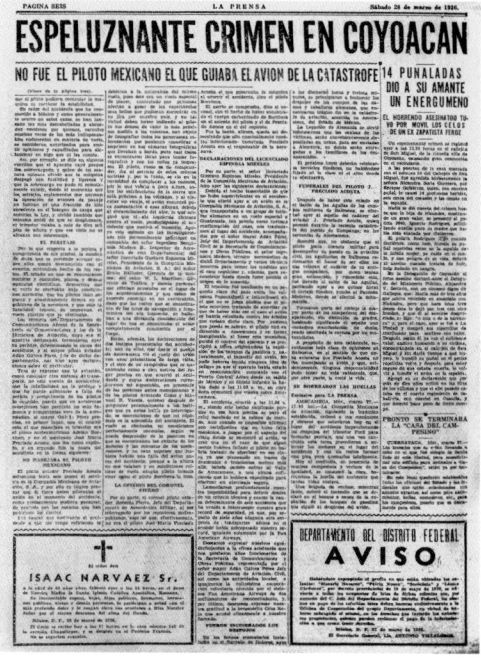

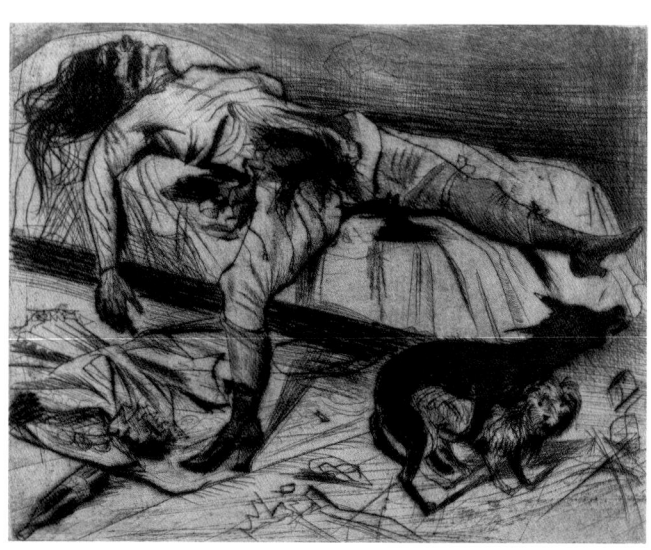

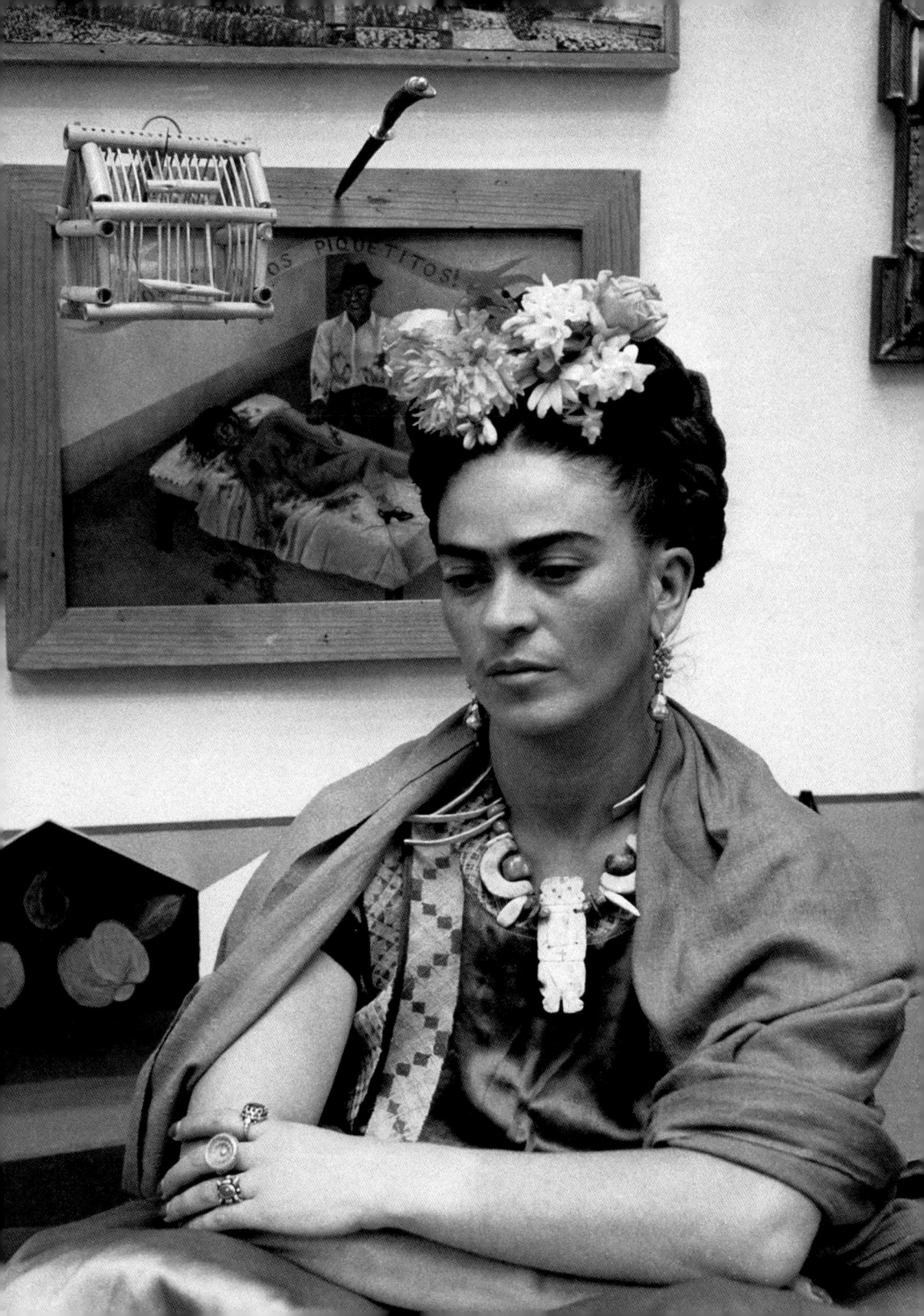

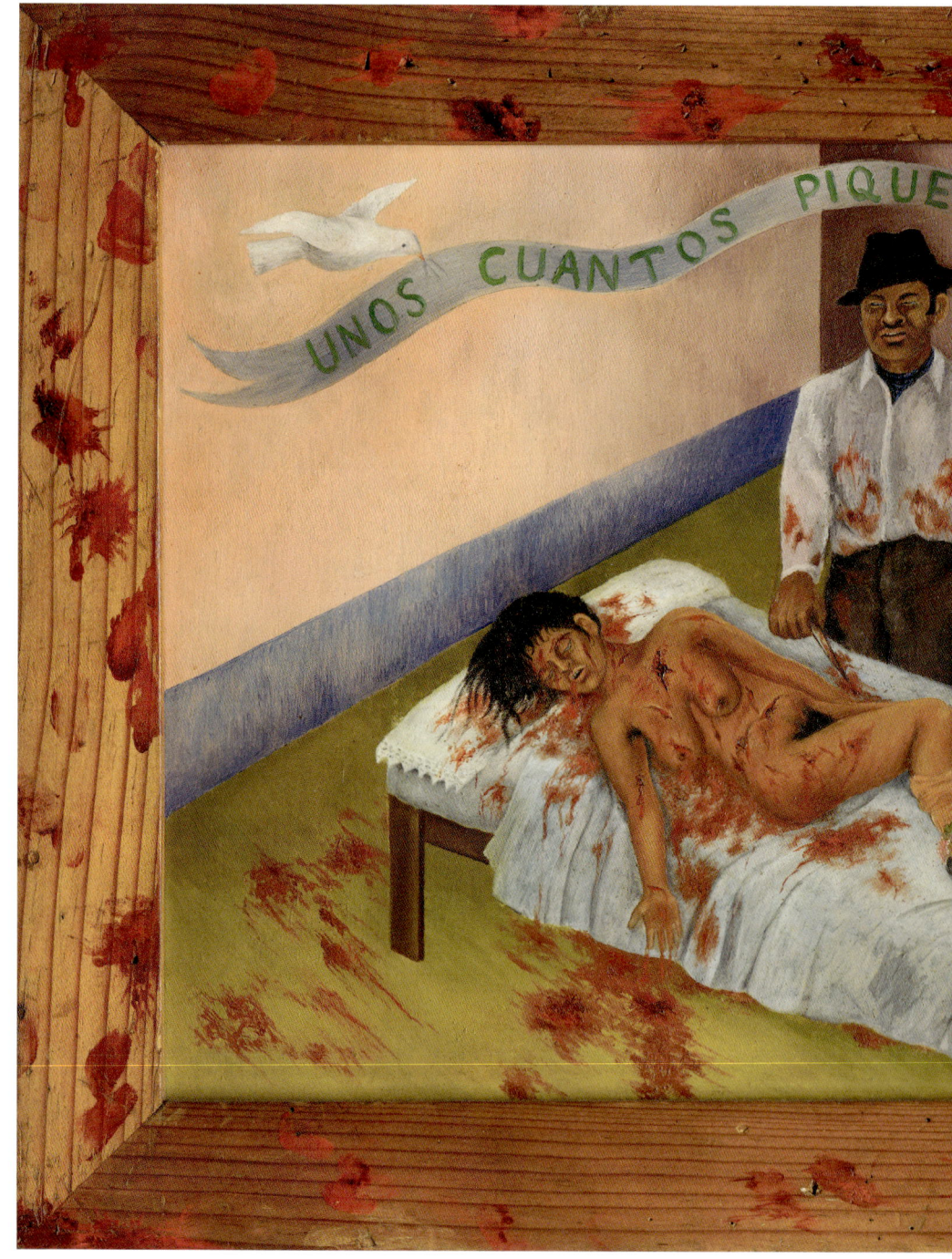

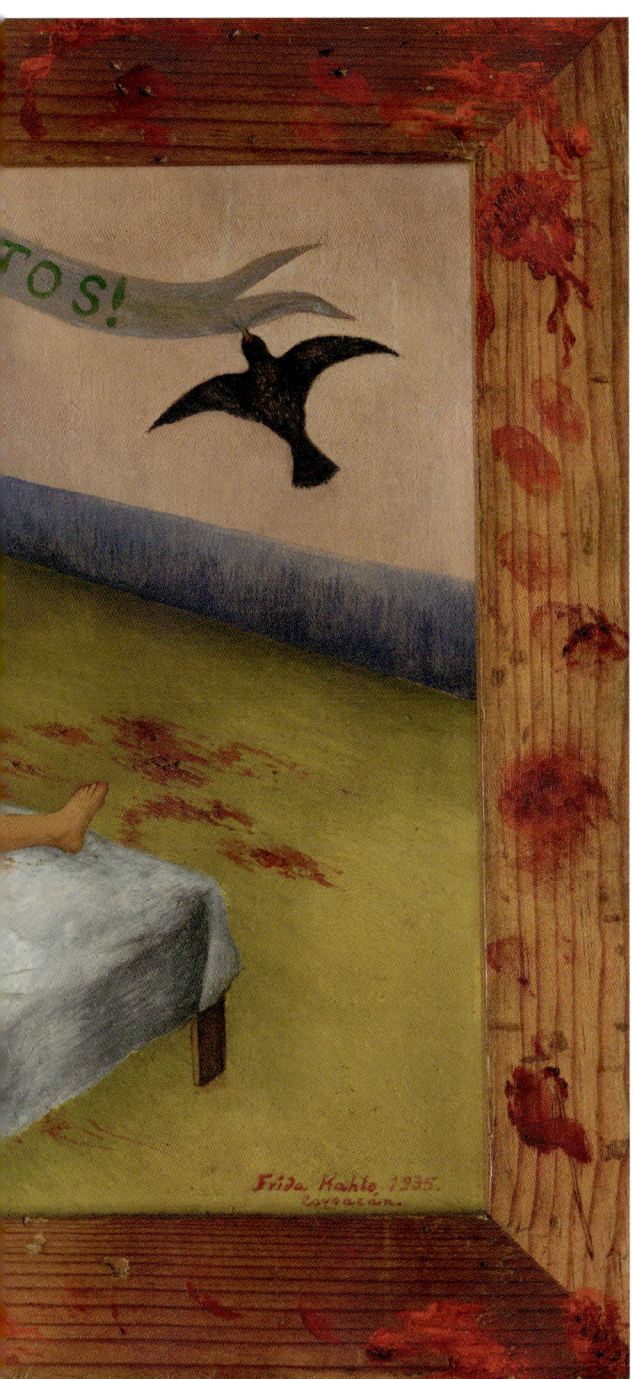

**A Few Small Nips
(Passionately in Love)**, 1935–1938
Oil on metal and wooden frame,
38 x 48.5 cm (15 x 19⅛ in.)
Mexico City, Xochimilco,
Museo Dolores Olmedo

Pages 158/159
The Square Is Theirs, 1937
Oil on canvas mounted on masonite,
31.4 x 47.9 cm (12⅜ x 18⅞ in.)
Private collection

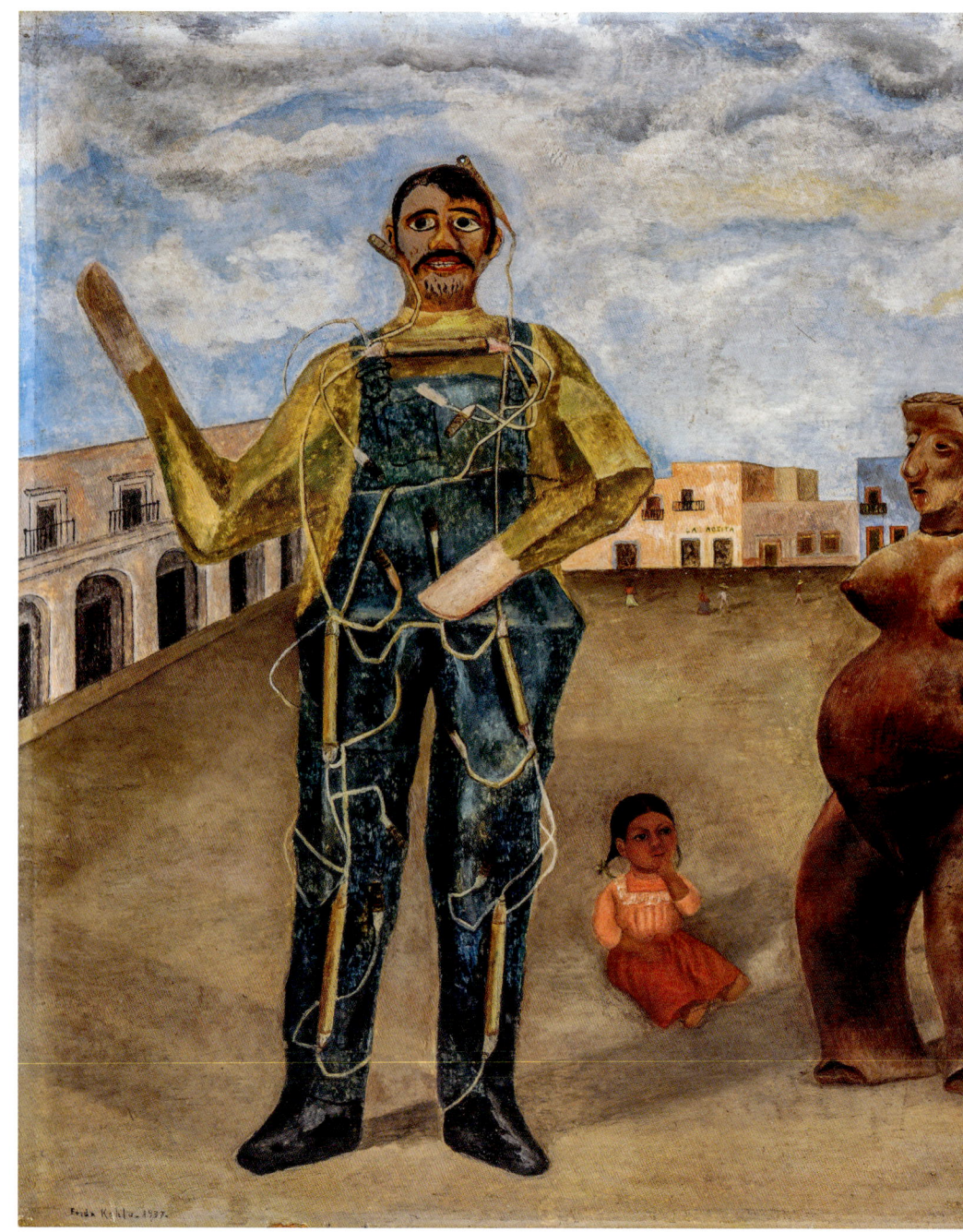

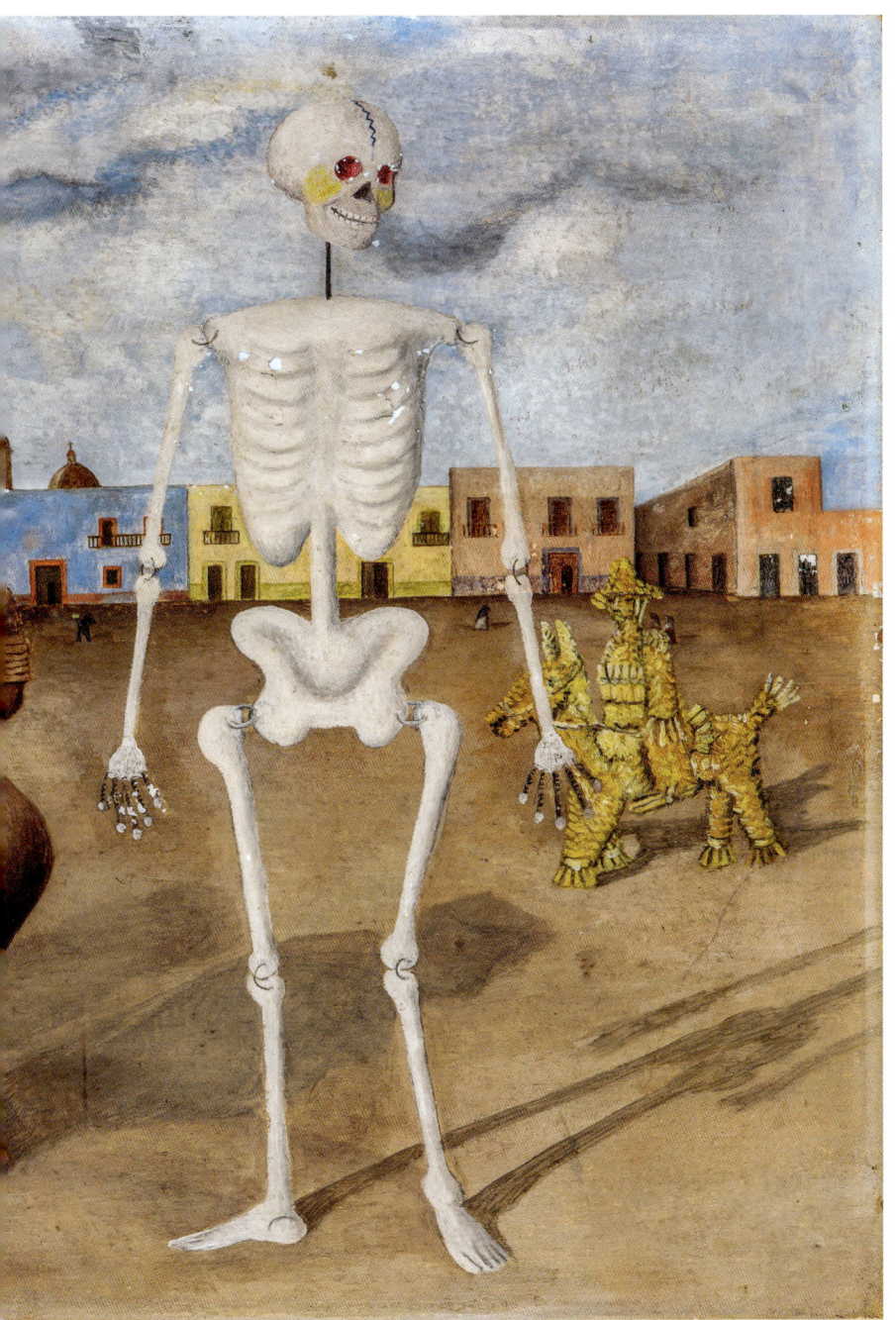

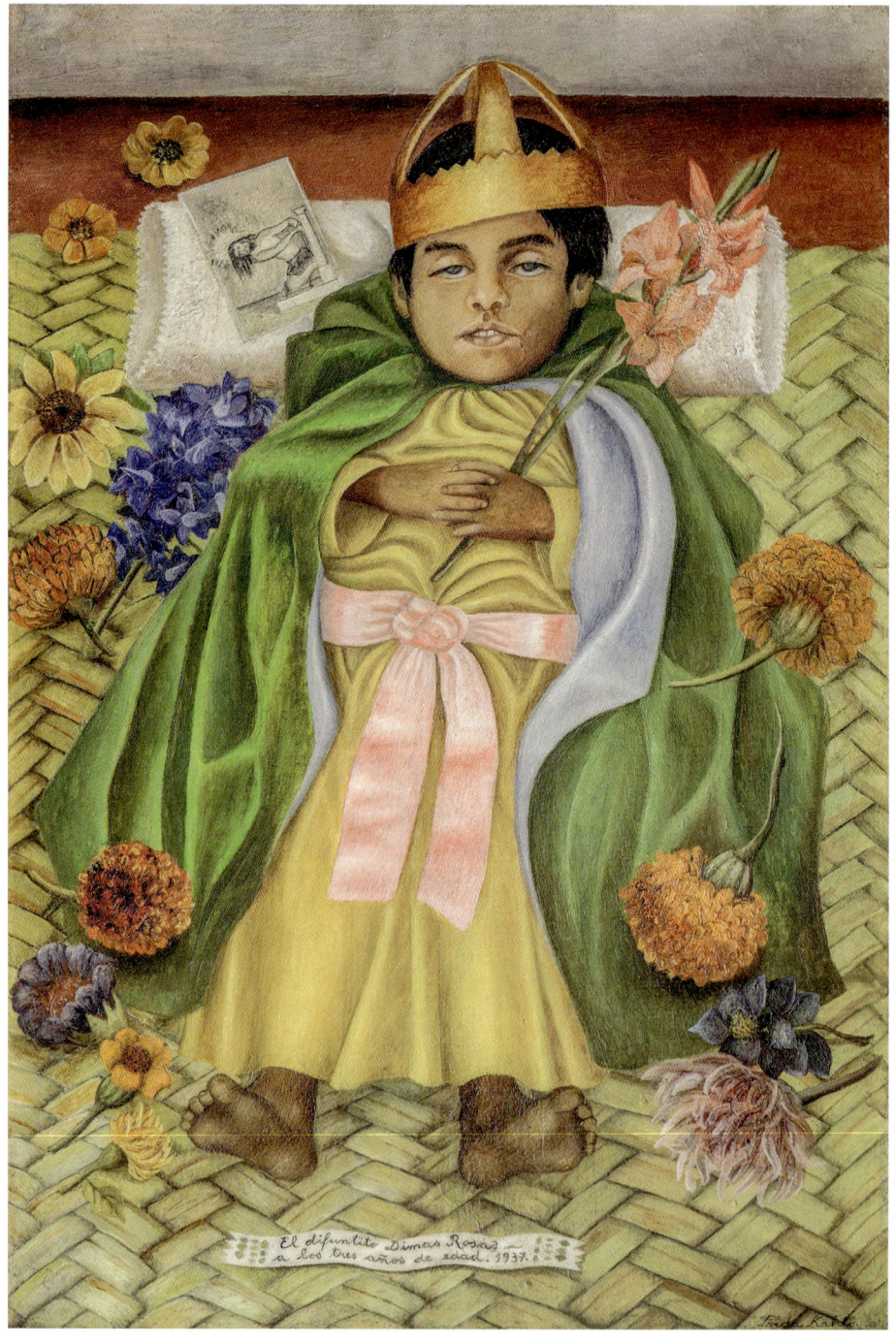

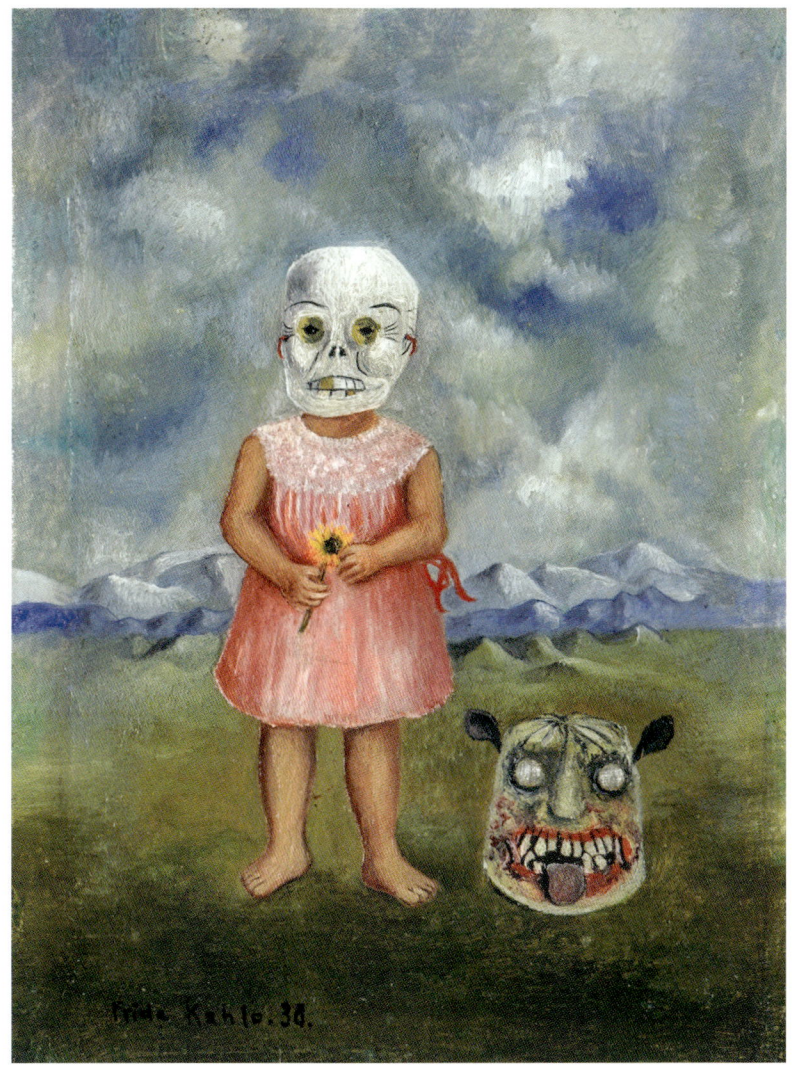

**Dressed Up for Paradise (The Deceased Dimas Rosas
at Three Years of Age)**, November 1937
Oil on masonite, 48 x 31.5 cm (18⅞ x 12⅜ in.)
Mexico City, Xochimilco, Museo Dolores Olmedo

Girl with Death Mask (She Plays Alone), 1938
Oil on tinplate, 14.9 x 11 cm (5⅞ x 4⅜ in.). Nagoya City Art Museum

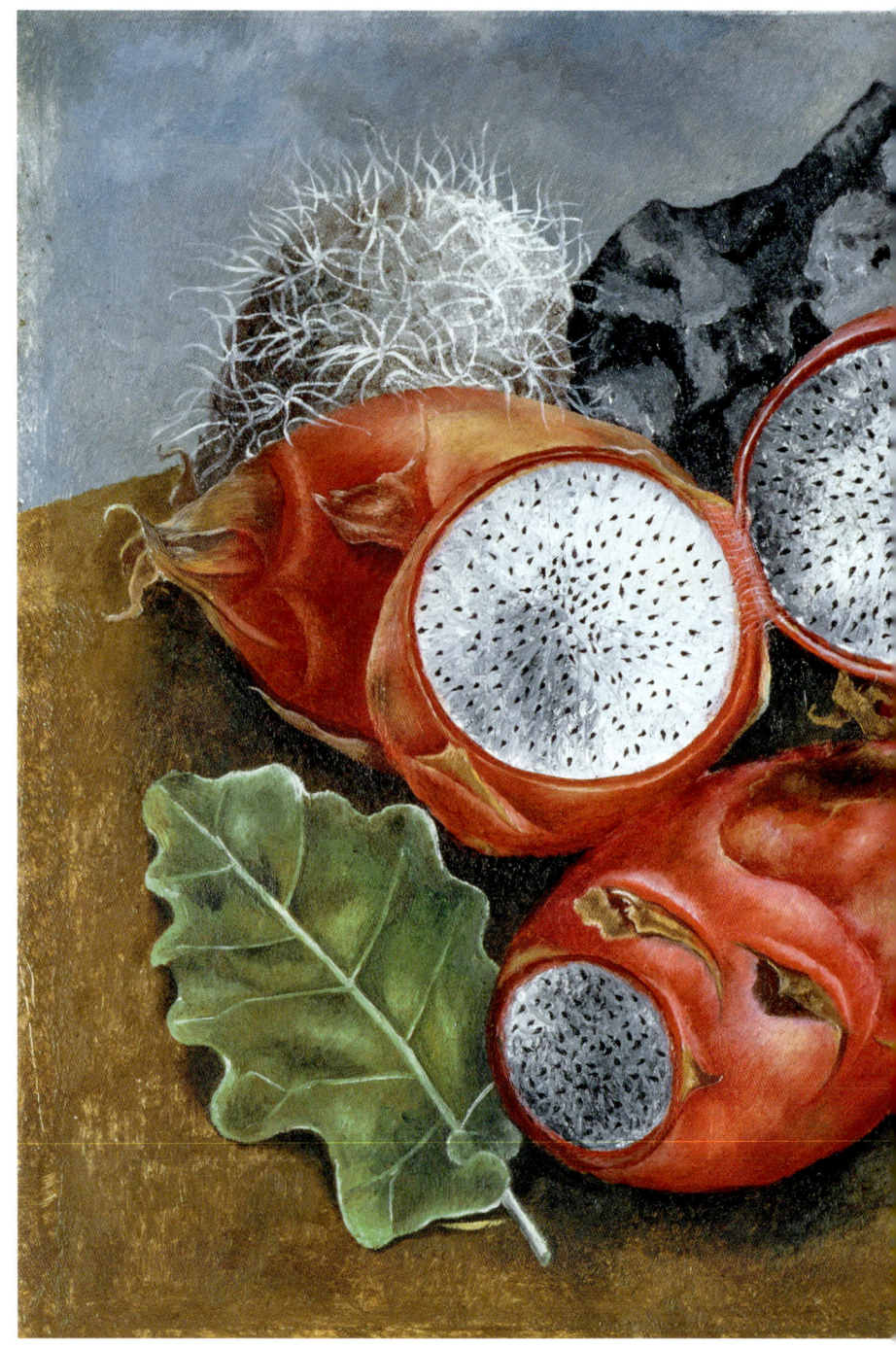

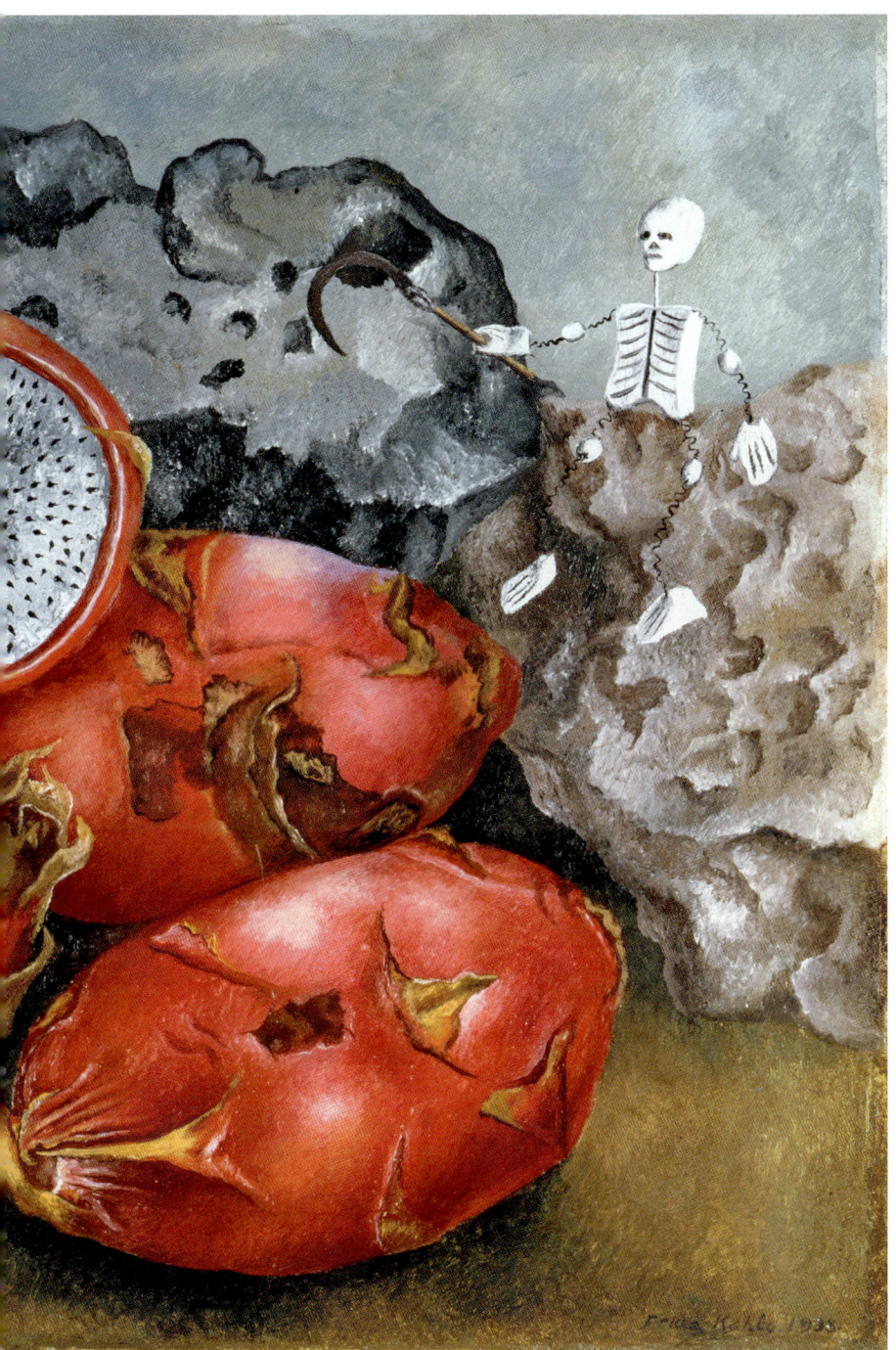

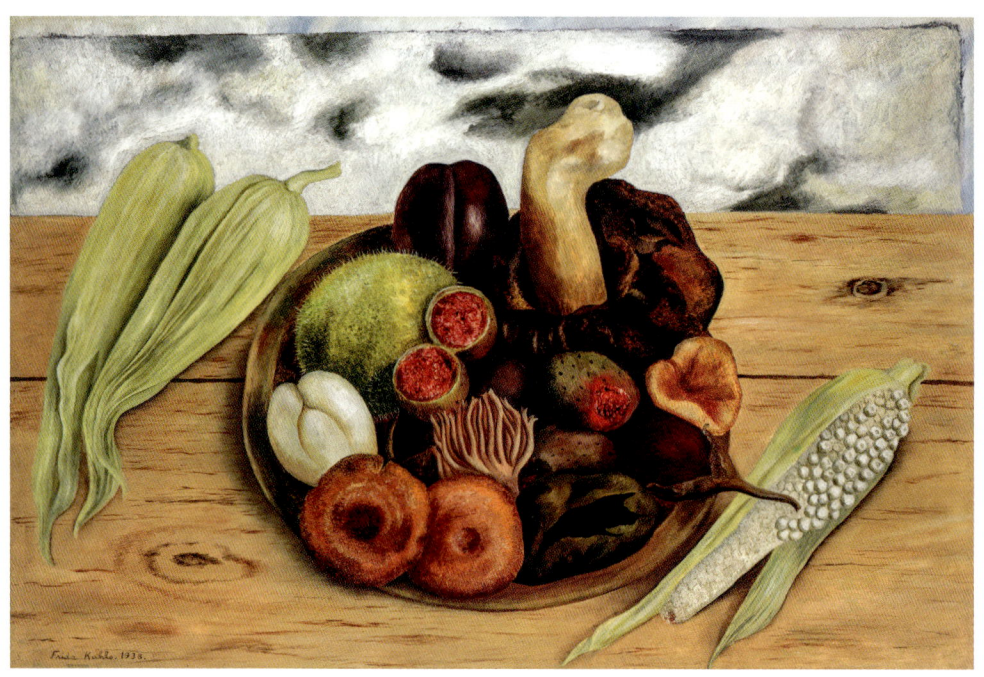

Pages 162/163
Pitahayas, 1938
Oil on aluminum, 25.4 x 35.6 cm (10 x 14 in.)
Wisconsin, Madison Museum of Contemporary Art,
Bequest of Rudolph and Louise Langer

Food from the Earth, 1938
Oil on masonite, 40.6 x 60 cm (16 x 23⅝ in.)
Mexico City, Banco Nacional de México collection

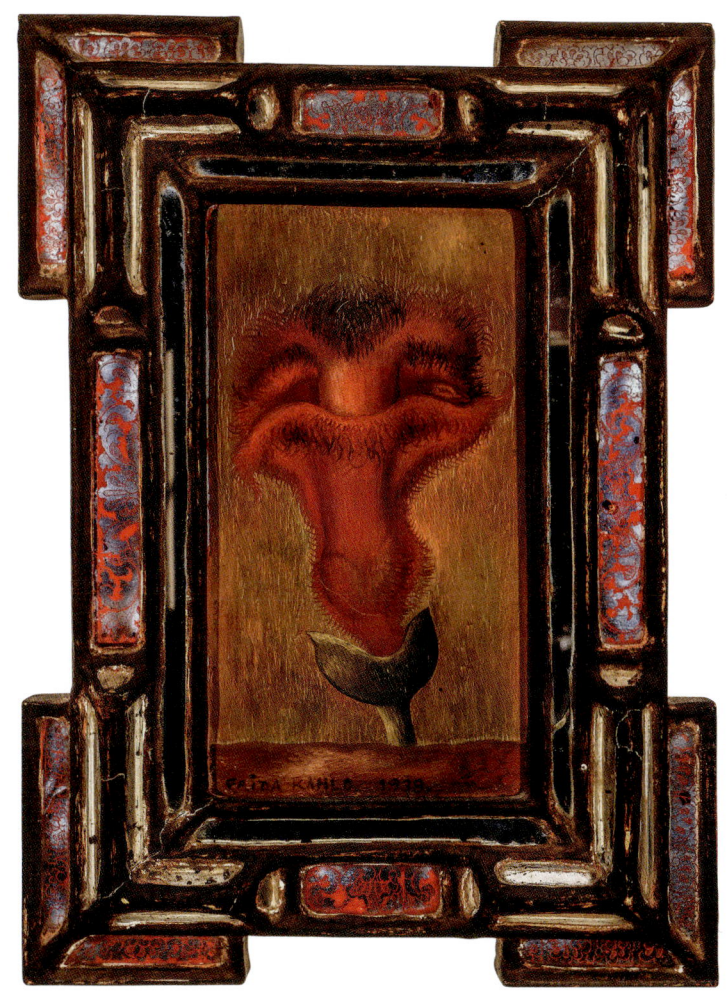

Xochitl (Flower of Life), 1938
Oil on metal, 18 x 9.5 cm (7⅛ x 3¾ in.), with painted mirror frame
Mexico City, private collection

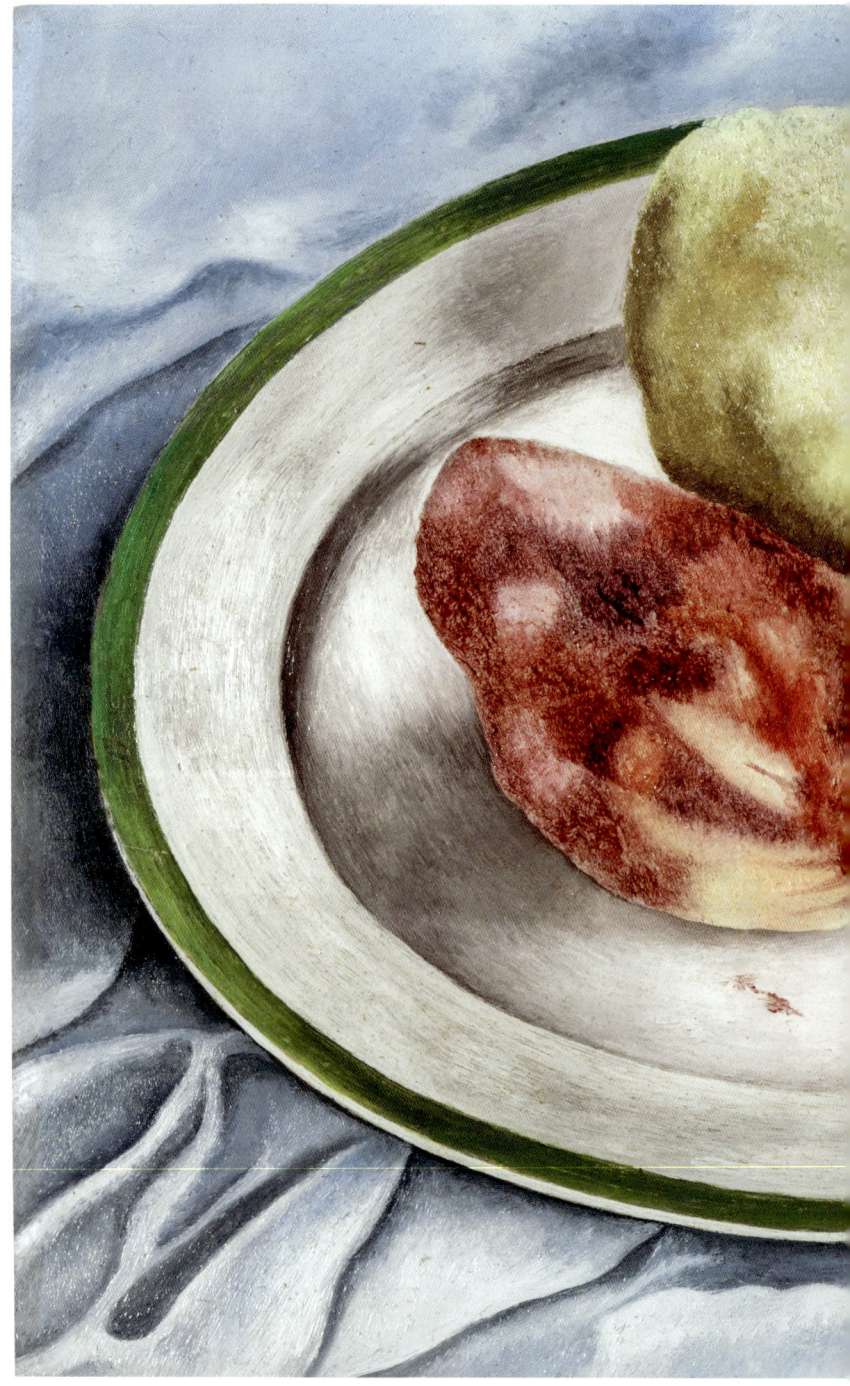

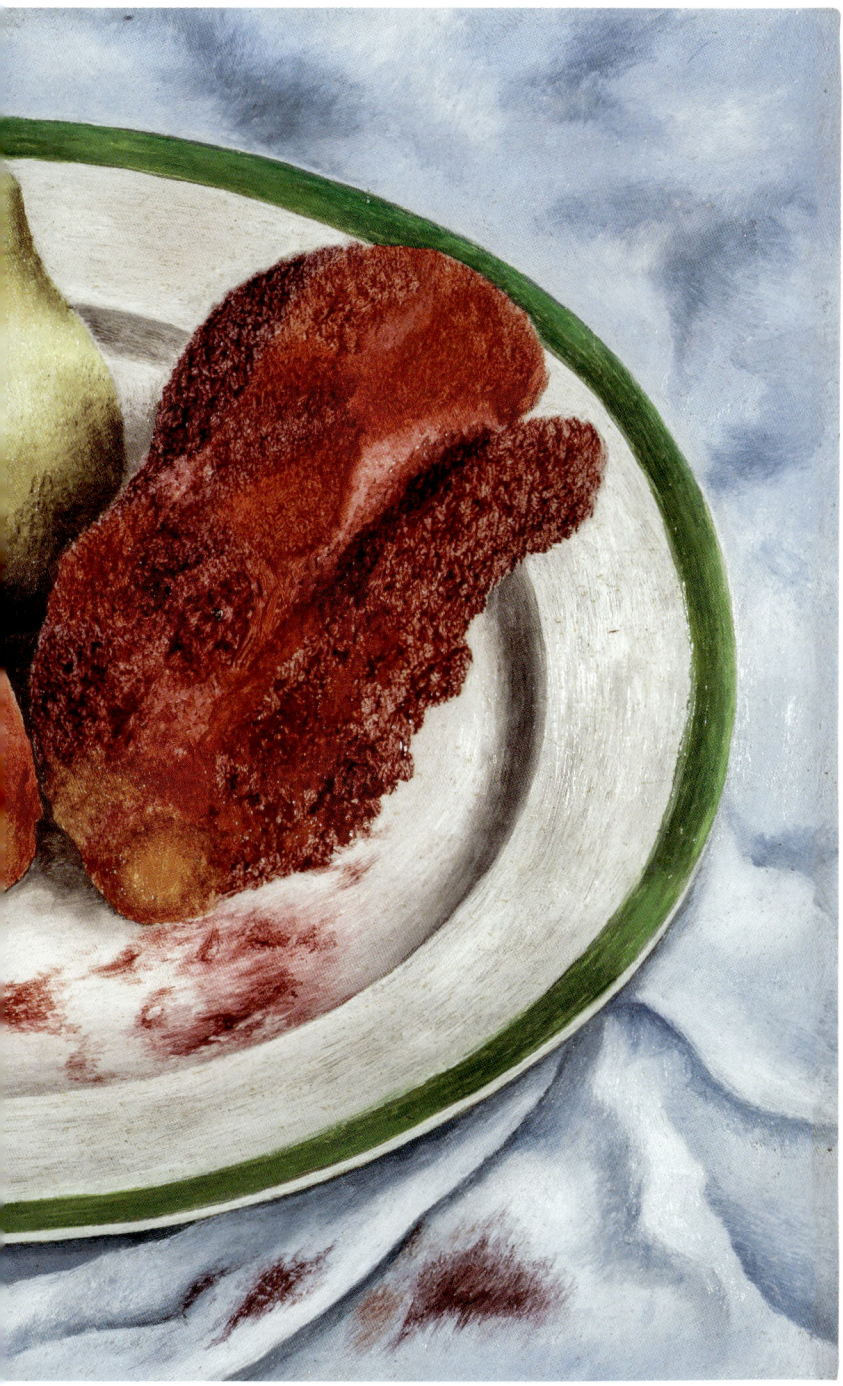

Pages 166/167
Tunas (Still Life with Prickly Pear Fruit), *c.* 1938
Oil on tinplate, 19.7 x 24.8 cm (7¾ x 9¾ in.)
Private collection, courtesy Pablo Goebel Fine Arts, Mexico City

Frida Kahlo and Diego Rivera with Fulang-Chang, Mexico City, 1934
Gelatin silver print, 10.2 x 12.7 cm (4 x 5 in.)
New York, collection of Spencer Throckmorton

Fulang-Chang and I, March 1937
Oil on masonite, 40 x 28 cm (15¾ x 11 in.)
New York, Museum of Modern Art,
Mary Sklar Bequest, inv. 277.1987.a-b

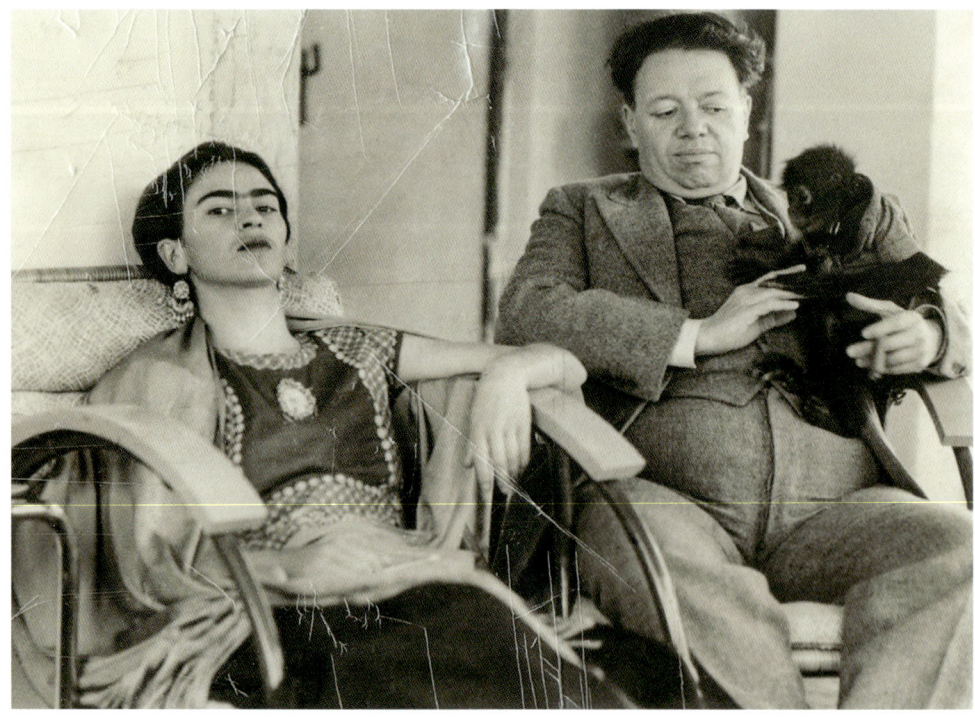

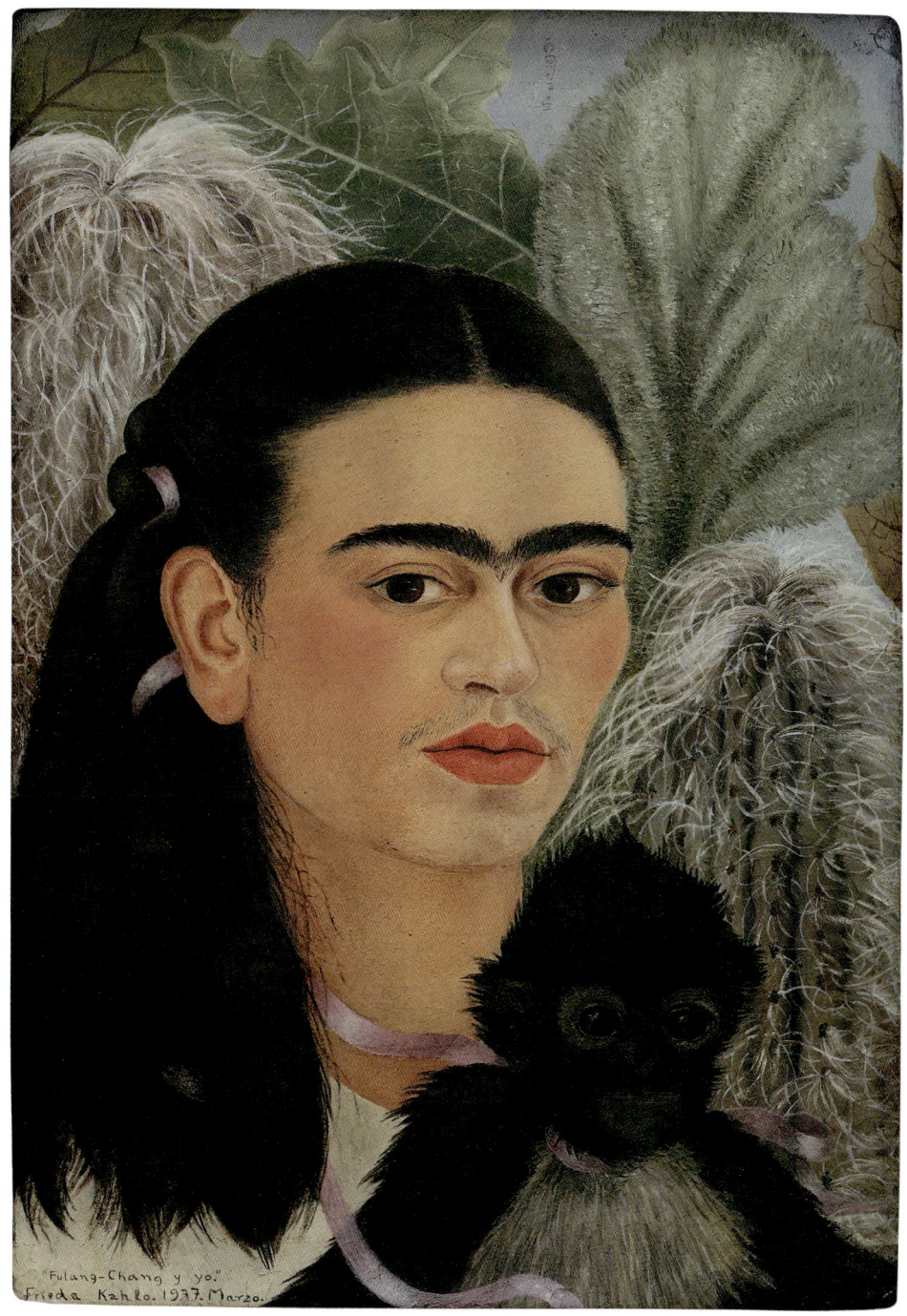

Self-portrait with Monkey, 1938
Oil on masonite, 40.6 x 30.5 cm (16 x 12 in.)
Buffalo, New York, Albright-Knox Art Gallery,
Bequest of A. Conger Goodyear, 1966, inv. 1966:9.10

Page 172
Lola Álvarez Bravo, **Frida Kahlo looking in the mirror
with two hairless dogs**, Casa Azul, *c.* 1944
Gelatin silver print, 26.7 x 35.9 cm (10½ x 14⅛ in.)
New York, collection of Spencer Throckmorton

Page 173
Ixcuhintli Dog with Me, *c.* 1938
Oil on canvas, 71 x 52 cm (30 x 20½ in.)
United States, private collection

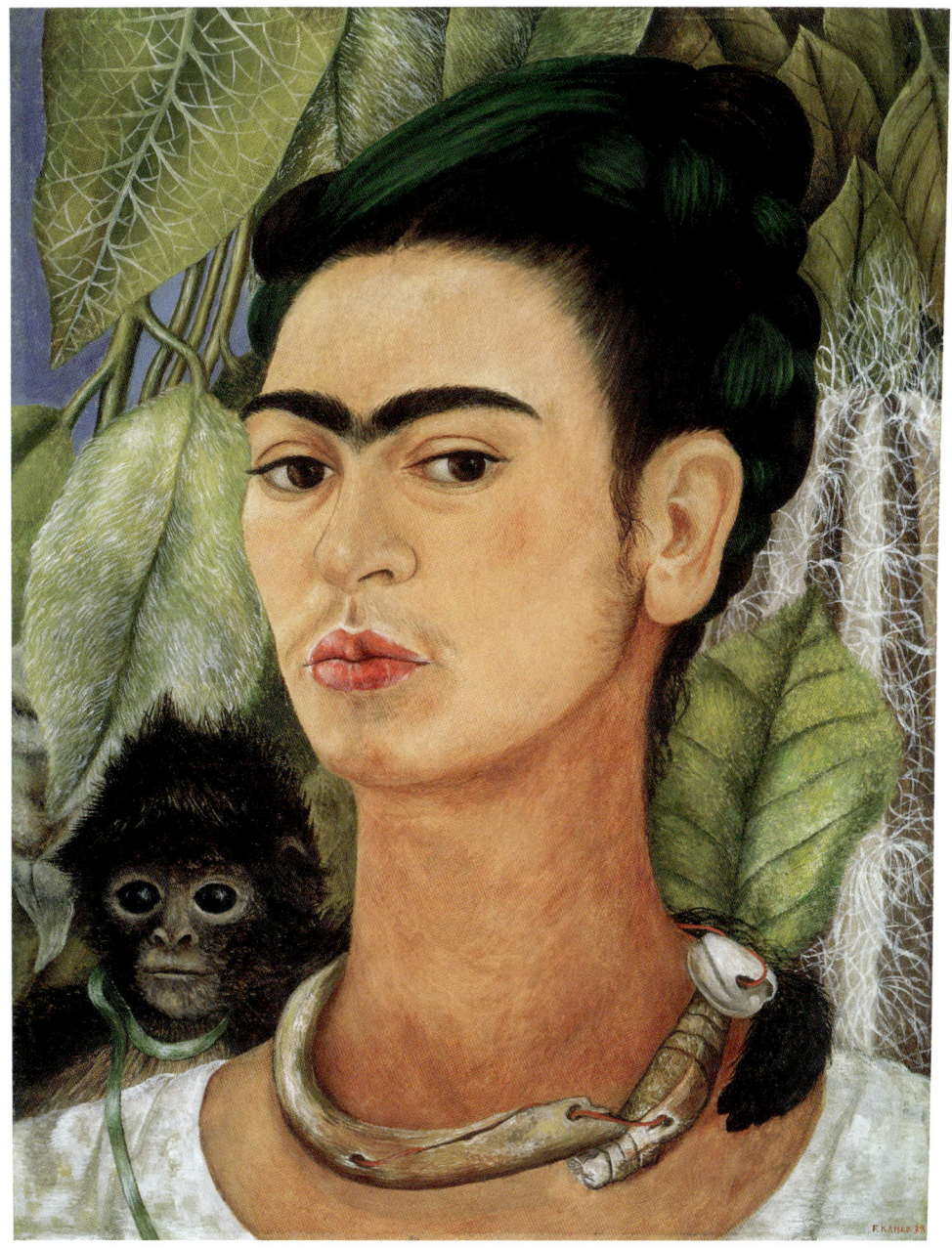

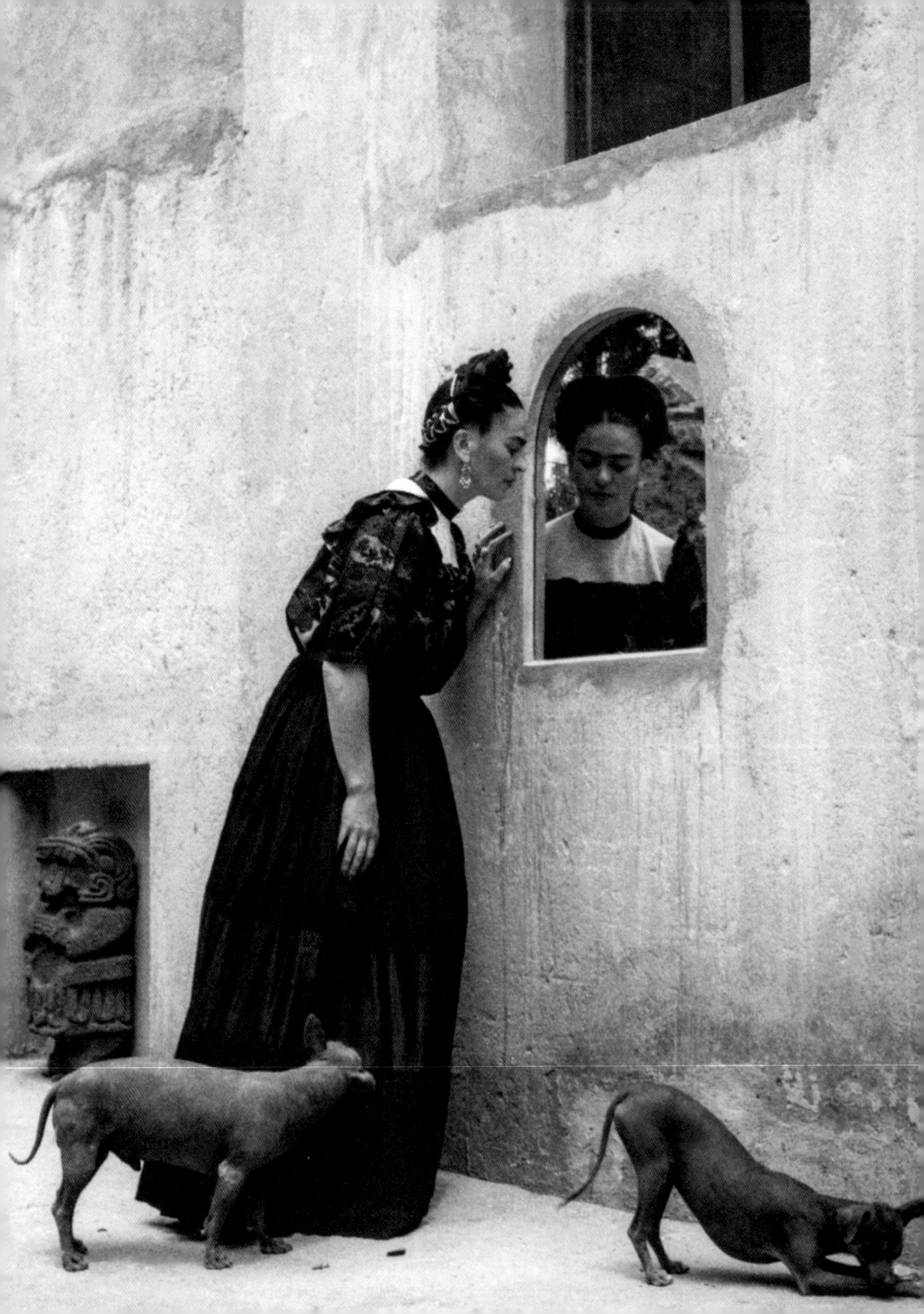

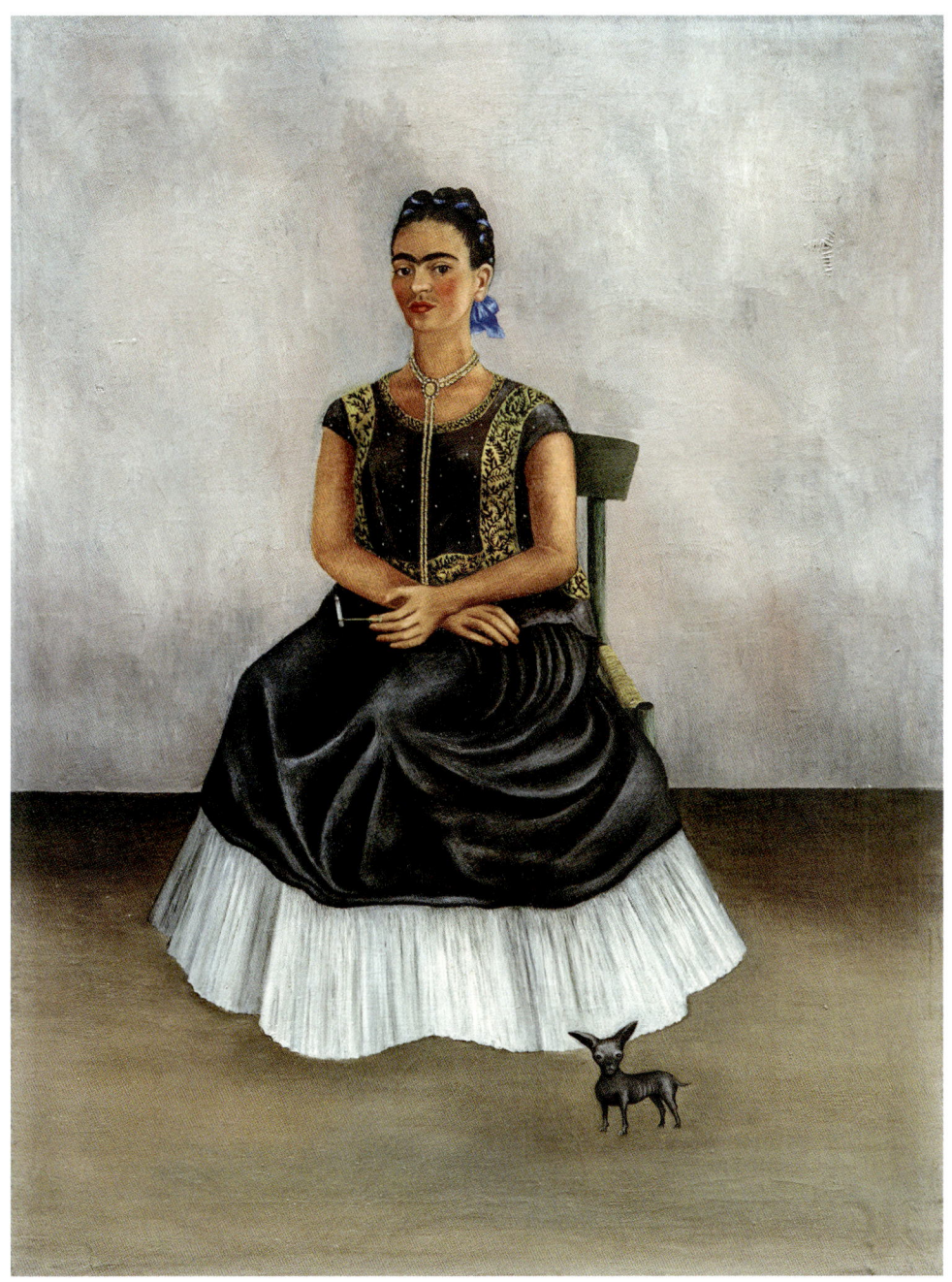

Self-portrait Dedicated to Leon Trotsky (Between the Curtains), November 1937
Oil on masonite, 76.2 x 61 cm (30 x 24 in.); inscription on paper at center:
Para Leon Trotsky / con todo cariño, / dedico ésta pin- / tura, el dia 7 / de Noviembre de / 1937. /
Frida Kahlo. / En San Angel. / México (For Leon Trotsky / with great affection, / I dedicate
this pain- / ting, the 7th / of November, / 1937. / Frida Kahlo. / In San Ángel. / Mexico)
Washington, D.C., National Museum of Women in the Arts,
gift of the Honorable Clare Boothe Luce *(detail p. 79)*

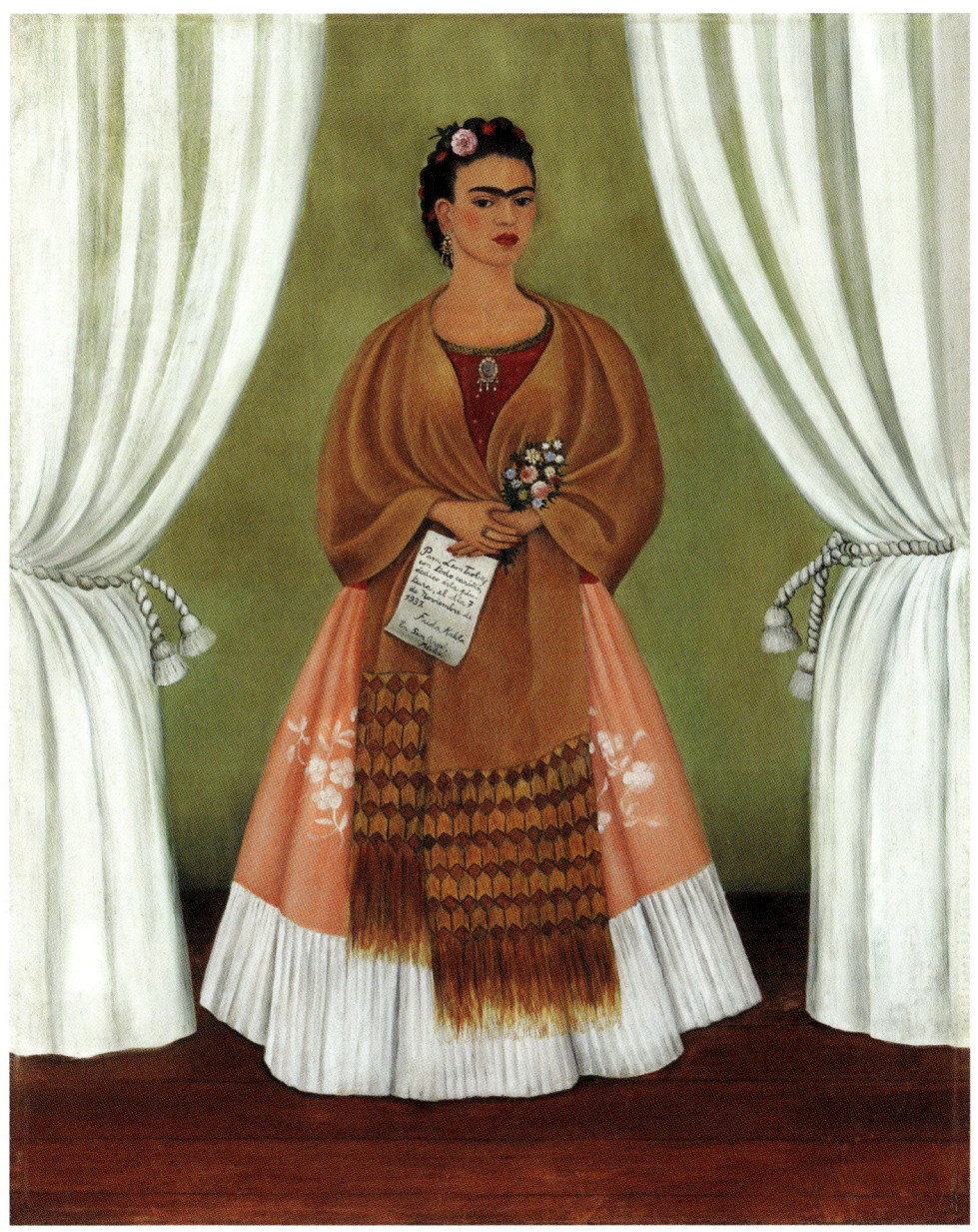

Lucienne Bloch, **Frida Kahlo and Cinzano**, New York, 1935
Gelatin silver print, 35.6 x 27.9 cm (14 x 11 in.)
New York, collection of Spencer Throckmorton

The Heart (Memory), 1937
Oil on metal, 40 x 28.3 cm (15¾ x 11⅛ in.)
New York, private collection

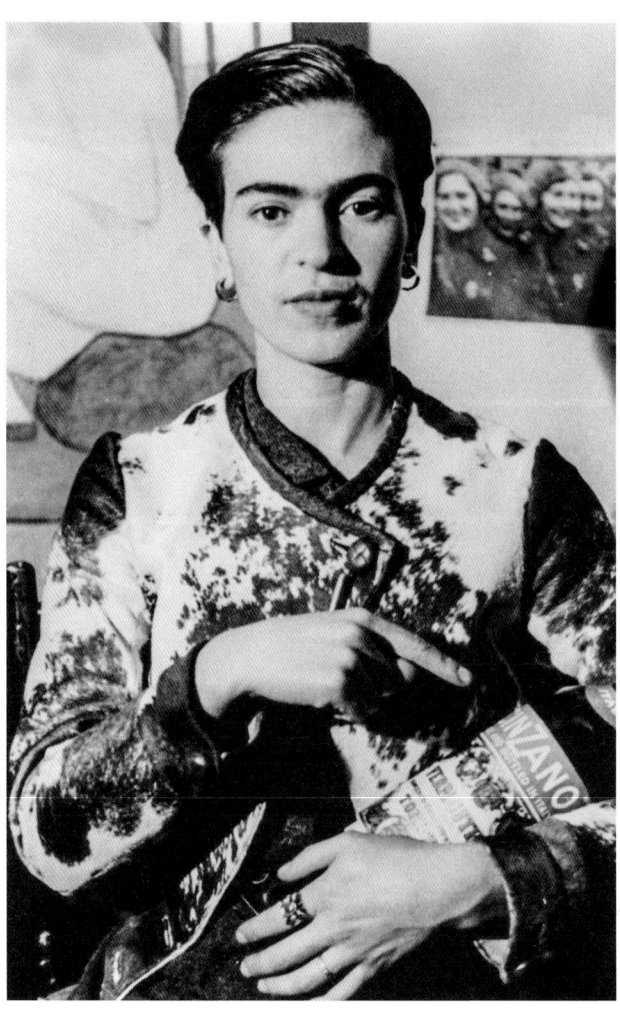

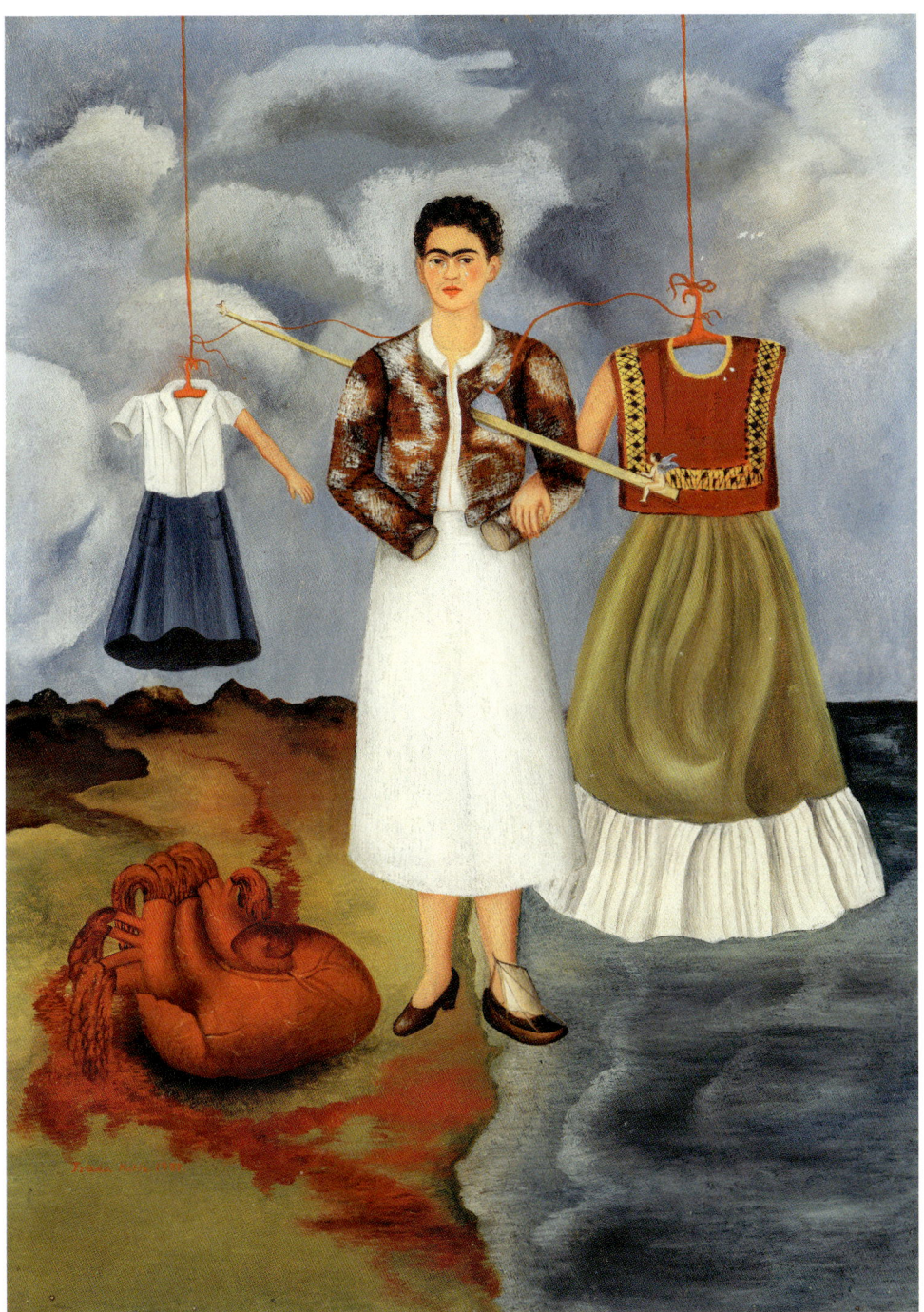

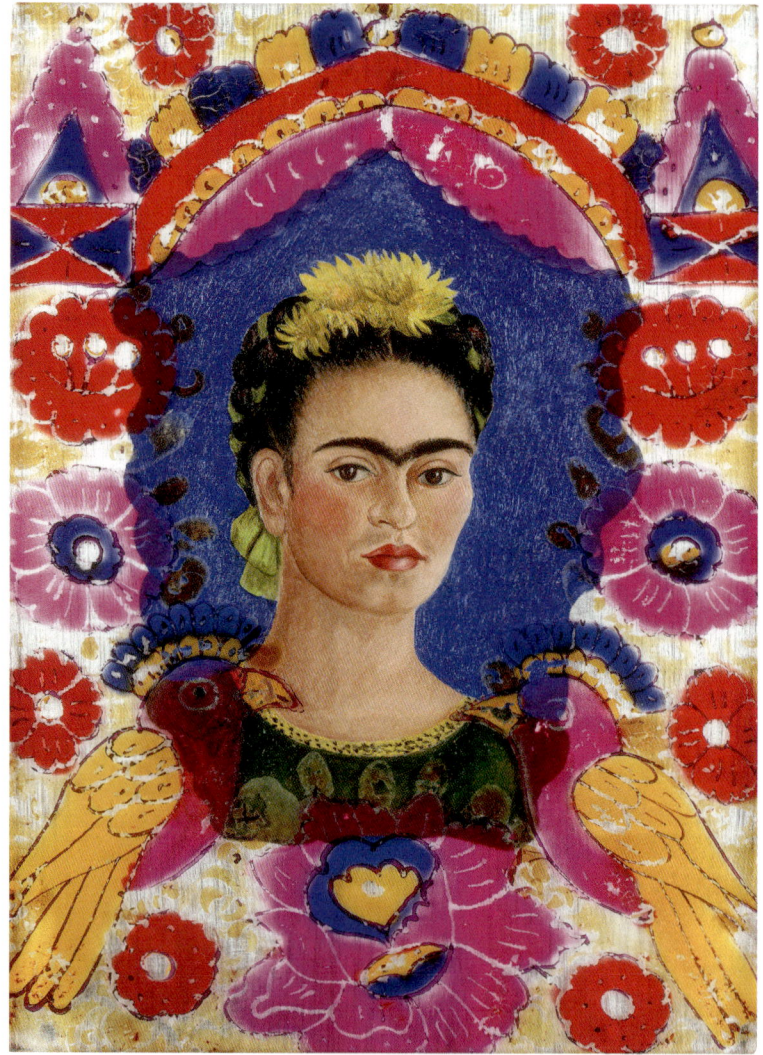

The Frame, *c.* 1938
Oil on aluminum, covered with painted glass, 28.5 x 20.7 cm (11¼ x 8⅛ in.)
Paris, Centre Pompidou, Musée national d'art moderne/
Centre de création industrielle, inv. JP 929 P

Julien Levy, **Frida Kahlo** (detail), 1938
Gelatin silver print, 23.9 x 16 cm (9⅜ x 6¼ in.). Philadelphia Museum of Art,
The Lynne and Harold Honickman Gift of the Julien Levy Collection, 2001

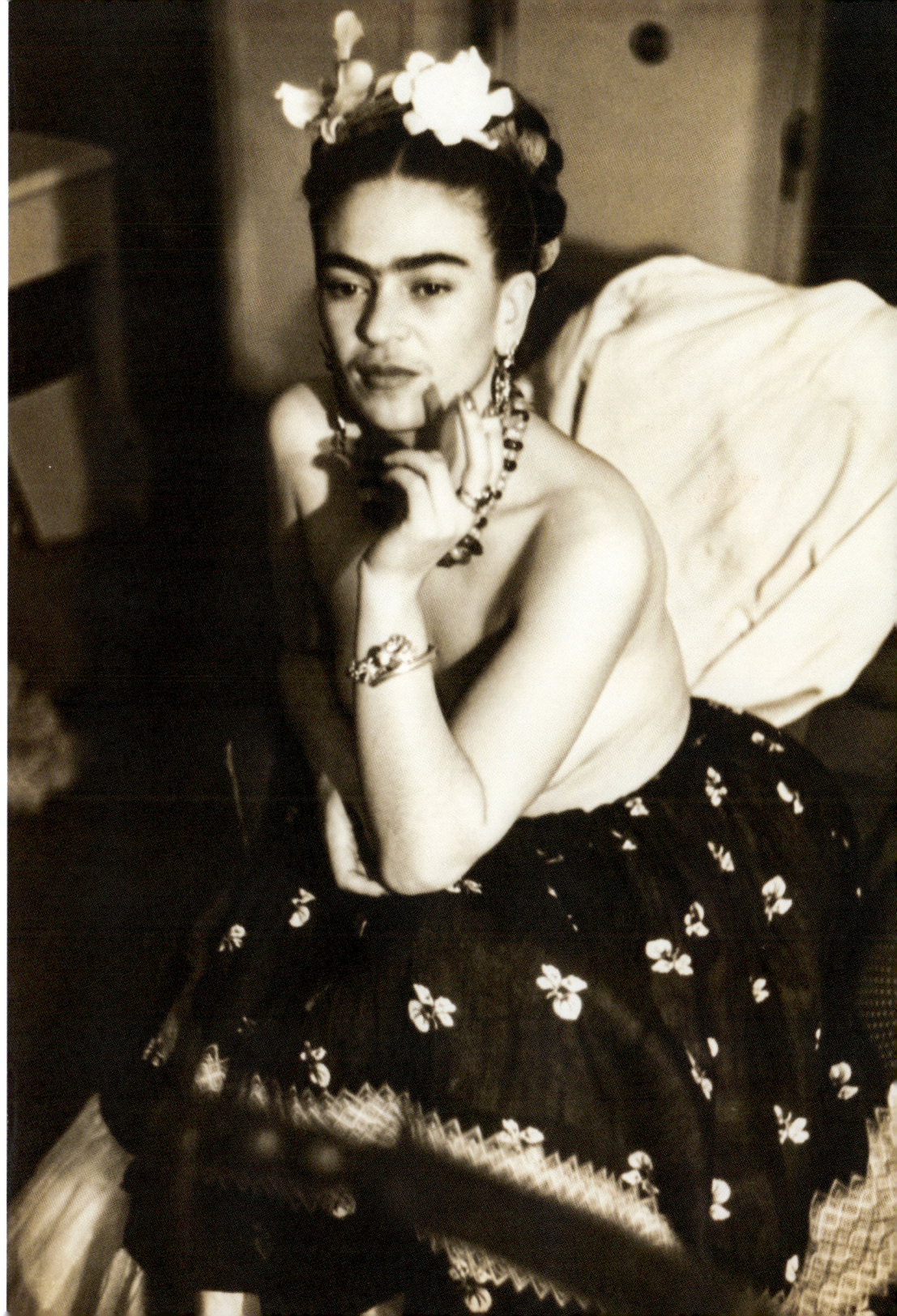

III.

I will paint pain, love, and affection.

The lessons of maturity and experience

1939–1946

> *"Her visual images were, almost always, veritable explosions out of the psychological depths: paintings and revelations. This can be said of very few artists. There is an impressive authenticity in Frida's visual metaphors. Looking at her paintings, we can say: this is true, this has been lived, suffered, and re-created."*
>
> — OCTAVIO PAZ, 1988

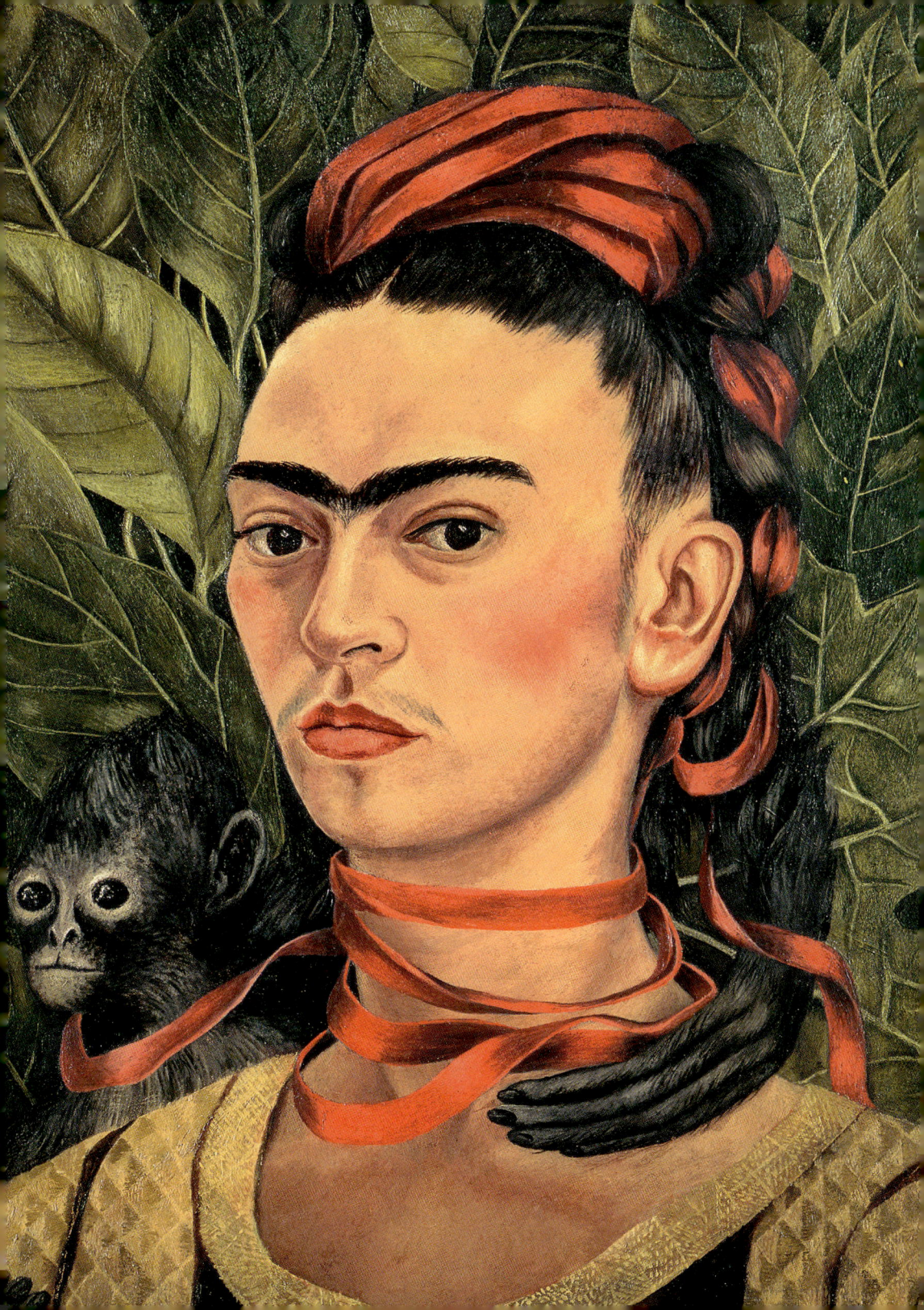

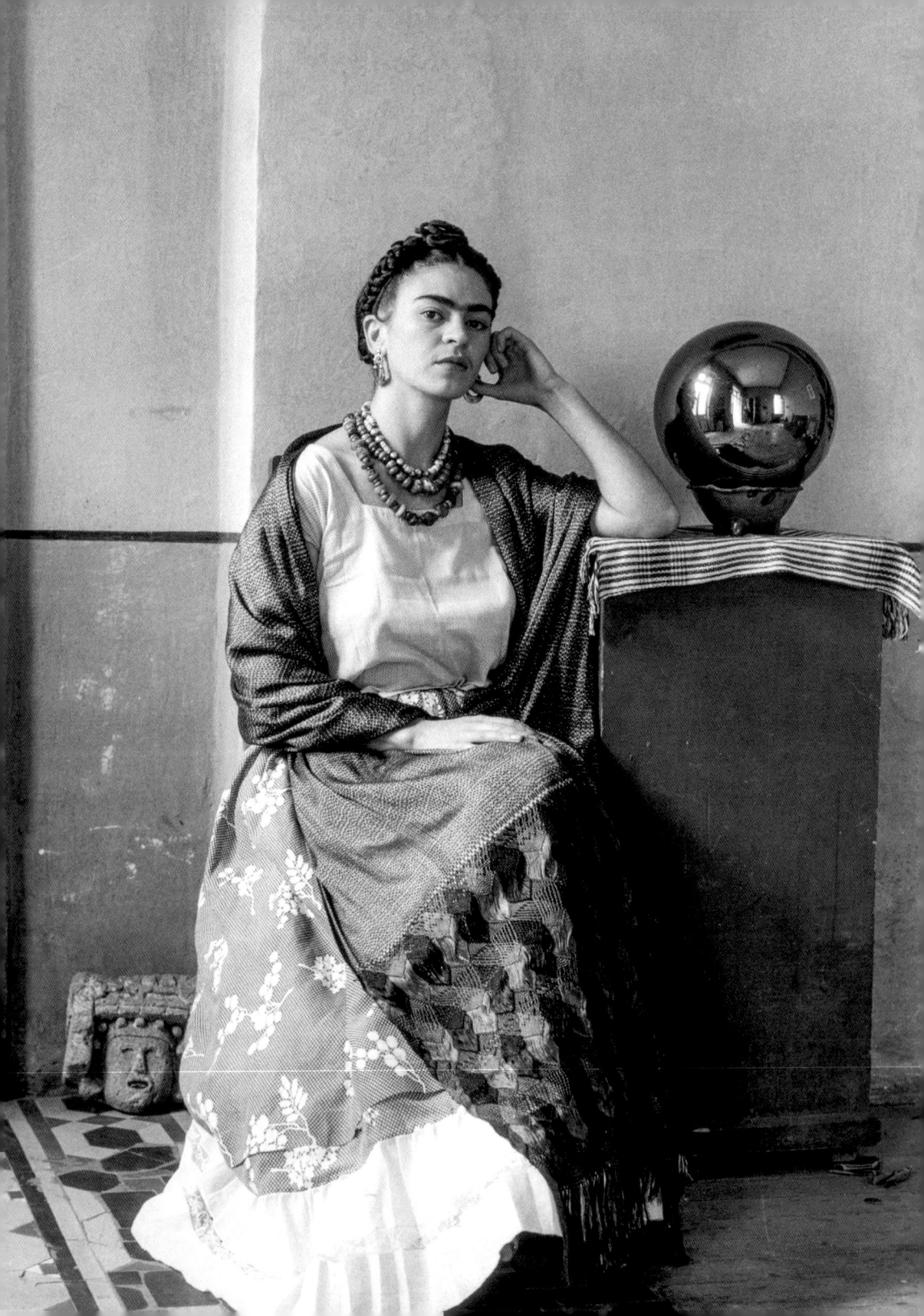

In the view of various authors writing about Kahlo's experience in Europe, based on only the few scattered words she wrote in 1939 to Rivera and to her lover Nickolas Muray (1892–1965), the opportunity to visit Paris and to show her work there did not altogether seem to turn out for the best. However, and as with much of what Kahlo wrote, where these letters talk about the time she spent in Paris they nevertheless relate only part of what actually happened. For one thing, it should not be forgotten that for a young painter who had never been to Europe and who had had no formal training in the fine arts, the very fact of being able to exhibit her work in Paris, let alone being introduced to avant-garde intellectuals and artists by the Surrealist writer André Breton himself, must have been something really quite extraordinary. Certainly, when Kahlo met Breton again in Paris it was very different from when she had met him the previous year in Mexico, when she was excited by the idea that he might be interested in her work and endorse what she had absorbed from Surrealism. In Paris, however, Kahlo was not at all happy with him on account of all the problems she had had to face during the preparations for the "Mexique" exhibition, and even more so because of the fact that her work was to be displayed mixed in with various traditional items he had bought from markets in Mexico.[1] In the end though her annoyance did not count for too much since the exhibition turned out to be a success, while one of her self-portraits, *The Frame* (p. 178), was even bought by the Louvre for the collection of the Musée du Jeu de Paume.[2]

In Paris, Kahlo also met Breton's wife Jacqueline Lamba again (p. 186). They had become kindred spirits during the time when they first met in Mexico since they both found themselves in similar situations, as women who were looking to establish their own path as artists but at the same time being married to men with strong personalities and great intelligence who were also internationally recognized artists. In the course of what was to be Kahlo's first and only visit to Europe her friendship with Lamba grew deeper, being based, quite independent of their respective marriages, on mutual admiration and a shared awareness of the appeal of their own personalities. On the other hand, in a few little-known photographs taken at the time by Dora Maar, who was then Picasso's lover and was a friend of Lamba's, the camera reveals the fears and insecurities Kahlo attempted to hide with her Tehuana costumes. This perception would seem to be borne out too in the drawings of Kahlo that Maar made at this time in Paris as well. Kahlo's intimate friendship

Page 181
Self-portrait with Monkey (detail), 1943 *(see ill. p. 237)*
Manuel Álvarez Bravo, **Frida with crystal sphere** (detail), Coyoacán, *c.* 1938
Gelatin silver print, 25.4 x 20.3 cm (10 x 8 in.)
Mexico City, Manuel Álvarez Bravo Archive

with Lamba had begun to take shape in the months they spent together in Mexico, where their playful behavior and exchanged glances approached the line of overt sexual attraction. Because of her background, Lamba was open to exploring her amorous desires without the need to choose between men and women or any sexual preferences, while Kahlo, of course, had explored her own bisexuality, although the two women responded to attraction in very different ways. Lamba admired Kahlo for what she had achieved as an artist and for the fact that she inhabited an artistic world that was her own, but must have been somewhat taken aback by her dependent relationship with Rivera. For her part, Kahlo found Breton too domineering and also perhaps not very supportive of the artistic needs of his wife and muse, who to a certain extent existed in the shadow of his genius and had not managed to establish herself independently as an artist.[3] Paradoxically, however, as the years passed Lamba went on to discover her potential as an artist and in doing so gained her independence, whereas Kahlo remained trapped in her emotional relationship with Rivera, which stifled her chances of achieving the complete autonomy she so fiercely desired.

Before Breton and Lamba left Mexico, Kahlo gave Lamba a small self-portrait on metal that was painted with such fine attention to detail that it makes the image look like a jewel or a religious icon (p. 203). In this painting it would seem that Kahlo wanted to express her feelings for Lamba as clearly as possible, and also how hard it was for them to be together, even though that was what she longed for most. The self-portrait is today in a frame made of shells but was originally mounted on a metal butterfly with magnificent wings especially made for Kahlo by a craftsman (p. 187). Underneath her self-portrait Kahlo left a space for Lamba to insert her own, so that in this way, with the two of them both on the butterfly's body, they could fly away from everything that was stopping them from being together and be reborn in each other's company, transformed into beings who were now completely free to feed on the nectar of their own flowers. However, things did not turn out that way. When they met again in Paris they certainly enjoyed being in each other's company as before, and spent time walking around the Place des Vosges together and the flea market at the Porte de Clignancourt.[4] While Kahlo was in Paris she had to be taken into hospital for a urinary tract infection; it is very likely that her condition made her feel vulnerable, in a country she did not know and with a language she did not speak, and that this was the reason she decided to return to Mexico and abandon her planned visit to London, where she had intended to meet Peggy Guggenheim to discuss the possibility of arranging a show at her gallery.[5]

Wallace Marly, **Frida Kahlo and Diego Rivera
in their studio in the Casa Azul**, Coyoacán, *c.* 1944

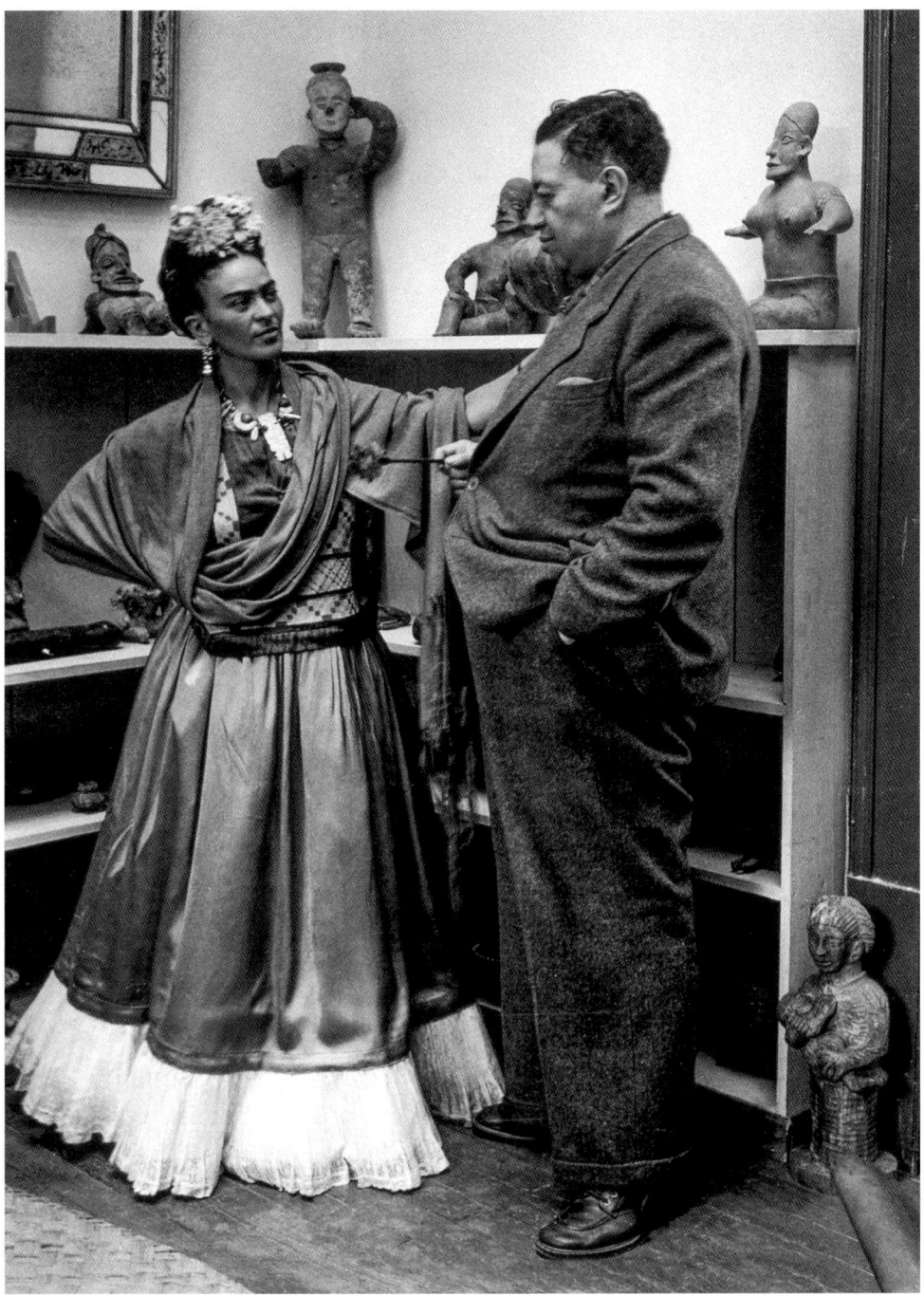

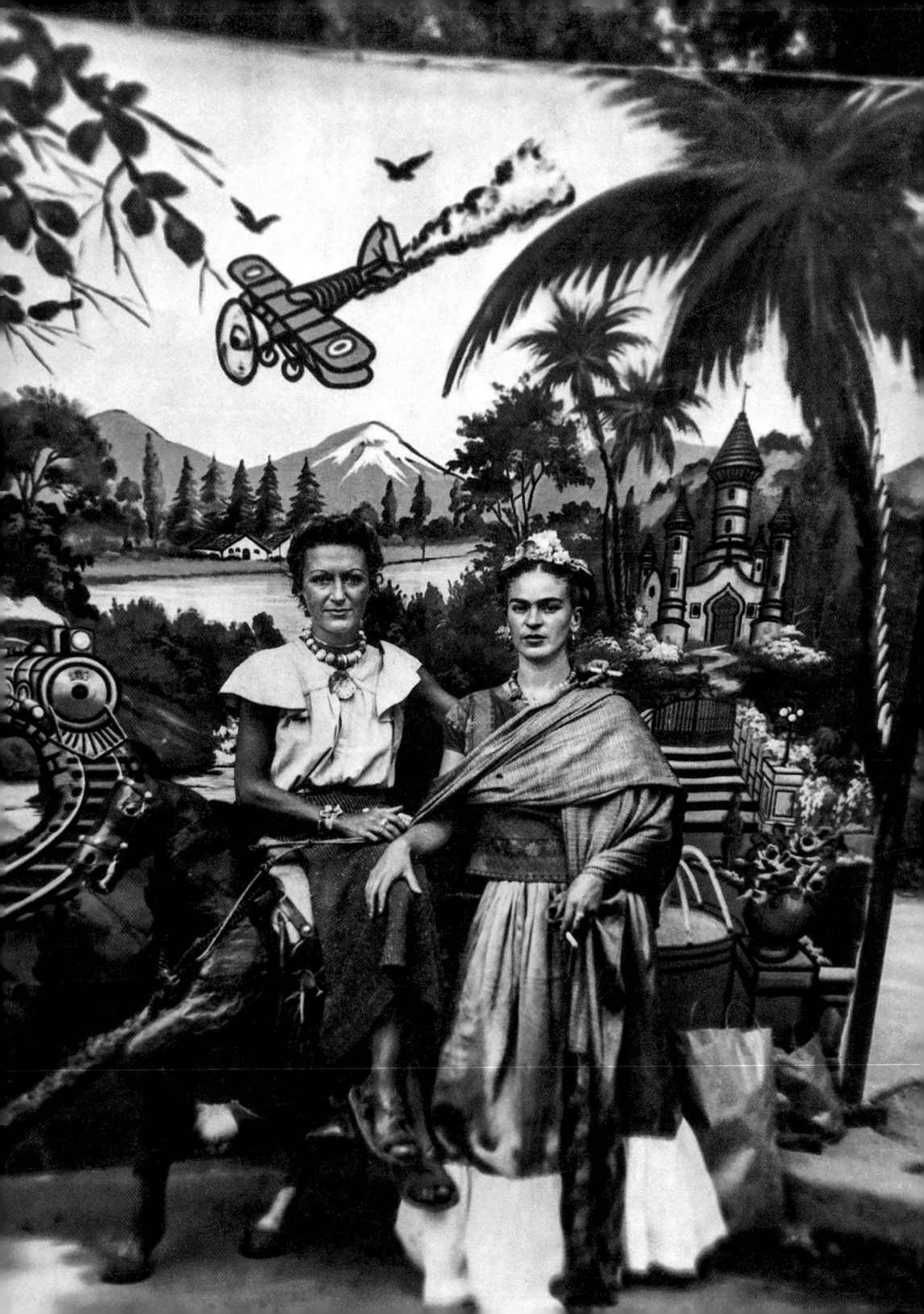

While preparations were under way for the "Mexique" exhibition, Kahlo met the handsome young man who was in charge of organizing and setting up the show at the Renou & Colle Gallery. Michel Petitjean was 29 and Kahlo was 32. Petitjean was the lover of Marie-Laure de Noailles, a rich patron of the Surrealists, while Kahlo was at the time involved in three separate relationships: her emotionally demanding relationship with Rivera in Mexico, her passionate affair with Nickolas Muray in New York, and, in Paris, her feelings of attraction for Lamba, which seem to have been mutual. From Paris, she wrote to her friends Ella and Bertram Wolfe that, "I have been behaving myself [...] I've not had any flings or fooled around, no lovers, nothing like that, and I miss Mexico more than ever; I love Diego more than life itself, and from time to time I miss Nick very much as well; I'm becoming straighter in my ways."[6] Yet even so, Kahlo had no qualms about getting involved with the young man who was helping to make the exhibition a success.[7] It would be easy to imagine how Petitjean could have fallen for Kahlo, but it should also be said that he was very familiar with the work of the Surrealists, including that of Breton himself, and had a genuine interest in Kahlo's paintings. When the exhibition ended, she gave him one of her most personal paintings, *The Heart (Memory)* (p. 177).

In Paris then, it could be said that Kahlo experienced a sense of freedom and self-esteem that she rarely felt when she was with Rivera. Meanwhile, Breton's exhibition had introduced her directly to the world of the Surrealists, who expressed their admiration for her work. As well as gaining their recognition she also became friends with some of these artists, such as Wassily Kandinsky (1866–1944), Joan Miró (1893–1983), and Wolfgang Paalen (1905–1959), among others; Picasso was one of these, who recalled his past

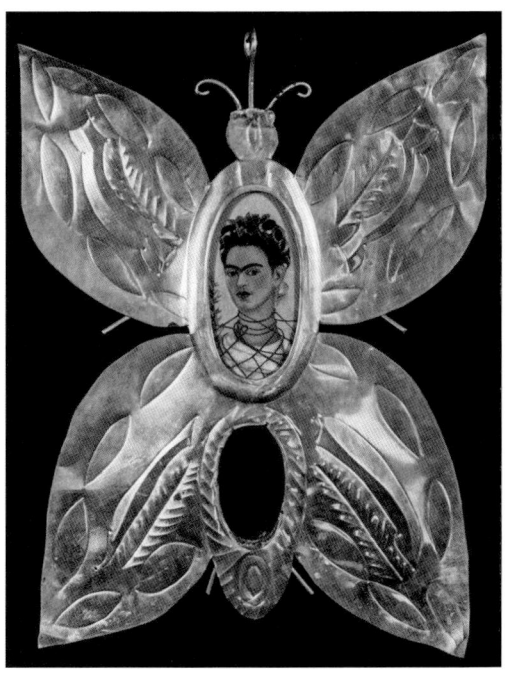

Jacqueline Lamba and Frida Kahlo,
Pátzcuaro, 1938
Gelatin silver print, 9.1 x 6.5 cm (3¾ x 2½ in.)
Formerly part of the collection of the
André Breton Archive, Paris

Self-portrait of Frida Kahlo, *c.* 1938
With tinplate frame in the shape of a butterfly.
Gelatin silver print, 25.4 x 20.3 cm (10 x 8 in.)
Formerly part of the collection of the
André Breton Archive, Paris

friendship with Rivera in Europe, between 1914 and 1916. Kahlo's time in Paris was clearly not all bad therefore, as some of the letters she wrote to her loved ones might seem to suggest. Of course, it is also possible that she simply preferred not to tell them how happy she was feeling without them, or about her fascinating new experiences which were all down to her own merits, as a woman and as an artist, traveling on her own, rather than being there as someone else's wife or lover.

Kahlo had come a long way since the first Surrealist drawings she had seen at the Julien Levy Gallery in New York in 1932, and had then started to make her own drawings in an attempt to tap the potential she saw in the world of dreams (pp. 142, 143). When Breton met her in Mexico, she had already developed a very refined Surrealist language of

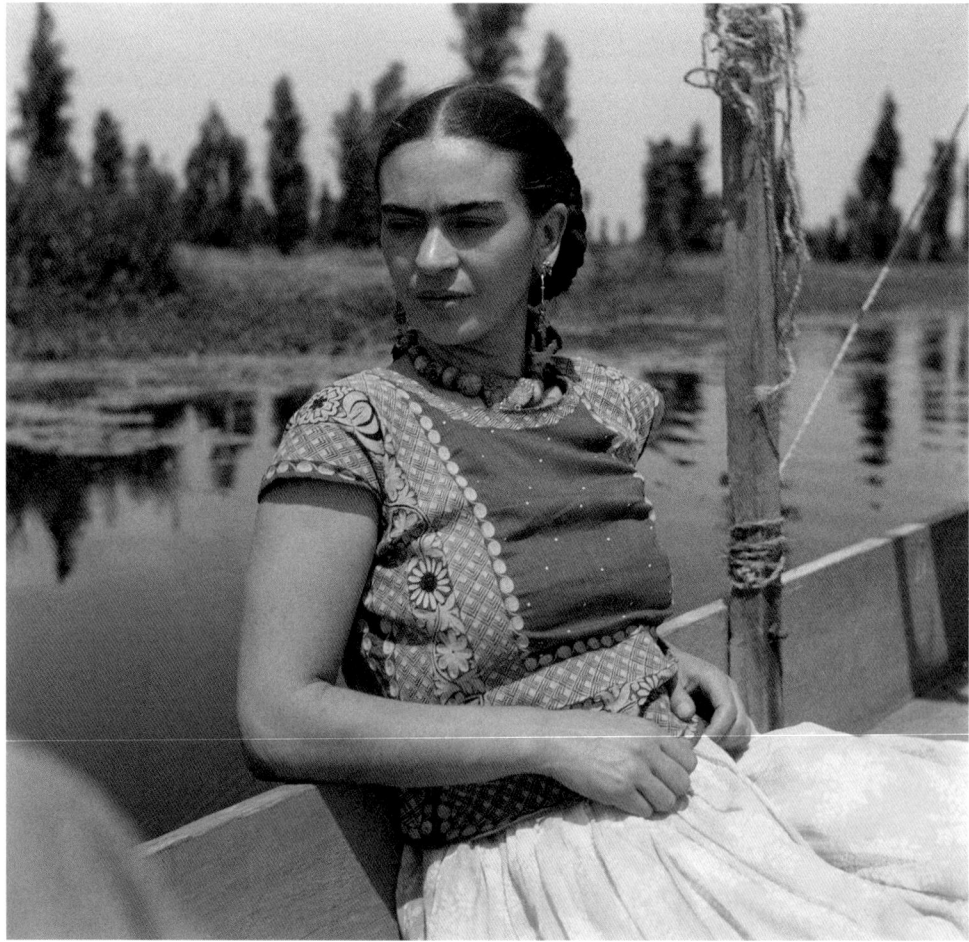

her own, which combined her obsessive pictorial technique (at times reminiscent of Dalí's) with an exploration of various subconscious states as manifested in the events of every-day life. Among the works Breton was able to admire when he visited her, and which was later included in the exhibitions in New York and Paris, was *What Water Gave Me* (p. 211). The intellectual sophistication of this self-portrait, in which Kahlo's body appears only as if through a veil, moved Breton to write that she had flourished in a state of "pure Surrealism," with no previous knowledge of the ideas that underpinned his own activities as leader of the Surrealists nor of the work of his colleagues in Paris. However, the truth is that this painting had been carefully planned by Kahlo, and in fact is her most deliber-ate attempt at working with the techniques of objective chance and the associative power of the subconscious. As Hayden Herrera has observed, "[Kahlo] was neither ignorant of this European movement nor was she truly part of it […] yet Surrealism encouraged Frida to follow her own fantasy."[8] Kahlo was certainly a highly educated painter, and was well informed about the history of art, being especially attracted to the work of the great masters of European painting and to that of the avant-garde in Europe. She had also, of course, studied the theoretical ideas of Surrealism through Breton's writings.

After 10 years of married life, Kahlo and Rivera had consolidated their relationship as a couple, which combined some of the conventions of a typical marriage alongside the similar outlook and ideology they shared through being involved with each other's work. At the same time, the fact that they both had new and exciting professional challenges certainly contributed to the working process they had in common as artists (p. 185). For Rivera, the experience of working on murals in the United States was in many ways one of the highlights of his career, while for Kahlo, having her first solo exhibition at a pres-tigious gallery in New York was the fulfillment of a dream she had cherished since she arrived in San Francisco in 1931, as she said over the years in a number of letters written to various friends.[9]

While countless pages have been written about Rivera's infidelities relatively little has been said about Kahlo's own extramarital relations, yet without wanting to engage in any arguments on the subject it was always clear that Kahlo was never going to have a marriage of the bourgeois, conventional type. It should be noted all the same though that while she and Rivera were both open-minded artists with left-wing ideological views and a natural inclination for new ideas, they nevertheless enjoyed some of the traditional aspects of mari-tal life together. For example, Rivera liked having a wife who would cook for him and look

Fritz Henle, **Frida in a Boat** (detail), 1936
Gelatin silver print, 5.1 x 5.1 cm (2¼ x 2¼ in.)
St. Augustine, Florida, Fritz Henle Estate

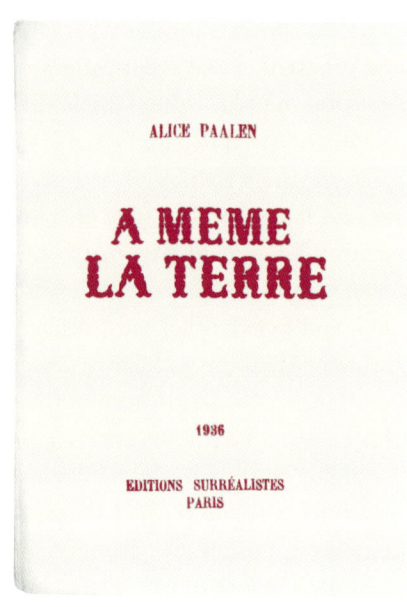

after the practical side of running a house, while Kahlo herself went out of her way to take care of all her husband's personal needs as lovingly as she could.[10] At the same time though they were both glad of the fact that they had a profound respect for each other's work, and for the mutual support that existed between them. Kahlo had great admiration for the social content and commitment of Rivera's art, but also for the love and dedication he showed for his profession, something that was not driven by his own personal ambition but to channel his energy so that his work would draw attention to the living conditions of the most vulnerable members of society. It is seldom acknowledged that this admiration Kahlo felt was based on something entirely real and must have been a powerful reason for her to remain with Rivera despite their differences, even if these would eventually lead to divorce. For his part, Rivera never lavished as much attention on any of his other wives, before or after, as he did on Kahlo and in particular as regards what she set out to achieve as an artist. He was the most vocal supporter of her chosen vocation, unselfishly opening doors to any contacts he had who might be able to help her develop her career. He was never condescending about Kahlo's achievements, and while they could of course not be compared with his much larger mural work that did not lead him to undermine her nor prevent him from making observations about her work when he thought it necessary, or if she asked him what he thought. In such cases, Rivera's response was always as objective as possible.

This sense of fellow feeling and trust has been largely overlooked in the art-historical writing about them, and consequently little is known about how they shared their common profession.[11] They are frequently described as inhabiting worlds that were diametrically opposed and being engaged with art for opposite reasons, when in fact they shared a great deal. One example in support of this is Kahlo's painting *The Suicide of Dorothy Hale* (p. 215), for which a number of letters and newspaper clippings that Kahlo sent to Rivera while she was traveling from New York to Paris and back to New York again confirm that she was keeping him updated, step by step, on her progress with the painting. At the

Alice Paalen, **À même la terre**, Paris, Éditions Surréalistes, 1936
Vienna, Universität für angewandte Kunst, Universitätsbibliothek

opening of Kahlo's exhibition at the Julien Levy Gallery, Clare Boothe Luce (1903–1987), the brilliant editor of *Vanity Fair* who had been invited to attend at Rivera's suggestion, fell in love with *Self-portrait Dedicated to Leon Trotsky* (p. 175) and duly commissioned Kahlo to paint a portrait for the mother of her dear friend Dorothy Hale (1905–1938), an actress from Pittsburgh who had died in dramatic circumstances.[12] Somewhat surprisingly, Kahlo chose to depict the moment of her suicide itself, using newspaper reports as her source (p. 214) in the same way as she had done with *A Few Small Nips* (pp. 156/157) and *The Airplane Crash* (Lozano 2021, cat. 48). For the composition, Kahlo took her model from the tradition of Mexican ex-votos since their expressive power resides in the way they capture a single, extraordinary image that creates a great impact with the viewer, and as work progressed she kept Rivera informed about how she intended to resolve the various details of the composition.[13]

The following year, in 1939, Kahlo made another painting suffused with the same sense of attraction exerted by female beauty that appeared in *The Suicide of Dorothy Hale*, and which is one of her most personal works, namely *The Earth Itself (Two Nudes in a Forest)* (pp. 216/217). Even though it is a small painting, it manages to present all the characteristic elements of the aesthetic universe Kahlo was capable of creating around her. It is also an intimate and enigmatic work that avoids the narrative character of her earlier paintings, since here, telling a story is no longer necessary. Instead, the image embraces an instant in all its fullness, without any explicit reference to insecurities, burdens, or dilemmas which, even though these are still present, do not determine the work's dramatic aspect. The scene appears to show a joyful, fleeting moment of love in the Garden of Eden, and of longed-for caresses amid the turbulence of existence. This is a woman's painting, made for another woman and crafted like a piece of jewelry for a lover, a ruby and emerald brooch with gold clasps and silver leaves, in which the goldsmith's work seals the impossible or unattainable relationship. It was painted specifically for Dolores Asúnsolo López Negrete (1904–1983), the actress generally known as Dolores Del Río and as Lolita to Rivera, and "*la maravillosa*" (marvelous) Dolores to Kahlo. She had been a great success in Hollywood in the 1930s and went on to have a distinguished career in the golden age of Mexican cinema in the 1940s. With one of the most beautiful faces in world cinema, Del Río was the personification of Mexican beauty in all its splendor and served as Mexico's cultural ambassador to important figures in the film industry, several of whom were also patrons of visual artists. She admired Rivera's painting and had a close and loving friendship with Kahlo.

The fact that the two women in this painting are shown naked while caressing and comforting each other has added to speculation about Kahlo's possible lesbian relationships. However, the title reveals what her motives and intentions actually were since it derives from *À même la terre*, the title of a collection of poems by Alice Rahon (1904–1987) (p. 190) who at the time was married to the Austrian painter Wolfgang Paalen. Kahlo had met them in Paris in 1939 and invited them to visit her in Mexico, and as well as being a poet Rahon was herself also a painter, and became close friends with Kahlo. *The Earth Itself* is a response to Rahon's poems, which are marked by a lyrical sadness that evokes the exotic paradises she saw on the many journeys she made, both real and imaginary, in search of the vital force so much desired by the Surrealists. The elusive and fragmented worlds and underworlds she described must have resonated strongly with Kahlo's most personal feelings, such as the touch she yearned for in the loneliness of her body, something quite apart from the fleeting contact of lovers and affairs that could not supply everything she wanted or were impossibly out of reach. Kahlo was swamped by the tidal wave of her emotions that were scattered so widely between Rivera, Muray, and Lamba, as fragmented as the bodies and landscapes cast adrift and evoked by Rahon in her poetry: "… you shall come through the forest, paying no heed to the signs and doorways, to the meeting place beneath the faded flowers."[14]

Such considerations aside, however, the real importance of this small painting within the context of the rest of Kahlo's work is that it introduces the notion of duality, a theme she went on to develop in much greater depth in the most ambitious painting of her whole artistic career, *The Two Fridas* (pp. 218/219). Kahlo's painting is a full-length, double self-portrait that acts as a manifesto describing how she conceived of herself and how she wanted her art to be understood by posterity. It was painted, together with *The Wounded Table* (pp. 224/225), for inclusion in the fourth International Exhibition of Surrealism, overseen from Paris by Breton and organized in Mexico by Paalen and the Peruvian poet César Moro (1903–1956). Existing photographs show Kahlo at work on the painting or posing next to it, and seeing her slender figure in this way reveals how much *The Two Fridas* is a work of monumental proportions, perhaps the closest she got to the epic figures Rivera painted in his murals in both Mexico and the United States. For the

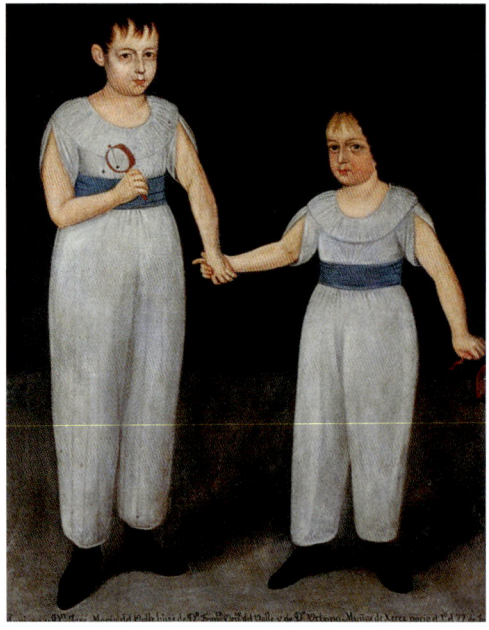

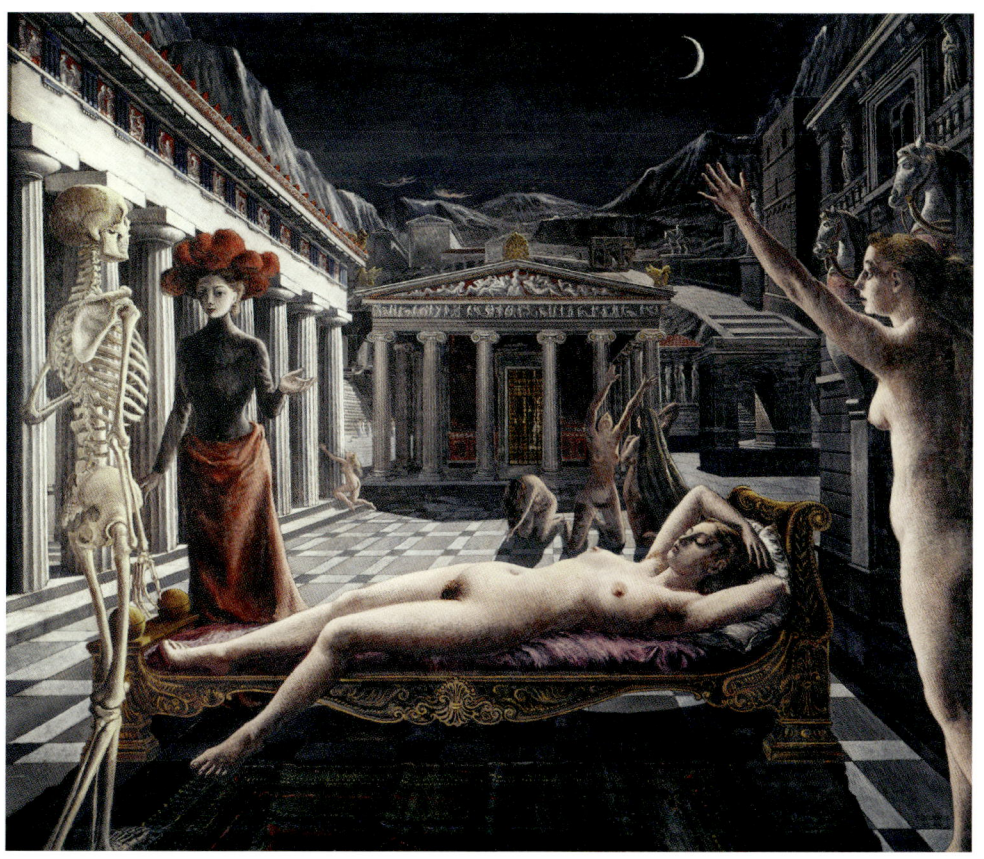

School of José María Estrada, **Portrait of the Children Mariano and
Don José María del Valle Muñoz de Jerez**, 19th century
Oil on canvas, 117 x 92 cm (46 x 36¼ in.); inscribed at the bottom:
Mariano and Dn José Maria del Valle, the children of Dn Franco Vencio
del Valle Da Urbana Munoz de Xerez, born June 22
Formerly part of the collection of the André Breton Archive, Paris

Paul Delvaux, **Sleeping Venus**, 1944
Oil on canvas, 173 x 199 cm (68⅛ x 78⅜ in.)
London, Tate Britain

viewer, this double portrait of Kahlo is at once overwhelming and enigmatic. As in the case of ex-voto paintings, she has included a supernatural and disturbing element: the exposed heart of each of the two women, which connects them to each other by way of a shared blood vessel. The model for this painting must certainly have been *Ángeles and Fuensanta* by Julio Romero de Torres (1874–1930), the most famous modernist painter in Spain (p. 222). However, in the course of my research on Kahlo's participation in the "Mexique" exhibition I chanced upon a group of photographs of 19th-century Mexican paintings that featured in the exhibition and which had been acquired by Breton in Mexico the previous year. One of them showed what may have been another source that inspired Kahlo to paint a double self-portrait, namely an oil painting on canvas from the school of José María Estrada (1810–1862), the whereabouts of which are currently unknown. The full-length image shows two children holding hands, both dressed alike in Empire-style clothing together with their toys (p. 192). Kahlo was an admirer of Estrada's work, and as well as owning one of his paintings she took ideas from his compositions when designing her own works, as in the case of *Self-portrait Dedicated to Leon Trotsky (Between the Curtains)* from 1937 (p. 175).[15]

Evidently, and as a number of authors have discussed, *The Two Fridas* is a painting that expresses the idea of duality in Kahlo's work. However, this duality also reveals a much deeper conflict by presenting two aspects of the same personality, created by Kahlo herself. Various writers have associated this painting with Rivera's decision to divorce her, and to the mixed emotions she felt as a result. Seen from another angle though, Rivera's decision to apply for a divorce may have had a more pragmatic basis, specifically to protect her, since the support they had given to Trotsky was reason enough to fear reprisals from the powerful GPU, the Soviet Union's secret police. At the same time, as Raquel Tibol pointed out, Rivera was indirectly implicated in the first failed attempt to assassinate Trotsky, by the mural painter David Alfaro Siqueiros (1896–1974) and his cohorts, who had used Rivera's truck during the attack.[16] Furthermore, during the investigations carried out afterward it emerged that Kahlo had met Trotsky's would-be killer while she was in Paris, and that he had tried to use her to get closer to his victim. Not surprisingly, after Trotsky's assassination had been carried out Kahlo was subjected to prolonged interrogation by the Mexican authorities, while Rivera's studio was ransacked in a search for compromising information. Rivera himself had fled to San Francisco with the help of the film actress Paulette Goddard (1910–1990).

Frida Kahlo (detail), *c.* 1940
Cibachrome print, 62 x 51 cm (24⅜ x 20⅛ in.)
Mexico City, Isolda P. Kahlo Archive

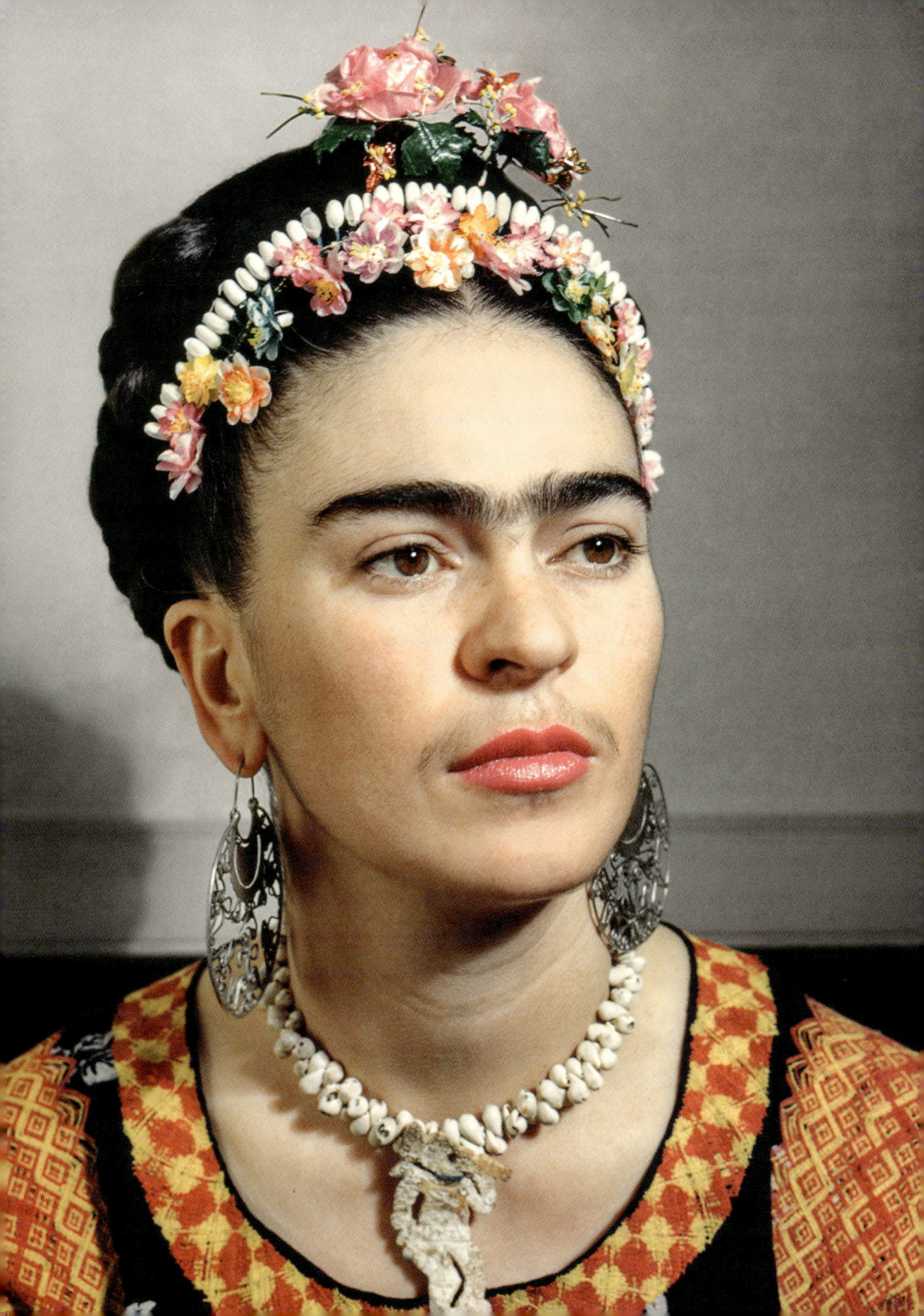

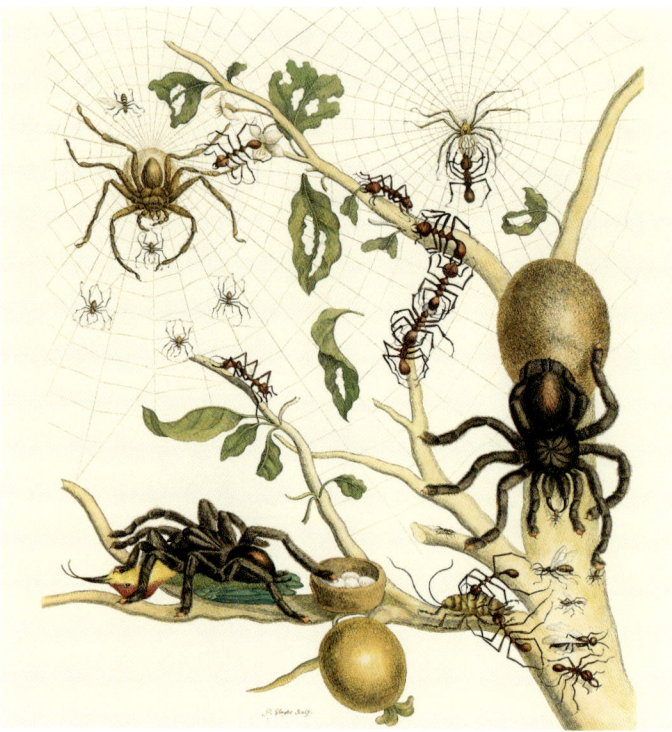

Whatever the actual reason for the divorce, it is certain that Kahlo's separation from Rivera left her deeply unsettled, as is clearly evident in *The Wounded Table*, the other work, also very large, that she presented at the Surrealist exhibition referred to earlier that was organized by Moro and Paalen at the Galería de Arte Mexicano.[17] The whereabouts of this painting are currently unknown.[18] Kahlo was in fact at work on *The Wounded Table* when the divorce was legally confirmed on November 6, 1939, and while *The Two Fridas* can be interpreted as a retrospective look at the 10 years she was married to Rivera, *The Wounded Table* is concerned with the immediate future as Kahlo imagined it after the divorce. It would be remiss, however, not to mention one other earlier work here as well, since it may have preceded the two large paintings in connecting pictorial content with the deterioration of Kahlo's emotional relationship with Rivera. The work in question is *Survivor* (p. 262), a small but powerful image that was probably the last painting Kahlo made in 1938 for inclusion in the exhibition at the Julien Levy Gallery since it appears at the end of the list of the works on display in the leaflet published to accompany the show. It was bought by the historian and critic Walter Pach, who was also an admirer of Mexican vernacular painting. The small composition is formally related to Mexican ex-votos, in the same way as several other of Kahlo's paintings from 1931 onward (as discussed in the previous chapter). In the figure of the warrior depicted she seems to be trying to establish a

Maria Sibylla Merian, ***Metamorphosis Insectorum Surinamensium***, 1705
Hand-colored copperplate engraving, Lámina 18

parallel with herself, in that just as the ceramic sculpture is shown standing alone in the landscape, so Kahlo also felt alone in her relationship with Rivera, which had been falling apart ever since his affair with her sister Cristina in 1935. She too is a survivor of the blows fate has dealt her, in the same way that the pre-Columbian figure is evidence of an enduring culture that has defied the passage of time.[19]

The inclusion of *The Two Fridas* and *The Wounded Table* in the Surrealist exhibition of 1940 consolidated Kahlo's status as an internationally recognized artist. Her success continued when she took part in two large group exhibitions in the United States, "20 Centuries of Mexican Art" at the Museum of Modern Art in New York and "Contemporary Mexican Painting and Graphic Art" at the Palace of Fine Arts in San Francisco. In little more than a decade, her development as an artist had been remarkable. Kahlo had not only managed to perfect her technique so that she was able to represent complex pictorial subject matter, but had also developed a symbolic and at times cryptic narrative style which allowed her to examine her different states of mind and view of life, yet without falling into an explicitly autobiographical mode of painting. The pictorial universe she had created provided a means for exploring her personal concerns and anxieties, using a language that was highly realistic and sincere but was recodified for the viewer's gaze, as if Kahlo wanted to set riddles that required a certain amount of mental agility for them to be understood.

By the 1940s, Surrealism had become a fully international movement. This was exactly what Breton had intended when he proposed that group exhibitions should be held in various different cities around the world, including the one in Mexico City in 1940 where Kahlo was asked to participate as an international representative of the Surrealists, rather than as one of the contingent of Mexican artists whose work was considered to have some connection or affinity with Surrealism. Kahlo's personal association with the theory and formal methods of Surrealism had been established during the time she was living in the United States, and had provided her with a very effective theoretical framework for setting free her own creativity. She discovered that by exploring different states of her subconscious she could put aside the restrictions of rational explanation with regard to her feelings, together with the difficulties resulting from her changing situation and the anxiety, pain, and sense of abandonment she then had to deal with. Throughout the 1940s, Kahlo used Surrealism as a way to explore her subconscious, a method that had already been adding to her work since the previous decade. Now, however, Surrealist imagery shared the pictorial space with more realistic representations of what was affecting her on the conscious plane, so that her paintings were no longer evasions of reality, as images of dreams or imaginary fantasies, but on the contrary had become eloquent representations of her difficult situation at the time.

From at least the date of the first Surrealist manifesto that was published in 1924, Breton had been looking to reassess the significance of dreams. For the Surrealists, dreaming was a way of freeing the imagination and achieving a state in which might be found "the revelation of the marvelous."[20] Freud's work had provided a foundation for the interpretation of dreams, and this was taken up as something that could be used by artists in the process of constructing their reality. The Surrealists, however, went further by placing the subconscious on the same level as conscious, rational experience, and as a result artists no longer needed to rationalize their dreams in order to incorporate them into their art. By acknowledging this, the subconscious took on a decisive authority. It is very possible that these theoretical ideas lie behind *The Dream (The Bed)*, from 1940 (pp. 226/227), in which Kahlo examined her personal problems with greater confidence following her remarriage to Rivera. Strictly speaking, the painting is a self-portrait, with Kahlo shown sleeping in the same way as she appears in several photographs taken of her sleeping in her house in Coyoacán. However, it is far from being a conventional self-portrait since Kahlo is represented floating in a metaphysical space full of clouds, which indicates that she is not simply asleep, but dreaming. This state of trance favors the free flight of imagination and the creative power of the subconscious, the same objectives that were sought by the artists and writers who were experimenting with the aesthetic techniques of Surrealism.

At this point in her career Kahlo joined the faculty of the Escuela de Pintura y Escultura (School of Painting and Sculpture) in Mexico City, commonly known as La Esmeralda, where her colleagues included such well-known artists as Antonio Ruiz, "El Corcito," María Izquierdo, and Francisco Zúñiga (1912–1998). For Kahlo, it must have been stimulating to teach painters who were only beginners, although because of her physical condition the classes ended up having to be taught in her own home in Coyoacán, and for this reason her students were referred to as "Los Fridos."[21] As well as being a source of motivation, Kahlo's work as a tutor must have given her a greater level of discipline and higher standards in her own work as an artist, as she moved away from painting under Rivera's wing to becoming a teacher in her own right.

By now Kahlo had already amply demonstrated that she had perfected her technical skills, as well as her ability to develop aesthetic and conceptual ideas, so as to examine her roots and her cultural identity while assimilating different aspects from various avant-garde movements. She had thoroughly mastered the skills required of a painter, as regards both form and content, and it seemed the only limits to what she was capable of doing were those she set herself. It was at exactly this stage that new paradigms began to emerge for her future as an artist. Had Kahlo truly realized her full potential? Was painting her main reason for living? It becomes increasingly clear that in the course of the 1940s she realized this was certainly not the case, and that her health was starting to impose real limitations on her physical abilities to the extent that devoting herself to painting could no longer be her main objective. Consequently, her aims as an artist may have had to be gradually reduced and instead she focused on certain ways in which she would be able to continue. While in the 1930s her work as an artist had proceeded

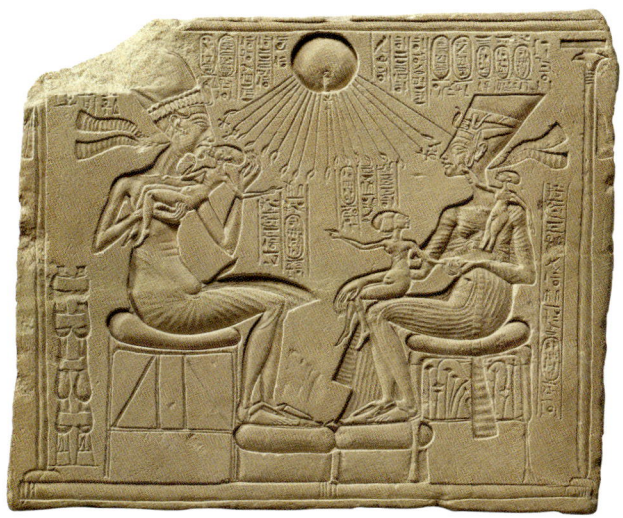

alongside Rivera's, in the 1940s she walked alone. No longer was she Frida Kahlo followed by the name "Frida Rivera" in brackets, as she had been introduced in the brochure printed to accompany her first solo exhibition in New York; and neither was she "Madame Frida Kahlo de Rivera," as she had been named in the catalogue for the "Mexique" exhibition in Paris. Now, and in confirmation of her new autonomy, one of her main tasks was to work so that painting might become a profession that would grant her freedom of choice and a measure of independence, both in relation to the possibility of making a living from her work but also deciding what she would be doing with her time.

Even so, while Kahlo was aware that she had reached the peak of her abilities as an artist, she also realized that her emotional relationships were having an adverse effect on her productivity, by plunging her into distressing periods of despair and hopelessness. She was now remarried to Rivera, but was determined to try not to be financially dependent on him. In practice, however, this proved not to be entirely possible since in order to cover her various medical expenses that began to accumulate in the 1940s she would have had to sell far more paintings than she was capable of producing. From the letters she wrote to her friends and clients it becomes clear that she went through phases where she had no will to paint, and felt depressed by the constant problem of having to find the

Domestic altar, showing Akhenaten, Nefertiti, and three of their daughters beneath the Aten sun disk, *c.* 1351–1334 BC
Limestone, 33.5 x 39.5 x 3.5 cm (13¼ x 15½ x 1½ in.)
Berlin, Staatliche Museen zu Berlin, Ägyptisches Museum und Papyrussammlung

"cash" to pay her debts. By now, there was no short-age of collectors interested in her work, but it is also known that she received commissions that were never fulfilled. Moreover, Kahlo did not work quickly enough because her technique was so very meticulous and because her illnesses, both physical and psychological, interfered with her having the necessary discipline and continuity to work consistently. It is thus somewhat paradoxical that at the very moment when she was at the peak of her artistic creativity, Kahlo did not always have the strength to paint. This was the reason she tried to obtain a Guggenheim Fellowship, as a means of establishing the financial stability that would allow her to paint without the pressure of having to sell her work. Yet despite her strong résumé and references from such highly regarded figures in the art world as Breton, Picasso (1881–1973), and Marcel Duchamp (1887–1968), among others, she was turned down. As a result, Kahlo's situation did not get any simpler, and not least because one area in which she was not prepared to make any concessions was in how to finish her paintings; she was proud of her ability as an artist, which she had achieved by herself, and thought nothing of retouching her paintings again and again until she felt they were properly true to her feelings and her state of mind. In this way she was bluntly stating what she wanted to express, while keeping hidden what she wanted to remain private, something that is especially apparent in her self-portraits from these years.

While Kahlo painted her self-portraits repeatedly throughout this decade, presenting herself with a poise that was distinguished yet seductive and seemingly wrapped in self-confidence, these images also reflect a persistent sense of vulnerability. "Reality is not as it is painted," as the popular saying goes – things are not as they seem. So, in the striking *Self-portrait* she dedicated to her friend and confidant Dr. Leo Eloesser (1881–1976), Kahlo

Self-portrait (for Bartolí with Love), *c.* 1938–1946
Oil and gold paint on wood with painted wooden frame, 5 x 4.2 cm (2 x 1⅝ in.)
United States, private collection, courtesy Weinstein Gallery, San Francisco

appears at her most beautiful (p. 233). In the painting she is perfect, but she cannot carry off the lie, and Eloesser is the unspeaking witness to the pain caused by her relationship with Rivera and which she has resolved to bear in silence. In *Self-portrait (with Bonito)* (p. 242), one of Kahlo's most eloquent works, she depicted herself in mourning, wearing a black embroidered *huipil* and with her hair braided in a simple indigenous style to express her grief at the recent death of her father and her sadness at the loss of Bonito, her beloved parrot that had died that year too.[22] As in traditional *vanitas* artworks, the entire painting speaks of sorrow and life, death and resurrection, transformation and regeneration. Nothing allows the viewer to see beyond her severe expression, the dark, intense eyes and thick, somber eyebrows acting as a barrier to the movements of our own gaze.

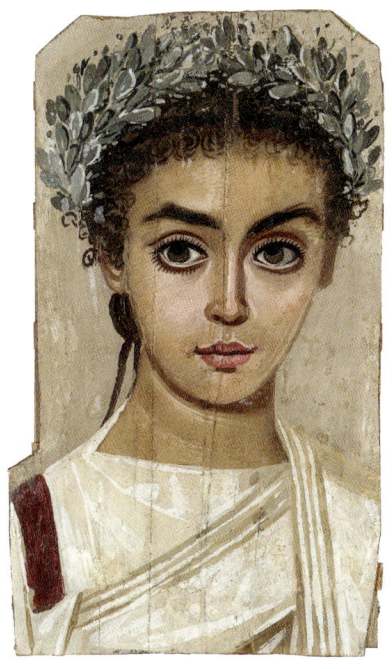

    The 1940s were especially plentiful for Kahlo in terms of self-portraits, and of the 43 paintings she is known to have made between 1940 and 1945, 22 were self-portraits. By doing this she was simply pursuing the interest she had in examining her own personality that had begun early on in her artistic career, but at the same time her patrons had now become particularly interested in these works, which to a certain extent limited her choice of subjects and also interrupted the process she had begun of seeking her own personal and financial independence from Rivera. Kahlo even went so far as to say how overwhelmed she felt at having to paint herself again and again with various different animals, regardless of whether they were parrots or monkeys and even if they were her own, pampered spider monkeys, Fulang-Chang and Caimito de Guayabal (pp. 235, 237, 241, 243).[23] There are at least eight self-portraits among Kahlo's works where she appears with monkeys, and of these, *Self-portrait (with Monkeys)* (p. 236) from 1943 is without a doubt the most seductive and disturbing.[24] In comparison with *The Earth Itself (Two Nudes in a Forest)* (pp. 216/217) from 1939, which also features monkeys in a jungle setting alongside the two naked women, in this later work Kahlo has

Roman Egyptian art from Fayum, **Portrait of a girl**, 120–150 BC
Encaustic on wood, height 35.5 cm (14 in.)
Frankfurt am Main, Liebieghaus Skulpturensammlung

abandoned the need for the dreamlike narrative and symbolic metaphors that connected her to Surrealism, preferring instead a direct and provocative approach. She appears to be implying that she is settled in this new phase of her marital relationship with Rivera, but that the priorities had changed where her feelings were concerned, such that there was no longer any place for sex between the two of them, nor for the passion of two decades ago, even though she was now more alone than she was before.

A further example of the many difficulties Kahlo encountered in seeking to make a career for herself as an artist without Rivera's support, and which has been little discussed, concerns an official commission from the office of the Mexican President in 1941 to paint five portraits of women celebrated in the country's history. These included images of Sister Juana Inés de la Cruz (1648–1695), Josefa Ortiz de Domínguez (1768–1829), and Leona Vicario (1789–1842).[25] Some time after she had already started the pictorial research, Kahlo was informed that there had been a change to the original commission, and she was now being asked to paint still lifes instead of portraits.[26] The first of these was *The Flower Basket*, dated 1941 (p. 265), a festive semicircular garland of flowers painted in a beautiful mix of colors, in the middle of which is a basket filled with roses, daisies, sunflowers, dahlias, and orchids that have attracted an industrious bumblebee, an iridescent butterfly, and a hungry hummingbird.[27] *Still Life* (p. 264) from 1942 was also part of this decorative commission, and both works were painted on copper and in the circular Renaissance *tondo* format, which Kahlo chose to use so that they would stand out amid the wooden architecture of the dining room in the National Palace. Unfortunately, the small amount of time allocated for the commission, and what seems to have been poor communication on the part of the president's staff in letting Kahlo know what he wanted, resulted in the project being called off, leaving her with two finished paintings, and probably a third one as well that was being worked on. Kahlo thus turned to her friend and patron, the engineer, to help her with this problem:

"Once again I find I have to disturb you concerning this business about the paintings the President commissioned me to make for the dining room in the National Palace, since the people in the Ministry of National Assets are no help at all, the work itself has been suspended, and frankly things aren't quite right. Both the engineer De la Sota Riva and Mr. Cházaro, the mayor, firmly insisted that I complete at least two of the paintings before September 15. I made a great effort and did what they asked, delivering the two

Self-portrait (for Jacqueline Lamba), July 28, 1938
Oil on tinplate, 12 x 7 cm (4¾ x 2¾ in.),
with frame decorated with shells, 19 x 13 cm (7½ x 5⅛ in.)
Paris, private collection, courtesy Galerie 1900–2000

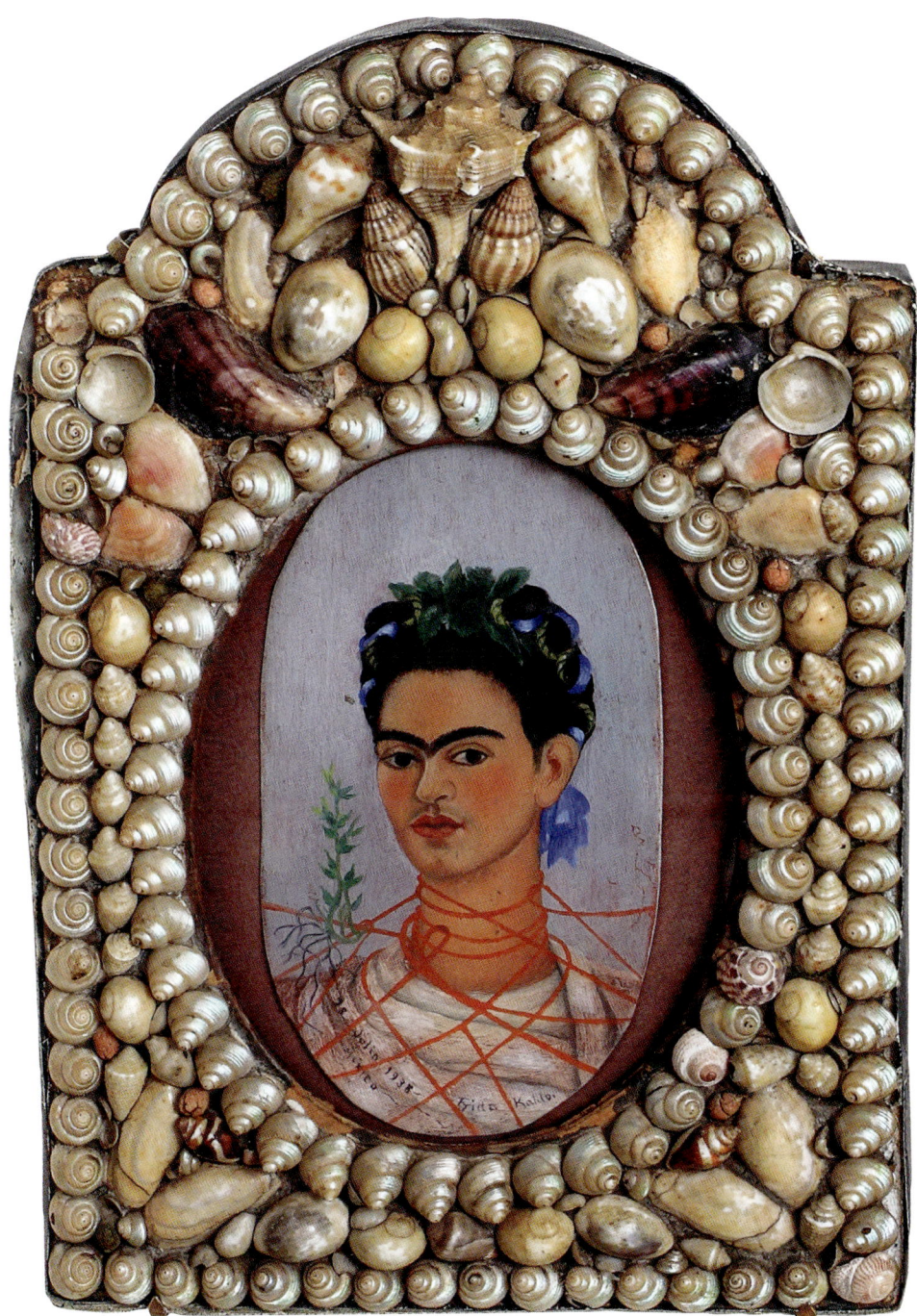

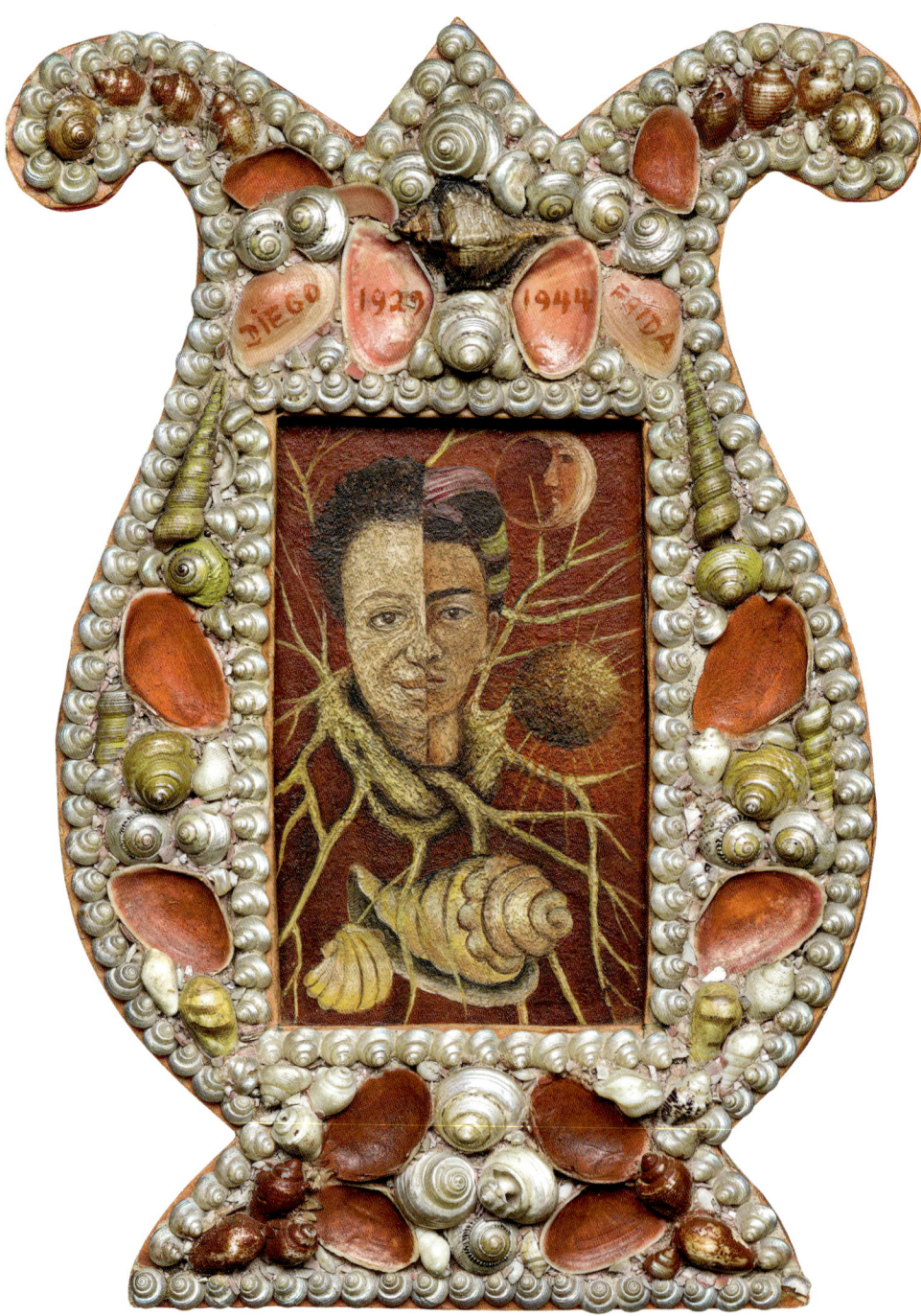

circular paintings and then hanging them where they were meant to go on the afternoon of September 13. I had forwarded my estimate to Mr. De la Sota Riva as of July 22, and charged them 900 pesos for each painting, making a total of 4,500 for all five […] I was wondering if it could be arranged for them to pay me for the two I have already completed (1,800 pesos) as I am really quite 'broke' […] but now it turns out that the lawyer Mr. Beteta is not going to authorize my invoice, so they have already done me out of my money."[28]

Gómez managed to get the two paintings back, even though they had indeed been installed in the presidential dining room.[29] It is possible that the third painting for this commission, which Kahlo had already started to paint, was another picture featuring exotic tropical vegetation which, after the order had been canceled, she used instead as the background for *Portrait of Marucha Lavín*, from 1942 (Lozano 2021, cat. 94). She was the wife of Kahlo's patron José Domingo Lavín, who commissioned several artists to paint a number of important works for his collection, including Kahlo's *Moses (The Birth of the Hero)* (pp. 272/273) from 1945.

The Chick (Spiders) (p. 258) also dates from this period, and in its detailed work it recalls the drawings of plants and insects by the illustrator and entomologist Maria Sibylla Merian (1647–1717) (p. 196). It is one of the most frequently exhibited of Kahlo's paintings, and yet one of the least analyzed. A closer look at this small work, however, confirms that throughout the 1940s Kahlo did not confine herself to painting self-portraits, but also found time to reflect on her career as an artist, the intellectual scope of her work, and her ability to develop a pictorial narrative that was filled with meanings and sophisticated metaphors. Although the picture shows what is essentially a bunch of flowers, there are a number of other pictorial elements, such as the spider's web that covers the flowers entirely and the small chick next to them, that make for a less conventional interpretation, and indeed suggest something more cryptic.[30]

In 1945, Kahlo was facing serious medical complications for which she had to undergo a number of difficult operations to attempt to relieve the pain in her spine and right leg. She also had to wear a corset, and a special insole in her shoe to compensate for her shorter leg. Her relationship with Rivera was at least more easygoing than it had been before the divorce, since they had agreed to accept each other's freedoms, although Rivera had started to seek the company of the editor and agent Emma Hurtado, with whom he ended up having a long-standing adulterous relationship.[31] Kahlo, however, refused to

Diego and Frida, 1944
Oil on masonite, 12.3 x 7.4 cm (4⅞ x 2⅞ in.);
with frame decorated with shells, 26 x 18.5 cm (10¼ x 7¼ in.)
Mexico City, private collection, courtesy Arvil gallery

allow her physical pain to prevent her from continuing to paint and fulfilling her professional obligations, whether as a teacher at La Esmeralda or in relation to her collectors. It would seem that she was trying not only to conserve her physical strength, but also to distance herself psychologically as a way of suppressing her pain and existential worries.

During her time as a student at the Escuela Nacional Preparatoria, Kahlo was witness to the beginnings of the Mexican muralist movement. The first time she met Rivera in fact was when he was working on *Creation* for the Simón Bolívar lecture theater, which was also his first mural. Kahlo's friendships at this time with writers and intellectuals enabled her to understand the significance of what muralism was seeking to achieve on aesthetic and artistic grounds, but as an artist she generally steered clear of the movement's engagements with history and ideology. However, it is important to note that in 1945 she designed a painting that shows strong compositional connections to Rivera's mural work. The collector José Domingo Lavín had bought a copy of Freud's book *Moses and Monotheism*, originally published in 1939 and which collected three of his essays; after discussing it at a dinner party at Lavín's house, Kahlo became very interested in finding out what the book was about, and after she had read it she agreed to a commission from Lavín to make a painting based on her interpretation of the texts.[32] In 1945, she duly presented him with *Moses* (pp. 272/273). Despite the fact that it was a painting done on an easel, Kahlo's approach to the composition was similar to that used by Rivera in some of his murals, particularly from *The History of Cardiology* which was painted between 1943 and 1944 at the National Institute of Cardiology in Mexico City.[33] She was inspired by this mural's layout to organize the many historical and mythical characters that made up her scene along horizontal and vertical axes, so as to create six thematic sections.

At the same time, she tried to give each of them individual identities and fit them into a hierarchical order. To deal with this complex content Kahlo had to carry out extensive research into pictorial sources in order to adapt images of the various gods and heroes to her own artistic interpretation. She felt a particular attraction for the pharaoh Akhenaten and his wife Nefertiti, as can be seen in passages she wrote in her diary (p. 361), which also echo some of Freud's views in his book since he too was drawn to Egyptian antiquities. Kahlo was especially inspired by the pictorial device of the sun's rays ending in human hands (pp. 272/273), which appears on a number of reliefs from Amarna depicting the 18th-Dynasty pharaoh with his family, from around 1334 BC (p. 199).

When Kahlo delivered the painting she agreed, contrary to her usual practice, to talk about it informally and explain to some of the Lavíns' guests who were there how she had found visual solutions to the difficulties of working with such a complex text, specifically in terms of Freud's historical perspective. She discussed his thesis that Moses had not actually been Jewish but Egyptian, and that the religion he had passed on to the Jews was based on the monotheism introduced by Akhenaten. Kahlo's comments were later collected in an article that appeared under her name in the magazine *Así* on August 18, 1945 with the title "Concerning one of my paintings, and how, based on a suggestion from the engineer José D. Lavín and the writings of Freud, I made a painting about Moses."[34] In the article she clarified that she "never" explained her paintings in public, pointing out that the same applied to other well-known modern painters too such as Picasso and José Clemente Orozco (1883–1949), to defend her view that artists were not required to explain or justify their work. Using simple language, if at times ironic, Kahlo's words revealed a great deal about how Freud's texts had made her think about Moses, as she explained:

"I read the book just the once, and began work on the painting based on the first impression it had made on me. Yesterday I reread it, and I must admit that I now find the painting very incomplete and quite different from what the interpretation should be as analyzed so wonderfully by Freud in his book *Moses*. But now there is nothing that can be done either to add to it or to take anything away, so I will talk about what I have in fact painted, such as it is, and as you can see it here.

"Of course, the main subject is *Moses*, or the *Birth of the Hero*. But in my own way (a very confused way), I have generalized the events or images that made the greatest impression on me when I read the book. As far as I'm concerned, to say it directly, you can all tell me if I've made a mess of it or not. What I was trying to express, more clearly and more forcefully, was that the reason people feel the need to invent or imagine heroes and gods is fear. Fear of life and fear of death.

"[…] Freud analyzes, in a very clear way but still very complicated for someone like me, the important fact that Moses was not Jewish but Egyptian, although in the painting I couldn't find a way to paint him that was either Egyptian or Jewish, and so I just painted a boy who, generally speaking, represents Moses as well as everyone else who, according to legend, had the same start in life and went on to become important figures, leaders of their people, heroes in other words (but smarter than the others, that's why I put the 'watchful eye' on him). In this case we also have Sargon, Cyrus, Romulus, Paris, etc.

"Freud's other very interesting conclusion was that Moses, since he wasn't Jewish, gave to the people he had chosen to be guided and saved a religion that also wasn't Jewish but rather Egyptian. This was specifically the religion revived by Amenhotep IV or Akhenaten, with its worship of Aten, that is the Sun, which had its roots in the ancient religion based in On (Heliopolis).

"So I painted the Sun as the central focus of all religions, as the *first god* and the creator and renewing force of life.

"Like Moses, there have been and always will be a large number of these 'big men,' who set about transforming religion and human society. You could say they are like messengers between the people they lead and the 'gods' they invent in order to control them.

"As is well known, there are still a few of these 'gods' around. Naturally, I couldn't fit them all in, so on either side of the Sun I placed the ones that, like it or not, have some direct relationship with the Sun. Those from the West are on the right, and those from the East are on the left.

"The Assyrian winged bull, Amun, Zeus, Osiris, Horus, Jehovah, Apollo, the Moon, the Virgin Mary, Divine Providence, the Holy Trinity, Venus and… the Devil.

"On the left is the Lightning, the Lightning Bolt, and the Lightning's trace that is, Huracán, Cuculcán, and Gukumatz, Tláloc, the magnificent Coatlicue, mother of all the gods, Quetzalcóatl, Tezcatlipoca, Centeótl, the Chinese dragon god and the Hindu god Brahma. I was missing an African god, but couldn't find him, I could have made a little space for him […] Having painted all the gods I could fit in, each in their respective heavens, I wanted to separate the celestial world of poetry and imagination from the earthly realm of the fear of death, and so there I painted skeletons, both human and animal, as you see them. The Earth is cupping her hands to protect them. There is no division between death and the group where the heroes are, because they die as well and the earth receives them openly and in the same way as anyone else.

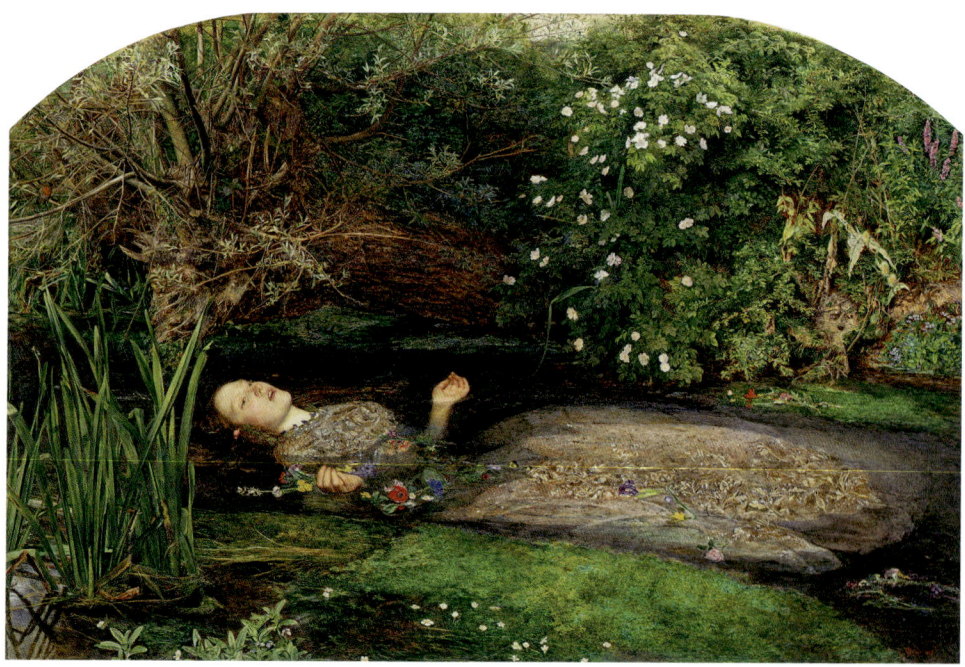

"On this same part of the earth, but painted with bigger heads to mark them out from the 'masses,' are the portraits of the 'heroes' (very few of these, but they are the chosen few), the ones who transform religions, who invent or create religions, the conquerors, the rebels… in other words, the 'big fish.'

"On the right (I should have painted this figure to be much more prominent than any of the others) is Amenhotep IV, later known as Akhenaten, a young pharaoh of the 18th Dynasty in Egypt (1370–1350 BC) who imposed on his subjects a religion that ran counter to tradition, which rejected polytheism and was strictly monotheistic, with distant echoes of the cult practised at On (Heliopolis), the religion of Aten, that is the Sun. They worshiped the sun not only in and of itself, but as the creator and protector of all living beings, both within Egypt and abroad, whose energy was made manifest in its rays, thus anticipating the most up-to-date scientific knowledge we have today about solar power.

"[…] Next is Moses, who according to Freud's analysis gave his adopted country the same religion as Akhenaten, changed just a little to suit the needs and circumstances of his time.

"Freud reached this conclusion following careful research, in the course of which he discovered how closely related the Aten religion was to that of Moses, both of them being monotheistic. (I couldn't figure out a way to convey all that part of the book in visual terms.)"[35]

The challenge involved in taking on this commission thus offers a glimpse of how Kahlo, who in 1945 was at the high point of her career as an artist, wanted to continue developing by exploring other ways of constructing her compositions, and other subjects. She decided to submit this painting in the Ministry of Public Education's open competition for the National Prize for Arts and Sciences, which had been established in the same year of 1945. A total of 192 painters sent in their works, and Kahlo was selected as a finalist alongside Francisco Goitia, Gerardo Murillo, Julio Castellanos, and the muralist José Clemente Orozco. She won the Public Education Prize, and Clemente Orozco won the National Prize for the Arts, which were presented to them by the President of Mexico. It must have been an even greater honor for Kahlo, however, to have received her award alongside her friend Clemente Orozco, one of the most important muralists in 20th-century Mexican art. Her painting was exhibited, with the title *Core of the Sun*, at the Palacio de Bellas Artes in July 1946, which was a mark of significant recognition for her.[36] It may thus be said that Kahlo had at last been properly recognized not only abroad but in her own country as well.

John Everett Millais, **Ophelia**, 1851/52
Oil on canvas, 76.2 x 111.8 cm (30 x 44 in.). London, Tate Britain

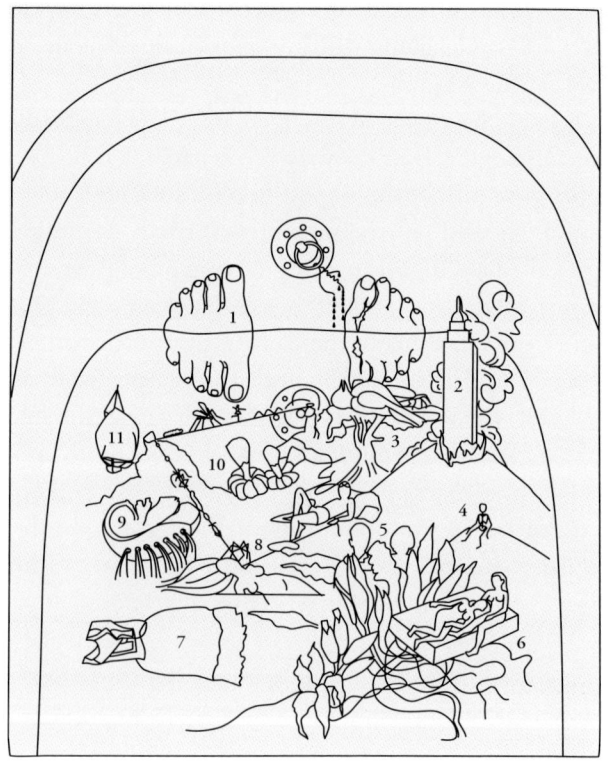

What Water Gave Me, 1938/39
Oil on canvas, 69 x 88 cm (27⅛ x 34⅝ in.)
Paris, private collection *(detail pp. 212/213)*

Diagram
1 The position of the body and feet correspond to *Lamentation over
the Dead Christ* by Andrea Mantegna, *c.* 1480
2 The New York skyscrapers are like those in *My Dress Was There Hanging*, 1933–1938, pp. 130/131
3 A robin, like the one in Millais's *Ophelia* from 1851/52
4 A skeleton, as in *Pitahayas*, 1938, pp. 162/163
5 The wedding portrait of Kahlo's parents, as in *My Grandparents, My Parents, and I*, 1936, pp. 118/119
6 The vegetation and naked women, as in *The Earth Itself*, 1939, pp. 216/217
7 An empty, floating dress, as in *My Dress Was There Hanging*, 1933–1938, pp. 130/131
8 A woman's body floating in the water, as in Millais's *Ophelia* from 1851/52
9 A shell inspired by the paintings of Hieronymus Bosch
10 Cactus plants, as in *Self-portrait (on the Border between Mexico
and the United States)*, 1931/32, pp. 110/111
11 A sailboat, as in *The Heart*, 1937, p. 177

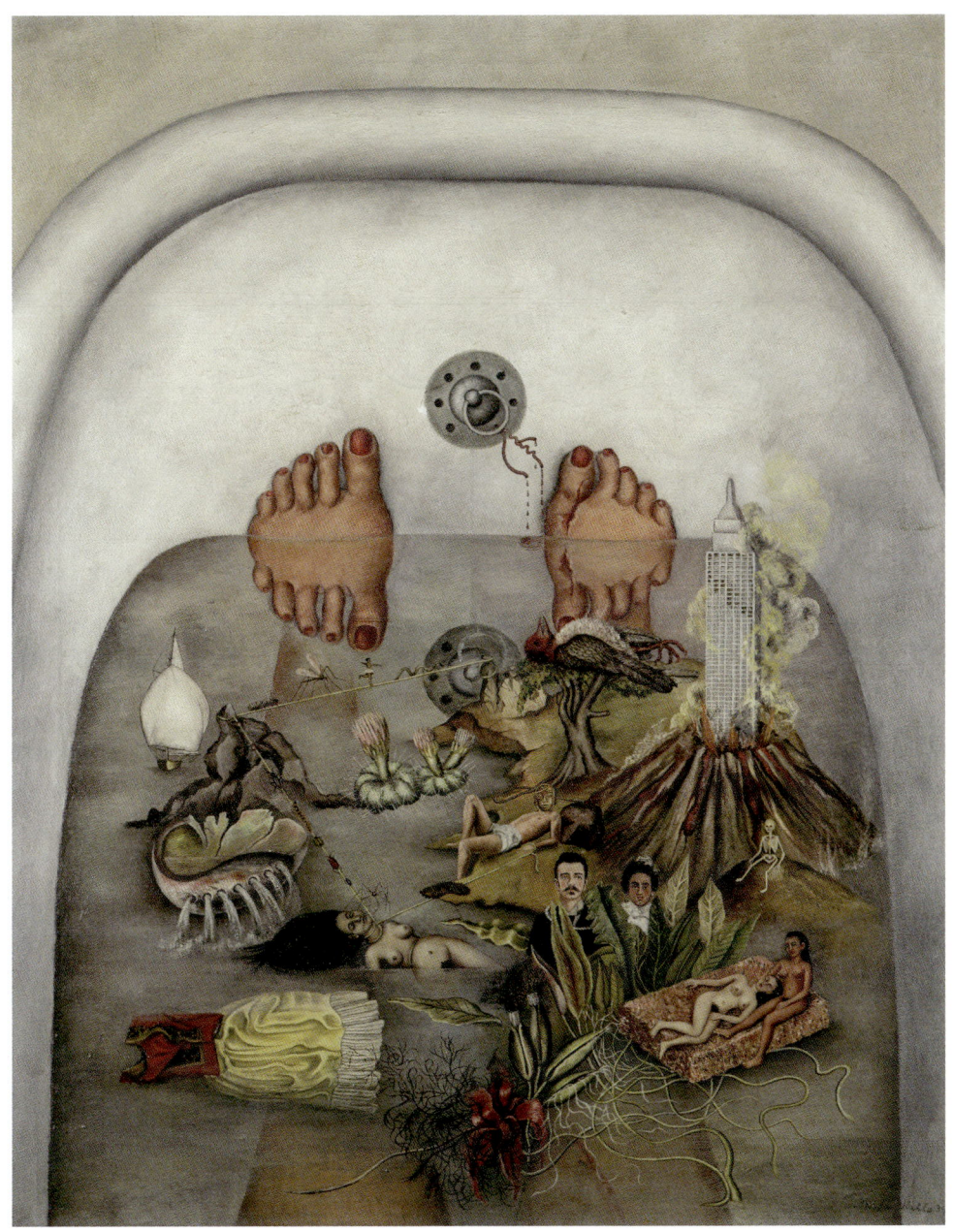

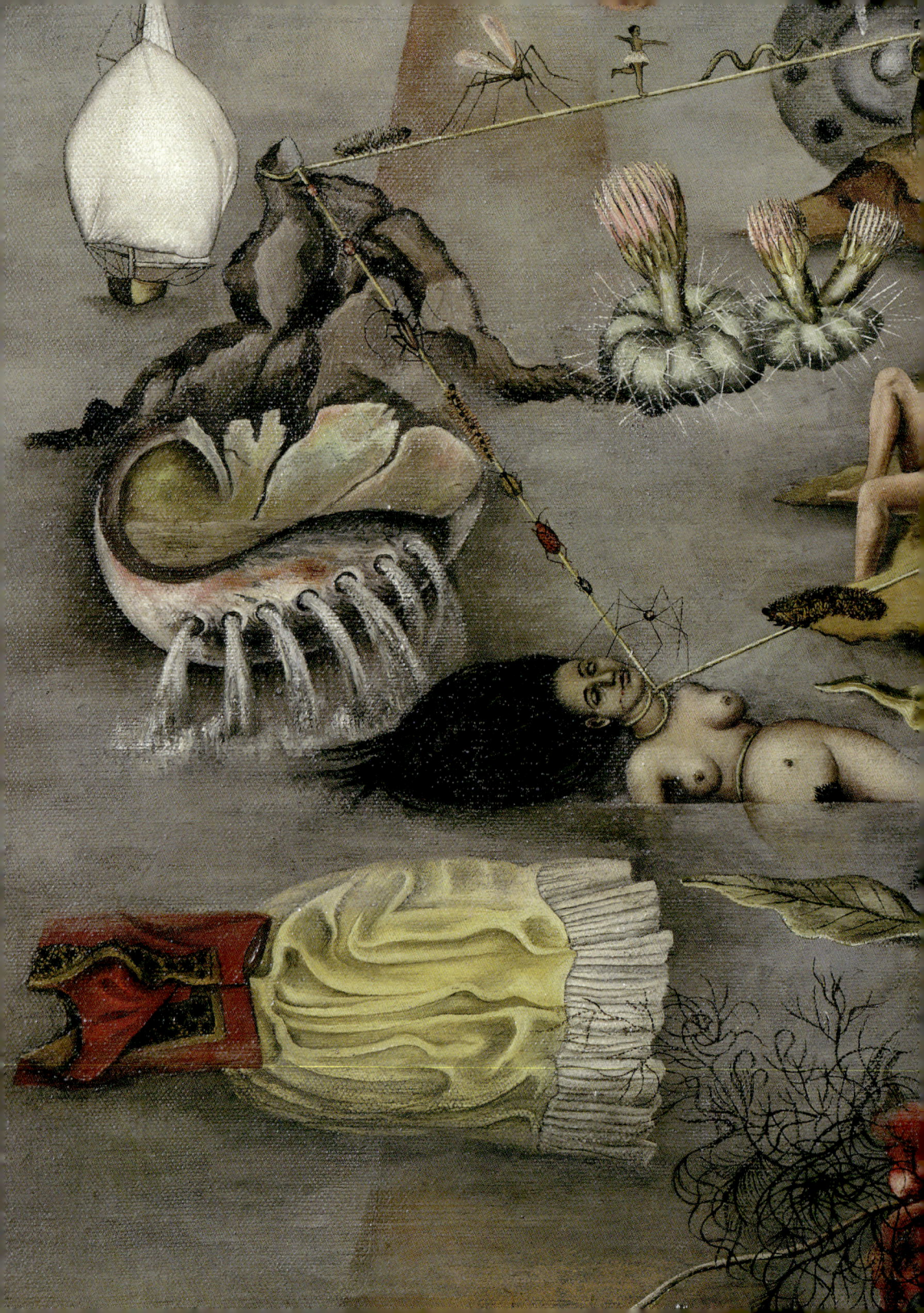

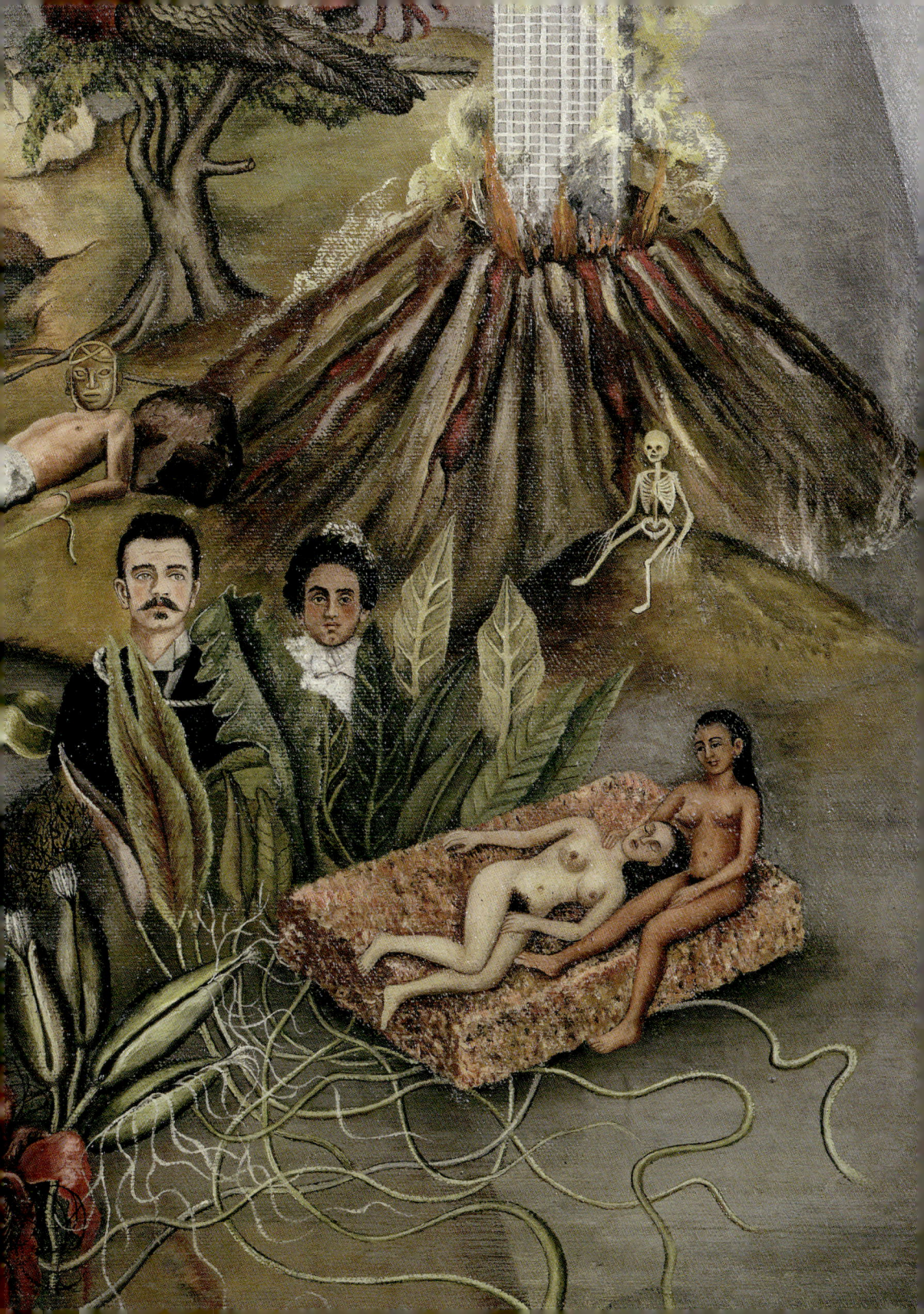

"Dorothy Hale Dies in 16-Story Plunge"
The New York Times, October 22, 1938

The Suicide of Dorothy Hale, 1938/39
Oil on masonite with painted wooden frame, 59.7 x 49.5 cm (23½ x 19½ in.)
Inscribed b.: En la ciudad de Nueva York el dia 21 del més de OCTUBRE de 1938,
al las seis de la mañana, se suicidó / la señora DOROTHY HALE tirándose desde
una ventana muy álta del edificio Hampshire House / En su recuerdo, [missing words]
éste retablo, habiendolo ejecutado FRIDA KAHLO. (In the city of New York on the
21st day of October 1938, at six o'clock in the morning, / Mrs. Dorothy Hale committed
suicide by throwing herself out of a very high window of the Hampshire House building /
[missing words] This retablo was painted in her memory by Frida Kahlo.)
Arizona, Phoenix Art Museum, anonymous gift, inv. 1960-20
(details pp. 1–3)

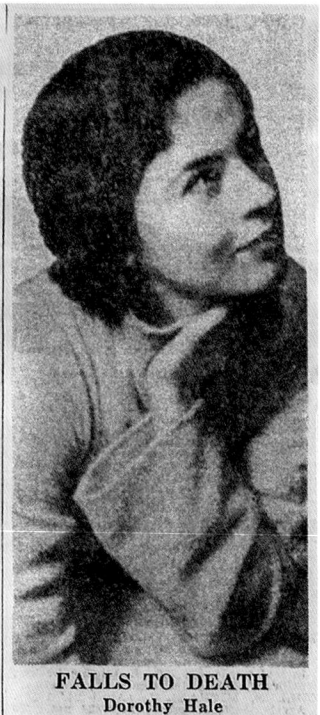

DOROTHY HALE DIES
IN 16-STORY PLUNGE

Actress Falls Out Window After
Entertaining Friends and
Attending Show

LEFT BURIAL DIRECTIONS

Painter's Widow Said to Have
Been Dissatisfied With Her
Progress on the Stage

Mrs. Dorothy Hale, widow of
Gardner Hale, noted fresco and
mural painter, and a close friend
of Harry L. Hopkins, WPA Ad-
ministrator, was instantly killed
early yesterday in a fall from the
window of her small apartment on
the sixteenth floor of Hampshire
House at 150 Central Park South.

Before she died, Mrs. Hale, whose
interest in the arts had progressed
from sculpture and roles in motion
pictures to an intense desire for a
career in the legitimate theatre, had
spent several apparently happy
hours with friends.

FALLS TO DEATH
Dorothy Hale

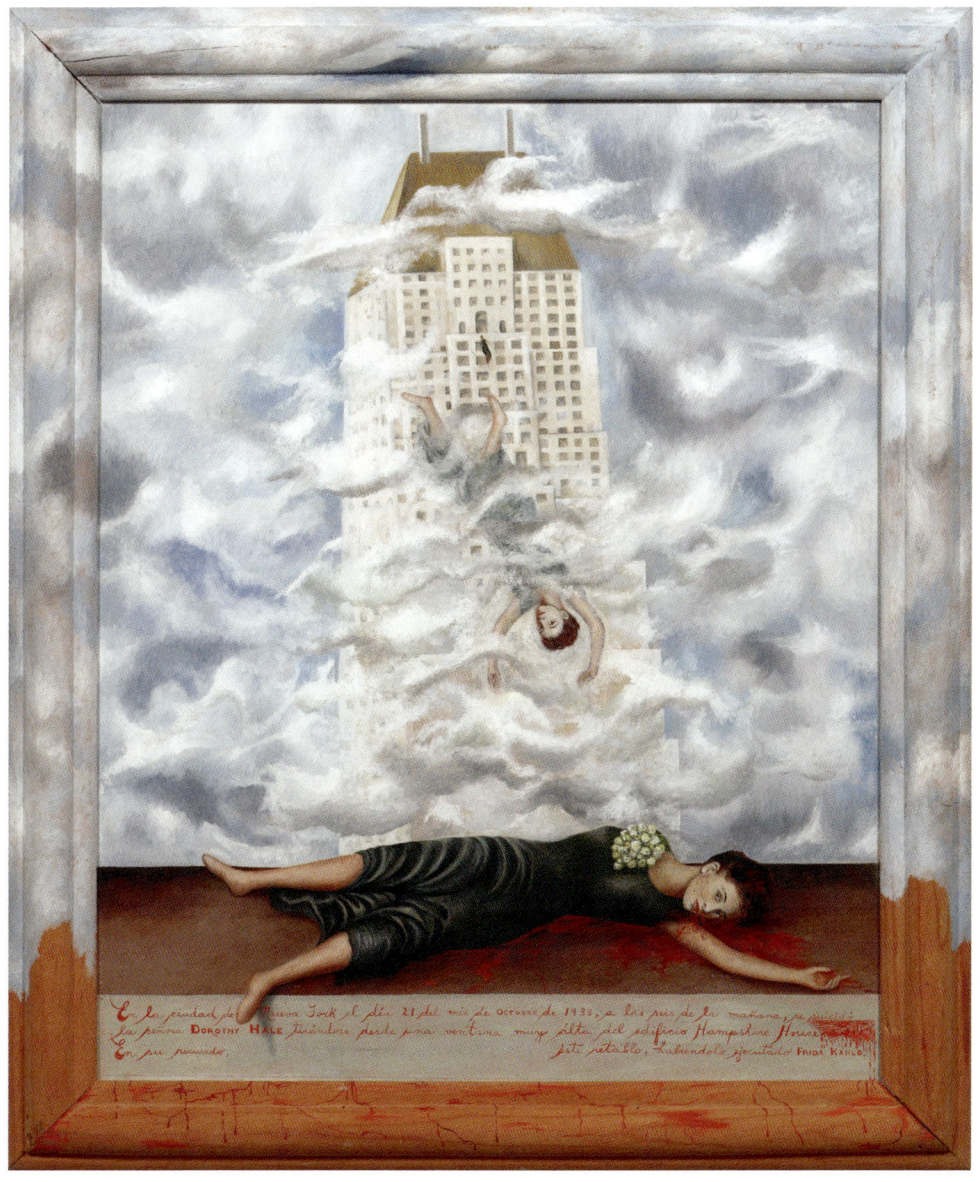

The Earth Itself (Two Nudes in a Forest), 1939
This work inspired by the poetry of surrealist
artist Alice Rahon Paalen was comissioned by
the Mexican actress Dolores Del Río.
Oil on metal, 25.1 x 30.2 cm (9⅞ x 11⅞ in.)
United States, private collection

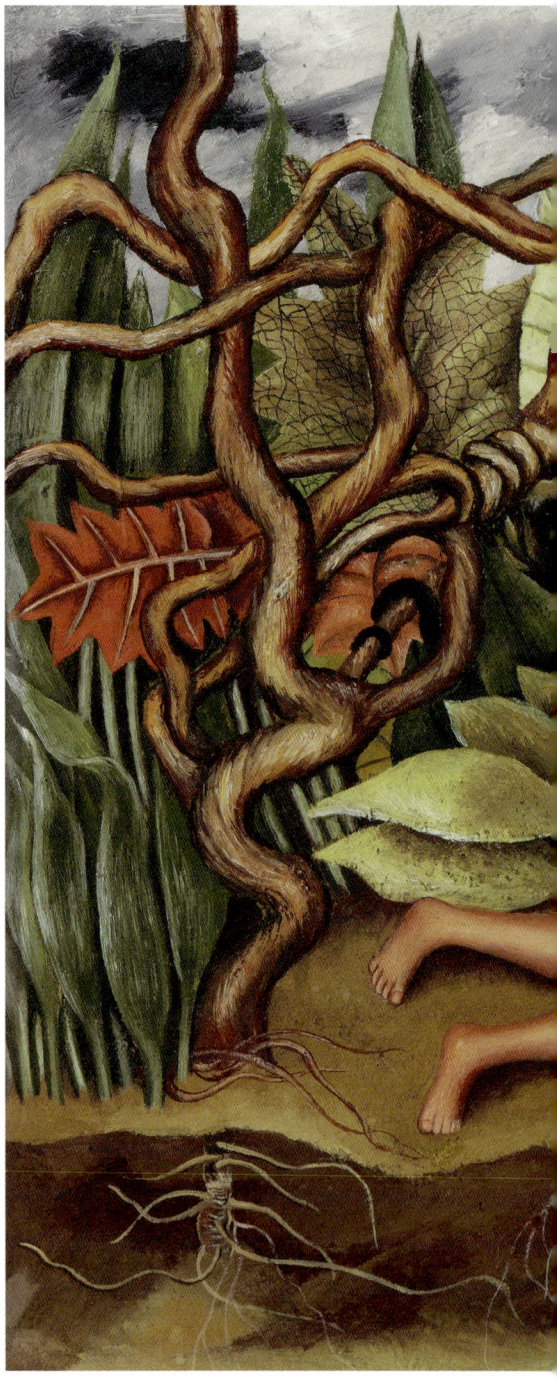

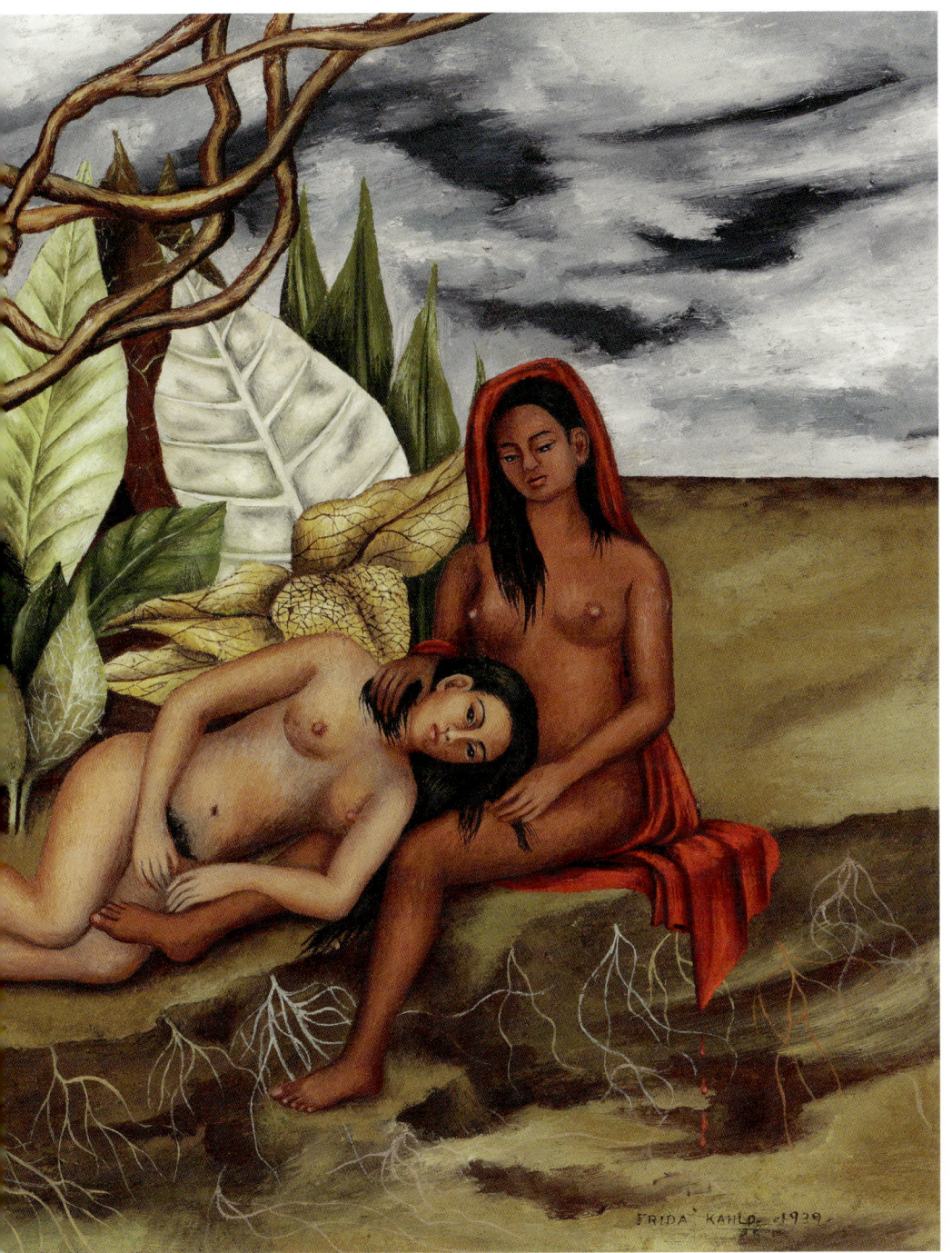

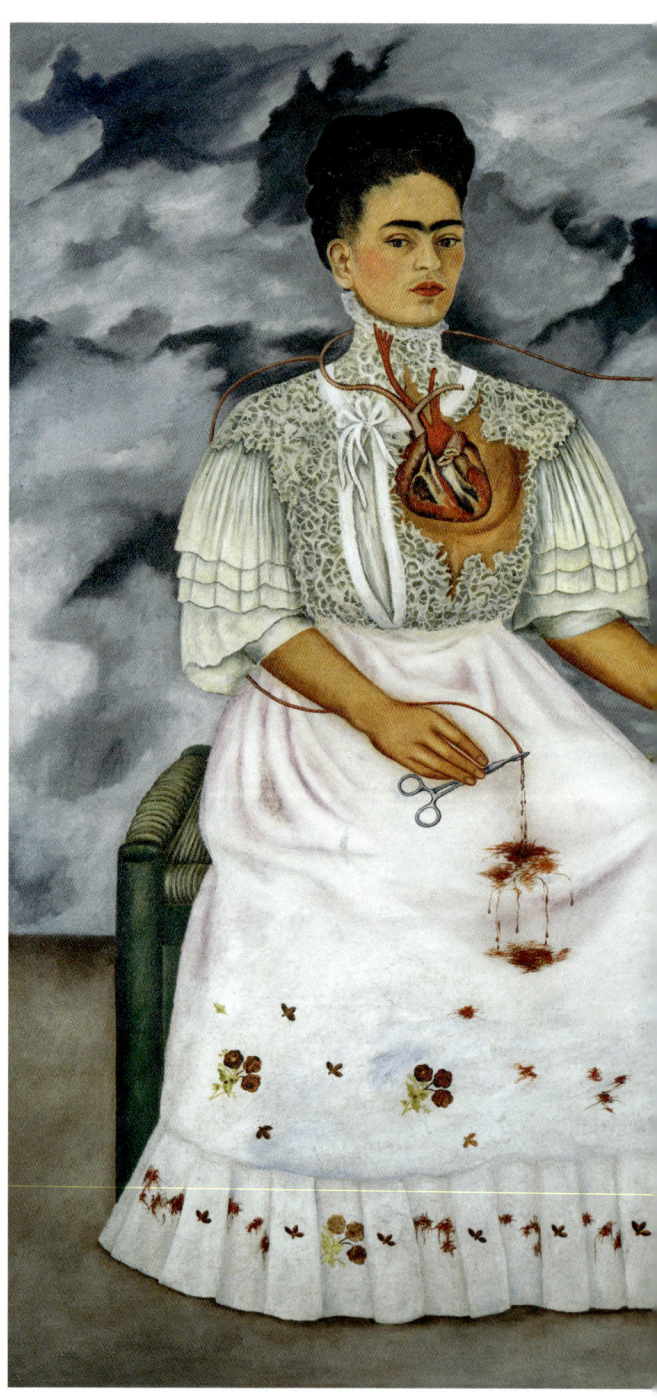

The Two Fridas, 1939
Oil on canvas, 173.5 x 173 cm
(68¼ x 68⅛ in.)
Mexico City, Secretaría de Cultura,
Instituto Nacional de Bellas Artes y
Literatura, Museo de Arte Moderno
(details pp. 221, 223)

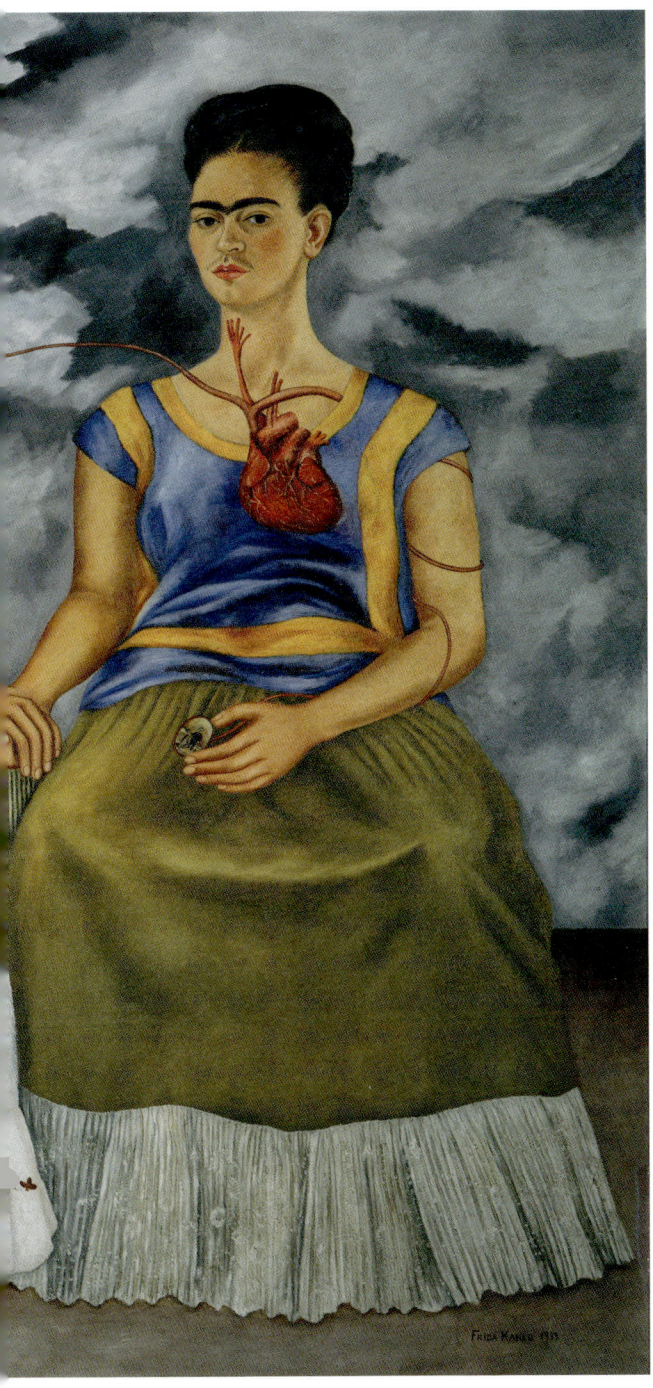

Wallace Marly, **Diego and Frida in their studio
in the Casa Azul**, *c.* 1944

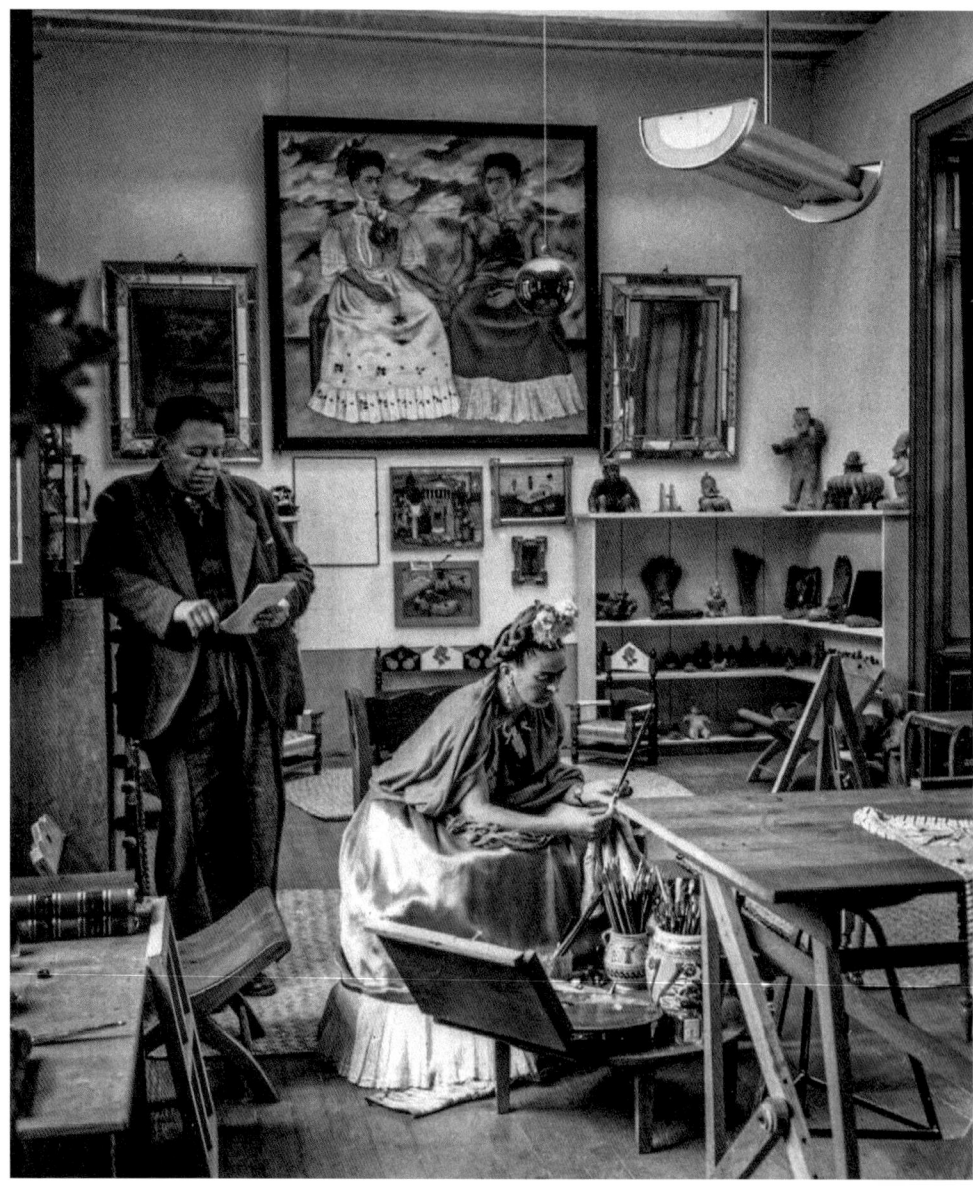

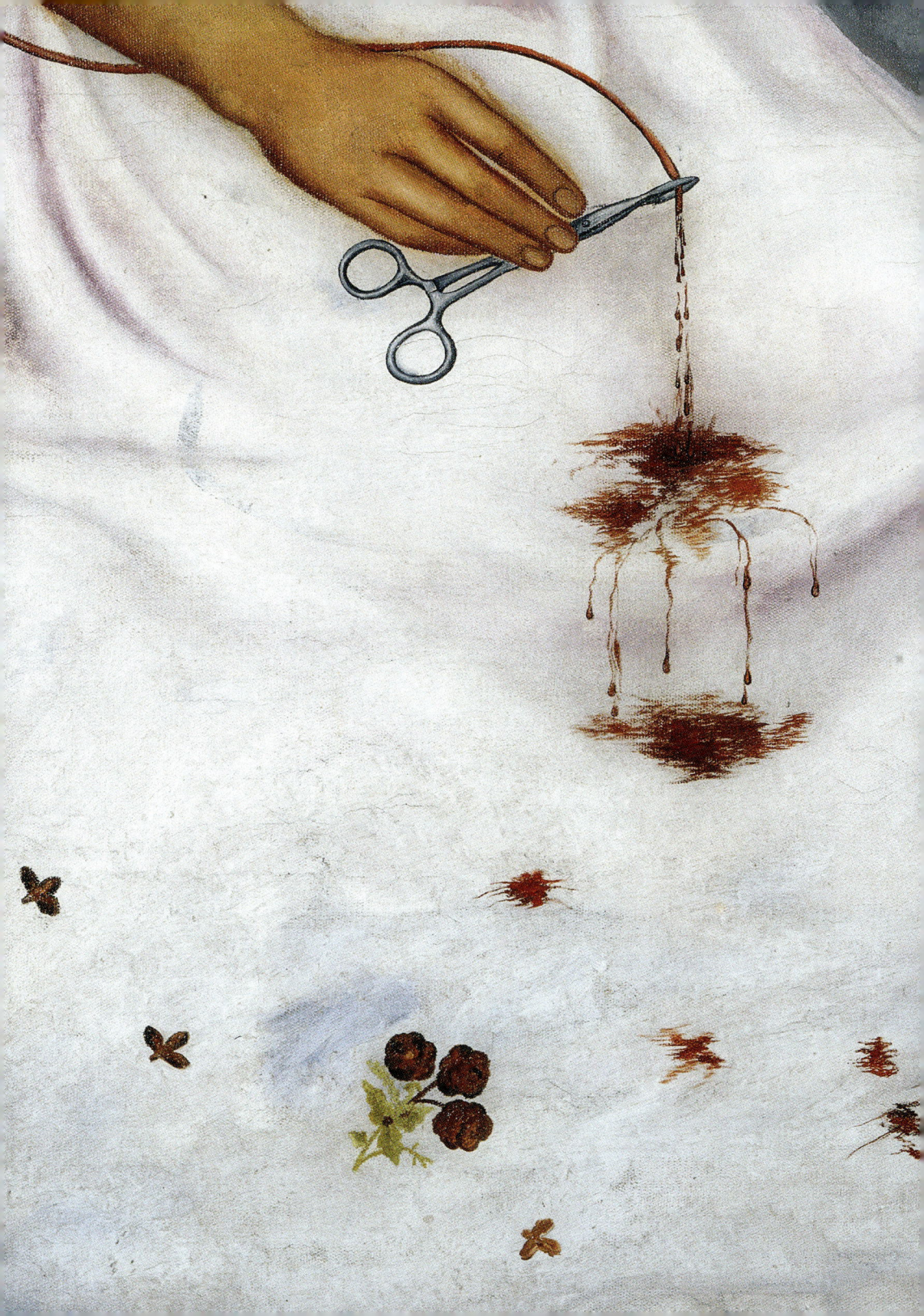

Julio Romero de Torres, **Ángeles and Fuensanta**, 1909
Oil and tempera on canvas, 99 x 119 cm (39 x 46⅞ in.)
Córdoba, Spain, Museo Julio Romero de Torres

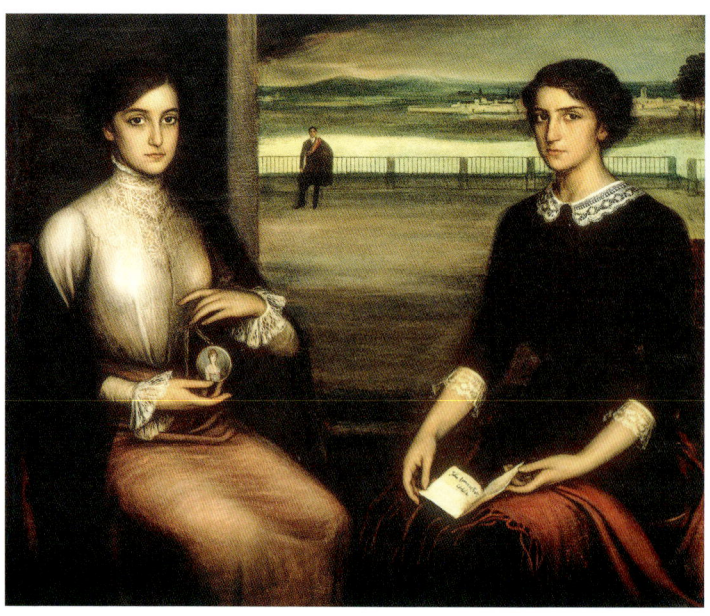

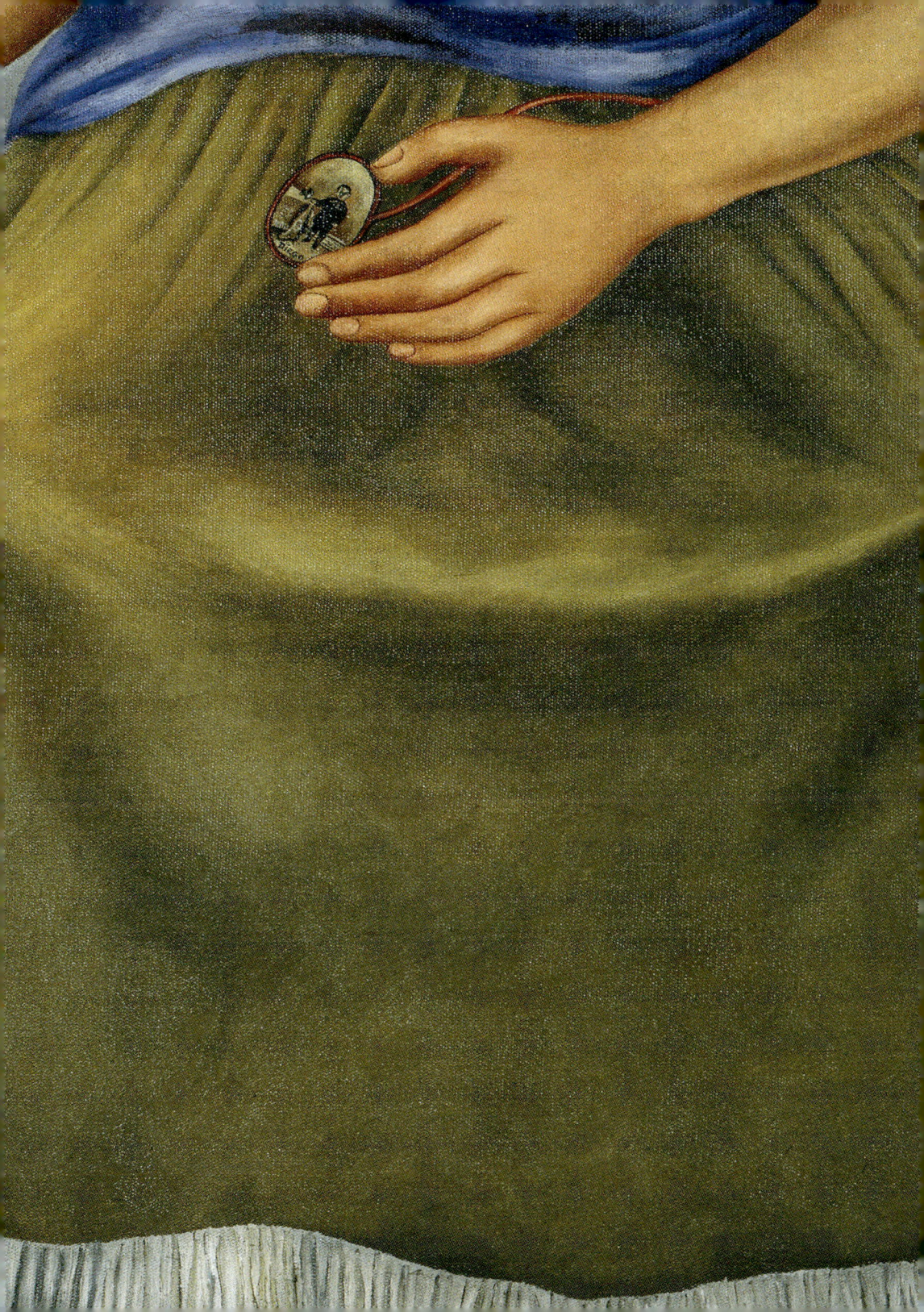

Bernard G. Silberstein,
Frida Kahlo painting
The Wounded Table, *c.* 1940
Gelatin silver print,
20.3 x 25.4 cm (8 x 10 in.)
Detroit Institute of Arts

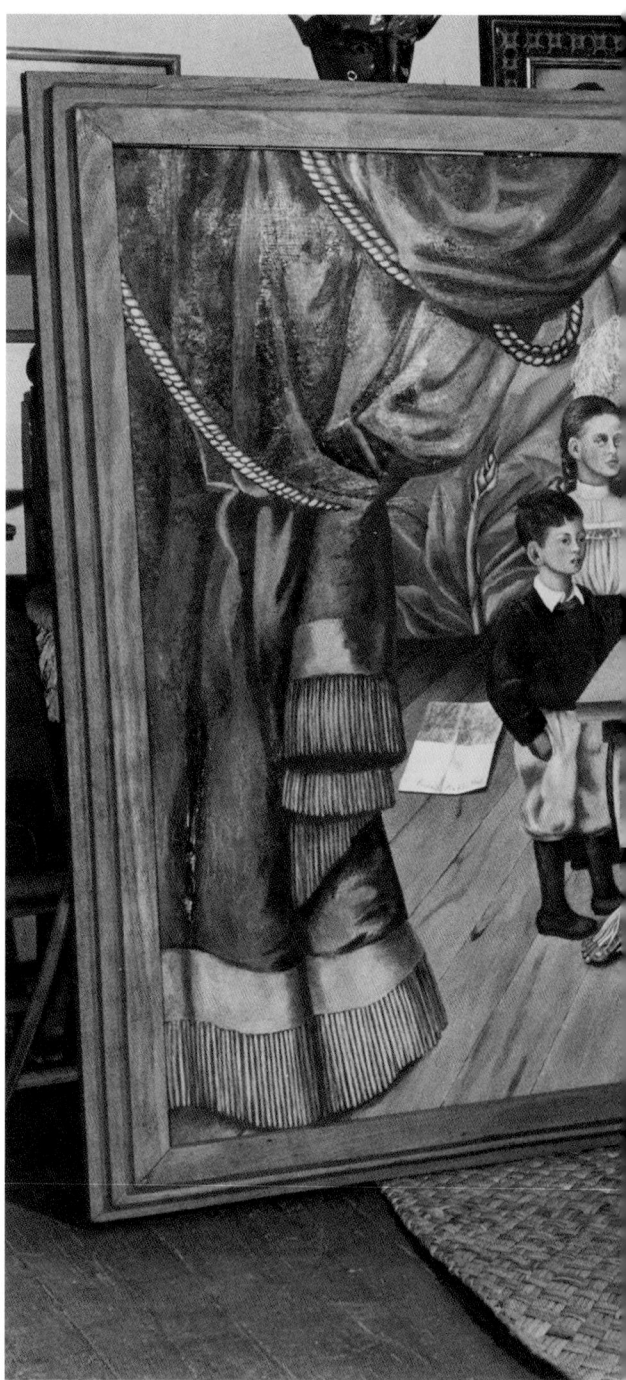

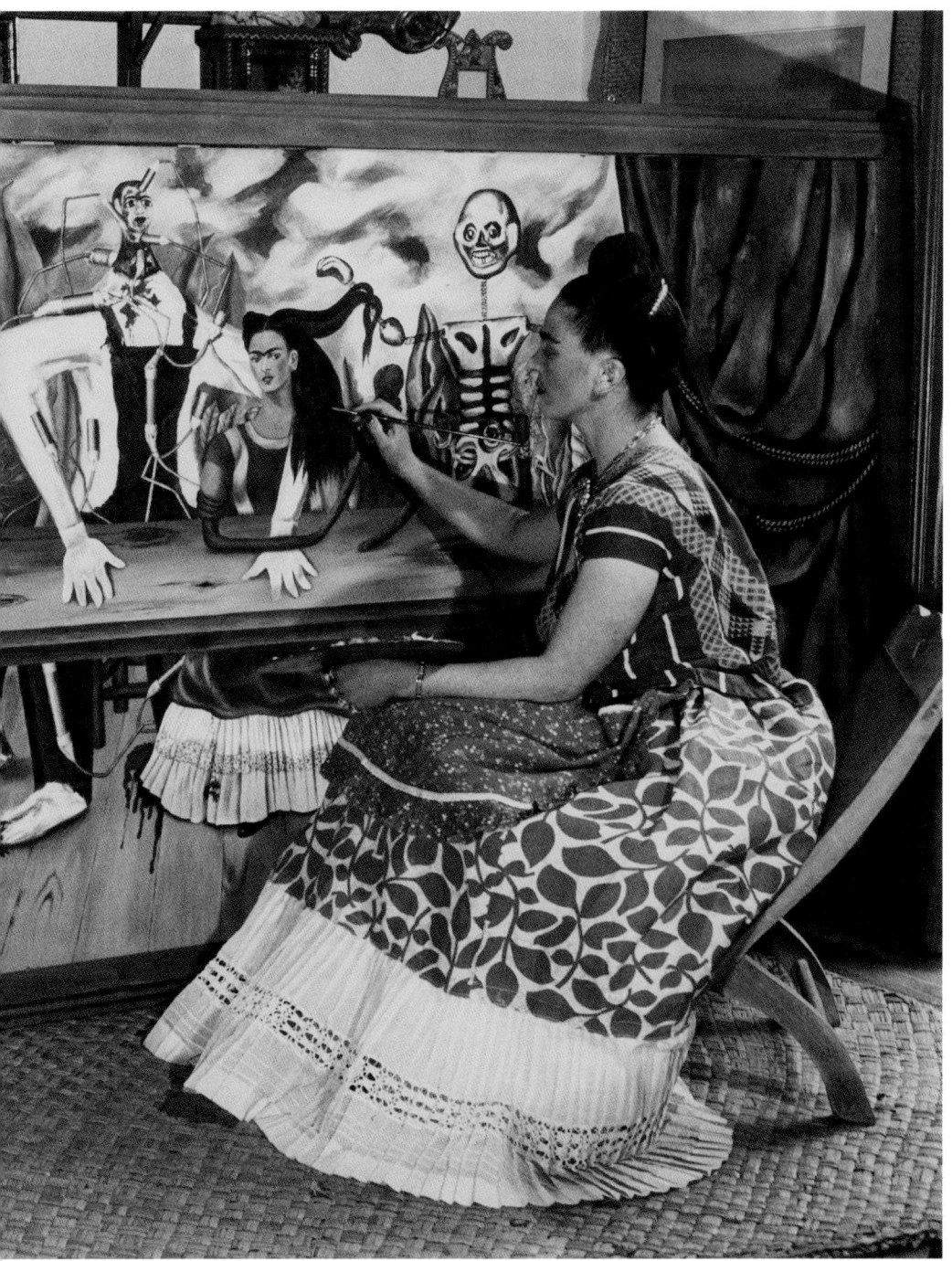

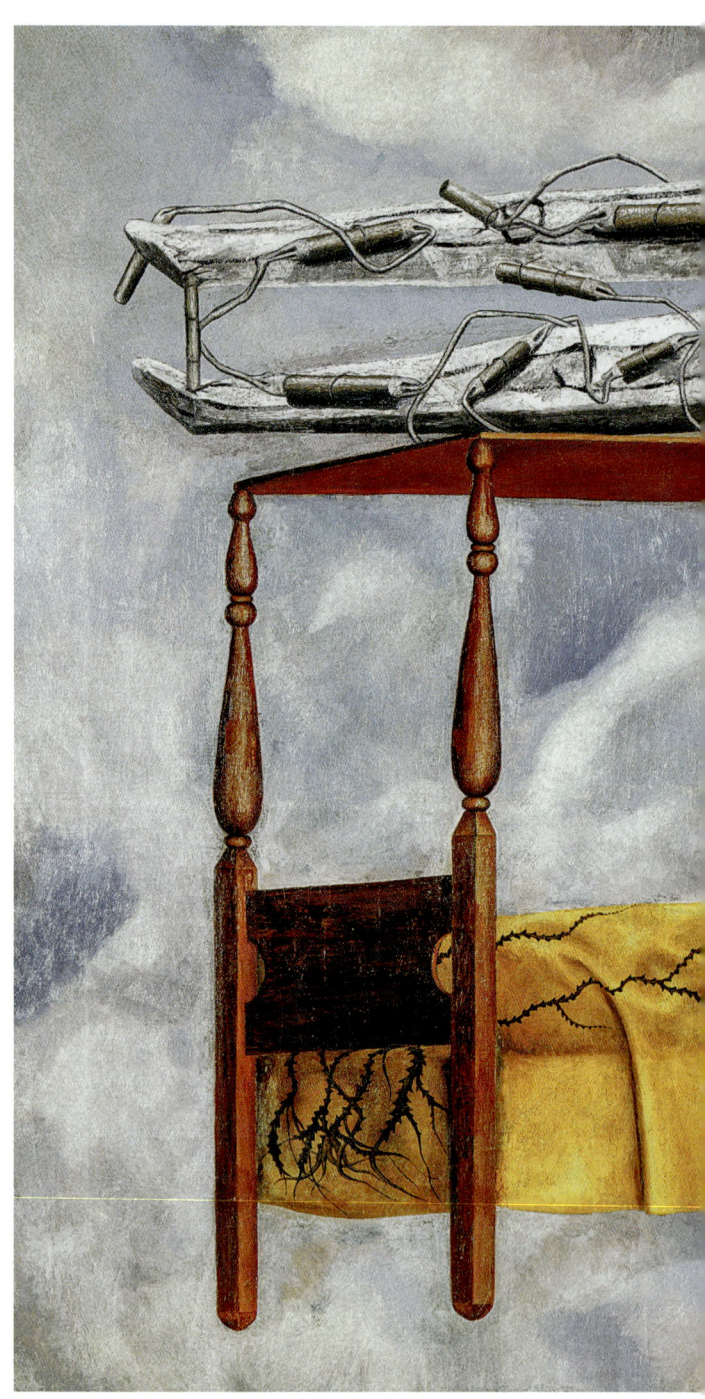

The Dream (The Bed), 1940
Oil on canvas, 74.3 x 97.2 cm
(29¼ x 38¼ in.)
New York, private collection

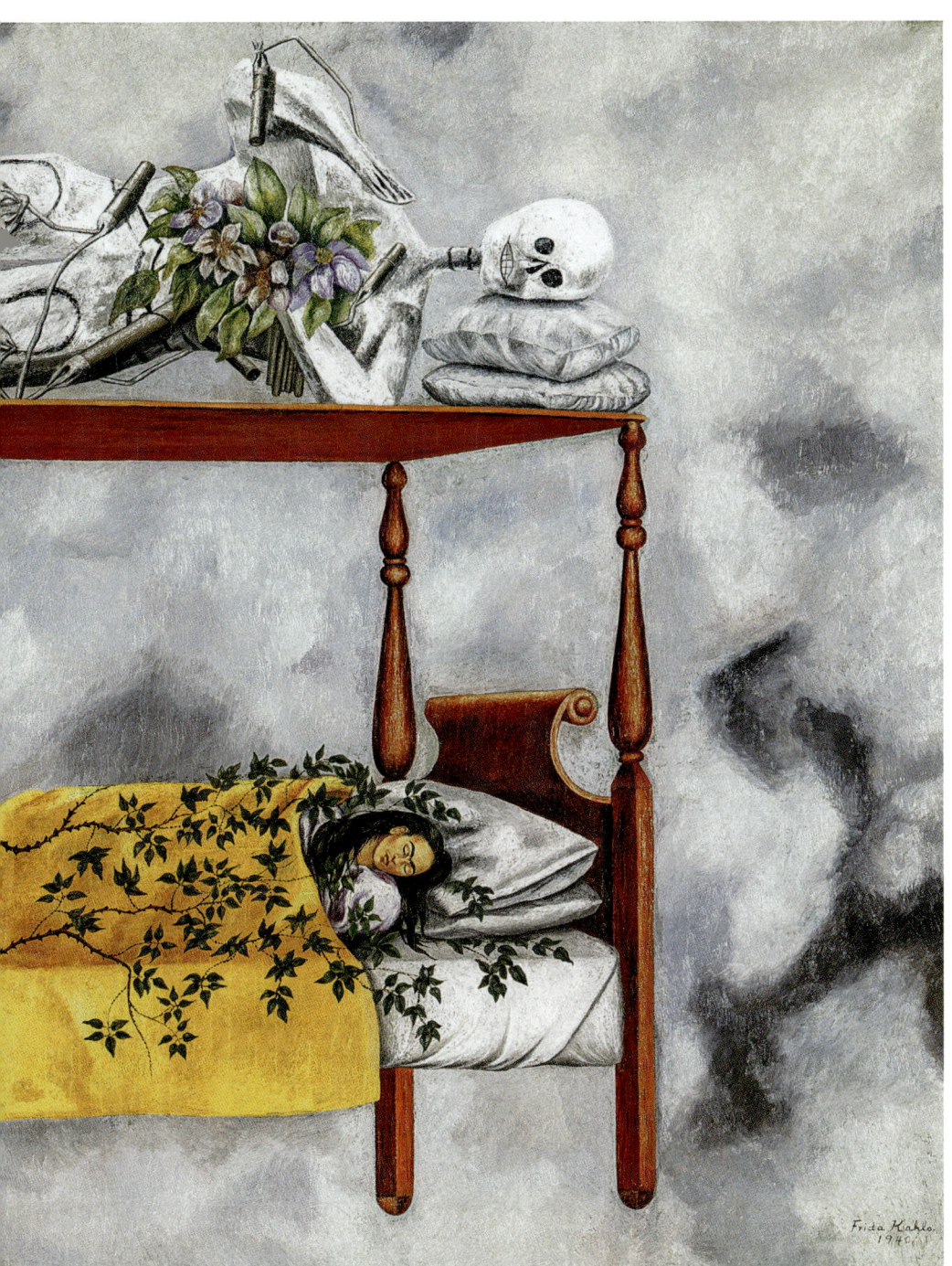

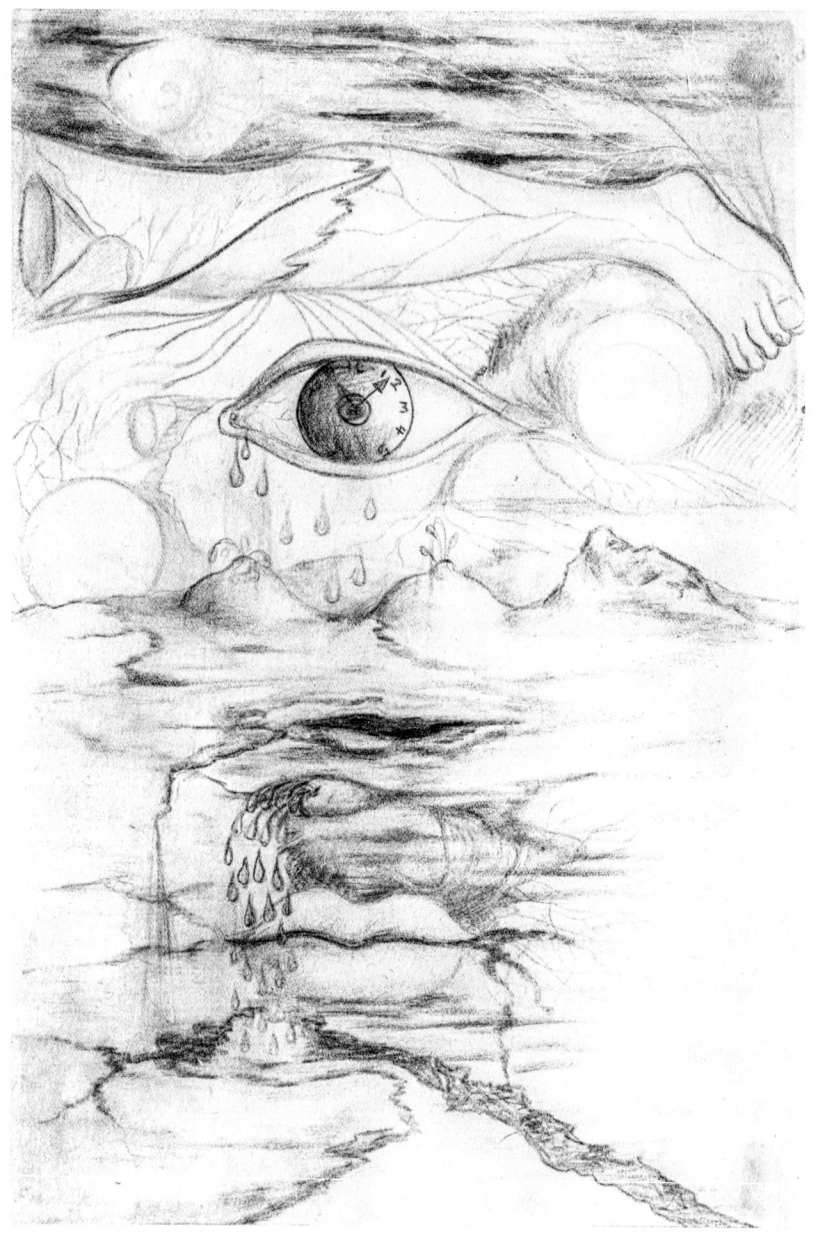

Fantasy (I), *c.* 1944
Graphite pencil and colored pencils on paper, 24 x 16 cm (9½ x 6¼ in.)
Mexico City, Xochimilco, Museo Dolores Olmedo

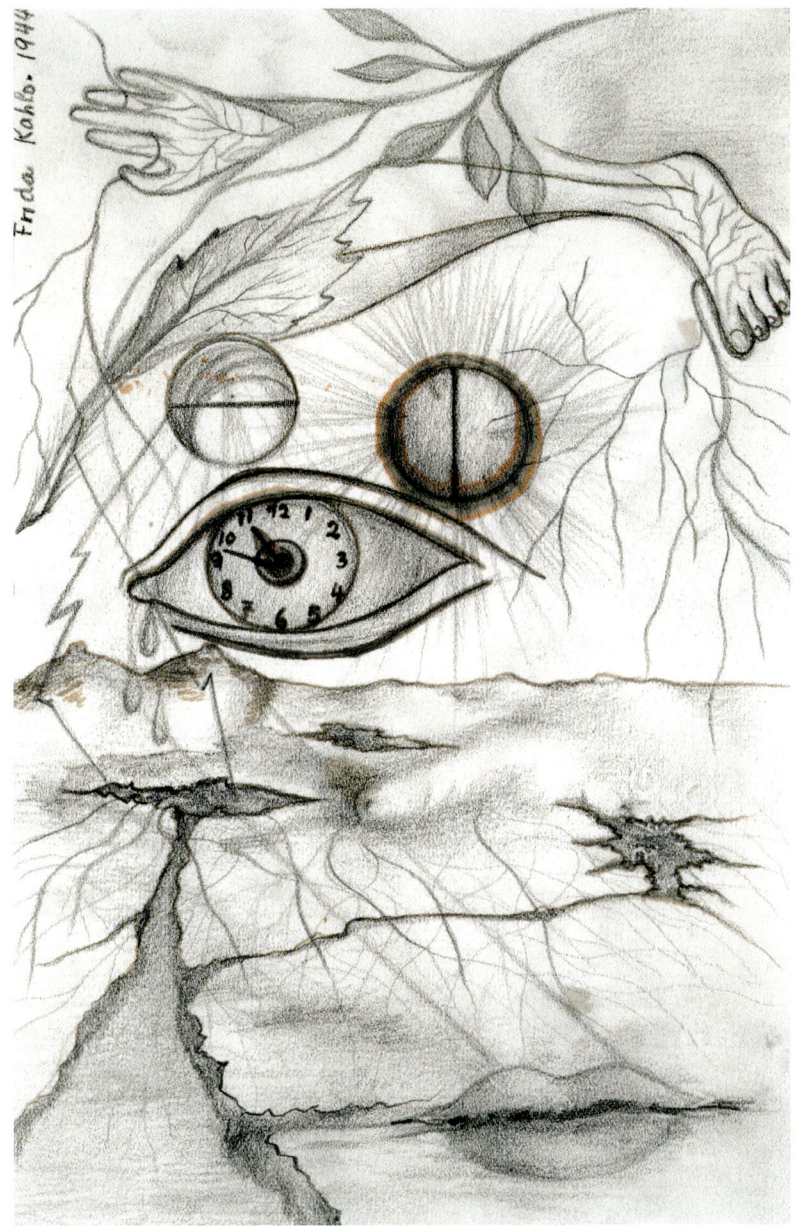

Fantasy (II), 1944
Conté crayon, graphite pencil, ink, and watercolor on paper,
24 x 16 cm (9½ x 6¼ in.). Mexico City, private collection

Self-portrait with Cropped Hair, 1940
Oil on canvas, 40 x 27.9 cm (15¾ x 11 in.); inscribed at the top:
Mira que si te quise, fué por el pelo, – / Ahora que estás pelona, ya no te quiero.
(Look, if I loved you it was because of your hair. – /
Now that you've cut it off, I don't love you any more.)
New York, Museum of Modern Art, gift of
Edgar Kaufmann, Jr., inv. 3.1943 *(detail pp. 8/9)*

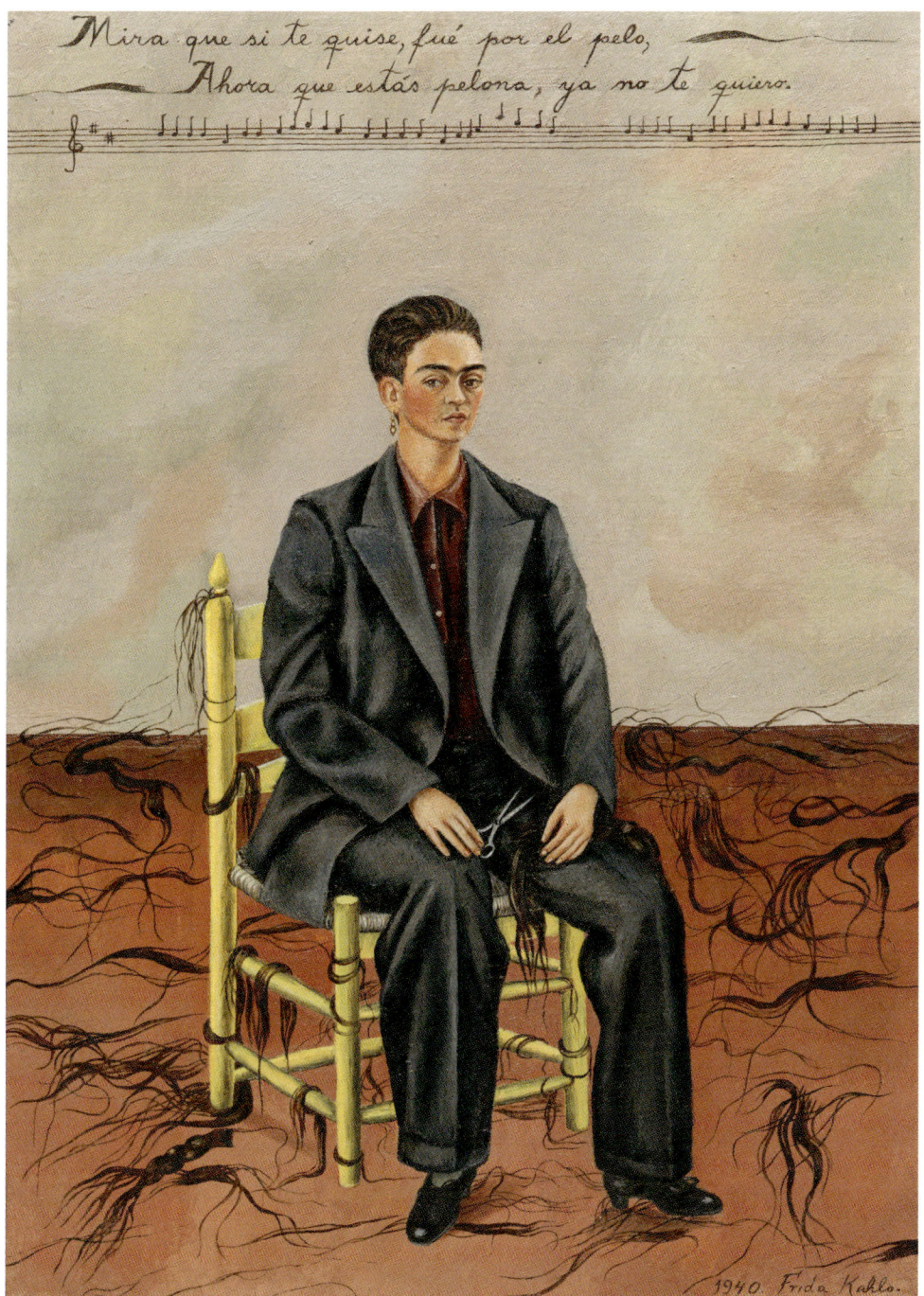

Wallace Marly, **Frida Kahlo in a hammock**, *c.* 1944

Self-portrait (Dedicated to Doctor Leo Eloesser), 1940
Oil on masonite, 59.7 x 40 cm (23⅜ x 15¾ in.); inscribed on the speech scroll:
Pinté mi retrato en el año de 1940 / para el Doctor Leo Eloesser, mi médico y /
mi mejor amigo. Con todo mi cariño. / Frida Kahlo (I painted my portrait in 1940 /
for Dr. Leo Eloesser, my doctor and / my best friend. With all my love. / Frida Kahlo.)
Private collection, Los Angeles, Lucas Museum of Narrative Art

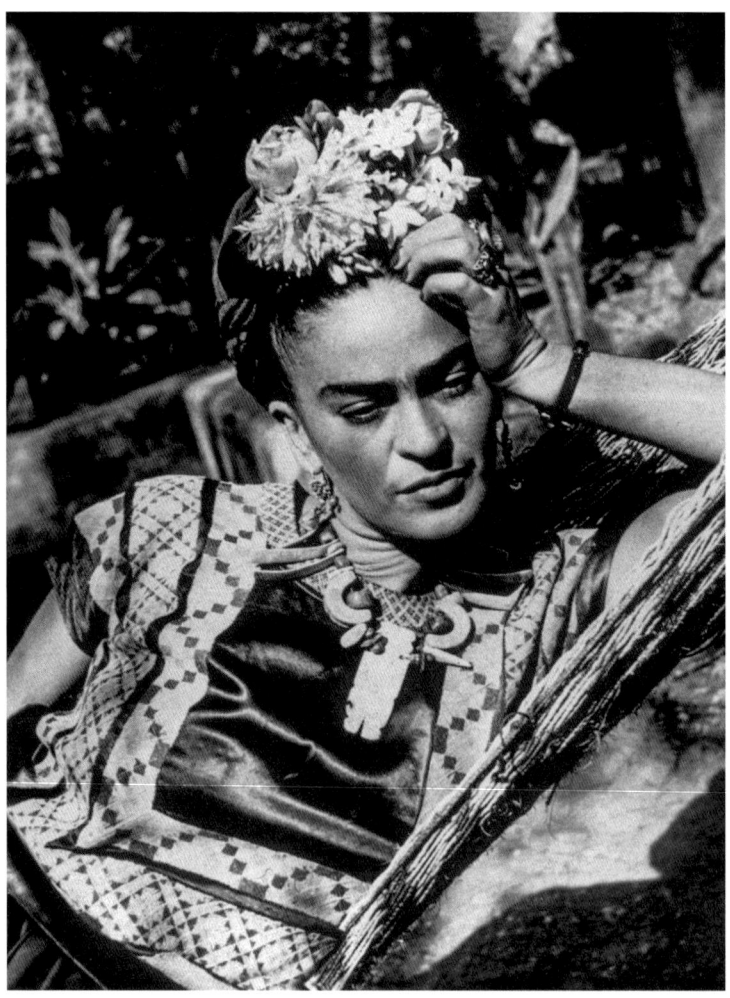

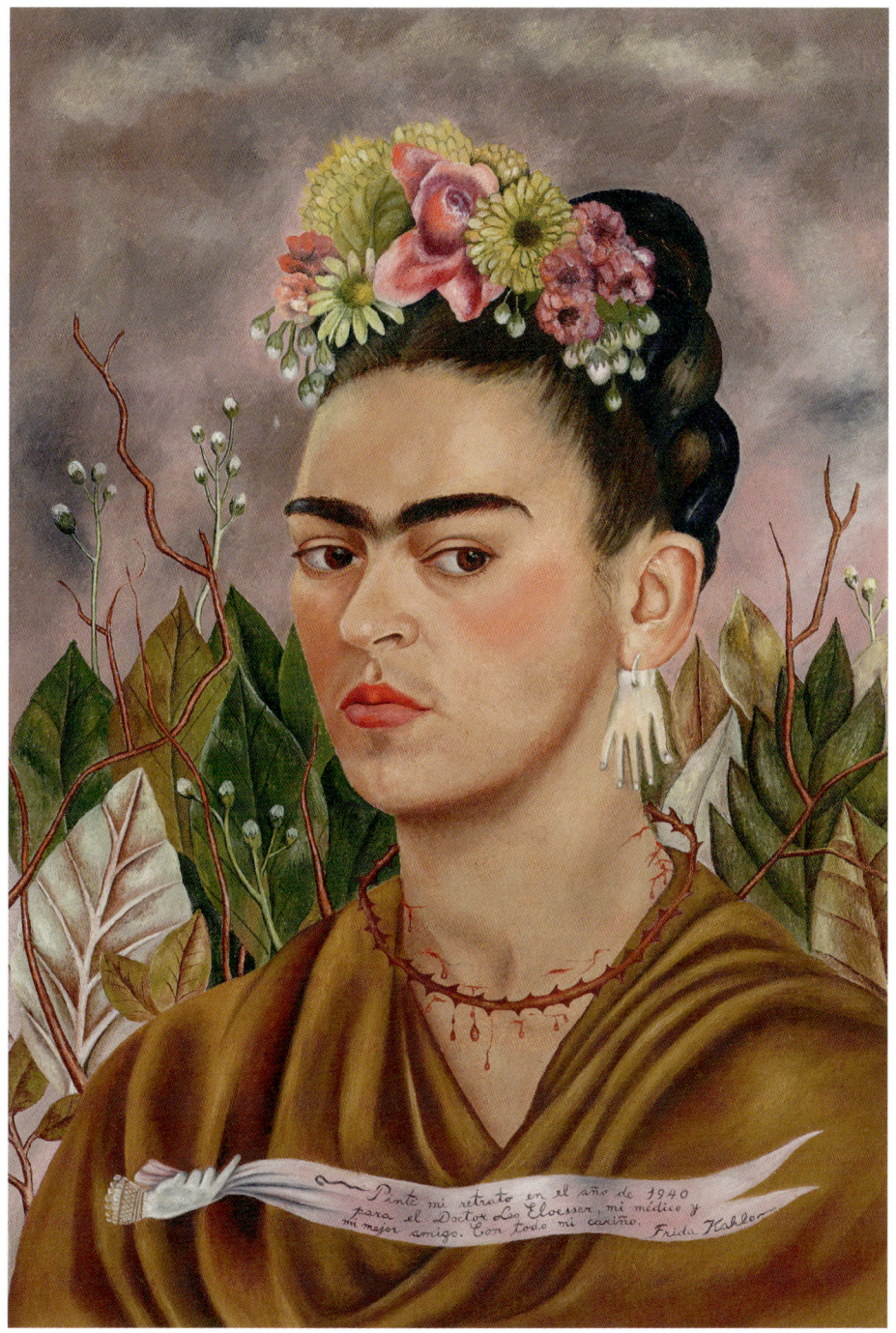

Self-portrait with Thorn Necklace and Hummingbird, 1940
Oil on canvas, mounted on wood, 62.5 x 48 cm (24⅝ x 18⅞ in.)
Austin, Texas, Harry Ransom Center, University of Texas,
Nickolas Muray Collection of Mexican Art, inv. 66.6

Page 236
Self-portrait (with Monkeys), 1943
Oil on canvas, 81.5 x 63 cm (32⅛ x 24¾ in.)
Mexico, The Jacques and Natasha Gelman Collection
of 20th-century Mexican Art/The Vergel Foundation

Page 237
Self-portrait (with Monkey), *c.* 1940
Oil on masonite, 55.2 x 43.5 cm (21¾ x 17⅛ in.)
Private collection of Madonna *(detail p. 181)*

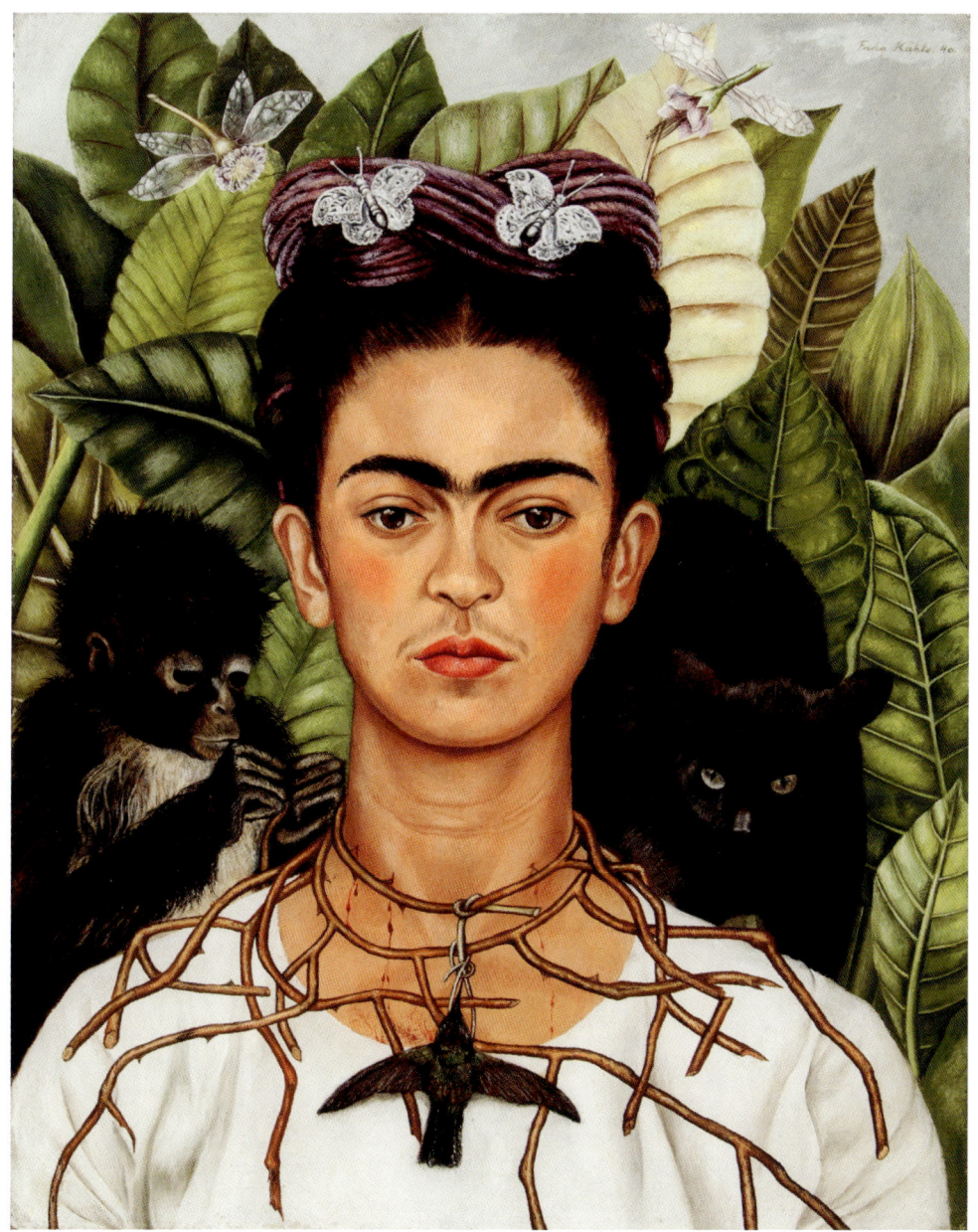

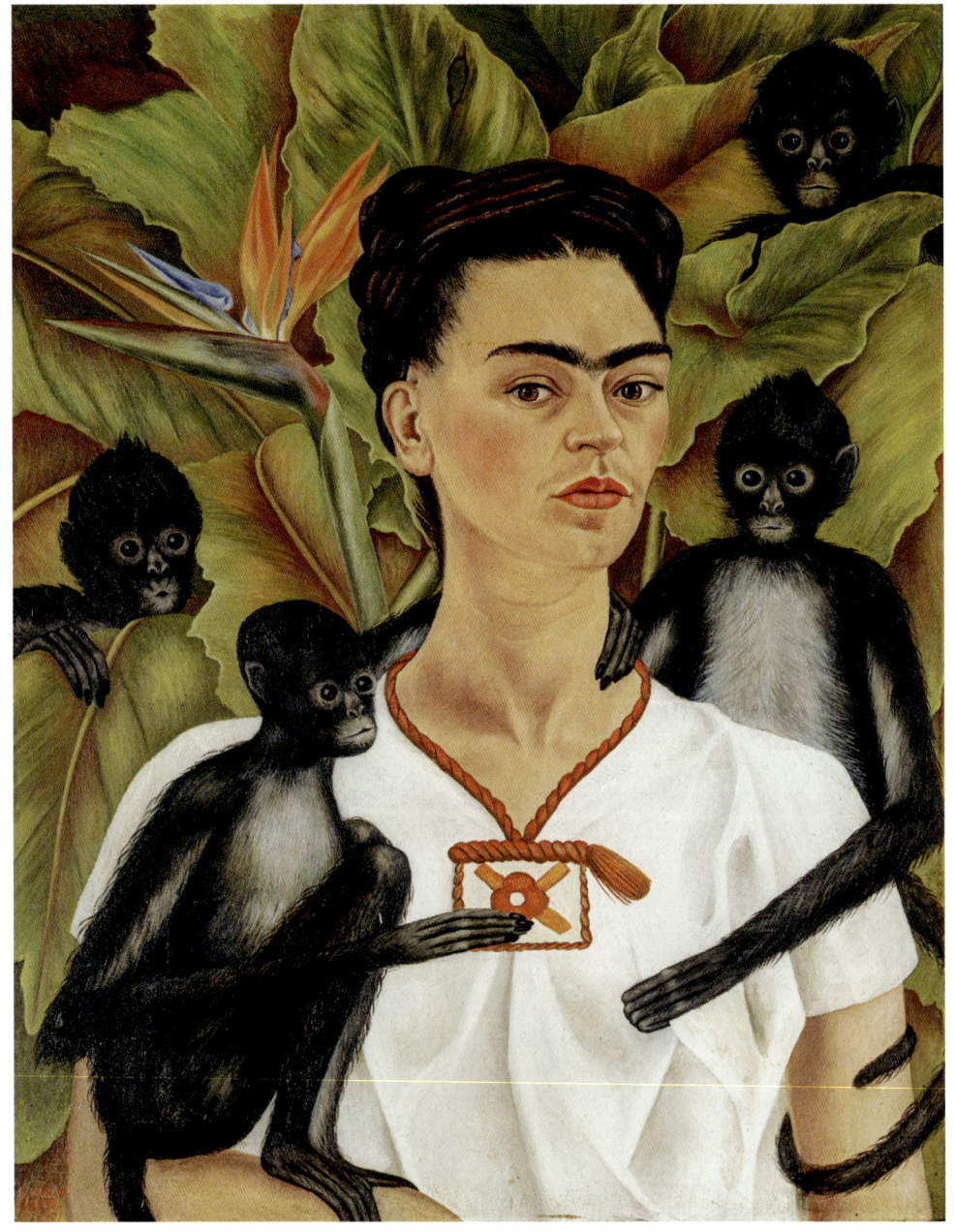

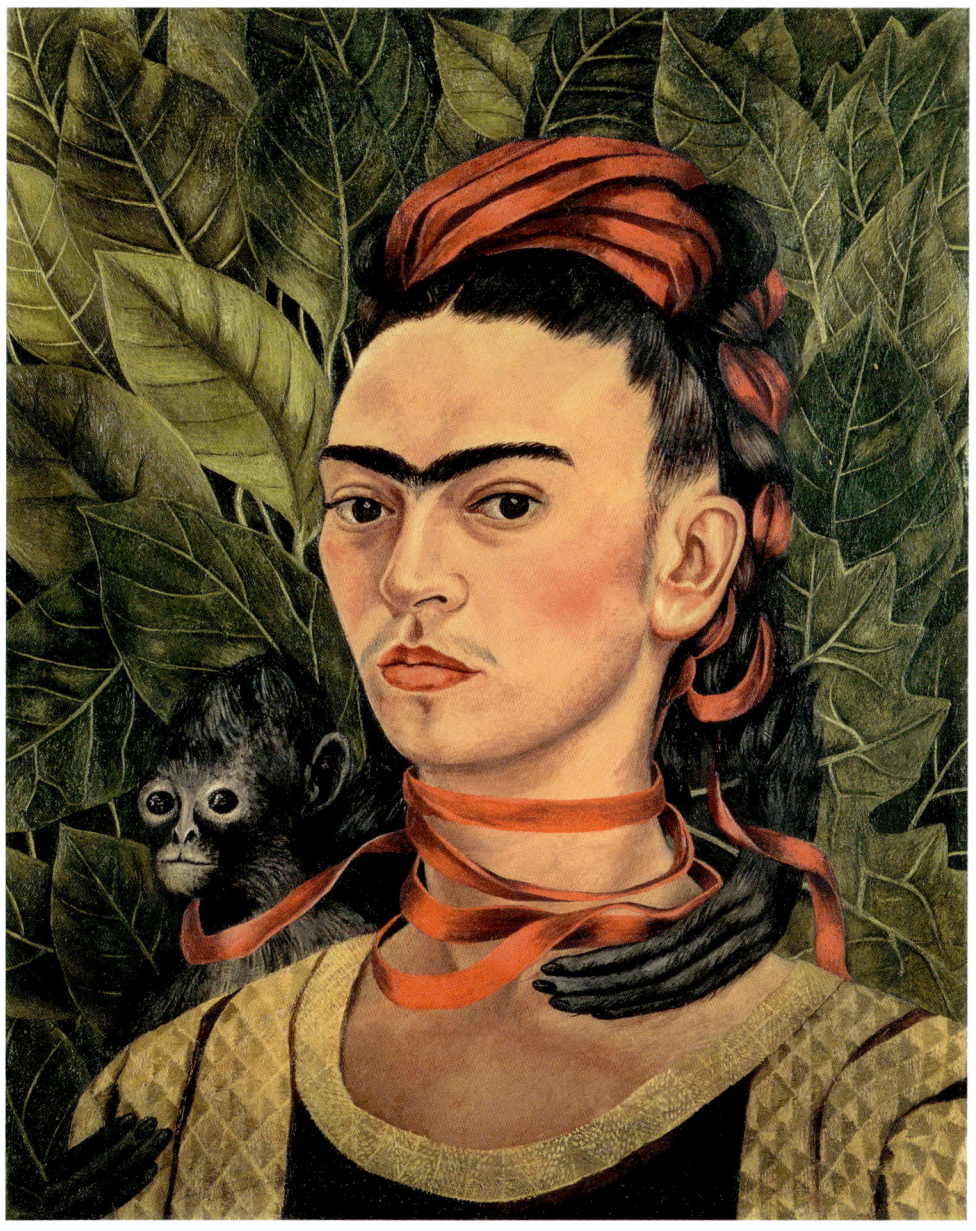

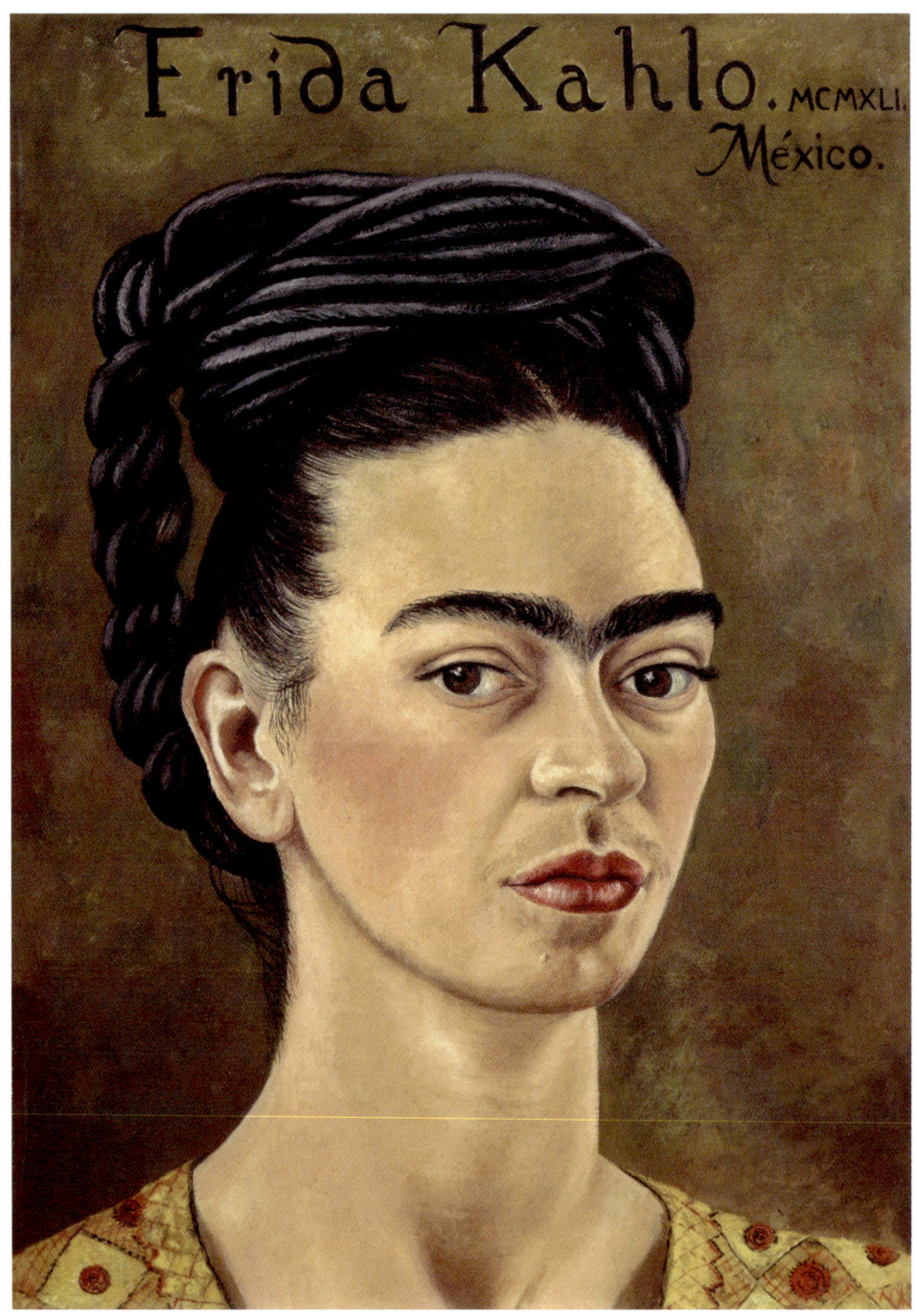

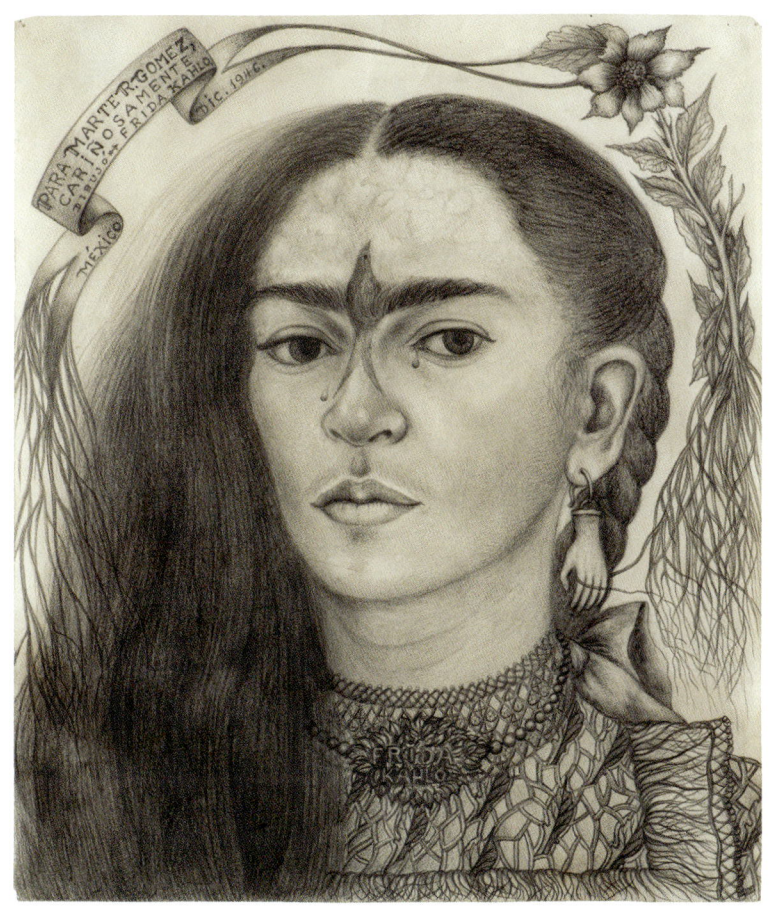

Self-portrait (MCMXLI), 1941
Oil on canvas, 39.5 x 29 cm (15½ x 11⅜ in.)
Mexico, The Jacques and Natasha Gelman Collection
of 20th-century Mexican Art/The Vergel Foundation

Self-portrait (Dedicated to Marte R. Gómez), December 1946
Graphite pencil on paper, 38.5 x 32.5 cm (15⅛ x 12¾ in.)
Berlin, Ulla and Heiner Pietzsch collection

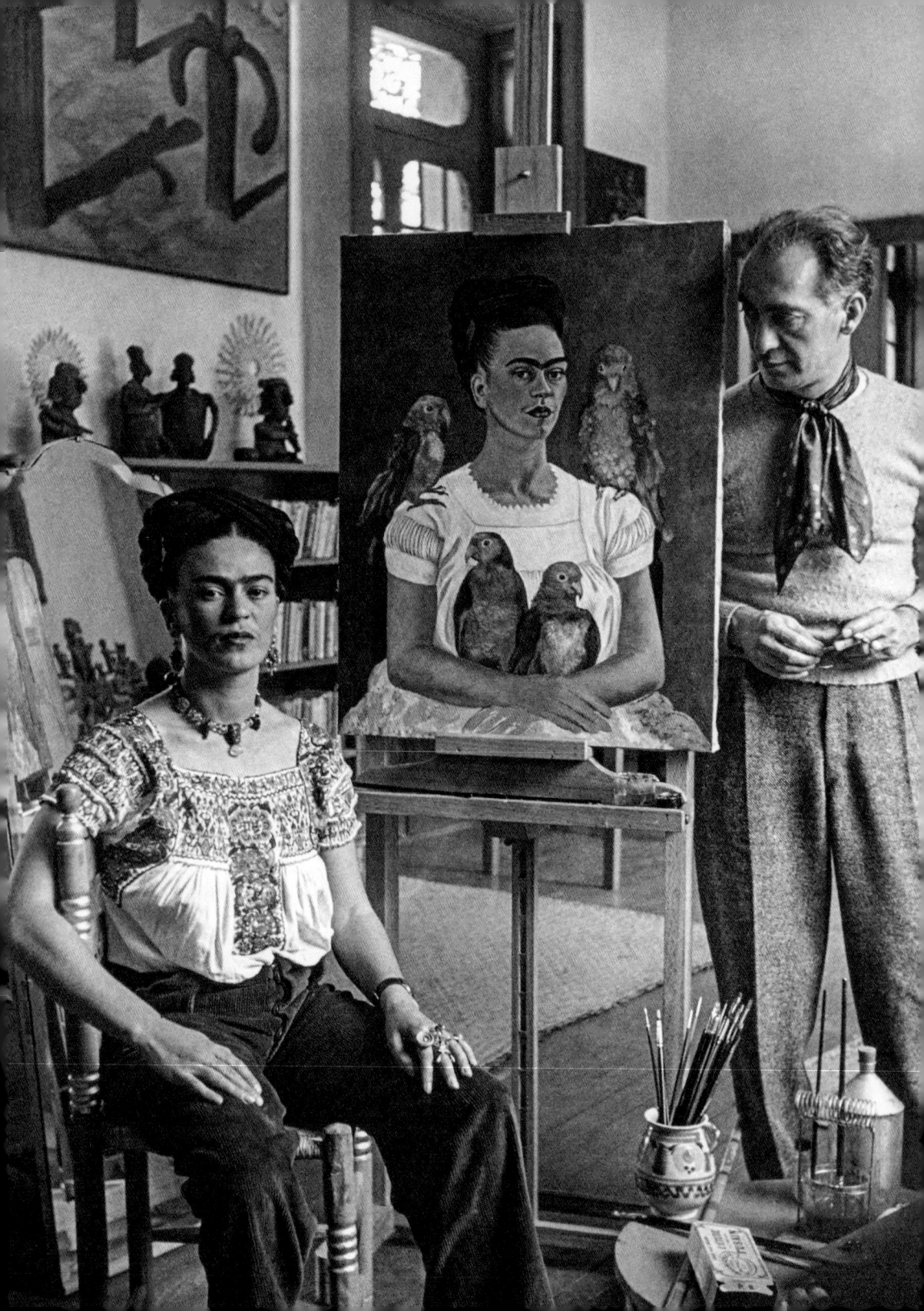

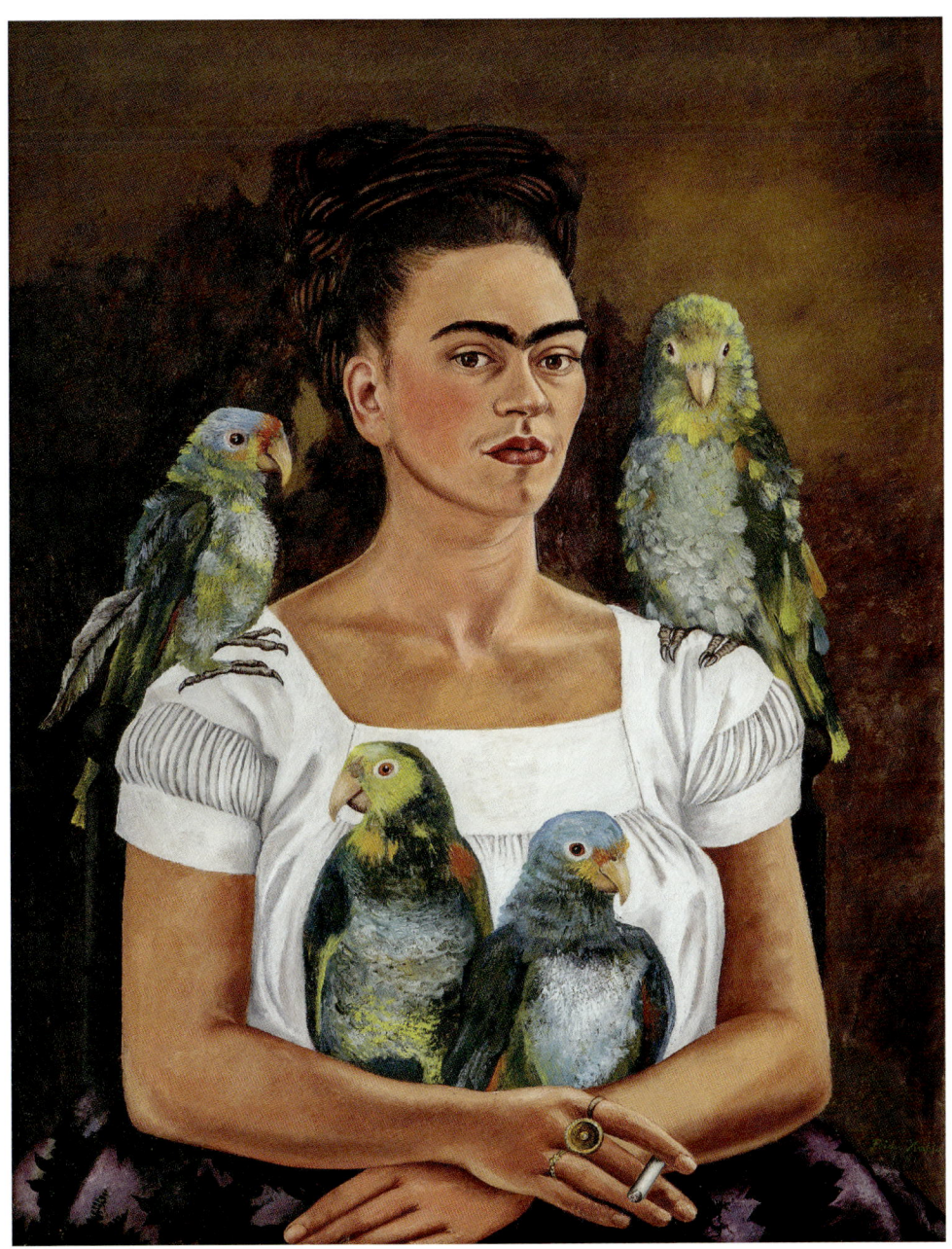

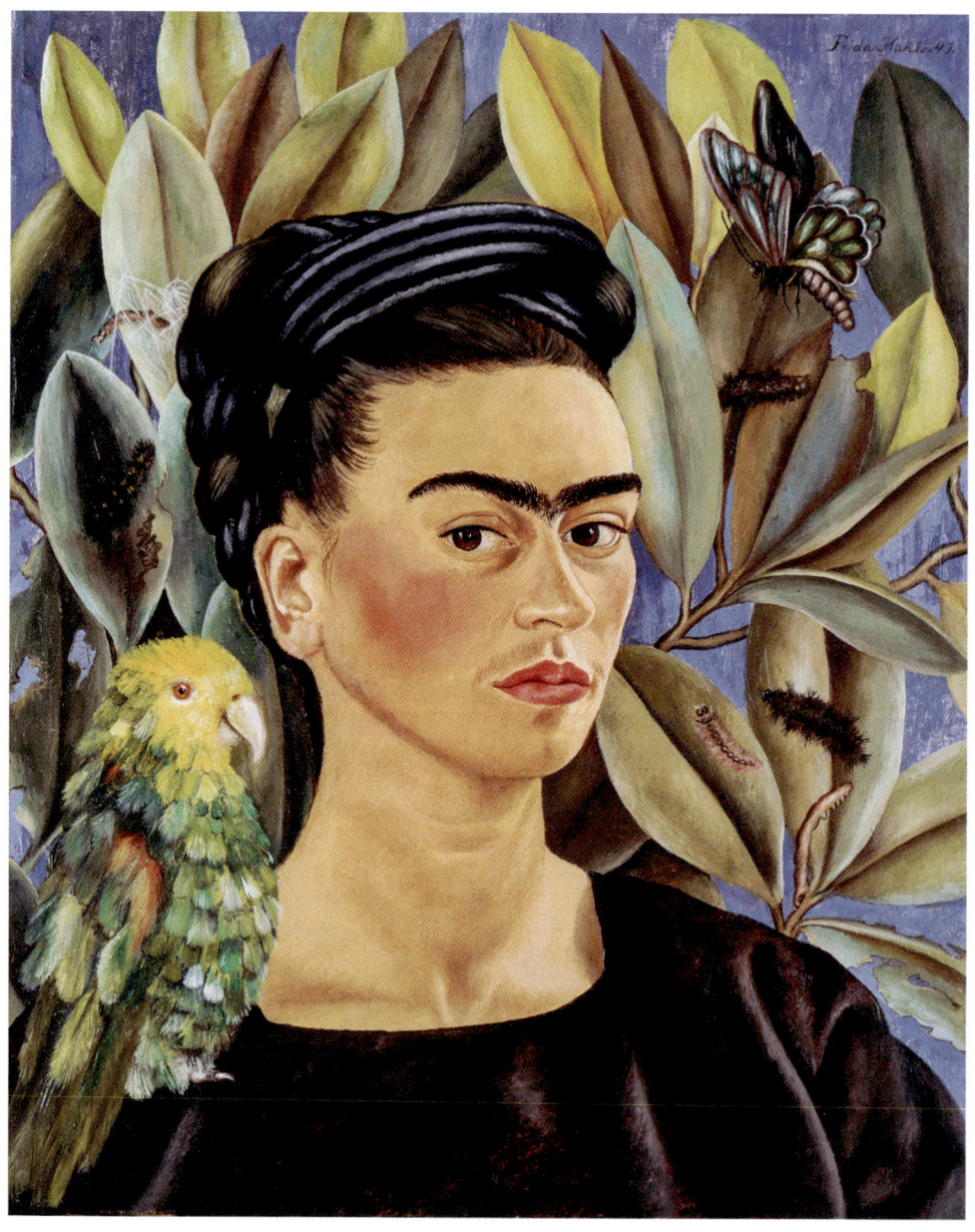

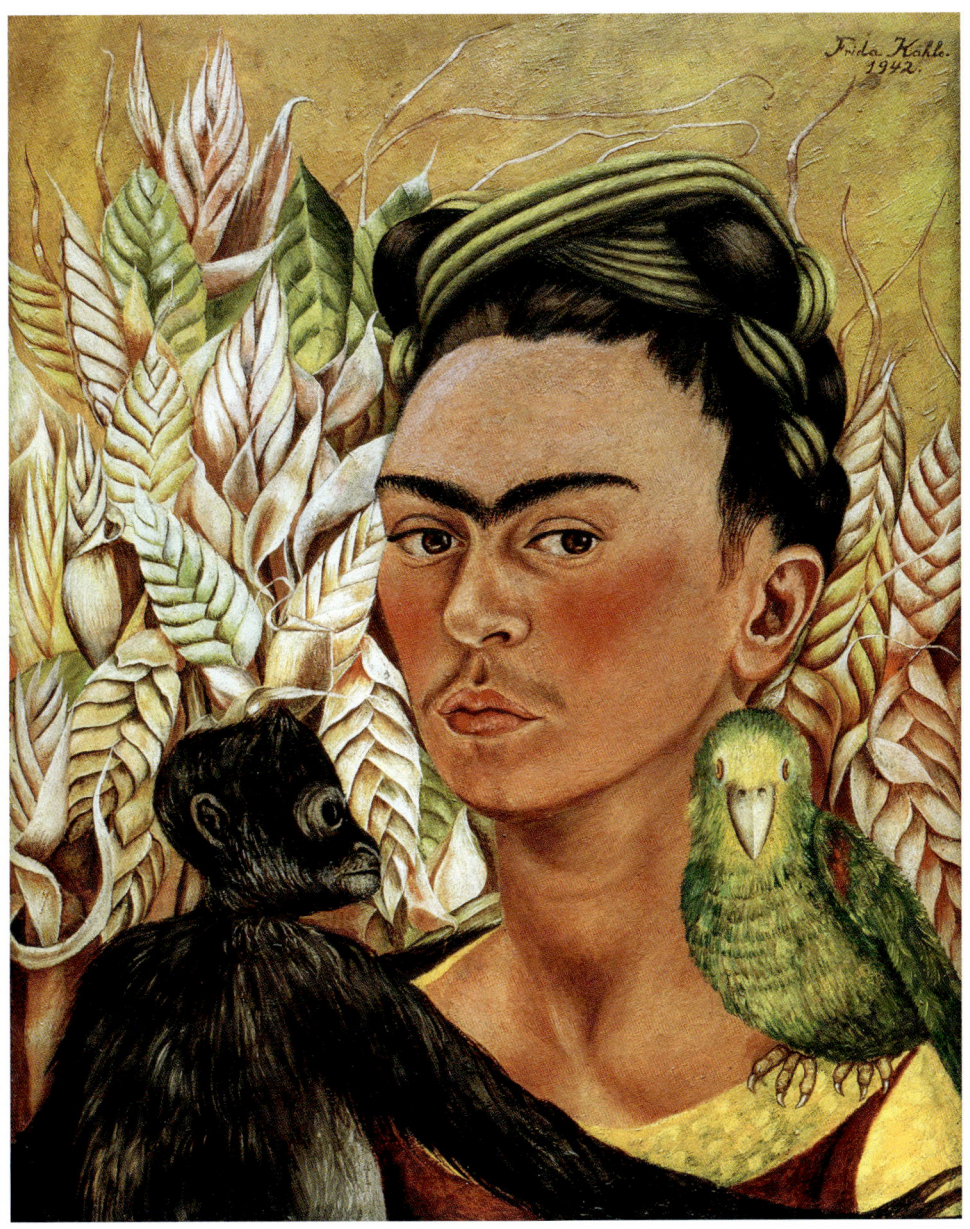

Page 240
Nickolas Muray, **Self-portrait with Frida Kahlo in her studio** (detail), Coyoacán, 1941
Gelatin silver print, 27.9 x 27.9 cm (11 x 11 in.)
New York, collection of Spencer Throckmorton/Nickolas Muray Photo Archives

Page 241
Self-portrait (Me and My Parrots), August 1941
Oil on canvas, 82 x 62.8 cm (32¼ x 24¾ in.). Private collection

Page 242
Self-portrait (with Bonito), 1941
Oil on masonite, 54.6 x 43.2 cm (21½ x 17 in.)
Private collection, courtesy Thomas Amman Fine Art, AG Zurich

Page 243
Self-portrait (with Monkey and Parrot), 1942
Oil on masonite, 54.6 x 43.2 cm (21½ x 17 in.)
Museo de Arte Latinoamericano de Buenos Aires, Fundación Costantini,
gift of Eduardo F. Costantini 2001, inv. 2003.34

Self-portrait (dedicated to Sigmund Firestone), February 1940
Oil on masonite, 61 x 43 cm (24 x 16⅞ in.); inscribed on the paper nailed to the wall,
t. r.: México, Coyoacán. / Para el Señor / Sigmund Firestone y / sus hijas Alberta y /
Natalia pinté éste / autorretrato con todo / cariño, en Febrero de / 1940. Frida Kahlo
(Mexico, Coyoacán. / For Mr. / Sigmund Firestone and / his daughters Alberta and /
Natalia, I painted this / self-portrait with great / affection, in February / 1940. Frida Kahlo)
Private collection, courtesy Mary-Anne Martin/Fine Art, New York

Pages 246/247
Roots, 1943
Oil on metal, 30.5 x 49.9 cm (12 x 19⅝ in.)
Private collection

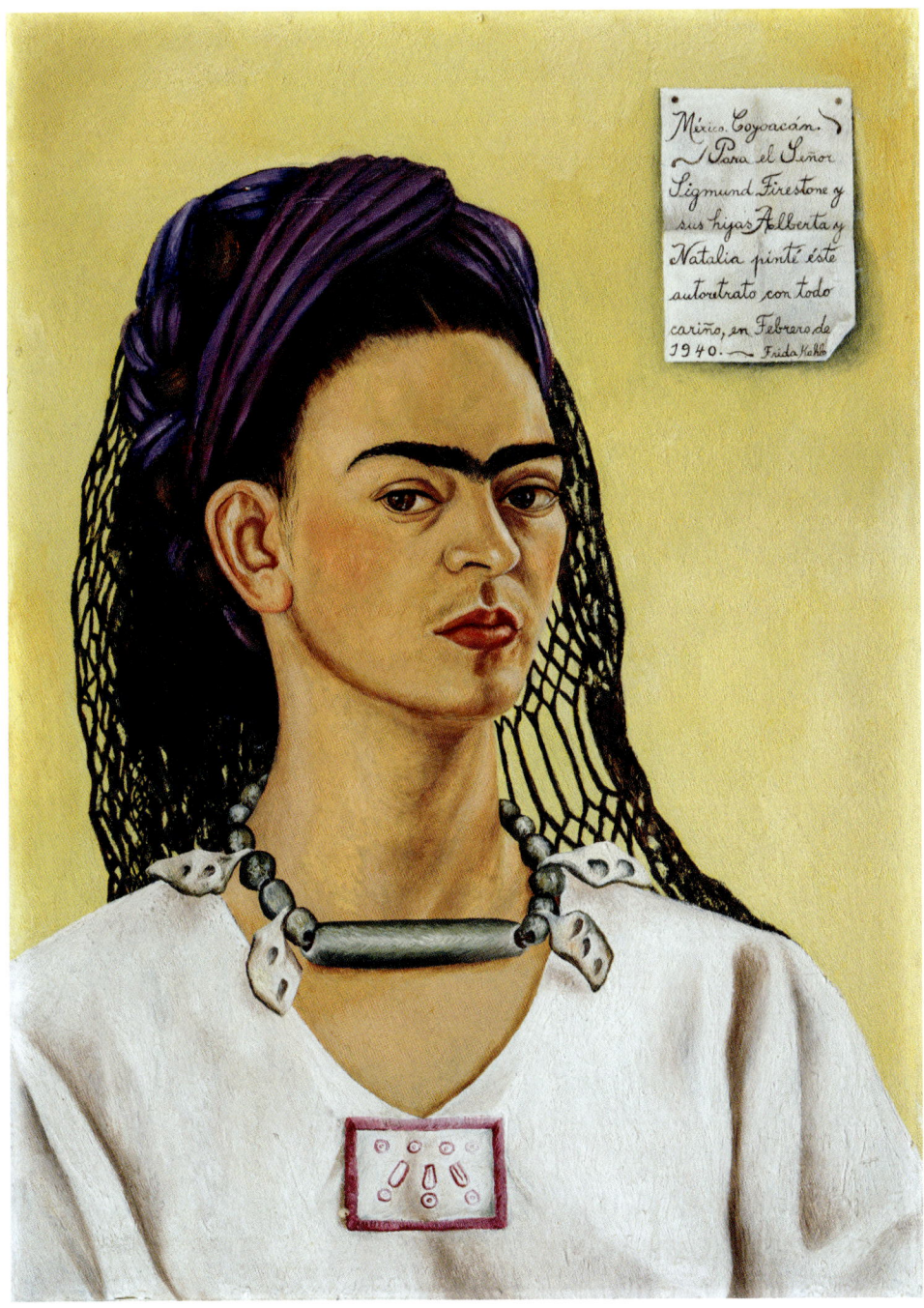

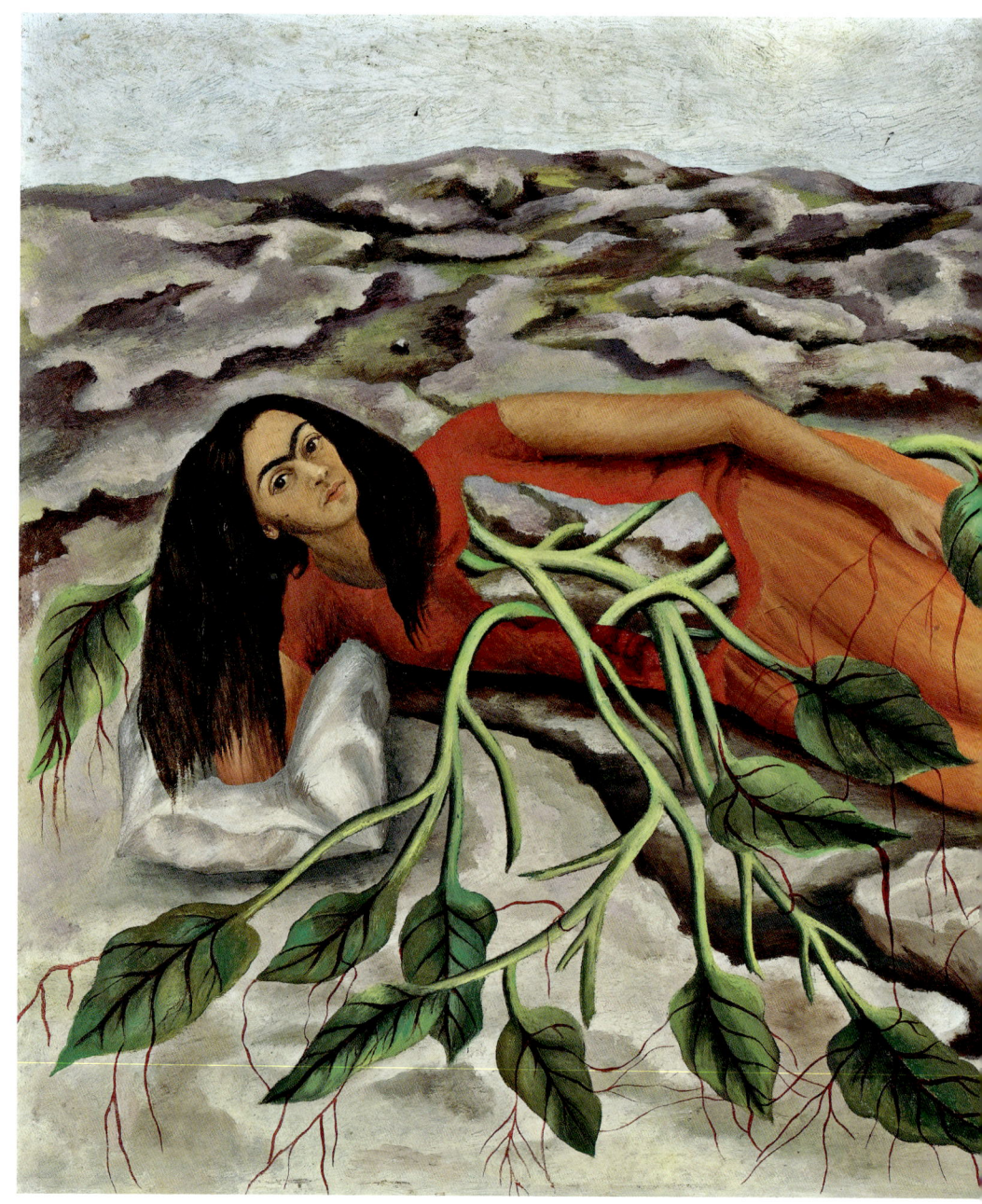

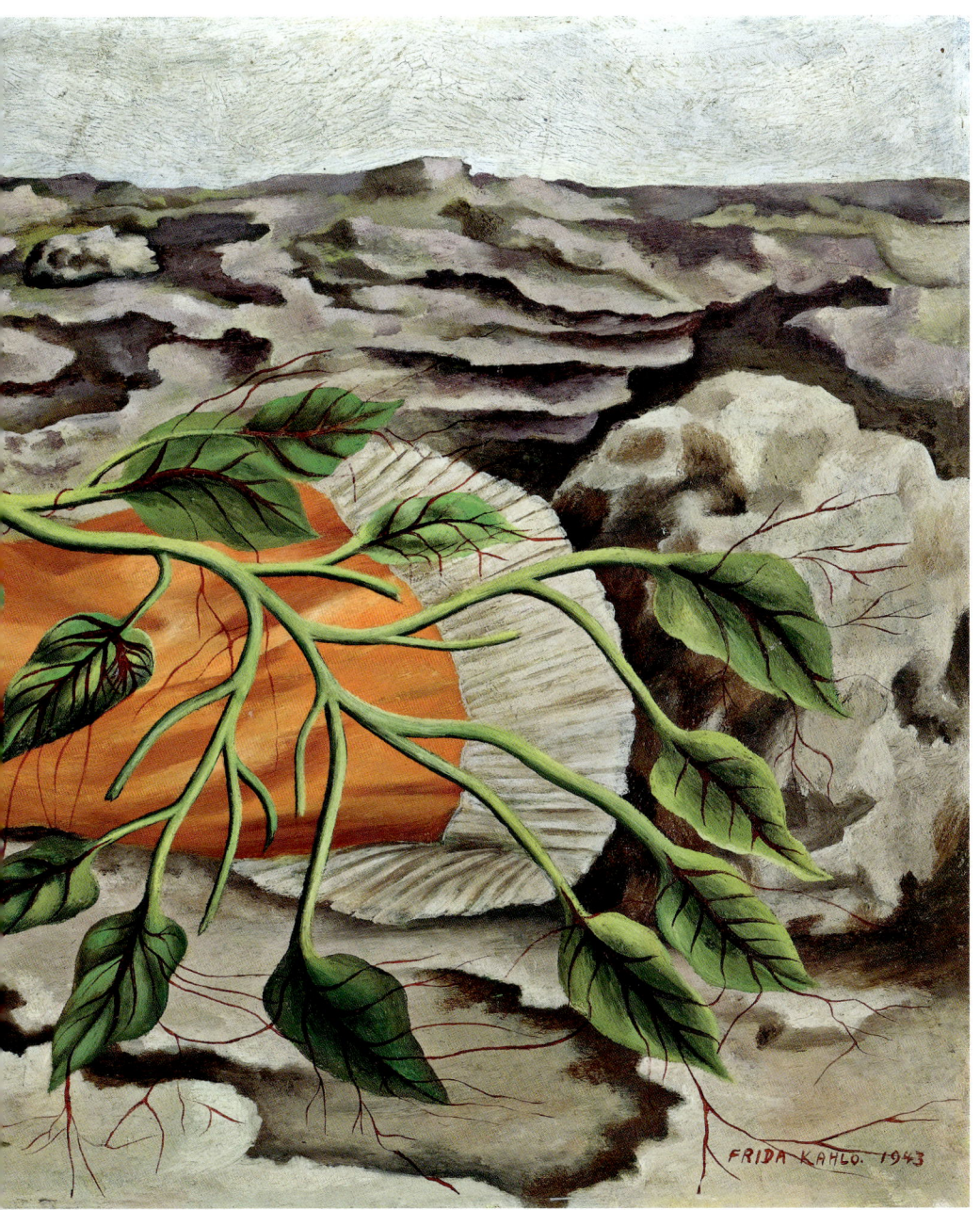

Thinking about Death, 1943
Oil on canvas, mounted on masonite, 44.5 x 36.3 cm (17½ x 14¼ in.)
Private collection, courtesy Sotheby's, Mexico

Page 250
Bernard G. Silberstein, **Diego Rivera watching Frida Kahlo
while she paints** *Self-portrait (Diego on My Mind)* (detail), c. 1940
Gelatin silver print, 24.4 x 19.4 cm (9⅝ x 7¾ in.)
New York, collection of Spencer Throckmorton

Page 251
Self-portrait (Diego on My Mind), 1943
Oil on masonite, 76 x 61 cm (30 x 24 in.)
Mexico, The Jacques and Natasha Gelman Collection
of 20th-century Mexican Art/The Vergel Foundation

Page 252
Self-portrait (with Braid), 1941
Oil on canvas, 51 x 38.5 cm (20⅛ x 15⅛ in.)
Mexico, The Jacques and Natasha Gelman Collection
of 20th-century Mexican Art/The Vergel Foundation

Page 253
Self-portrait with Small Monkey (and Señor Xolotl), 1945
Oil on masonite, 56 x 41.5 cm (22 x 16⅜ in.)
Mexico City, Xochimilco, Museo Dolores Olmedo

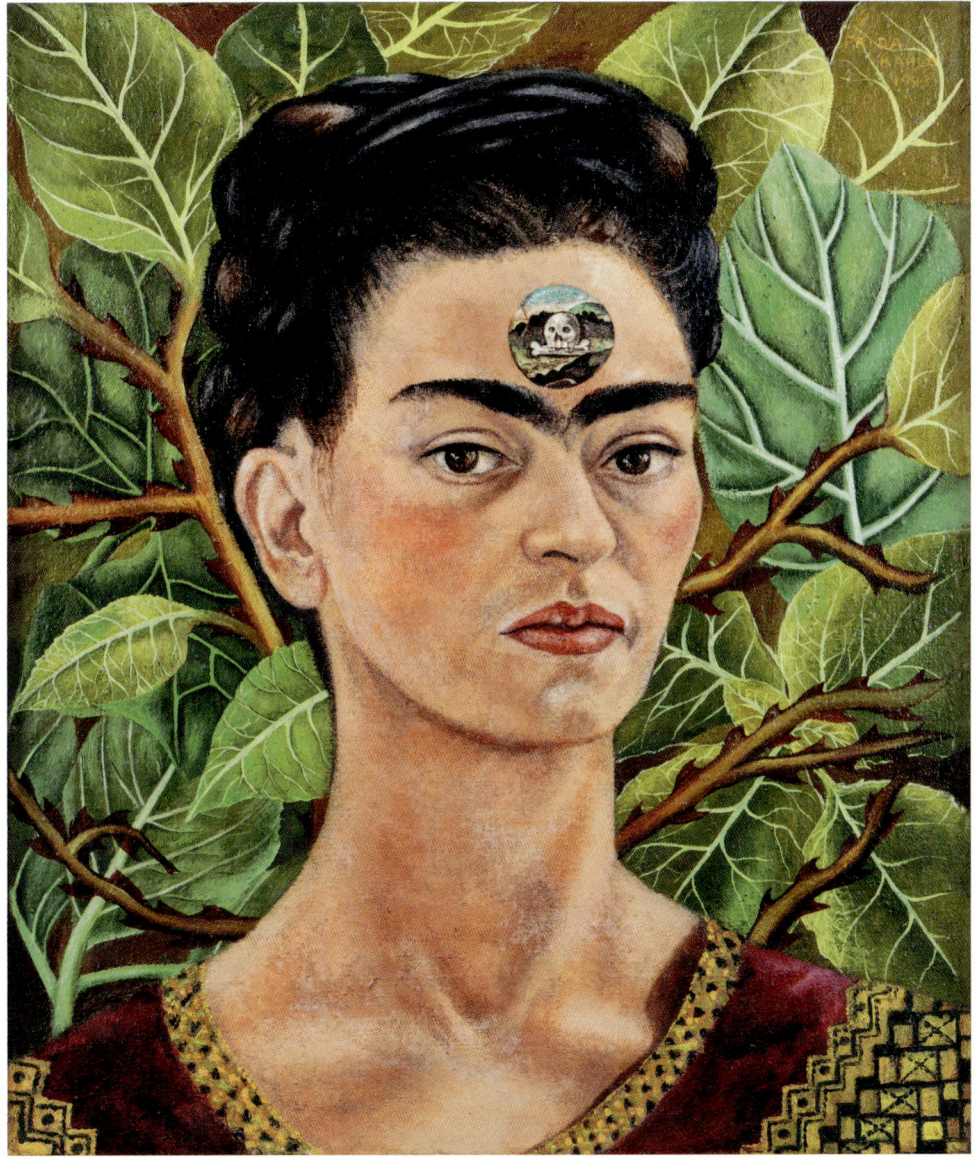

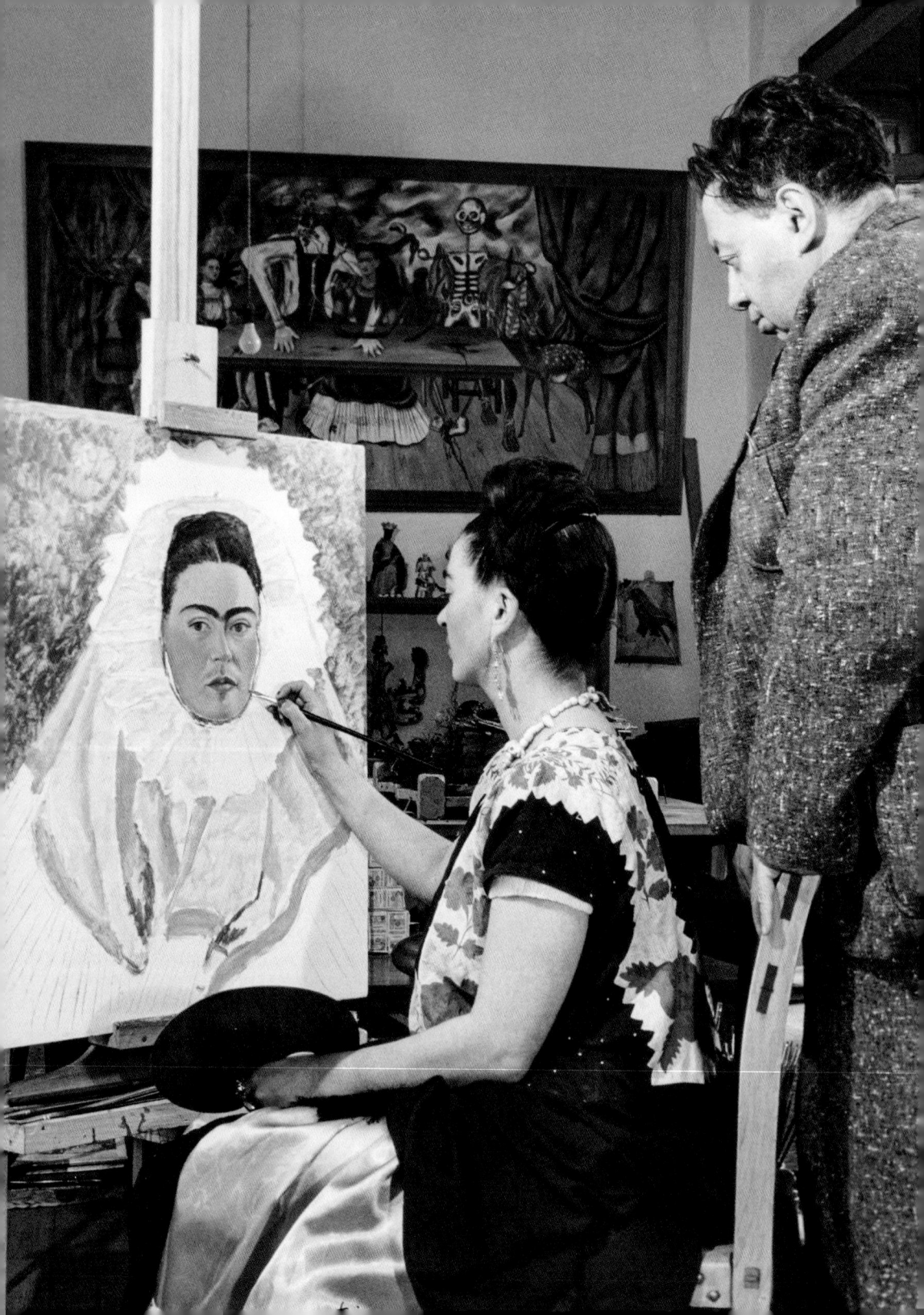

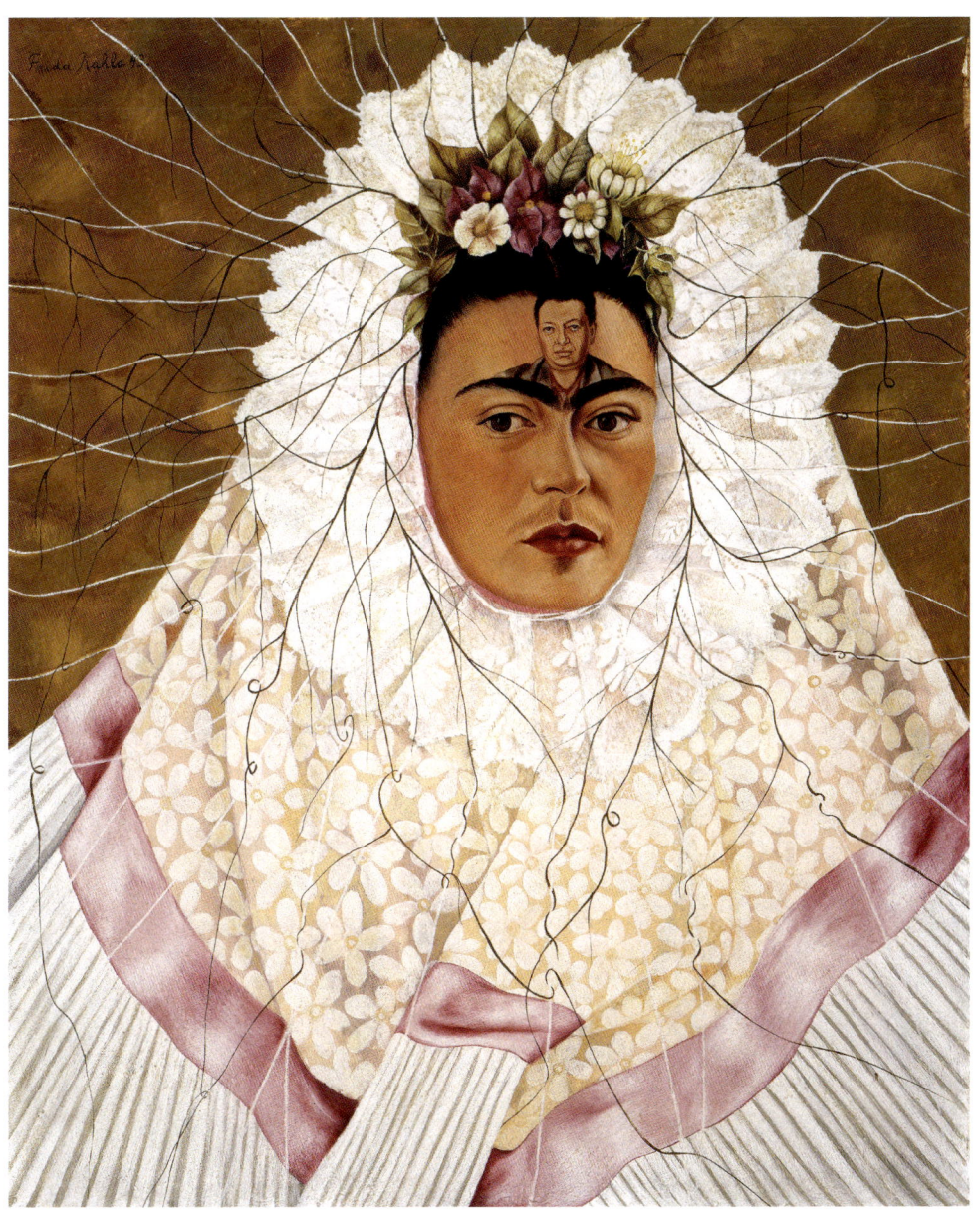

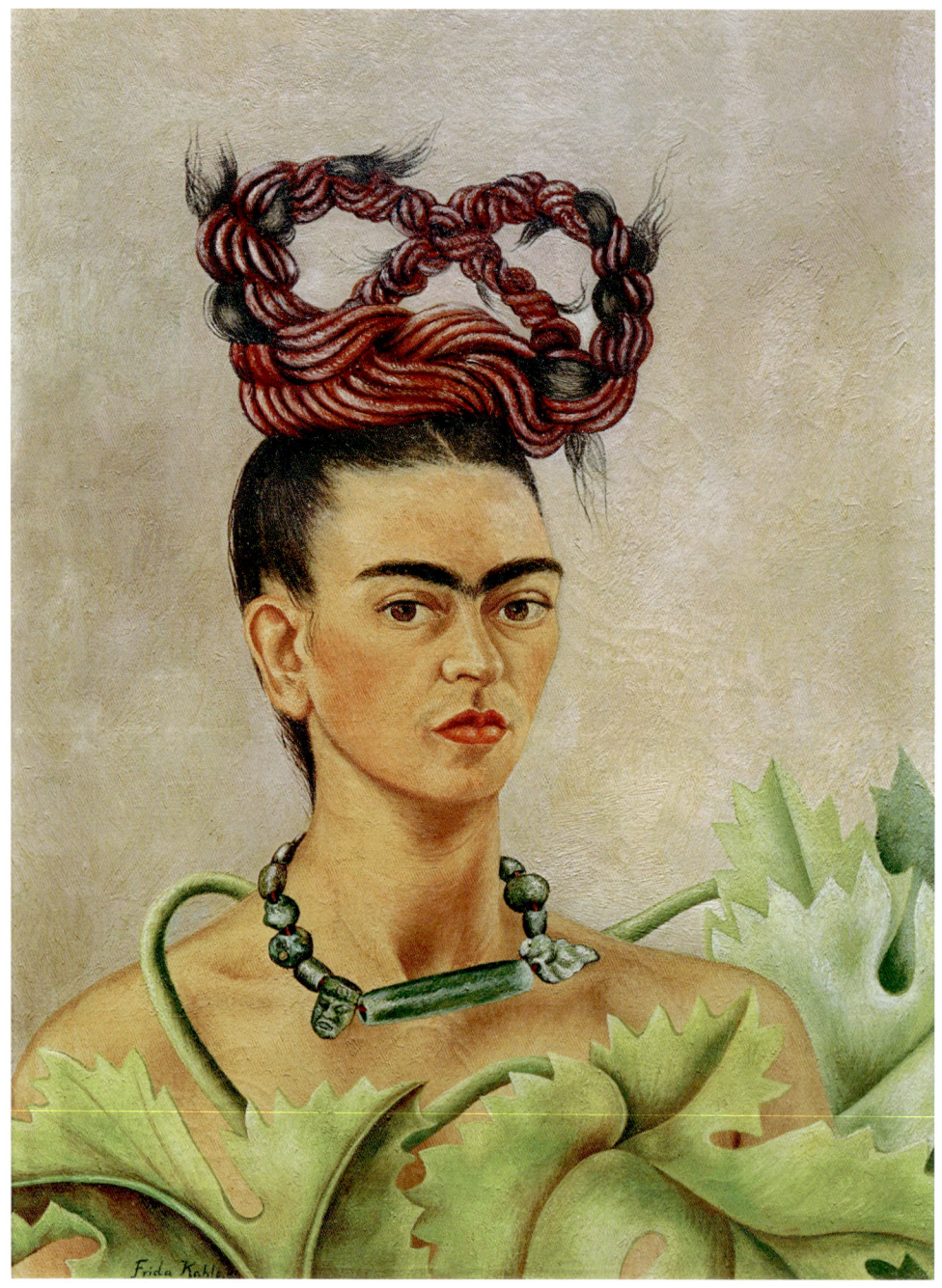

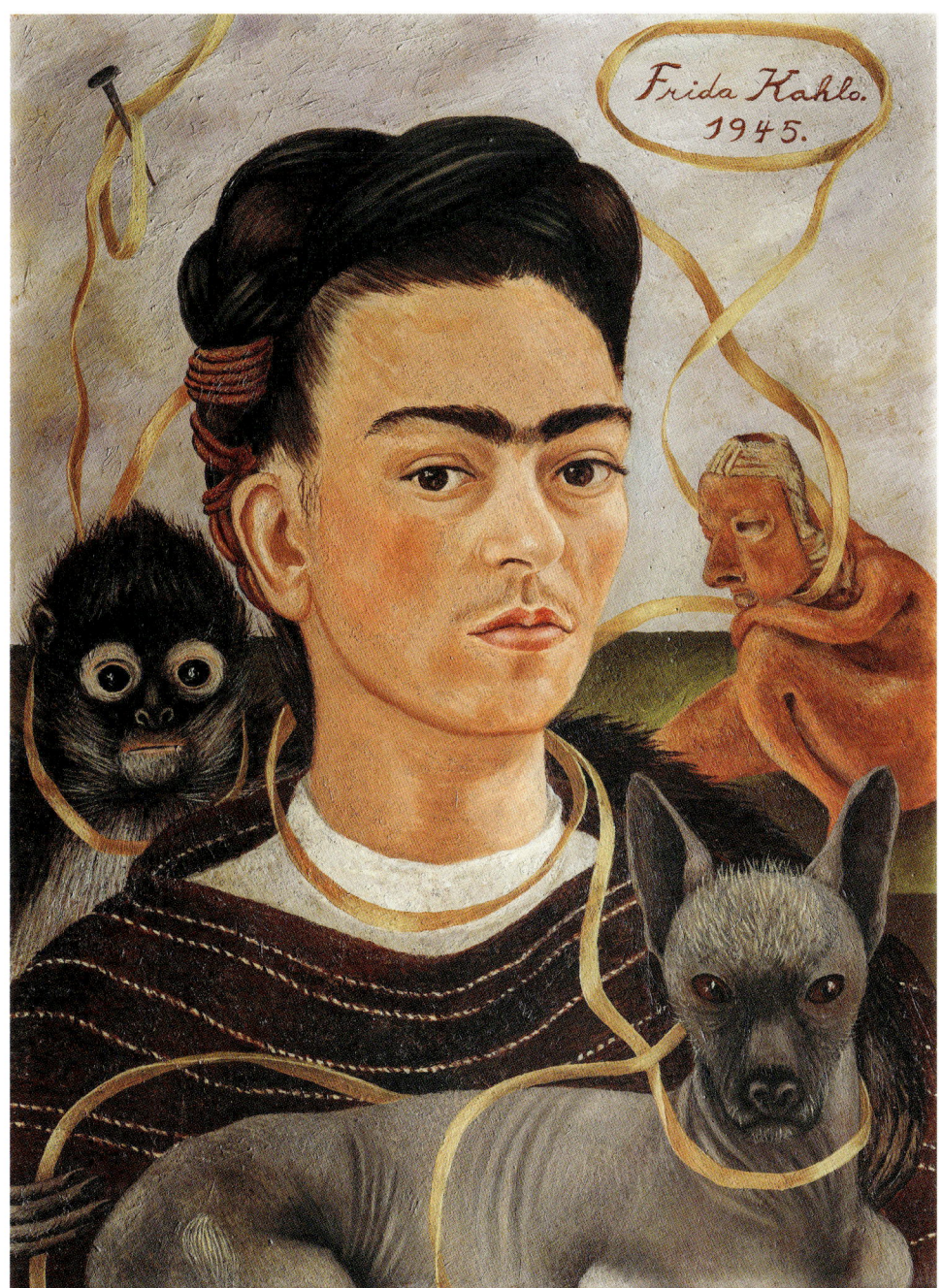

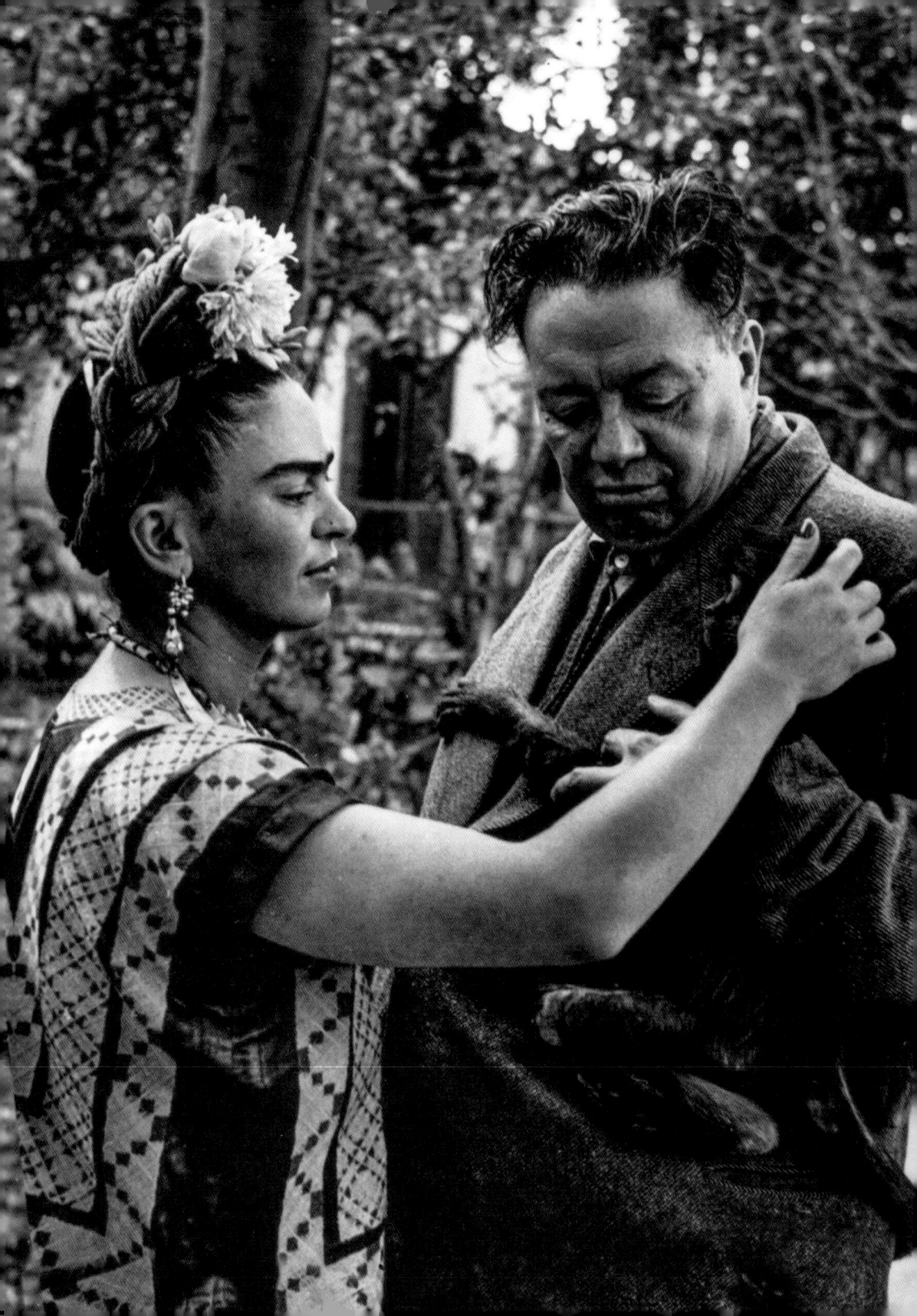

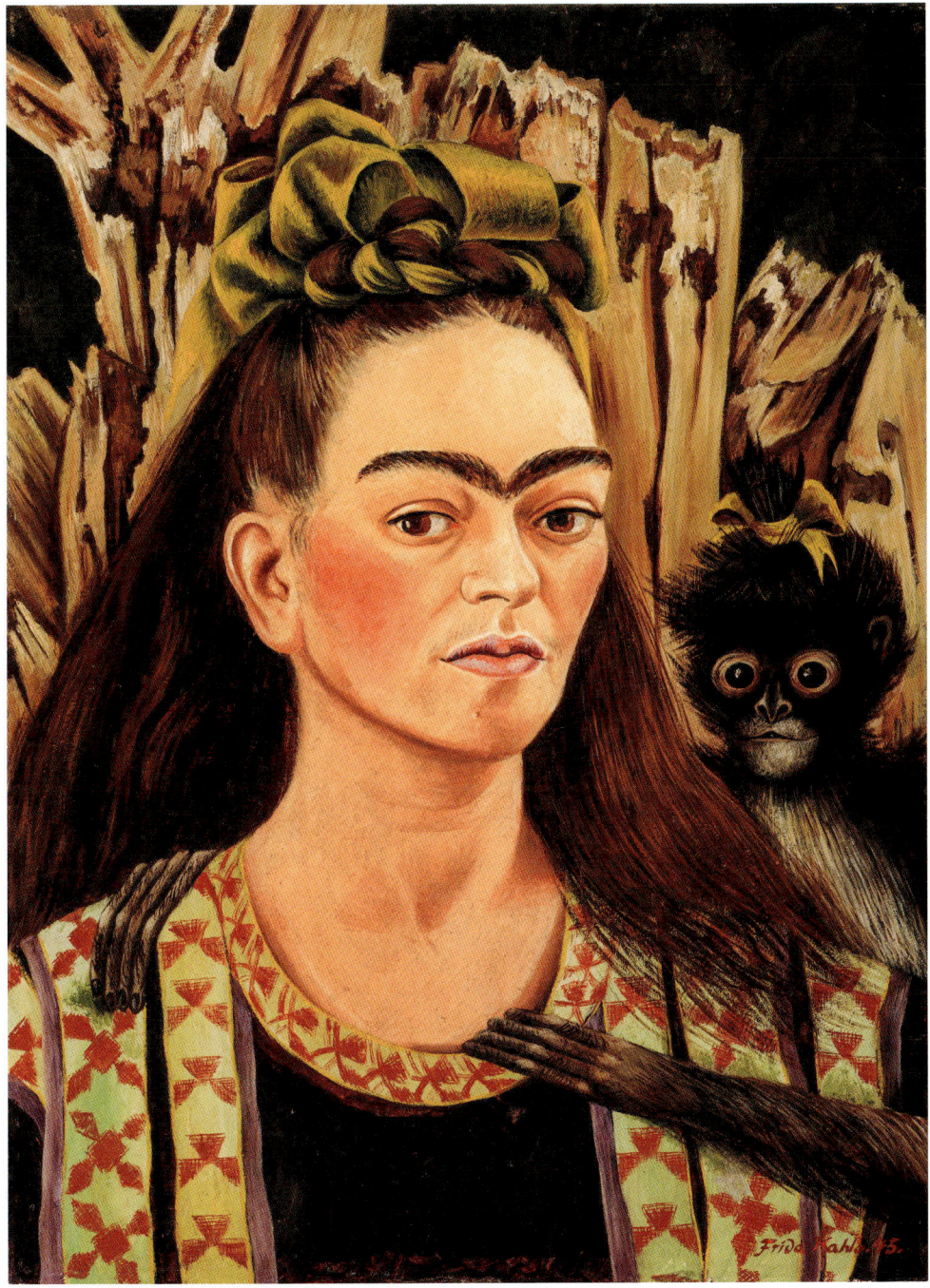

Page 254
Wallace Marly, **Kahlo and Rivera with pet monkey**, c. 1944

Page 255
Self-portrait with Monkey, 1945
Oil on masonite, 60 x 42.4 cm (23⅝ x 16¾ in.)
Cuernavaca, Museo Robert Brady

The Broken Column, c. 1944
Oil on plaster corset with straps
Mexico City, Coyoacán, Museo Frida Kahlo

The Broken Column, 1944
Oil on canvas, mounted on masonite, 39.8 x 30.5 cm (15⅝ x 12 in.)
Mexico City, Xochimilco, Museo Dolores Olmedo

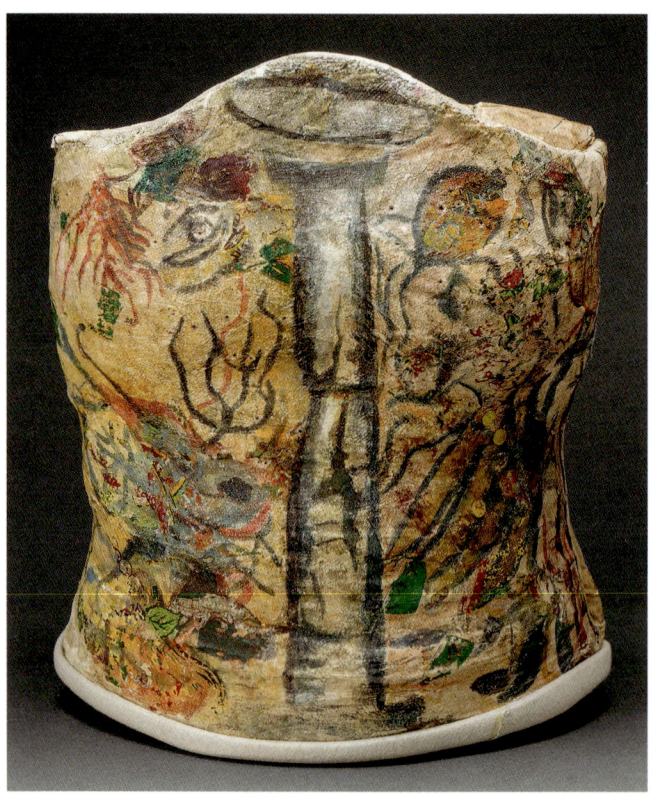

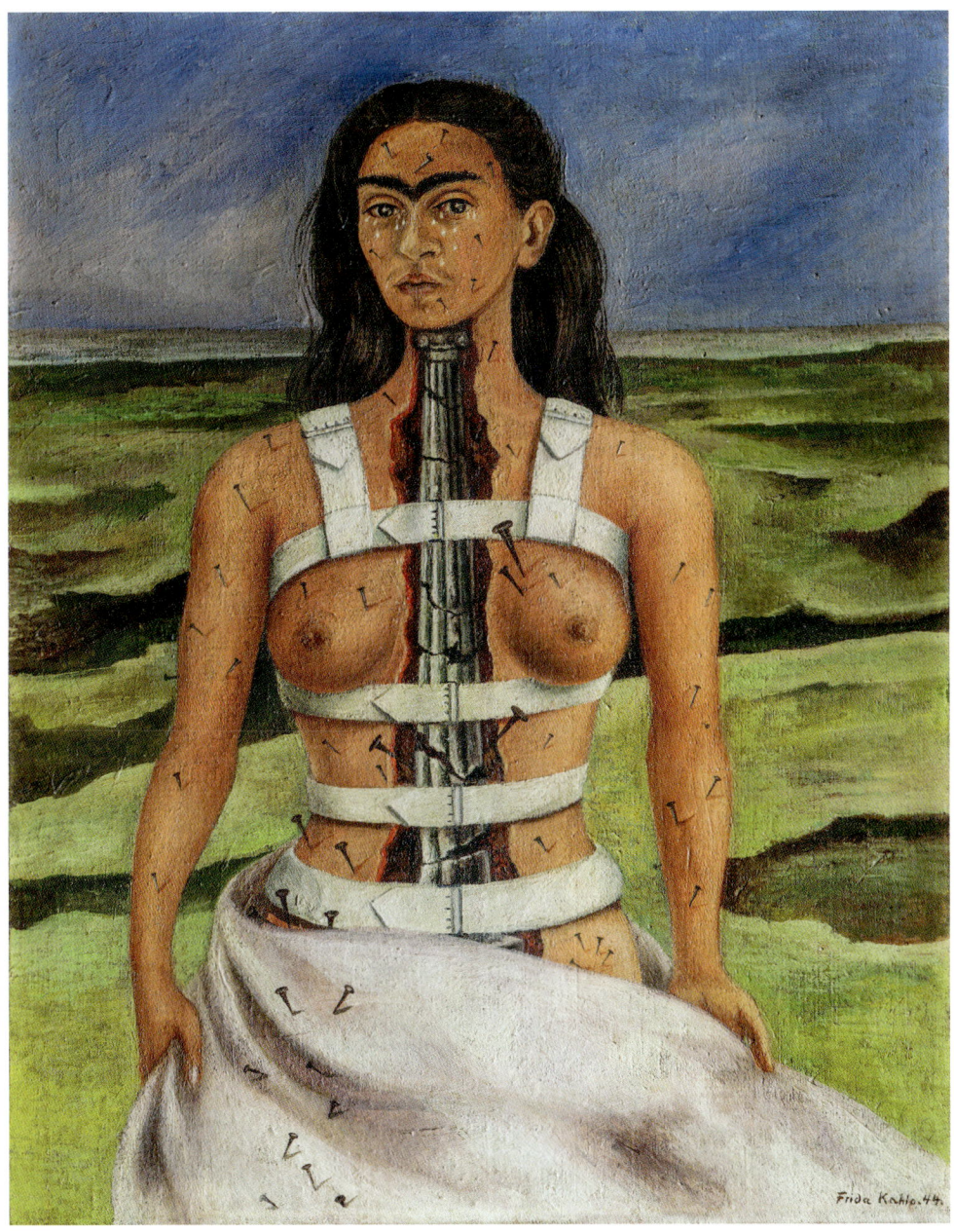

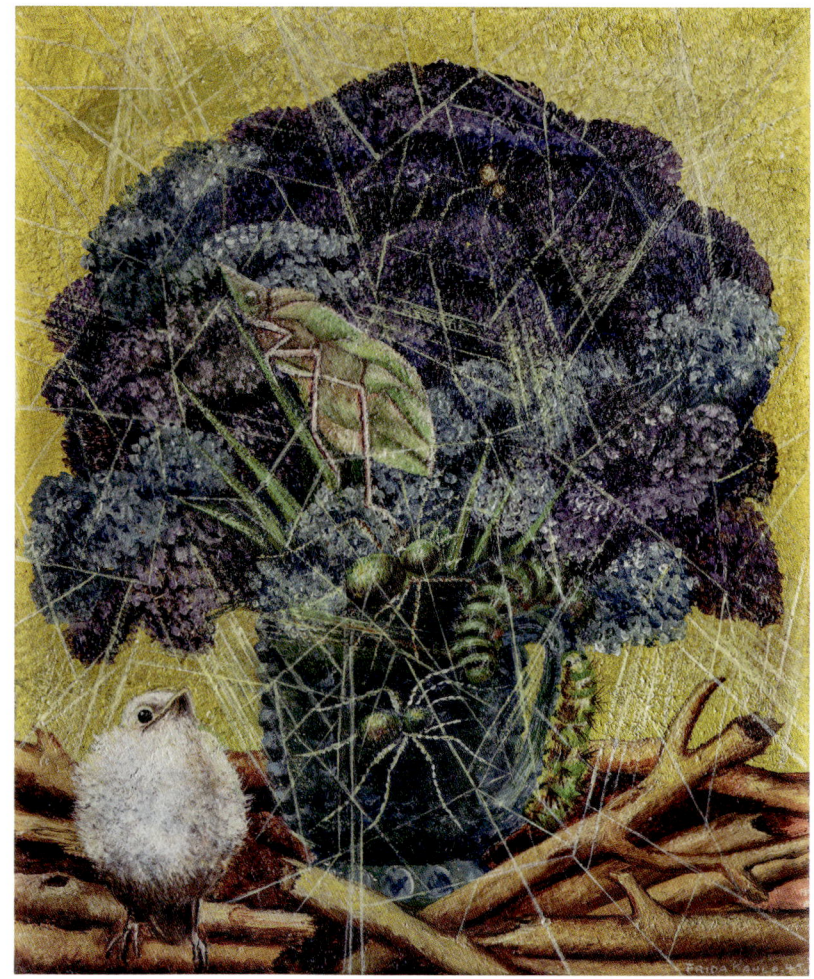

The Chick (Spiders), 1945
Oil on masonite, 27.2 x 22.2 cm (10¾ x 8¾ in.)
Mexico City, Xochimilco, Museo Dolores Olmedo

The Mask, 1945
Oil on canvas, 40 x 30.5 cm (15¾ x 12 in.)
Mexico City, Xochimilco, Museo Dolores Olmedo

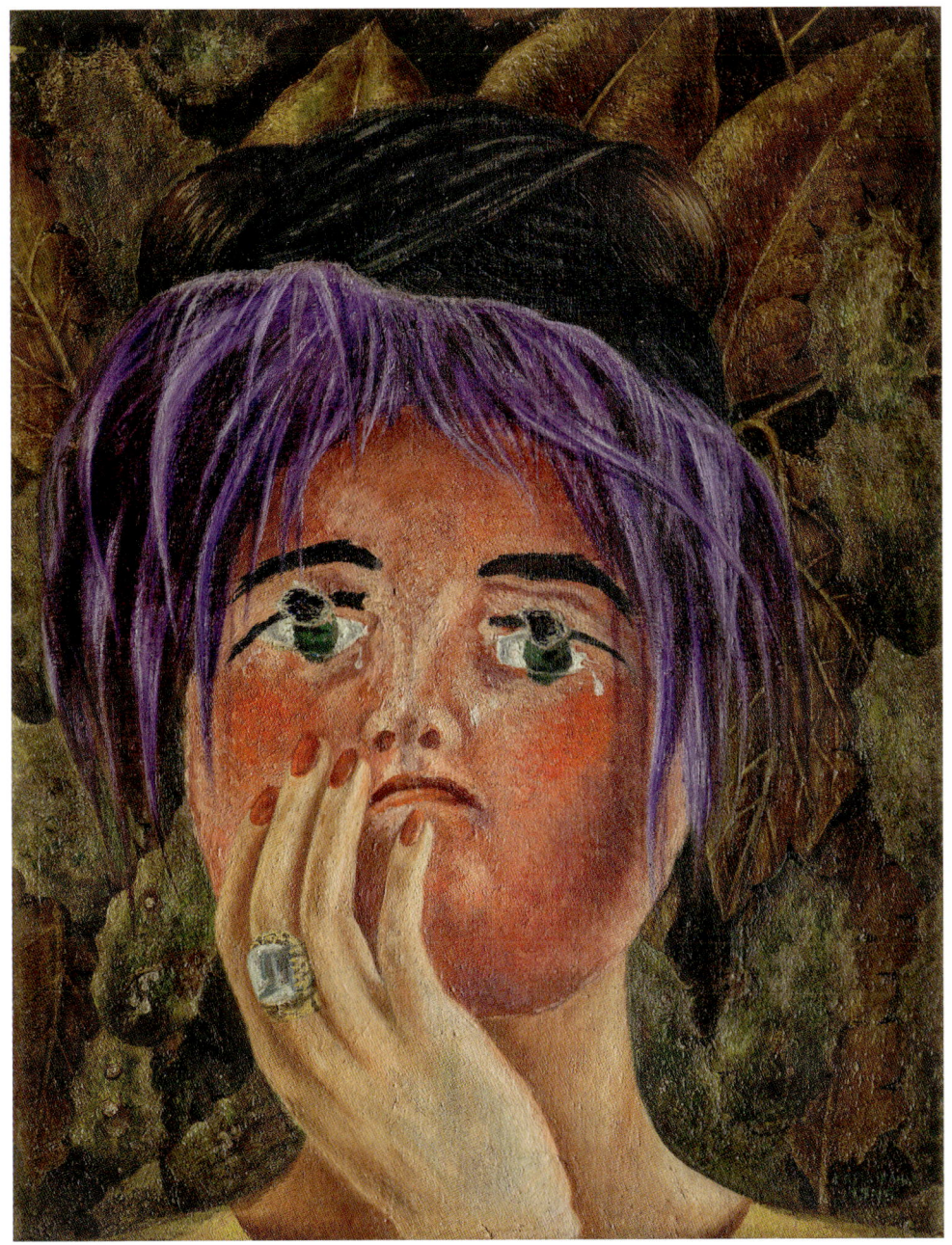

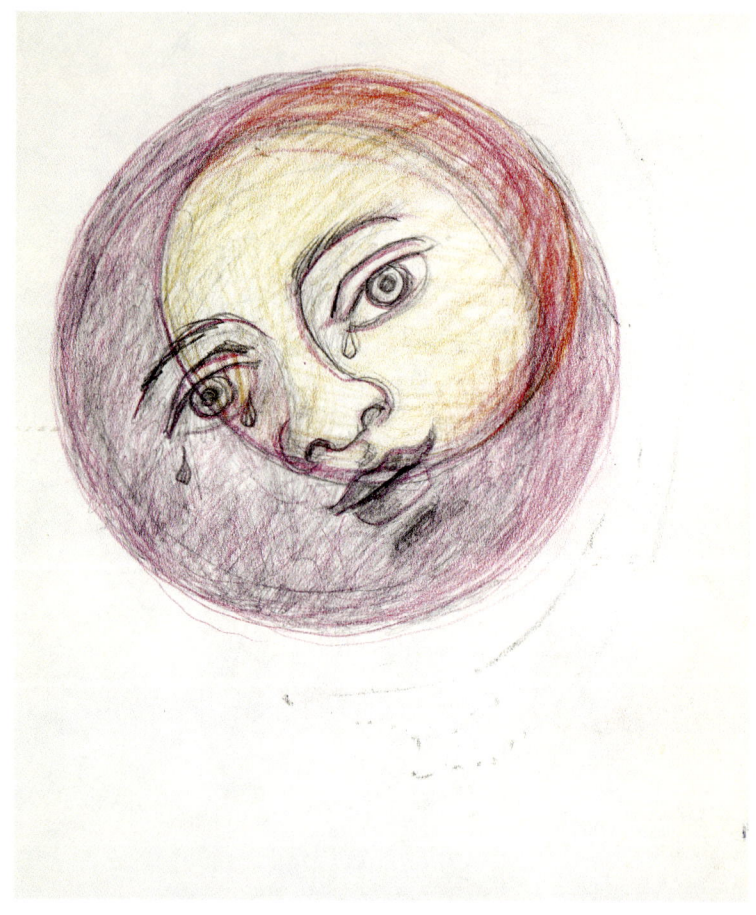

Sun and Moon, *c.* 1946
Graphite pencil, colored pencils, and Conté crayon on paper,
19.5 x 16 cm (7⅝ x 6¼ in.). Private collection
(recto of page 261)

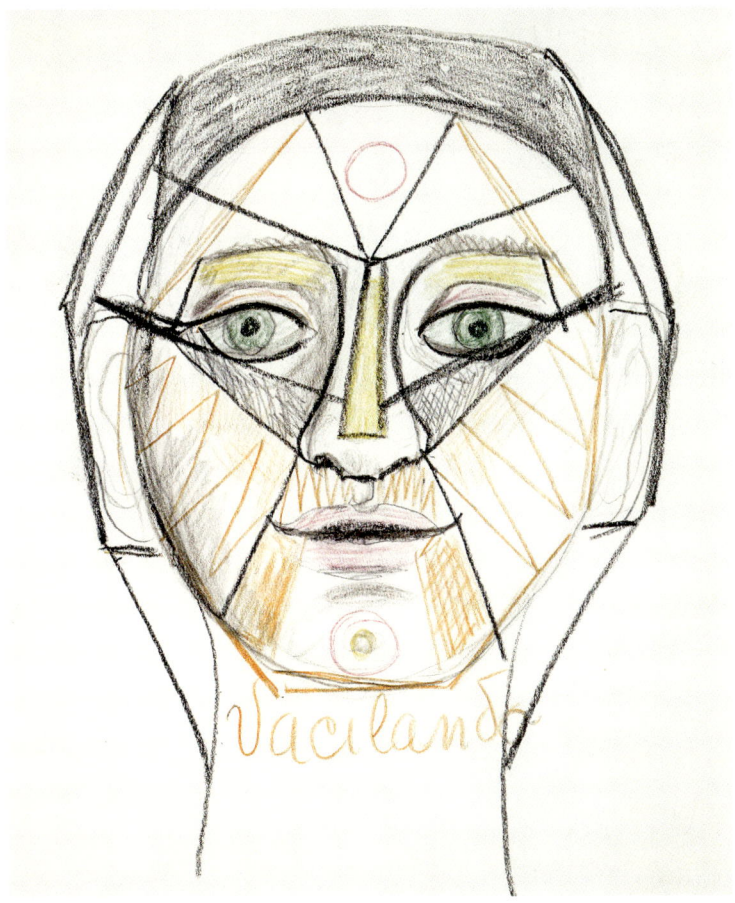

Wavering, *c.* 1946
Conté crayon, colored pencils, and graphite pencil on paper,
19.5 x 16 cm (7⅝ x 6¼ in.). Private collection
(verso of page 260)

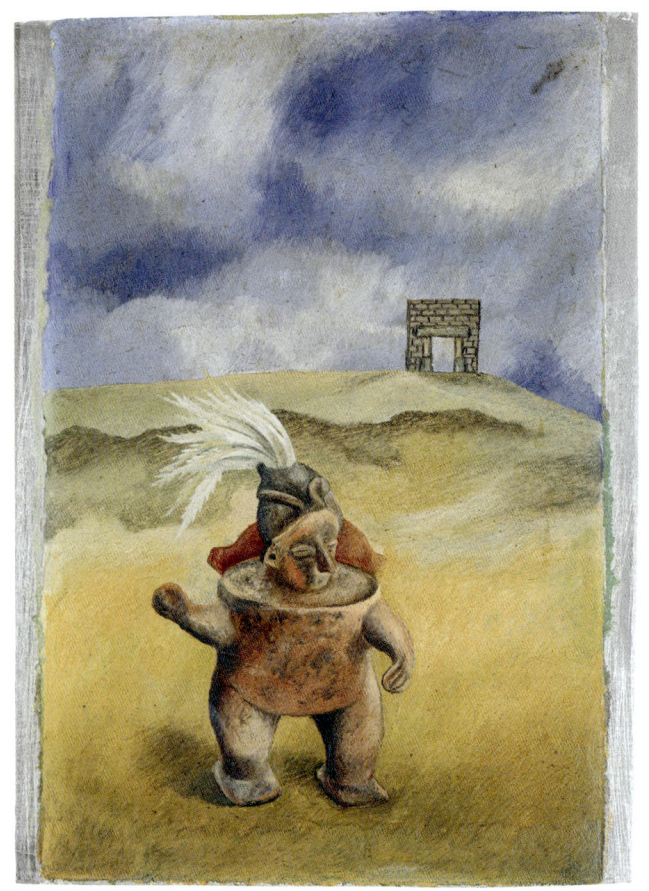

Survivor, *c.* 1938
Oil on tinplate, 17 x 12 cm (6¾ x 4¾ in.)
Juan Antonio Pérez Simón collection

The Girl, the Moon, and the Sun, 1942
Oil on masonite, 54.6 x 43.1 cm (21½ x 17 in.)
Mexico City, Juan Antonio Pérez Simón collection

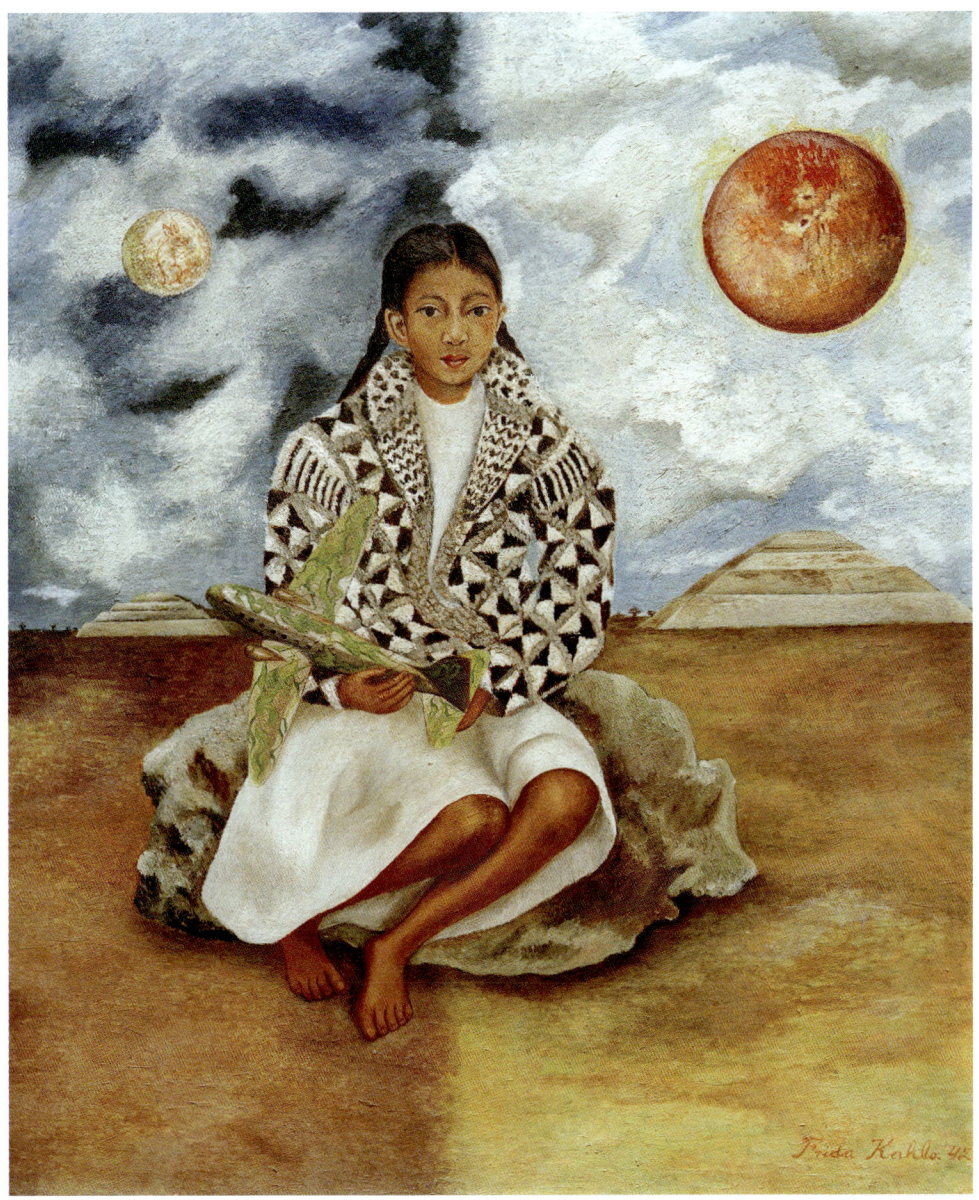

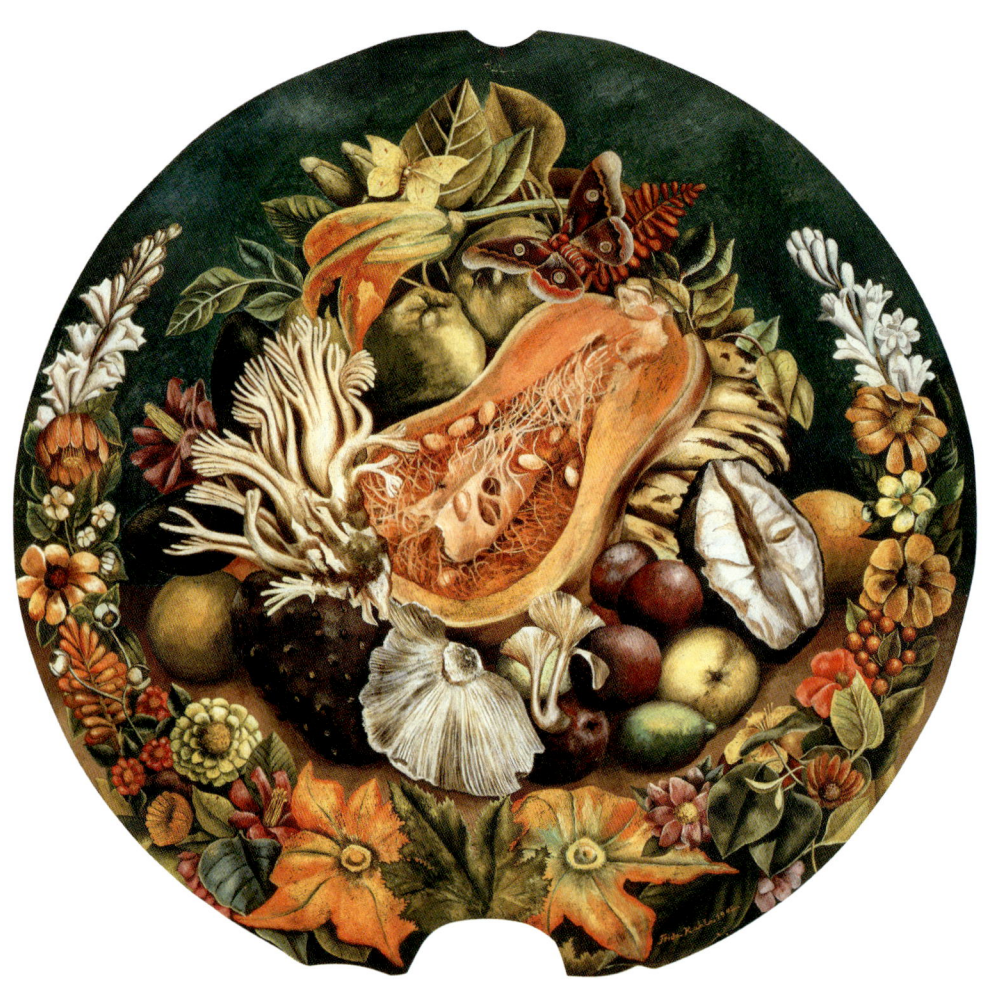

Still Life, 1942
Oil on copper, diameter 63 cm (24¾ in.)
Mexico City, Coyoacán, Museo Frida Kahlo

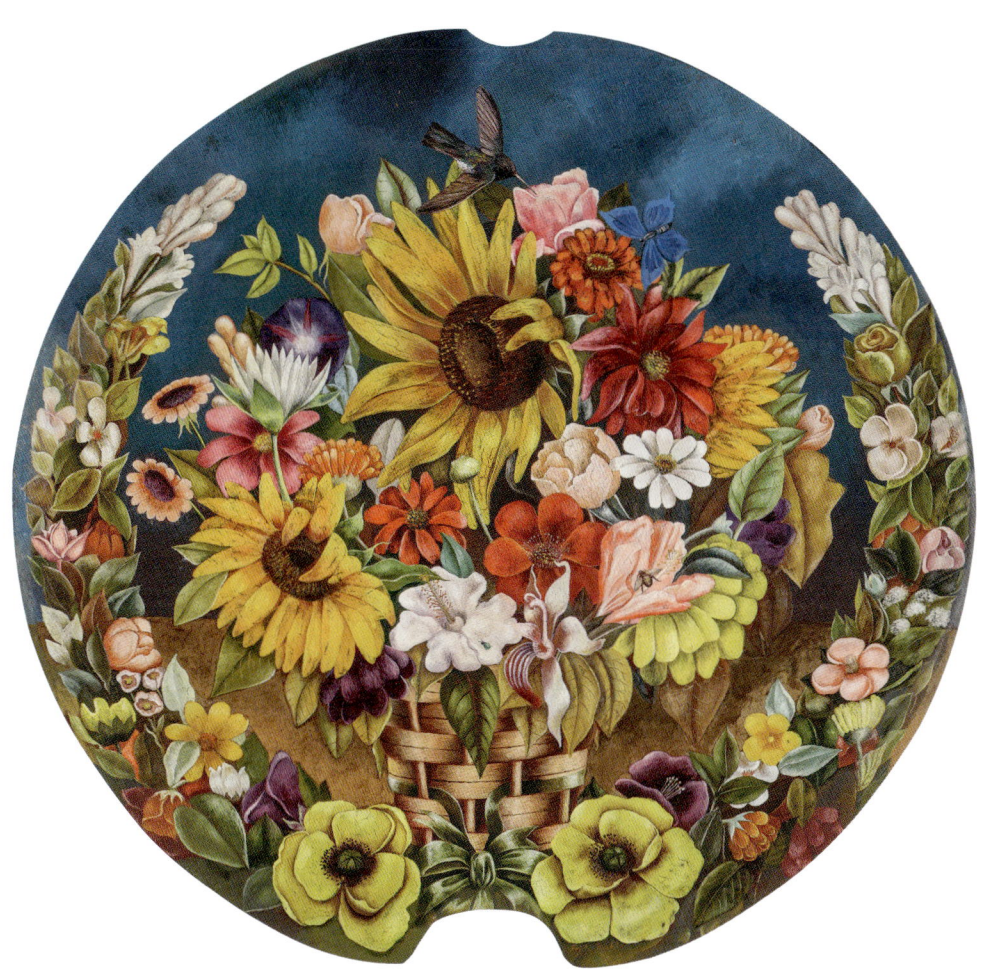

The Flower Basket, 1941
Oil on copper, diameter 65 cm (25⅝ in.)
United States, private collection, courtesy Christie's, New York

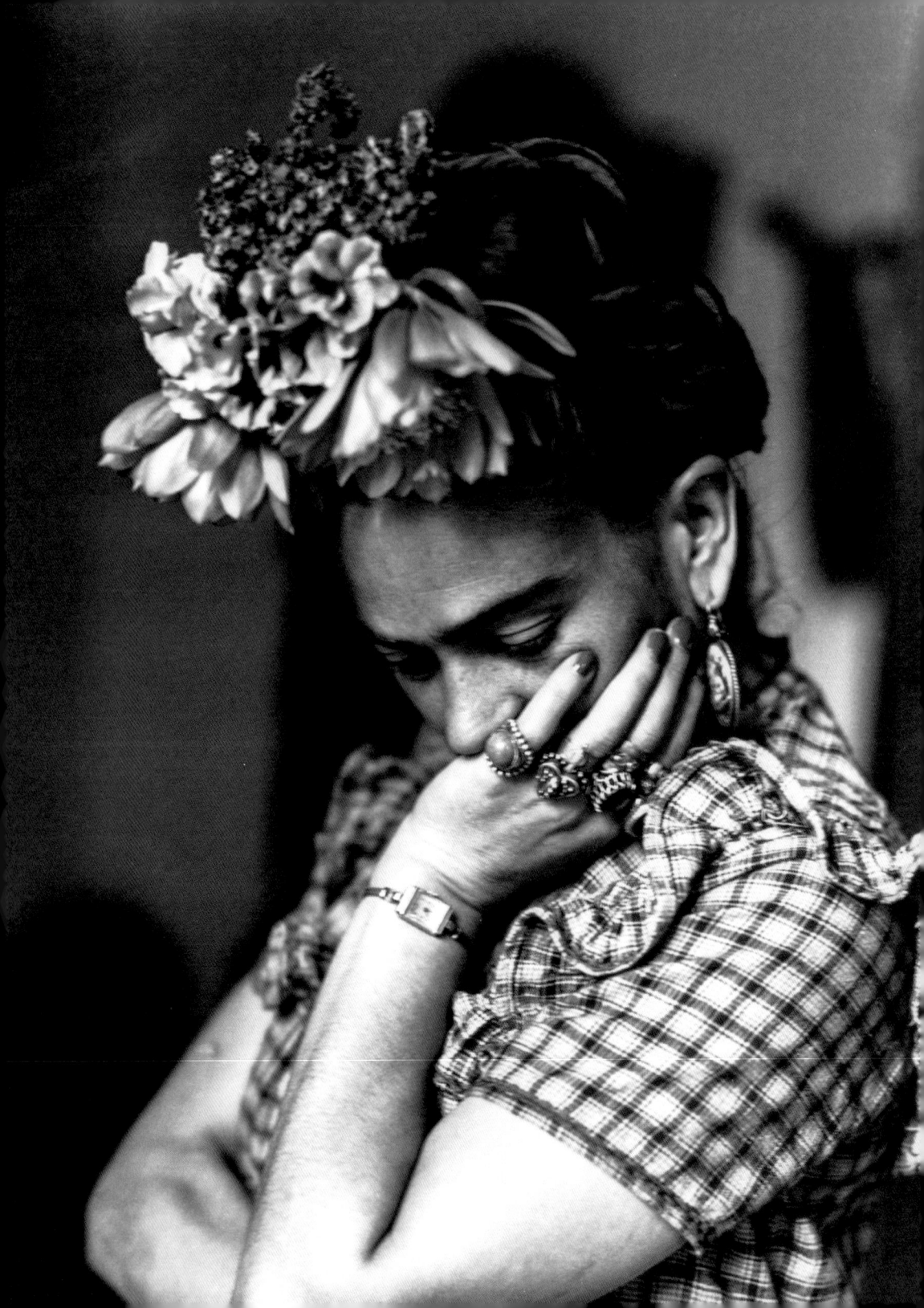

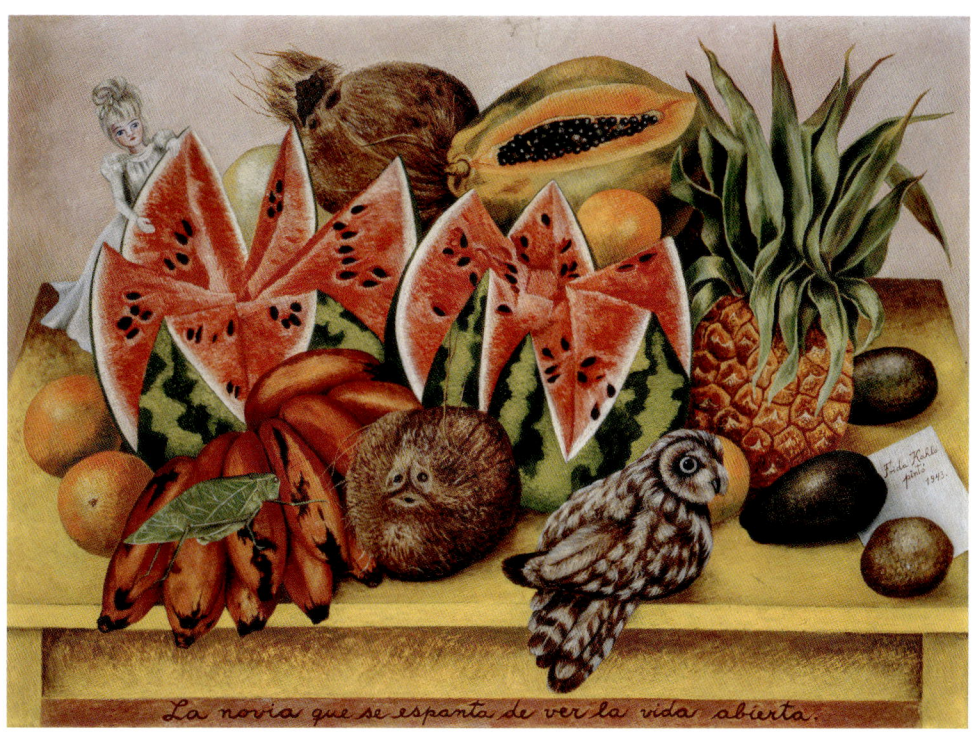

Sylvia Salmi, **Frida Kahlo**, 1944

The Bride Frightened at Seeing Life Opened, 1943
Oil on canvas, 63 x 81.5 cm (24¾ x 32⅛ in.)
Mexico, The Jacques and Natasha Gelman Collection
of 20th-century Mexican Art/The Vergel Foundation

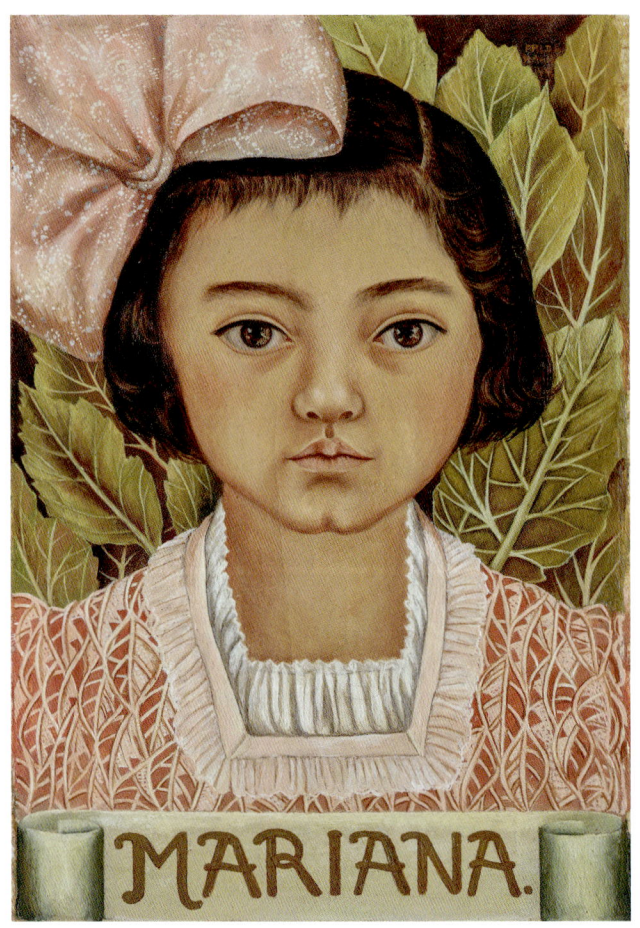

Mariana, 1944
Oil on canvas, 40 x 28.5 cm (15¾ x 11¼ in.)
New York, private collection

Portrait of Doña Rosita Morillo, 1944
Oil on canvas, mounted on masonite, 76 x 60.5 cm (29⅞ x 23⅞ in.)
Mexico City, Xochimilco, Museo Dolores Olmedo

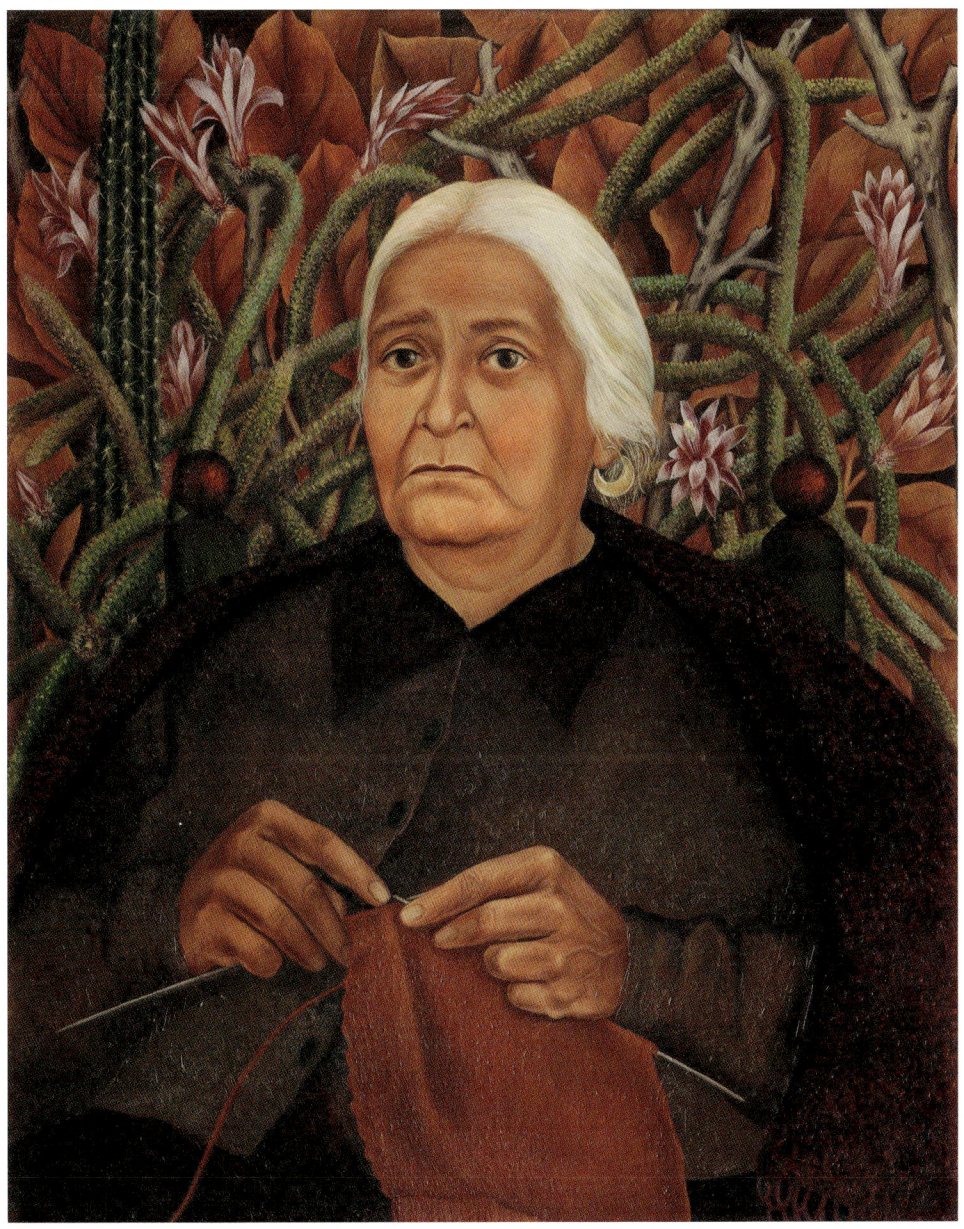

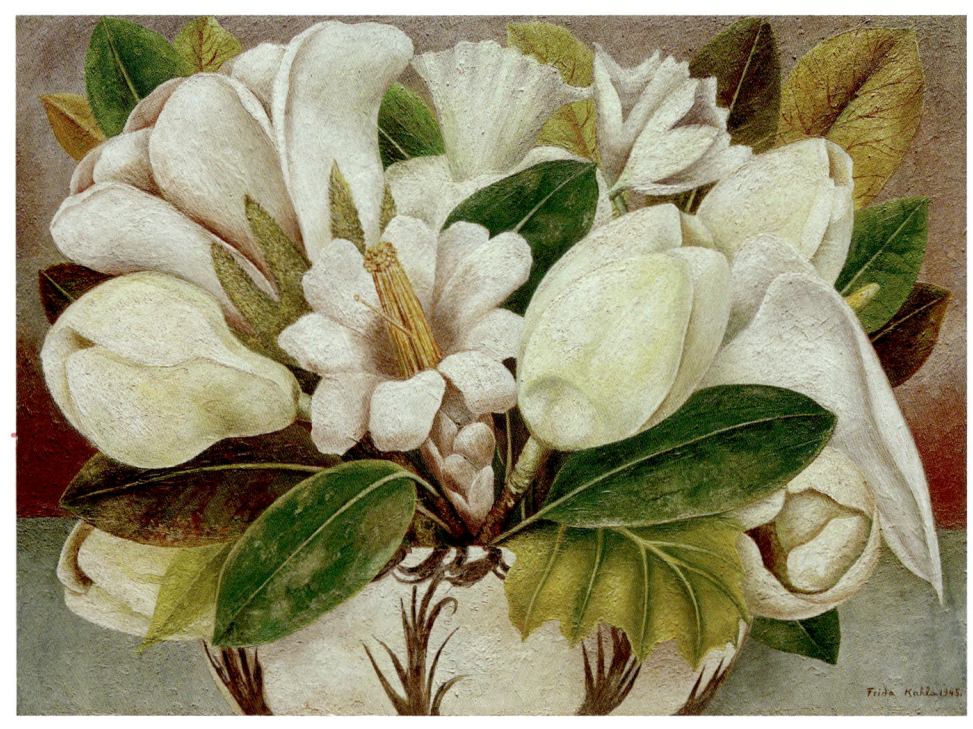

Magnolias, 1945
Oil on masonite, 41 x 57 cm (16⅛ x 22½ in.)
Mexico, private collection

The Flower of Life, 1944
Oil on masonite, 27.8 x 19.7 cm (11 x 7¾ in.)
Mexico City, Xochimilco, Museo Dolores Olmedo

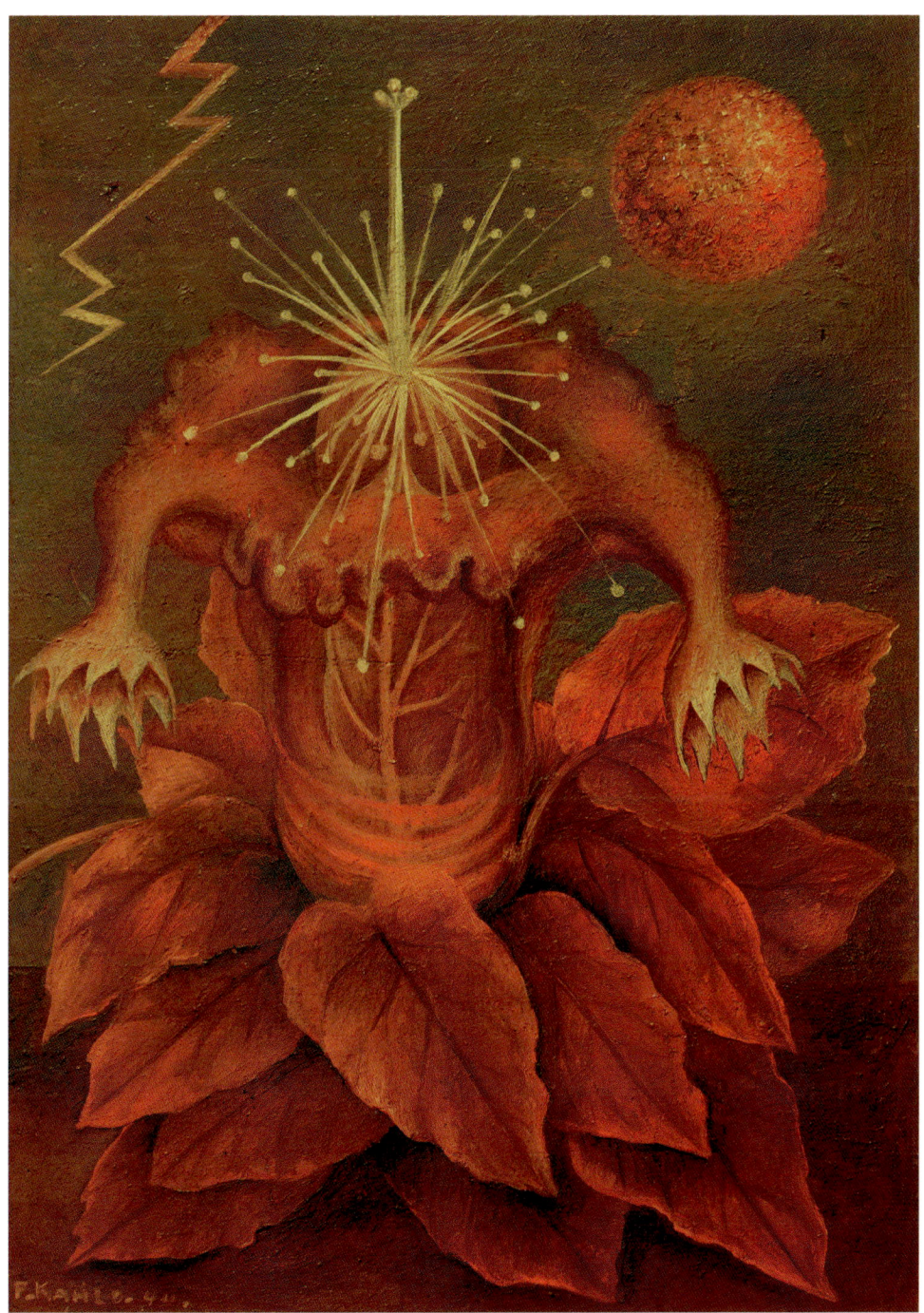

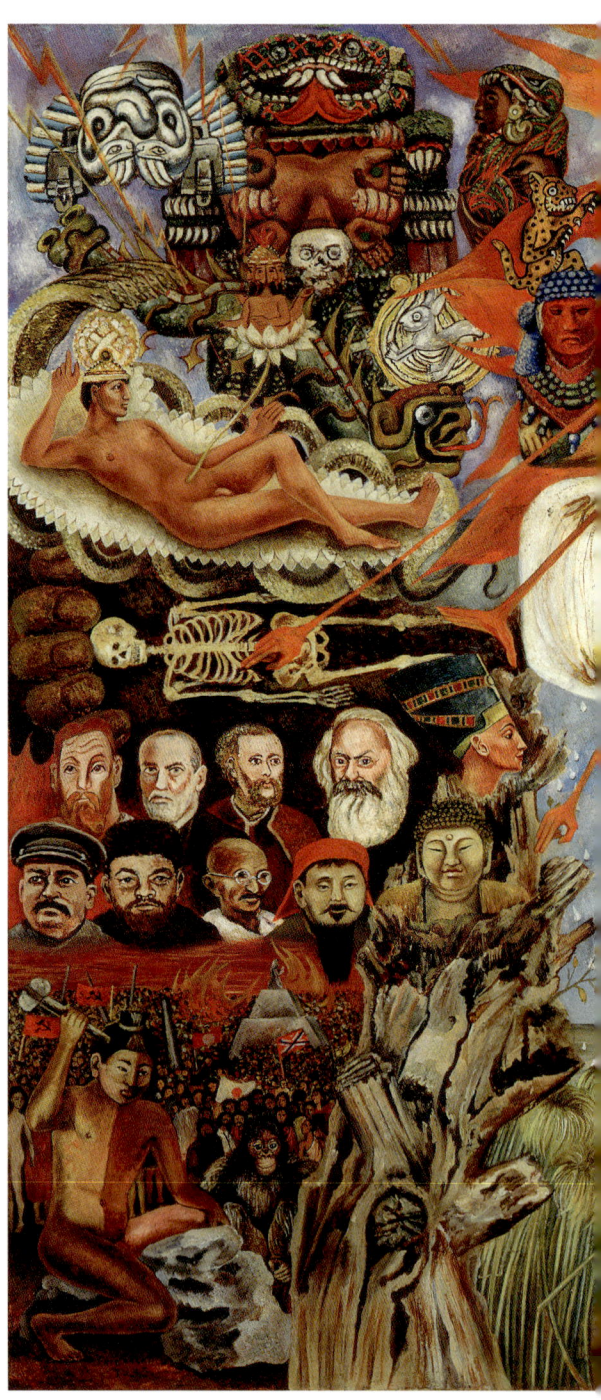

Moses (The Birth of the Hero), 1945
Oil on masonite,
61 x 75.6 cm (24 x 29¾ in.)
United States, private collection

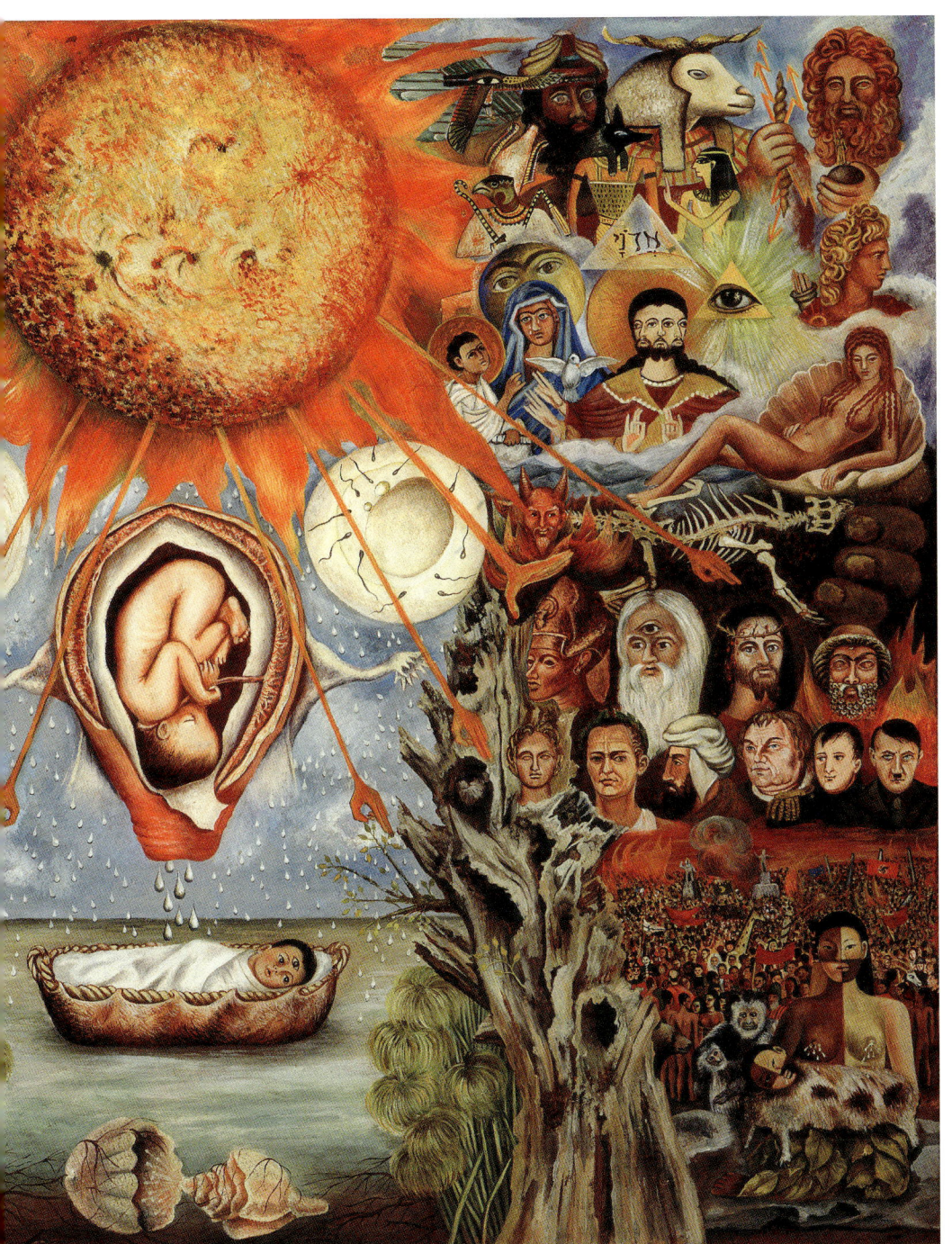

Detail 1, The Gods of the East
The celestial world of imagination and poetry
1 The Lightning, the Lightning Bolt, and Lightning's trace (the clap of thunder):
Huracán, Cuculcán, and Gukumatz **2** Tláloc (mask) **3** Coatlicue, mother of all
the gods **4** Quetzalcóatl **5** Chinese dragon god **6** Brahma (emerging from the lotus
flower that grows from the ocean in Vishnu's navel) **7** Vishnu, who is reclining on
Shesha, the divine serpent (not mentioned by Kahlo) **8** Human skeleton

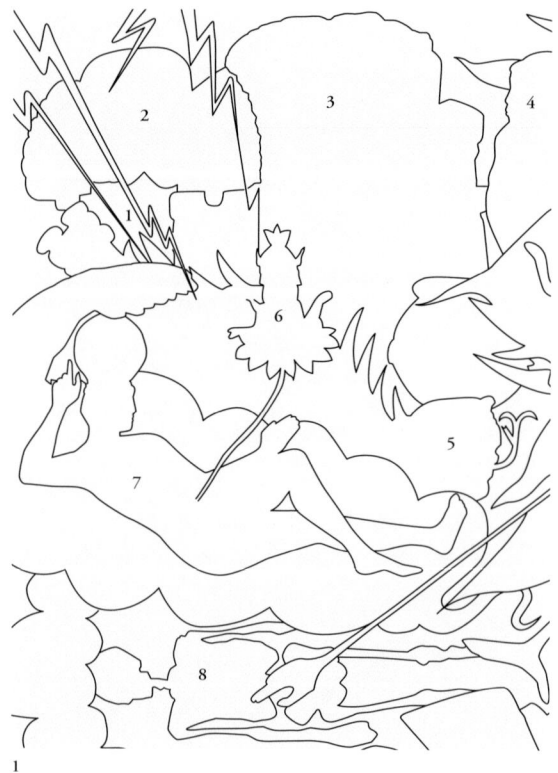

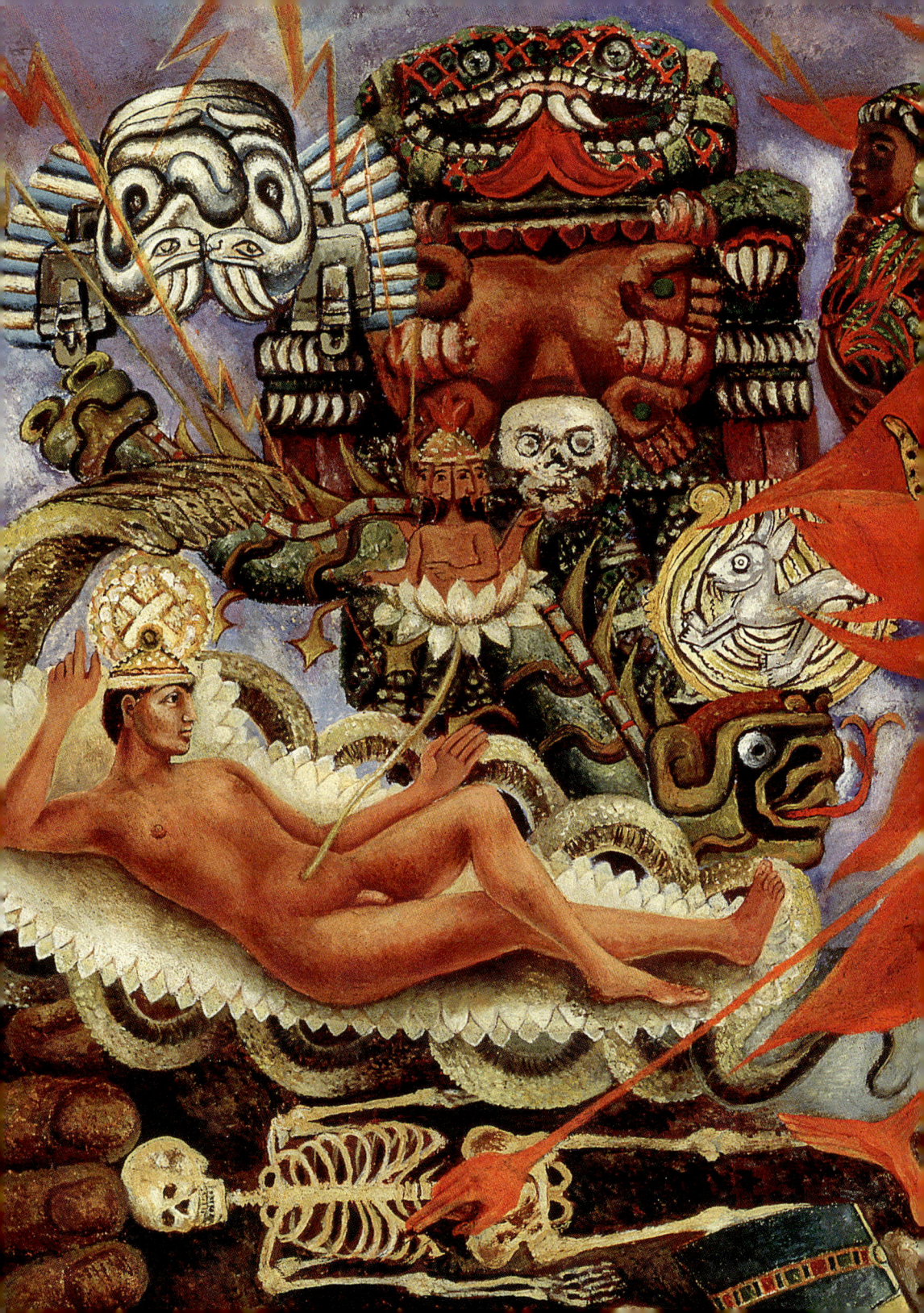

Detail 2, The Gods of the West
The celestial world of imagination and poetry
9 An Assyrian winged bull (Lamassu) **10** Amun **11** Zeus **12** Horus
13 Anubis (not mentioned by Kahlo) **14** Jehovah **15** Apollo **16** The Moon
17 The Virgin Mary **18** Divine Providence **19** The Holy Trinity
20 Venus **21** The Devil **22** Animal skeleton

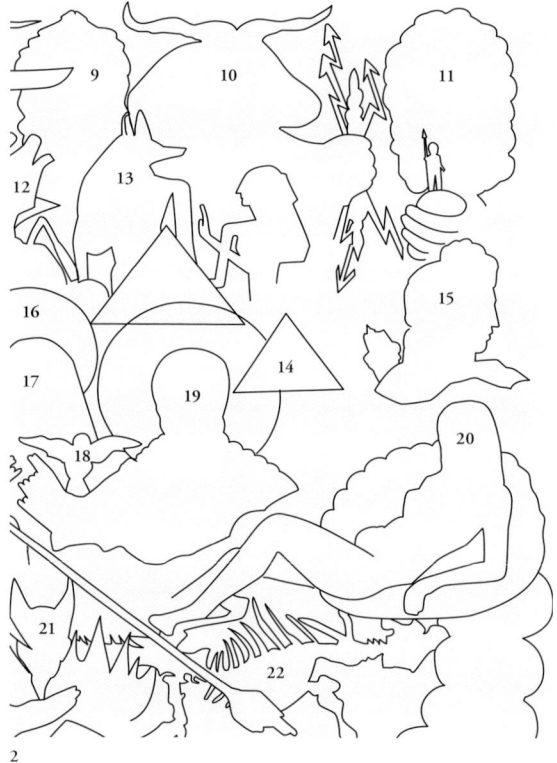

2

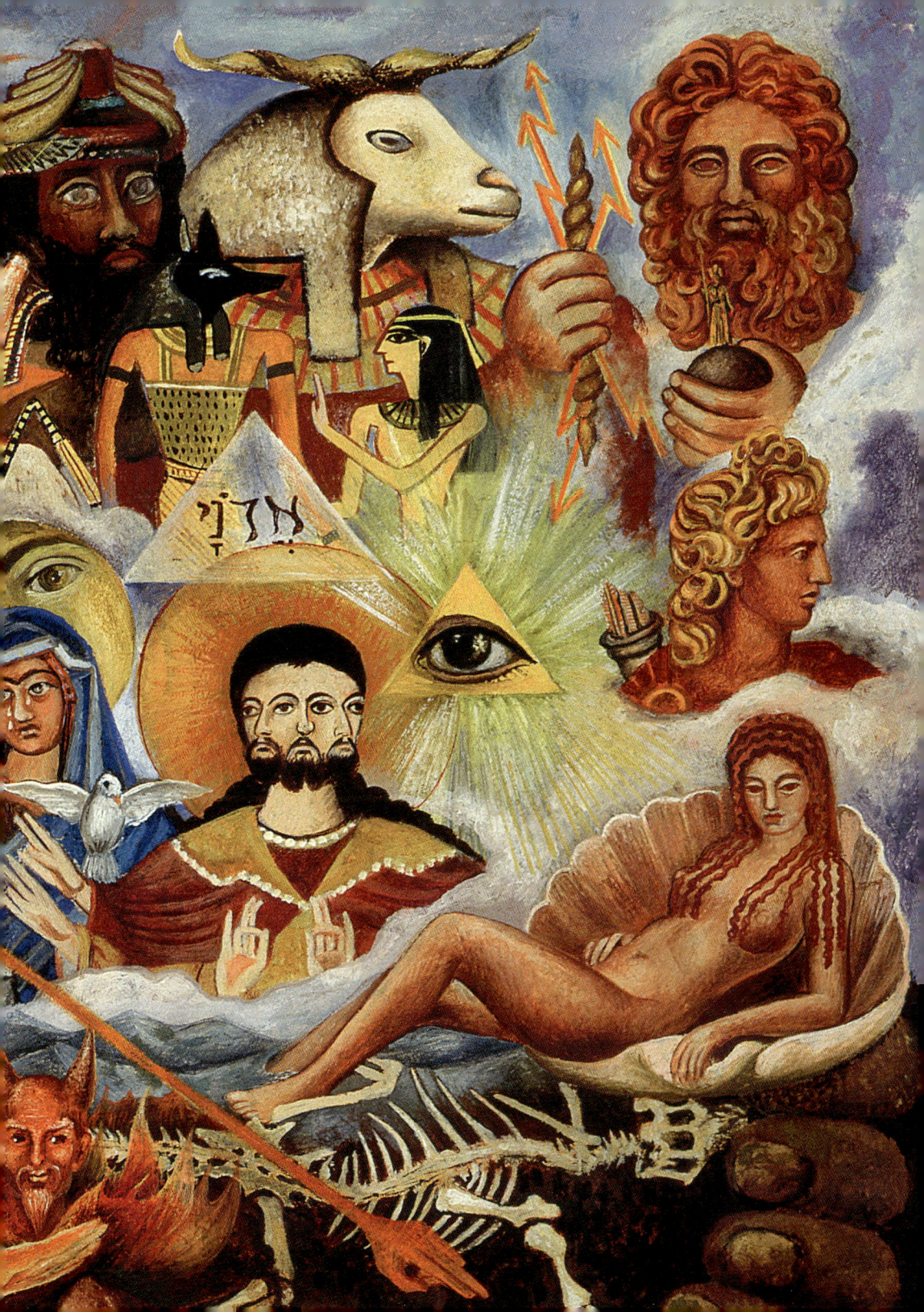

Detail 3

The earthly realm of the fear of death

23 Epicurus **24** Freud **25** Paracelsus **26** Marx **27** Nefertiti **28** Stalin
29 Lenin **30** Gandhi **31** Genghis Khan **32** Buddha **33** Man,
the maker, in his four colors (the four races) **34** A monkey

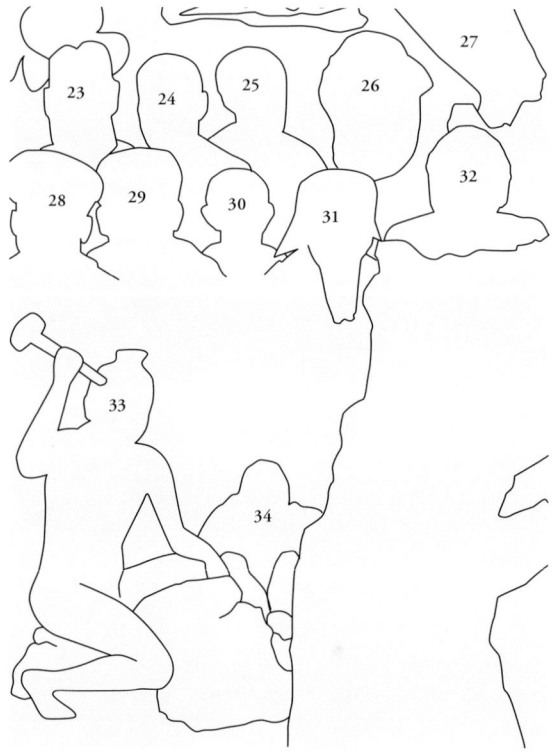

3

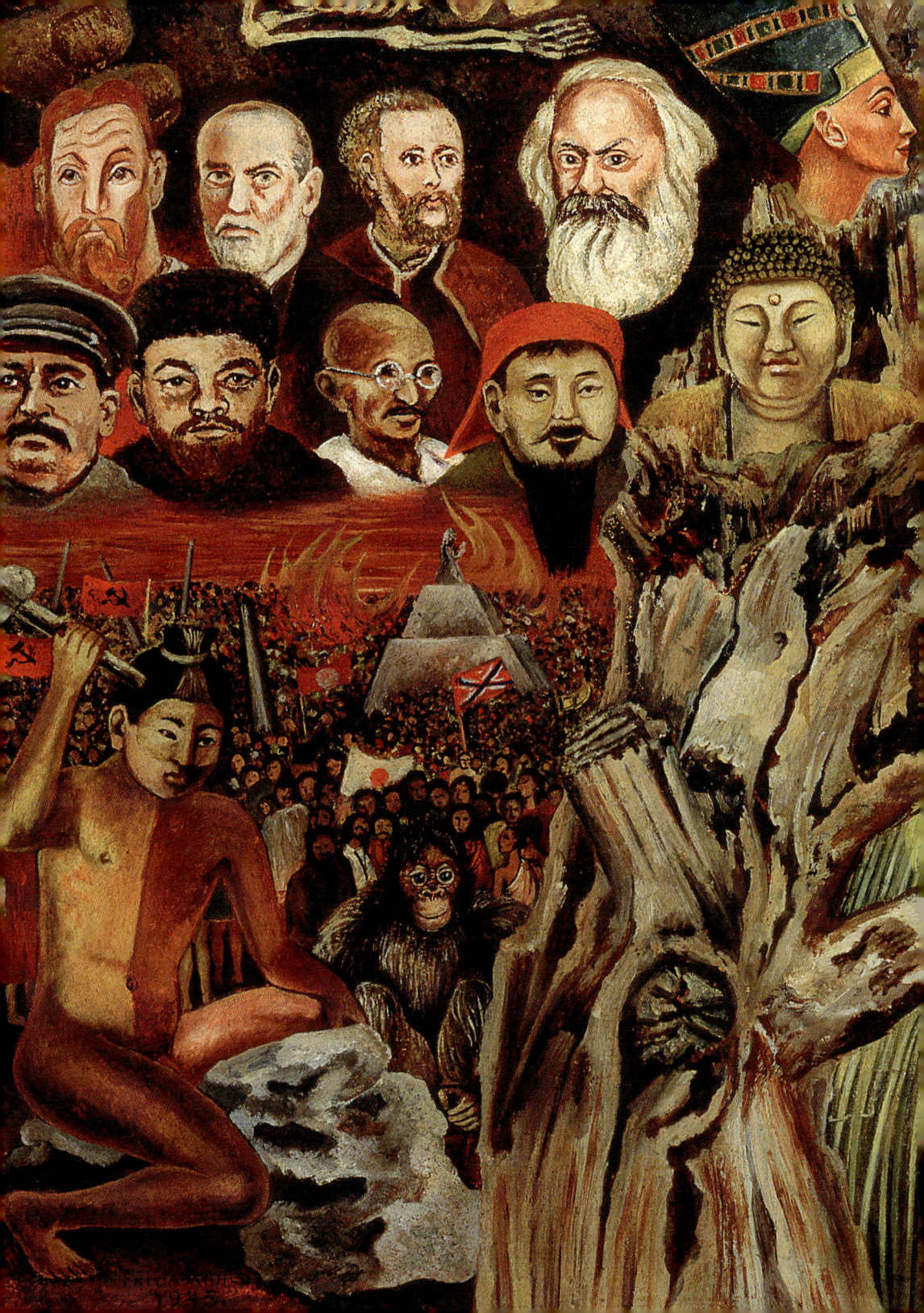

Detail 4
The earthly realm of the fear of death
35 Akhenaten **36** Moses **37** Christ **38** Zoroaster **39** Alexander the Great
40 Julius Caesar **41** Muhammad **42** Martin Luther (Kahlo originally
intended to have Timur here) **43** Napoleon **44** Hitler **45** The mother,
the creator with her child in her arms **46** A monkey

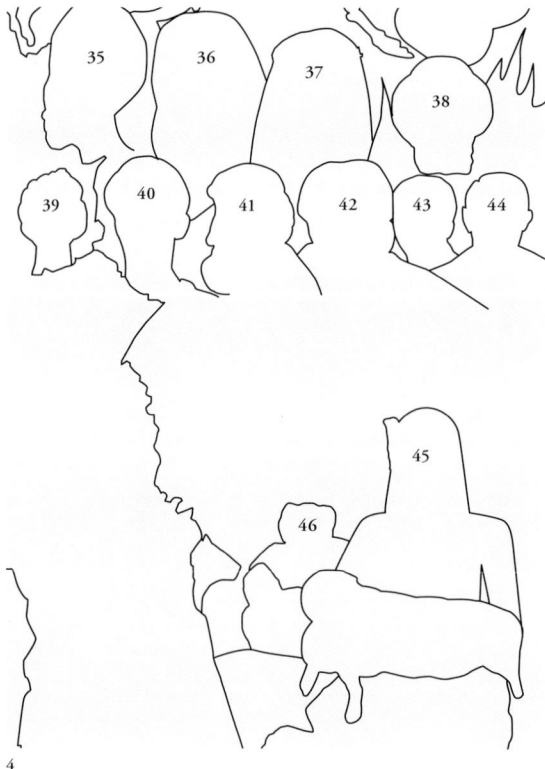

4

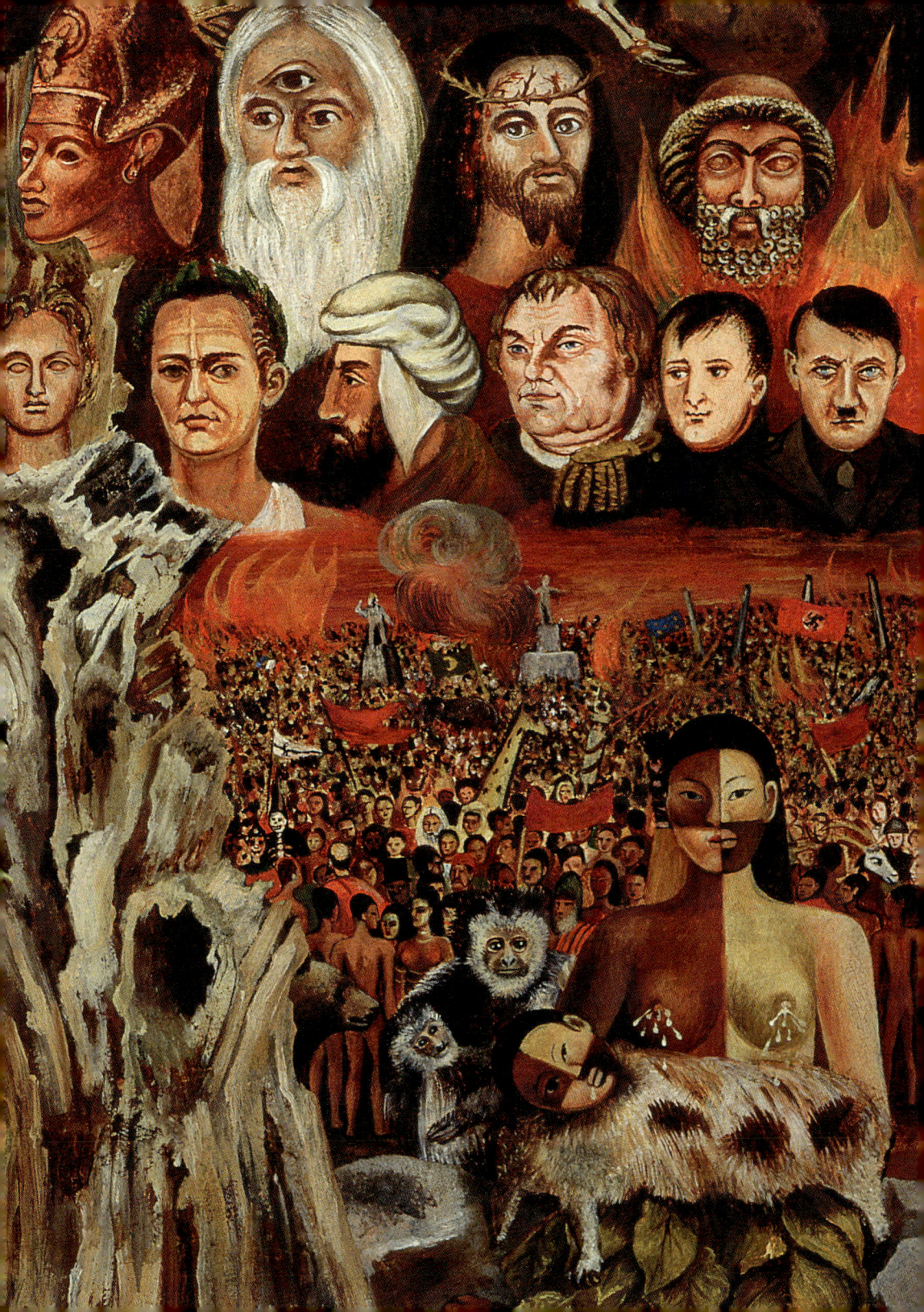

Detail 5
47 The Sun **48** Cellular division **49** An egg being fertilized
50 Human fetus **51** The deification of the sun (Aten)
52 The infant Moses **53** Shell and snail (Love, the two sexes)

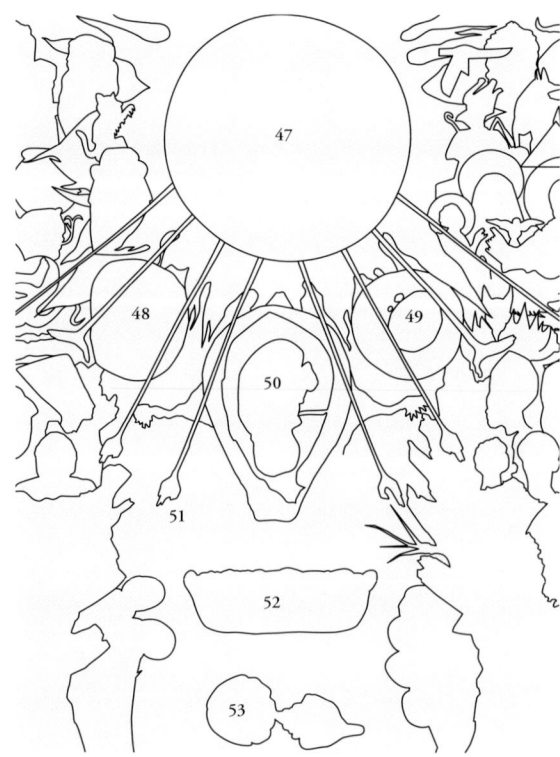

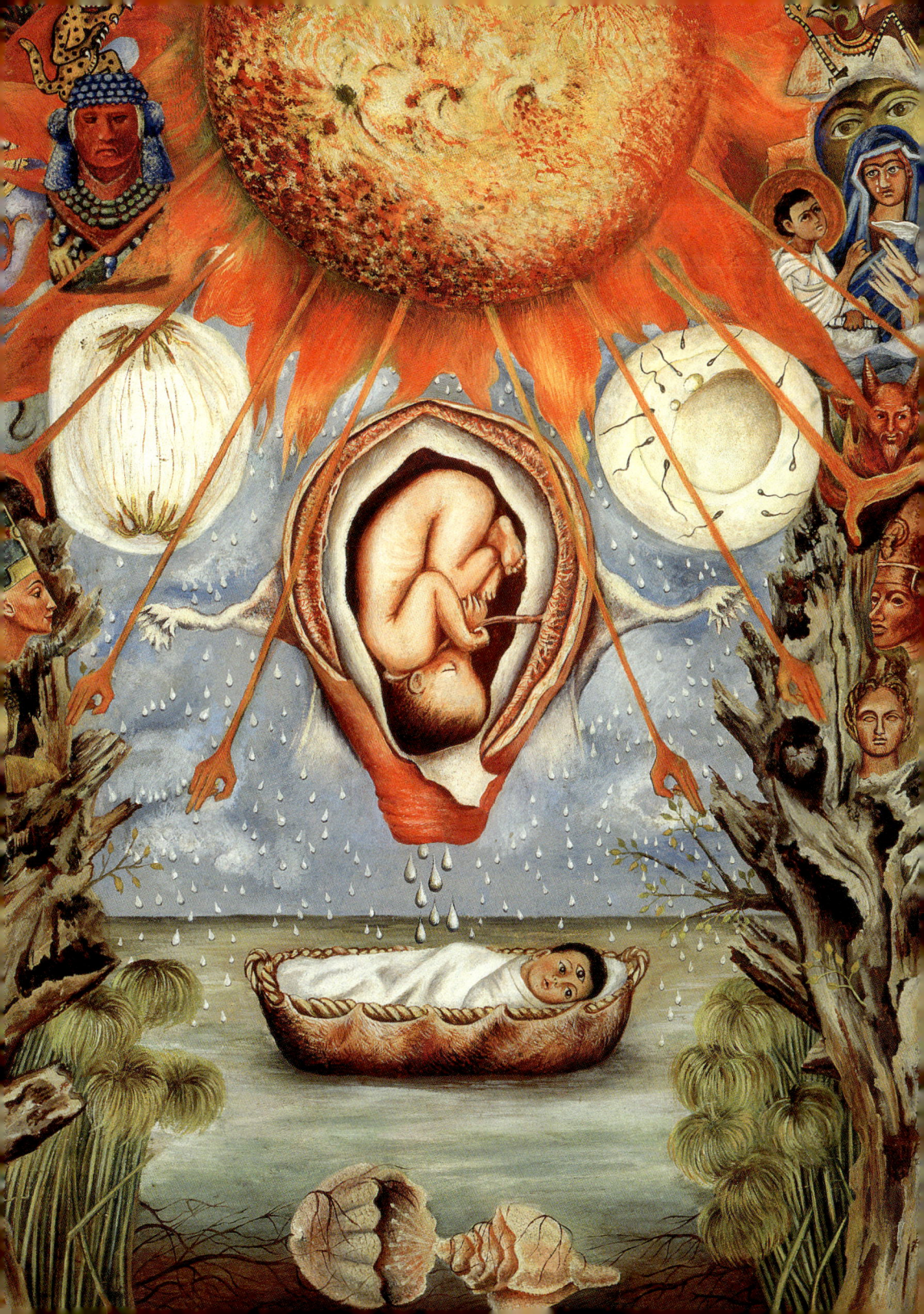

IV.

I no longer feel the slightest hope.
I hope never to return.

The will to continue painting right up until the end

1947–1954

"*The tragedy in Frida's work is not its dominant theme [...] the darkness of her pain is only the velvety background for the marvelous light that pours out from her biological strength, her exquisitely refined sensitivity, magnificent intelligence, and her invincible compulsion to fight for life.*"
— DIEGO RIVERA, 1953

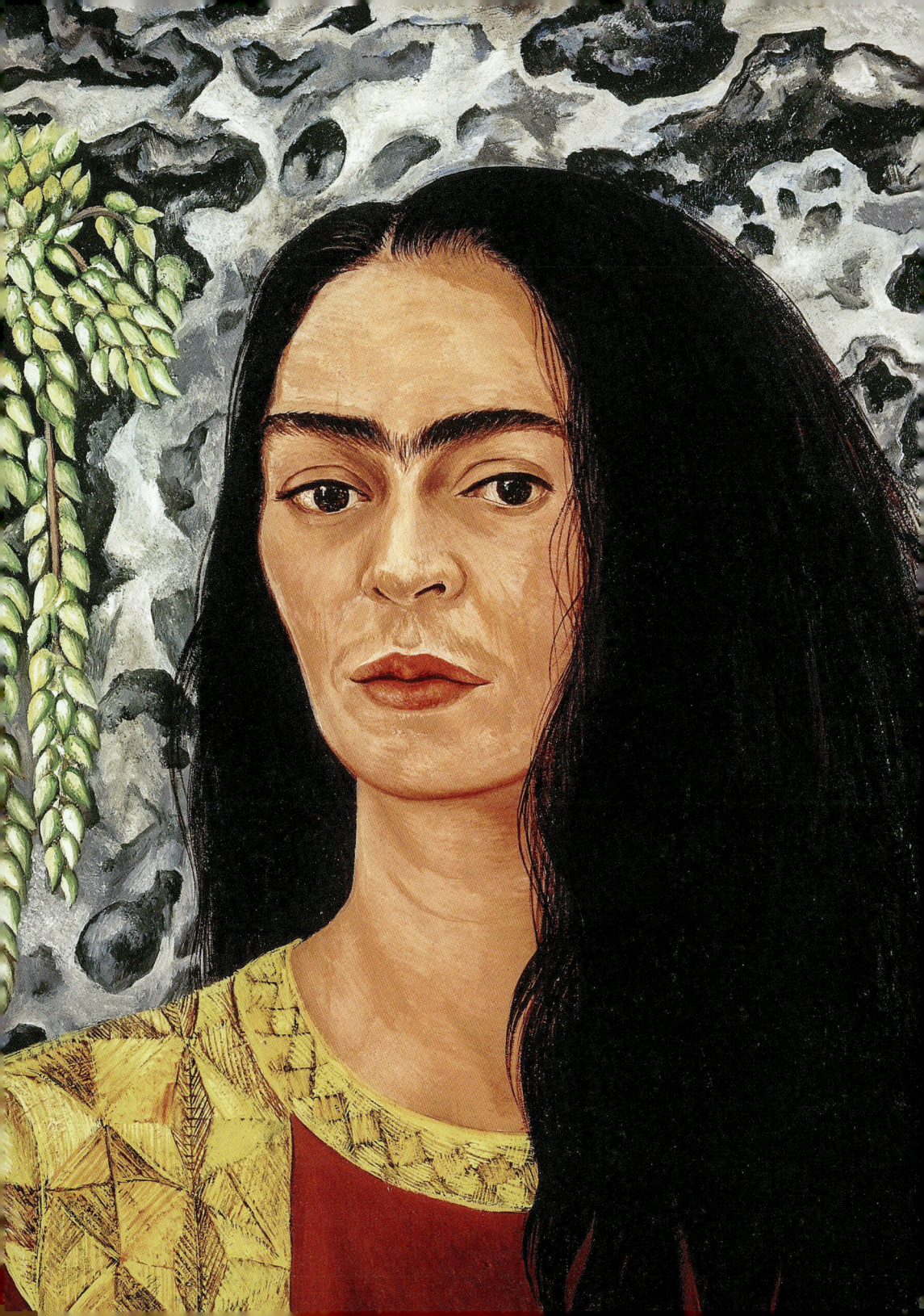

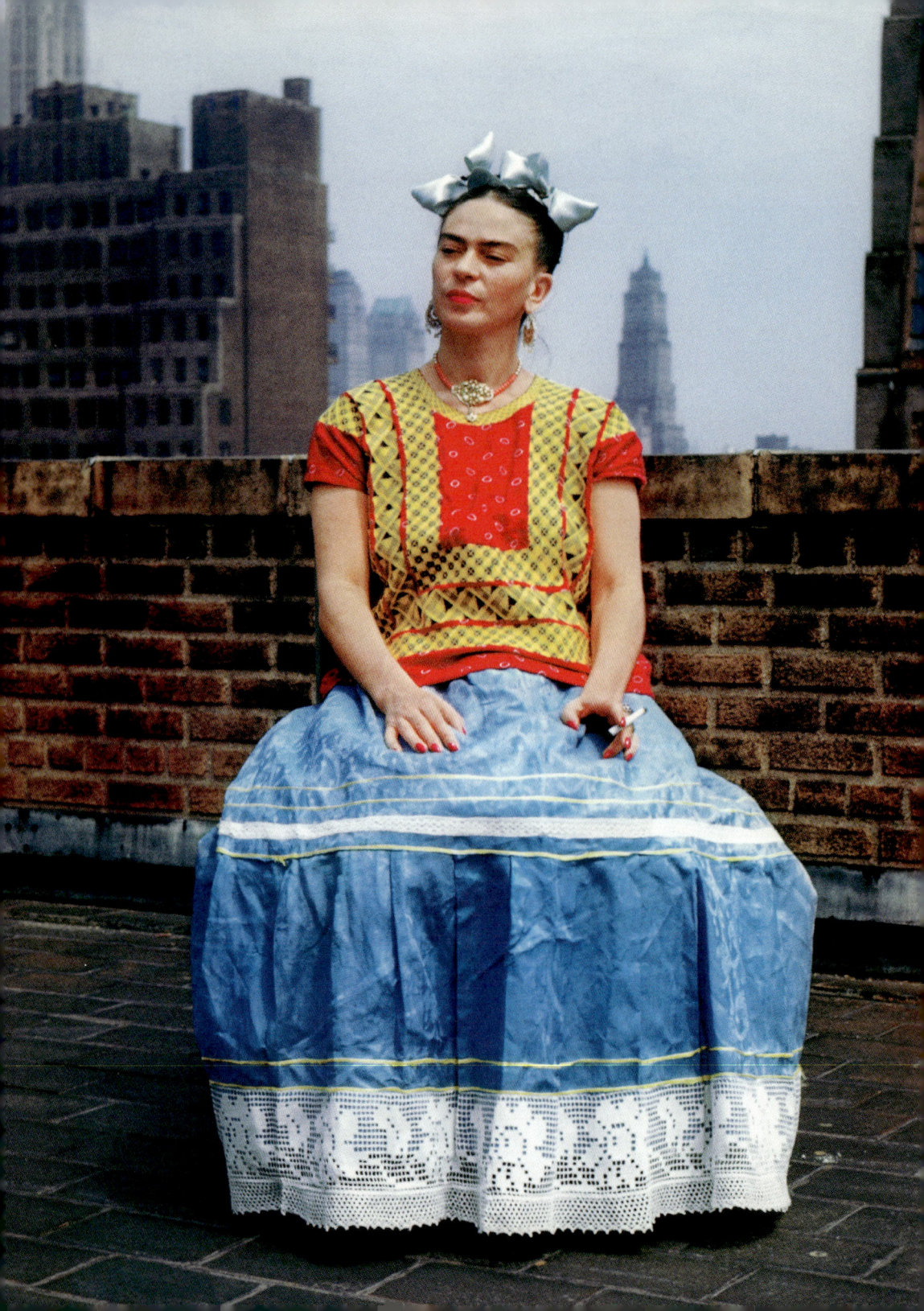

The last years of Kahlo's life were marked by the absolute certainty that she had achieved what she had set out to do as an artist, yet at the same time by her physical and emotional inability to overcome her various illnesses, which would eventually lead to her death. However, the end of her artistic career was shaped above all by the fact that she was losing the ability to look after herself and to retain her mental faculties, making it less and less possible for her to continue to paint.

A look at the works from Kahlo's final creative period shows them to be a summary of her artistic achievements. While her capacity to express herself through her painting had certainly diminished as her health and emotional state declined, these late works neverthe-less demonstrate that her creative will remained a powerful force until the end.

Throughout these last years she continued to make paintings in the genres she had been working with since the beginning of her career as an artist, namely portraits of friends and loved ones; self-portraits that dealt with her feelings and her fears about death; still lifes that she preferred should be pictures brimming with life and which invited thought because of their symbolism and hidden meanings; and, along with all of these works, a number of scenes in obvious celebration of Stalinist propaganda, which was something totally new in her work. In this way then, and far from giving up, Kahlo con-tinued to paint and wanted her paintings to reflect the most recent developments in her process of introspection and revision as an artist.

In 1944, Kahlo painted two double self-portraits in which she merged together half of her own face with half of Rivera's. Since the paintings are almost identical, to distin-guish them they have generally been referred to simply as *Diego and Frida I* (p. 204) and *Diego and Frida II* (Lozano 2021, cat. 112). They were both originally in beautiful hand-crafted frames made of small shells, although the owner of the second one, the actress María Félix (1914–2002), removed the frame from hers as its handmade style was not to her taste. There are small variations in the size and brushwork of the two paintings, but essentially the composition is the same. However, early photographs of them, in which the second painting still appears in its original frame, reveal that there was a subtle but decisive difference between the two. For the painting which is today still in its frame, writ-ten on four shells in a row above the portrait are the words "DIEGO 1929 1944 FRIDA"

(p. 204), while on the original frame of the other painting (Lozano 2021, cat. 112) the shells are separated, with the words "1929 FRIDA" written on two shells to the left of the picture and "1944 DIEGO" to the right. Following discussions with my colleague Andrea Kettenmann, it is my opinion that by reversing the order of the names like this Kahlo wanted to indicate that, after 15 years of marriage that also included their divorce, in other words the very years given by the dates on the shells, she and Rivera had now become united as two halves of one and the same person. Not only this, but in spite of their disagreements and infidelities they were, more than ever, a couple and a partnership with shared concerns and ideologies, just like the thorny branches that are shown growing from the same trunk and surrounding their faces in both paintings.

If these two self-portraits are compared with those Kahlo painted in the following year, it can be seen that her image gradually fades into the background until her face disappears behind a mask (p. 259). In 1944 though, in the self-portrait *The Broken Column* (p. 257), Kahlo had already decided to bring the various sufferings of her body to the fore, as represented metaphorically by the tight corset she is wearing, the nails driven into her unflinching skin, and the Classical column broken into sections so that it resembles the bones of her spine. These elements, however, are in opposition to Kahlo's strength of spirit and will to carry on living, which in turn are represented by her figure standing upright in a desolate landscape that stretches off into the distance. From this point onward, Kahlo's injuries and declining health became the subject of a number of her paintings, even to the extent that she painted on the different plaster corsets she had to wear (p. 256).

After being racked with pain for four months so that she was not even able to leave her bed, Kahlo asked her friends Ella and Bertram Wolfe, on the advice of her patron, the film producer Arcady Boytler, to get in touch with Dr. Philip Wilson, a well-respected orthopedic surgeon working in New York. After examining her, Wilson advised that she should have an operation as soon as possible to fuse the vertebrae in her spine.[1] The procedure would then require Kahlo to remain totally immobile for several weeks. As a result, she was admitted to the Hospital for Special Surgery in New York, accompanied by her younger sister Cristina, who also cared for her during the very difficult period of her convalescence.[2]

The letters Kahlo sent, by way of Cristina, to her sisters Matilde and Adriana in Mexico reveal something of her terrible ordeal. From the letters that have survived it is known that she was visited by a number of friends, including Ella Wolfe, Mary Sklar, Nickolas Muray, who introduced Kahlo to his new wife Margaret Schwab, and also Alice

Gisèle Freund, **Frida Kahlo and Dr. Farill with her self-portrait**, 1951

Rahon, who brought her sweets and ice cream to brighten her days. Even so, Kahlo began to suffer from panic attacks, which pushed her to the brink of her sanity. Cristina and her other sisters were concerned that her mental health would continue to deteriorate, and succeeded in getting Dr. Wilson to allow her to go up to the terrace on the sixth floor of the hospital where she could sit in a small sunroom there that was open to the air. Little by little, she began to recover her spirits, and in fact in some of the photographs that Muray took of her while she was in hospital at this time Kahlo appears to be reborn, dressed in her traditional Mexican costumes and with brightly colored ribbons in her hair (p. 286).[3]

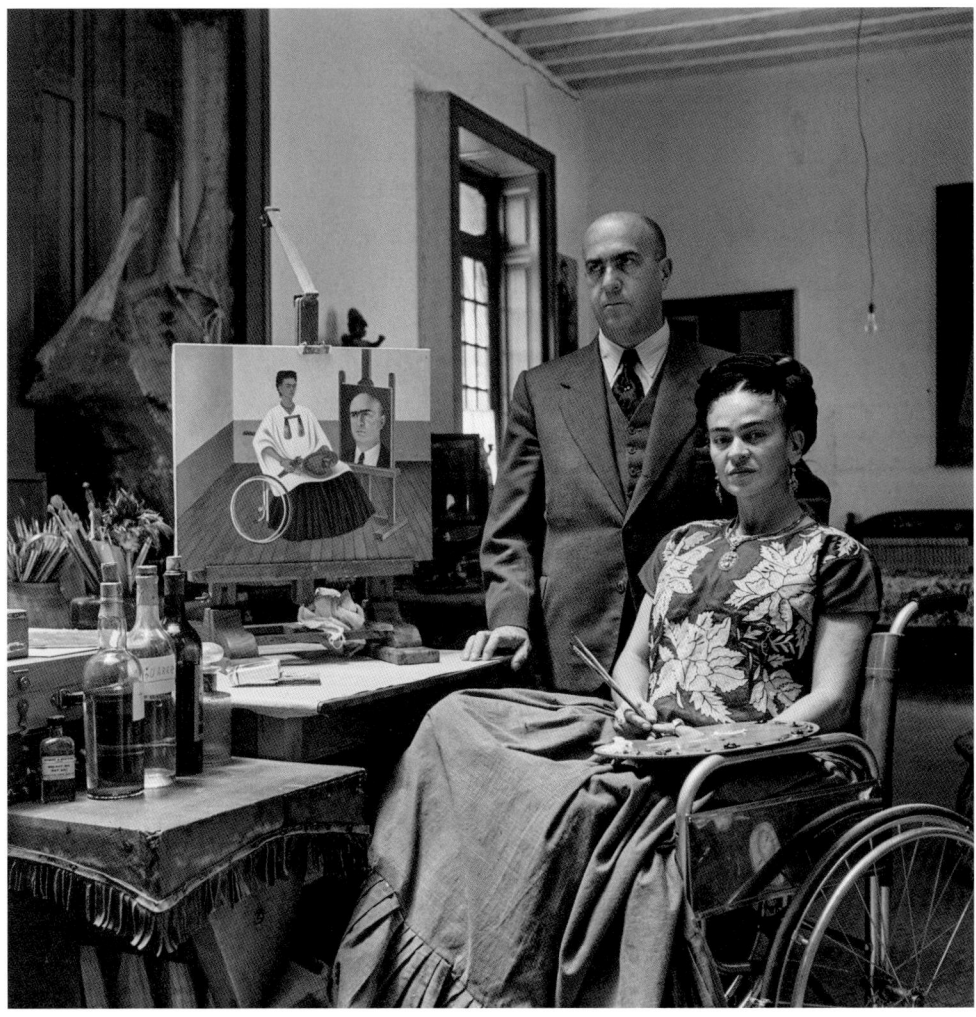

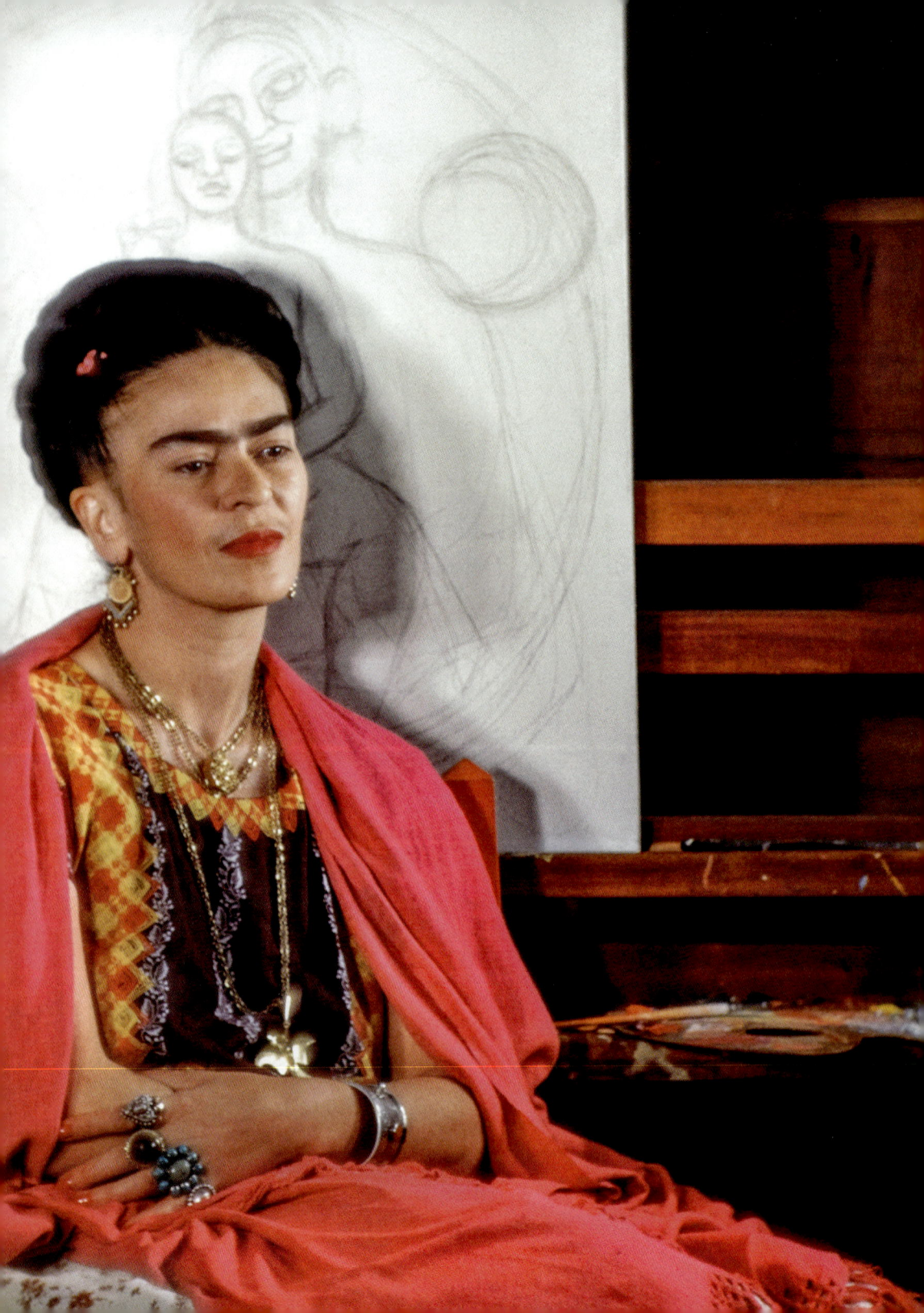

During the weeks she spent in hospital, Kahlo occupied herself by making large numbers of drawings in which she let all the pain of her tragic situation spill out, although they can also be regarded as Surrealist experiments in projecting her subconscious. However, it was not long before she began to depict these difficult periods in her life in her paintings as well.

Even before her operation though, some of Kahlo's paintings were showing her response to the days that passed visiting doctors and undergoing various treatments. On occasion this could be somewhat sarcastic, such as the time when Dr. Carbajosa told her she could eat whatever she wanted. Kahlo then took this recommendation and translated it by portraying herself in *Without Hope* (pp. 308/309) lying in bed, with her body held fast by the bedsheets as tears run down her face while she is force-fed offal through an enormous funnel. The following year, with the operation behind her, she put her wounds on display in the double self-portrait she entitled *Tree of Hope (Remain Strong)* (p. 307), which in the image on the left shows Kahlo from behind with the incisions Dr. Wilson had had to make around the level of her waist to fuse her vertebrae together. Some of the marks on her skin seem to repeat the lines of the fissures in the lava in the rocky landscape where this imaginary scene is set, a device Kahlo had also used previously (pp. 216/217, and pp. 246/247).

In the painting therefore, the sterile surroundings of the New York hospital have been replaced by a landscape in Mexico, the source of all her tragedies. Kahlo is stretched out on a hospital gurney with her face turned away, while the sheet is wrapped around her upper body as if it were a shroud from which only her loose hair emerges. The other Kahlo is seated alongside on a plain wooden chair, and is shown free of the orthopedic corset which she is holding in one of her hands. She is dressed in the style of the women of the Isthmus of Tehuantepec, with her full skirt and *huipil* from the town of Juchitán, and this Kahlo is the one who has triumphed over death. The duality between the two figures is repeated in the rest of the scene, which is divided between day and night with the sun and the moon both being present at the same time. The picture thus implies that although Kahlo has survived the operation and has found the strength to keep going, she is nevertheless still stuck in the desolation and melancholy of this harsh and lifeless landscape. And yet, in her other hand she is holding a small flag on which is written "Tree of Hope, Remain Strong" as a sign that she has indeed resolved to carry on fighting.

Before Kahlo went to New York, and while she was still at the peak of her artistic ability, in spite of the pain she was in she painted one of her most celebrated works, *The*

Gisèle Freund, **Frida Kahlo in front of a sketch for** *The Love Embrace of the Universe,* *the Earth (Mexico), Me, Diego, and Señor Xólotl* (detail), *c.* 1948

Little Deer (pp. 310/311). In its hybrid visual form it identifies Kahlo's anxieties about the deterioration of her body with the survival instinct of an animal fleeing for its life. Kahlo lived surrounded by animals in her house in Coyoacán and had a good understanding of the feelings of the spider monkeys, parrots, and even fawns she kept, such as her beloved Granizo, which she included in the painting *The Wounded Table* (pp. 224/225). In *The Little Deer*, however, she decided to take a step beyond the mere empathy that can exist between human and animal feelings, and created a portrait of herself as a defenseless animal being hounded by the pain and disturbance of her medical treatment and by the misfortunes of her life. Kahlo's idea of representing herself as a fleeing deer may have been inspired by 17th-century emblems, specifically the engraving "Et piu dolsi" ("It hurts more"), one of the love emblems that appeared in the book *Quaeris quid sit amor* (What Is Love, You Ask?) by Daniel Heinsius, published in around 1601.[4] However, instead of a deer's head on the body of this stag with antlers Kahlo painted her own, with the face looking impassively out at the viewer. Meanwhile, nine arrows have struck the deer's body and blood flows from the wounds. The animal has tried to flee from its hunters, but the dead trees of the forest are blocking its escape, so that this Kahlo-deer no longer has anywhere to turn. In the distance, a pool of crystal-clear water can be seen, but above it a storm is gathering. This was the state of Kahlo's feelings in May 1946, worn down by the burden of her physical condition and longing to escape the pain it was causing her, yet without, so it would seem, being able to see a way out, or to find happiness again. She finished the painting just before her operation in New York and gave it to Arcady and Lina Boytler, with great affection and accompanied by a poem she had written which included the lines: "Sadness haunts my paintings, it's in them through and through, and so it is for me today, as calm has left me too […] Please take this little portrait, with tenderness for you."[5]

Taking a moment to study these three paintings, all completed immediately before and after her operation, it is very apparent that in spite of Kahlo's worsening health her intellectual ability had not declined and in fact she had expanded the artistic ideas she had been exploring by looking at new sources and subjects. Considered together, these three paintings from 1945 and 1946 enabled her to develop a new approach with regard to the conceptual modernity of her painting. The central theme of all three self-portraits is a woman's body, and specifically her own body, punished by medical procedures, hurt by operations, and wounded by the trials of life. It is the same body that appeared in *What Water Gave Me* from 1938/39 (p. 211), except that there it was submerged and obscured by visions from her unconscious; it is the same body that longs for tenderness and affection in the small but important painting *The Earth Itself (Two Nudes in a Forest)* from 1939 (pp. 216/217); and it is the same body Kahlo cut open to expose her insides in both

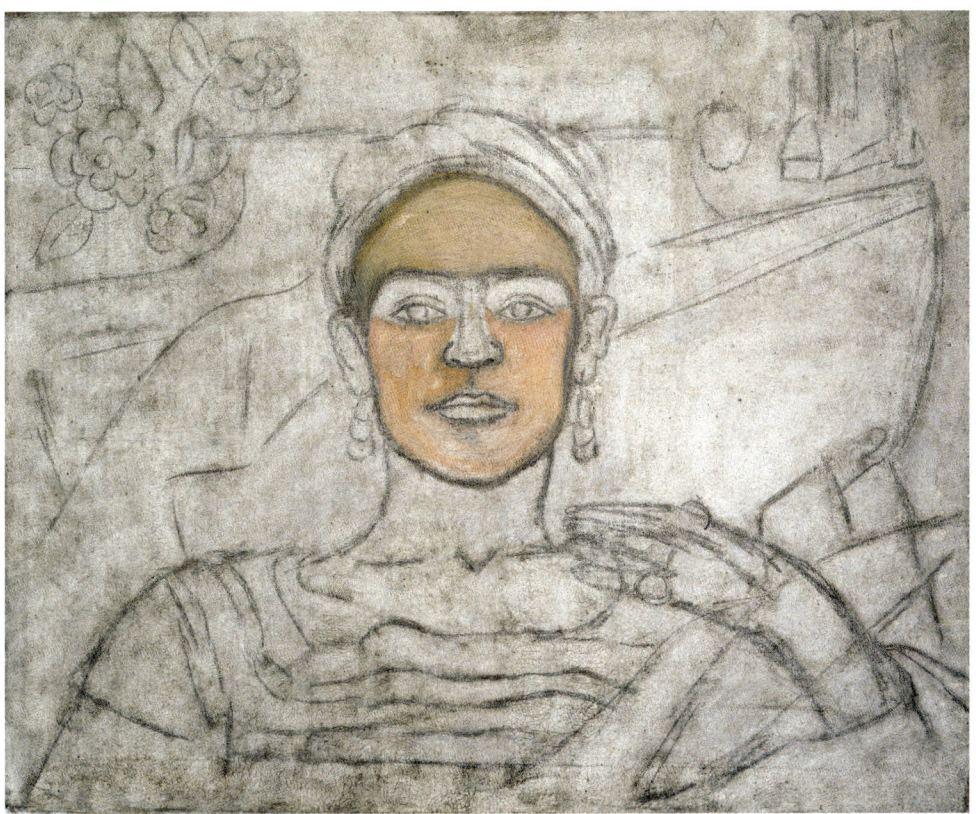

The Heart (Memory) from 1937 (p. 177) and *The Broken Column* from 1944 (p. 257). Now, however, the body that Kahlo had turned into a source of reflection for her paintings has become a body manipulated by others, objectified by men and transformed to the extent that it has turned into a male deer complete with antlers. Up until Kahlo there had not been a female artist who employed such a conceptual approach that ranged from portraits of her face to exhibiting the organs from inside her own body. No woman art- ist had dared to make her own body into a pictorial subject by means of incisions and the body's pain and powerlessness. This process, which had first begun in response to a desire to capture her own likeness with the self-portrait Kahlo painted as a present for

Self-portrait (unfinished), *c.* 1952
Oil and charcoal on canvas, 55 x 65 cm (21⅝ x 25⅝ in.)
Mexico City, Coyoacán, Museo Frida Kahlo

her boyfriend Alejandro Gómez Arias in 1926 (p. 53), ended up by becoming a separation from her own body. She was at once the living person and the subject of her works, but also the painter who made the female body a discrete entity or object for analysis in modern art. The deconstruction of the female archetype has here prevailed over the construction of individuality, and Kahlo's body has become the instrument for analysis, critique, and condemnation.

The lengthy process of construction and then deconstruction of Kahlo's artistic personality seems to have been directly shaped by the knocks she sustained throughout her life, as if it were some rigid structure which in the end must yield to ideological discourse. Moreover, it no longer needed to be painted in order to manifest itself, the pages of a diary were enough, where Kahlo wrote and made drawings from 1943 up until the year she died. This is evidently what Raquel Tibol found to be so invaluable in Kahlo's letters: they were her voice speaking without any intermediaries, in which she could express directly some of what was happening to her. As such, her painting and her diary merge to become a single channel for her art in which the writing was rooted in the paintings but also complemented by the large number of drawings (not all of which have yet been catalogued), and in turn further supported and offset by the exceptionally rich pictorial source of the photographs that survive, from the time Kahlo was a child until her final days.

The young woman of the 1920s had worked hard to learn about and try out for herself the new aesthetic ideas that emerged in Mexico following the revolution, while also experimenting with the techniques of early avant-garde movements such as Stridentism, Cubism, and Germany's New Objectivity. By the early 1930s she had become a stronger painter, as a result of having to confront the question of her Mexican identity while she was living in the United States, a country that did not recognize her values and customs. After she had returned to Mexico Kahlo continued to explore the ideas of the avant-garde, Surrealism in particular, but now also sought to incorporate conceptual and narrative elements from traditional Mexican culture that illustrated the collective unconscious of a country in pursuit of modernity. In Paris, she had mingled with the Surrealists in person, chief among them Breton, and had been fêted by some of the most famous painters in the world, including Picasso. However, her development and success as an artist was not always matched by stability in her emotional relationships.

In consequence, by the late 1930s, following her brief divorce from Rivera and at a time when her health was beginning to decline, Kahlo decided to take a deep and

Juan Guzmán, **Frida Kahlo in the American British Cowdray Hospital**, *c.* 1951
Gelatin silver print, 24 x 19 cm (9½ x 7½ in.)
Mexico City, Fundación Televisa, Collection and Archive

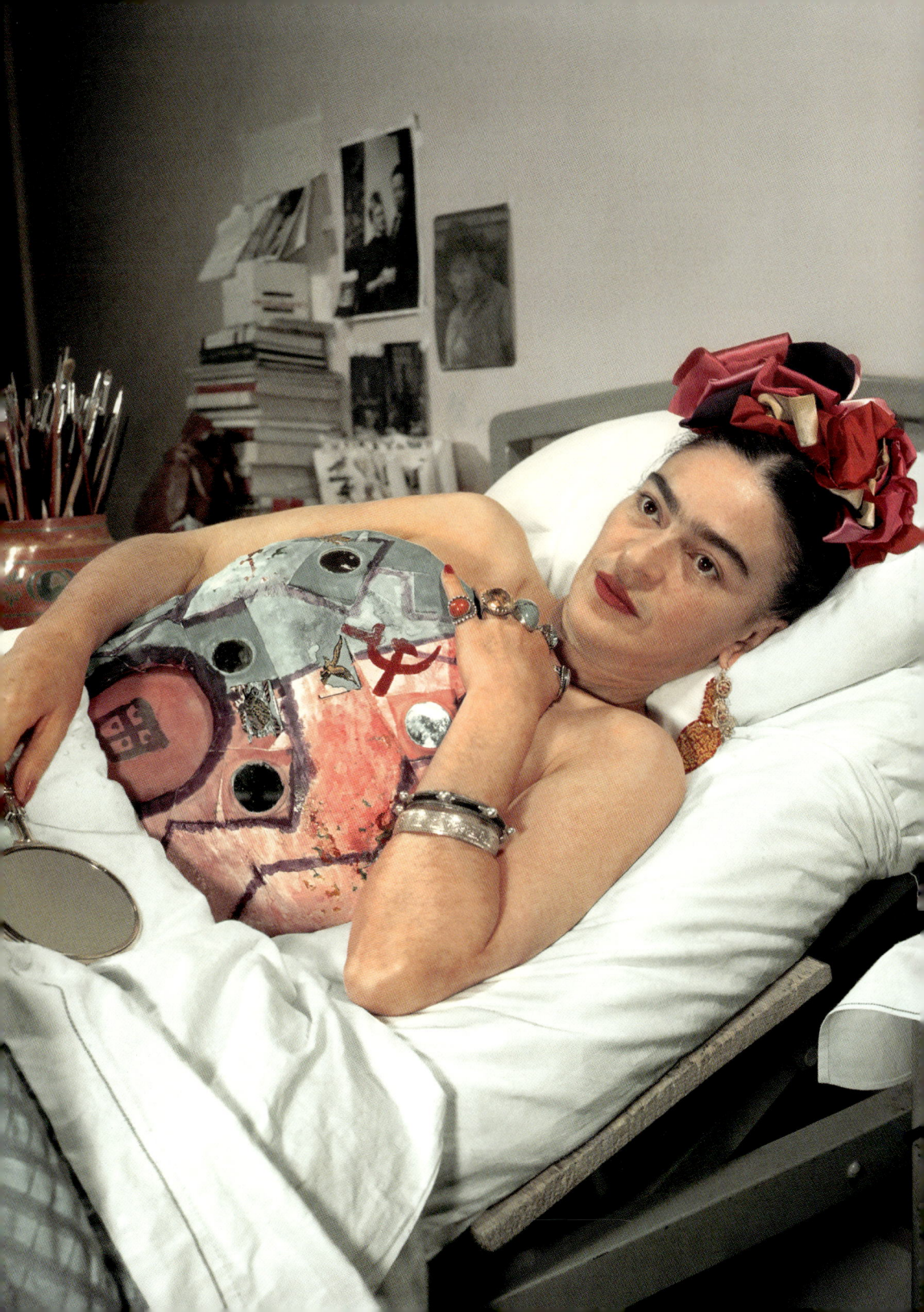

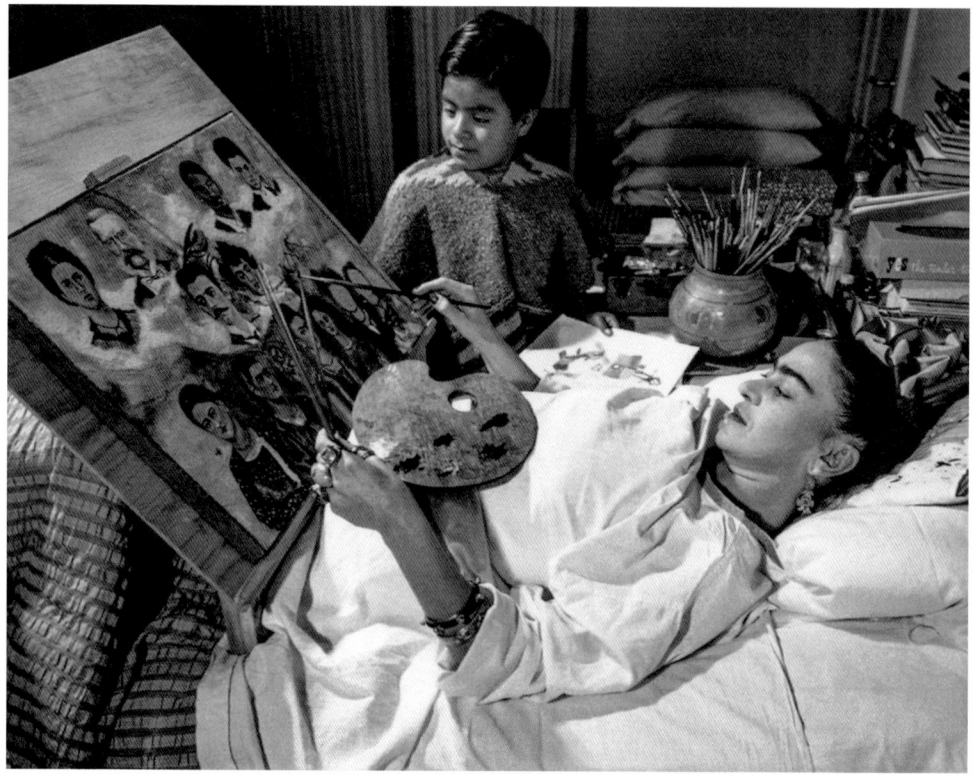

Juan Guzmán, **Vidal Nicolas, a fortune teller boy, watching Frida paint**
Portrait of Frida's Family (Family Tree) **at the American British Cowdray Hospital,** *c.* 1951

introspective look at herself and present the results of this self-analysis in a series of
unsettling self-portraits, starting with *What Water Gave Me* (p. 211), *The Two Fridas*
(pp. 218/219), and *The Wounded Table* (pp. 224/225), which are among her most intellectually ambitious paintings.

It should hardly need saying that Kahlo was not only a painter but a multidisciplin-
ary artist. Even her clothing and various accessories were part of an ongoing performance
piece, within an artistic narrative that concealed certain truths while at the same time
exploring a multitude of possibilities by means of the character she had created. Kahlo
continued to shape and adjust this character each time she portrayed herself, but also
through writing her diary and the personal, cryptic drawings she made there, not to mention of course every time she arranged her hair or selected her clothing and jewelry before
presenting herself in public.

Around 1950, in a process that ran parallel to this integration of Kahlo's character into her artistic narrative, her painting reached a point of no return when the painted self-portrait ceased to be the sole element in the narrative and Kahlo divided into two forms, or changed into some other form, as, for example, a deer or a sunflower. In 1949 she painted two works that clearly demonstrate the process of deconstruction that was taking place in her painting during the final years of her life. In *The Love Embrace of the Universe, the Earth (Mexico), Me, Diego, and Señor Xólotl* (p. 317) Kahlo depicted herself as a maternal figure cradling Rivera's naked body in her arms, embracing him and caressing the soft skin of his rosy and effeminate flesh, as if he had just landed on the island governed by Sappho, as she once wrote of him.[6] At the same time she is also weeping here, and blood gushes from an open wound in her neck and chest that resembles the channel cut by a river into the earth. Both she and Rivera are in turn held by the Earth Mother who, in the form of a pre-Hispanic idol, supports them between her arms to protect them and has surrounded them with an abundance of cacti and succulents; these allude to the endless cycle of life which she in turn nourishes with the milk that trickles from her own wounded breast and falls into the crevices of the fertile earth. This universe is dominated by a cosmic vision in which the sun and the moon, day and night relate to Nahuatl mythology and its dialectic of life and death. The painting is, however, not only a portrait of the complex, codependent relationship between Kahlo and Rivera, which was certainly strong as well as loving, since Kahlo also seems to be acknowledging the emotional and dysfunctional union their marriage had become, for all its complicity and loyalty, and also the fact that Rivera was her central focus, even more so than her painting and her own artistic personality. He is the child she is holding in her arms, but also the unfaithful lover who has betrayed her, a reality she gives in to in the end as if it were some kind of inescapable karma and which, nearing the end of her days, she has come to accept in an act of reconciliation with the forces of the universe.

The second painting Kahlo made in 1949 was a portrait commissioned by the American painter and art critic Florence Arquin (1900–1974). Kahlo had originally made a sketch for a self-portrait in which she was dressed in a Tehuana costume, but this most likely ended up as the self-portrait she sold to Dr. Samuel Fastlicht once it was finished (p. 315). She then began work on a second, smaller painting that perhaps better reflected her state of mind and restated the process of the deconstruction of her personality (p. 313). It is a powerful self-portrait, in which Rivera once again appears merged with Kahlo's likeness. Fixed on to Kahlo's forehead, his portrait sits above her converging eyebrows as an explicit metaphor that he dominates her thoughts and her future days. He is painted with a third eye on his forehead, in recognition of his imagination, intelligence, and astute observation of life. In contrast, Kahlo's face is gaunt, while her long dark hair is

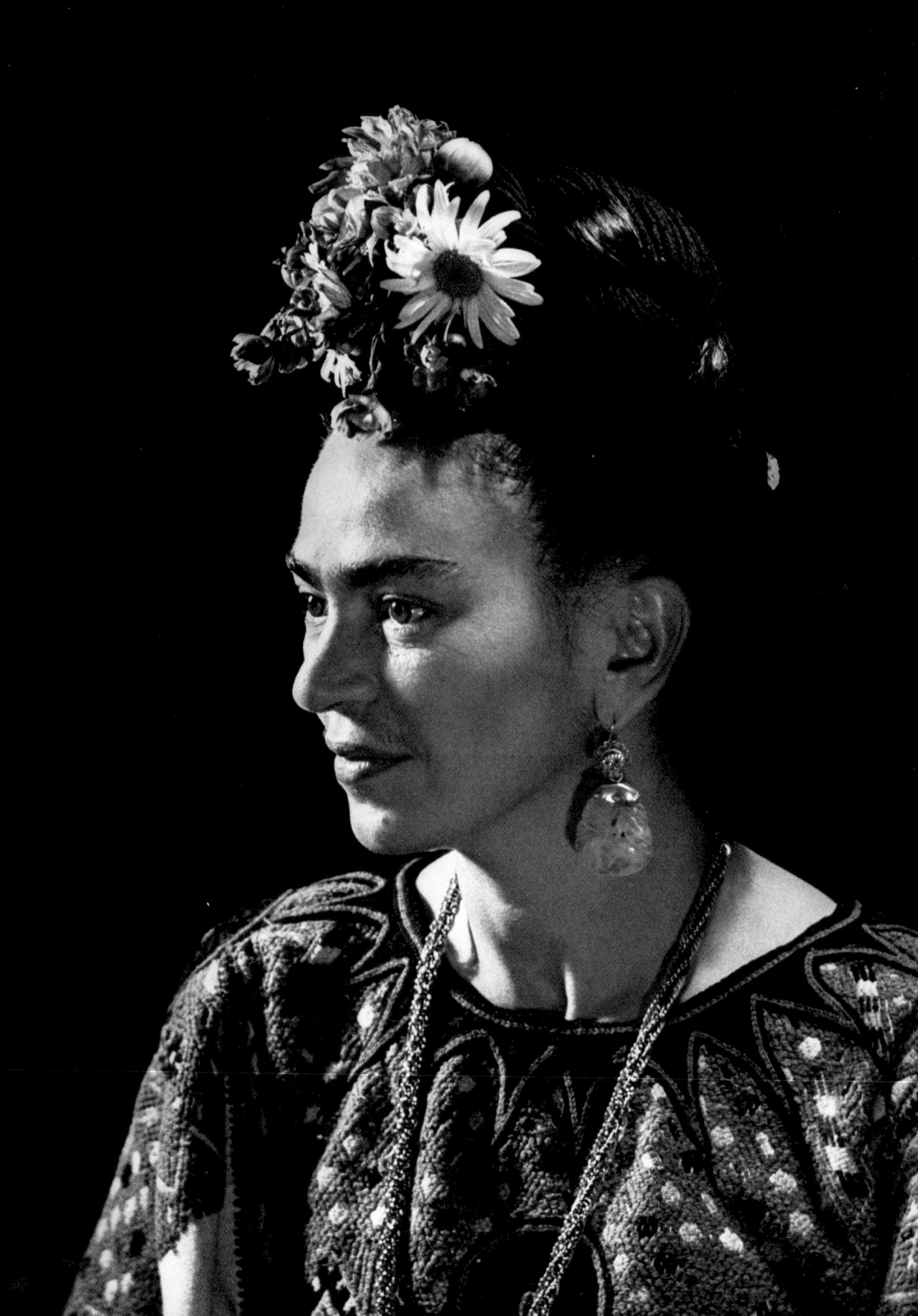

pulled back from her temples and then falls loosely over her shoulders, some of it coiling around her neck as if silently suffocating her. In the top-right corner of the painting, Kahlo wrote "Diego and I" which thus made him the primary subject, even to the point where she omitted her own name. Her gaze looks out at the viewer in an appeal for empathy, expressing her restraint in the face of her suffering and her resignation to the fact that Rivera, in spite of his unfaithfulness, is the center of her existence, "*el niño de sus ojos*" (the apple of her eye) as she used to tell him in her letters.

There is something very disturbing about this image. A sense of emotional instability is apparent that suggests an extreme narcissism in Kahlo's affliction and a delusional obsession to keep Rivera beside her. This aspect of her character has taken over the self-portrait, while the wounded aspect has had to stand back. Kahlo's powerlessness has become what supports her painting, and it is thus not her wounded self but Kahlo the painter who claims Rivera as her own, and to whom she has given herself, body and soul. In this same year of 1949, Kahlo wrote a few words about Rivera for the catalogue to the major retrospective exhibition mounted in honor of his 50 years' work as an artist: "Diego is not constrained by any limited or particular personal relationships. Contradictory, like everything that moves life onward, his relationships are at one and the same time a huge embrace and a violent release of powerful and individual forces [...] In my difficult and hidden role, as the ally of this extraordinary man, I am rewarded like the green dot that exists within a sea of red, the reward that makes for equilibrium."[7] *Diego and I* (p. 313) was to be Kahlo's last great self-portrait painted with that fine and precise brushwork in the style of a Flemish painter. A new period of illness and pain was about to begin, that would last right through until 1954.

Four years after having placed herself in Dr. Wilson's care, Kahlo was once again in poor health. Following a series of visits to different doctors, all with their own ideas for how she should be treated, in January 1950 part of Kahlo's right foot had to be amputated, as had been originally diagnosed by her longstanding friend and confidant, Dr. Eloesser. While she was still in hospital recovering, she had to undergo another operation for a bone graft to correct the fusion of her vertebrae that Dr. Wilson had carried out a few years previously. As Matilde Kahlo Calderón explained to Dr. Eloesser in a letter she wrote on Kahlo's behalf, this second operation had resulted in Kahlo suffering from feverish episodes, intestinal paralysis, and constant vomiting, and meant that she had had to wear an orthopedic corset. Kahlo had suffered great pain all over her body, and because she was

Marcel Sternberger, **Frida Kahlo**, 1952
Gelatin silver print, 50.8 x 40.6 cm (20 x 16 in.)
New York, collection of Marcel Sternberger

intolerant to morphine she had to be injected with high doses of Demerol. On April 4, she had to have yet another operation on her spine because of a serious bone infection. As Kahlo's sister put it, she was going through a terrible ordeal, as if she were in a bed filled with broken glass.

Even so, it was not all pain for the nine months she stayed in the American British Cowdray Hospital. The character of Kahlo, as the painter, can be seen posing in several photographs taken by Juan Guzmán (Hans Gutmann; 1911–1982), a photographer born in Cologne who had fled to France with the rise of National Socialism and later moved to Spain, before eventually arriving in Mexico in 1939 as an exile from the Spanish Civil War. As an experienced photographer, Guzmán took a number of pictures of Kahlo in her bed and room at the hospital. In these photographs, Kahlo is shown painting on an easel that had been specially designed so that she could work while she was in bed (p. 296), or in the plaster corset she had to wear which she had decorated with an image of the Communist hammer and sickle (p. 295). With braids and red ribbons in her hair, wearing makeup and jewelry with bracelets and rings on each finger, she looks like a princess. She was also kept entertained by the various people who came to visit her, including the famous actress María Félix, and also put on puppet shows and made drawings of the models of little figures that Rivera had sent her. She became something of a celebrity during her stay at the hospital, and it became like a theater set, with Kahlo on the stage. Once again then, the force of her character was imposed on the pain being endured by the physical person.

While Kahlo was convalescing at the hospital she also began to paint again, although it is clear from the photographs and unfinished paintings now in the Museo Frida Kahlo in Coyoacán that her physical strength was much reduced. One portrait that was left unfinished shows her family (pp. 318/319); it was partly based on the composition of *My Grandparents, My Parents, and I (My Family)* from 1936 (pp. 118/119), but now included her sisters Matilde, Adriana, and Cristina, as well as her niece and nephew Isolda and Antonio. She also started work on a self-portrait (pp. 320/321) that she gave to Dr. Farill for having saved her life, and, as she said herself, for giving her back her joy in life. It is a carefully painted work, and shows Kahlo already in a wheelchair with a visibly exhausted face and frail body beneath her traditional indigenous clothing.

At this time as well she decided to go back to painting still lifes, but now with a different approach from what she had used in the late 1930s and early 1940s. The first works in this new series can be interpreted as songs in praise of life after she had been discharged from hospital and had returned to her home in Coyoacán. The fruits are ripe and full of color, and the paintings play freely with the volume of their forms and the seductiveness of their colors; some of the fruits are also cut open to expose the richness

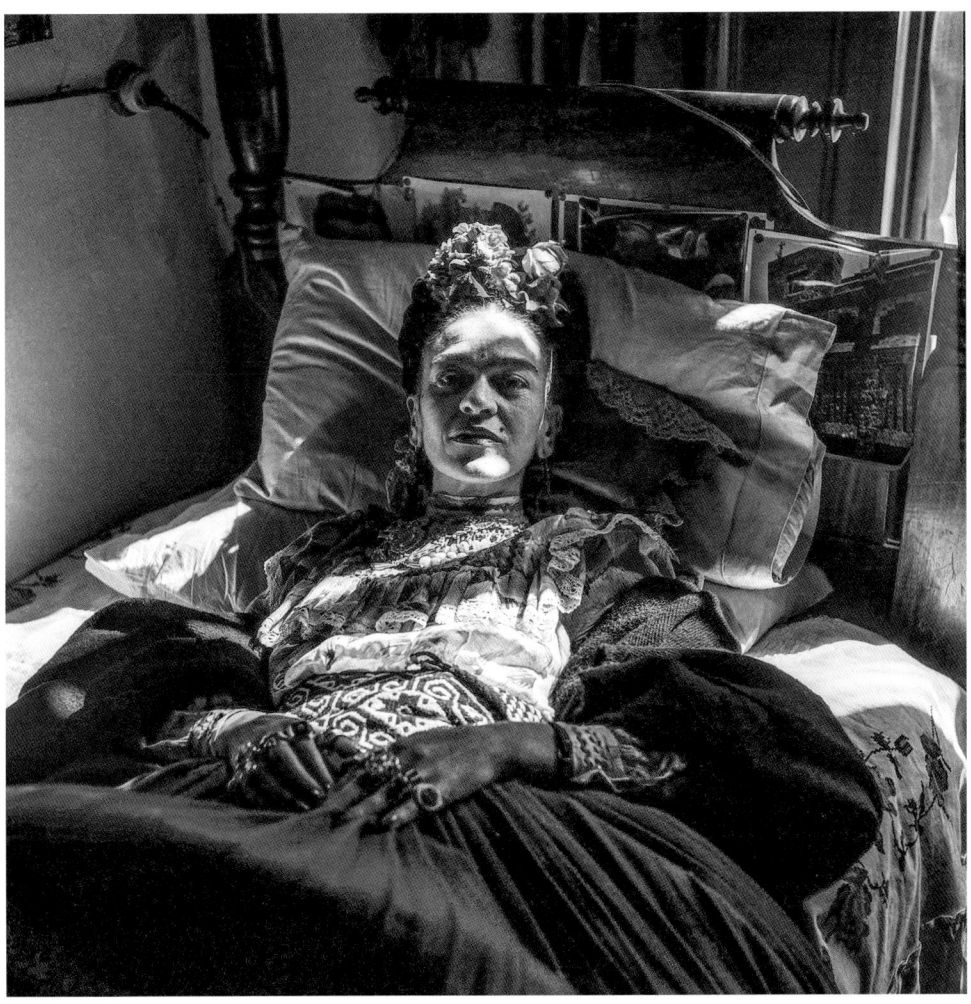

Bernice Kolko, **Frida Kahlo in her bedroom
in the Casa Azul**, Coyoacán, *c.* 1952
Gelatin silver print, 24.8 x 19.5 cm (9¾ x 7⅝ in.)
Mexico City, Fundación Zúñiga Laborde

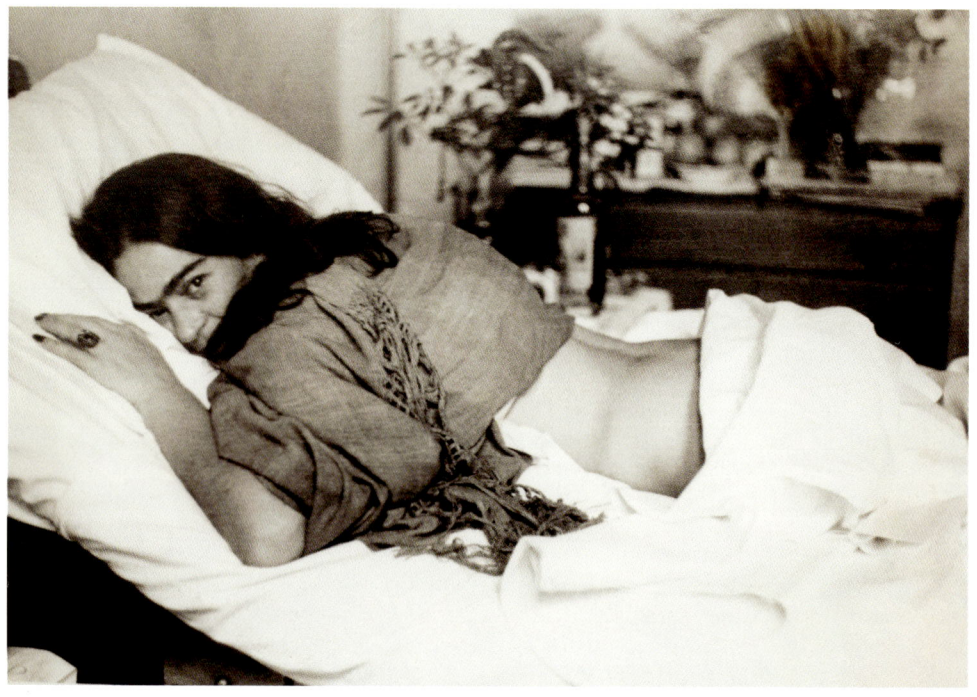

Nickolas Muray, **Frida**, New York, 1946
Gelatin silver print, 8.3 x 16 cm (3¼ x 6¼ in.)
Nickolas Muray Photo Archives

of their insides, as if they were human organs full of health and vitality (pp. 334/335, 336/337, and 338). Just two years later, however, the feeling of exuberance in these small still lifes was beginning to fade, as a reflection that Kahlo's health was deteriorating once again and as she felt that her body was beginning to give up. These still lifes had become a means for her to express her emotions, and an outlet for the distress and anguish that was taking hold of her. As a result, the fruits take on human characteristics, with eyes that seem to look at us and even cry, as in *Weeping Coconuts* (p. 341). The range of colors becomes more limited and the fruits look overripe, in a sort of parallel development to what had happened to Kahlo's own body. These still-life paintings are like small self-portraits, the last metaphors of Kahlo's state of mind in this difficult, terminal stage of her life (see also pp. 342/343).

During this final creative phase, Kahlo's left-wing ideology became fully explicit in her work, which had not been the case in the two previous decades she had been painting (pp. 335, 356). In the postwar period both Kahlo and Rivera felt deeply concerned by the arms race that had been set in motion between the major powers of the new world order, and in 1949 Kahlo became actively involved as a member of the Mexican Committee sponsored by the American Continental Congress for World Peace. She and Rivera had also become involved in pro-Soviet activities, in conjunction with the international peace movement, and for the Congress due to be held in Vienna in 1952 Kahlo painted a small composition to highlight the dangers of a global disaster, part landscape and part still life, with the title *Congress of the Peoples for Peace* (pp. 344/345). In the center of the painting is a tree symbolizing life, knowledge, and harmony between nations, on either side of which two nuclear explosions indicate the apocalyptic threat hanging over the future of humanity. Not only is the subject matter new within the context of the rest of Kahlo's work, but so too the manner in which it was painted. The brushwork is thick and textured, in an expressionistic style that is quite uncharacteristic of Kahlo and is further enhanced by the acidic colors used. She seems to have lost her touch for the fine and delicate short brushstrokes that previously marked her style, perhaps as a result of all her new anxieties, together with the simple inability to carry on painting as before. She still managed, albeit with some difficulty, to finish a portrait of her father (p. 322), which turned out to be the last of her works to express her usual pictorial spirit, in tribute to the man who had guided her artistic talent. At this time too Kahlo was giving considerable thought to what her own legacy would be as an artist, since although her work was seemingly little more than an intimate look at her own human condition, she recognized that there was a need for it to go beyond the limits of her person and that this could only be done by means of what had always been her main occupation, namely a painter. Consequently, in the still lifes she painted in 1952 and 1953 a dove of peace makes its appearance. As still lifes they are also framed within a context of cosmogonic visions, with titles that directly communicate the message Kahlo wanted to convey: *Still Life (Living Nature)* (pp. 348/349), *Fruit of Life (Light)* (p. 346), and *Still Life (Long Live Life)* (p. 350).

In 1953, Kahlo once again had to put herself in the care of her doctors, and in August part of her right leg had to be amputated. This would be the final blow, and Rivera proved to be right when he warned that the operation, far from saving her, would lead to her death. Neither her will to live nor her desire to remain with Rivera were enough to enable her to survive. Fate had finally caught up with her. In her diary she wrote, in the plainest language, "I am disintegration" (p. 367), and it was evident that the conceptual deconstruction which had begun in her painting was now on the point of claiming her physical self.

Kahlo's character had now fallen silent. From the night before this operation, she stopped speaking; she had nothing more to say. Her body was about to be cut up yet again, so as to try and save her life. The paradox of such a situation is that, in many ways,

Kahlo did indeed die with the amputation itself, for though alive, she was dead inside. Her zest for life had disappeared, as had her passion for painting, for loving and being loved, lost amid a deep depression that took months to subside. In some of the paintings she was able to complete in 1953 and 1954, all her former strengths as an artist can be seen to have been completely destroyed, for example, in *Still Life with Flag* (p. 352), in which Kahlo's touch cannot be discerned. Painting would seem to have become a form of torture for her, and neither she herself nor the character she had created were recognizable any longer. She developed a strange ideological obsession with Stalin, and painted a portrait of him in a style that seems inexplicably rhetorical and academic, although this was left unfinished.

In her final days, it is probable that she felt overcome by moments of hysteria and loss of control. The drugs and medication were keeping her in a daze, while the people who were now looking after her were gradually isolating her from her friends, and even her family. She was slowly fading, and being attended to mostly by nurses. For Rivera, it was unbearable to see her like this. Kahlo may well have tried to take her own life, and unleashed her final expressions of rage and unconditional love for Rivera on the pages of her diary. Her last two self-portraits are testaments to this period of shutting down, with regard to her mental faculties as well as her image. In *Marxism Shall Give Health to the Ill* (p. 356), Kahlo appears standing on her own two feet, wearing a corset yet freed from having to rely on using her crutches. Although this painting was left unfinished, she had originally decided on a much longer title for it: *Peace on Earth so that Marxist Science May Save the Sick and those Oppressed by Criminal Yankee Capitalism.* In the spring of 1954 Kahlo made her last two paintings, both of them small works for which she used a palette knife that made them visually very powerful. Of the two, *Frida in Flames*, or *Self-portrait inside a Sunflower* (p. 357), carries a sense of foreboding. The painting shows her seated next to a brick kiln amid a desolate landscape, while her face is surrounded by what would appear to be a headdress of some sort in the form of a sunflower. The whole picture is painted with anger and a certain violence, using thick, expressionistic colors that lack any shading or tonality and with the shapes only crudely outlined, thus revealing Kahlo's frustration

Self-portrait (with Loose Hair), July 1947
Oil on masonite, 61.5 x 45.5 cm (24¼ x 17¾ in); inscribed on the speech scroll:
Aqui me pinté yo, Frida Kahlo, con / la imágen del espejo. Tengo 37 años, /
y es el mes de Julio de mil novecientos / cuarenta y siete. En Coyoacán, México, /
lugar donde nací. (I, Frida Kahlo, painted myself here from / my image in a mirror.
I am 37 years old / and it is July, nineteen hundred / forty-seven.
In Coyoacán, Mexico, / the place where I was born.)
Private collection *(detail p. 285)*

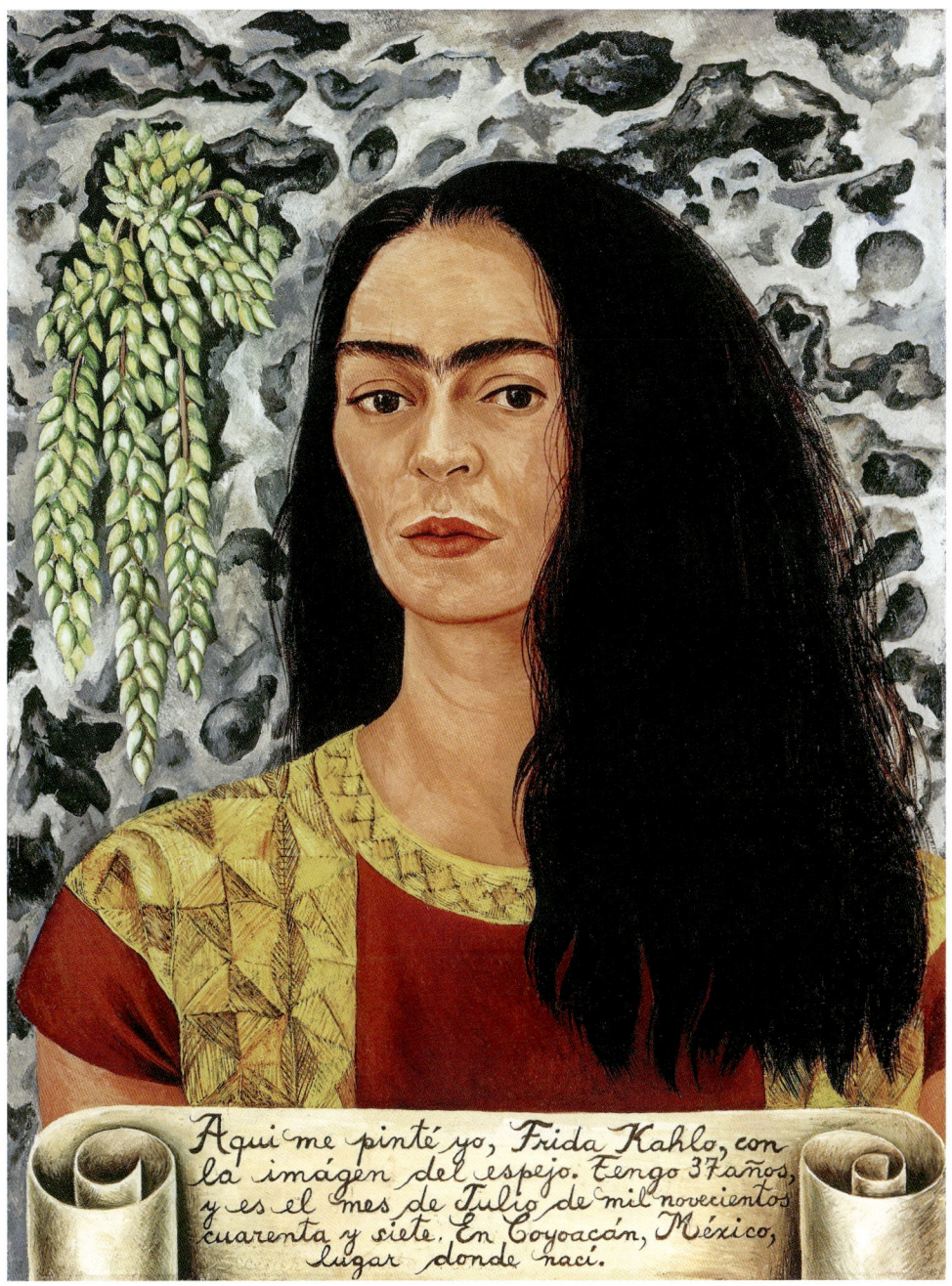

at not being able to paint exactly what she wanted to convey: her infinite loneliness and the absence of affection, and her feeling that she was lost in an uncertain end to her life that she no longer wanted to prolong. It is known that she tried to destroy the painting, scraping away at the surface with a straight-edged knife. It survived though, and as such serves as a reliable witness to the literal deconstruction of her painting, together with the deconstruction of her character and her personal self.

Kahlo's physical torture at last came to an end on the night of July 13, 1954. She was honored with an open casket at the Palacio de Bellas Artes, and hundreds of mourners attended to pay their last respects while a Communist flag was draped over her coffin. Her body was cremated and a number of those who were there reported that, at the moment when it entered the furnace, her hair and the flowers and ribbons in it all caught fire, making it look as though her face was inside a sunflower.[8] She had finally found her rest, but the legend of Frida Kahlo was only just beginning. Her career as an artist was marked by exceptional opportunities, and she was able to develop her pictorial talent because of her great intellectual ability to question and analyze art. She always had Rivera's unconditional support, and he was perhaps the first to see that she could become a great artist. As a couple together they had many artistic and political concerns in common, and their views and shared ideology made them comrades as well as accomplices. They also loved and admired each other. Kahlo found her own path as an artist, and did so with a directness and intensity of purpose, taking Mexico, New York, and Paris by surprise with the art she made, and within her own time gaining the recognition of the international art world. Kahlo was also a beloved figure in Mexican culture, yet above all else, she was a free human being who allowed herself to love and to explore the world, ever since her childhood. She had enormously strong willpower, and in the course of her life had to deal with a series of very difficult obstacles. But she fought her battles, and won them. She suffered and was loved in equal measure. However, and more than anything else, I believe that her painting deserves to be much better known, and hope that this book may make some contribution to that end.

Tree of Hope (Remain Strong), 1946
Oil on masonite, 56 x 41 cm (22 x 16⅛ in.)
Chicago, private collection

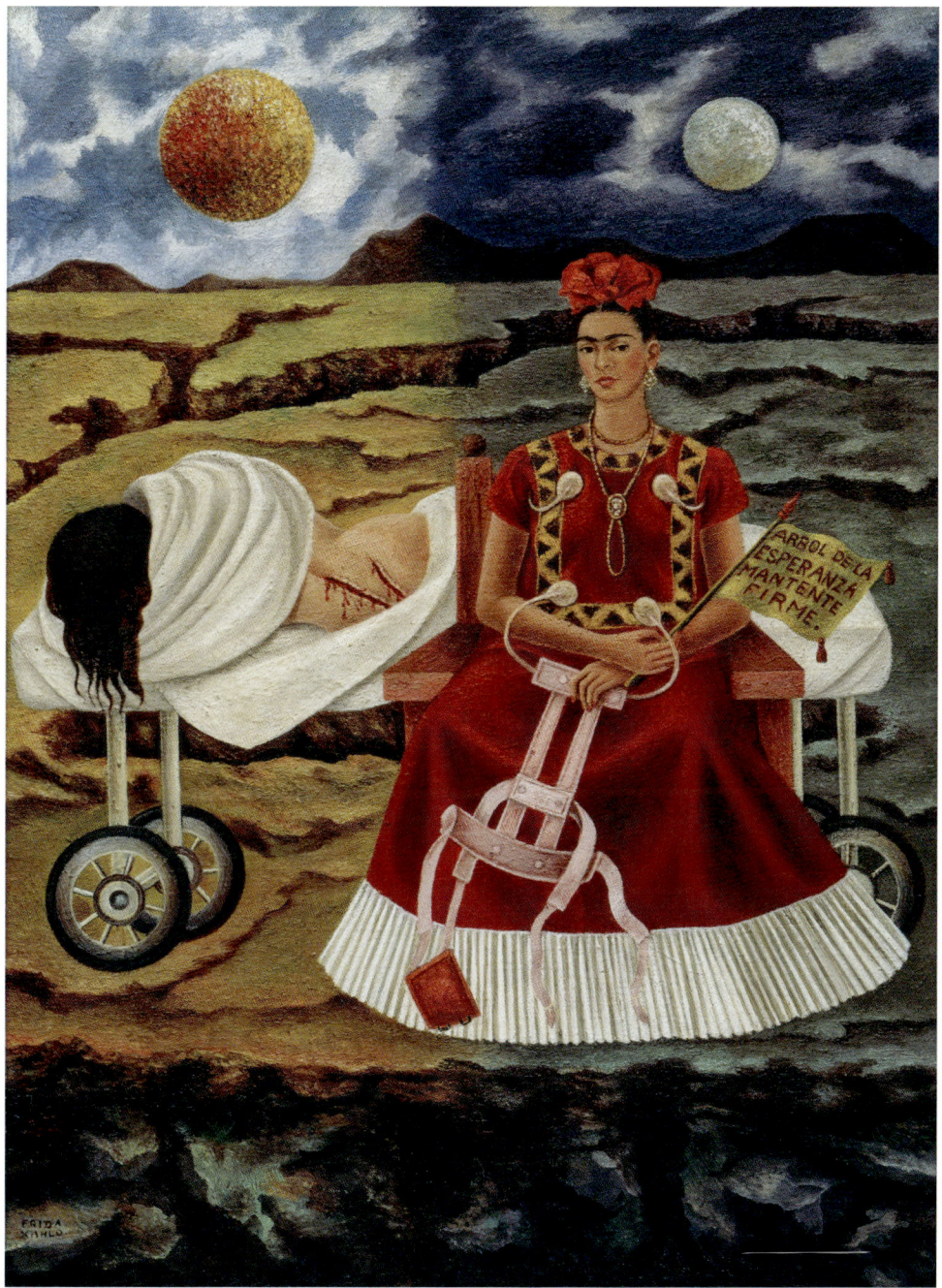

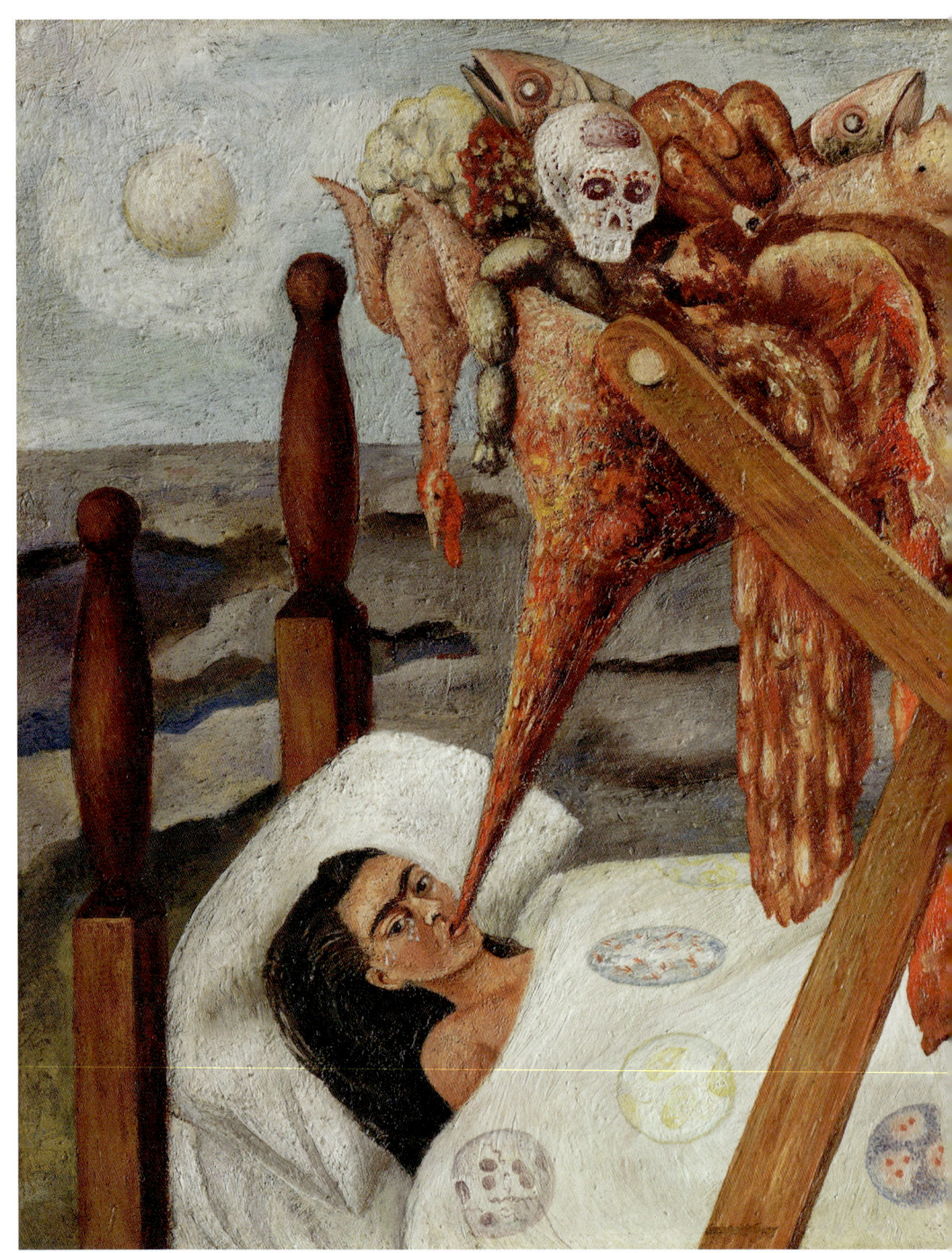

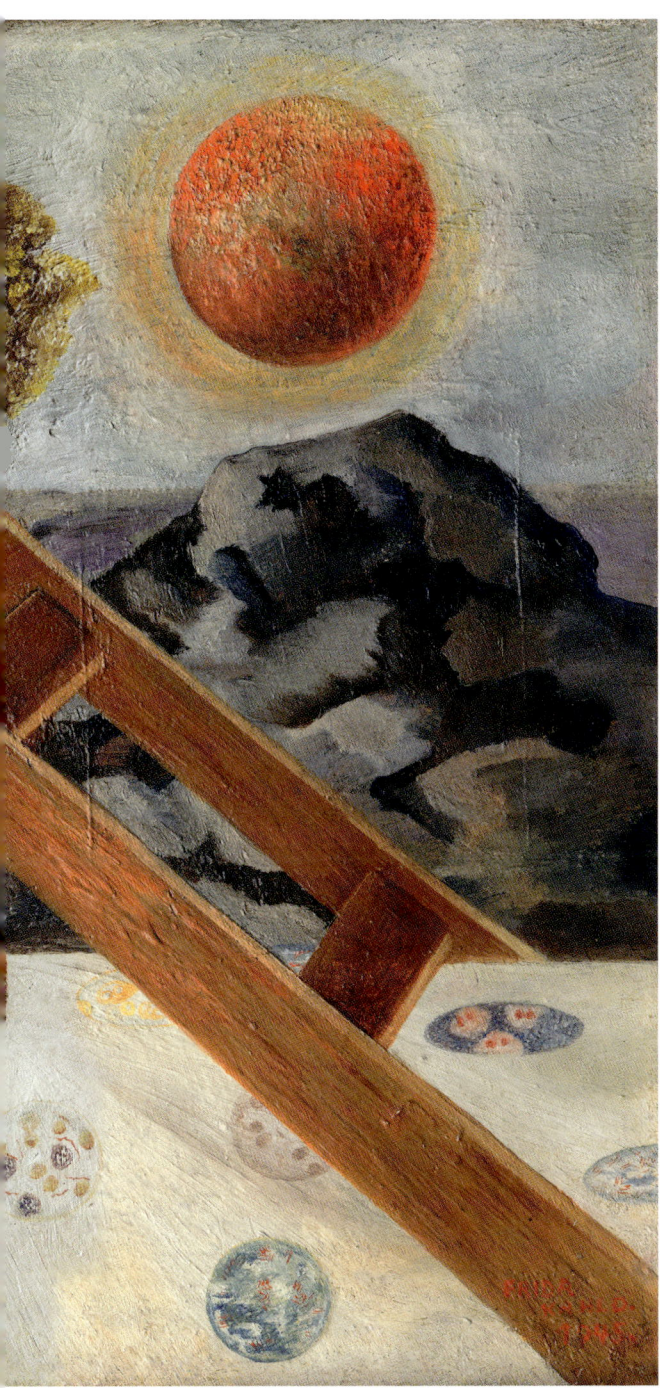

Without Hope, 1945
Oil on canvas, mounted on
masonite, 28 x 36 cm (11 x 14⅛ in.)
Mexico City, Xochimilco,
Museo Dolores Olmedo

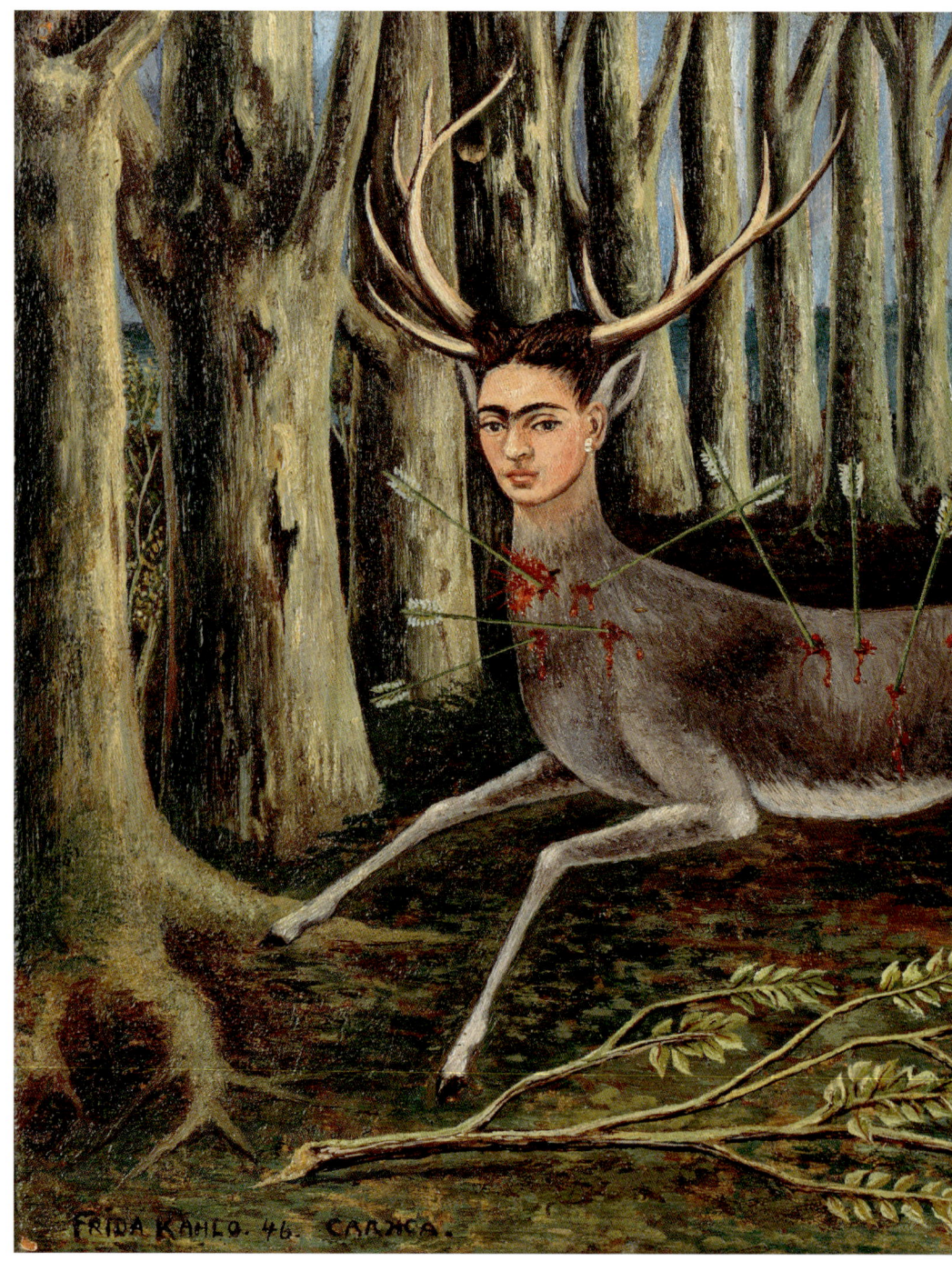

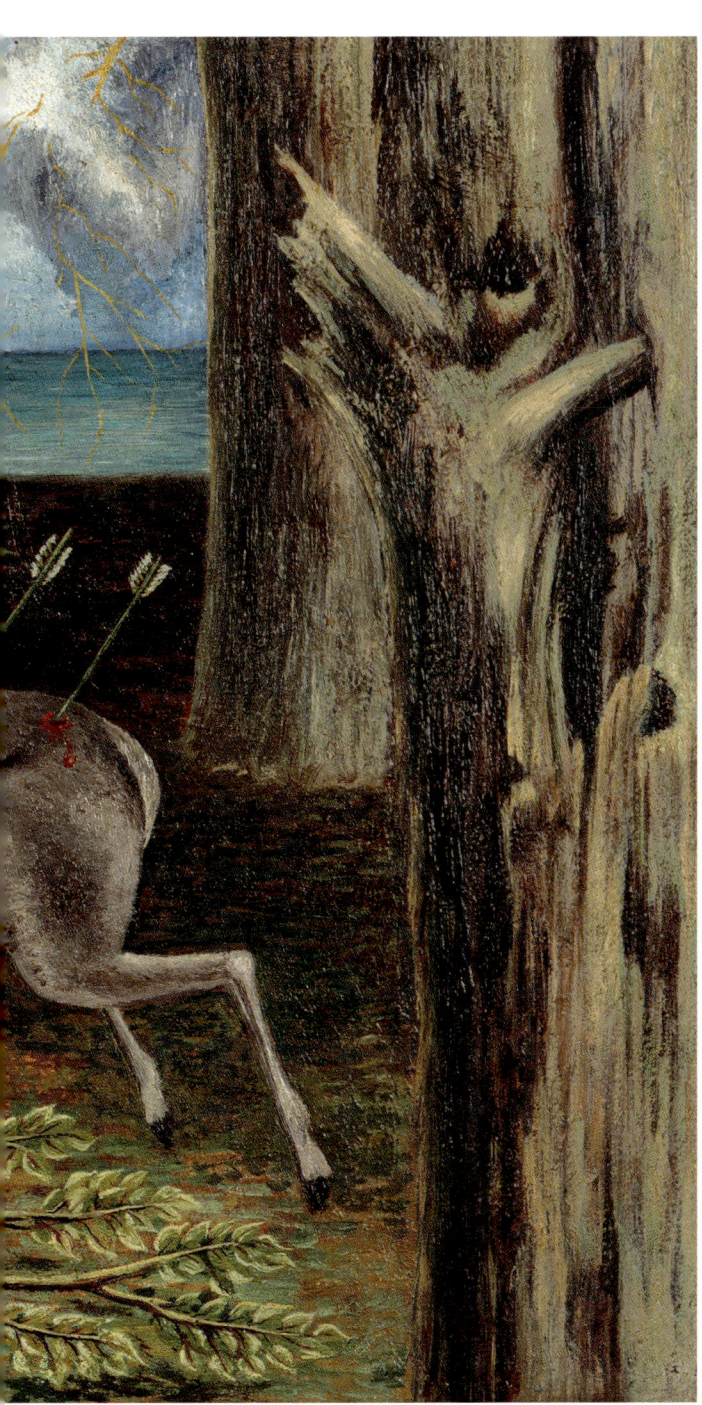

The Little Deer,
April–May 3, 1946
Oil on masonite, 22.4 x 30 cm
(8⅞ x 11¾ in.)
Chicago, private collection

Diego and I, June 1949
Oil on canvas, mounted on wood, 29.8 x 22.4 cm (11¾ x 8⅞ in.)
Buenos Aires, collection of Eduardo F. Costantini

Page 314
Bernard G. Silberstein, **Frida Kahlo in Tehuana costume**, *c.* 1940
Gelatin silver print, 43.2 x 35.6 cm (17 x 14 in.)
New York, collection of Spencer Throckmorton

Page 315
Self-portrait (for Samuel Fastlicht), 1948
Oil on masonite, 50 x 39.5 cm (19¾ x 15½ in.)
Mexico City, private collection

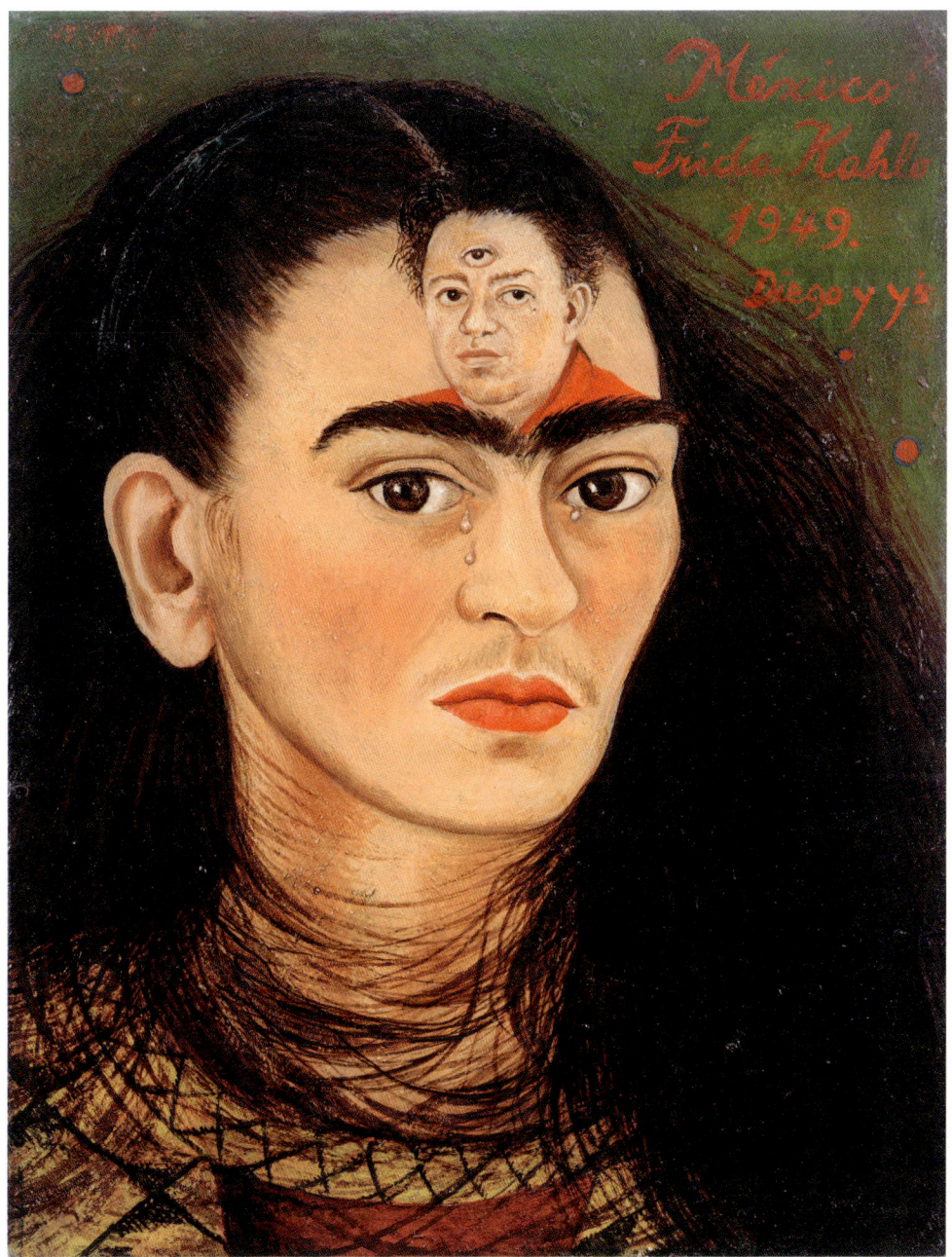

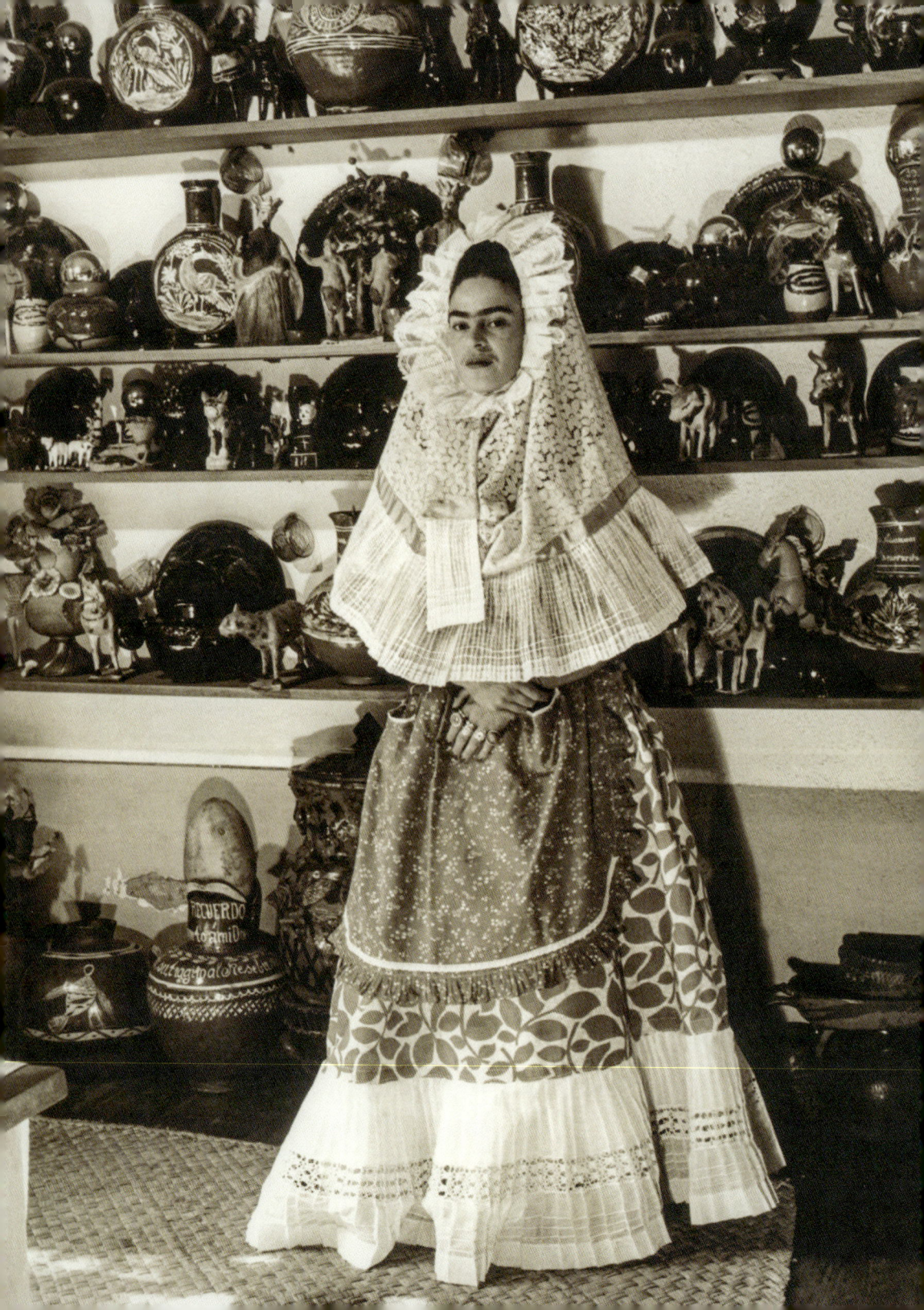

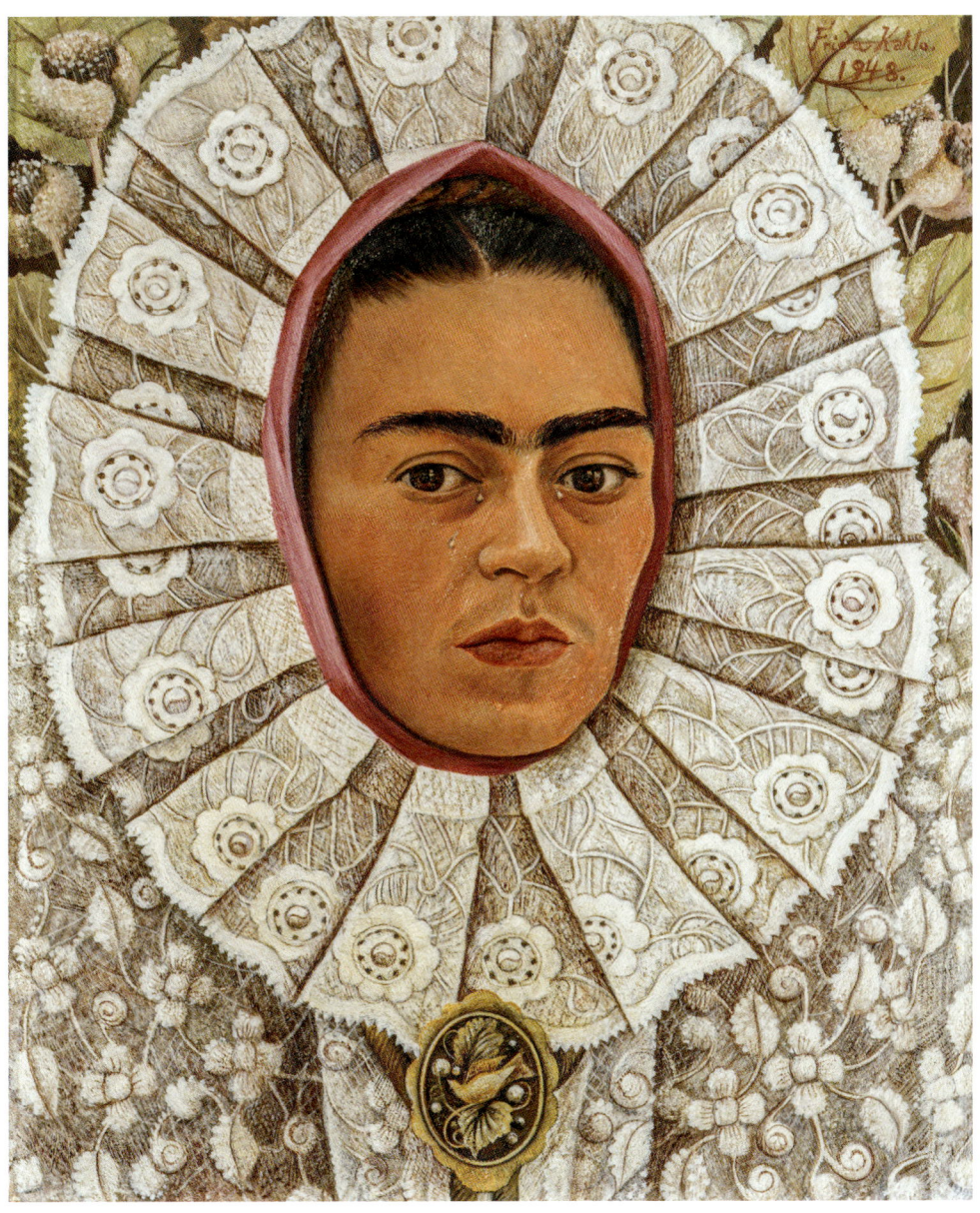

Florence Arquin, **Frida Kahlo in the courtyard of the Casa Azul posing beside** *The Love Embrace of the Universe, the Earth (Mexico), Me, Diego, and Señor Xólotl, c.* 1948
Gelatin silver print, 12.3 x 17 cm (4⅞ x 6¾ in.)
Washington, D.C., Smithsonian Institution, Archives of
American Art, Florence Arquin Papers, 1923–1985

**The Love Embrace of the Universe, the Earth (Mexico),
Me, Diego, and Señor Xólotl**, 1949
Oil on canvas, 70 x 60.5 cm (27½ x 23⅞ in.)
Mexico, The Jacques and Natasha Gelman Collection
of 20th-century Mexican Art/The Vergel Foundation

Pages 318/319
Portrait of Frida's Family (Family Tree) (unfinished), *c.* 1950–1954
Oil on masonite, 41 x 59 cm (16⅛ x 23¼ in.)
Mexico City, Coyoacán, Museo Frida Kahlo

Bottom row, on the left: Matilde and Adriana, Frida's sisters; *center*: Frida and a newborn baby, very likely Wilhelm, her brother (1906), who died shortly after he was born; *on the right*: Isolda, Frida's niece, Cristina, Frida's sister, and Antonio, Frida's nephew, shown both as a small boy (Kahlo rejected this original sketch) and then much older. *Center row*: Guillermo Kahlo, Frida's father, and her mother, Matilde Calderón. *Top row, on the left*: Frida's paternal grandparents, Rosine Marie Henriette Kaufmann and Johann Heinrich Jakob Kahlo; *on the right*: her maternal grandparents, Antonio Calderón and Isabel González y González

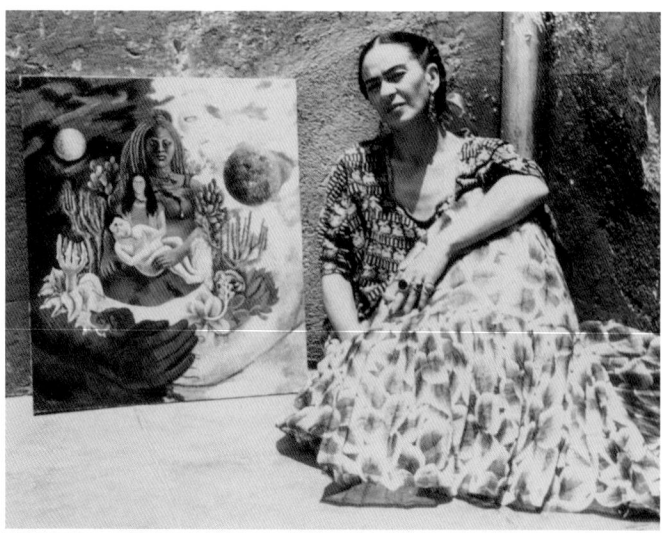

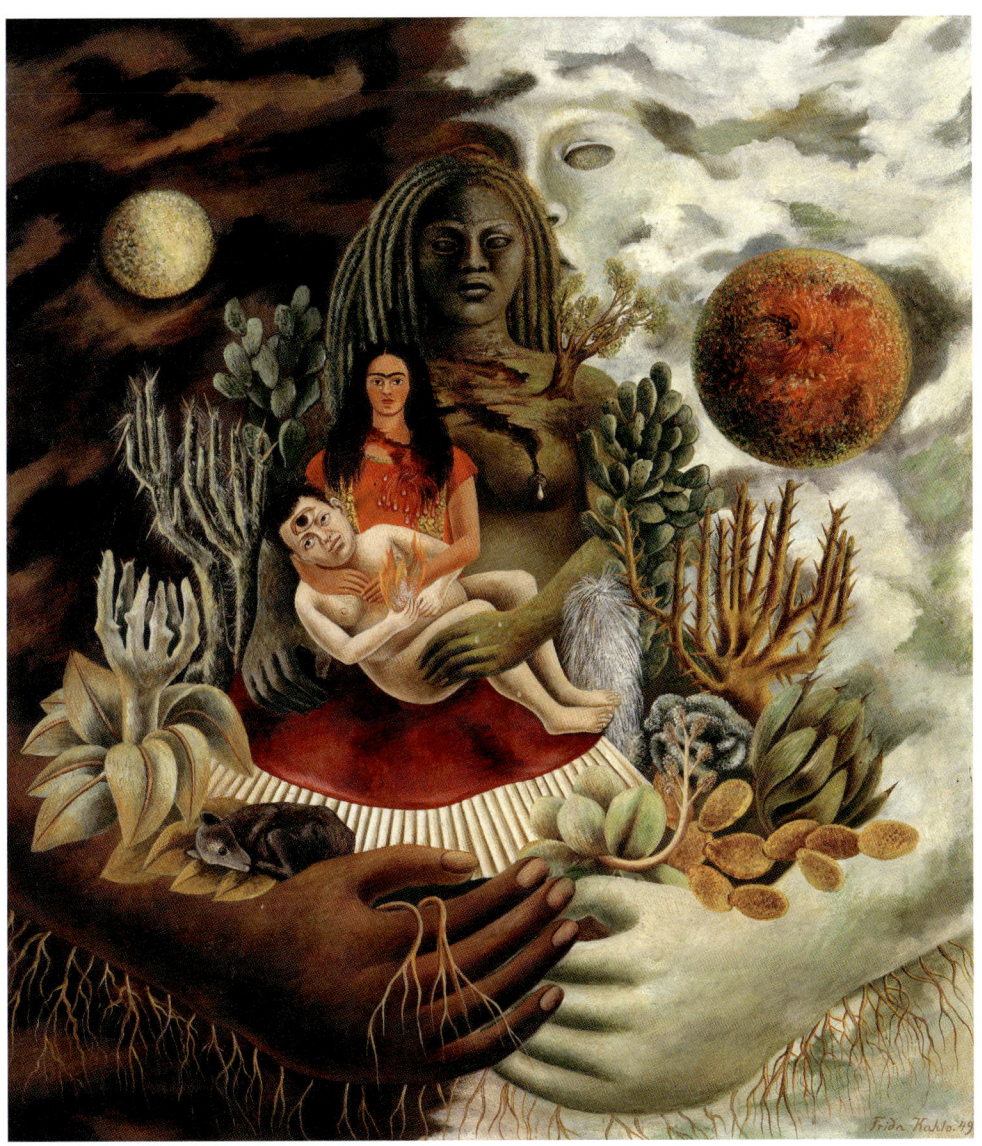

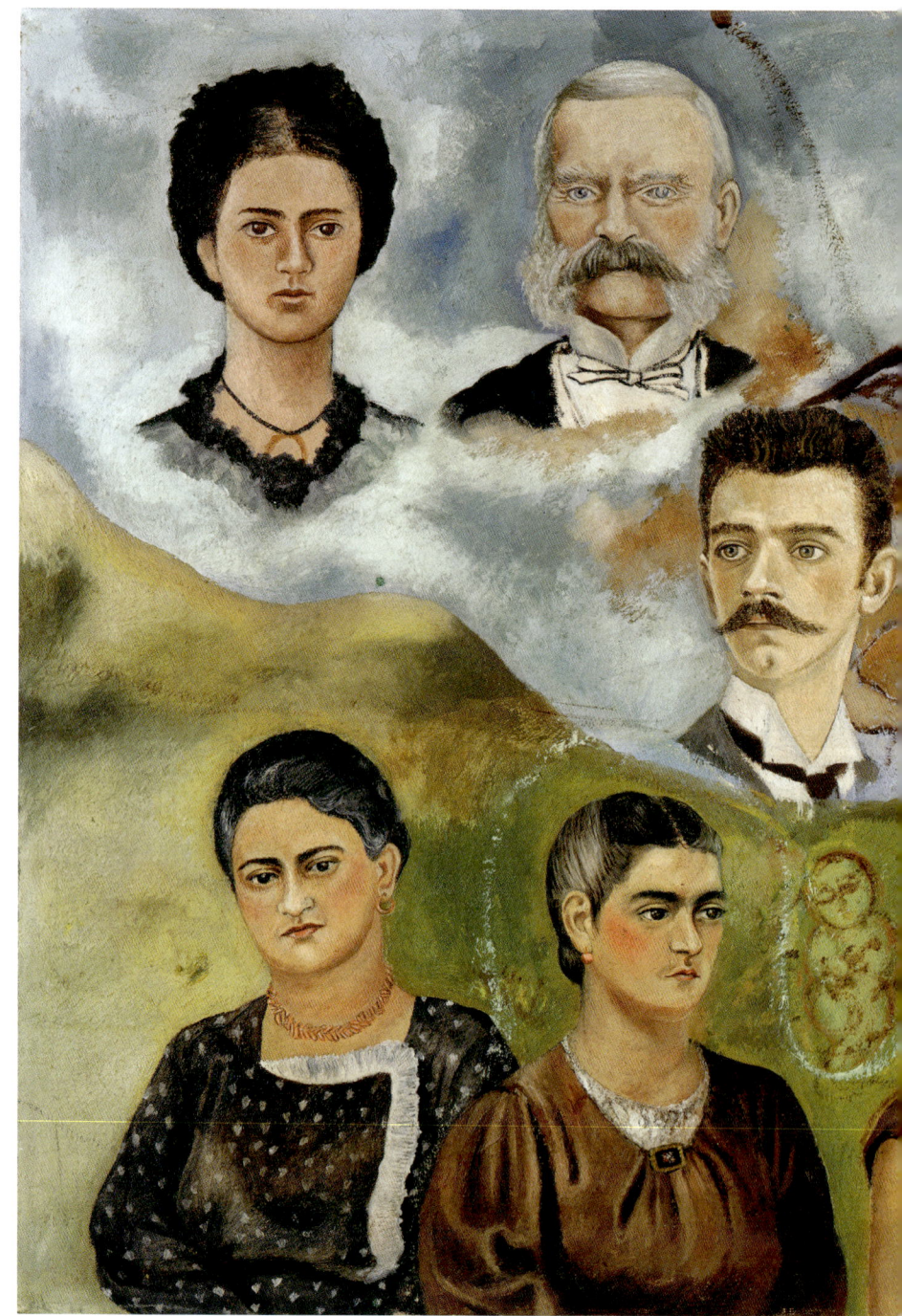

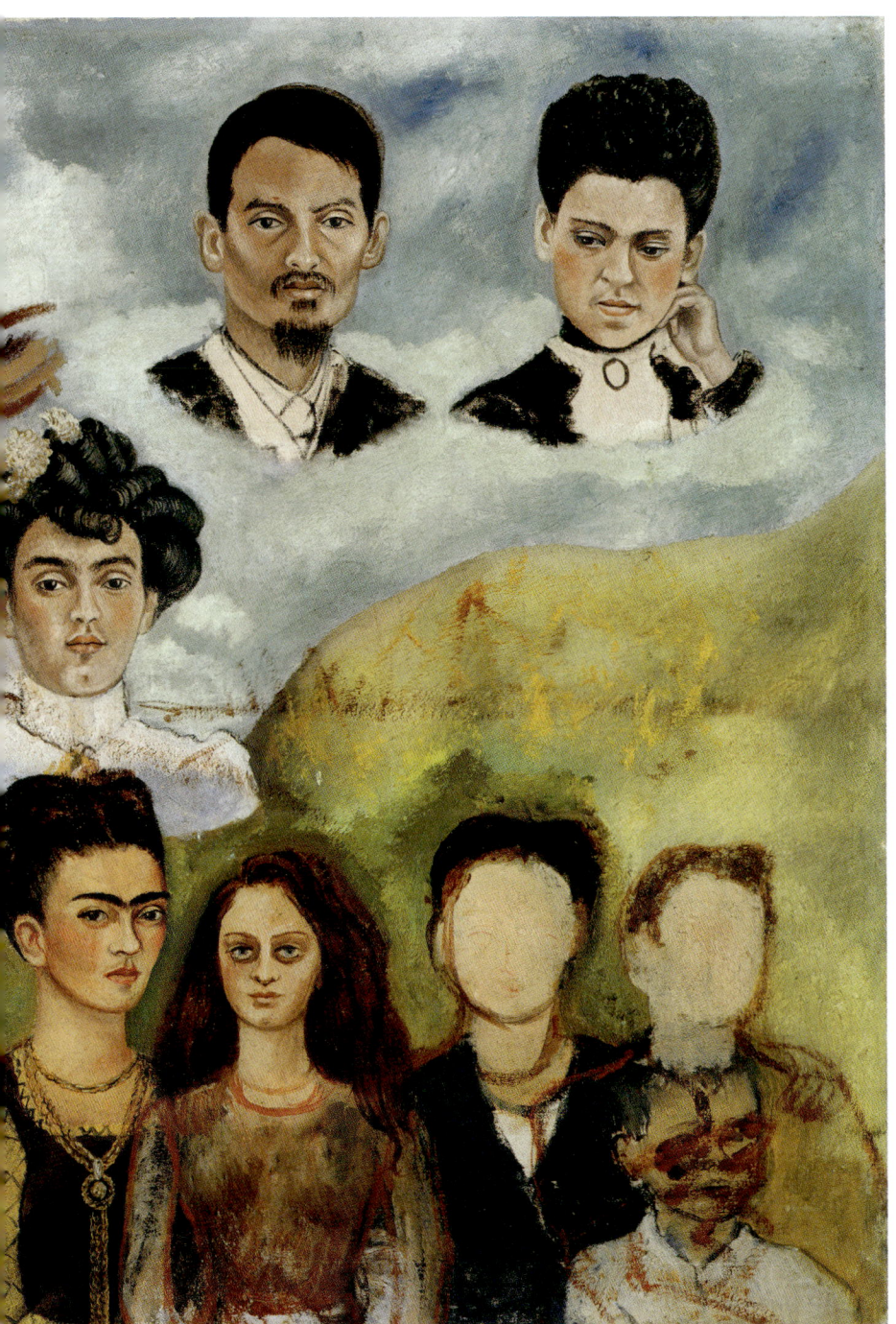

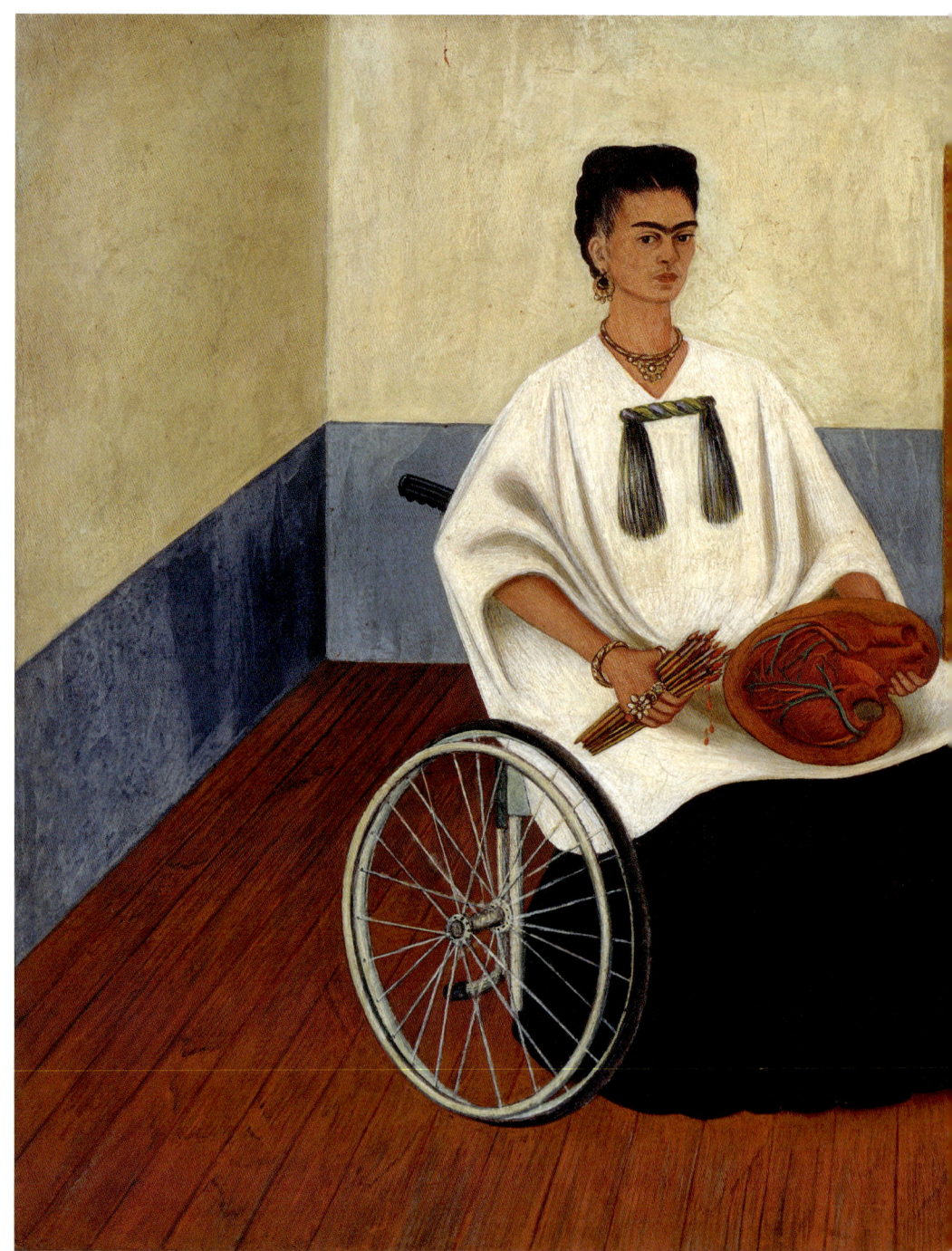

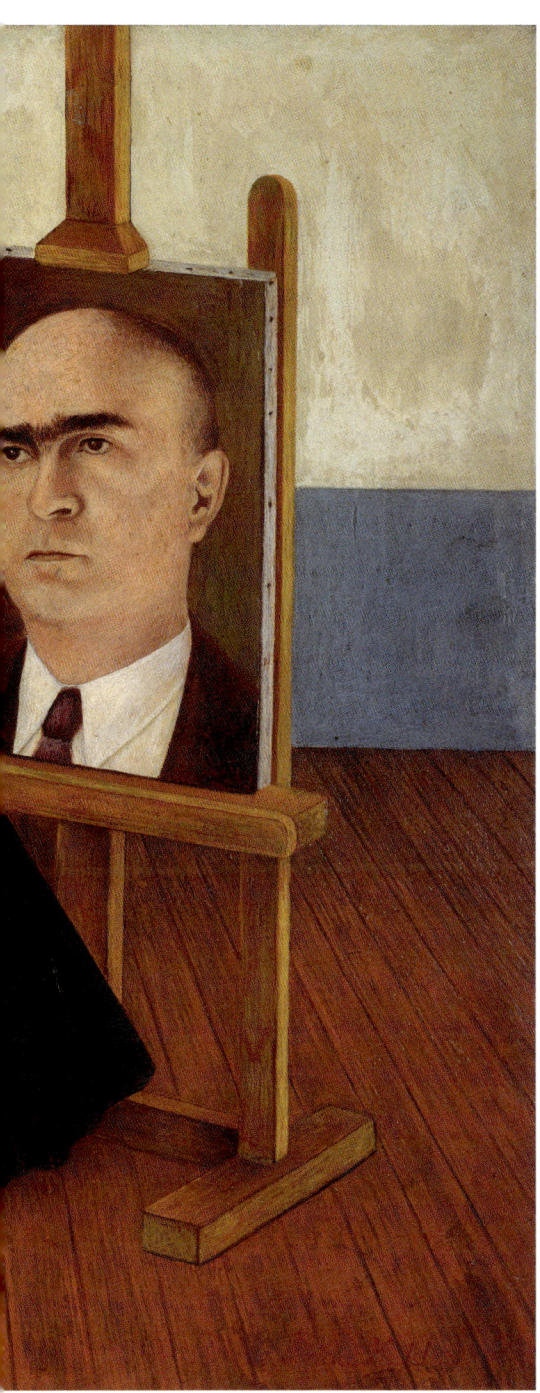

Self-portrait (with Dr. Farill), 1951
Oil on masonite, 41.8 x 50.2 (16⅜ x 19¾ in.)
Private collection, courtesy
Hauser & Wirth Collection Services

Page 322
Portrait of My Father, 1949–1951
Oil on masonite, 60.5 x 46.5 cm (23⅞ x 18¼ in.);
inscribed along the bottom: Pinté a mi padre
Wilhelm Kahlo de origen húngaro alemán artista
fotógrafo de / Profesión, de carácter generoso
inteligente y fino valiente porque padeció durante
/ Sesenta años epilepcia *[sic]*, pero jamás dejó de
trabajar y luchó contra Hitler, con adoración.
Su hija Frida Kahlo. (I painted this portrait of my
father Wilhelm Kahlo, who was of Hungarian-
German origin and an artist and photographer
by / profession, he was kind, intelligent, and
very brave because he suffered / from epilepsy
for 60 years, but he never stopped working and
also fought against Hitler,/ with devotion,
his daughter, / Frida Kahlo.)
Mexico City, Coyoacán, Museo Frida Kahlo

Pages 323
Gisèle Freund, **Frida painting the portrait
of her father** (detail), *c.* 1950

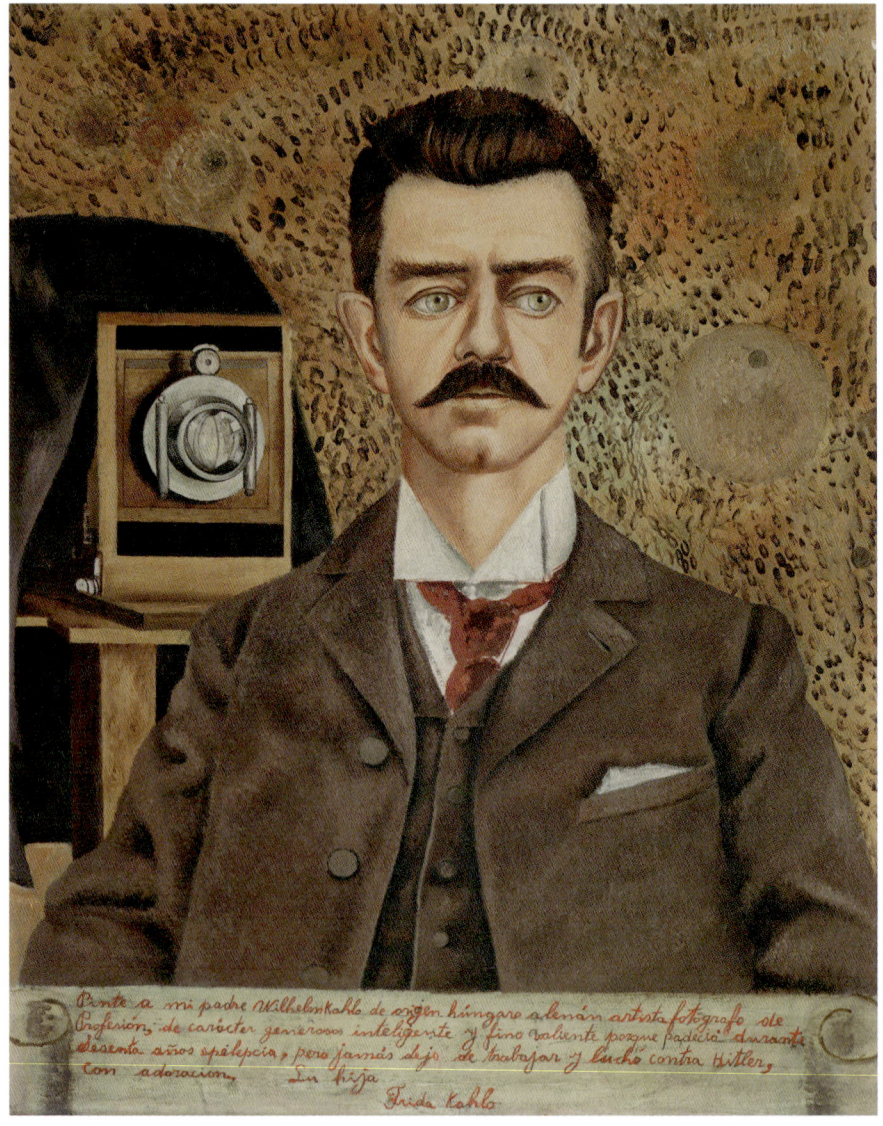

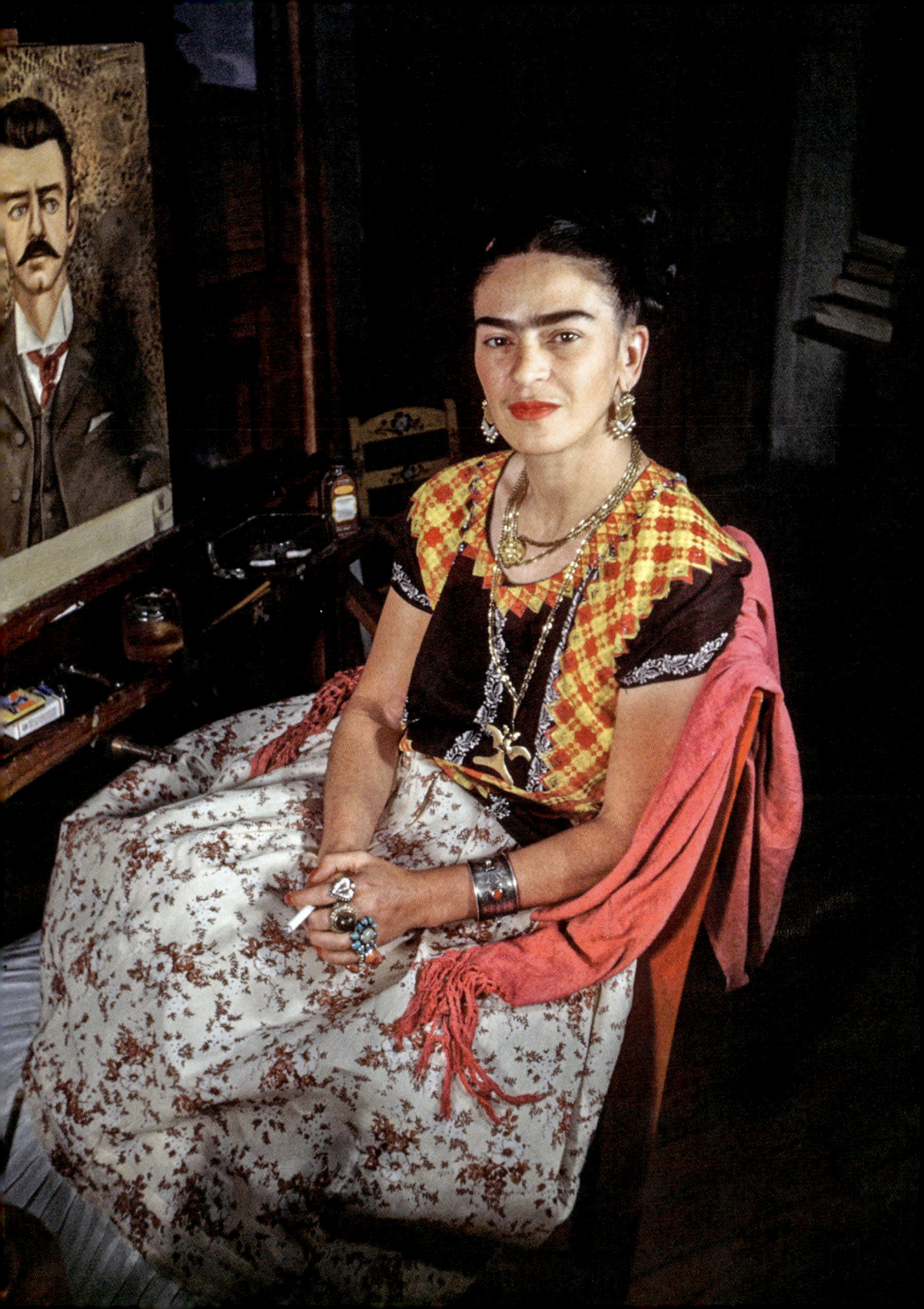

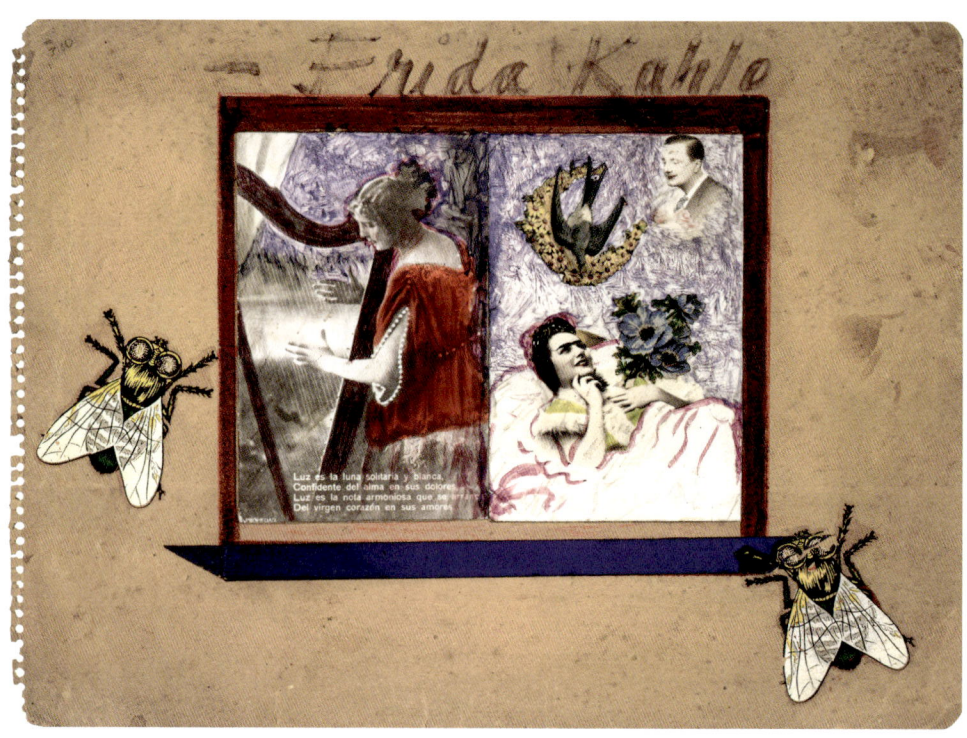

Light Is the Lonely Moon (Collage with Two Flies), *c.* 1953
Watercolor and collage on card stock, 12.7 x 16.8 cm (5 x 6⅝ in.)
Mexico, The Jacques and Natasha Gelman Collection
of 20th-century Mexican Art/The Vergel Foundation

Chromophore-Auxochrome, 1944
Collage of overlaid illustrations from anatomical drawings
of the human body, 42 x 36 cm (16½ x 14⅛ in.)
Mexico, The Jacques and Natasha Gelman Collection
of 20th-century Mexican Art/The Vergel Foundation

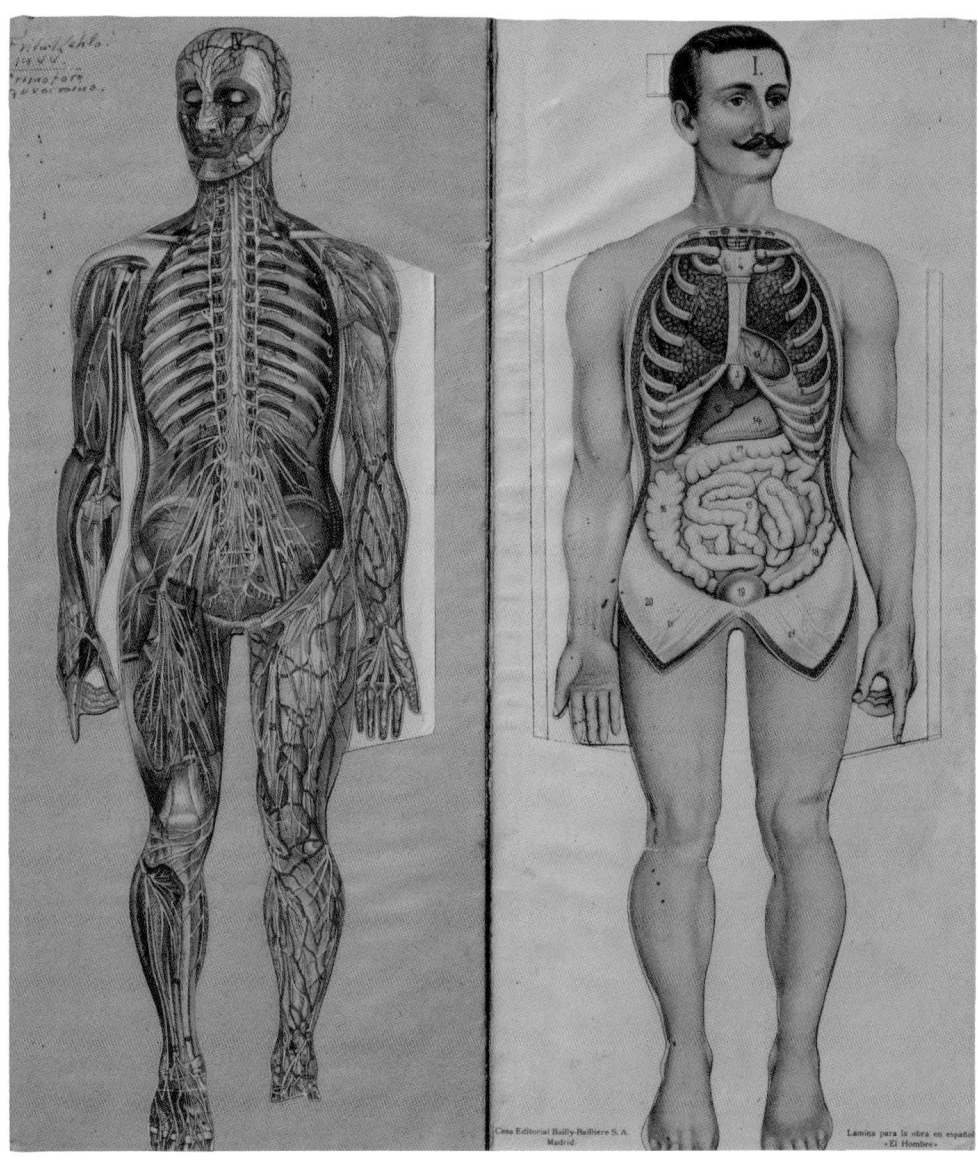

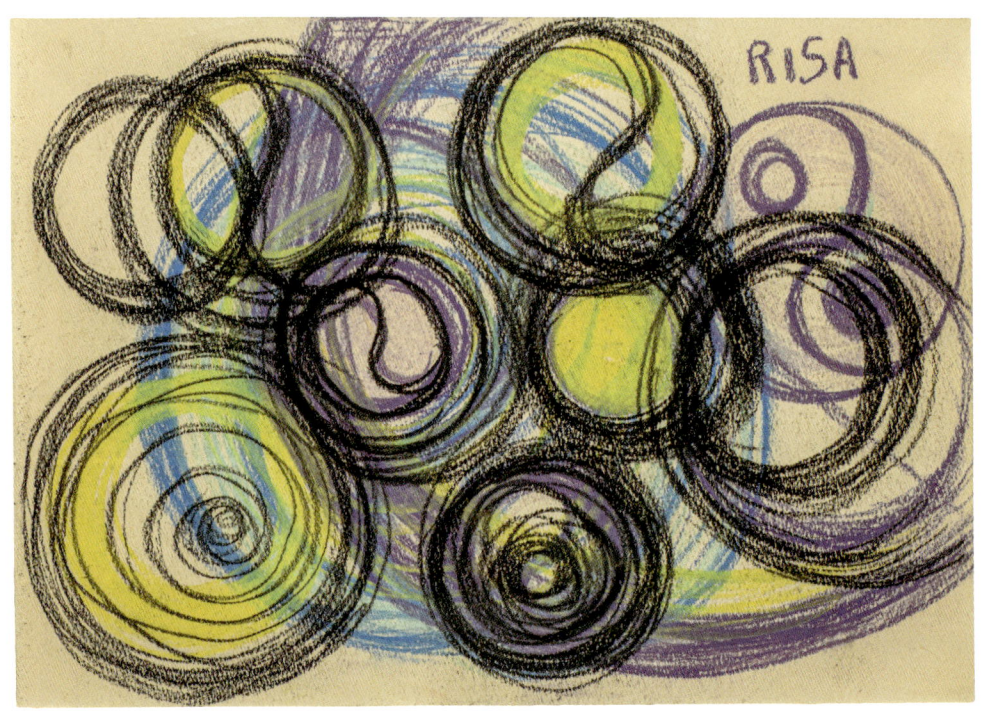

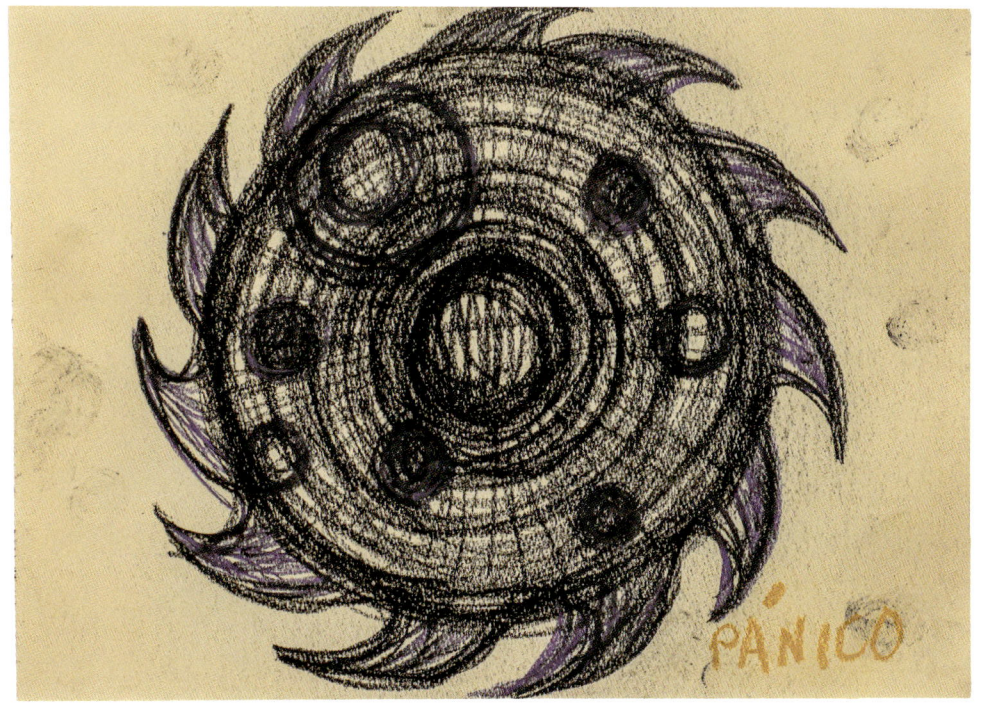

Panic
Conté crayon, colored pencil, and pastel on paper,
22.9 x 31.8 cm (9 x 12½ in.)

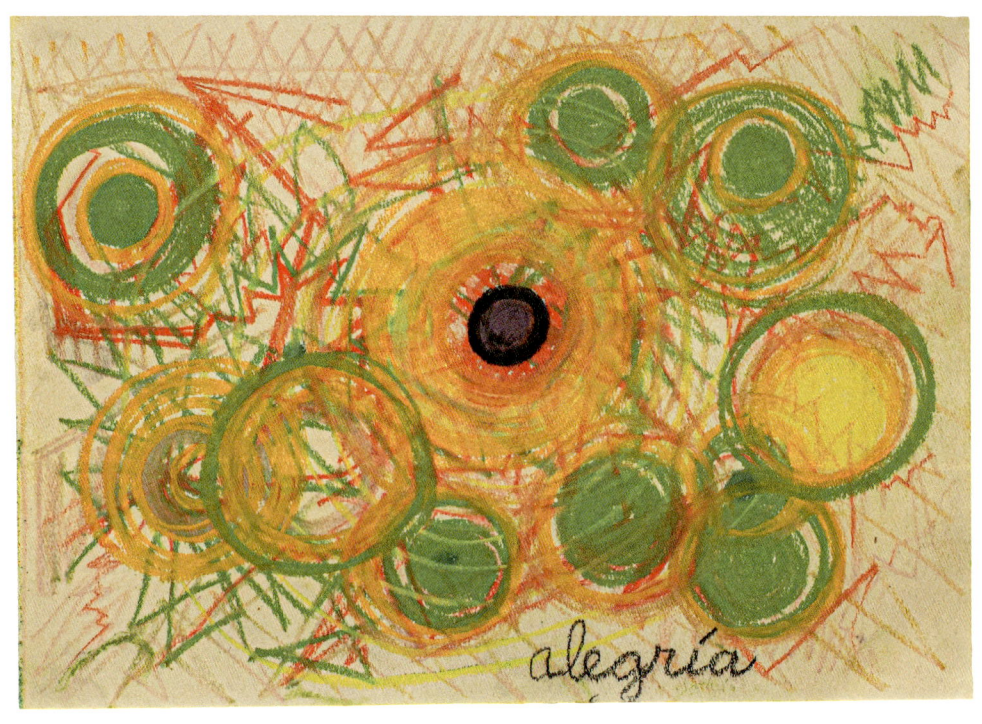

Joy
Pastel, colored pencils and charcoal on paper,
22.9 x 31.8 cm (9 x 12½ in.)

Anguish
Charcoal, crayon, pastel, and colored pencils on paper,
31.8 x 22.9 cm (12½ x 9 in.)

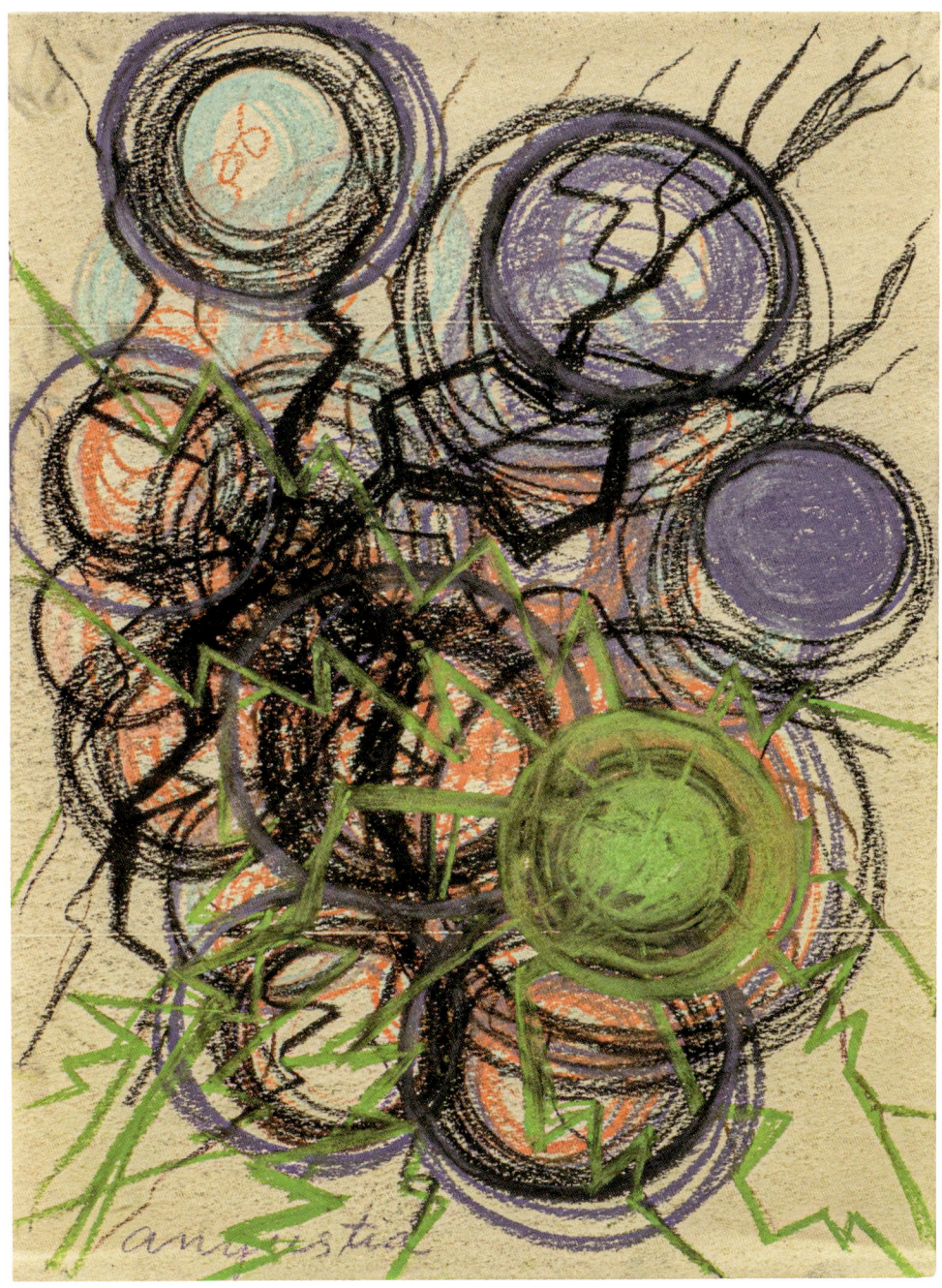

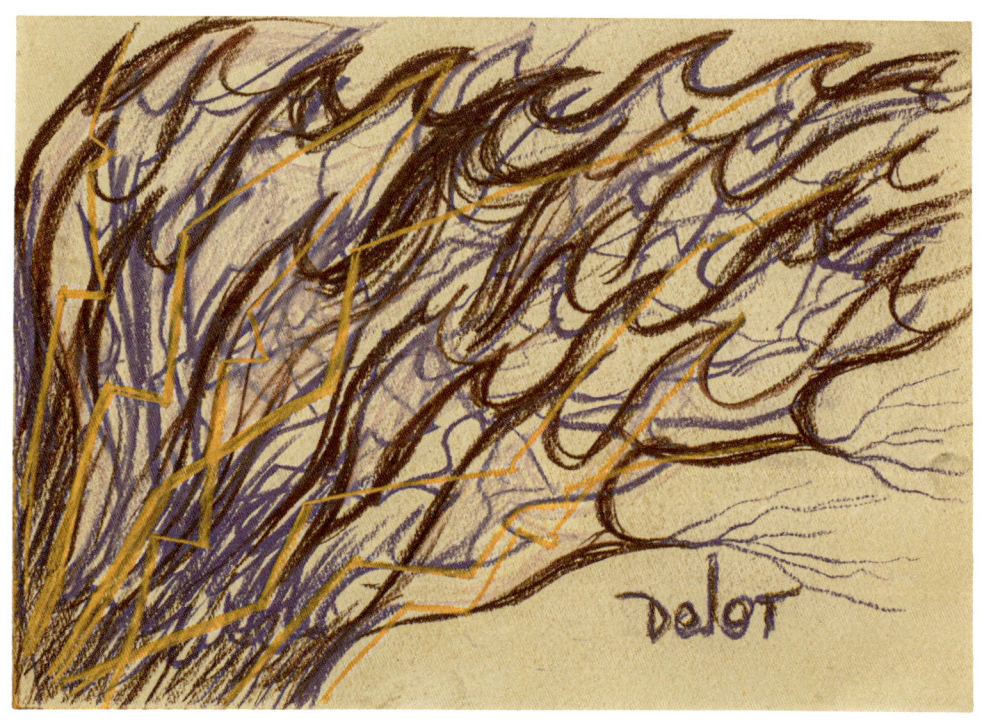

Pain
Crayon, charcoal, pastel, and colored pencils on paper,
22.9 x 31.8 cm (9 x 12½ in.)

Portrait of Juan Rohl, 1947
Ink on paper, 28 x 21 cm (11 x 8¼ in.); inscribed b. r.:
Para Juanito Rohl cariñosamente Frida Kahlo 47.
(For Juanito Rohl fondly Frida Kahlo 47.). Private collection

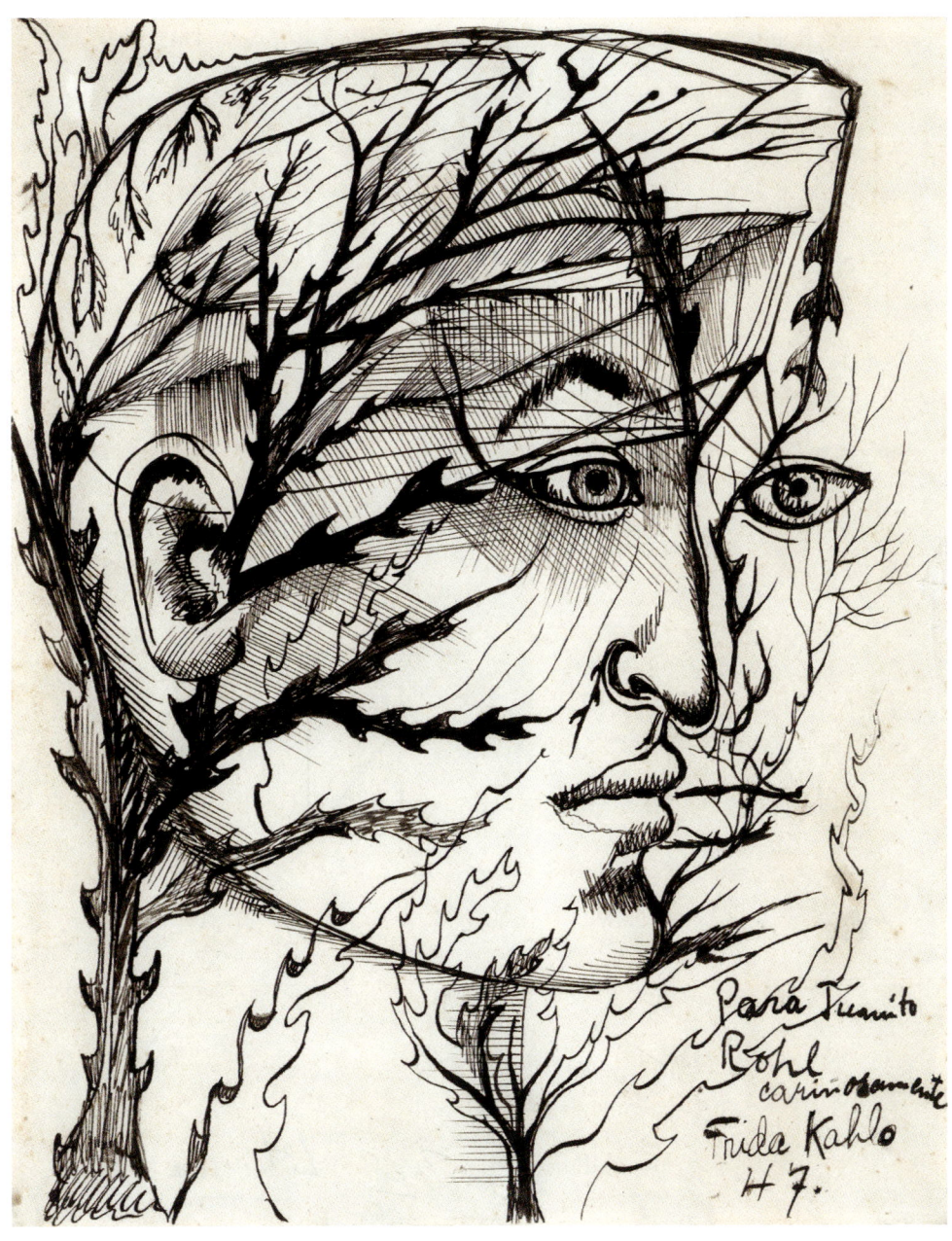

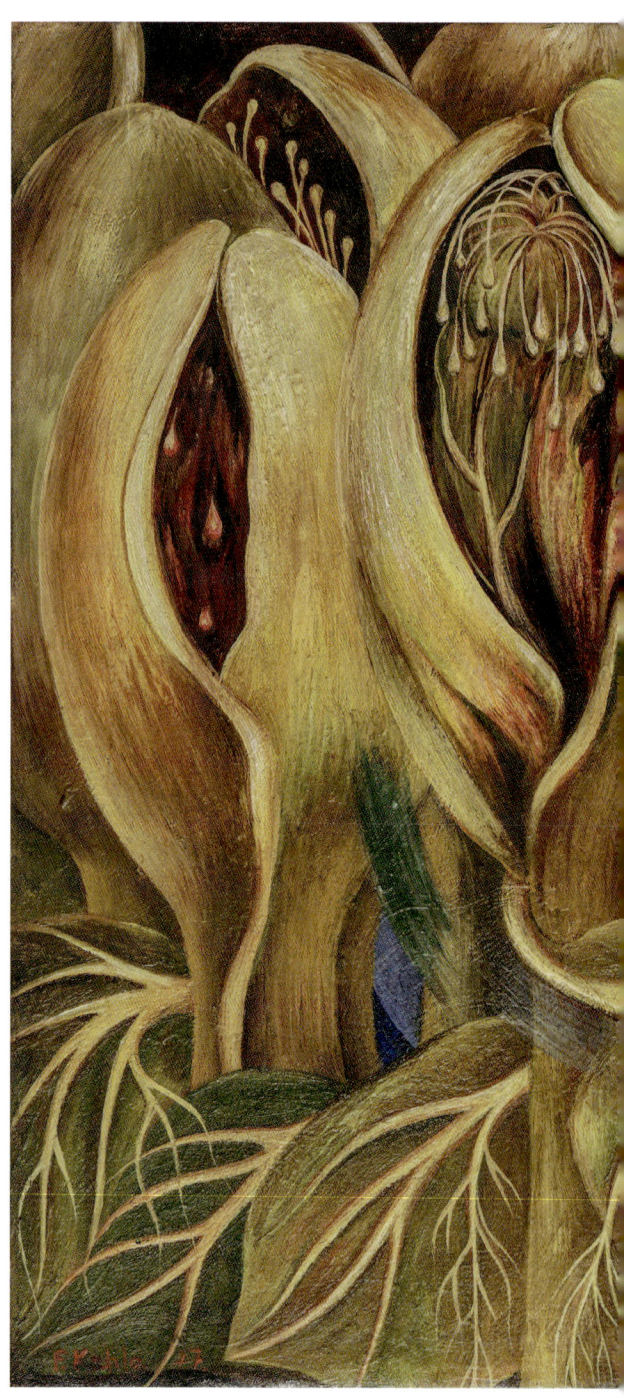

Sun and Life, 1947
Oil on masonite, 40 x 49.5 cm
(15¾ x 19½ in.)
Mexico City, private collection,
courtesy Arvil gallery

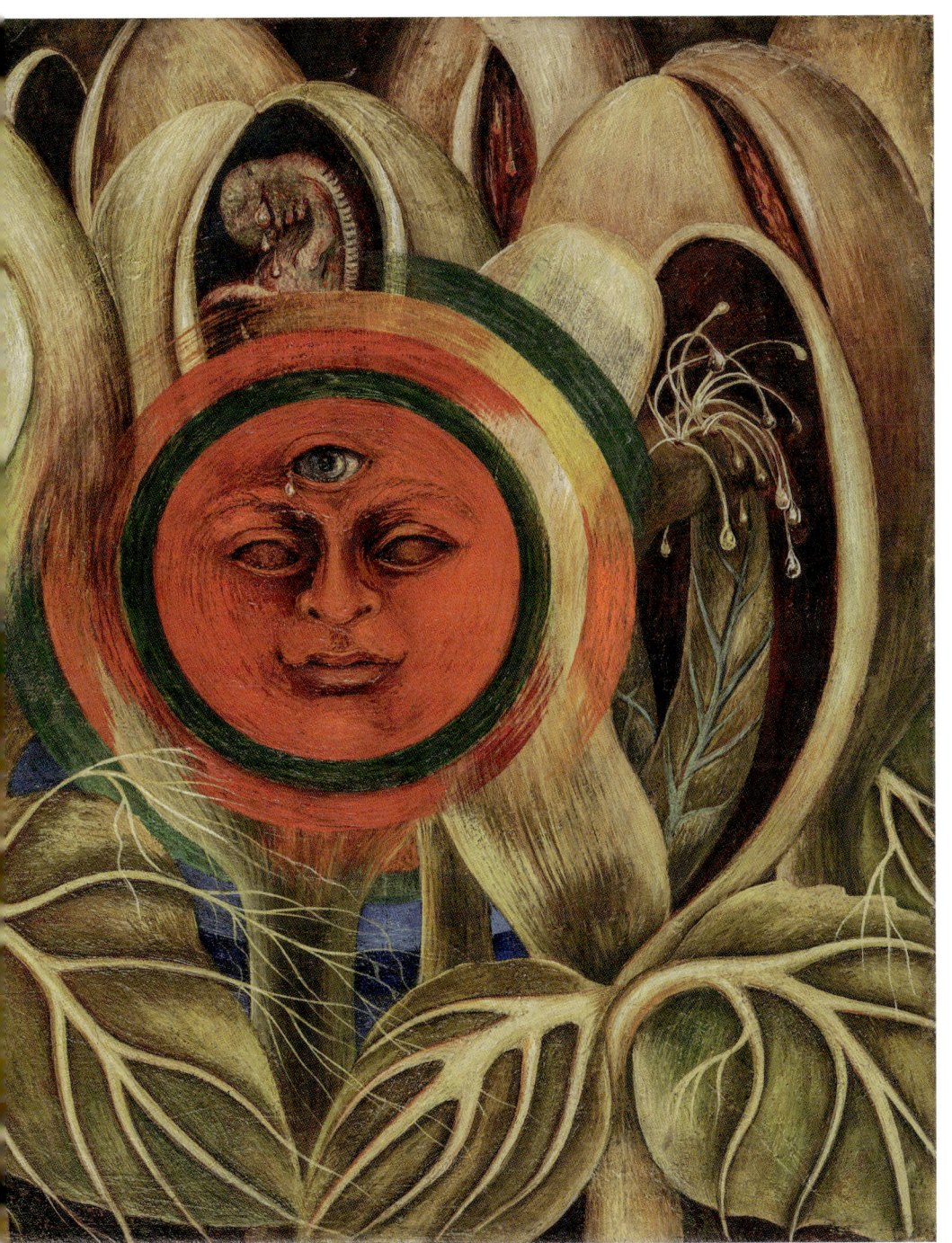

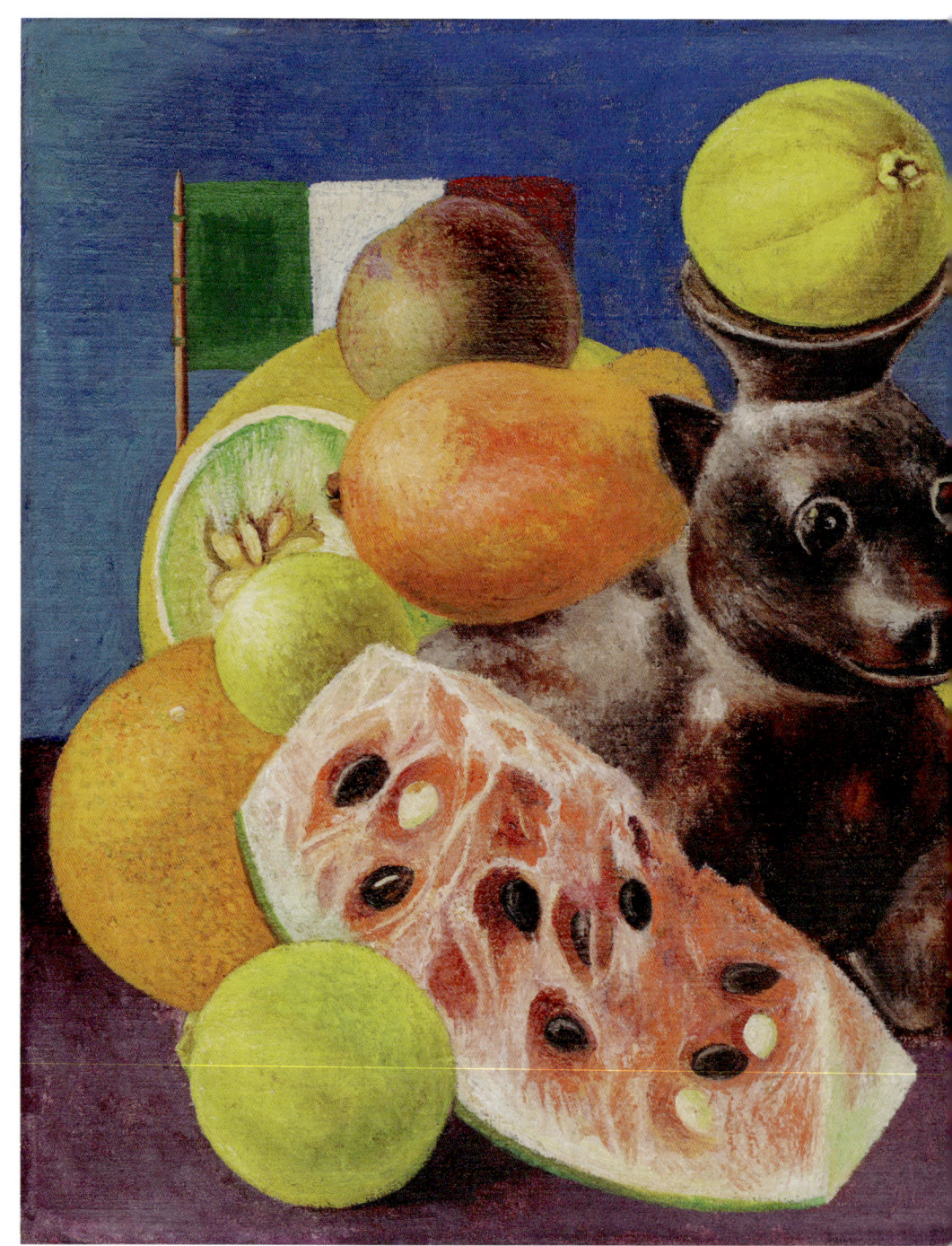

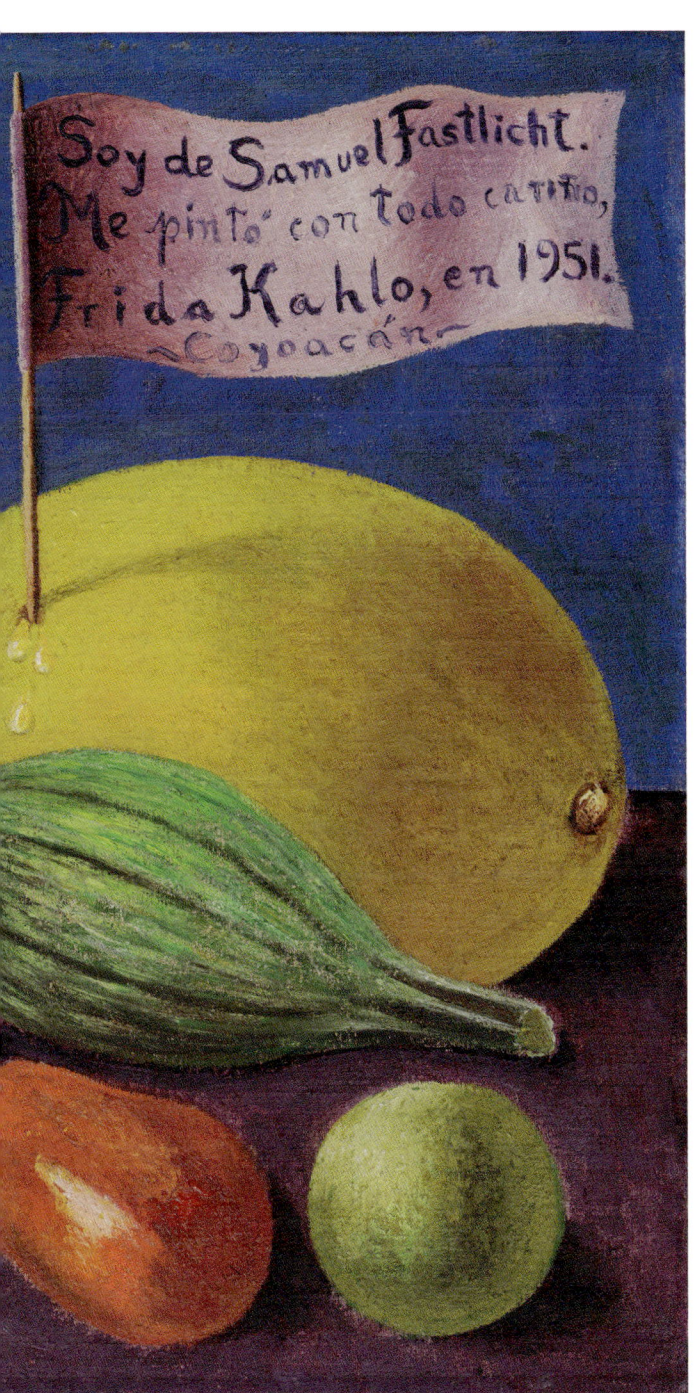

Still Life ("I Belong to Samuel Fastlicht"), 1951
Oil on canvas, mounted on wood,
28.6 x 35.9 cm (11¼ x 14⅛ in.);
inscribed t. r.: Soy de Samuel
Fastlicht. / Me pintó con todo
cariño, / Frida Kahlo,en 1951. /
Coyoacán (I belong to Samuel
Fastlicht. / I was painted with
great affection, / Frida Kahlo,
in 1951. / Coyoacán)
Mexico City, private collection,
courtesy Arvil gallery

Pages 336/337
**Still Life (with Parrot
and Flag)**, 1951
Oil on masonite,
28.1 x 40 cm (11 x 15¾ in.)
Mexico City, private collection,
courtesy Christie's, New York

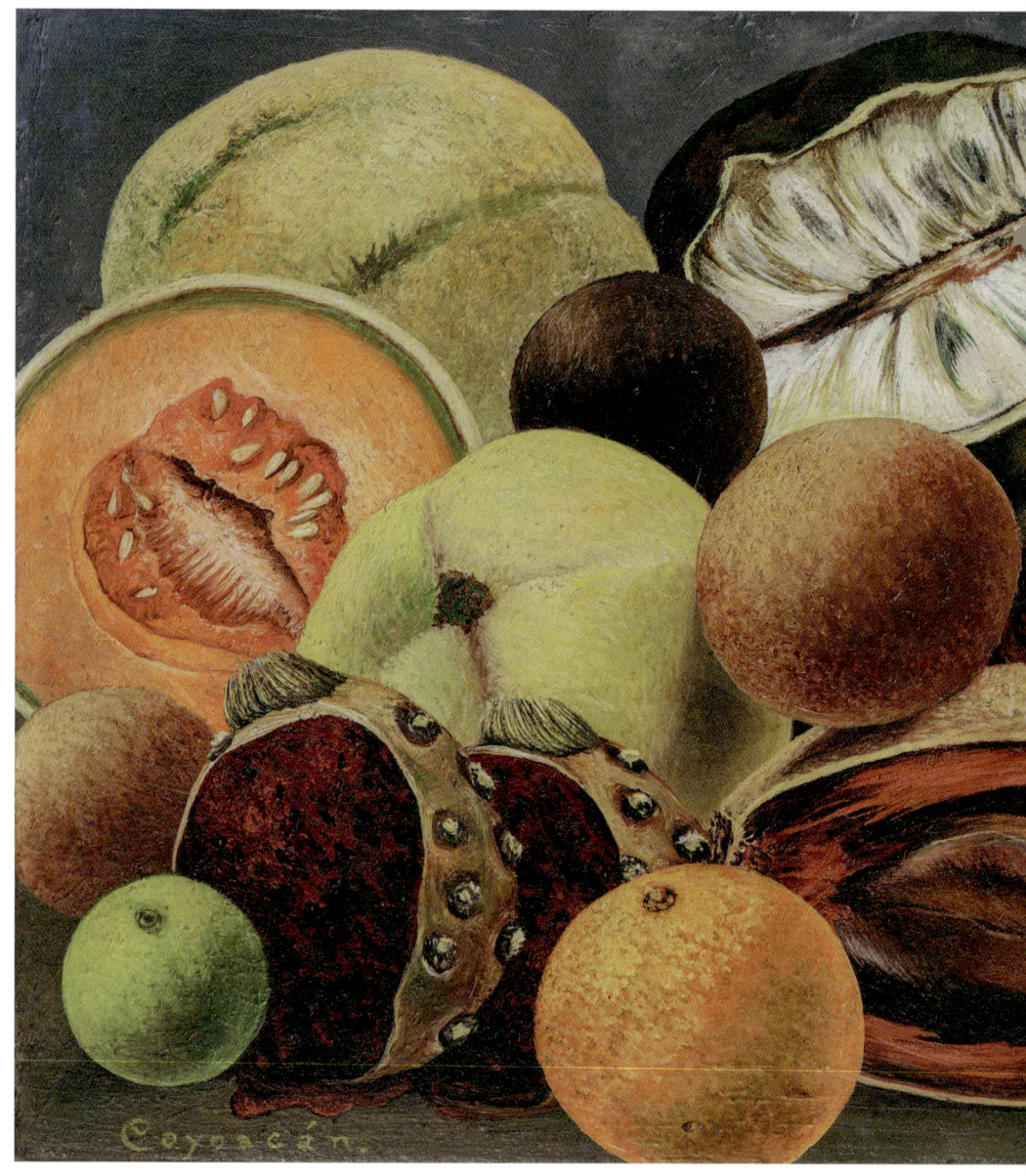

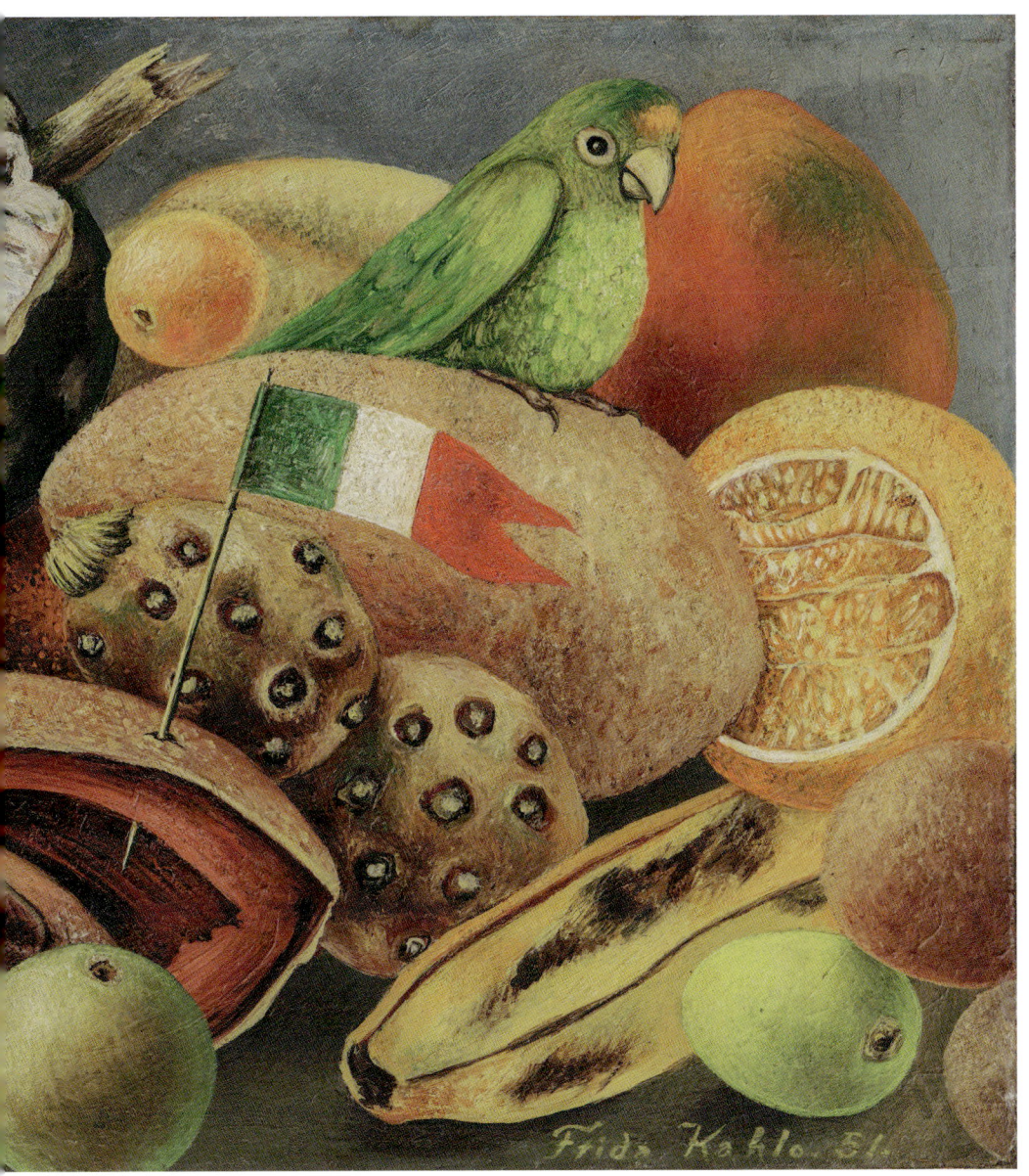

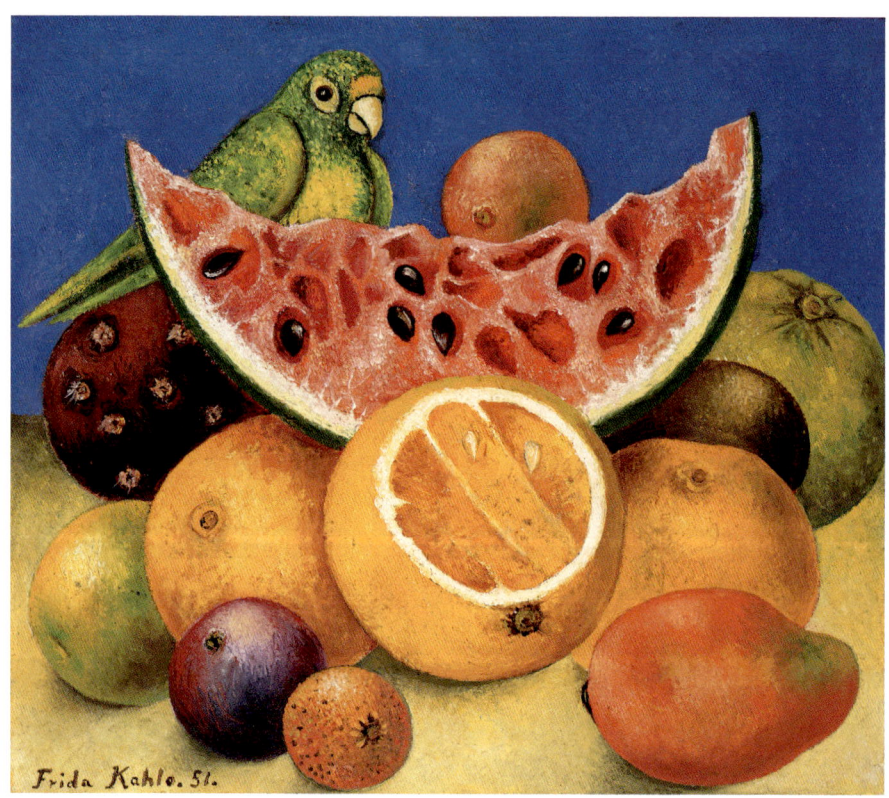

Still Life (with Parrot and Fruit), 1951
Oil on canvas, 25.7 x 28.2 cm (10⅛ x 11⅛ in.)
Austin, Texas, Harry Ransom Center, University of Texas,
Nickolas Muray Collection of Mexican Art, inv. 66.7

Frida Kahlo in the Casa Azul (detail), Coyoacán, 1951
Gelatin silver print, 14.9 x 11.7 cm (5⅞ x 4⅝ in.)
New York, collection of Vicente Wolf, courtesy
Mary-Anne Martin/Fine Art, New York

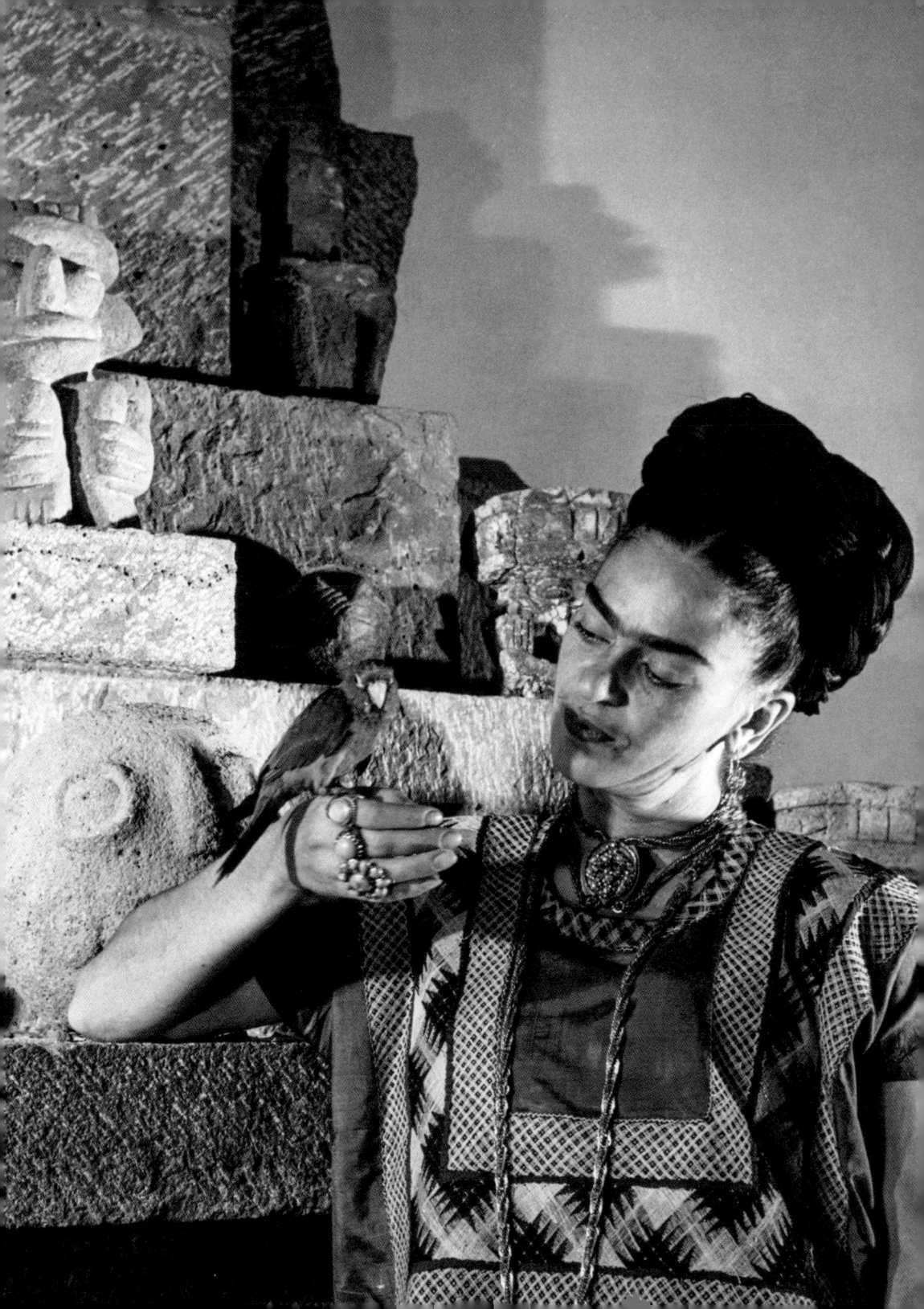

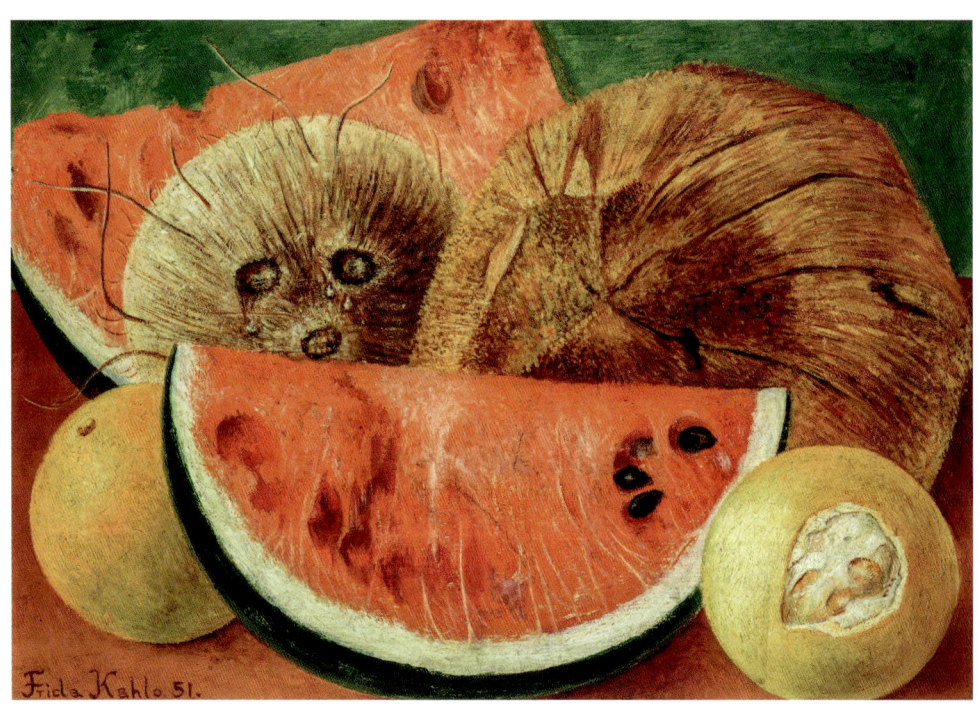

Coconuts, 1951
Oil on masonite, 25.4 x 34.6 cm (10 x 13⅝ in.)
Mexico City, Secretaría de Cultura, Instituto Nacional
de Bellas Artes y Literatura, Museo de Arte Moderno

Weeping Coconuts, *c.* 1951
Oil on masonite, 35.6 x 42.5 cm (14 x 16¾ in.); inscribed on the flag:
PINTÓ CON TODO / CARIÑO. FRIDA KAHLO
(Painted with great / affection. Frida Kahlo)
Los Angeles County Museum of Art, The Bernard and Edith Lewin
Collection of Mexican Art, inv. M.2004.283.2

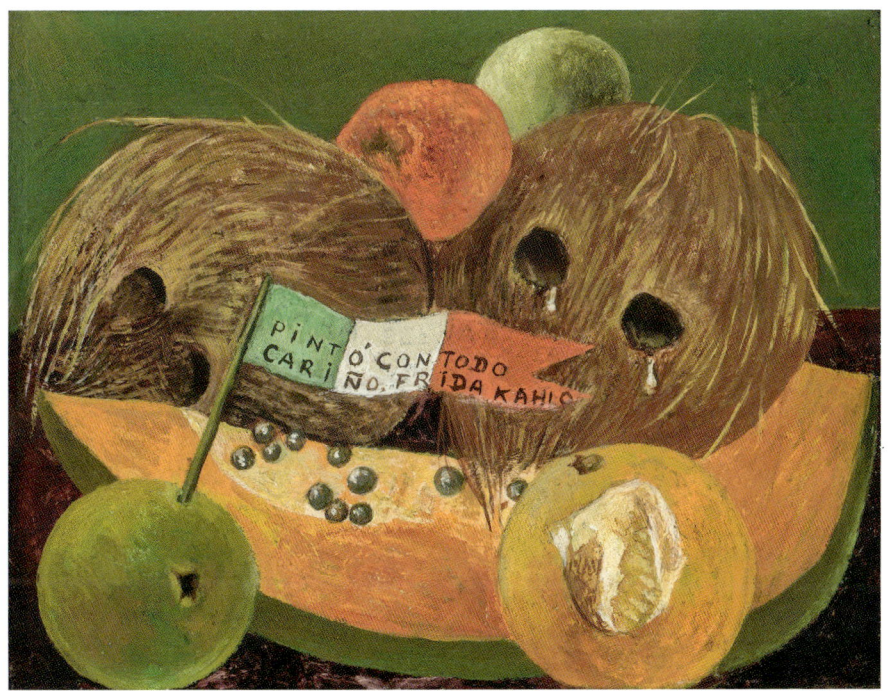

Pages 342/343
Still Life (for Samuel Fastlicht, "with all my love"), 1952
Oil on canvas, mounted on wood, 25.8 x 44 cm (10⅛ x 17⅜ in.); inscribed
on the flag: PARA SAMUEL FASTLICHT / *PINTÓ CON TODO AMOR /*
FRIDA KAHLO. EN LA / CIUDAD DE PUEBLA. 1952 (For Samuel Fastlicht /
painted with all my love / Frida Kahlo. In the / city of Puebla. 1952)
Mexico City, private collection

Pages 344/345
Congress of the Peoples for Peace, October 1952
Oil and tempera on canvas, mounted on masonite, 20.3 x 25.4 cm (8 x 10 in.)
Private collection, courtesy Sotheby's, New York

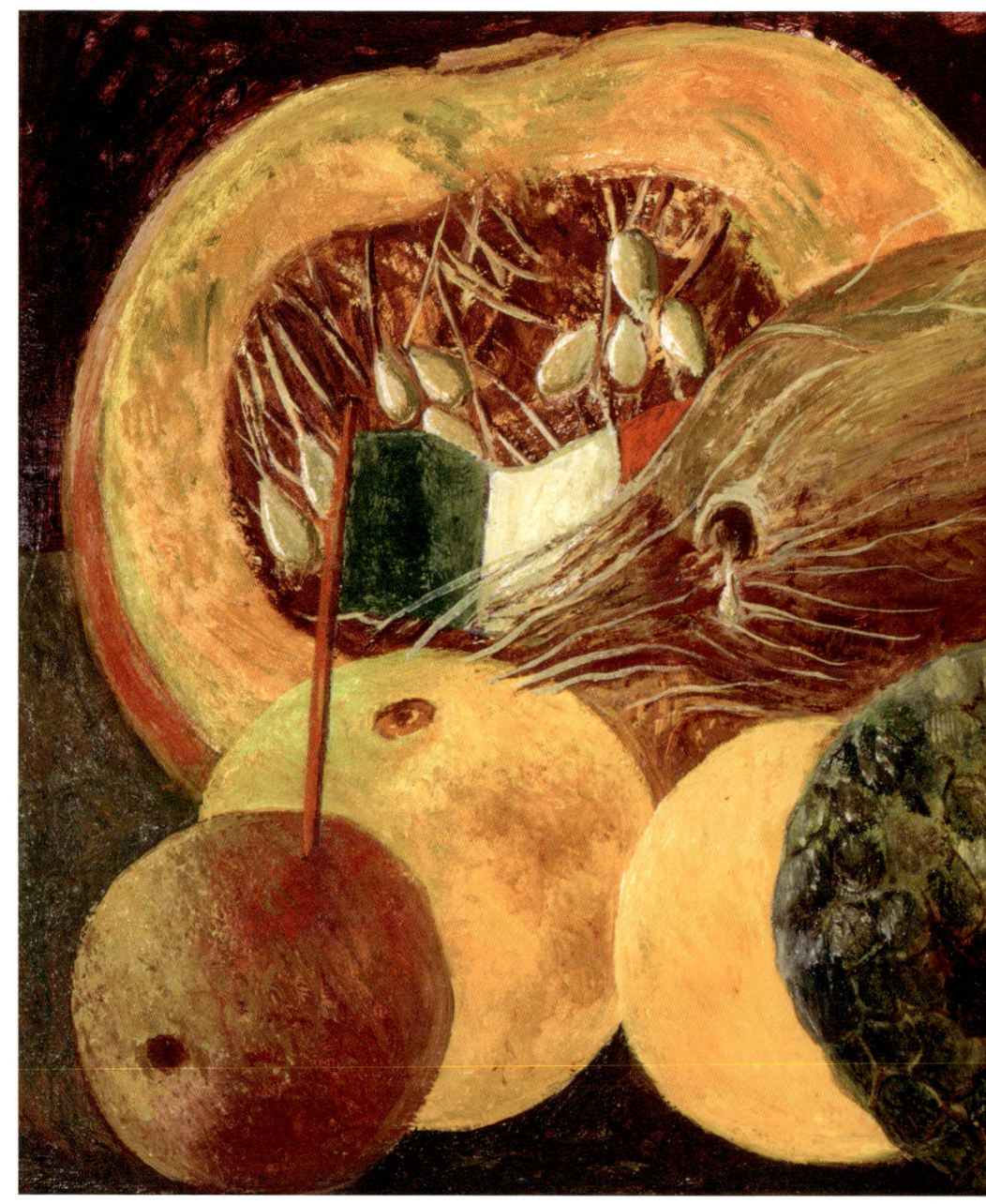

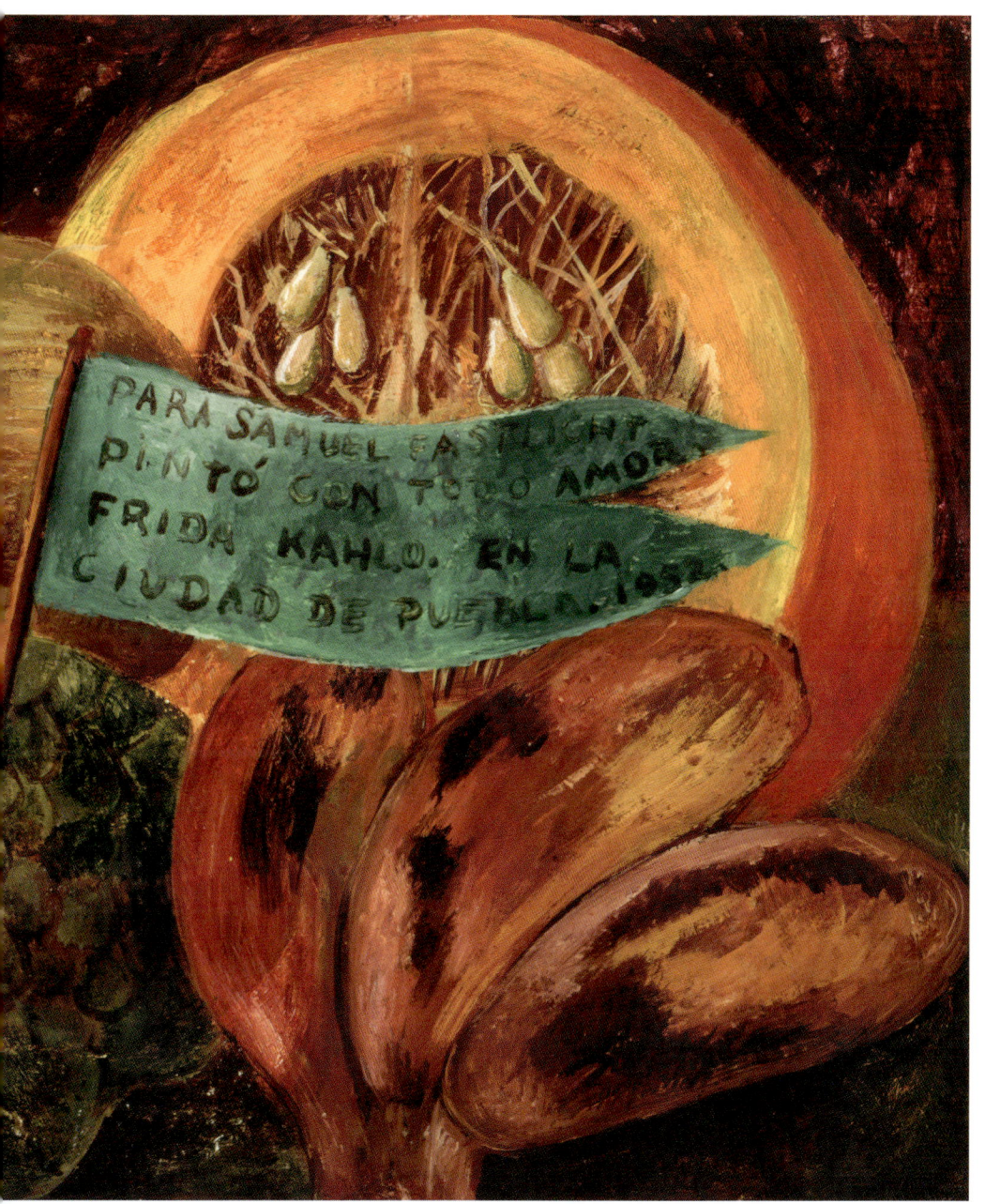

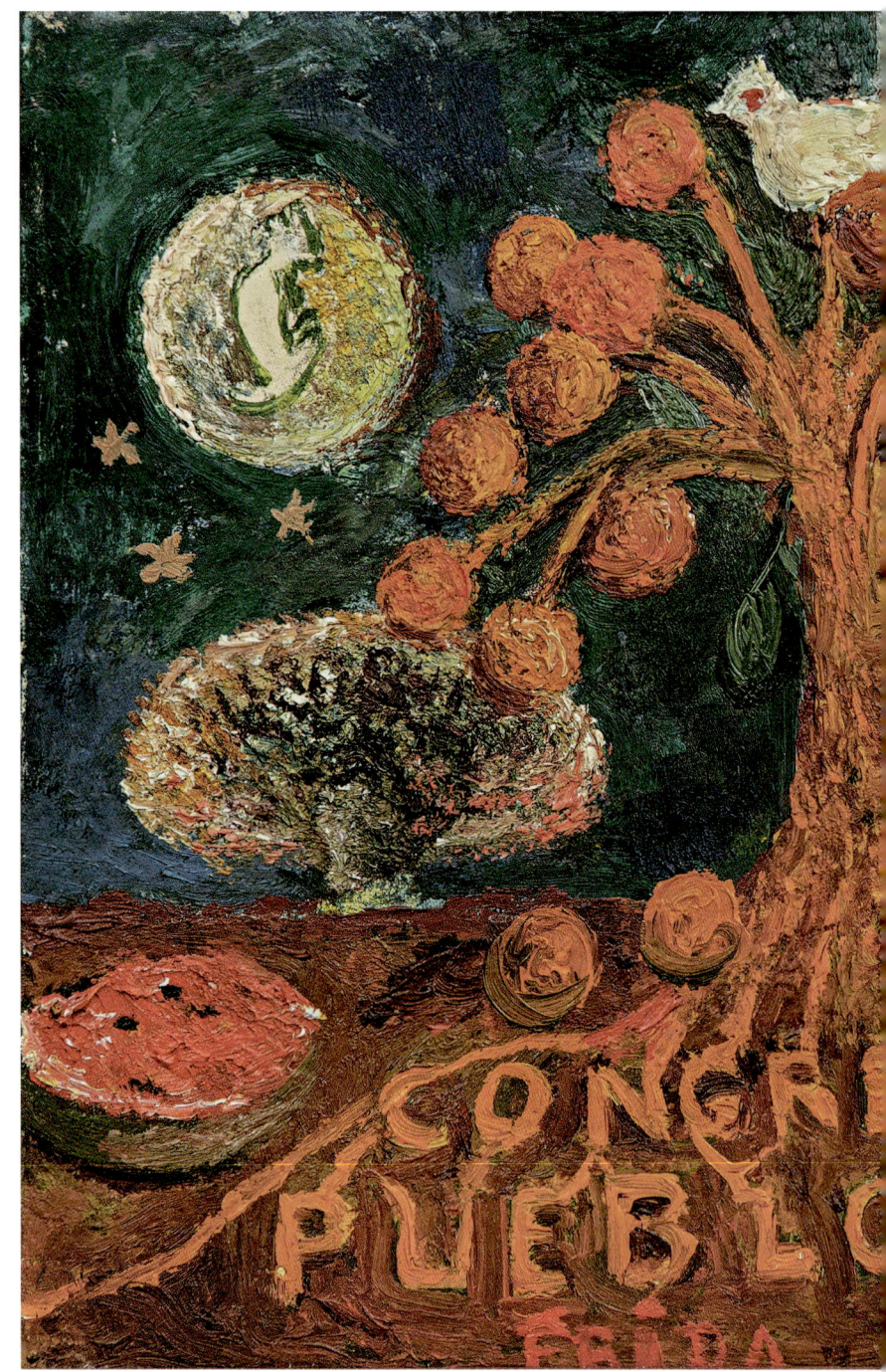

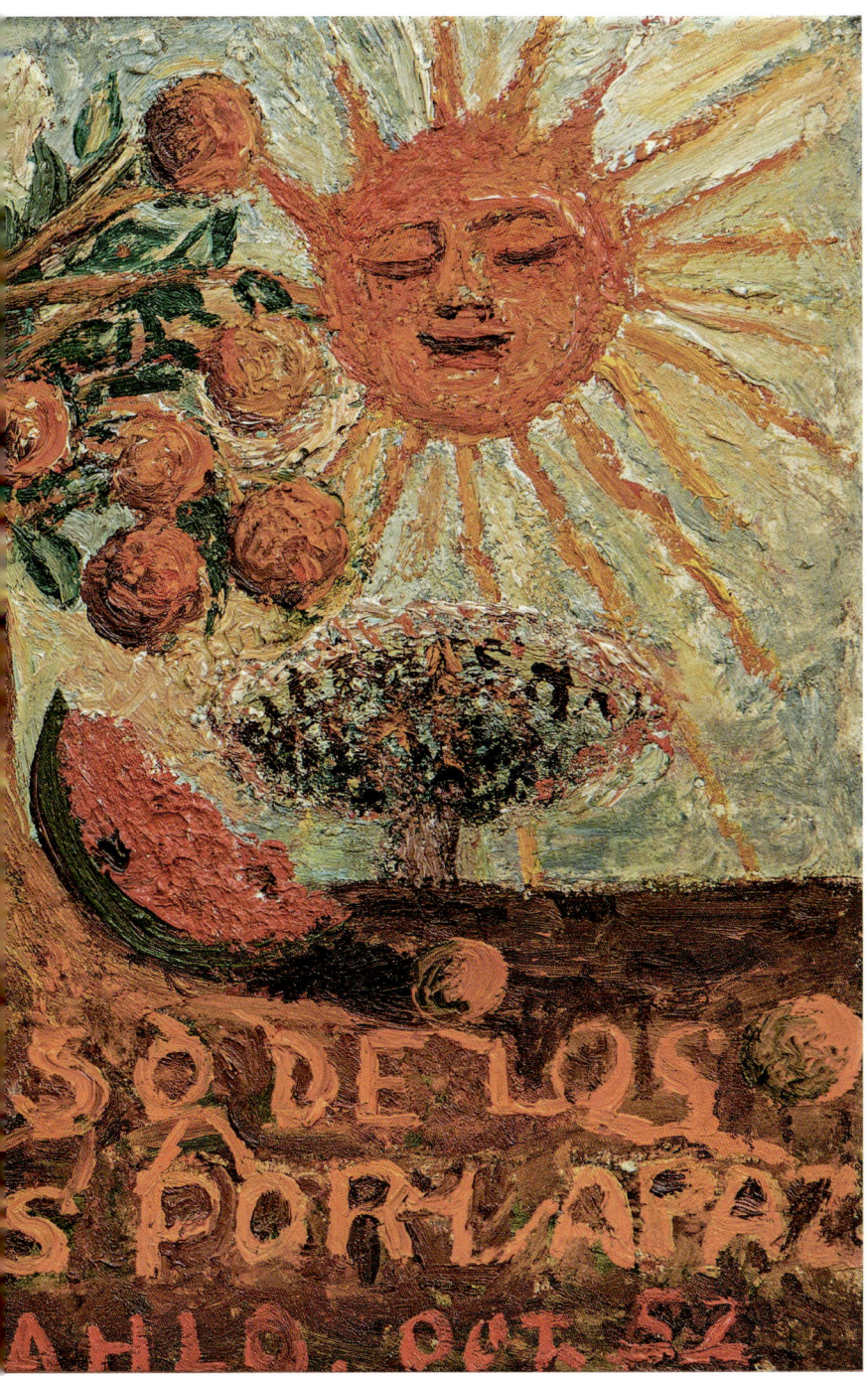

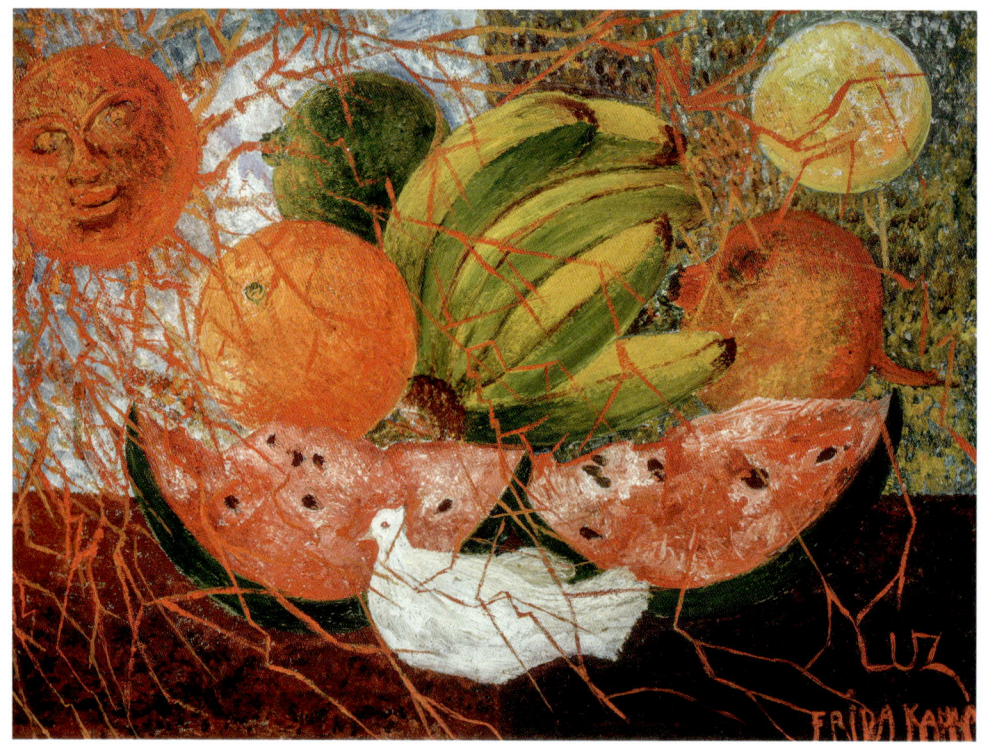

Fruit of Life (Light), *c.* 1953
Oil on masonite, 47 x 62 cm (18½ x 24⅜ in.)
London, private collection

Juan Guzmán, **Frida Kahlo with two birds** (detail), 1951
Gelatin silver print, 23.5 x 19 cm (9¼ x 7½ in.)
New York, collection of Spencer Throckmorton

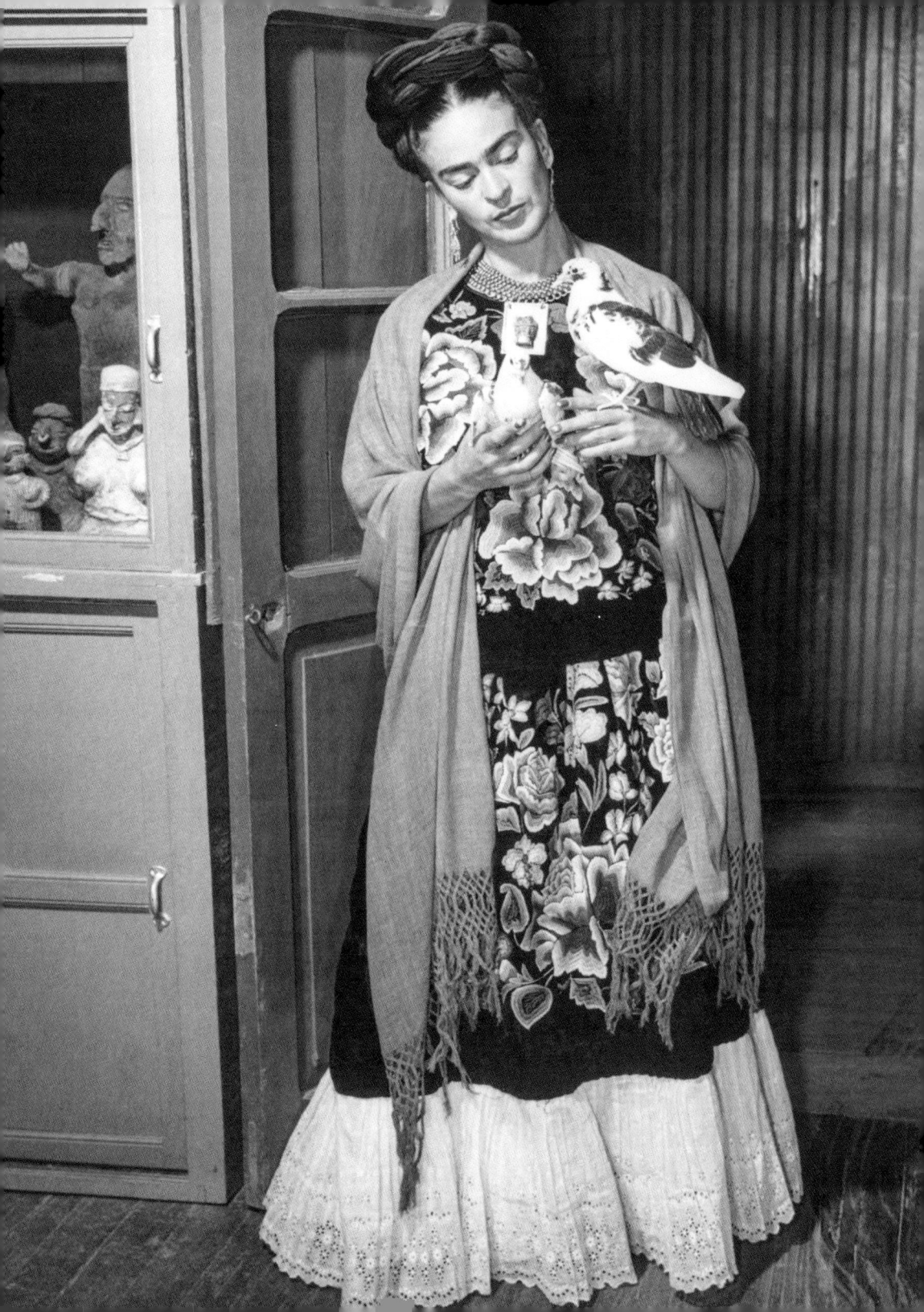

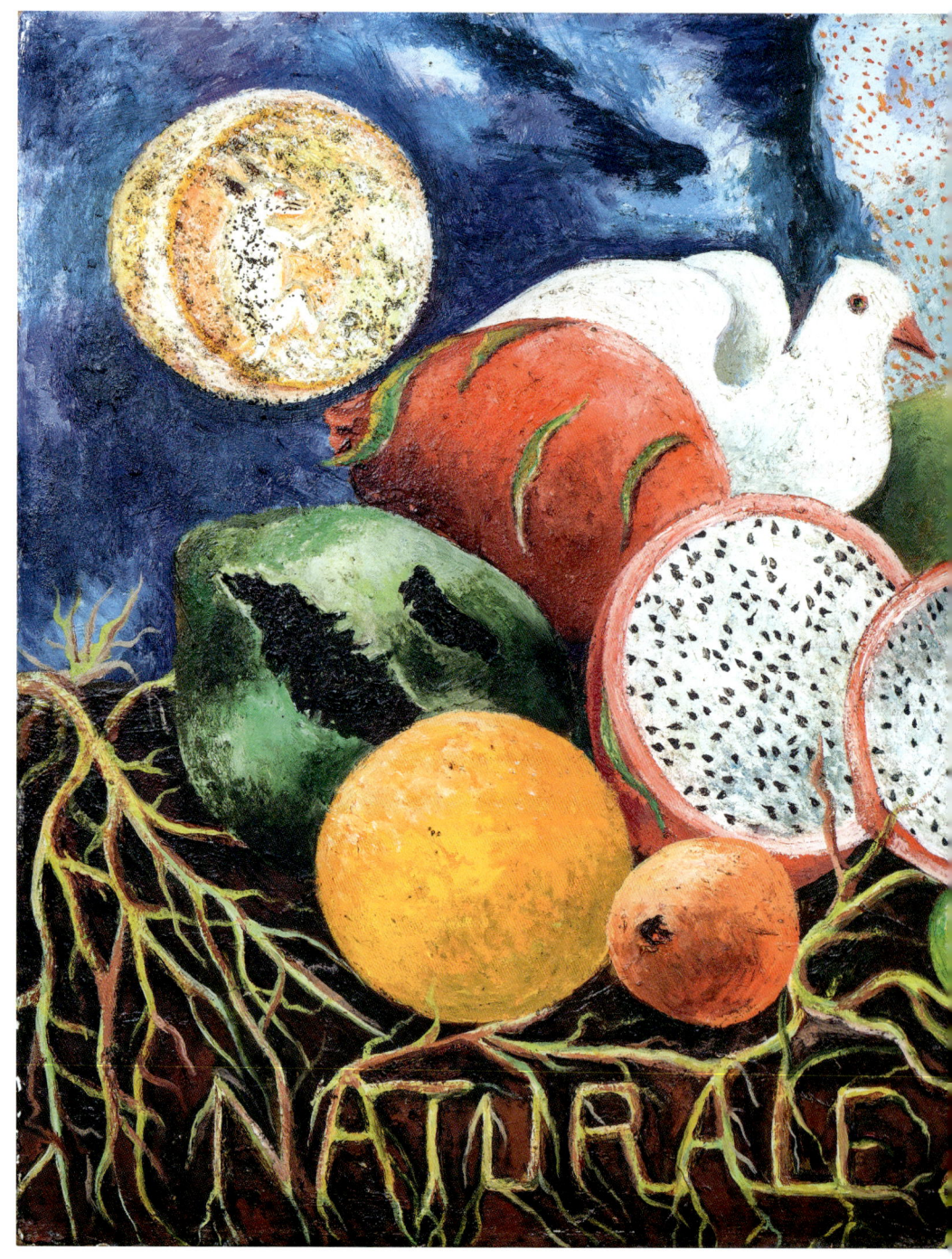

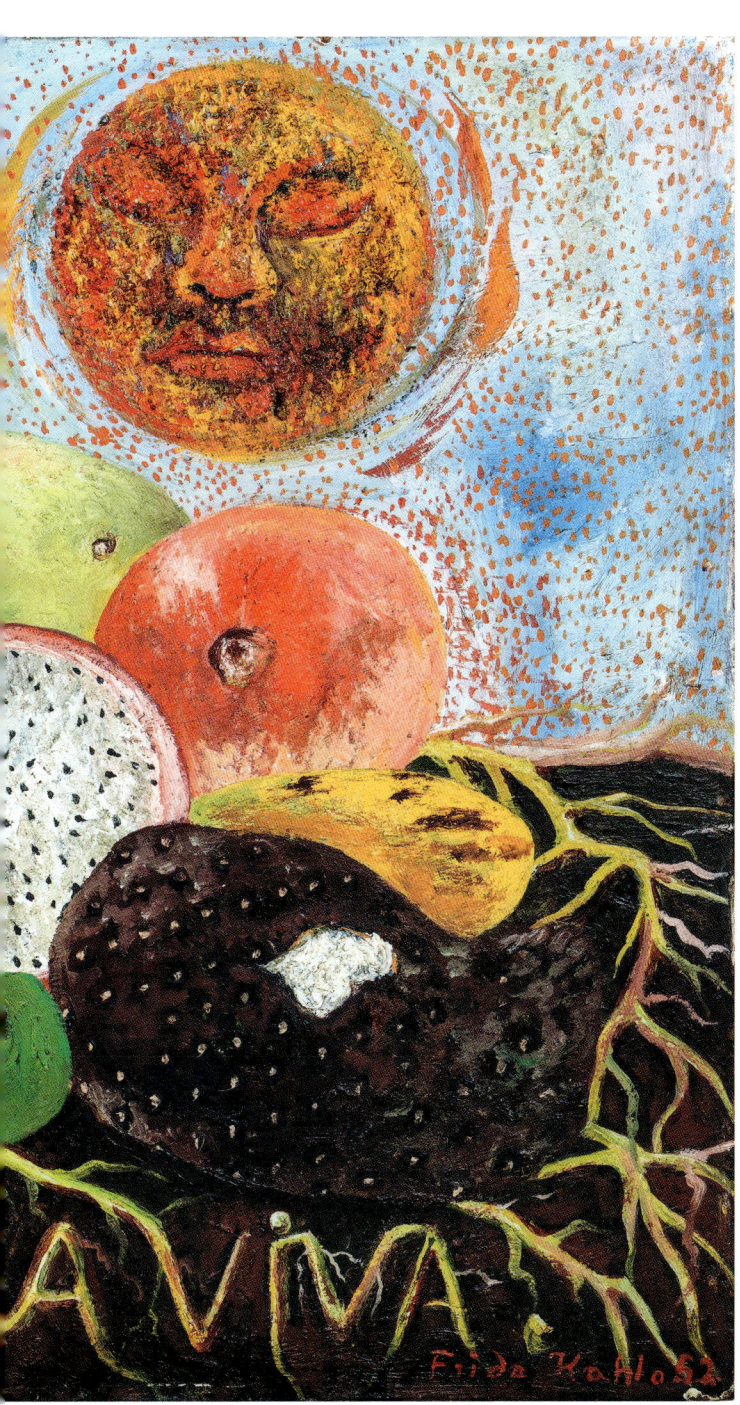

**Still Life
(Living Nature)**, 1952
Oil on masonite,
44.1 x 60 cm (17⅜ x 23⅝ in.)
Monterrey, private collection,
courtesy Sotheby's,
Mexico City

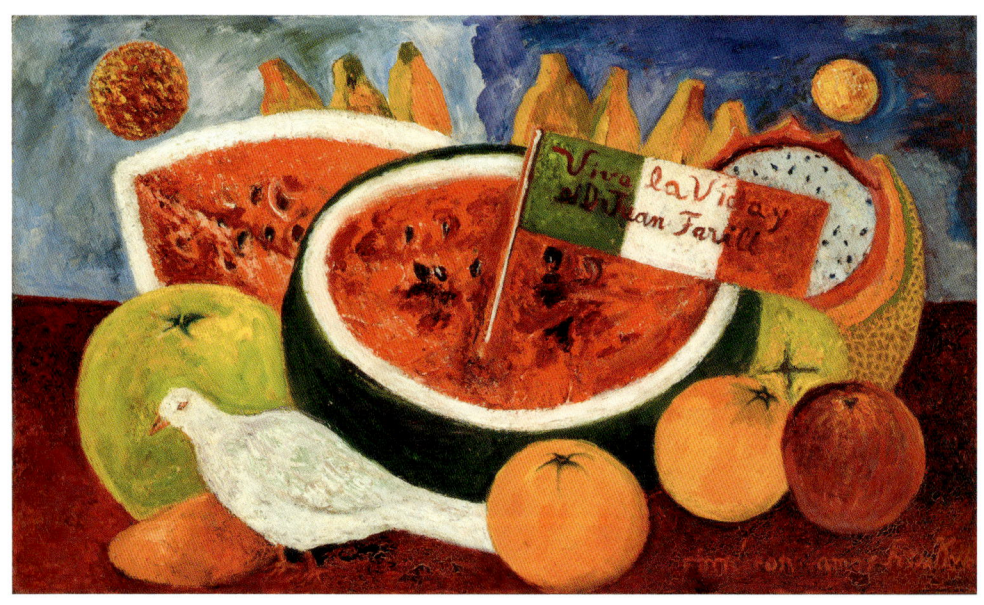

Still Life (Long Live Life), *c.* 1953/54
Oil on masonite, 39 x 65 cm (15⅜ x 25⅝ in.)
Inscribed on the flag: Viva la Vida y / el D. Juan Farill
(Long Live Life and D. Juan Farill)
Mexico, private collection

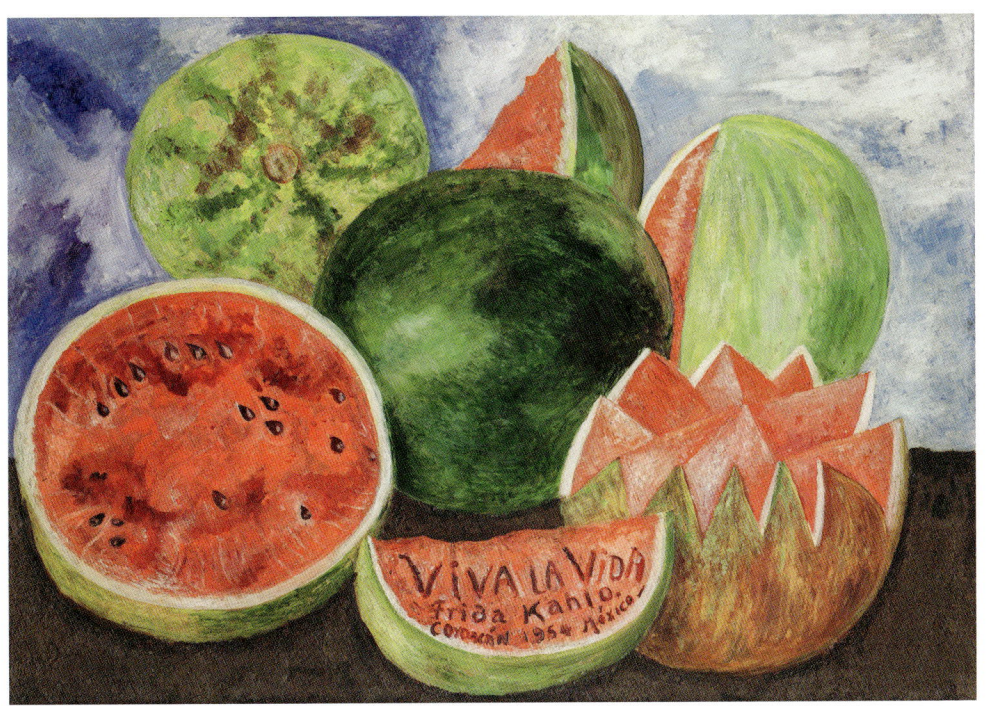

Long Live Life, 1954
Oil and sand on masonite, 52 x 72 cm (20½ x 28⅜ in.); inscribed on the
watermelon slice: VIVA LA VIDA / Frida Kahlo. / COYOACÁN 1954 México –
(Long live life / Frida Kahlo. / Coyoacán 1954 Mexico –)
Mexico City, Coyoacán, Museo Frida Kahlo

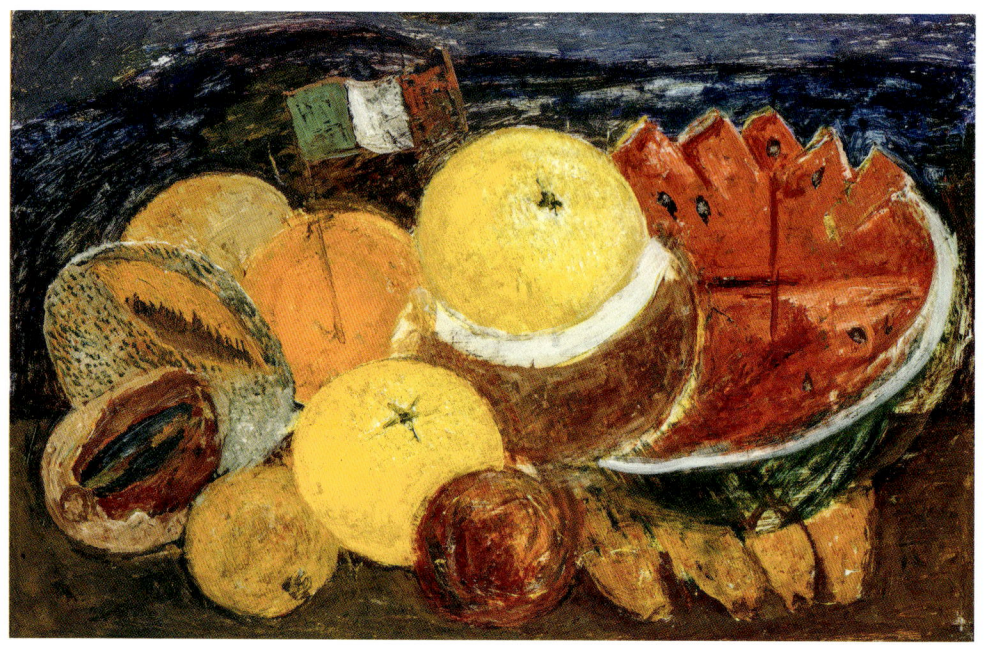

Still Life with Flag (Still Life with Mexican Flag), *c.* 1953/54
Oil on masonite, 38 x 58 cm (15 x 22⅞ in.)
Mexico City, Coyoacán, Museo Frida Kahlo

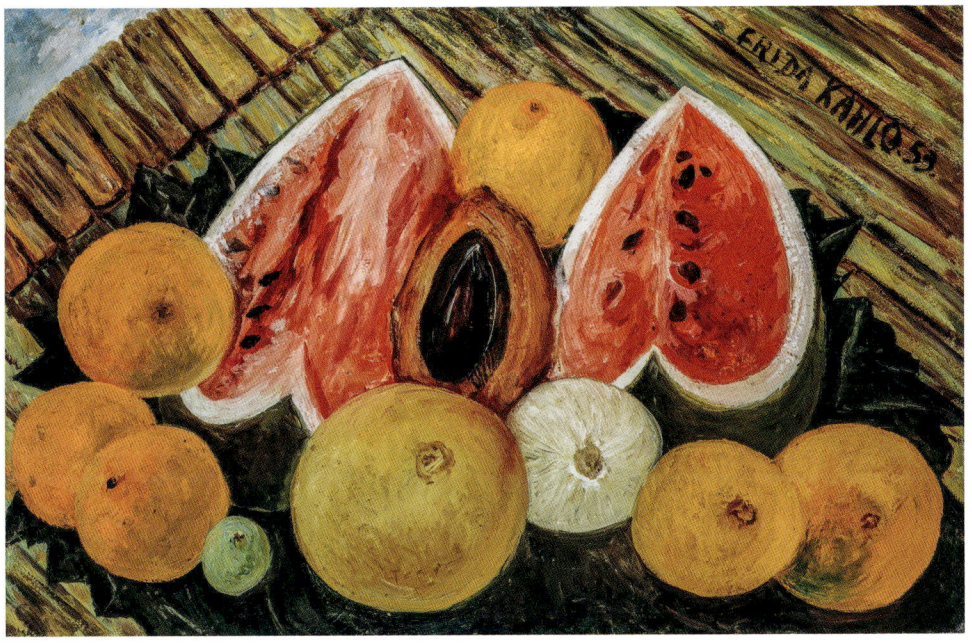

Still Life with Watermelons, 1953
Oil on masonite, 39.8 x 59.6 cm (15⅝ x 23½ in.)
Mexico City, Secretaría de Cultura, Instituto Nacional
de Bellas Artes y Literatura, Museo de Arte Moderno

Page 354
Florence Arquin, **Frida Kahlo in a plaster corset decorated
with the hammer and sickle**, *c.* 1951
Platinum print, 10.8 x 7.6 cm (4¼ x 3 in.)
New York, collection of Spencer Throckmorton

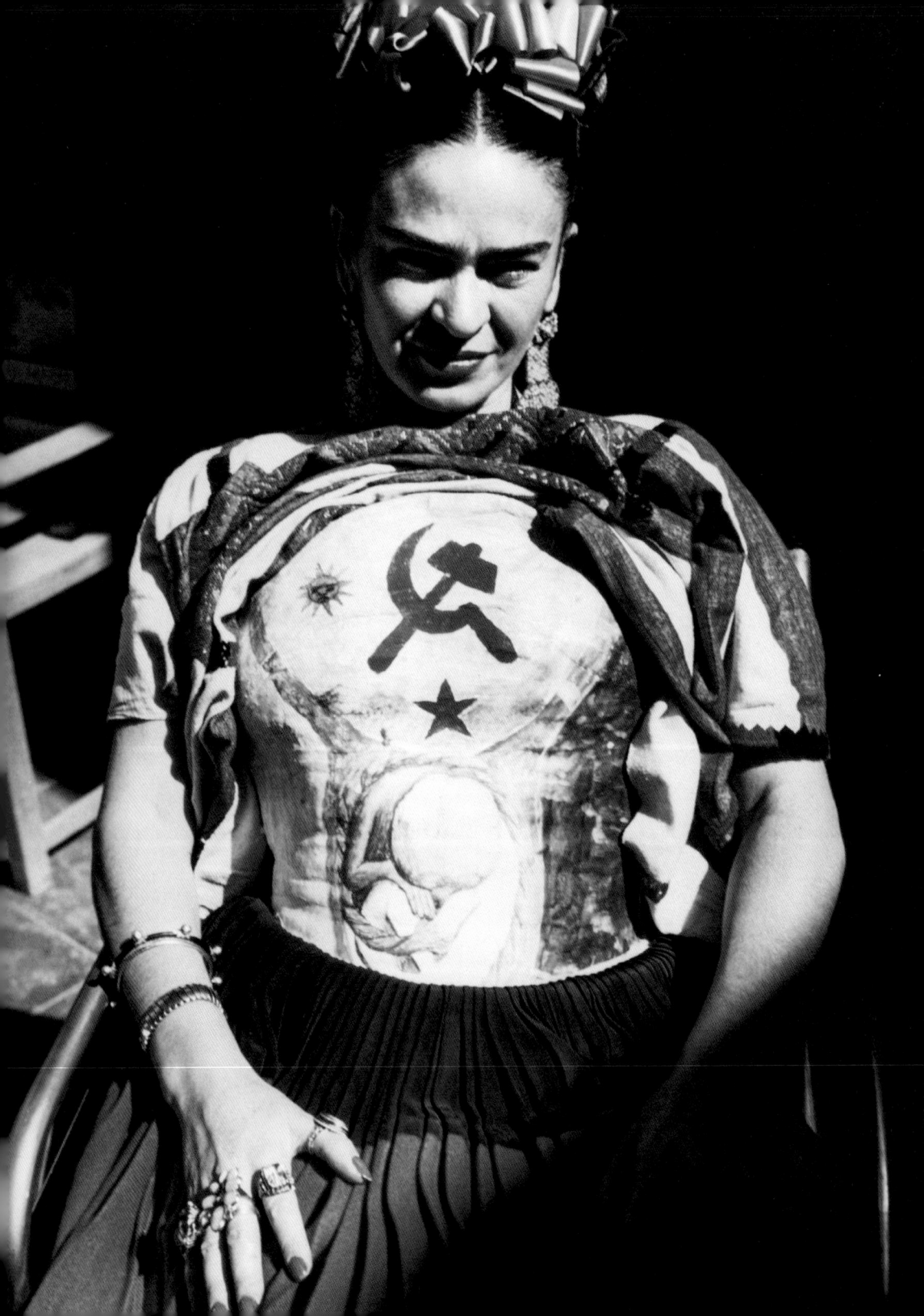

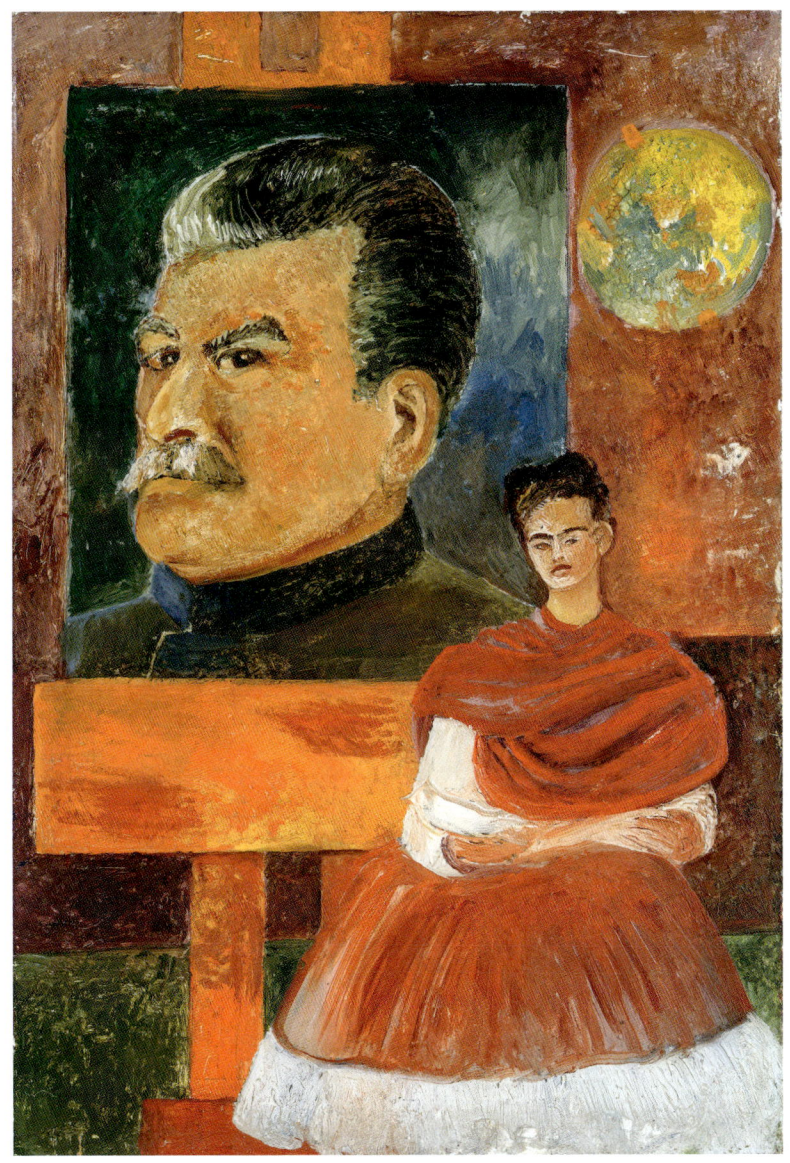

Frida and Stalin (unfinished), 1954
Oil on masonite, 59 x 39 cm (23¼ x 15⅜ in.)
Mexico City, Coyoacán, Museo Frida Kahlo

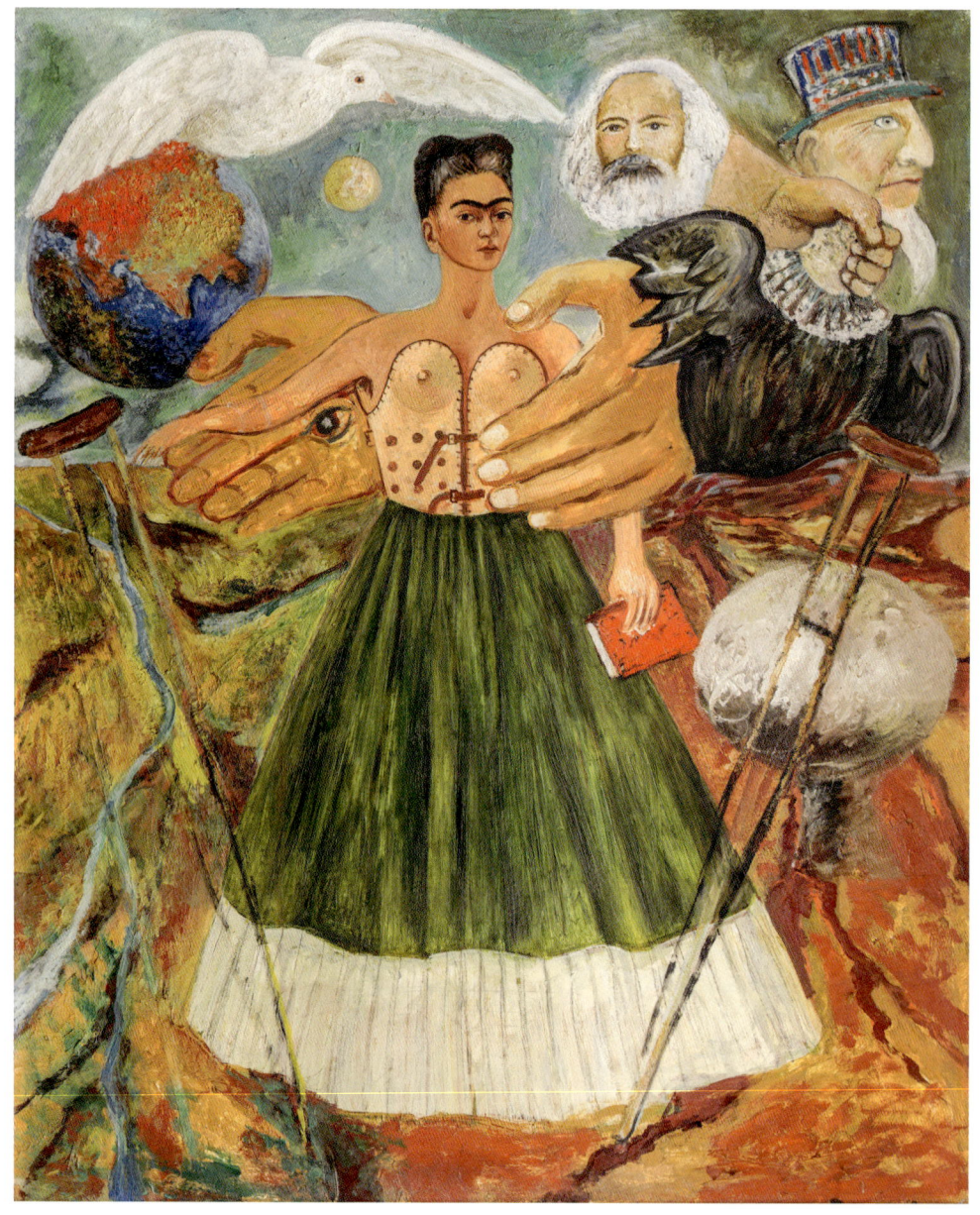

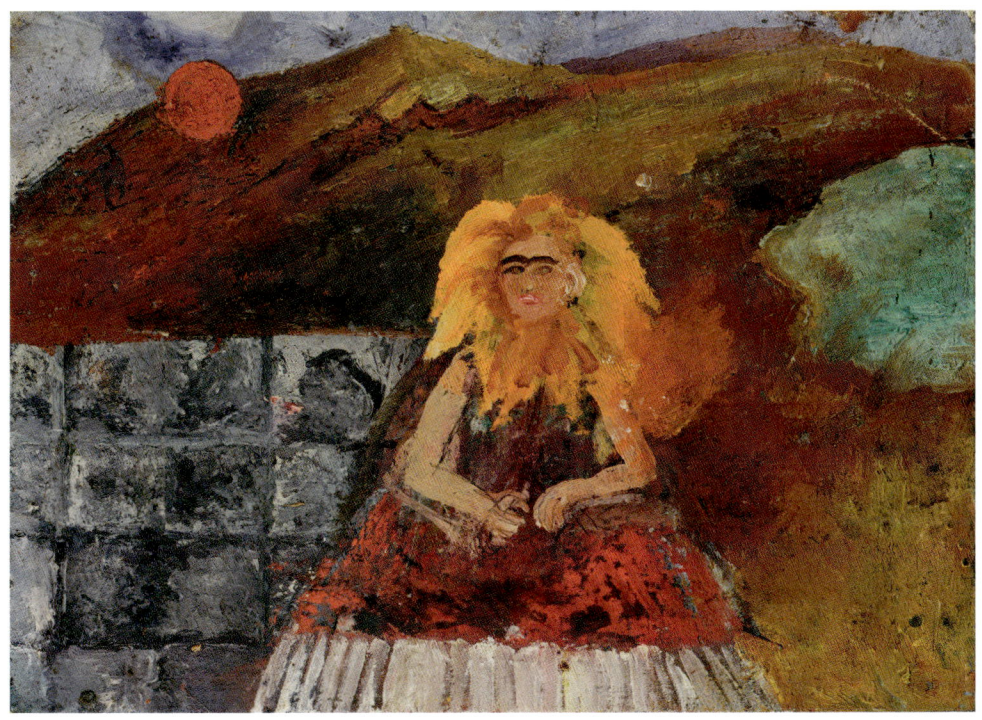

Marxism Shall Give Health to the Ill (unfinished), *c.* 1954
Oil on masonite, 76 x 61 cm (30 x 24 in.)
Mexico City, Coyoacán, Museo Frida Kahlo

Frida in Flames (Self-portrait inside a Sunflower) (unfinished), 1953/54
Oil on canvas, mounted on wood, 23.8 x 32.4 cm (9⅜ x 12¾ in.)
United States, private collection, courtesy Mary-Anne Martin/Fine Art, New York

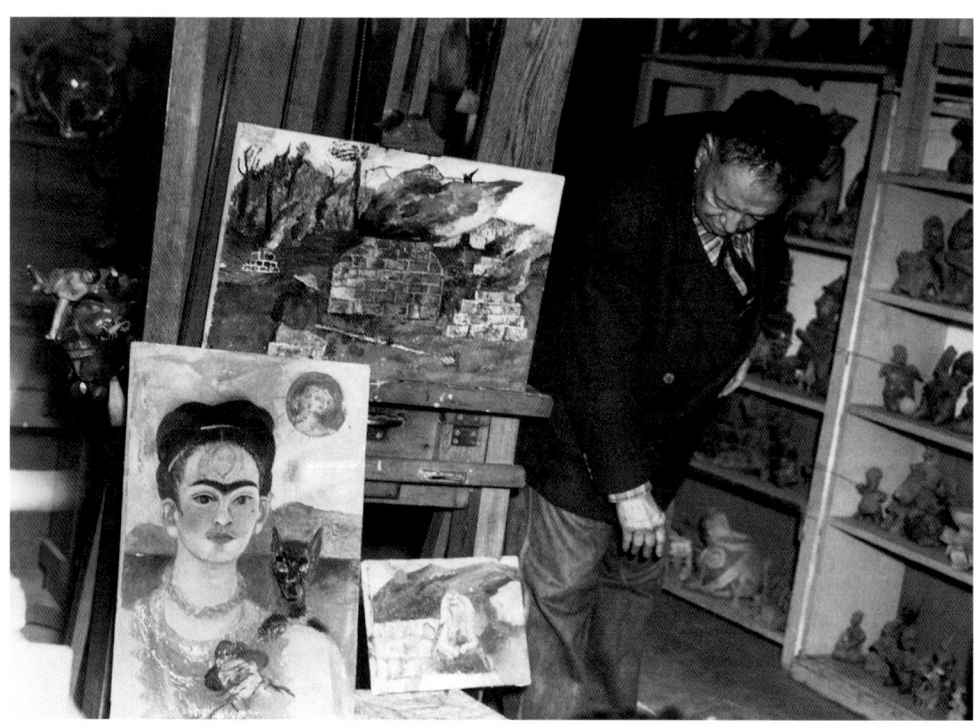

Photograph from the newspaper *La Prensa*, **Diego Rivera in Kahlo's studio
in the Casa Azul** (detail), Coyoacán, July 14, 1954
Gelatin silver print, 12.9 x 20.7 cm (5⅛ x 8⅛ in.)
Buenos Aires, collection CEDODAL, Diego Rivera Photographic Archive

**Self-portrait (with Diego's Image on the Breast and
María between the Eyebrows)** (unfinished), *c.* 1953/54
Oil on masonite, 59.7 x 40 cm (23½ x 15¾ in.)
California, private collection

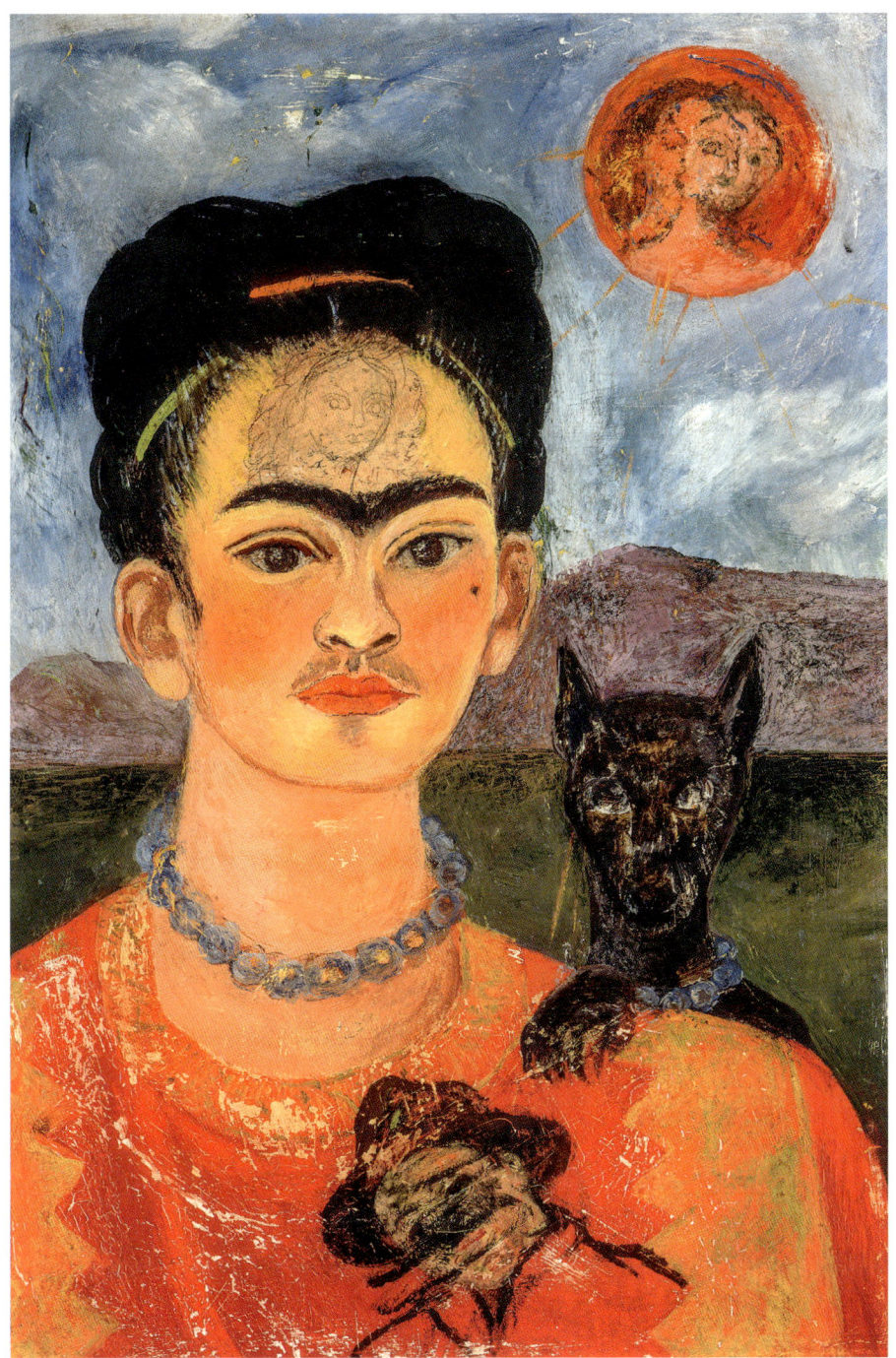

V.
Kahlo's Diary

*"Who would ever have thought that dots
are alive and in fact can help us to live? [...]
They are distant suns that call to me,
because I am a part of their core."*

— FRIDA KAHLO, c. 1945

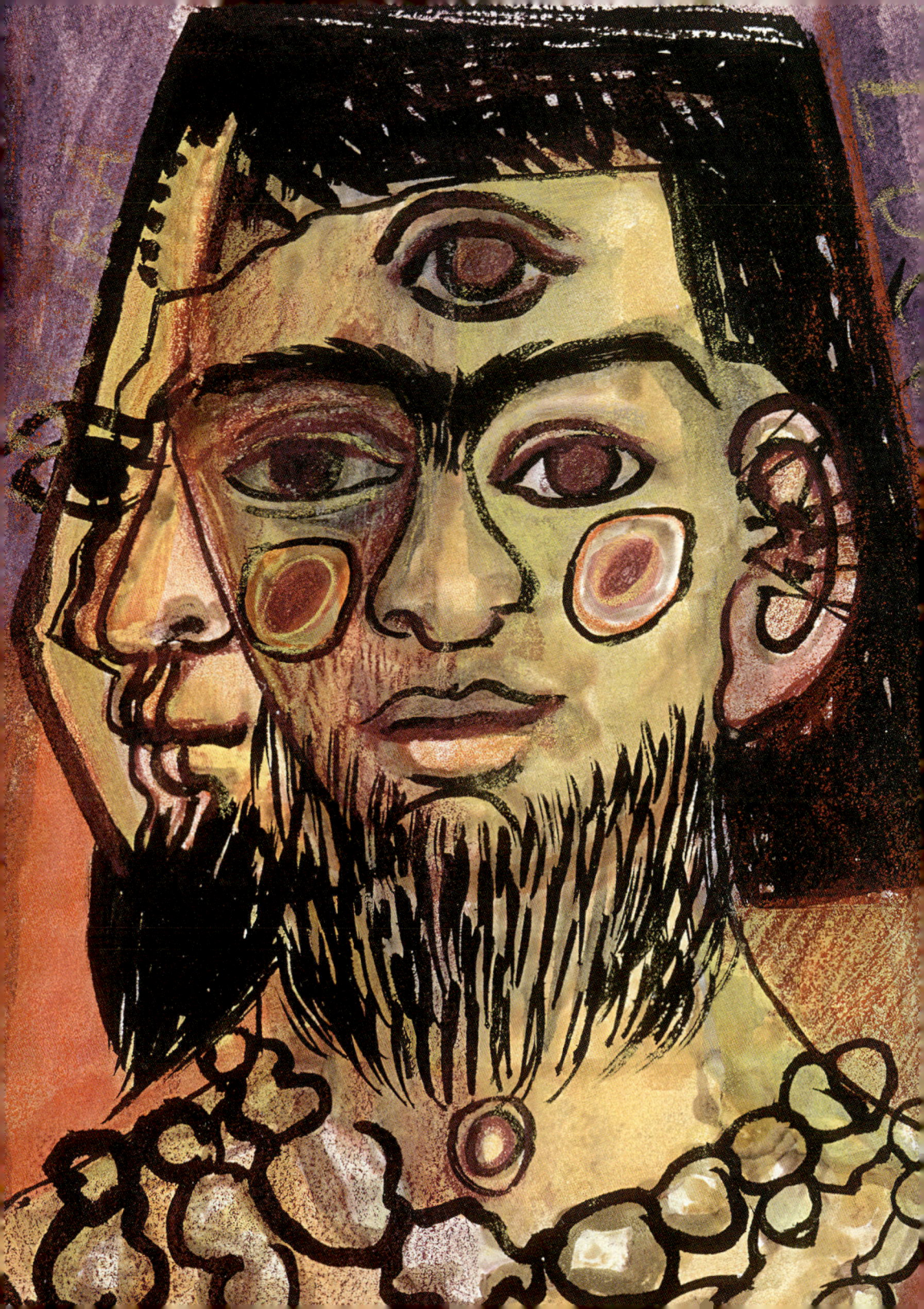

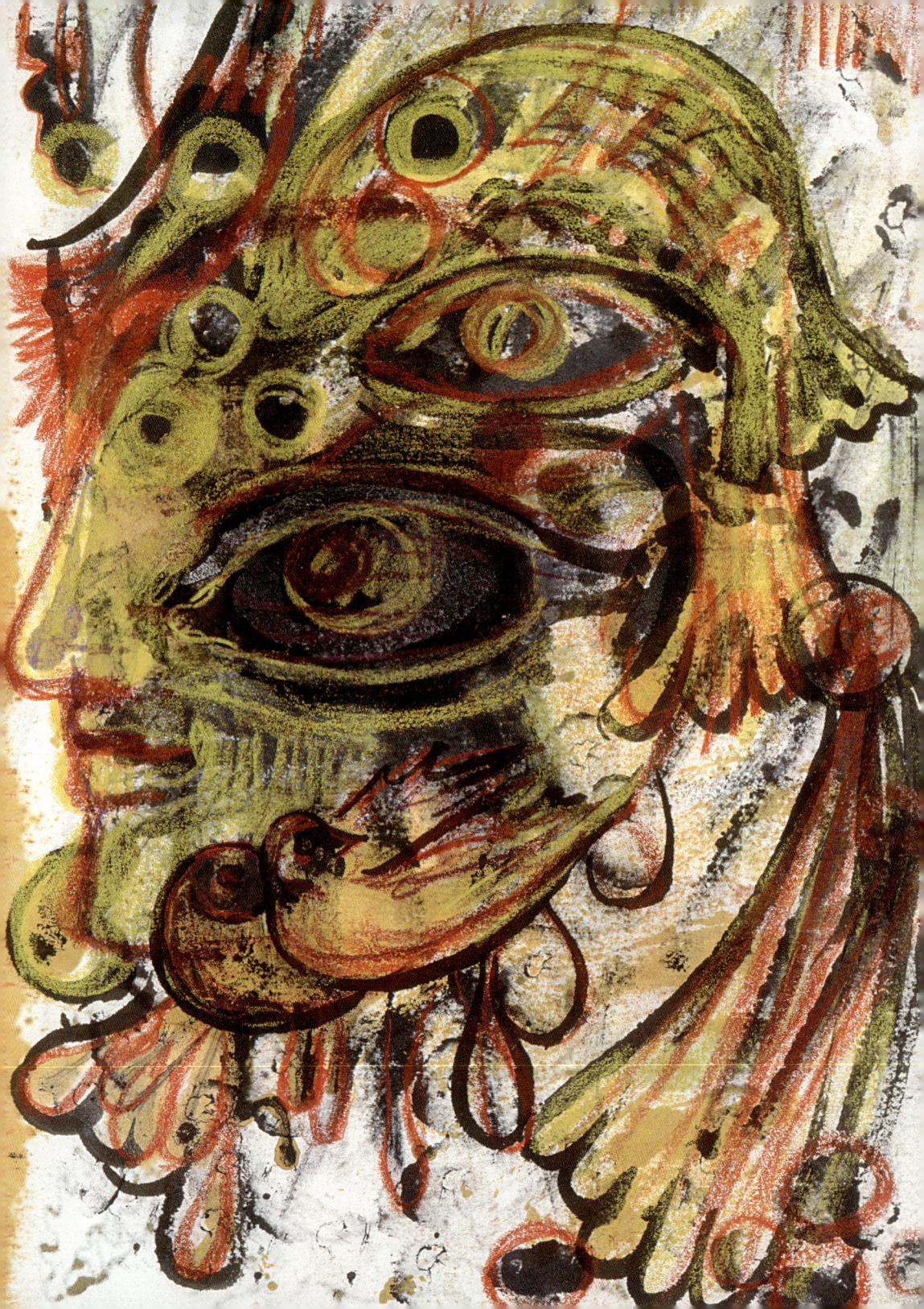

Kahlo's diary might naturally be assumed to be a record of her daily activities, but this is not in fact the case and indeed it was never her intention to write such an everyday account. What the diary is instead is a testament to the extraordinary world she created for herself. It was begun in the early 1940s, although the earliest date that is actually mentioned is 1944; even so, Kahlo did also refer to various details concerning her earlier personal history, such as her father's arrival in Mexico in the 19th century (he arrived in 1890) and that she was born in 1910 (in fact, she was born in 1907), while she also copied out and included part of a letter she had been sent by her friend Jacqueline Lamba, possibly from 1939.

Some of the pages consist of written content only, and in these cases they are mostly poems and snippets of wordplay, jotted down with a creativity and wit that recalls the literary quality of some of Kahlo's letters. However, the diary is in the main more of an artist's sketchbook, since most of the pages feature the various drawings she made to express or comment on different moments in her life. These illustrations, with added watercolor in vibrant tones or in India ink, convey a sense of absolute creative freedom and are full of inventiveness and interesting shapes.

On a few pages Kahlo made reference to her own paintings, such as *The Two Fridas* (p. 383, no. 15) and *The Love Embrace of the Universe, the Earth (Mexico), Me, Diego, and Señor Xólotl* (p. 317), and she also included a diagram of the golden mean for use in some of the still lifes she painted between 1951 and 1954. There are notes as well about some of the artists who inspired her, such as Pieter Bruegel (1525–1569) and Hieronymus Bosch (1450–1516), but more than anything else the diary was Kahlo's intimate confidant, a place where she found solace in her sorrow and loneliness and where she could express her "sadness in silence, her pain out loud." Her diary was the companion she could turn to and ask for answers about what she called the "cosmic truths that exist in silence."

The diary also represents a direct parallel to Kahlo's extensive correspondence, in the letters that she wrote from the 1920s through until the end of her life. The importance of Kahlo's writing was identified early on by Raquel Tibol, and was the reason why she then devoted several years of her life to tracking it down in all the collections and archives to which she was able to obtain access. The wealth of material Tibol managed to assemble in this way is extraordinary, although the work does need to be continued since new letters

Page 361
Portrait of Neferúnico, Founder of Lokura
(detail of diary page), 1945

Face in profile with two doves (detail of diary page)

still turn up on occasion at auctions in the United States and in Europe and these must be carefully studied, not least because a number of letters have also surfaced whose authenticity is open to question.

Tibol's research reveals Kahlo as a literary figure as well as being a painter. Moreover, in these writings she speaks directly, in her own words, and without any mediation on the part of other people or their interpretation. Kahlo's letters, like her diary, also shed light on the development of some of her paintings. In her earliest letters from the 1920s, when Kahlo was at school and seeing Alejandro Gómez Arias, she included small drawings with what she wrote together with humorous little scenes and elaborate calligraphy. This playful interaction between the drawn image and the written thought carried over into the diary Kahlo kept as an adult, in which her extraordinary artistic ability was used to intertwine words and line drawings, photographs and collages, portraits and stories, and amid this collection of labyrinthine daydreams are found her beliefs and ideals, reflections on her past and present, her life and her sorrows.

On some of the diary pages the meeting between poetry and drawing becomes a single conceptual unit, whereby the lines of the poem appeal to the reader's senses while the words in turn are surrounded by the gestural lines of the illustrations, as if they were flickering stars in a world without sound (p. 371). Kahlo painted this particular page around 1945, as is indicated by the fact that the last sentences relate to the content of her painting *Without Hope* (pp. 308/309), which is dated to that year: "Not the slightest hope remains for me, everything moves in time with what is in my belly."

On July 13 of the same year, Kahlo began to write a love story about two characters called Chromophore and Auxochrome with the title *Xocolatl*, the elixir of the gods that is made from cocoa beans and is believed to be an aphrodisiac. Auxochrome is the one who captures color, in other words Rivera, while Kahlo is personified as Chromophore, the one who provides color. For her they were an inseparable unit, "an odd couple from the land of dots and lines." The story originated in the research Kahlo undertook for *Moses* (pp. 272/273), the painting she produced in response to certain of Freud's writings and in which she developed an interpretation of the myth of the "birth of the hero," by contextualizing it within different cultures and moments in history. These included the pharaoh Akhenaten and his wife Nefertiti, who in the pages of Kahlo's diary were transformed into the beautiful Neferisis, "She Who Is Immensely Wise," and "Ojo-único" ("One-Eye"), these being the parents of Neferúnico who would go on to establish the city of "Lokura" (p. 361),. Each of these characters was a projection of Kahlo herself, either as self-portraits or versions of her that existed somewhere between the real world and other, imaginary worlds (pp. 372–373, no. 4–5), and were all drawn with a sense of freedom and delight that is unmatched in her painting.

The artistic quality of the drawings found alongside most of the written content in Kahlo's diary is precisely what makes them worthy of greater examination. Sarah M. Lowe produced the first full, page-by-page study of the diary in 1995, and a number of other scholars have also had the opportunity to assess it, yet none of them have concentrated in any detail on the drawings' artistic merit. However, Kahlo's sense of poetry and her use of the written word are fully complemented by the visual and conceptual richness of some of her illustrations. There are indeed some pages where the writing serves as an underlying narrative but the drawing is so skillful that the art dominates the text (p. 374). The graphic line is magnificent, both confident and sublime, with a fluidity that succeeds in integrating bodily forms in a somewhat whimsical manner (pp. 376–378,

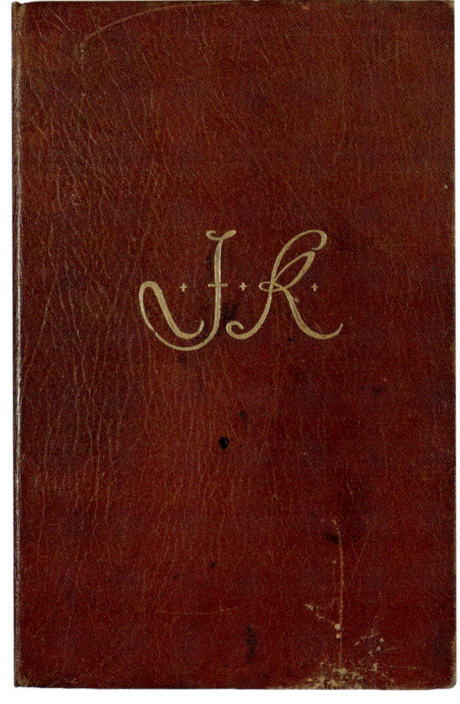

nos. 8–10) that is not unlike the work of William Blake, the 18th-century English poet, painter, and illustrator of mystical texts. Close reading of Kahlo's diary also reveals the literary references in several passages, so that, as Lowe discovered, it becomes clear that Kahlo used Lewis Carroll's *Through the Looking-glass* as a source in her account of the genesis of *The Two Fridas*.

In the last 15 years of Kahlo's artistic career, which correspond to the period when she was writing the diary, she was at the height of her abilities and had unquestionably found her own language as an artist. It is therefore no accident that in a number of these drawings she was exploring how various unconscious states might be revealed by means of Surrealist techniques, such as through the automatic drawing of lines or by evoking her dreams to release the creative potential of the subconscious (p. 379).

By their nature, personal diaries are private, and because of this the person writing is able to express their feelings freely and openly. Even so, the writing is at the same time implicitly aimed at a potential reader, in the hope that what is being written about,

Cover of Kahlo's diary (with the initials F. K.; leather-bound)
Mexico City, Coyoacán, Museo Frida Kahlo

and the writer's own individual way of being and thinking, might become known. This leads to the question of what purpose Kahlo had in mind for her diary. It would seem quite likely that, as with many of her paintings, she would have wished that her deepest thoughts might reach beyond the place where they were recorded. Given that, her wish would be that anyone who did eventually read what she had written would come to know her feelings and her sorrows, her great love for Rivera but also her fears and the loneliness she increasingly felt toward the end of her life.

As noted above, the pages of Kahlo's diary served as somewhere for her to set out her problems and as a companion in her misfortunes. This might explain why several pages have been torn out and why in other places words have been changed and overwritten, while elsewhere some pages are so covered with drawings that the writing disappears completely. Some of this was also perhaps the result of editing decisions made with the eventual reader in mind. And yet, if Kahlo did open up in her diary about her most intimate thoughts she also did so cryptically (as was the case in some of her paintings), by making use of numerical codes or words in other languages. This occurs, for example, with the number "379" and the name "Sadja" (p. 382, no. 14), which appears three times in the diary and is a reference to the main character Nadja in André Breton's autobiographical novel of that title from 1928. Nadja, which is the shortened form of the word for "hope" in Russian, is, like Kahlo, a seductive and marvelous character, who is possessed by desire and demands the ultimate proof of love, which is life itself. As Kahlo wrote to Rivera in her diary, "we shall see, and we shall learn. There is always something new. Always connected to what lived in the past. Oh winged one – my Diego, my love of a thousand years. Sadja."

In 1950, Kahlo's health began to decline, and the change is reflected in her diary. The pages are also marked with the political views she held in her final years, and a renewed commitment to left-wing ideology is evident in her praise of Stalin, Lenin, Marx, and Engels, in the same way as can be seen in the paintings she made between 1952 and 1954 (p. 380). At this late stage Kahlo's conceptual approach to her art was also undergoing a process of deconstruction, in response to both her psychological and her physical condition. Since the mid-1940s there had been a transformation in the way Kahlo's body was depicted in her self-portraits, with wounds and hollows frequently being shown as metaphors for the emotional vulnerability she was feeling. At other times her face was altered, even to the point where Rivera's portrait was set on her forehead or else where her face formed half of one two-sided image, as in the double self-portraits *Diego and Frida* and

I am DISINTEGRATION
(detail of diary page)

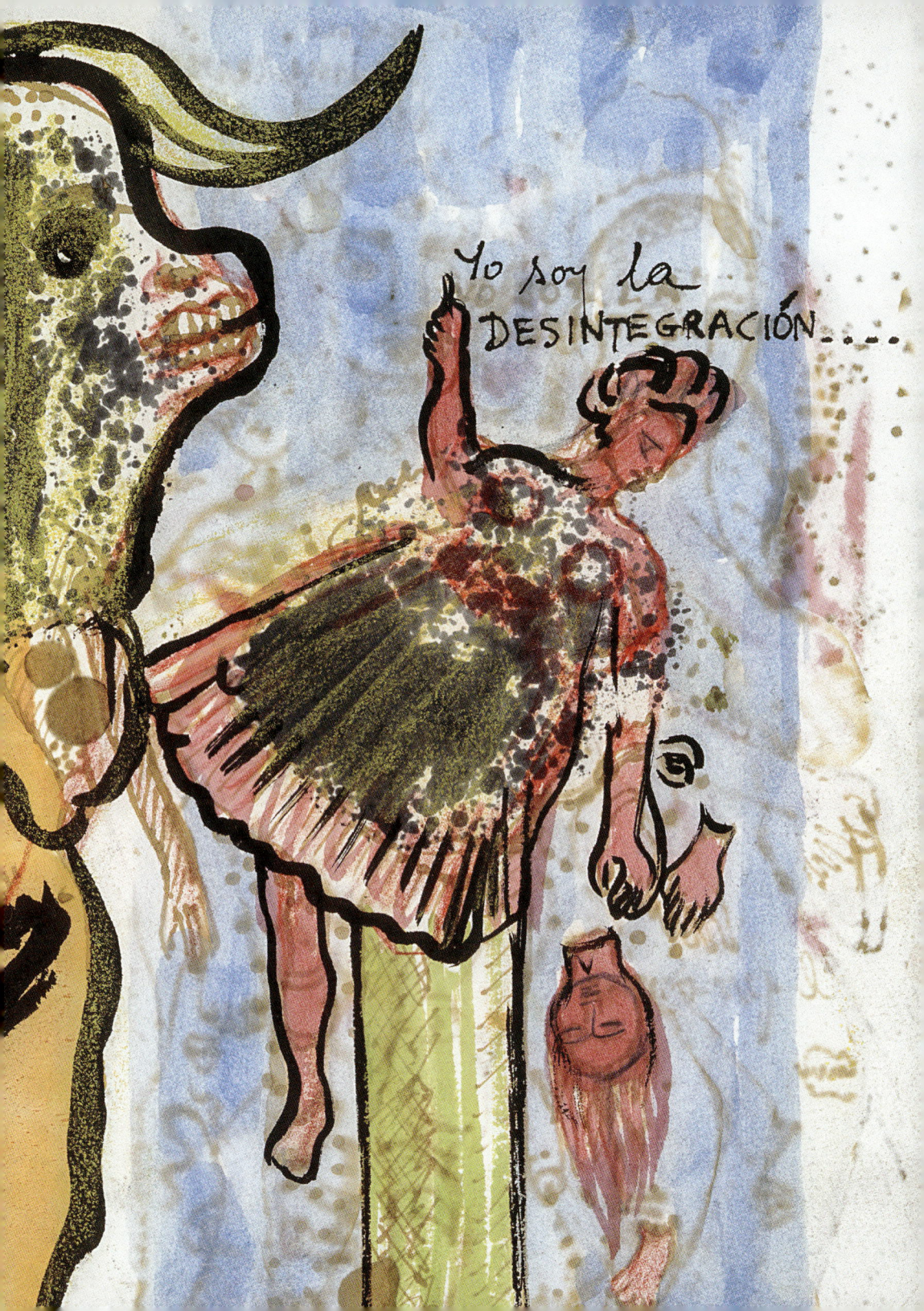

Diego and Frida (p. 204, and Lozano 2021, cat. 112). Kahlo's face was also hidden altogether, as in her self-portrait *The Mask* (p. 259) from 1945.

The process of deconstruction affected not only her body but also her spirit, and in the diary it is noticeable how Kahlo projected her personality according to that of other people, so as to satisfy her own needs through those she loved. Kahlo lived for Rivera, and in her diary she wrote: "Diego the beginning. Diego the maker. Diego my child, Diego my man. Diego the painter. Diego my lover, Diego 'my husband' Diego my friend. Diego my mother. Diego my father. Diego my son. Diego = Me" (p. 375, no. 7).

The deconstruction of Kahlo's body, meanwhile, is presented on several pages in the diary, such as when, for example, she depicted herself naked and with broken wings like a butterfly that wanted to be transformed before it could take flight, while at the same time asking herself if she was ready to leave: "Are you going?" she asked, but the reply was: "No" (p. 384, no. 16).

Similarly, when the pain in Kahlo's leg had become so severe that her doctors had to amputate part of her right foot, and again in 1953 when her greatest fear came to pass and her gangrenous leg had to be amputated, defiant in the face of her fate

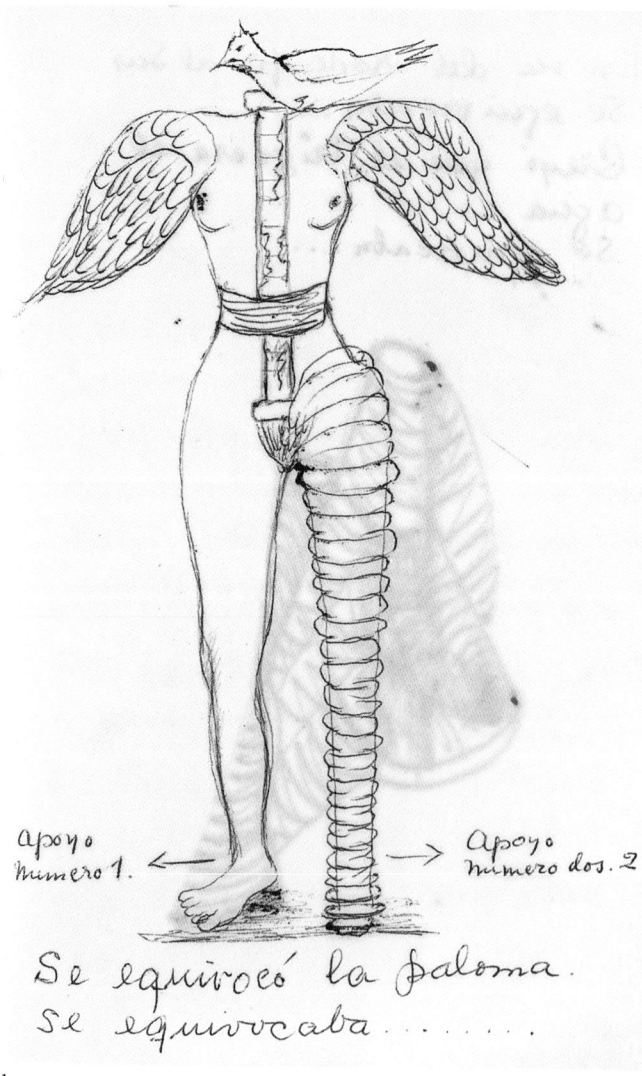

apoyo
número 1. ←   → apoyo
                        número dos. 2

Se equivocó la paloma.
Se equivocaba.......

1

Kahlo drew in her diary a picture of her feet separated from her body, with the admonition: "What do I want feet for if I have wings to fly" (p. 385). On another occasion she drew herself naked again, but this time with one leg missing and with a broken spine, like a *Winged Victory of Samothrace* accompanied by a dove, and evoking lines from a poem by Rafael Alberti (1902–1999): "The dove was wrong. It was mistaken. Instead of north, it went south. It was mistaken […] It thought the wheat was water. It was mistaken…" (p. 368, no. 1).

The following year, having lost her strength and her hope, Kahlo became dependent on prescription drugs to help her cope with her physical pain. Her deconstruction was now complete. "My leg was amputated six months ago, they have put me through centuries of torture and at times I almost lost my mind. I kept wanting to kill myself […] I'll leave it a while" (p. 386 no. 18). In the last pages of her diary Kahlo began saying her farewells, thanking those who had cared for her while she was ill and writing a brief summary of her life. Finally, alongside a drawing of herself shown naked and front on, completely honest and stripped of all the personal paraphernalia she had adopted throughout her life (pp. 388–389, no. 20), Kahlo embraced the fact that her time had come: "I look forward to my departure – and I hope never to return – FRIDA". And with that, I bring my own thoughts on the pages of Kahlo's diary to a close.

1.
Support number 1.
Support number two. 2
The dove was wrong.
It was mistaken ……

2.
Title-page
Painted in 1916

3.
Numbers, their economy
and the farce of words,
nerves are blue.
I don't know why – also red,
but full of color.

Through round numbers
and colored nerves
the stars are made
and worlds are sounds.

Not the slightest hope remains for
me, everything moves in time with
what is in my belly

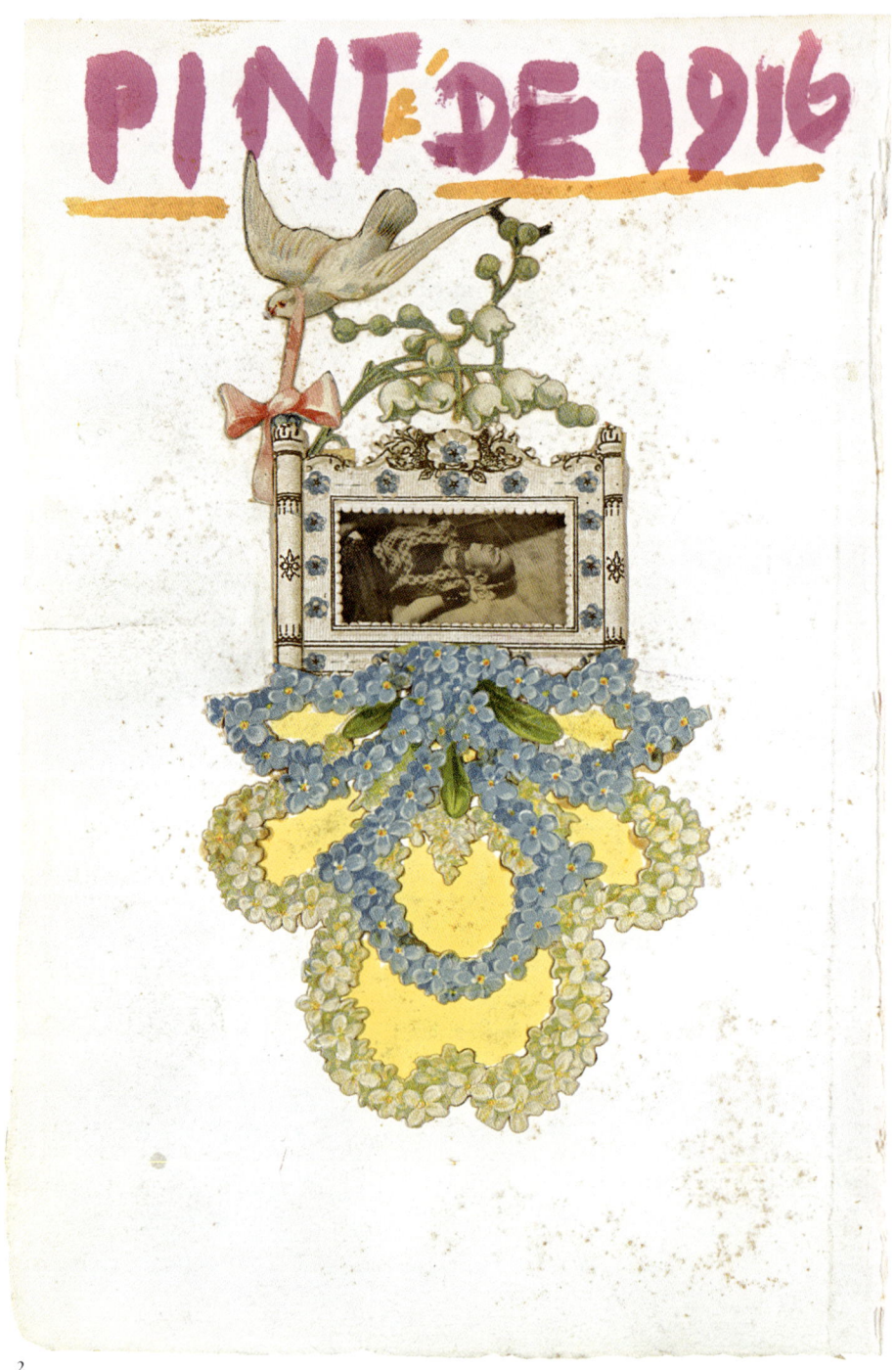

2

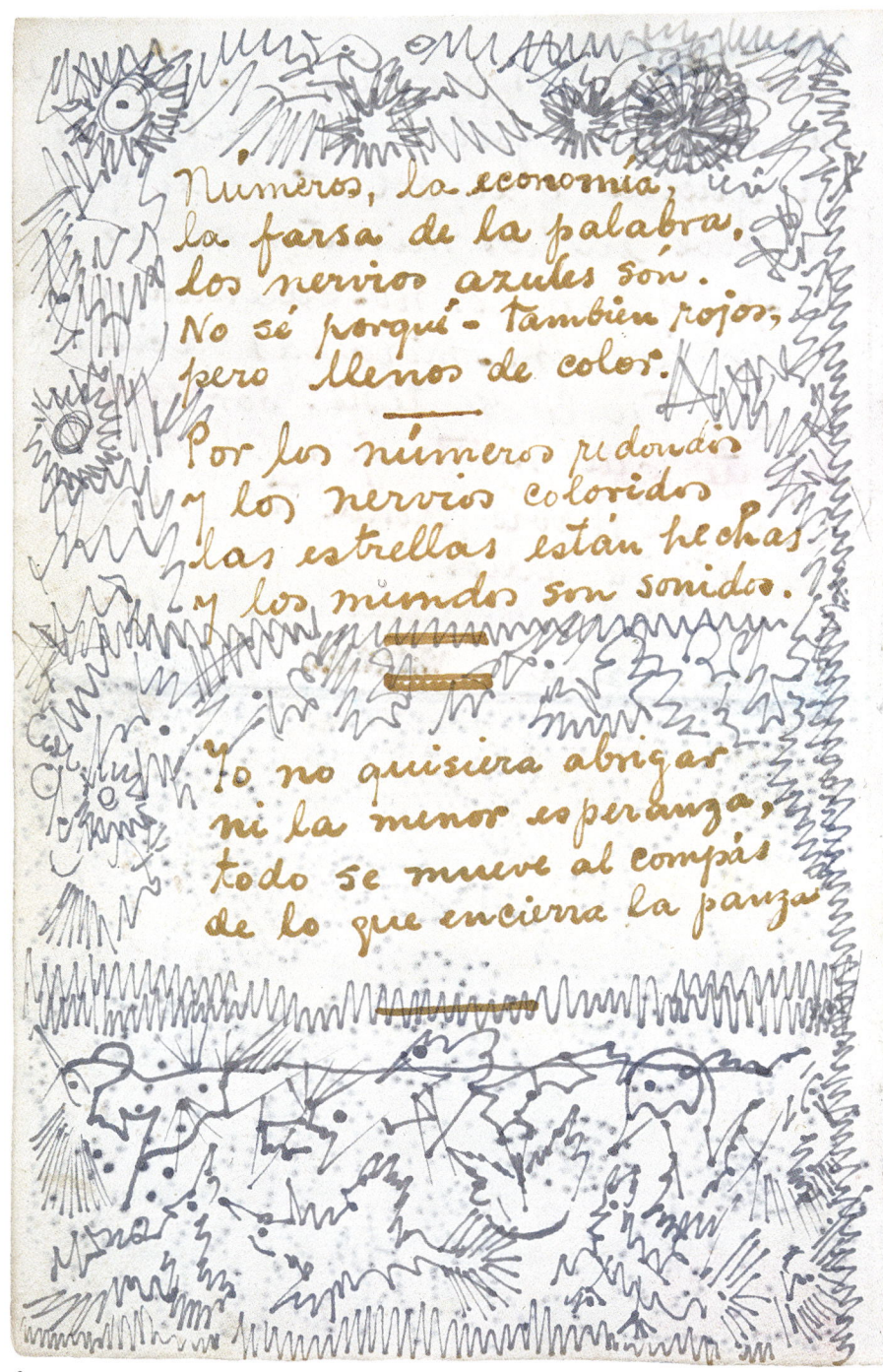

Números, la economía,
la farsa de la palabra,
los nervios azules són.
No sé porqué – también rojos,
pero llenos de color.

Por los números redondos
y los nervios coloridos
las estrellas están hechas
y los mundos son sonidos.

Yo no quisiera abrigar
ni la menor esperanza,
todo se mueve al compás
de lo que encierra la panza

3

4.
real world

5.
dance to the sun

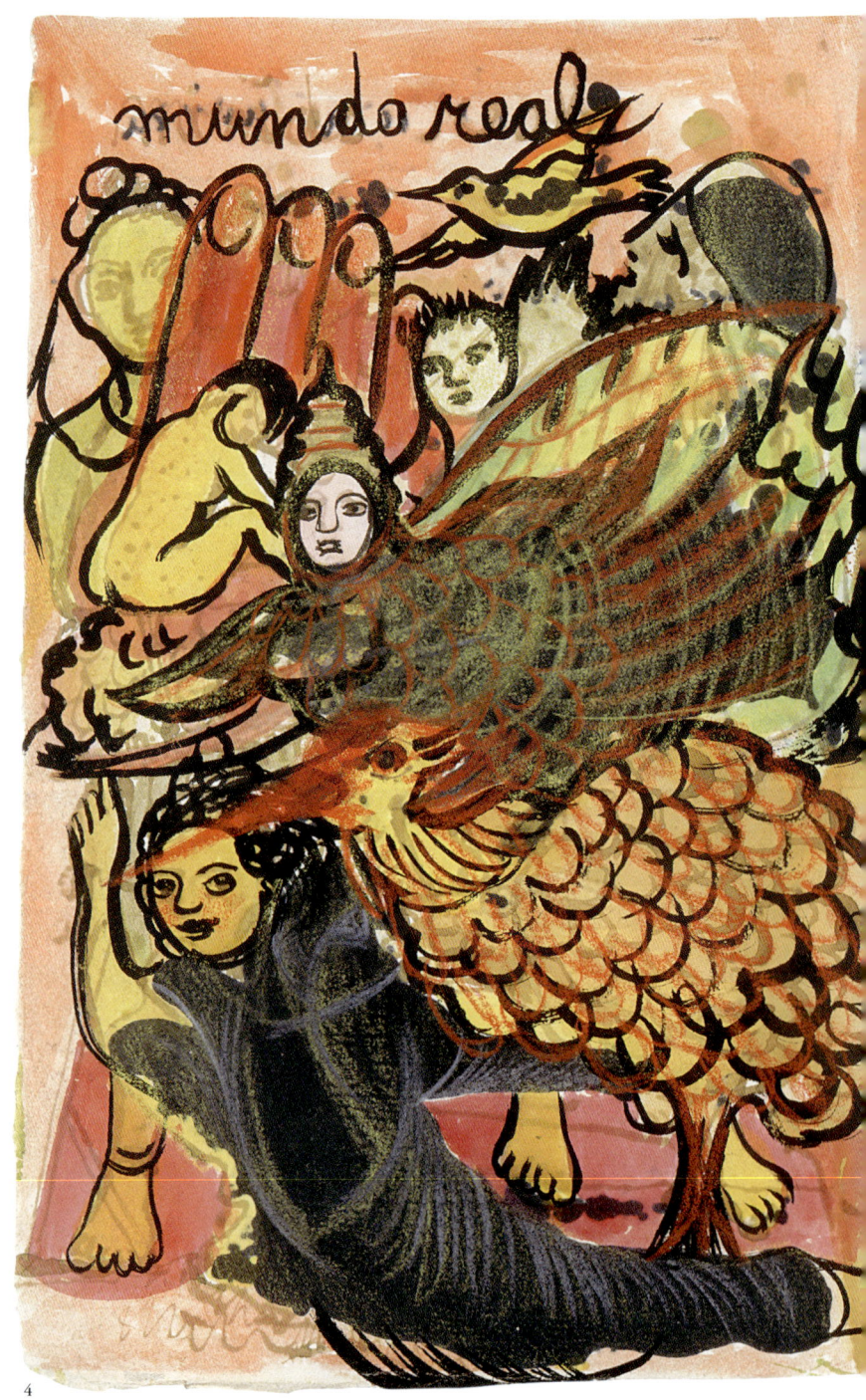

4

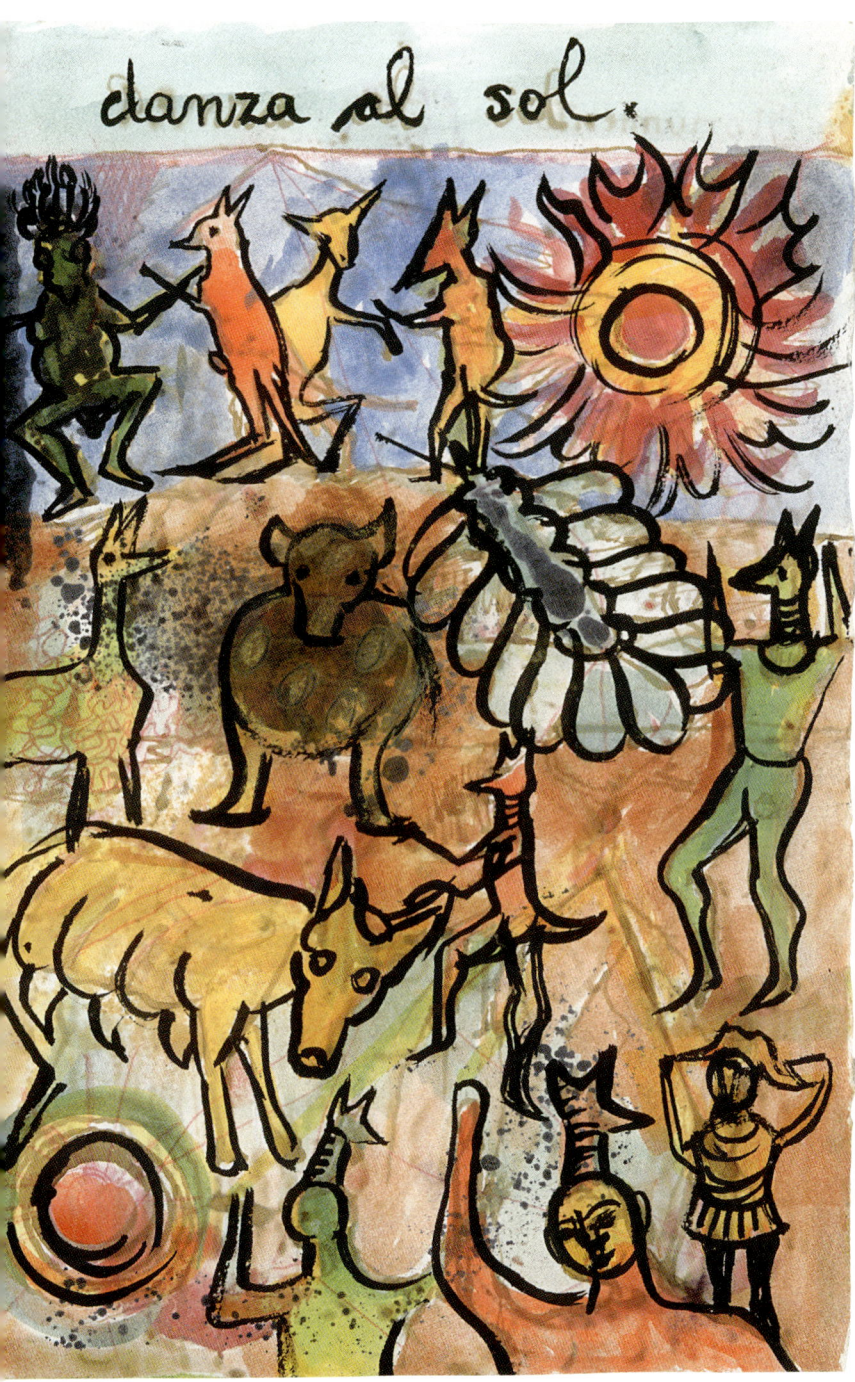

danza al sol.

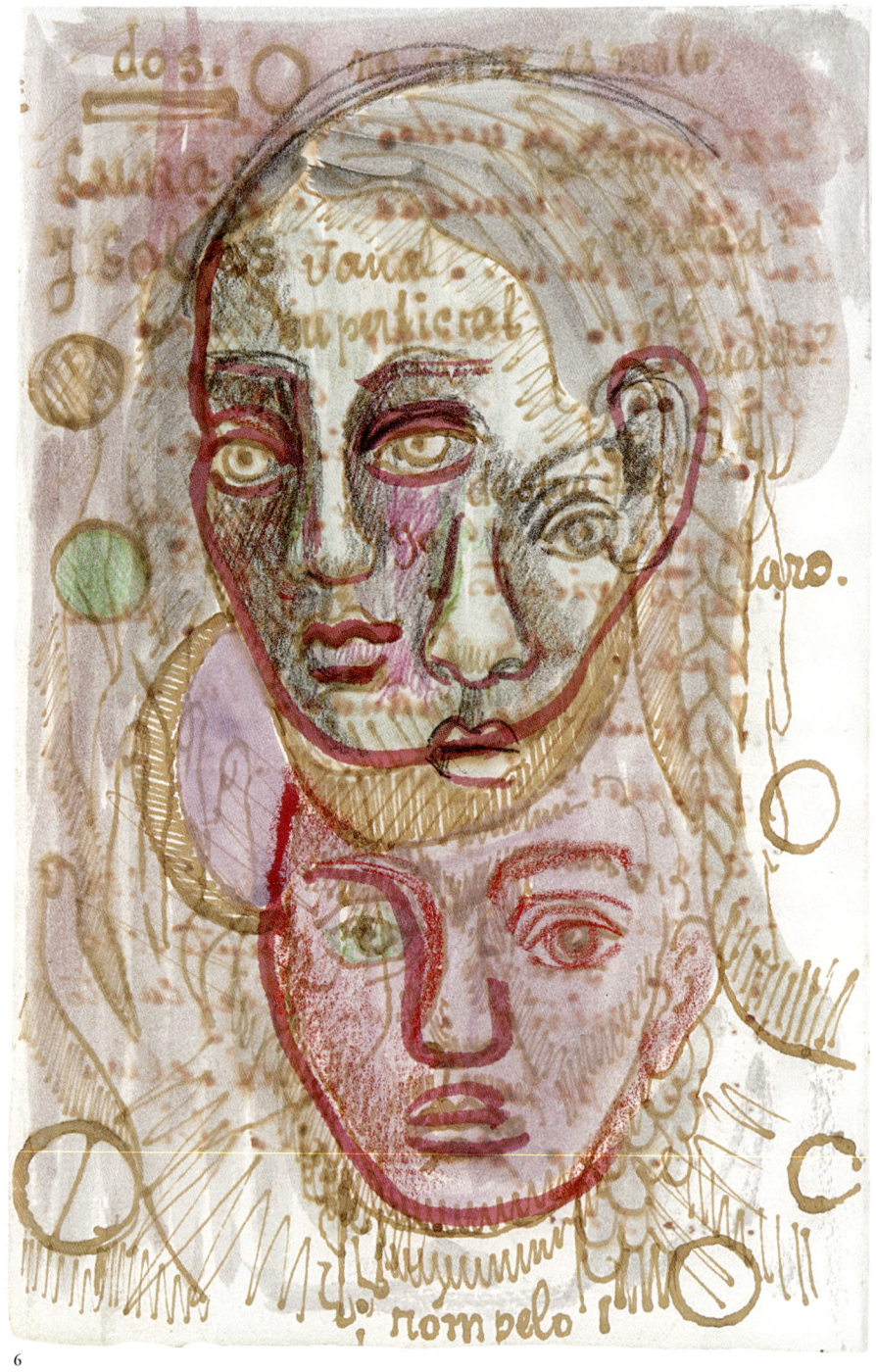

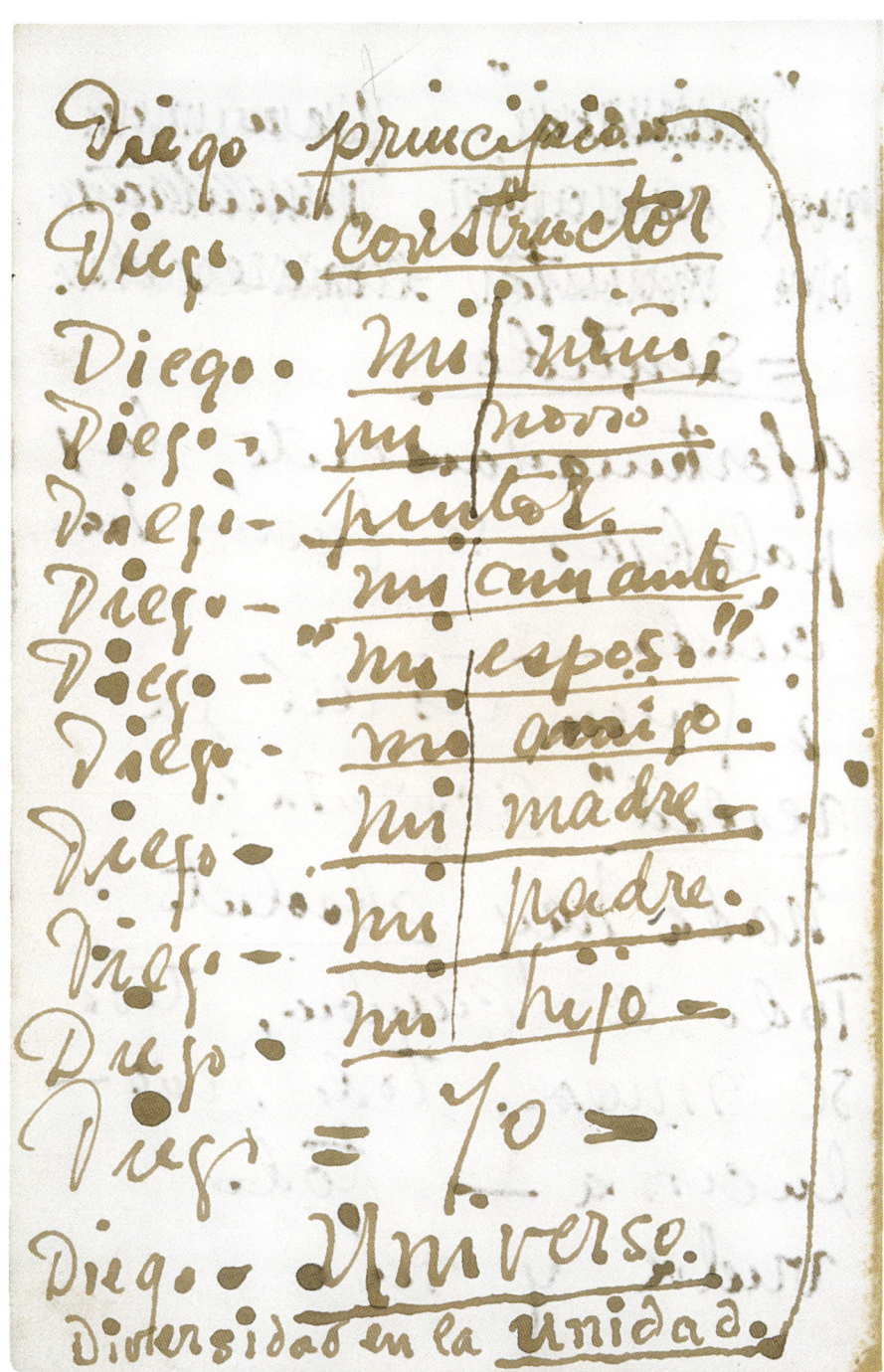

Diego principio..
Diego constructor
Diego. mi niño
Dieg. mi novio
Diegi- pintor
Diego- mi amante
Dieg. "mi esposo"
Dieg- mi amigo.
Diego. mi madre
Dieg- mi padre
Dieg- mi hijo =
Diego = YO =
Diego. Universo.
Diversidad en la unidad.

7

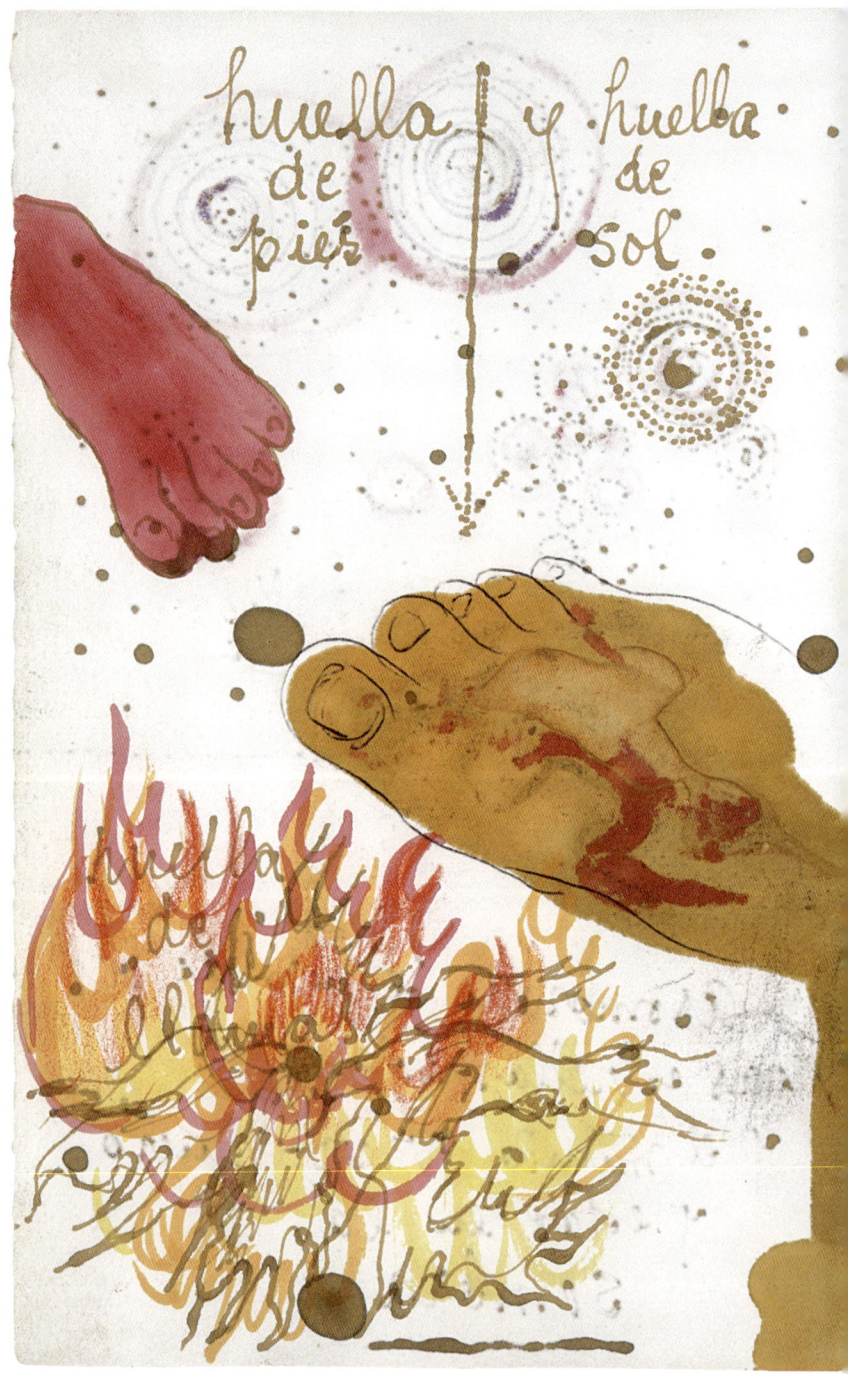

8

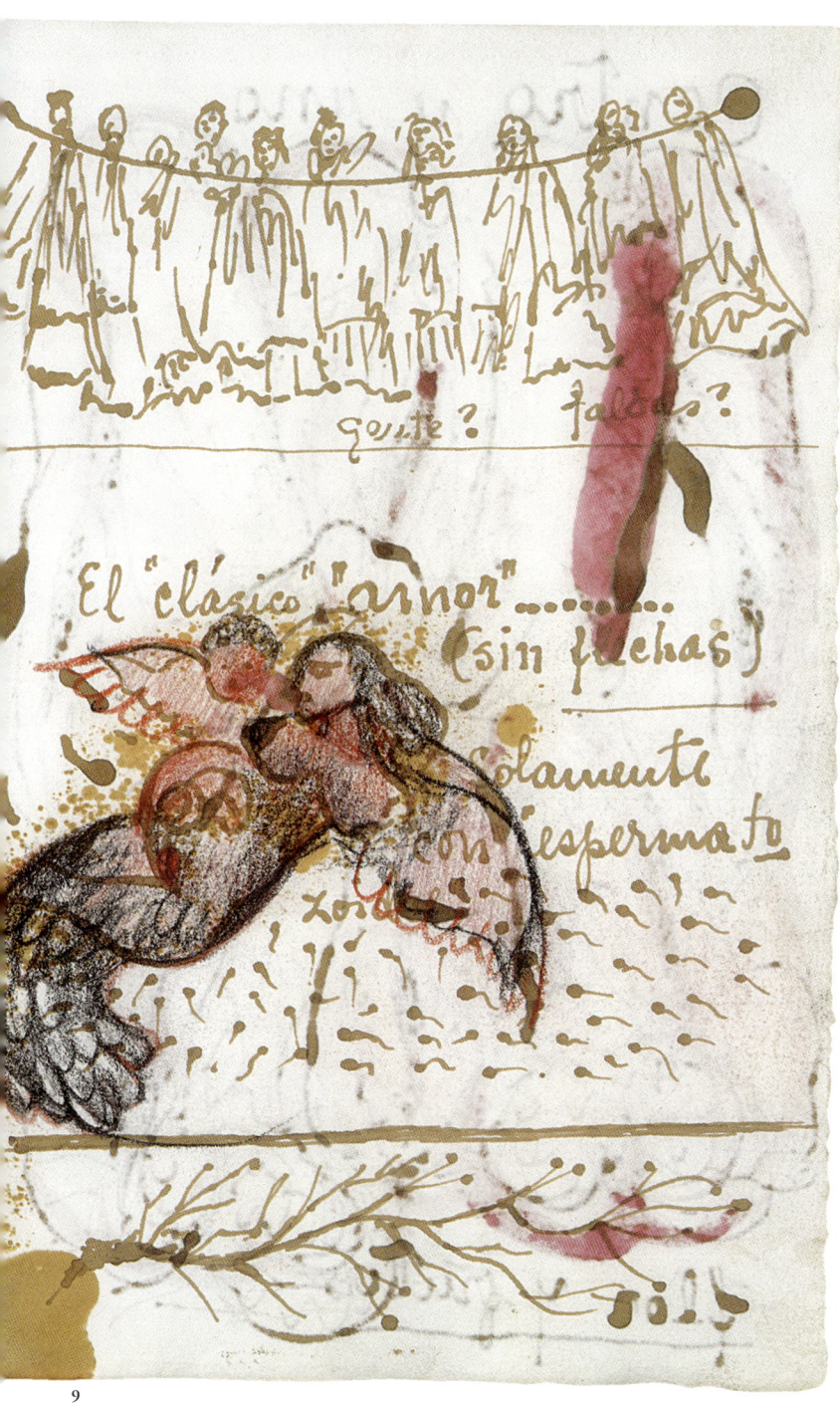

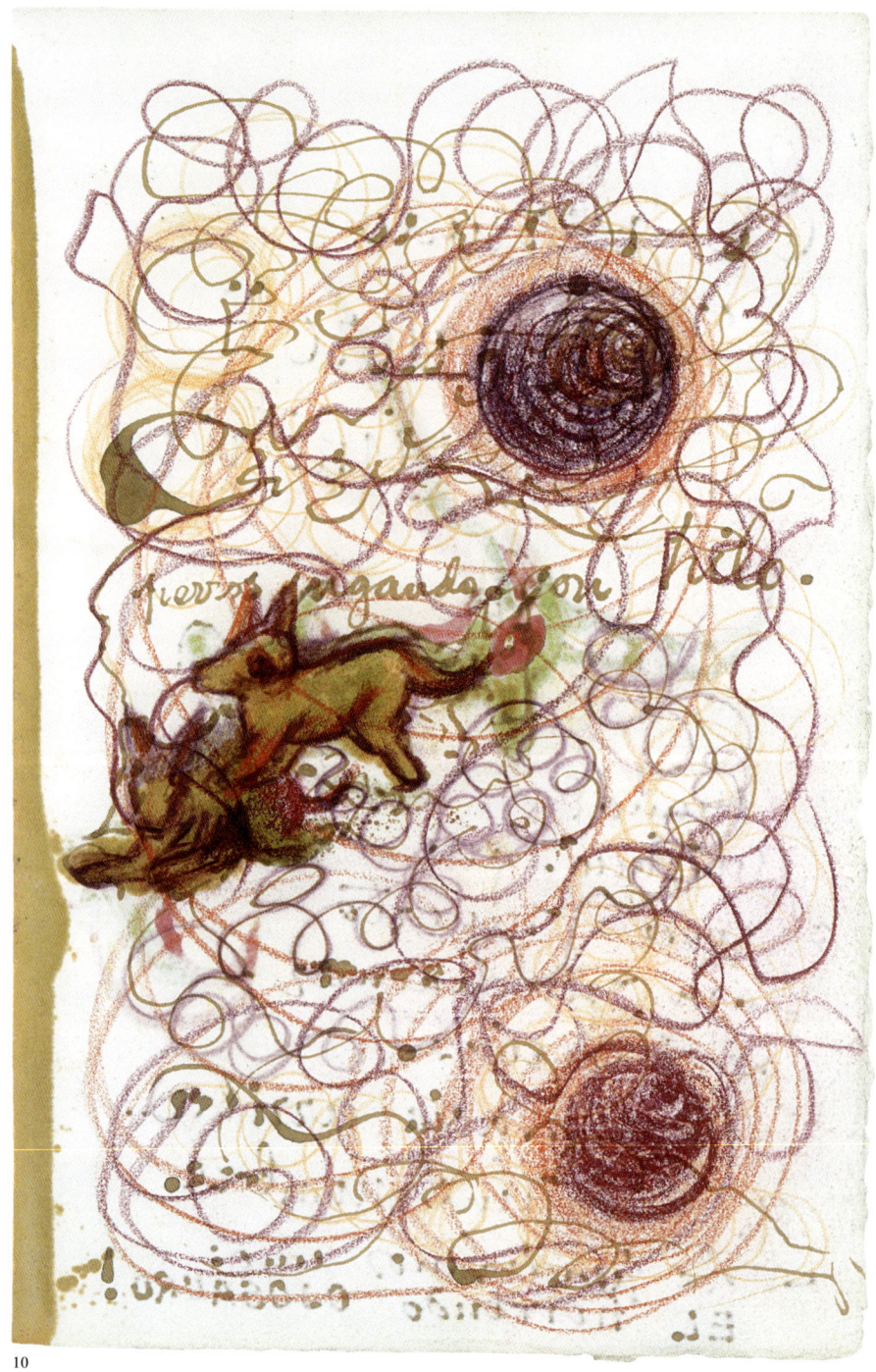

10

6.

two.
it doesn't work, it's bad.
dreadful
isn't it?
Moons
and Suns
banal.
superficial
don't you think so?
YES
I want…
Me
Of course.
tear it up!

7.

Diego the <u>beginning.</u>
Diego the <u>maker</u>
Diego <u>my child,</u>
Diego <u>my man.</u>
Diego the <u>painter.</u>
Diego <u>my lover,</u>
Diego <u>"my husband"</u>
Diego <u>my friend.</u>
Diego <u>my mother.</u>
Diego <u>my father.</u>
Diego <u>my son.</u>
Diego = Me =
Diego <u>the Universe.</u>
Diversity in <u>unity.</u>

8.

Footprints
and sun print
flame print

9.

people? skirts?
The "classic" type of "love"
……
(without arrows)
just with sperm

10.

Dogs playing with string.

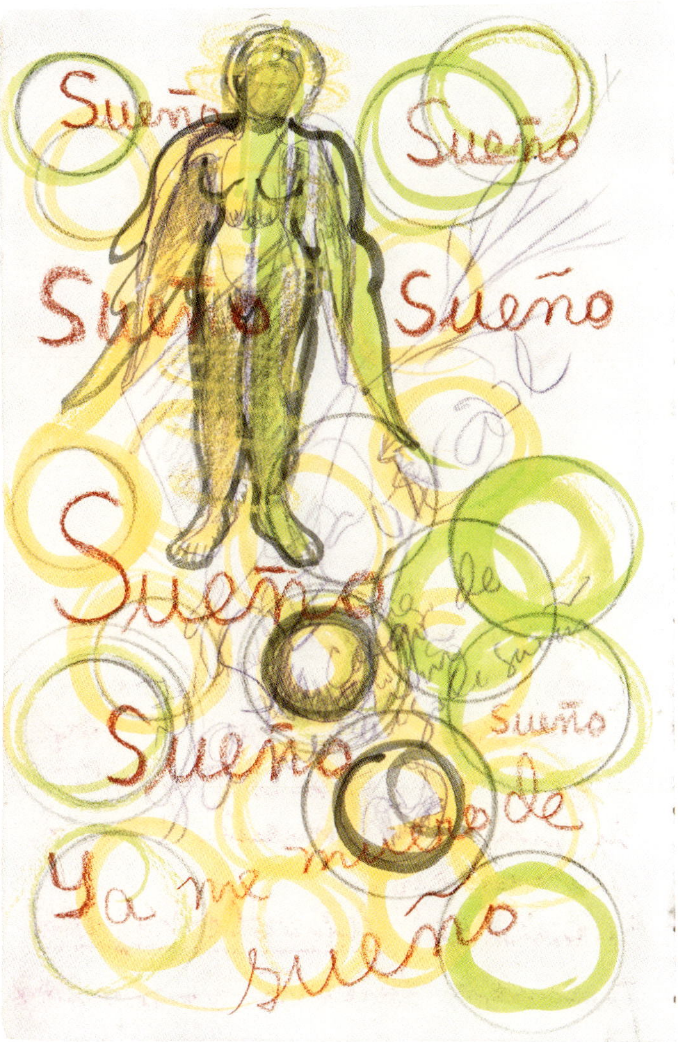

11

11.

Dream Dream
Dream Dream
Dream
Dream Dream
My dreams are killing me

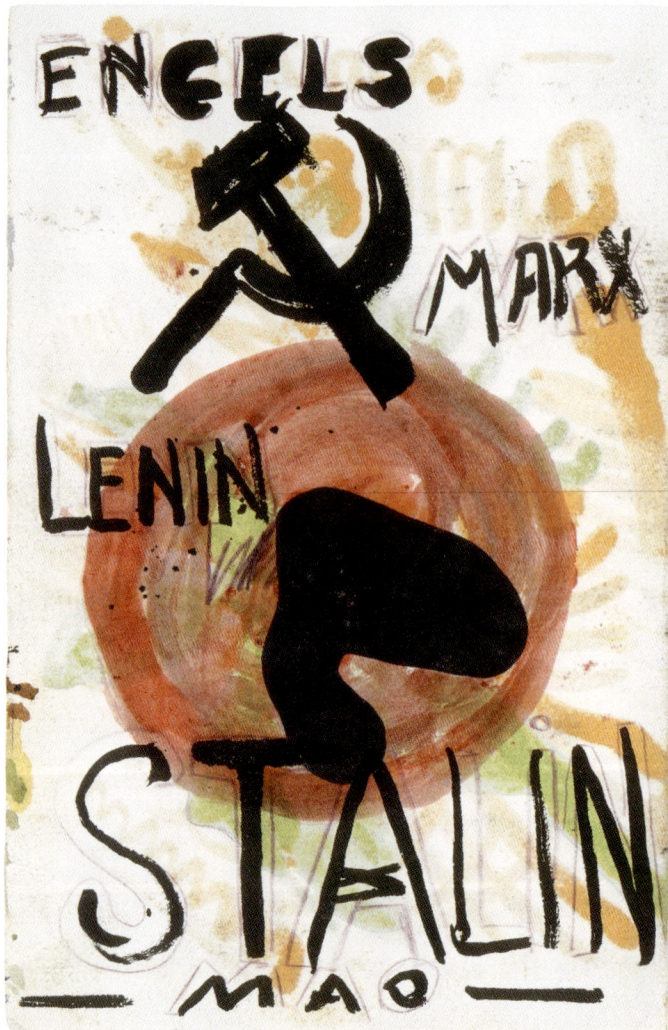

12

12.
ENGELS
MARX
LENIN
STALIN
– MAO –

13.
[…] lí
[…] villa.
[…] TREE ed
[…] YOURS
[…] ALONE laughed
[…] VOY age
[…] rame
[…] lways…
[…] mozo
SMILE
drop, jack, speck.
MYRTLE, SEX, broken,
KEY, SOFT, EMERGES
TENDERNESS
LIQUOR firm hand
LOVE strong chair
THANKS TO LIFE
FULL LIFE
FILLED
ARE…

14.
Sadja
Sadja
379
for ever

15.
Alone with my great happiness
and the very vivid memory of
the little girl. It has been 34
years since I lived that magical
friendship and every time
I remember it the image
comes more alive and grows
more and more inside my
world.

FINCH 1950. Frida Kahlo
FINCH
THE
TWO
FRI-
DAS
Coyoacán
Allende 52

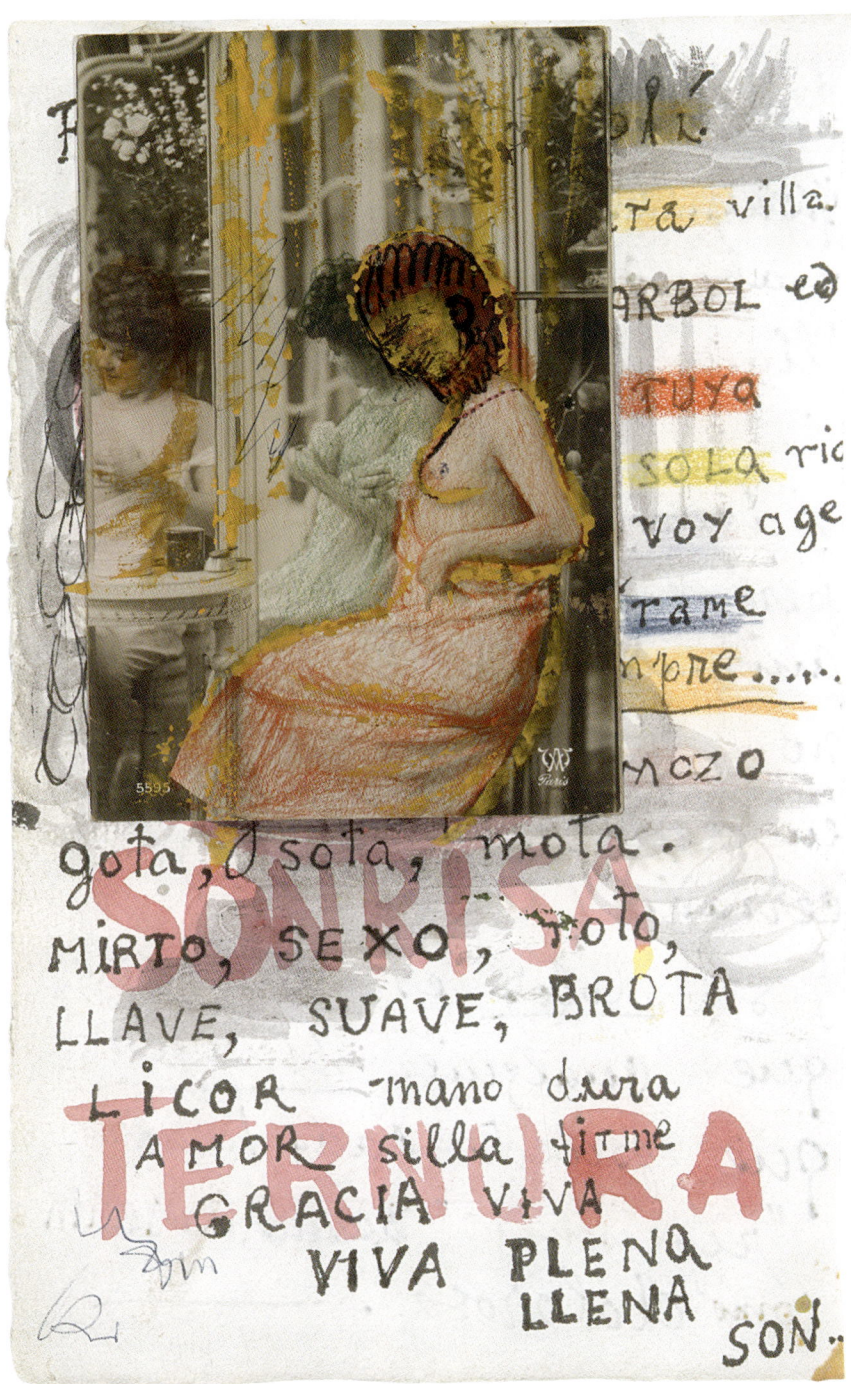

gota, sota, mota.
MIRTO, SEXO, foto,
LLAVE, SUAVE, BROTA
LICOR mano dura
AMOR silla firme
GRACIA VIVA
VIVA PLENA
LLENA
SON.

SONRISA

TERNURA

13

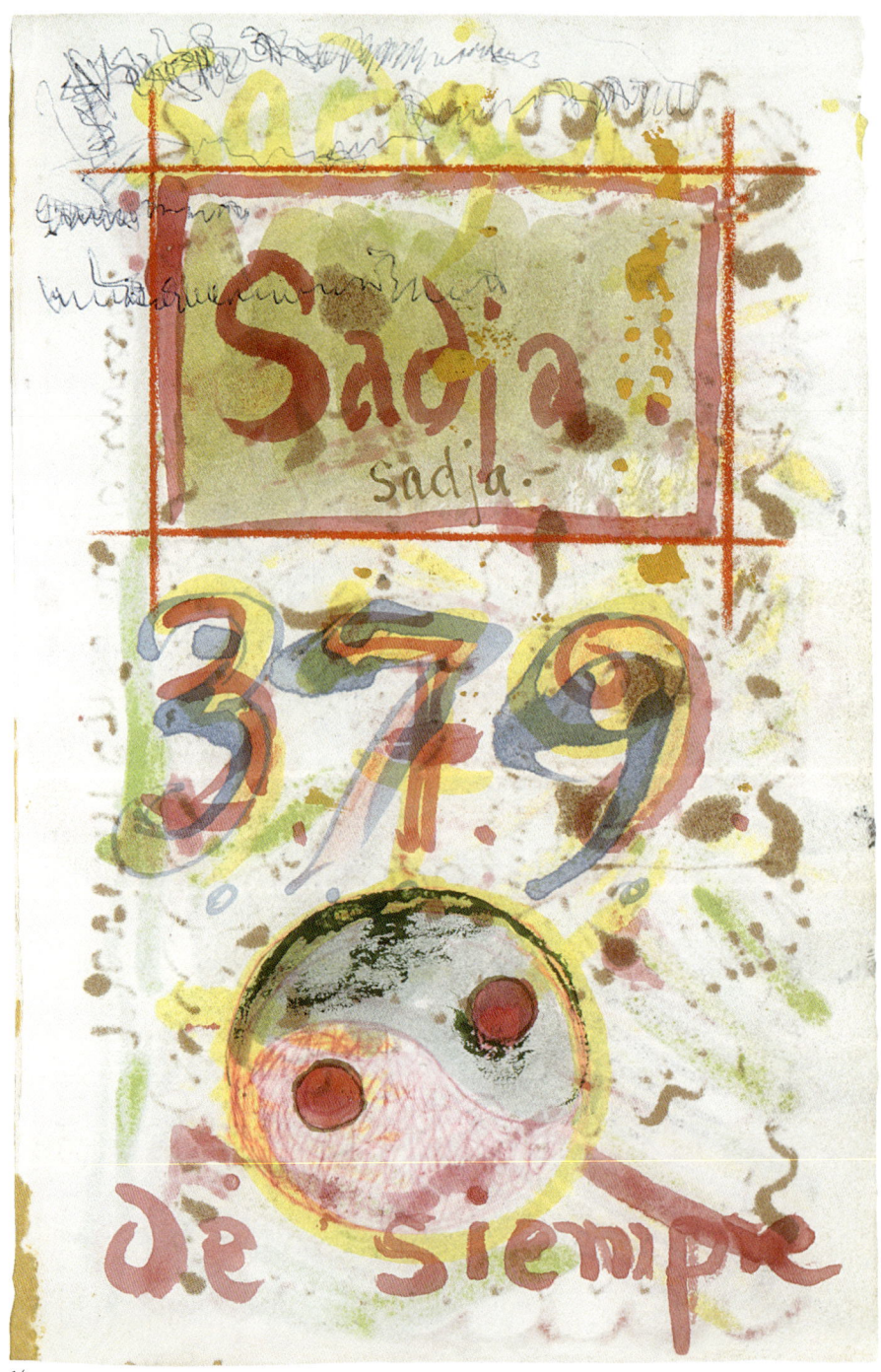

14

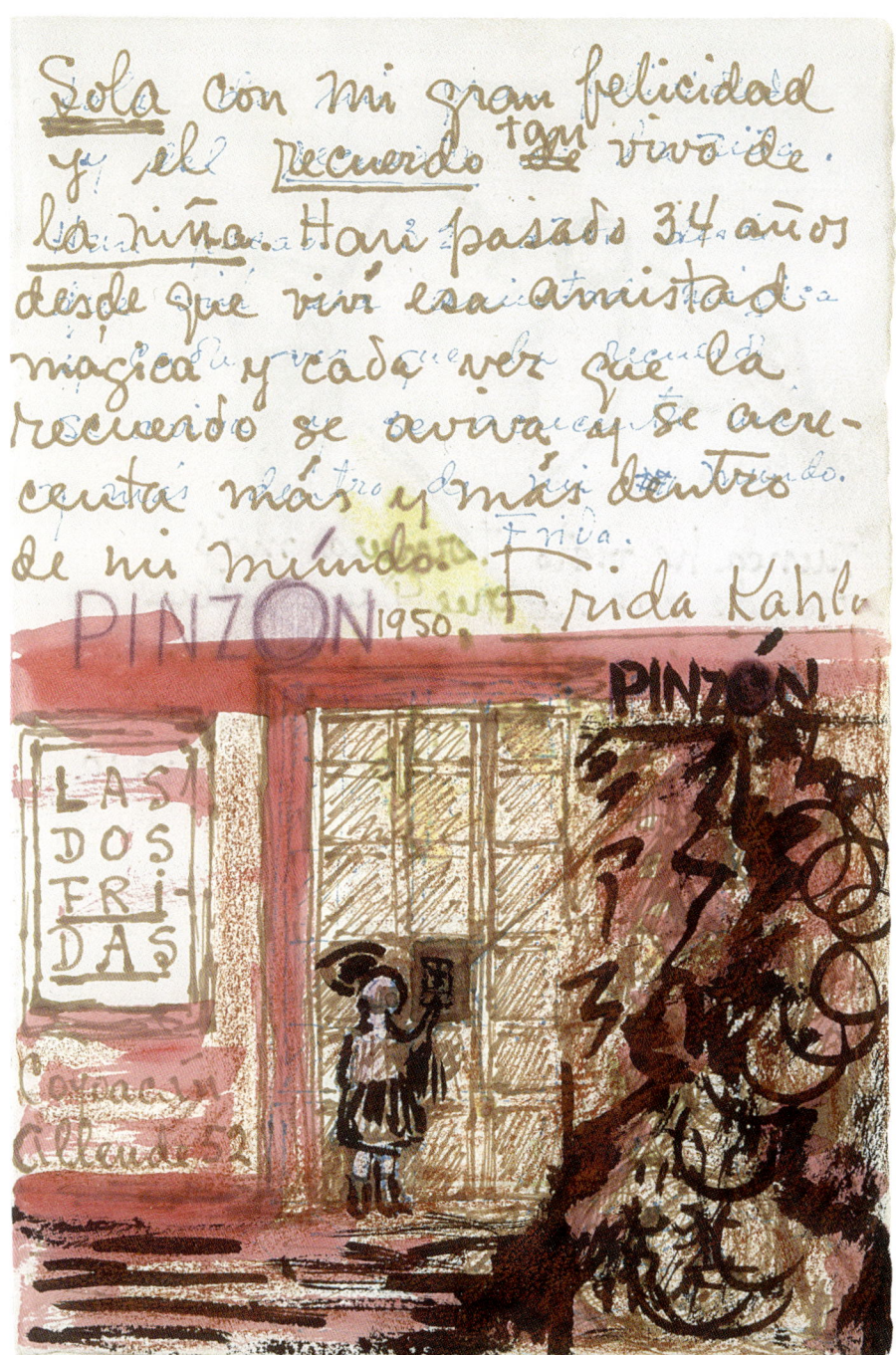

Sola con mi gran felicidad
y el recuerdo tan vivo de
la niña. Han pasado 34 años
desde que viví esa amistad
mágica y cada vez que la
recuerdo se aviva y se acre-
centa más y más dentro
de mi mundo. Frida. Frida Kahlo
PINZÓN 1950.

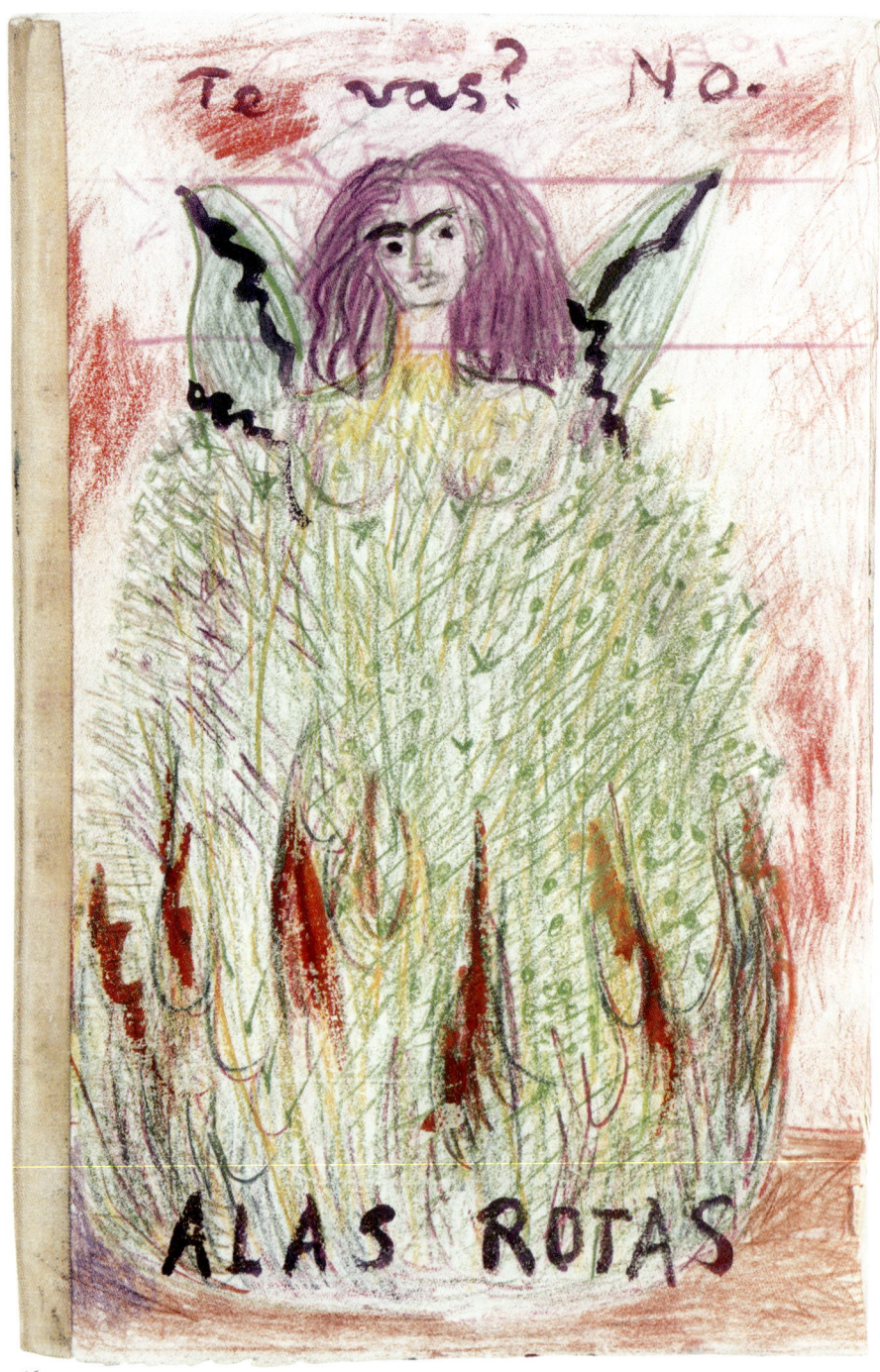

16

16.
Are you going? No.
BROKEN WINGS

17.
What do I want feet for
If I have wings to fly.
1953.

18.
February 11, 1954
My leg was <u>amputated</u>
six <u>months</u> ago
They have put me through
centuries of torture and
at times I almost lost
my mind. I kept wanting
to kill myself
Diego stops me doing it
in the vain
belief that he might
need me. That's what
he said and I believe him. But
never in my life have I
suffered more.
I'll leave it a while.

19.
It's already March
<u>Spring</u> 21.
I've managed to get a lot done.
Walking confidently
Painting confidently.
I love Diego more
even than myself.
My will is strong
my will endures.
Thanks to Diego's won-
derful love.
And the honest and
thoughtful care of
Dr. Farill. And the earnest
and loving efforts
of Dr. Ramón Parrés
and to the kindness of
David Glusker who has
been my doctor all my
life and thanks to Dr.
Eloesser.

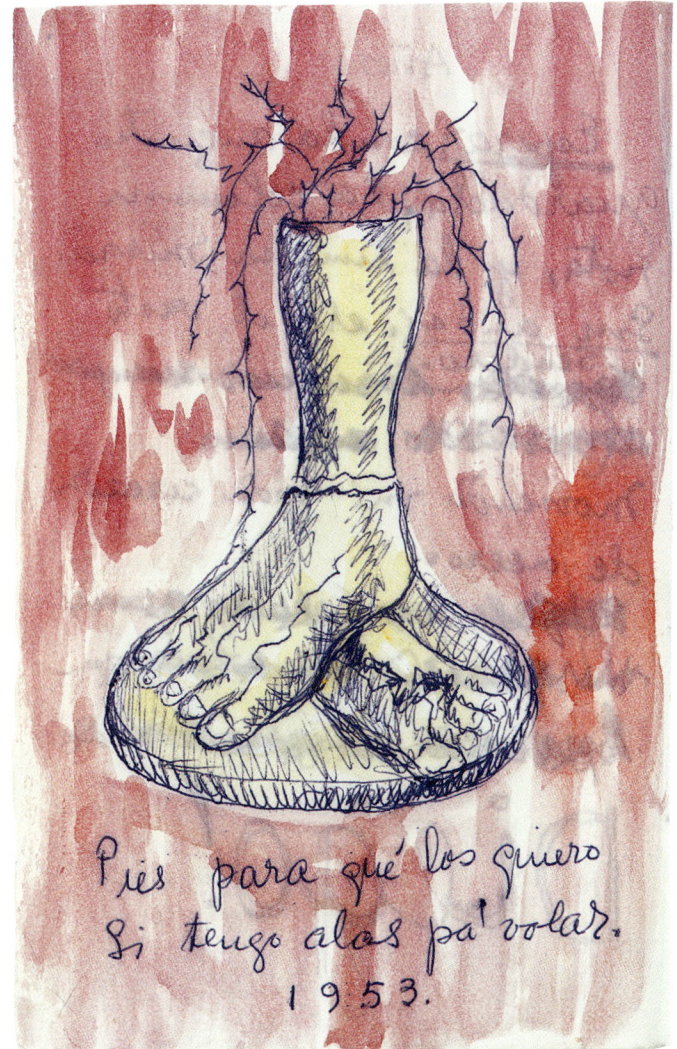

17

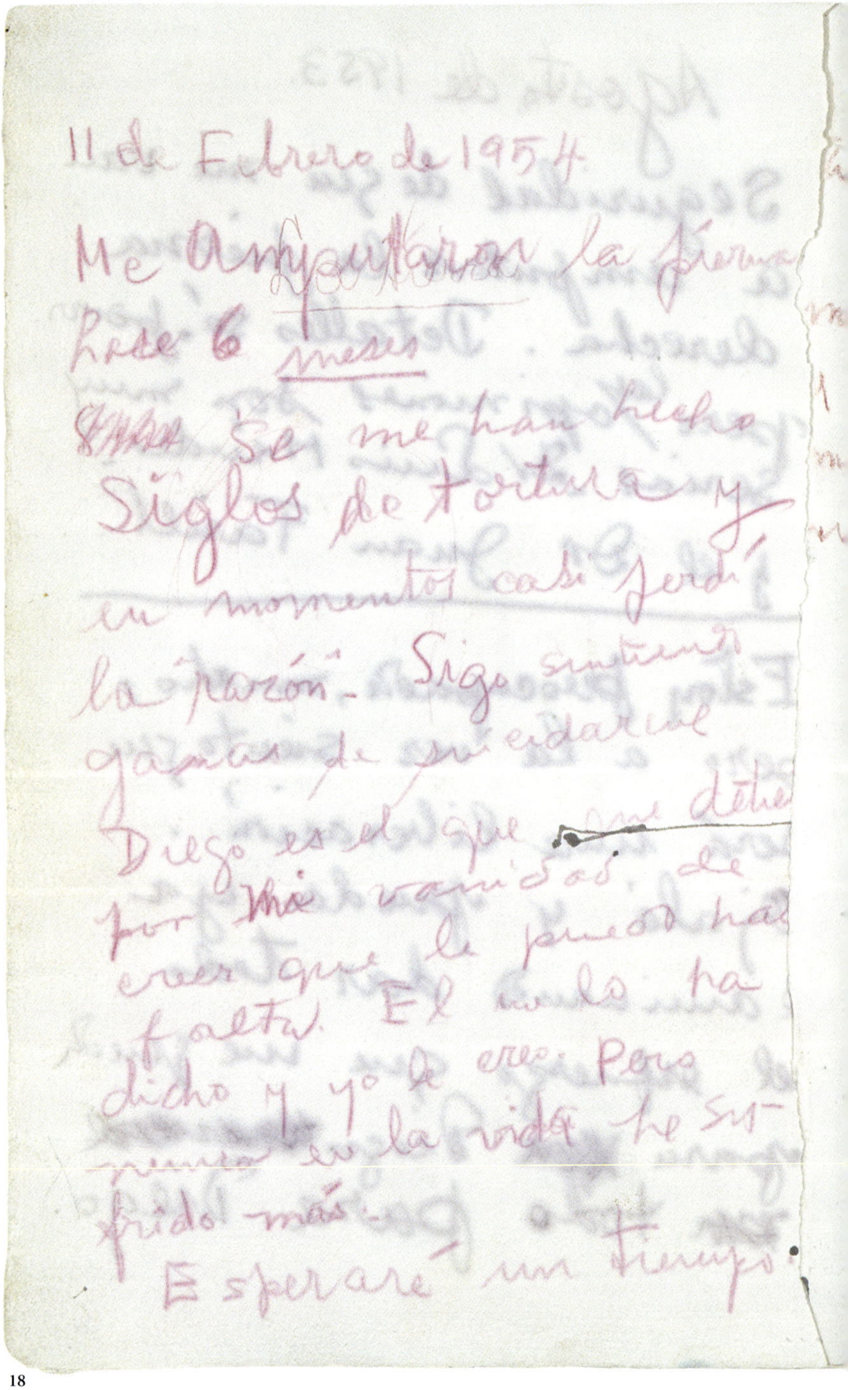

11 de Febrero de 1954

Me Amputaron la pierna
hace 6 meses
se me han hecho
Siglos de tortura y
en momentos casi perdí
la "razón". Sigo sintiendo
ganas de suicidarme.
Diego es el que me detiene
por mi vanidad de
creer que le puedo hacer
falta. El me lo ha
dicho y yo le creo. Pero
nunca en la vida he su-
frido más. Esperaré un tiempo.

18

386

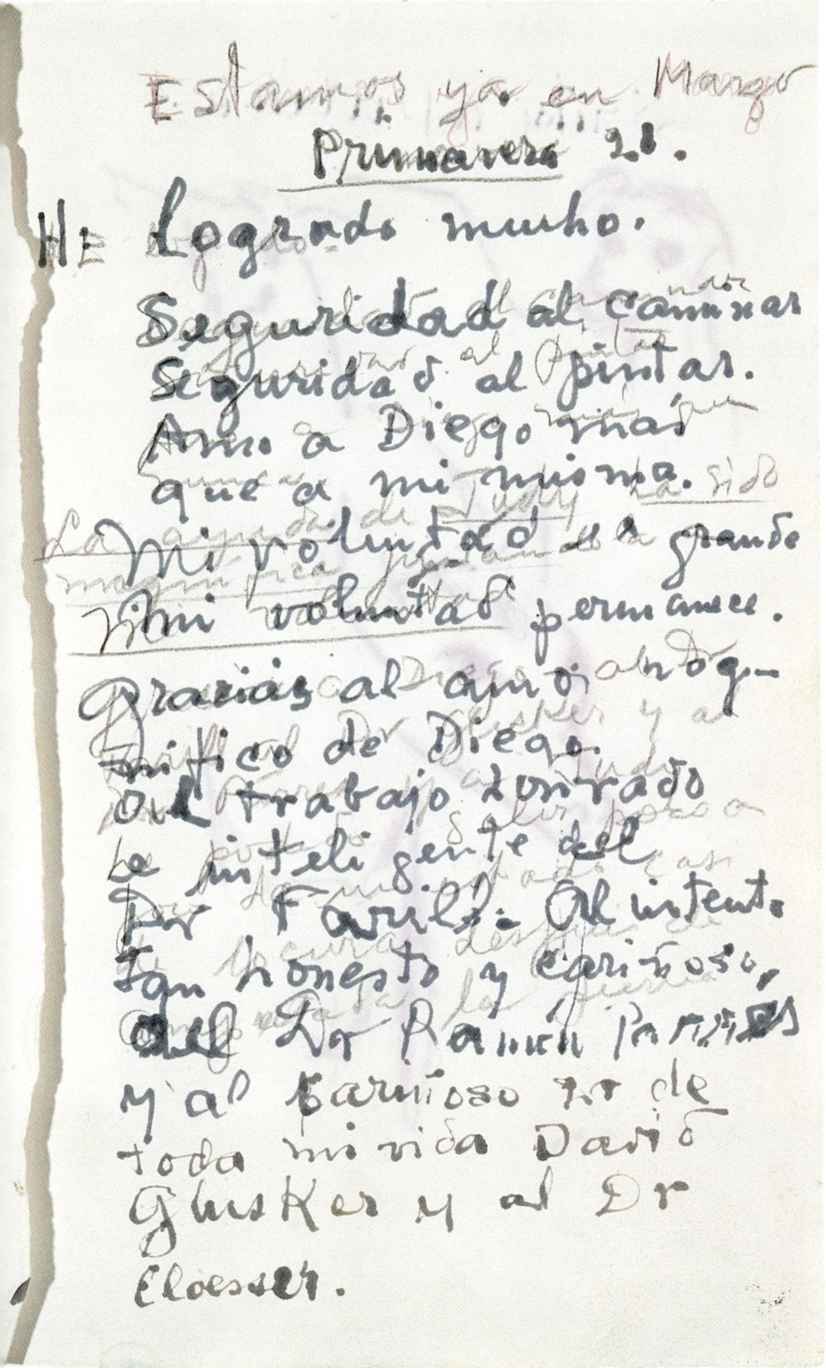

Estamos ya en Marzo
Primavera 21.

HE logrado mucho.

Seguridad al caminar
Seguridad al pintar.
Amo a Diego más
que a mi misma. Sido
Mi voluntad es la grande
Mi voluntad permanece.

Gracias al ayudante mag-
nífico de Diego, y al
trabajo honrado
de inteligente del
Dr Farill. Al intento
tan honesto y cariñoso,
del Dr Ramón Parres
y al cariñoso no de
toda mi vida David
Glusker y al Dr
Eloesser.

19

20.
Thanks to the
doctors
Farill – Glusker
– Párres
and Doctor Enrique
Palomera
Sanchez Palomera.
Thanks to the nurses
to the orderlies to the
cleaners and staff
at the
English Hospital –
Thanks to Dr. Vargas
to Navarro and Dr.
Polo
and to my strength
of will.
I look forward to
my departure – and
I hope
never to return –
FRIDA

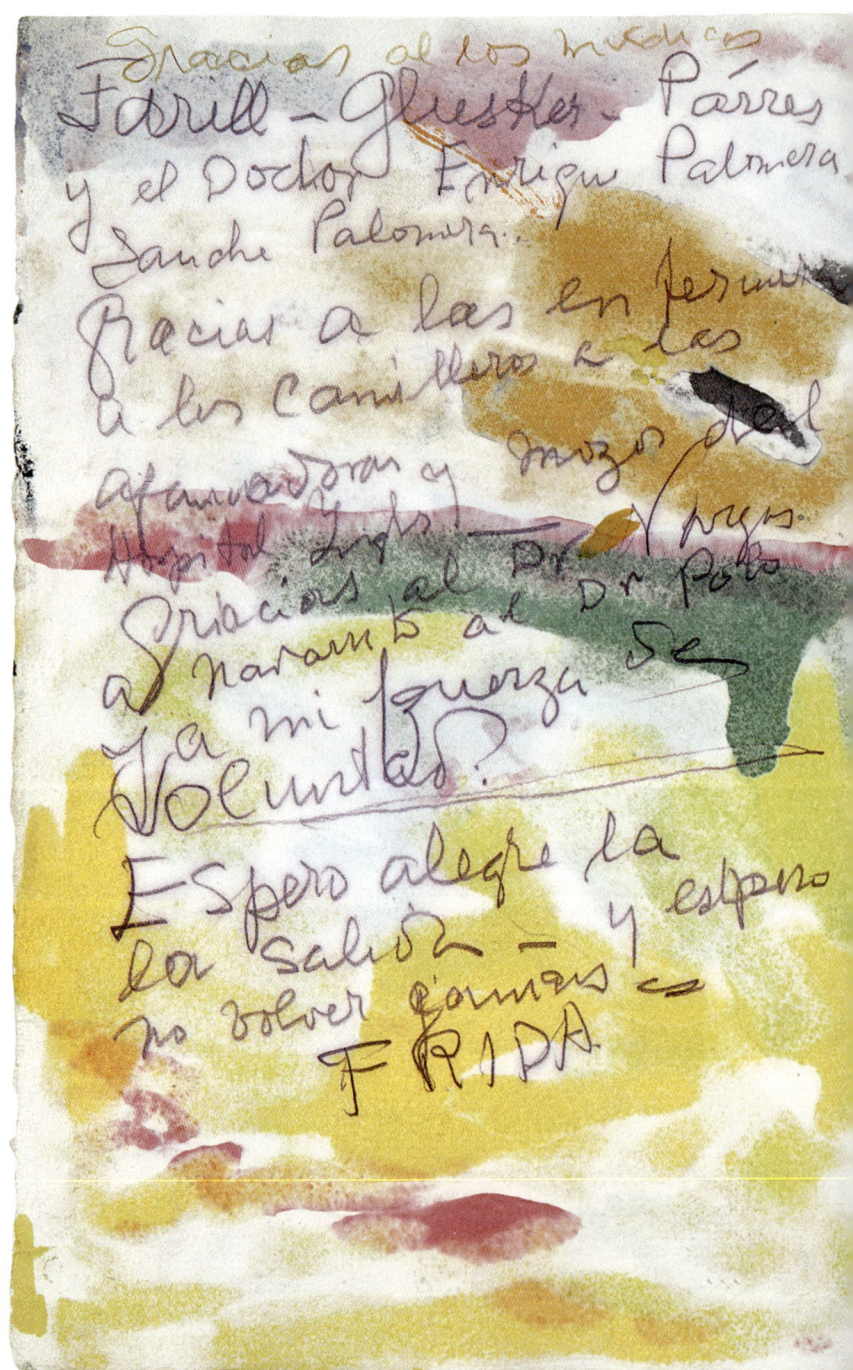

20

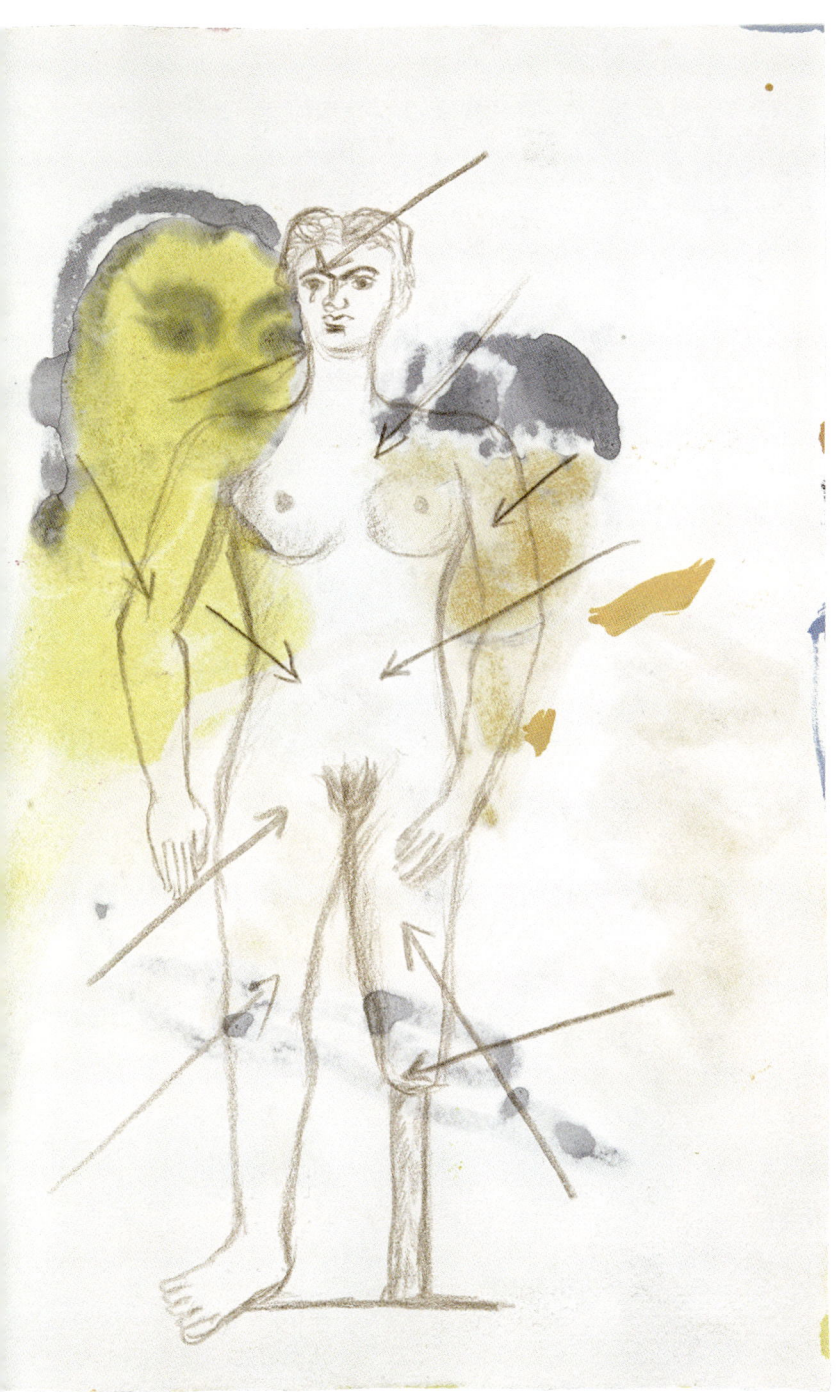

VI.

Biography

1904–1954

Luis-Martín Lozano
Marina Vázquez Ramos

*"Who was Frida Kahlo? It's not possible to find an
exact answer. The personality of that woman is
so contradictory, so many-faceted, that one can say
there were many Fridas."*

— ALEJANDRO GÓMEZ ARIAS, 1977

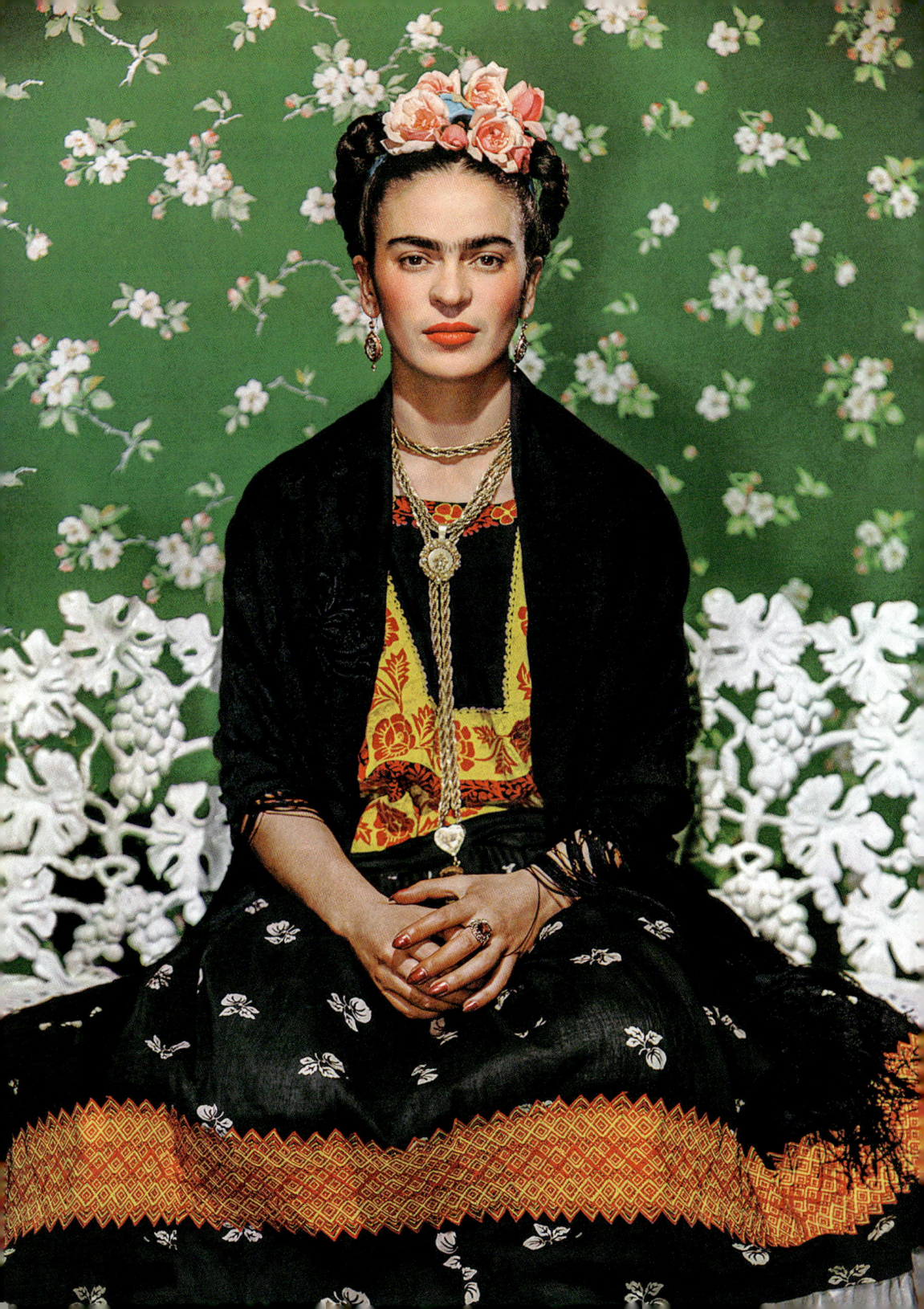

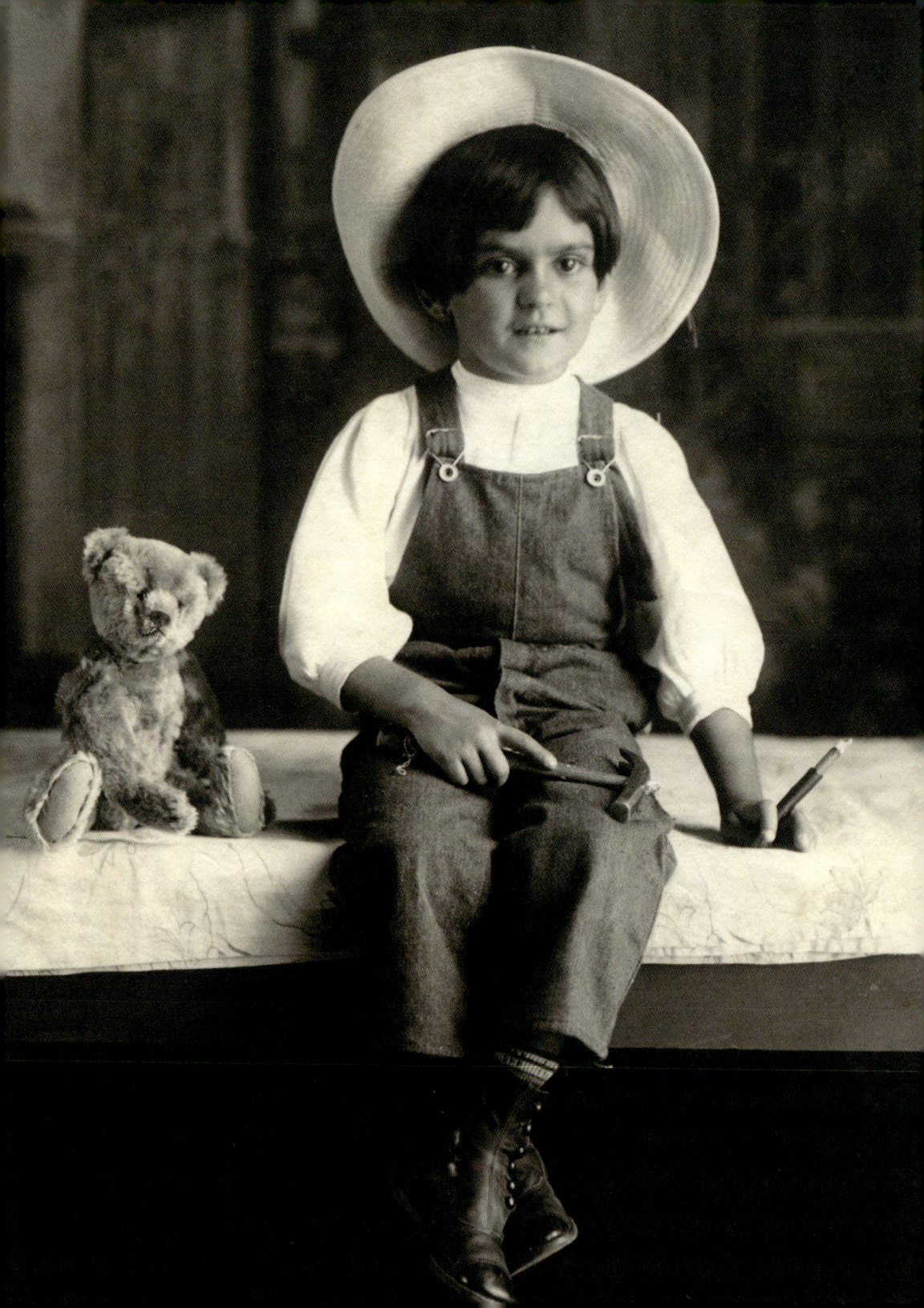

1904 Frida's father, Carl Wilhelm Kahlo, who was born in Pforzheim, Germany, buys a plot of land that was previously part of the former hacienda of San Pedro Mártir and had been ceded by another German immigrant, Sigismund Wolff Lowenstein. Here he builds the house that will later be known as the Casa Azul, where Frida Kahlo will live for the greater part of her life.

The painter Gerardo Murillo (known as Dr. Atl) returns from Europe, bringing new ideas for the arts in Mexico.

1906 The magazine *Savia Moderna* organizes an exhibition of work by Mexican painters which demonstrates the aesthetic connections between Mexico and Europe.

1907 Frida Kahlo is born on July 6, at 8:30 a.m.

On July 28, her name is entered in the civil register by her father and maternal grandmother, Isabel González, as Magdalena Carmen Frieda Kahlo y Calderón.

1908 President Porfirio Díaz announces in an interview with the Canadian-American journalist James Creelman that Mexico is ready for democracy.

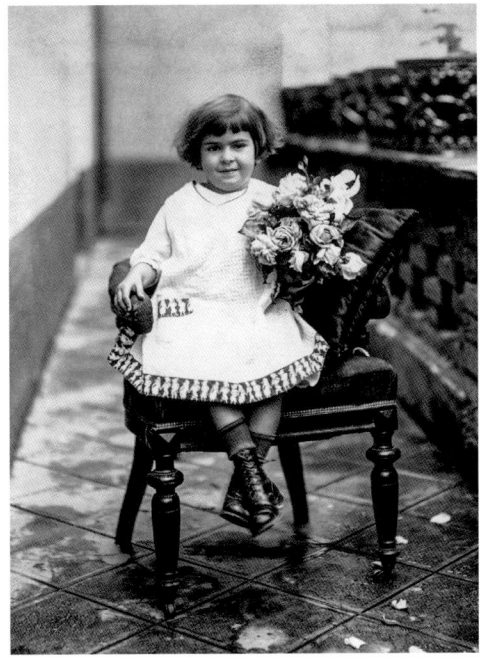

1909 The Ateneo de la Juventud is founded in Mexico City. This association, consisting of young writers, philosophers, and others, made an important contribution to Mexican intellectual culture.

1910 On September 19, the exhibition "Exposición de Pintura, Escultura y Dibujo" opens at the Escuela Nacional de Bellas

Page 391
Nickolas Muray, **Frida** (detail), 1939
Carbon pigment print, 48.2 x 36.8 cm (19 x 14½ in.)
New York, collection of Spencer Throckmorton/Nickolas Muray Photo Archives

Guillermo Kahlo, **Frida Kahlo Calderón** (detail), 1913
Gelatin silver print, 17 x 12 cm (6¾ x 4¾ in.)
Mexico City, Isolda P. Kahlo Archive

Guillermo Kahlo, **Frida at four years old**, September 1911
Gelatin silver print, 19 x 13.4 cm (7½ x 5¼ in.)
New York, collection of Spencer Throckmorton

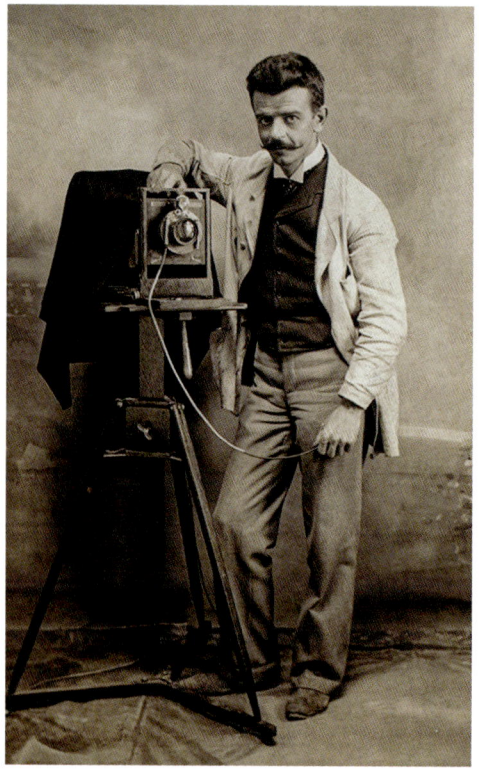

de Bellas Artes. The same day, the Mexican Revolution breaks out.

1913 Kahlo takes her First Communion.

Alfredo Ramos Martínez starts the first Open-air School of Painting, the Barbizon, in Santa Anita, Iztapalapa. It stays open for one year.

1914 In October, the Convention of Aguascalientes takes place, a meeting held by revolutionary factions to determine what political and social reforms are needed in Mexico. In the same month, Murillo is appointed director of the Escuela Nacional de Bellas Artes. He modifies the curriculum in order to make artists work for the propagation of revolutionary ideals.

1918 Kahlo contracts polio at the age of 11, and as a result her left leg will be thinner for the rest of her life and her right leg shorter. Some of the doctors who examine her diagnose a "white tumor" and slight atrophy in her right leg.

Adolfo Best Maugard's "drawing method" begins to be implemented at the Escuela de Artes Industriales de La Corregidora in Querétaro.

1919 Best Maugard and Jaime Martínez del Río stage the ballet *Mexican Fantasy (La fantasía mexicana)* which opens at the Arbeu Theater in Mexico City with the Russian ballerina Anna Pavlova's company.

Artes (formerly the Academia), organized by the Society of Painters and Sculptors. This group show was presented at the same time as the official celebrations for Mexico's Centennial of Independence, and presented a full range of visual arts in the country at the start of the 20th century.

On November 20, Diego Rivera's first solo exhibition opens at the Escuela Nacional

Guillermo Kahlo, **Self-portrait**, *c.* 1907

Guillermo Kahlo, **Frida at five years old, with her sisters Matilde and Adriana, two of her cousins, and her uncle**, 1912
Frida is seated on the left, with Matilde standing on the right, and Adriana seated on the right.

Pavlova herself performed the *Jarabe Tapa-tío*, also known as the Mexican hat dance, dressed in the traditional *china poblana* costume of a woman from Puebla and with the colors of the Mexican flag.

1920 Frida Kahlo starts studying at the Escuela Normal Primaria. While there, she becomes friends with Miguel N. Lira and meets Alejandro Gómez Arias.

The "post-revolutionary" Mexican state is born and a non-radical middle class takes control.

1921 In May, the painter David Alfaro Siqueiros's manifesto *3 Llamamientos de orientación actual a los pintores y escultores de la nueva generación americana* (Three Appeals for a New Direction for the New Generation of American Painters and Sculptors) is published in Barcelona in the magazine *Vida Americana*.

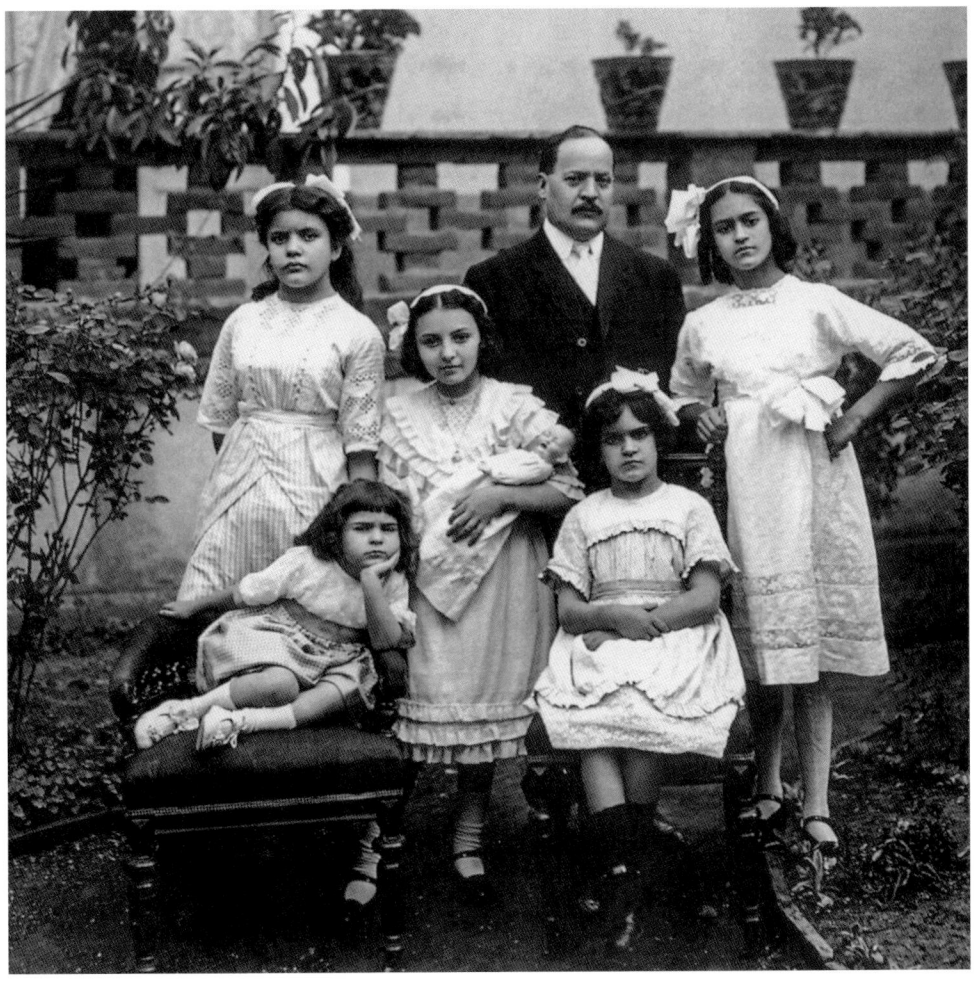

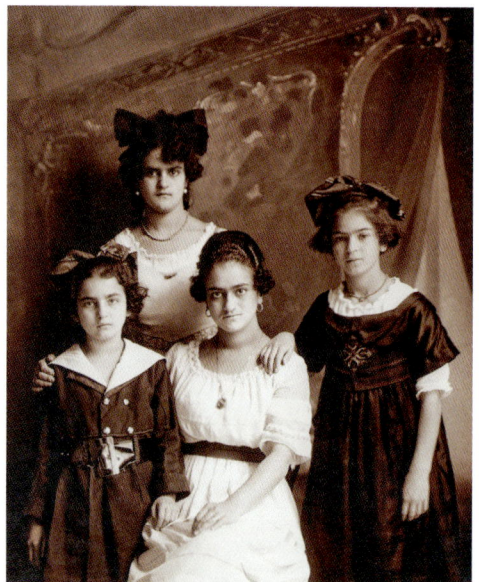

José Vasconcelos is appointed First Secretary of Public Education.

Ramos Martínez returns to the post of director at the Escuela Nacional de Bellas Artes and restarts the Open-air School of Painting program.

Best Maugard launches the Pro-Mexican Art Movement.

In December, the poet Manuel Maples Arce publishes the first manifesto of the Stridentist movement, *Actual No. 1*.

1922 Kahlo enrolls at the Escuela Nacional Preparatoria where she hopes to go on to study medicine. She joins a group of young people there known as Los Cachuchas, which along with Gómez Arias and Miguel N. Lira includes José Gómez Robleda, Manuel González Ramírez, Carmen Jaime, Agustín Lira, Ernestina Marín, Alfonso Villa, and Jesús Ríos Ibáñez y Valles.

To help out at home Kahlo works at a lumberyard, tallying the wood as it comes in and goes out.

She learns how to touch up photographs using a brush at her father's photography studio in the La Perla jewelry shop, at the junction of Madero and Motolínia streets.

On November 30, Kahlo's prose poem "Recuerdo" (Memory) appears in the weekly newspaper *El Universal Ilustrado*.

In December she and Gómez Arias begin writing letters to each other.

Vasconcelos, the Secretary of Education, commissions Murillo and Roberto Montenegro to paint the first murals in the former church and cloister of the Colegio Máximo de San Pedro y San Pablo.

1923 Kahlo's letters reveal that she has now started having a relationship with Gómez Arias.

An avid reader since childhood, Kahlo is excited to begin reading Oscar Wilde's *The Picture of Dorian Gray*.

On March 9, Rivera's first mural, *Creation*, is unveiled in the Simón Bolívar lecture theater of the Escuela Nacional Preparatoria.

Guillermo Kahlo, **Frida with her sisters Matilde, Adriana, and Cristina**, *c.* 1914

Guillermo Kahlo, **Frida dressed as a man (center), with her sisters Adriana and Cristina, Carmen Romero, and Carlos Veraza**, Coyoacán, February 7, 1926
Mexico City, Isolda P. Kahlo Archive

Best Maugard's *Método de dibujo. Tradición, resurgimiento y evolución del arte mexicano (Drawing Method: Tradition, Renewal, and Evolution of Mexican Art)* is published.

A group of artists including Rivera, Alfaro Siqueiros, and Xavier Guerrero form the Union of Technical Workers, Painters, and Sculptors.

1924 Kahlo frequently goes to read in the Ibero-American Library at the Ministry of Public Education.

In March, the Union of Technical Workers, Painters, and Sculptors launches *El Machete*, a newspaper that serves as its voice in matters of art and politics. On April 12, the exhibition "Tarde del Movimiento Estridentista" (Afternoon of the Stridentist Movement) opens at the Café de Nadie.

1925 Kahlo learns shorthand and typing at the Academias Oliver and starts work as an apprentice engraver with Fernando Fernández.

On September 17, she is involved in a horrific accident while returning home from school when the bus she is traveling in collides with a streetcar. As a result of the crash she suffers fractures to her third and fourth lumbar vertebrae, her pelvis is broken in three places and there are 11 fractures

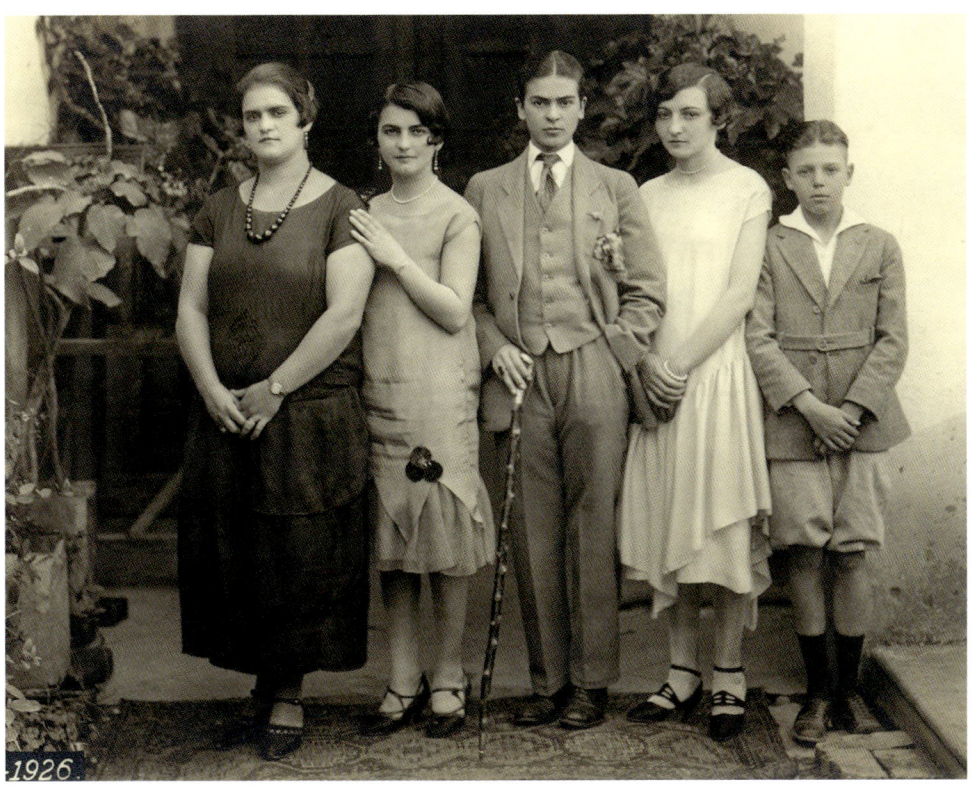
1926

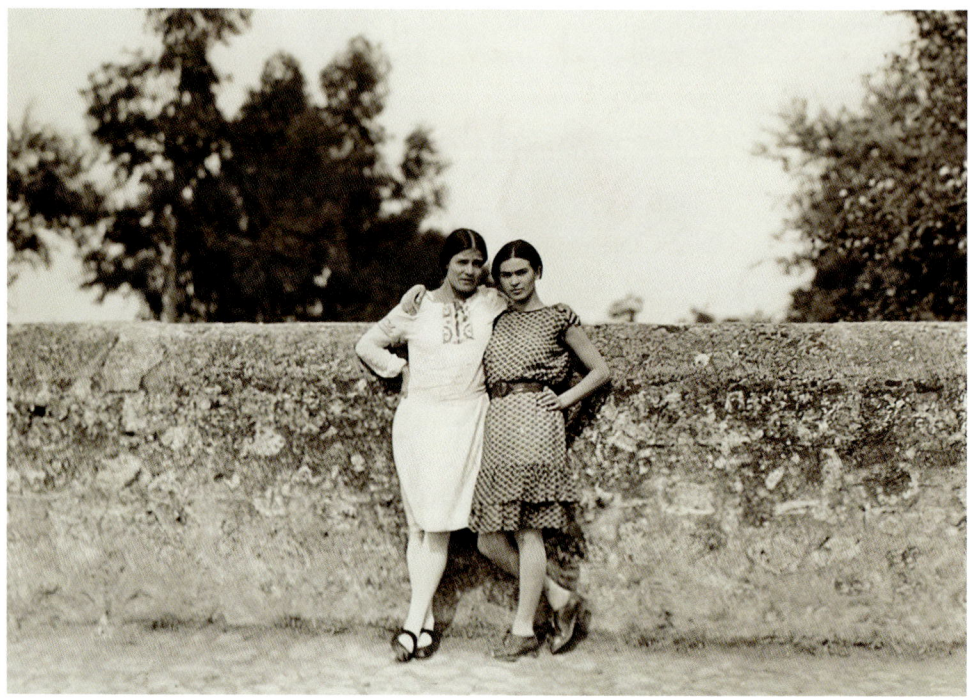

in her right foot, her left elbow is dislocated, and there is a serious wound in her abdomen caused by a metal rod which pierced her body at her hip and exited through her vagina.

On October 13, Kahlo writes to her boyfriend Gómez Arias the first of the letters she sends him while she is in the Red Cross Hospital.

On October 17, after being kept in hospital for a month, Kahlo is discharged and goes to stay with her parents where she spends three months recovering. She is then moved to her sister Matilde Kahlo Calderón's house in Mexico City so that she is able to continue with her medical treatment at the hospital.

She abandons her studies at the Escuela Nacional Preparatoria.

Kahlo moves back to Coyoacán, where she is cared for by Dr. Pedro Calderón.

Her mother places a full-length mirror

Kahlo and Tina Modotti (detail), 1920s
Gelatin silver print, 20.8 x 27 cm (8¼ x 10⅝ in.). Private collection

Kahlo in the inner courtyard of the Casa Azul (detail), 1930
Photographic print, 10.8 x 8 cm (4¼ x 3⅛ in.)
Boston, Museum of Fine Arts

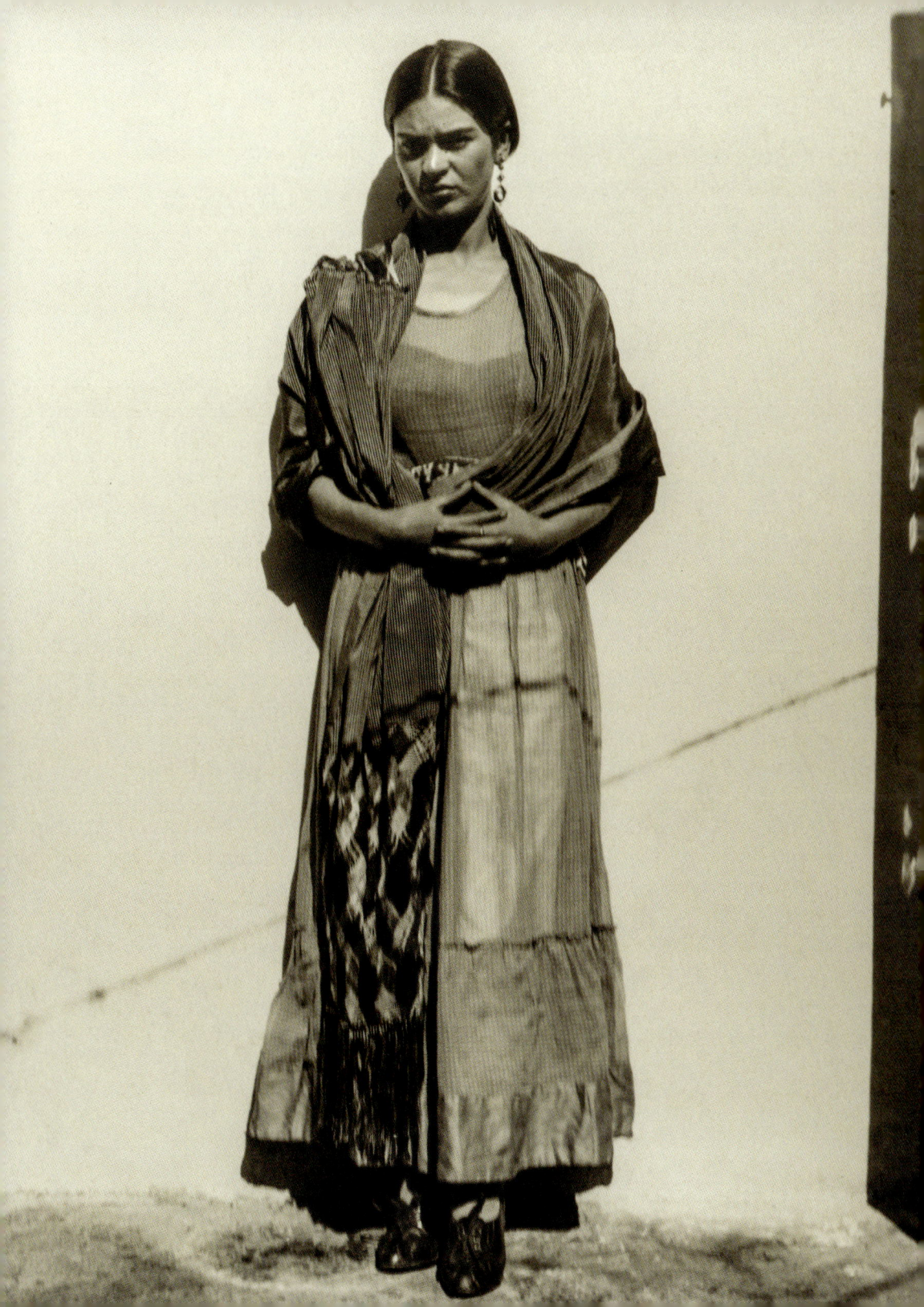

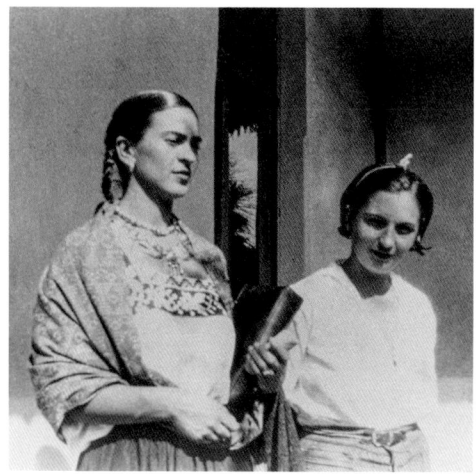

around lay priests and Mexican Catholics who oppose what was known as the Calles Law, a decree which sought to limit and control the influence of the Catholic Church in Mexico.

An exhibition of works by the students of the Open-air Schools of Painting travels to Berlin, Paris, and Madrid.

1927 Gómez Arias departs for Europe where he is to travel for a few months, which causes his relationship with Kahlo to cool down. She attempts to keep it alive through her letters and on March 29 tells him that she is painting a self-portrait for him in a style influenced by Sandro Botticelli.

On April 19, Kahlo is fitted with a plaster corset at the Hospital de las Damas Francesas, and is subjected to a strenuous two-hour stretching session.

In October, she decides to end her relationship with Gómez Arias.

Kahlo becomes involved with a number of young Communists who are organized around the Federación Juvenil Comunista de la ciudad de México (Mexico City Communist Youth Federation) and the Asociación de Estudiantes Proletarios de la Universidad Nacional de México (Association of Proletarian Students of the National University of Mexico).

above her bed so that Kahlo can see herself. She begins drawing, using herself as a model.

By December 18, she is sufficiently well recovered to be able to travel back and forth to Mexico City. However, from now on Kahlo will endure constant pain in her spine and right foot.

The magazine *Mexican Folkways* is first published (it runs until 1937), edited by the American anthropologist and ethnographer Frances Toor.

1926 In September, Kahlo begins painting *Self-portrait (in a Velvet Dress)* (p. 53) for her boyfriend Gómez Arias.

Start of the Cristero War (1926–1929), in which government forces are in armed conflict with various militia groups formed

Frida and Cristina Kahlo, *c.* 1930
Gelatin silver print, 20.3 x 25.4 cm (8 x 10 in.)
New York, collection of Spencer Throckmorton

Rivera and Kahlo at an exhibition, *c.* 1930
Gelatin silver print, 12.7 x 16.5 cm (5 x 6½ in.)
New York, collection of Spencer Throckmorton

1928 Germán de Campo y Castillo, one of Kahlo's classmates at the Escuela Nacional Preparatoria, introduces her to the group associated with Julio Antonio Mella. He was the lover of the photographer Tina Modotti, who was the secretary of both the Italian Board of the Mexico-California Committee for the Defense of Victims of Fascism and the group of political refugees from the International Red Aid in Mexico City.

Kahlo and Modotti become friends and comrades. As Kahlo recounted years later, it was also at Modotti's house that she first properly met Rivera.

Kahlo begins to visit the Ministry of Public Education, where Rivera is painting murals, to ask his opinion about her paintings. She tells him she is just a young woman who has to work to make a living.

In July, a community of artists, mostly from the Open-air Schools of Painting, forms the anti-academic group ¡30–30! and publishes its manifesto, *1er Manifiesto Treintatrentista*, which is followed in due course by four further manifestos.

1929 On August 21, Kahlo and Rivera are married in a civil ceremony at the old Town Hall in Coyoacán. She is 22 and he is 42, and at first they live together at Reforma 104.

Kahlo sells her first painting, *Two Women (Portrait of Salvadora and Herminia)*

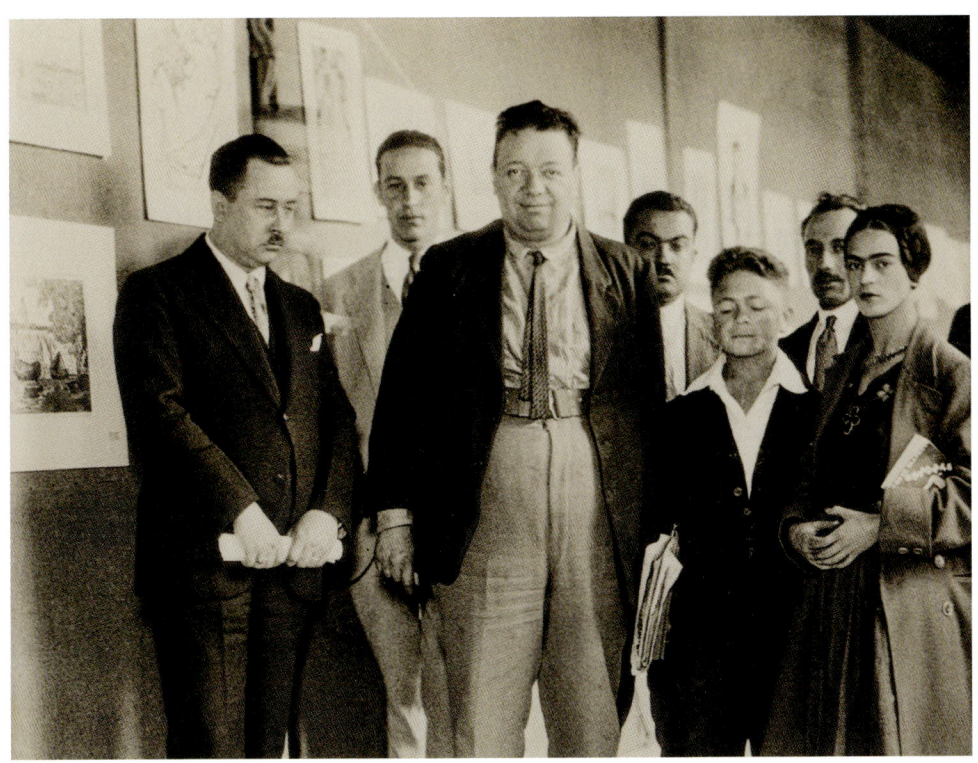

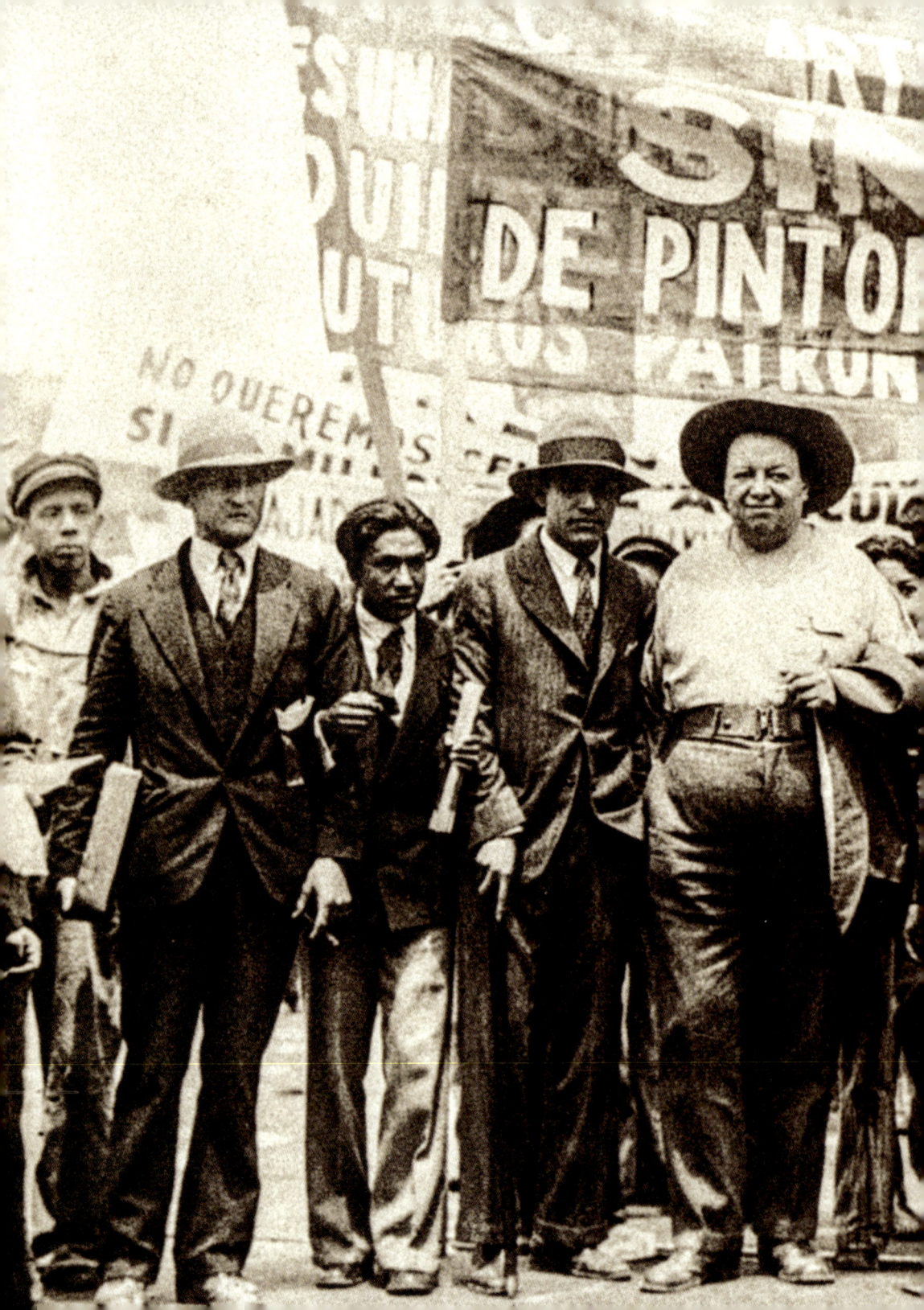

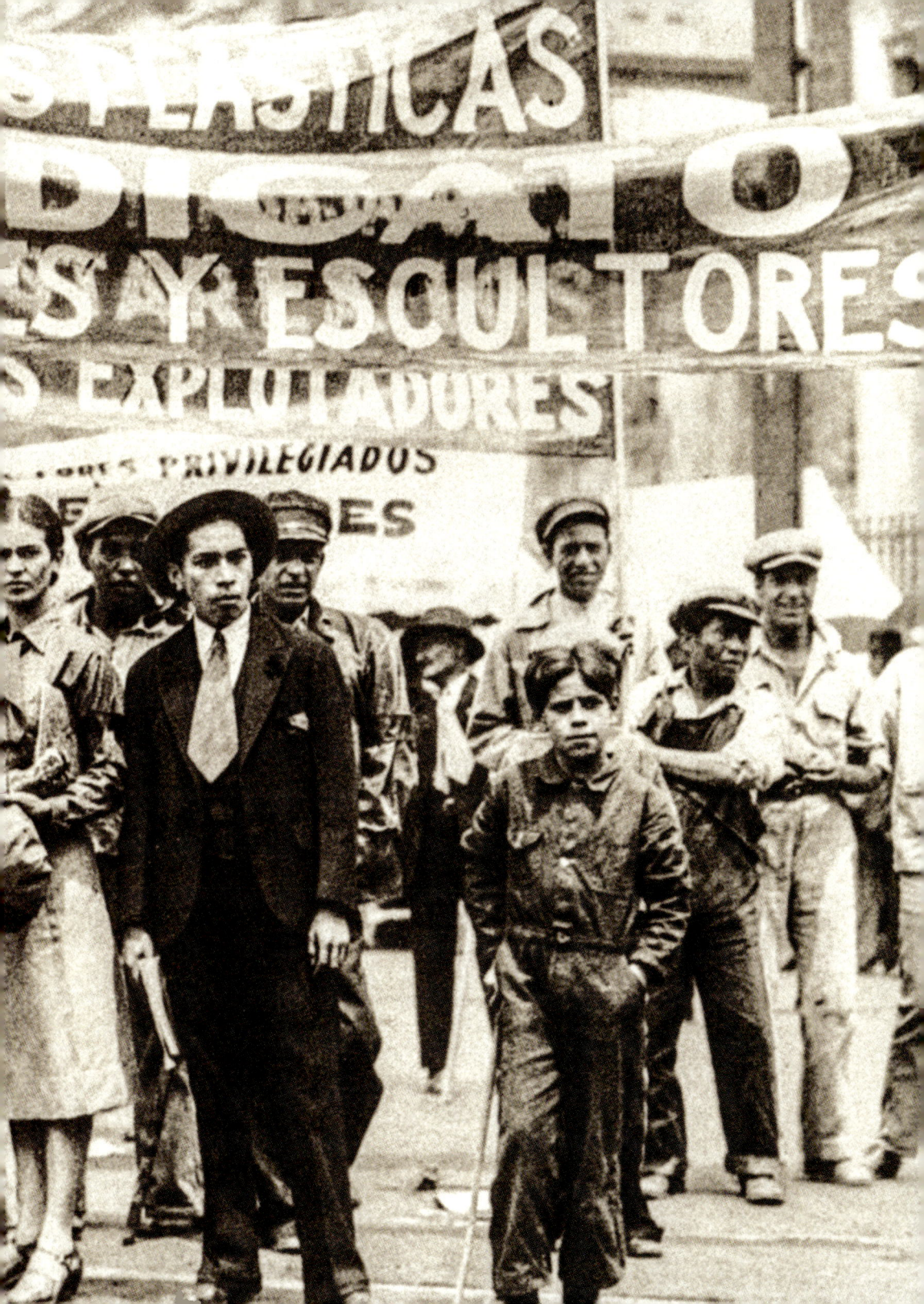

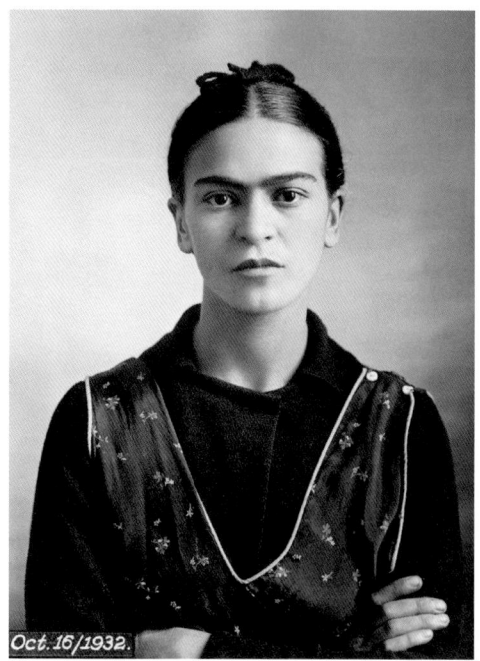

Oct. 16/1932.

On January 25, the ¡30–30! group's "Primera Exposición de Grabado en Madera en México" (First Exhibition of Mexican Woodcuts) opens at the Carpa Amaro.

In August, Rivera is appointed director of the Escuela Nacional de Bellas Artes, which he renames the Escuela Central de Artes Plásticas and introduces a new curriculum and a new way of understanding artists that sees them as workers whose technical training is in the arts.

1930 On November 10, Kahlo and Rivera arrive in San Francisco, where Rivera has been asked to paint a mural for the California School of Fine Arts (today: San Francisco Art Institute). They stay in the studio of the artist Ralph Stackpole, at 716 Montgomery Street.

In December, Kahlo meets the photographer Edward Weston. In the same month she goes to see Dr. Leo Eloesser, who diagnoses lumbar scoliosis. He becomes a close friend for the rest of her life.

(p. 65), which is bought by Jackson Cole Phillips.

Kahlo's first pregnancy ends in an abortion she is advised to have, because of her misshapen pelvis.

Rivera is asked to paint a mural at the Palacio de Cortés in Cuernavaca, so he and Kahlo divide their time between there and Mexico City.

1931 Kahlo exhibits her work for the first time, with *Frida and Diego Rivera* (p. 125) at the "Sixth Annual Exhibition of the San Francisco Society of Women Artistas."

Pages 402/403
Tina Modotti, **Diego Rivera and Frida Kahlo leading a delegation on behalf of the Union of Technical Workers, Painters, and Sculptors on a march on May 1**, 1929

Guillermo Kahlo, **Portrait of Frida following the death of her mother**, Mexico City, October 16, 1932
Gelatin silver print, 16.5 x 11.4 cm (6½ x 4½ in.)
New York, collection of Spencer Throckmorton

Peter A. Juley & Son, **Diego Rivera with Lucille E. Blanch and Frida Kahlo with Arnold Blanch**, San Francisco, 1931

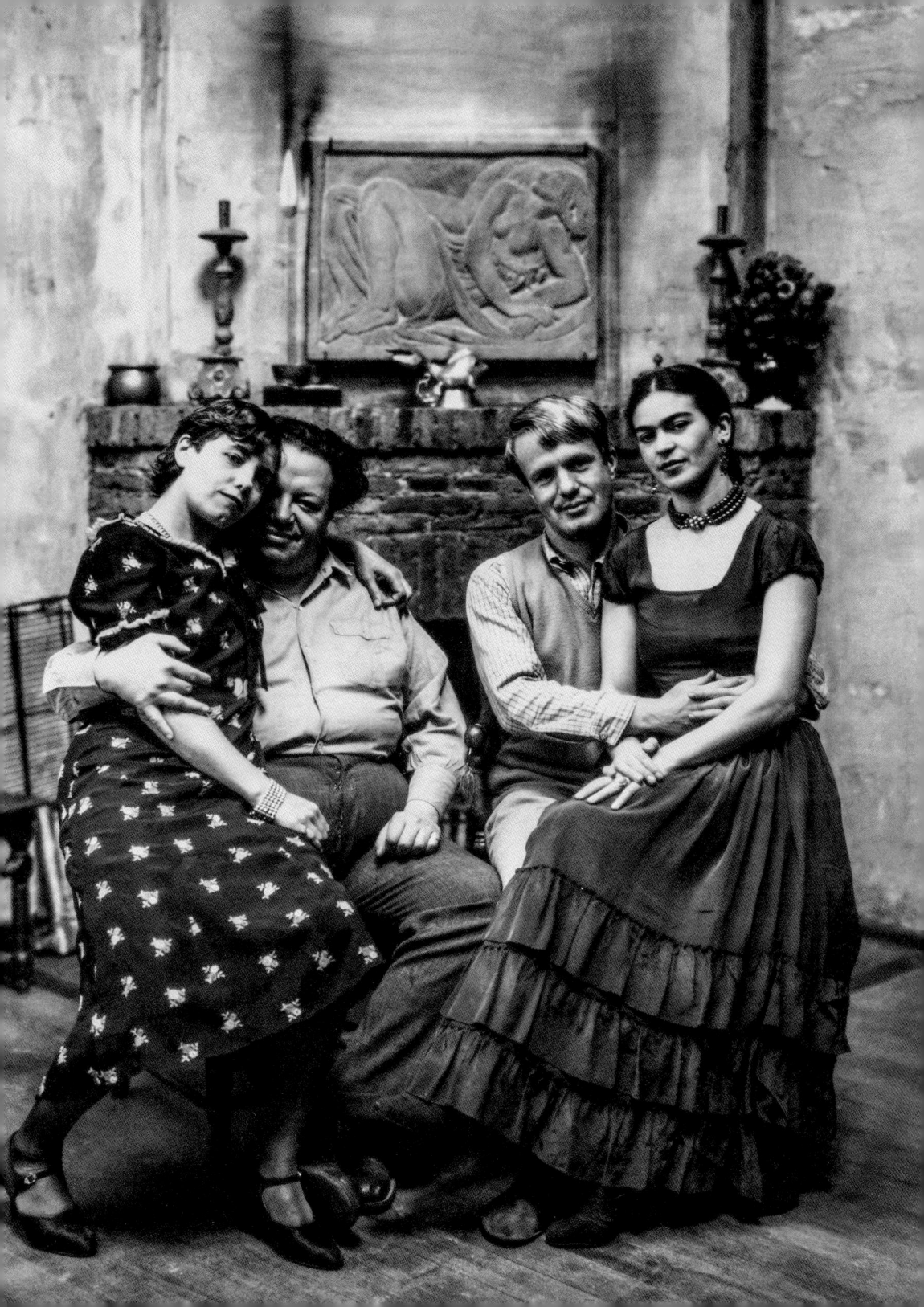

On June 8, they both return to Mexico for a short time.

On November 6, Kahlo and Rivera set out for New York for Rivera's retrospective exhibition at the Museum of Modern Art. While in New York, Kahlo is able to see the work of a number of Surrealist artists, and makes her first drawings influenced by Surrealist ideas. On April 10, the ¡30–30! group presents its final exhibition, "De la vida del Café," in a Chinese café in Mexico City.

The La Tolteca cement factory organizes a competition for which Mexican painters and photographers are asked to send in works that represent the building of a new and modern Mexico.

1932 At the end of March, Kahlo and Rivera travel by bus to Philadelphia to attend the premiere of the ballet *H. P. (Horsepower)*, with music by Carlos Chávez and set design and costumes by Rivera.

On April 21, Kahlo and Rivera travel by train to Detroit, where Rivera has been asked to paint a mural at the Detroit Institute of Arts.

On July 4, Kahlo suffers a miscarriage and is admitted to the Henry Ford Hospital in Detroit, where she stays for two weeks in the care of Dr. Jean Paul Pratt. While in

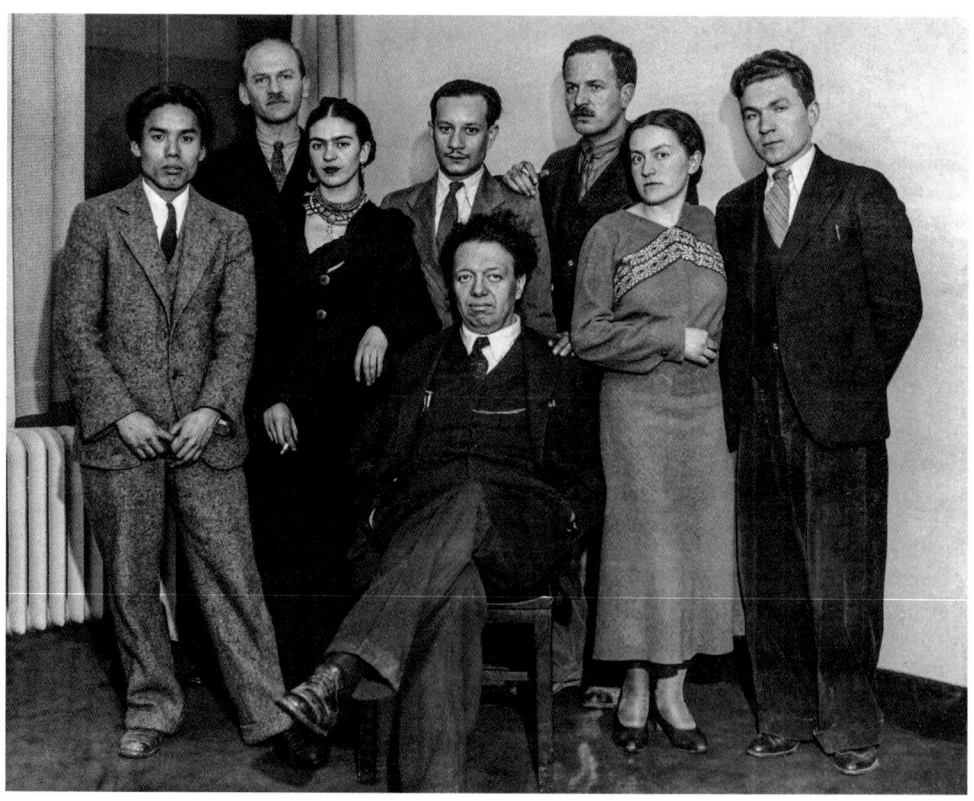

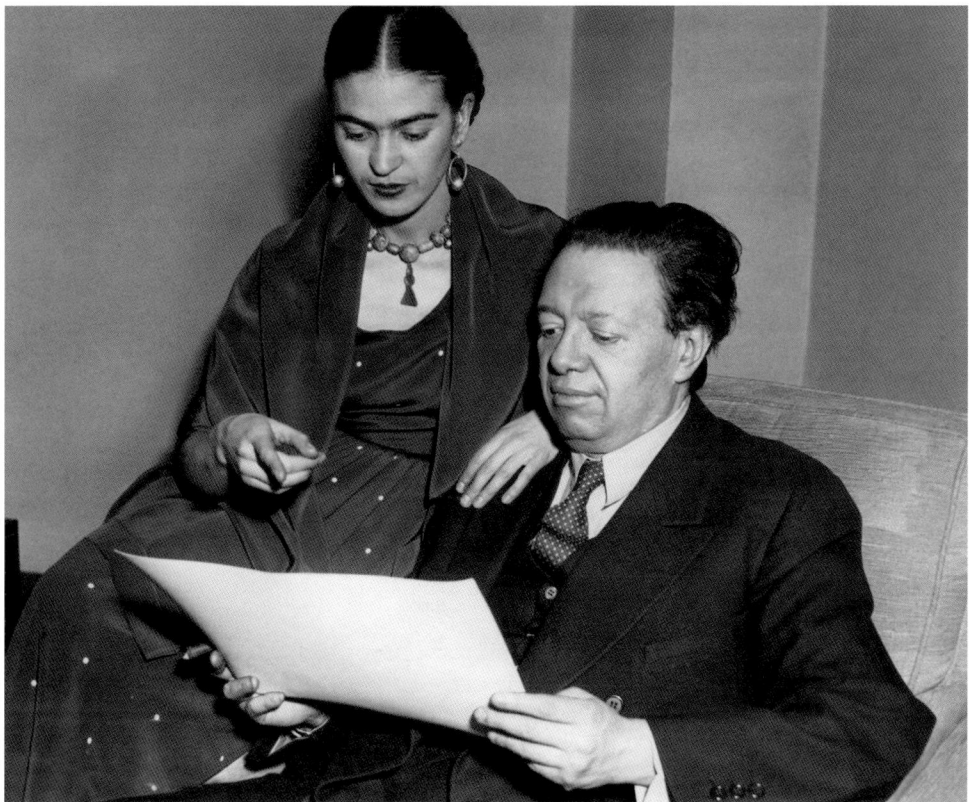

hospital she begins to paint *Henry Ford Hospital* (pp. 112/113).

Also in July, accompanied by her friend Lucienne Bloch, Kahlo visits a little arts and crafts guild where she is able to use its lithography press to make her only known lithograph, *Frida and the Miscarriage* (p. 114).

On September 3, Kahlo receives news that her mother is seriously unwell. The following day she and Bloch leave for Mexico by train, and arrive in Mexico City at 10:00 p.m. on September 9.

On September 15, Kahlo's mother, Matilde Calderón, dies at the age of 58.

Kahlo and Rivera, seated, together with his assistants, Detroit, 1932
From left to right: Hideo Noda, Lou Block, Andrés Sánchez Flores, Lord John Hastings,
Lucienne Bloch, and Stephen Dimitroff. Gelatin silver print, 16.8 x 20.6 cm (6⅝ x 8⅛ in.)
New York, collection of Spencer Throckmorton

Kahlo and Rivera, Detroit, *c.* 1933
Gelatin silver print, 16.8 x 21.6 cm (6⅝ x 8½ in.)
New York, collection of Spencer Throckmorton

On October 21, Kahlo returns to Detroit, and on November 15 travels to New York with Rivera, who is making the trip in order to finalize details for a new mural project he is to paint at the Rockefeller Center.

1933 On March 14, once Rivera's mural painting work at the Detroit Institute of Arts has been completed, he and Kahlo return to New York.

Rivera starts painting *Man at the Crossroads*, the mural commissioned by the Rockefeller family for the lobby of the Radio Corporation of America (RCA) Building. The following year it is censored and then destroyed, and as a result the plans for him to paint murals for the Chicago World's Fair are also canceled.

With his mural projects now suspended, Rivera decides to use the money paid to him by Rockefeller to paint *Portrait of America*, a series of his own murals at the New Workers School of the Communist Party (Opposition) in New York.

On December 20, Kahlo and Rivera leave for Mexico.

They move into one of the new houses designed in a functionalist style by Juan O'Gorman in Mexico City in the suburb of San Ángel.

In Mexico City, the Liga de Escritores y Artistas Revolucionarios (League of Revolutionary Writers and Artists) is established.

1934 Kahlo is pregnant again but suffers another miscarriage, this time being cared for by Dr. Zollinger. She is diagnosed with premature ovarian failure, and also has to have an appendectomy; the phalanges in the toes of her right foot then have to be amputated because of trophic ulcers that would not heal.

1935 Kahlo discovers that Rivera has been having an adulterous relationship with her sister Cristina. They separate, and she moves into a modern apartment at 432 Avenida de los Insurgentes in downtown Mexico City.

In early July, Kahlo travels to New York with Anita Brenner and Mary Schapiro. She stays at the Holly Hotel on Washington Square.

On July 23, she writes to Rivera in a letter saying that she loves him more than her own skin. Once back from New York she begins to paint *Passionately in Love* (pp. 156/157), one of her most disturbing paintings.

A second operation is needed for her right foot, which then takes six months to heal.

Kahlo gets back together with Rivera and moves back into the house in San Ángel.

1936 She has to have a third operation on her right foot, which this time entails a

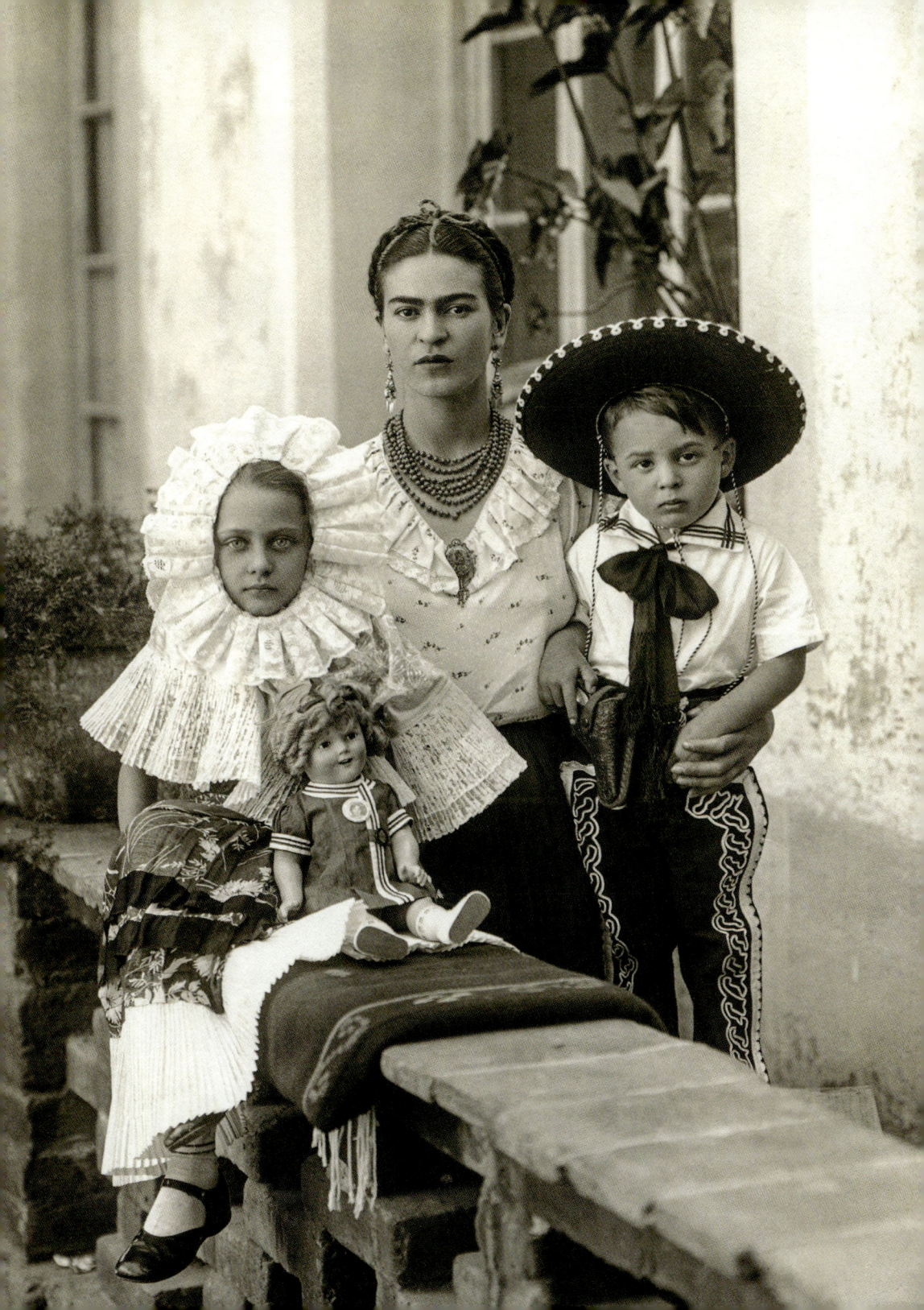

periarterial sympathectomy with sesamoid excision.

On November 23, Kahlo and Rivera take part in an anti-fascist demonstration in Mexico City.

1937 On January 9, Kahlo travels to the port of Tampico to meet Leon Trotsky and his wife Natalia Sedova. Trotsky has arrived in Mexico as an exile after being persecuted by Stalin, and after Rivera made appeals to the Mexican President Lázaro Cárdenas to grant him political asylum.

Trotsky and Sedova stay in Coyoacán, at Kahlo's parents' house. Kahlo and Trotsky have a brief affair, which she ends abruptly.

On September 23, Kahlo's painting *My Grandparents, My Parents, and I* (pp. 118/119) is included, with the title *Family Tree*, in the inaugural exhibition held by the gallery of the Art Department of Social Action at the Universidad Nacional Autónoma de México, organized by the painter Julio Castellanos.

Kahlo is invited by the gallery owner Julien Levy to exhibit her work in New York.

On November 7, she presents Trotsky with *Self-portrait Dedicated to Leon Trotsky (Between the Curtains)* (p. 175) as a gift for his birthday.

A group of artists led by Leopoldo Méndez establish the Taller de Gráfica Popular, to promote the use of engraving for socially committed ideological purposes.

1938 The Surrealist André Breton visits Mexico, with his wife Jacqueline Lamba, where he is to deliver a series of lectures.

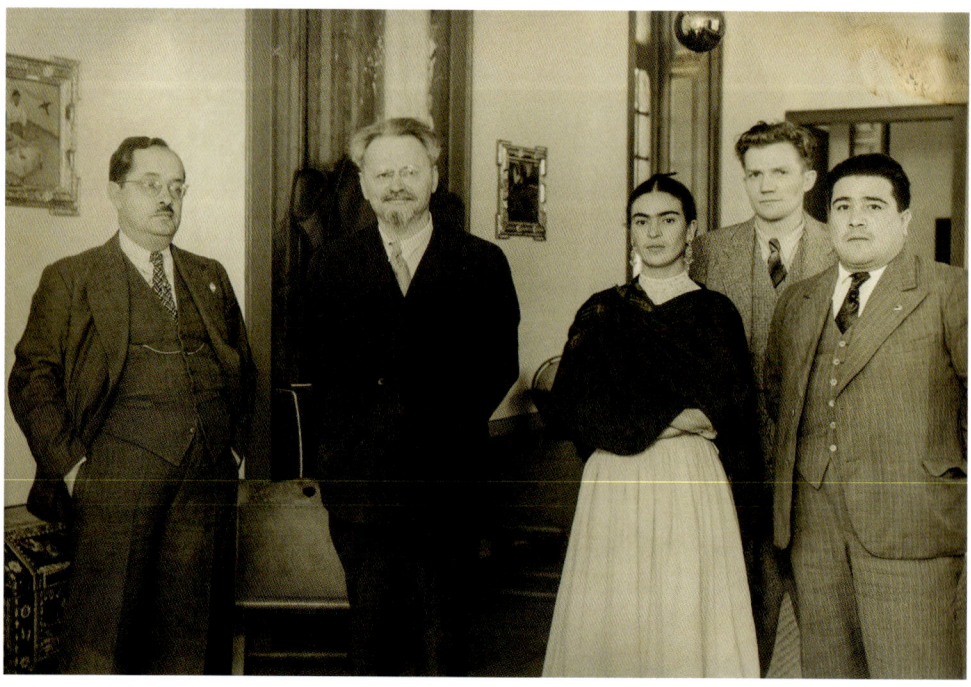

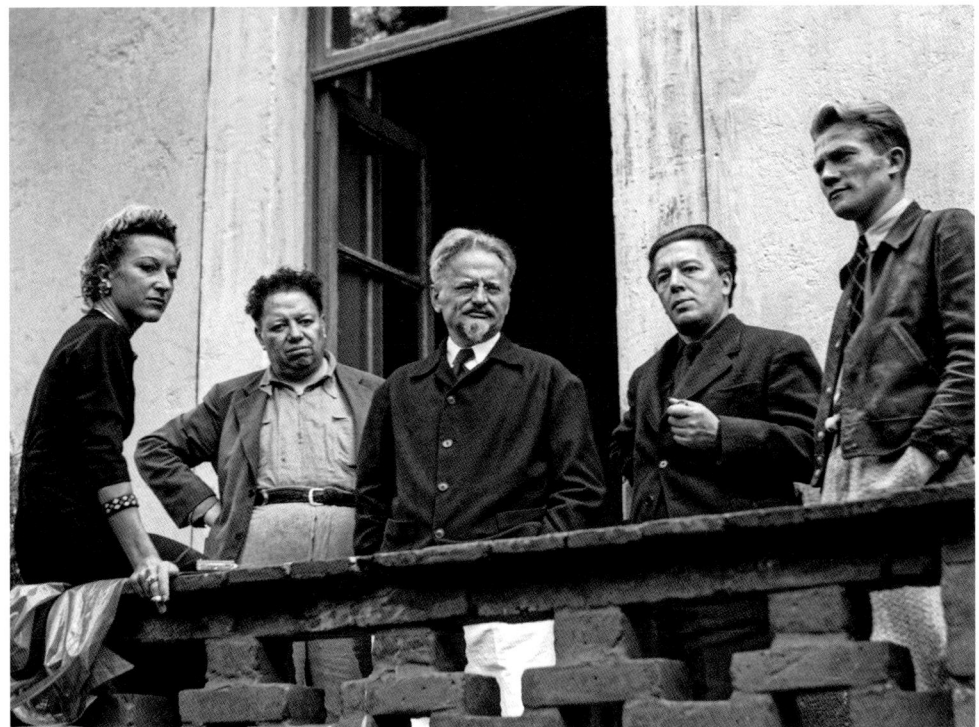

Breton is keen to meet Trotsky and becomes interested in Kahlo's work, heaping praise on her paintings which he considers to be fundamentally Surrealist.

The actor and collector Edward G. Robinson visits Mexico and is introduced to Kahlo and Rivera. He acquires four of Kahlo's paintings for his collection of modern art.

In July, Kahlo, Rivera, Trotsky, Sedova, Breton, and Lamba all travel together to Michoacán. At Pátzcuaro a number of conversations take place that provide the basis for the *Manifesto for an Independent Revolutionary Art*, which is signed by Breton and Rivera.

In October, Kahlo travels to New York for her first solo exhibition, which runs

Antonio Villalobos, Leon Trotsky, Frida Kahlo, Jean van Heijenoort, and José Escudero Andrade (detail), Coyoacán, *c.* 1937
Gelatin silver print. Collection of Paul Stapleton, courtesy Escudero family

Manuel Álvarez Bravo, **Jacqueline Lamba, Diego Rivera, Leon Trotsky, André Breton, and Jean van Heijenoort** (detail), Coyoacán, 1938
Gelatin silver print, 13 x 18 cm (5⅛ x 7⅛ in.)
Mexico City, Manuel Álvarez Bravo Archive

from November 1 through 15 at the Julien Levy Gallery at 15 East 57th St. The exhibition is reviewed in *Time*, *Vogue*, and *The New Yorker* magazines.

Kahlo is treated by Dr. David Glusker, who is able to heal the ulcers on her right foot.

In November, Kahlo and Rivera sign a letter of complaint in protest at the destruction of the murals painted by Juan O'Gorman in the departure lounge of Mexico City airport, which were strongly critical of the German government.

1939 In January, Kahlo leaves New York for Paris aboard the ocean liner SS *Paris*. It is her first and only trip to Europe. She disembarks at Le Havre on January 21, where she is met by Lamba and the photographer Dora Maar.

In Paris, she stays first with Lamba and Breton at 42, Rue Fontaine, but then moves to the Hotel Regina on the Place des Pyramides.

On February 16, Kahlo is admitted to the American Hospital in Neuilly-sur-Seine, close to Paris, for a urinary tract infection.

On March 10, the group exhibition "Mexique," organized by Breton and featuring some of Kahlo's art, opens at the Renou & Colle gallery. Her paintings are praised by a number of artists, including Picasso, Kandinsky, and Duchamp.

The Louvre acquires Kahlo's painting *The Frame (Self-portrait)* (p. 178), which is delivered to the Galerie Nationale du Jeu de Paume on July 4. In Paris, Kahlo becomes friends with the painters Wolfgang Paalen and Alice Rahon, and invites them to visit her in Mexico.

On March 25 she departs for Mexico by way of New York, having canceled her plans to travel to London with a view to showing her work at Peggy Guggenheim's gallery.

In the spring, Kahlo is reunited with Rivera, who asks her for a divorce. She agrees to it, and returns to live in Coyoacán, transforming her parents' house into the Casa Azul.

On November 6, the divorce is finalized.

Kahlo is suffering from severe pain in her spine and Dr. Juan Farill puts her through a stretching routine using 20kg weights. A number of other doctors at the time advise surgical intervention to fuse some of her vertebrae together, following the method developed by Dr. Fred Albee and which also requires a bone graft.

1940 On January 17, the fourth International Exhibition of Surrealism, organized by Breton, Paalen, and César Moro, opens at the Galería de Arte Mexicano. Two of Kahlo's most famous paintings are included: *The Two Fridas* (pp. 218/219) and *The Wounded Table* (pp. 224/225).

In September, Kahlo takes a flight to San Francisco for treatment at St. Luke's Hospital. She is seen by Dr. Leo Eloesser, who recommends complete rest.

Kahlo later travels to New York to discuss the dates for a new exhibition with Julien

Kahlo arriving in New York, October 1938

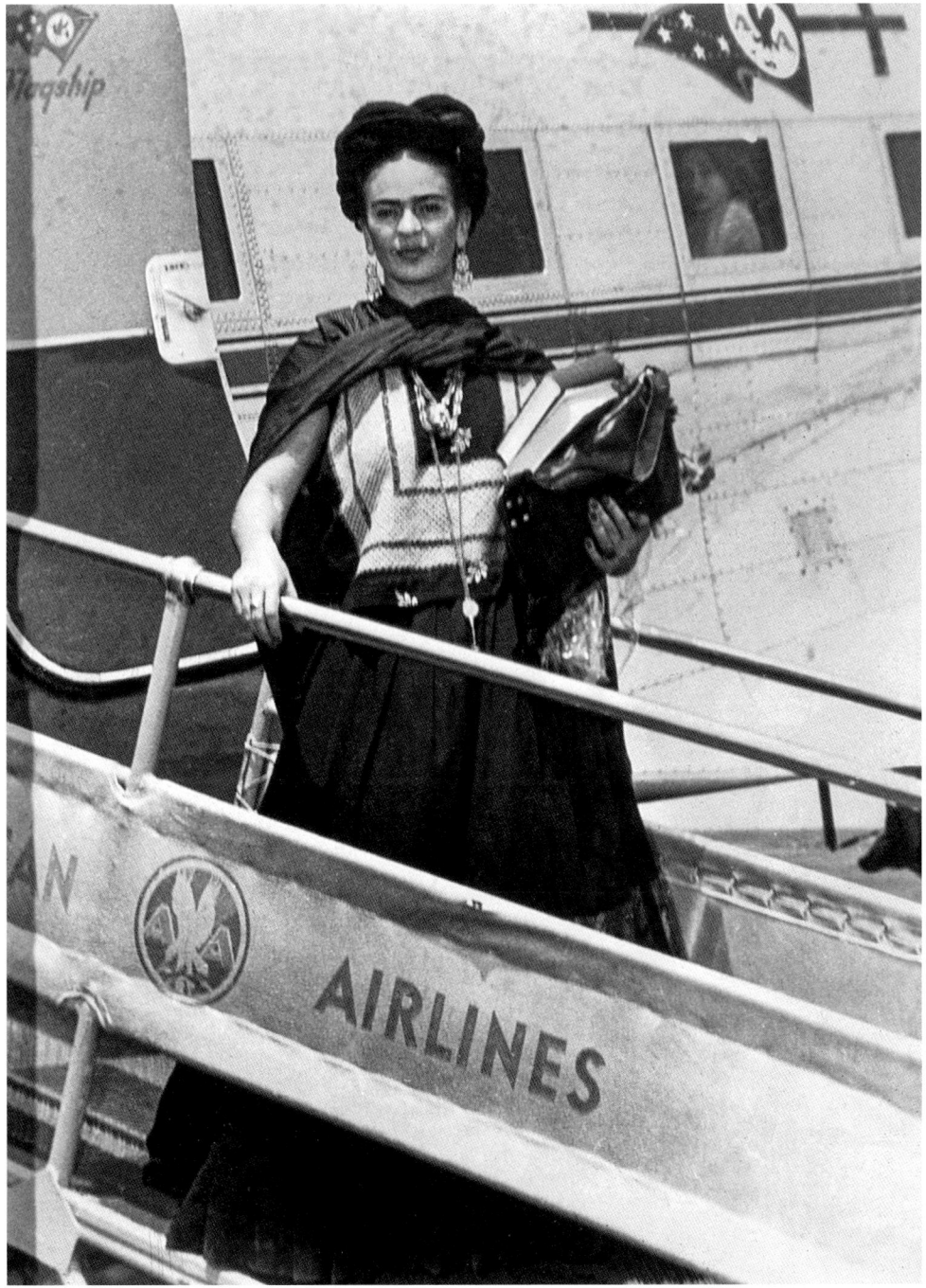

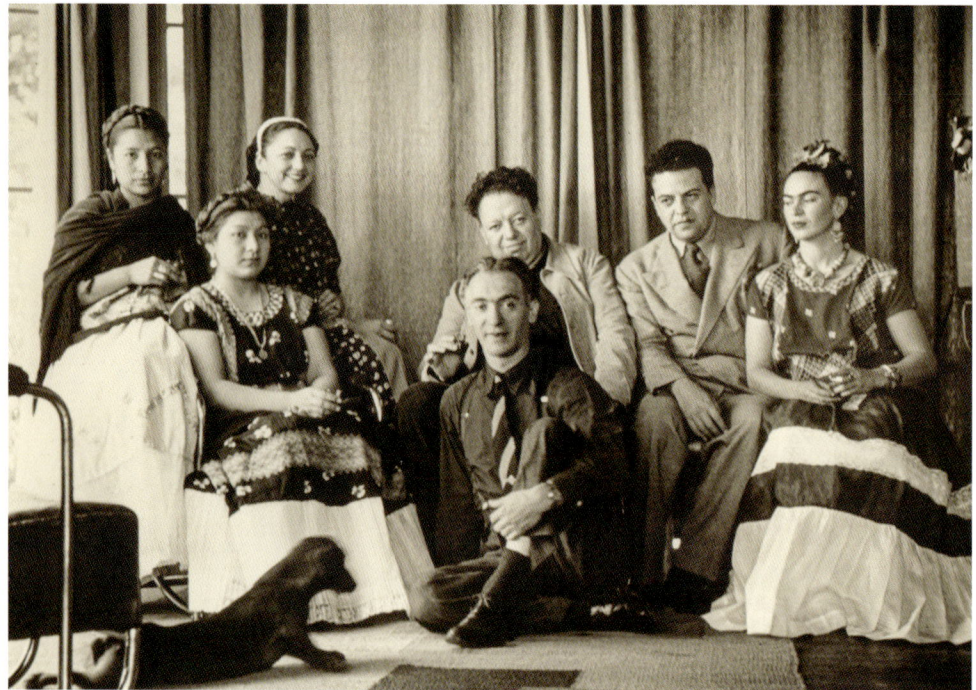

Levy, and on November 28 returns to San Francisco to join Rivera there.

On December 8, Rivera's birthday, they get married again in San Francisco City Hall.

Kahlo applies for a fellowship from the Guggenheim Foundation, but is unsuccessful.

1941 On April 14, her father Guillermo Kahlo dies.

1942 Under the direction of Antonio Ruiz, "El Corcito," the Escuela Libre de Escultura y Talla Directa is restructured and relocates to Callejón de la Esmeralda where it opens under the new name of the Escuela de Pintura y Escultura. The following year, Kahlo is asked to give painting classes there.

1943 In January and February, Kahlo's work appears in an exhibition of portraits

Friends gathered in Rivera's studio (detail), San Ángel, 1938
Alfa and Nereida Ríos Pineda, Rosa Rolanda, Diego Rivera, Nickolas Muray,
Miguel Covarrubias, and Frida. Gelatin silver print, 20 x 25 cm (7⅞ x 9⅞ in.)
Washington, D.C., Smithsonian Institution, Archives of American Art

Bernard G. Silberstein, **Frida in her bedroom holding a baby goat**, Coyoacán, 1940
Gelatin silver print, 41.9 x 35.6 cm (16½ x 14 in.)
New York, collection of Spencer Throckmorton

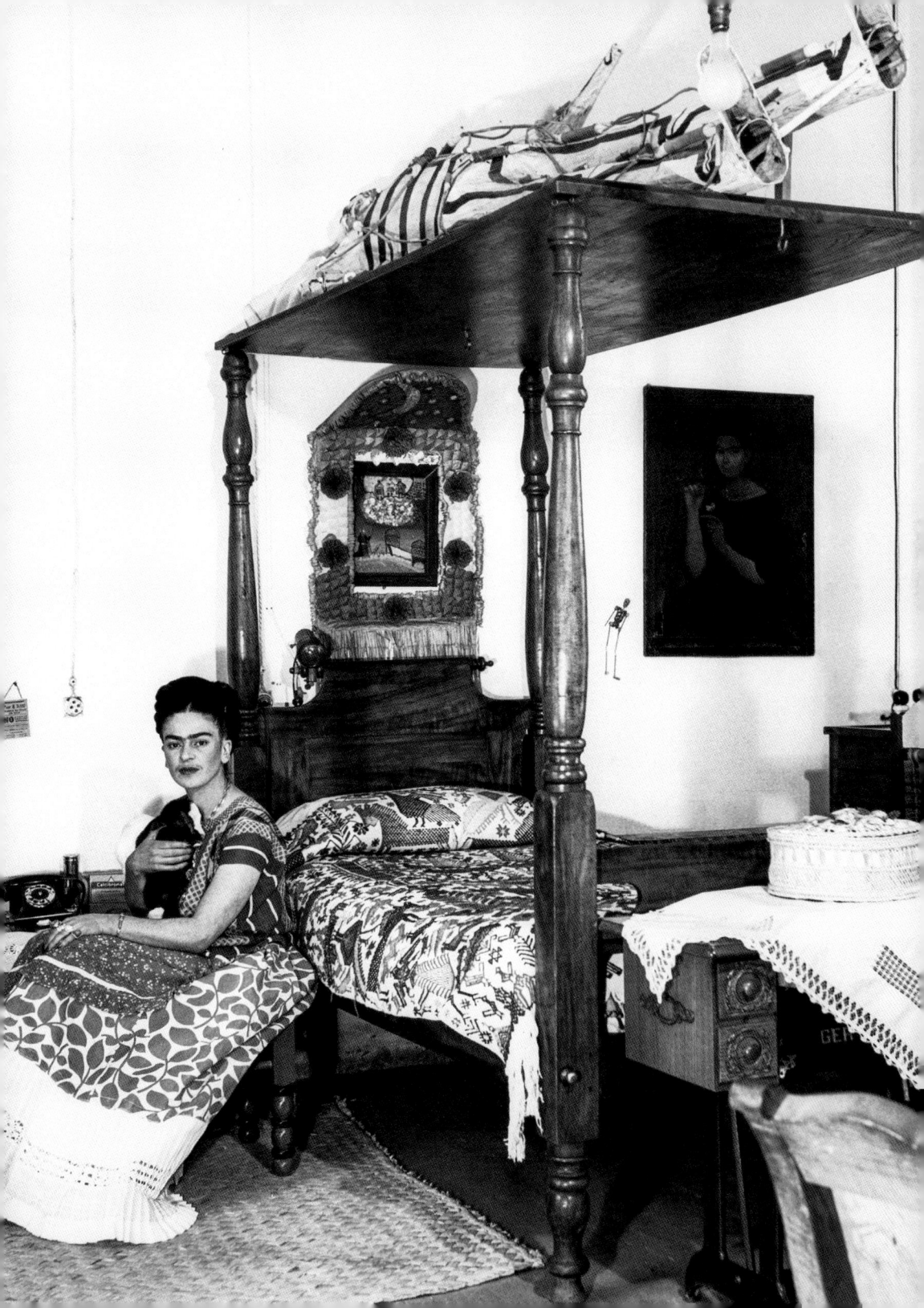

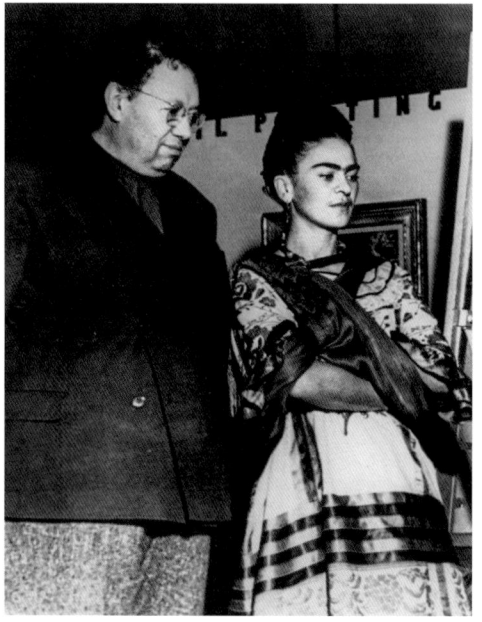

of her most complex works in terms of both its iconography and its composition.

On June 19, a number of murals painted by Kahlo's students, who are known as "Los Fridos," are displayed at the *pulquería* or *pulque* bar La Rosita in Coyoacán.

1944 On June 24, Kahlo writes to Dr. Eloesser complaining of severe pains in her spine. This is also the year in which she paints one of her best-known works, *The Broken Column* (p. 257).

Kahlo is asked to paint a mural in the banquet hall of the Posada del Sol Hotel, but declines and instead passes the work on to her students.

Kahlo and Rivera start work on the construction of the Anahuacalli ("house surrounded by water" in Nahuatl) on a plot of land in El Pedregal in San Pablo Tepetlapa. The building is based on pre-Hispanic designs by Rivera and is intended to house his collection of pre-Columbian art.

David Alfaro Siqueiros opens his Centro Realista de Arte Moderno (Realist Modern Art Center) on June 7.

On July 24, an exhibition of Picasso's work opens at the Sociedad de Arte Moderno (Modern Art Society) in Mexico City.

1945 On February 1, Kahlo presents a group exhibition of work by her students from La Esmeralda in a visual arts space on Calle de la Palma in Mexico City.

The pain in Kahlo's spine has still not gone away, and on the orders of Dr. Alejandro Zimbrón she is fitted with a steel corset to keep her back in a fixed position. She is also given injections of lipiodol in her

at the Benjamin Franklin Library in Mexico City.

Peggy Guggenheim includes a self-portrait by Kahlo in the "Exhibition by 31 Women" she organizes for the Art of this Century gallery in New York.

Owing to problems with her health Kahlo is unable to fulfill her teaching schedule at the Esmeralda Escuela de Pintura y Escultura, but continues working with her students from her house in Coyoacán.

The industrialist José Domingo Lavín talks to Kahlo about his interest in Freud's *Moses and Monotheism*, and commissions a painting from her based on her interpretation of the book. In 1945, she presents him with the painting *Moses (The Birth of the Hero) (Core of the Sun)* (pp. 272/273), one

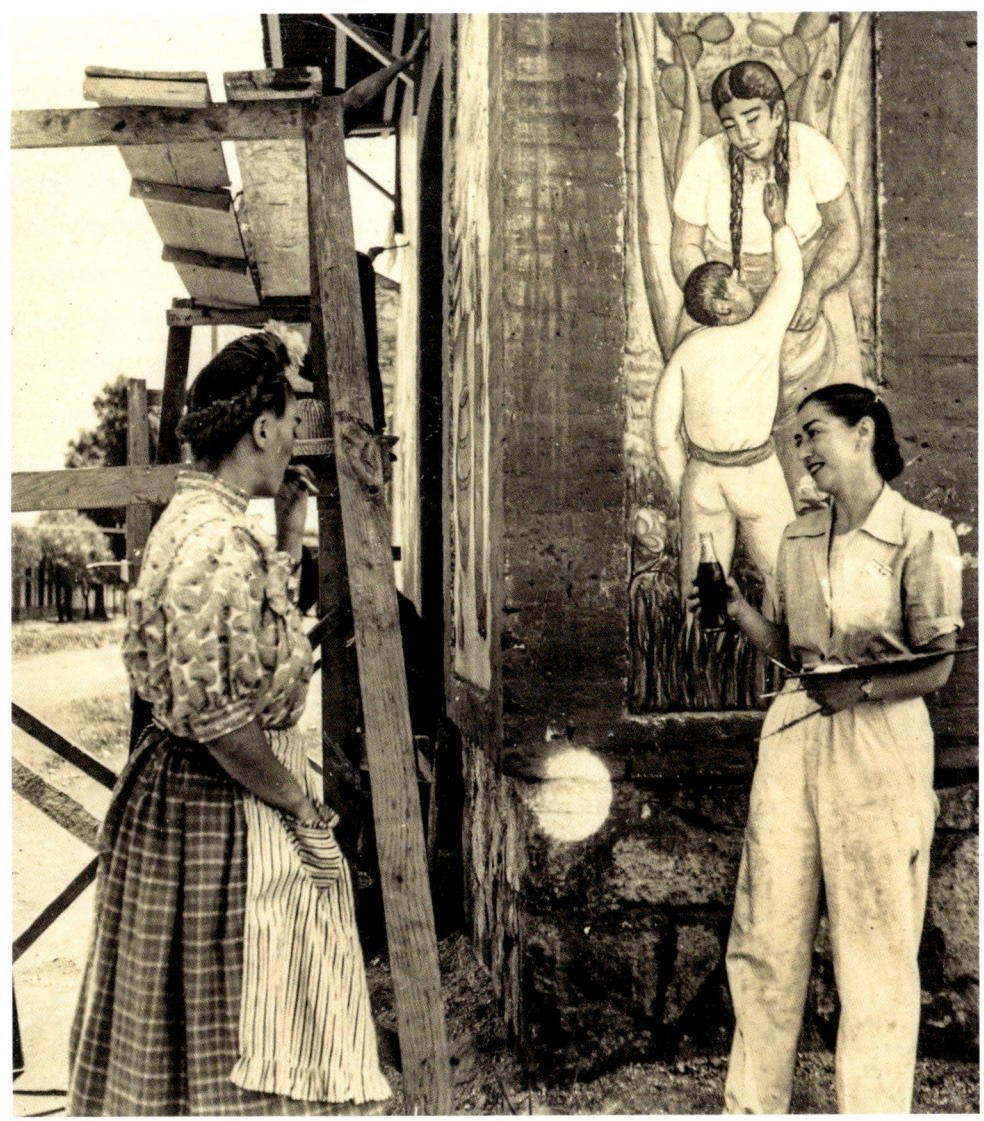

**Rivera and Kahlo at their second marriage at
San Francisco City Hall** (detail), December 8, 1940
Gelatin silver print, 24 x 19.7 cm (9½ x 7¾ in.). New York, collection of Spencer Throckmorton

Leo Matiz, **Kahlo and María Ángeles Ramos, one of her students from the Esmeralda Escuela de
Pintura y Escultura, painting murals on the walls of the *pulque* bar La Rosita** (detail), Coyoacán, 1943
Gelatin silver print (contact sheet), 14.3 x 12.7 cm (5⅝ x 5 in.)
New York, collection of Spencer Throckmorton

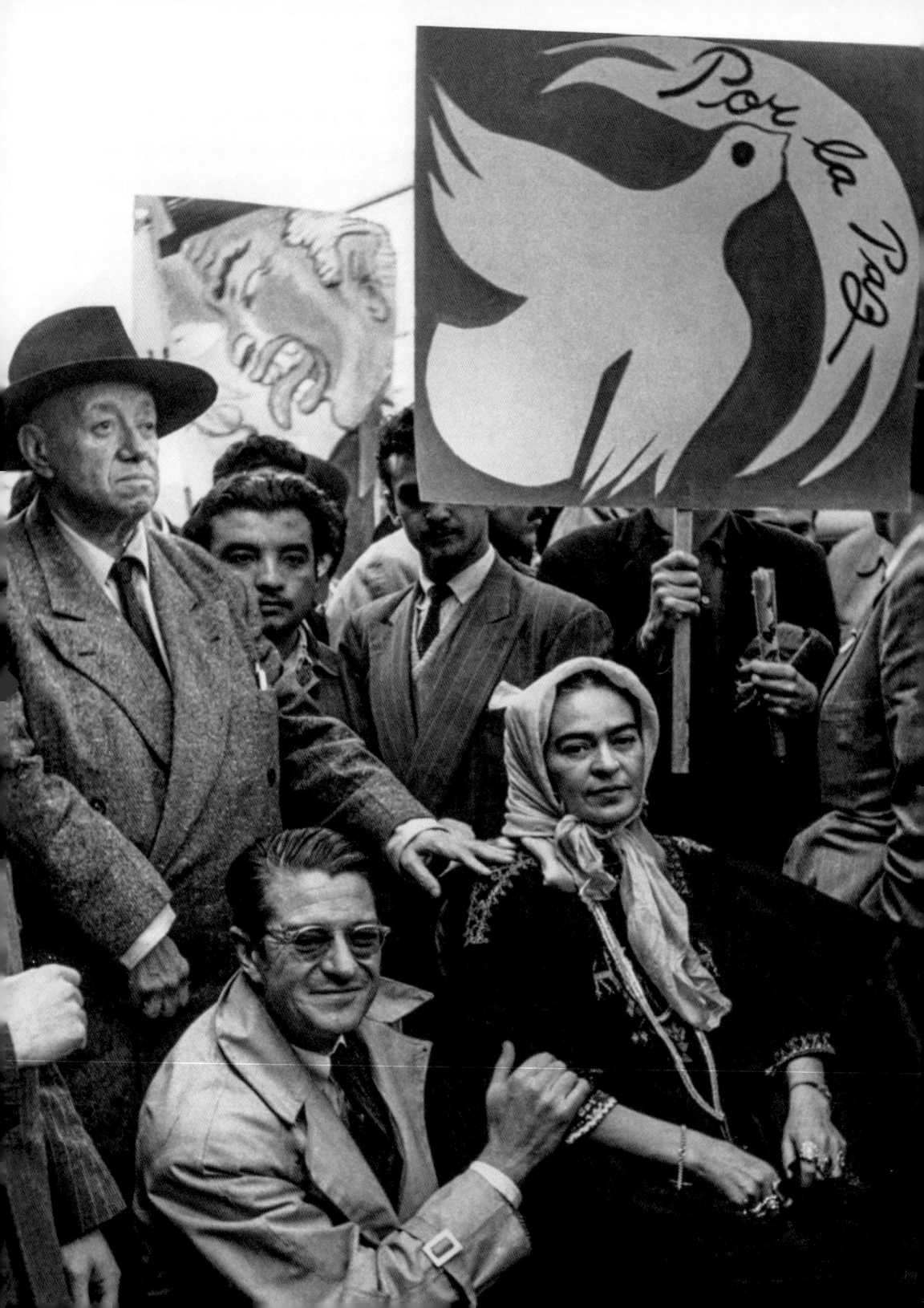

spinal canal, which cause severe headaches and pressure in her skull.

1946 After being bedridden for four months, Kahlo agrees to have an operation with Dr. Philip Wilson. Before she travels to New York to do so she paints *The Little Deer* (pp. 310/311), and on May 3 gives it to her friends and patrons, the producer Arcady Boytler and his wife Lina.

In May as well, she makes the journey to New York so that Dr. Wilson can assess her condition. The operation involves fusing four of her lumbar vertebrae together and grafting bone to her spine from her pelvis, as well as inserting a 15-centimeter metal plate.

Cristina remains by her sister's side throughout the difficult and painful period of her convalescence.

On July 29, the two of them return to Mexico.

Kahlo submits her painting *Moses* (pp. 272/273) for inclusion in the exhibition organized by the committee of the National Prize for Arts and Sciences. It is exhibited with the title *Core of the Sun* and she receives a painting prize from the Ministry of Public Education.

1947 Kahlo takes part in the exhibition "45 Autorretratos de pintores mexicanos:

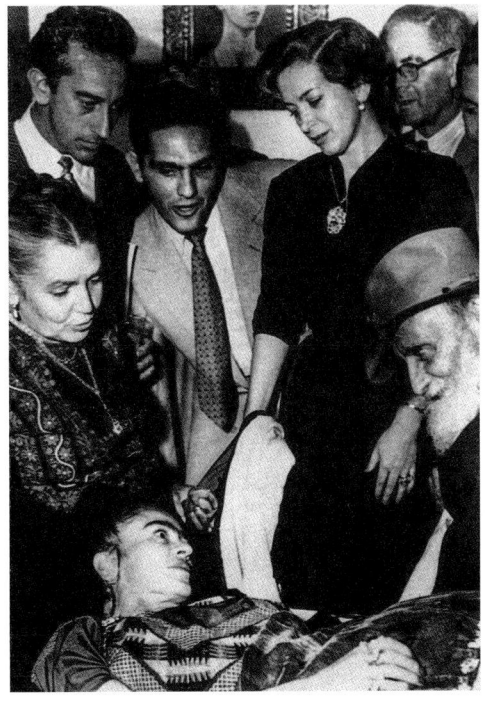

siglos XVII al XX" organized by the Instituto Nacional de Bellas Artes (National Institute of Fine Arts), where her painting *Self-portrait (Diego on My Mind)* (p. 251) is shown with the title *Tehuana*.

On November 6, the Museo Nacional de Artes Plásticas opens at the Palacio de Bellas Artes in Mexico City. A painting by Kahlo is exhibited in the Gran Galería de Arte Moderno.

Kahlo in a wheelchair with Rivera and Juan O'Gorman at the march protesting against US intervention in the overthrow of the legitimate government of Guatemala (detail), July 2, 1954
Gelatin silver print, 25.4 x 20.3 cm (8 x 6 in.). New York, collection of Spencer Throckmorton

Kahlo at the opening of her exhibition at the Galería Arte Contemporáneo, April 13, 1953
From left to right: Concha Michel, Antonio Peláez, Roberto Garza, Carmen Farell, and Dr. Atl

1948 Kahlo takes part in a group exhibition organized to mark the founding of the Sociedad para el Impulso de las Artes Plásticas (Society for the Promotion of Visual Arts).

She rejoins the Communist Party.

1949 Kahlo takes part in the inaugural exhibition at the Salon de la Plástica Mexicana with *The Love Embrace of the Universe, the Earth (Mexico), Me, Diego, and Señor Xólotl* (p. 317).

1950 Kahlo's health continues to deteriorate and she is admitted to the so-called English Hospital in Mexico City. She remains there for almost a whole year and has to have seven operations on her spine and two toes of her right foot amputated.

1952 Kahlo arranges for her students to work on new decoration for the façade of the *pulquería* La Rosita.

Ciudad Universitaria (University City) is officially opened, to the south of Mexico City. The sculptor Mathias Goeritz designs the Museo Experimental El Eco, in Mexico City, while the painter Rufino Tamayo is commissioned by the government of Miguel Alemán to paint two murals at the Palacio de Bellas Artes.

1953 The exhibition "Mexican Art" runs from March to May at the Tate Gallery in London, and includes five paintings by Kahlo.

On April 13, Kahlo's only solo exhibition to be held in Mexico, "Primicias para un homenaje," opens at the Galería Arte Contemporáneo run by the photographer Lola Álvarez Bravo.

In May, Rivera returns to Mexico after making a trip to South America. He arrives from Chile accompanied by the journalist Raquel Tibol, who stays at the Casa Azul.

Kahlo talks to Tibol about the personal details of her life story, with a view to it being published as her autobiography as proposed by Rivera. The project remains unfinished.

On August 11, Kahlo's right leg has to be amputated below the knee because of gangrene.

On October 17, the Mexican president Adolfo Ruiz Cortines enacts reforms in the constitution to grant women the right to vote.

1954 On February 11, Kahlo admits that she wants to take her own life.

On April 24, she begins saying goodbye to her friends.

In a wheelchair and while recovering from pneumonia, against the advice of her doctors Kahlo takes part in a march to protest the overthrow of the democratic government of Jacobo Árbenz in Guatemala following a coup instigated by the US government and conducted by the CIA.

Kahlo dies on July 13.

On July 14, her body is cremated at the Panteón Civil, the state cemetery in Mexico City.

Her ashes are transferred to a pre-Hispanic urn that is kept at the Museo Frida Kahlo in the Casa Azul in Coyoacán, where Kahlo was born and lived for most of her life.

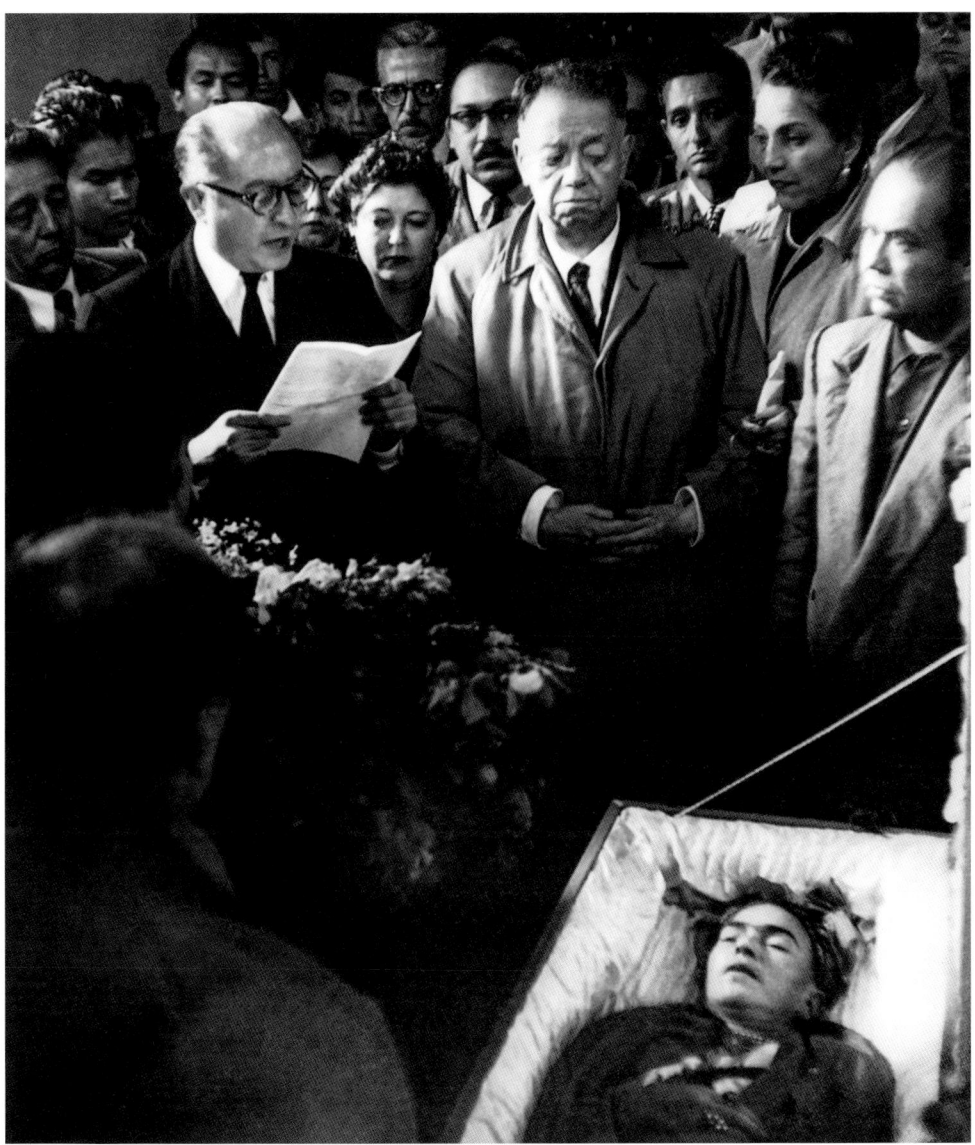

Héctor García, **Andrés Iduarte, Director of the Instituto Nacional de Bellas Artes,
reading the eulogy beside Frida Kahlo's open coffin** (detail), July 14, 1954
Gelatin silver print, 17.8 x 12.7 cm (7 x 5 in.)
New York, collection of Spencer Throckmorton

VII.

Frida and Diego

*"[...] this gives her great powers of inventive creation
within a reality that remains entirely real even as
it soars to a marvelous, yet logical expression of the
imagination in the realm of the unexpected, where
the sudden appearance of dialectical associations are
as surprising as they are undeniable."*

— DIEGO RIVERA, *c.* 1953

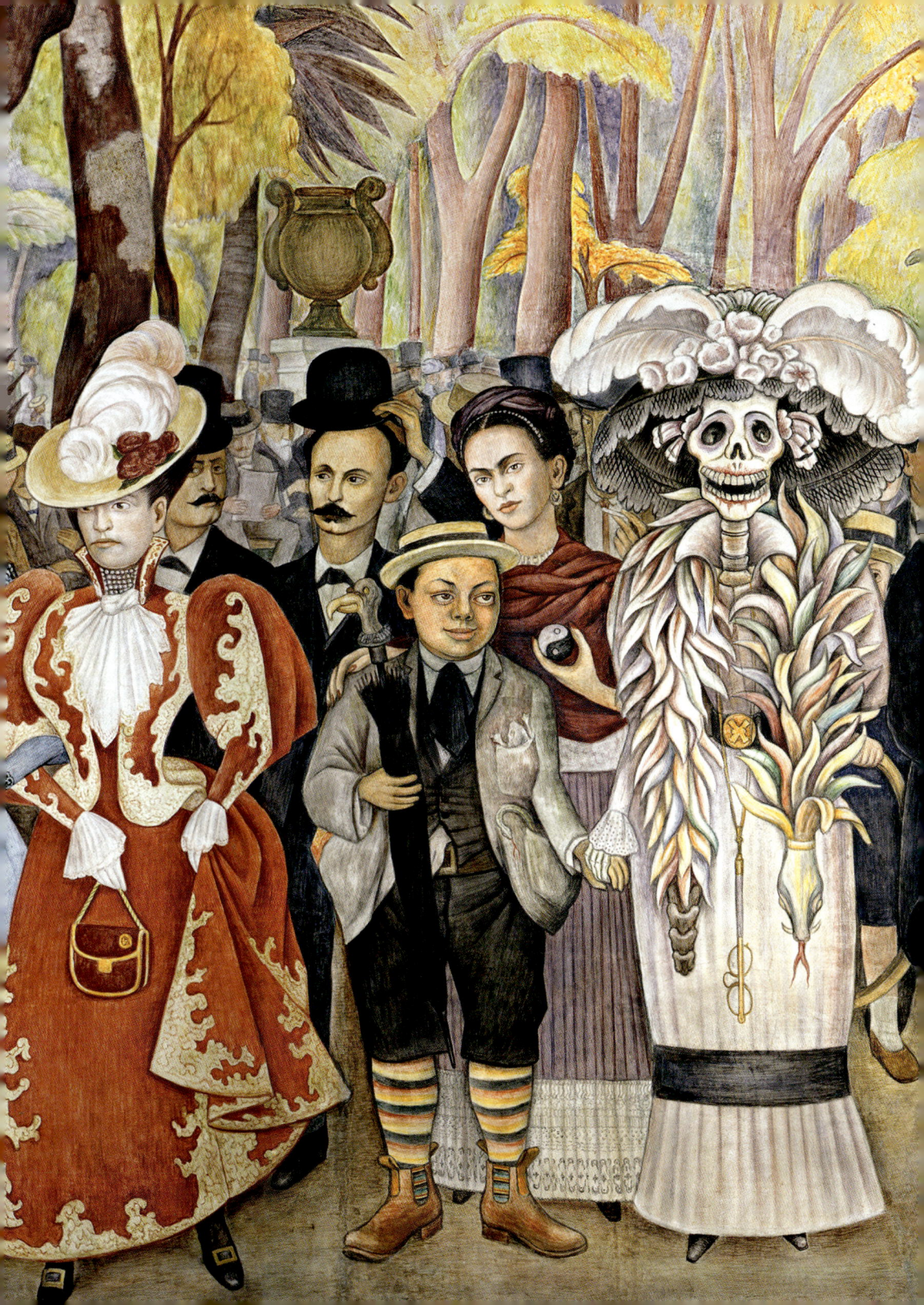

Portrait of Diego
by Frida Kahlo

I must warn you to begin with that I will be painting this portrait of Diego using colors that are unfamiliar to me, words, and because of that the portrait will be a poor one. I love Diego so much that I cannot be a "spectator" looking in on his life and am instead a part of it, which is why, perhaps, I will exaggerate the positive aspects of his unique personality and try, even if only a little, to minimize any aspects that may be hurtful to him. This will not be a biographical account either, since I think it is more honest simply to write about the Diego I feel I have come to know to some extent in the course of the 20 years I have lived with him. I will not speak of Diego as "my husband," because that would be ridiculous; Diego has never been and never will be anyone's "husband." Neither will I speak of him as my lover, inasmuch as he transcends the limitations of sex; and if I spoke of him as I might speak of a child I would only be describing or painting my own emotions, and thus end up with something that was more a portrait of me than one of Diego. And so, with complete honesty, I will try to relay this singular truth, which is mine, of making a sketch, to the best of my abilities, of his image.

HIS FORM: he has an Asian head, with dark hair that is so thin and fine that it seems to float in the air. Diego is a great big child, enormous even, with a pleasant face and a gaze that is slightly sad. His dark, bulging eyes, so intelligent and so large, are difficult to keep in place (they are almost bursting out of their sockets) so that the eyelids are swollen and the eyes protrude like those of a frog. They are very far apart from each other, more than other people's eyes are, and because of this he is able to take in a much broader field

Page 423
Diego Rivera, **Frida Kahlo with Diego Rivera as a boy and "Catrina" the image of death**, 1947/48. Detail from the mural *Dream of a Sunday Afternoon in Alameda Park* Mexico City, Secretaría de Cultura, Instituto Nacional de Bellas Artes y Literatura, Museo Mural Diego Rivera

Diego Rivera, **Frida Kahlo representing the creative forces of the southern American continent**, 1940. Detail from the mural *Panamerican Unity* San Francisco, City College

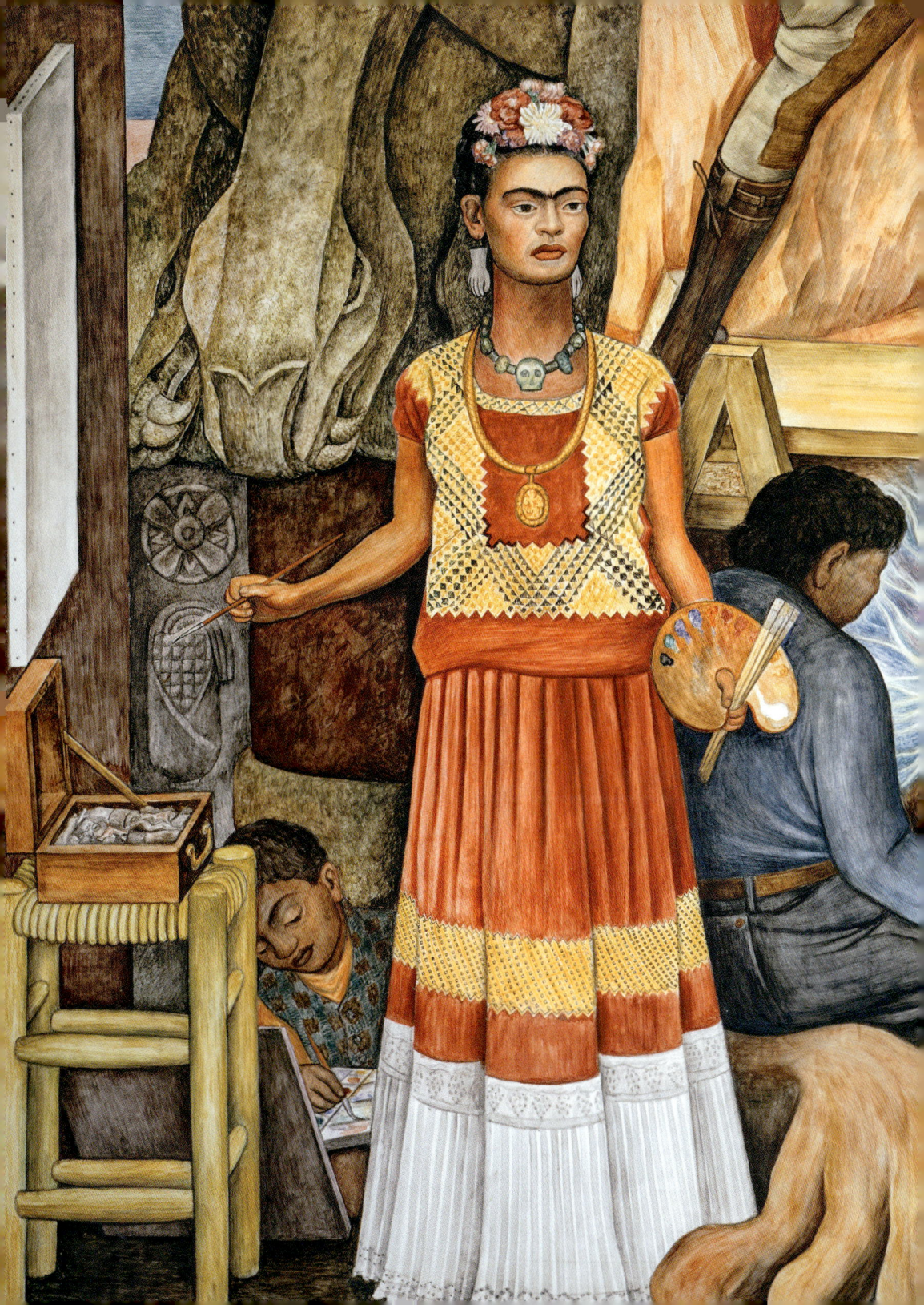

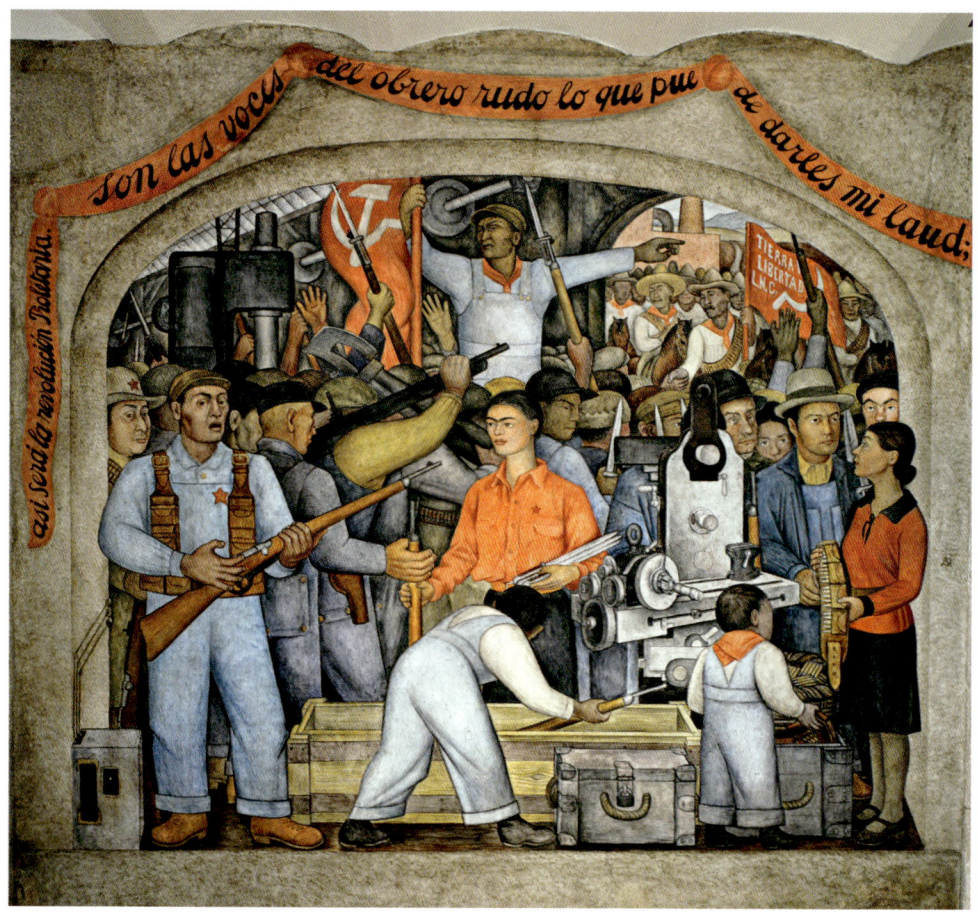

of vision, as if these eyes had been made especially for a painter of big crowds and spaces. Between them, in the wide distance that separates them, an invisible Eastern wisdom can be perceived, and at times an ironic yet tender smile escapes from his Buddha's mouth, a gift of his countenance.

To see him naked instantly evokes the image of a boy-frog standing upright on its back legs. His skin is greenish-white, like an aquatic creature. Only his hands and face, being tanned by the sun, are darker. His childlike shoulders, which are narrow and

Diego Rivera, **Frida distributing weapons**
In the Arsenal (detail from the mural *Ballad of the Proletarian Revolution*), 1928/29
Mexico City, Secretaría de Educación Pública

rounded, are joined without angles to female arms that end at his marvelous hands, which are small and finely made, the sensitive and discerning antennae that communicate with the whole universe. It is astounding how much these hands have painted, and that they still work on without ever tiring. Concerning his chest, it has to be said that had he ever landed on an island ruled by Sappho he would not have been executed by her warriors. The sensuality of his magnificent breasts would have ensured as much. Nevertheless, his unusual personal virility would make him an object of desire in the lands of empresses devoted to the love of men. His huge stomach, taut and smooth as a sphere, sits atop strong legs that are as beautiful as columns and at the lower ends of which his large feet point outward at an obtuse angle. It is as if they intend to span the globe and hover, fixed and unmoving, above it, making him like some antediluvian creature from which, from the waist up, a specimen of future humanity is to emerge, two or three thousand years from now. [...]

Diego's figure is that of an endearing monster, whose grandmother, Antigua Ocultadora [Ancient Concealer] – the essential and eternal matter, the mother of all humankind and the gods they invented in their delirium, prompted by fear and hunger, by WOMANKIND, and among all of them, ME – wants to cradle him for ever, like a newborn child.

HIS CONTENT: Diego is not constrained by any limited or particular personal relationships. Contradictory, like everything that moves life onward, his relationships are at one and the same time a huge embrace and a violent release of powerful and individual forces. These forces live inside him, like the seeds cherished by the earth, and outside, like landscapes. There are probably some people who will be expecting a very personal portrait of Diego from me, a "feminine" one that is good-natured and anecdotal, full of complaints and a little gossip as well, but of the "decent" kind that is understandable and serves a purpose in proportion to the morbid interest of the reader. Others may wish to hear me complain about "how much I have suffered" living with a man like Diego. However, the banks of the river seem not to suffer from the river's flow, or the ground when it rains, nor do I think an atom suffers when it releases its energy... for me, everything has its natural reward. In my difficult and hidden role, as the ally of this extraordinary man, I am rewarded like the green dot that exists within a sea of red, the reward that makes for equilibrium. The sorrows and joys that are always present in this world in which I live, though it is rotten with lies, are not mine. If I have prejudices, if other people's actions hurt me, even Diego's, I take responsibility for not being able to see clearly; but while that may be the case, I admit all the same that it is entirely natural for red blood cells to wage war against white ones without the slightest prejudice, and that this phenomenon is in fact a sign of health.

I will not devalue Diego's fantastical personality, for which I have the deepest respect, by saying stupid things about his life. On the contrary, what I would like to say, in a way that does him justice and with a kind of poetry I do not possess, is what Diego really is. […]

In a portrait of him there are three main angles or qualities I consider to be fundamental. First and foremost he is a revolutionary in everything he does, being dynamic and filled with vital energy but also extraordinarily sensitive; he is an indefatigable worker within his profession, and has a knowledge matched by few other painters in the world; he possesses a phenomenal enthusiasm for life, and at the same time feels dissatisfied that he has not learned more, built more, or painted more. Secondly, there is his constant curiosity, which makes him a tireless student of all things. Thirdly, his utter lack of prejudice, and therefore faith, since Diego accepts (as Montaigne did) that "where doubt ends stupidity begins" and that the person who has faith in something is thereby admitting to their unconditional submission, and the loss of their freedom to analyze or to influence the course of facts. Having such a clear view of reality, Diego is a rebel. And because he has a magnificent understanding of the materialist dialectic of life, Diego is a revolutionary. Out of this triangle, which is also the source of Diego's other forms, there emanates a kind of aura which envelops the whole. This fluid atmosphere is love, but love as a general structure, as motion that creates beauty. I imagine the world he would like to live in. It would be a huge party in which each and every thing would be involved, from human beings to stones, sun, and shadows, all as one and yet with their own beauty and their own creative power. It would be a celebration of shape, color, movement, sound, intelligence, knowledge, and emotion; a spherical, intellectual, and loving celebration, that would cover the entire surface of the earth. Diego continuously strives to hold this celebration with all that he has: his genius, his imagination, his words, and his actions. He strives, at every moment, to rid humankind of fear and stupidity.

Because of his profound desire to help transform the society in which he lives into a more beautiful place – a healthier, less painful, and more intelligent place – and because he has given the Socialist Revolution, which is as positive as it is inevitable, all his creative strength, constructive genius, penetrating sensitivity, and constant work, Diego is forever being attacked. Throughout the last 20 years I have seen him fight against the unbelievably complex mechanisms of the negative forces that oppose his push for freedom and change. The world is hostile because his enemy is in the majority, but this does not

Diego Rivera, **Frida Kahlo depicted as an *ahuianime*, a sacred prostitute,
in the *tianguis* (market) of Tenochtitlán,** 1945
Detail from the mural *Pre-Hispanic and Colonial Mexico*
Mexico City, Palacio Nacional

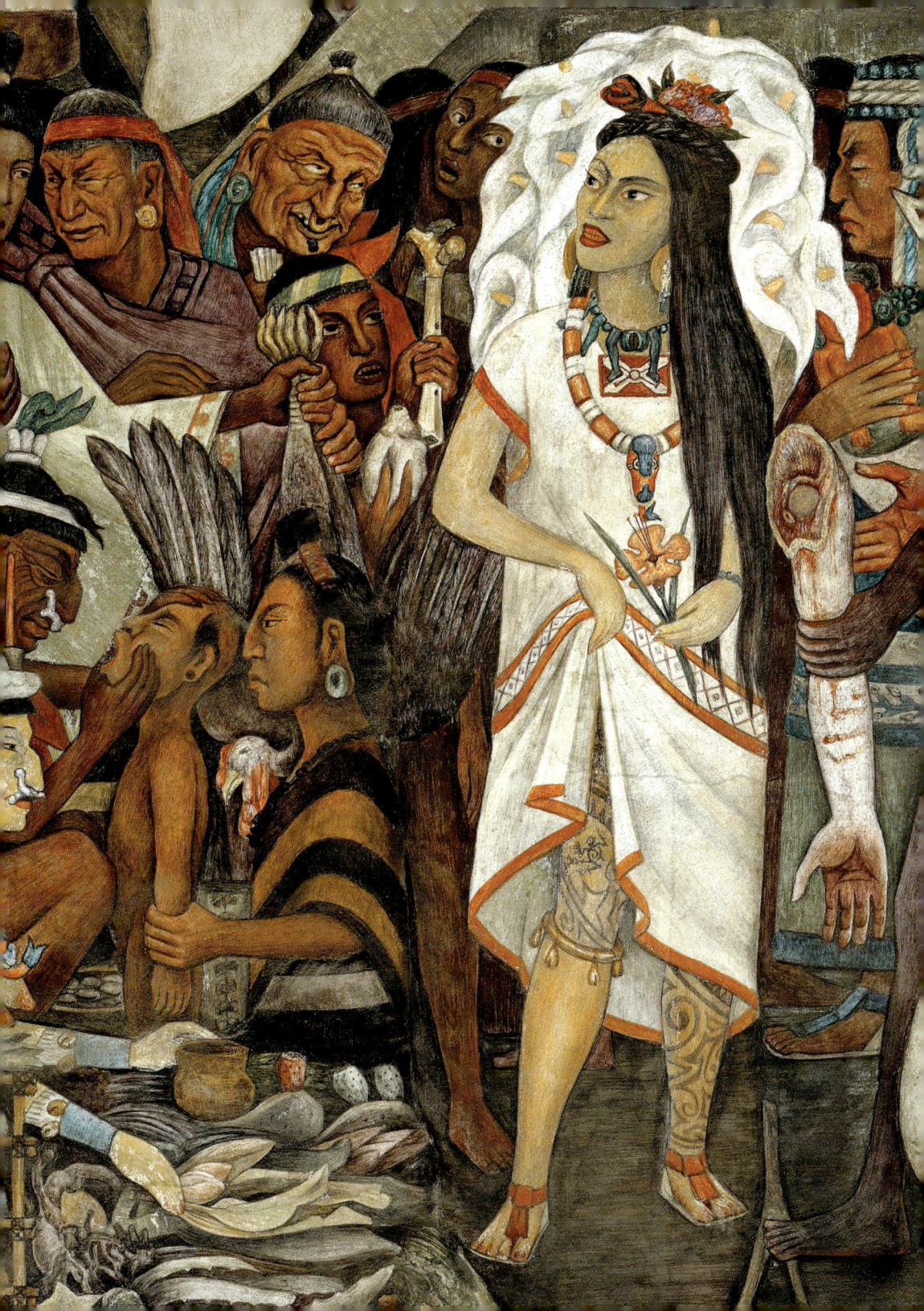

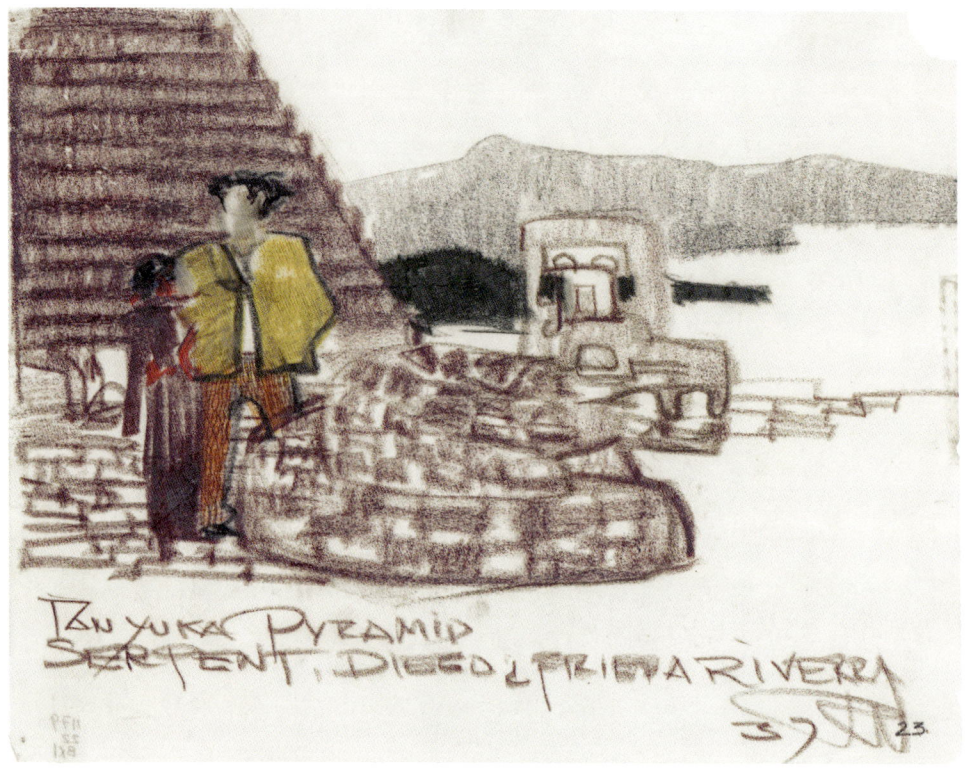

intimidate him; and as longs as he lives, new, vibrant, and courageous means of doing battle will flow from his hands, lips, and his entire being.

In the same way as Diego, others who have brought light to this world have endured struggle; and like them too, Diego has no "friends," only allies. All that flows from Diego is magnificent: his dazzling intelligence, his deep and clear understanding of the humanity he works with, his experience, and his great sophistication, which does not come from books, but is instead inductive and deductive; also his genius and his will to build, as founded in reality and in a world scrubbed clean of cowardice and lies. Those of us who,

Richard Neutra, **Frida and Diego in front of the pyramid of Tenayuca**, 1937
Colored chalks, 22 x 28 cm (8⅝ x 11 in.). Los Angeles, University of California, Special Collections Library at the Charles E. Young Research Library, Richard and Dion Neutra Papers

Emmy Lou Packard, **Frida and Diego at mealtime in the Casa Azul** (detail), Coyoacán, September 1941. Palladium print, 12.7 x 12.7 cm (5 x 5 in.) New York, collection of Spencer Throckmorton like him, are aware of the urgent need to destroy the false foundations of the present world, are all his allies.

To those who make cowardly attacks against him Diego always responds with conviction and with a great sense of humor. He never compromises, nor does he concede; he confronts his enemies, most of whom are underhand in their ways though some of them are bold, openly and always with reality on his side, never resorting to "hopes" or "ideals." This intransigence and rebelliousness are the essence of Diego, and thus complement his portrait. [...]

And people say he is a millionaire... the truth about Diego's millions is this and only this: being a craftsman and not a member of the proletariat, he owns the tools of his

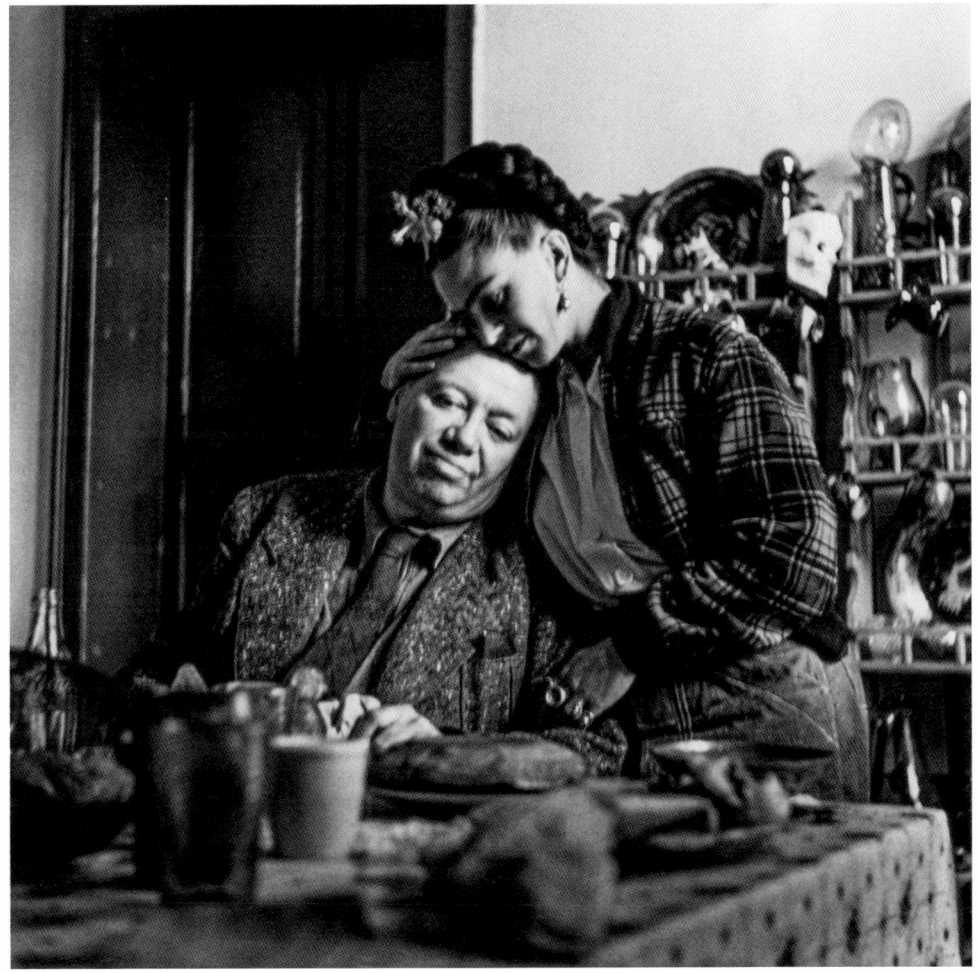

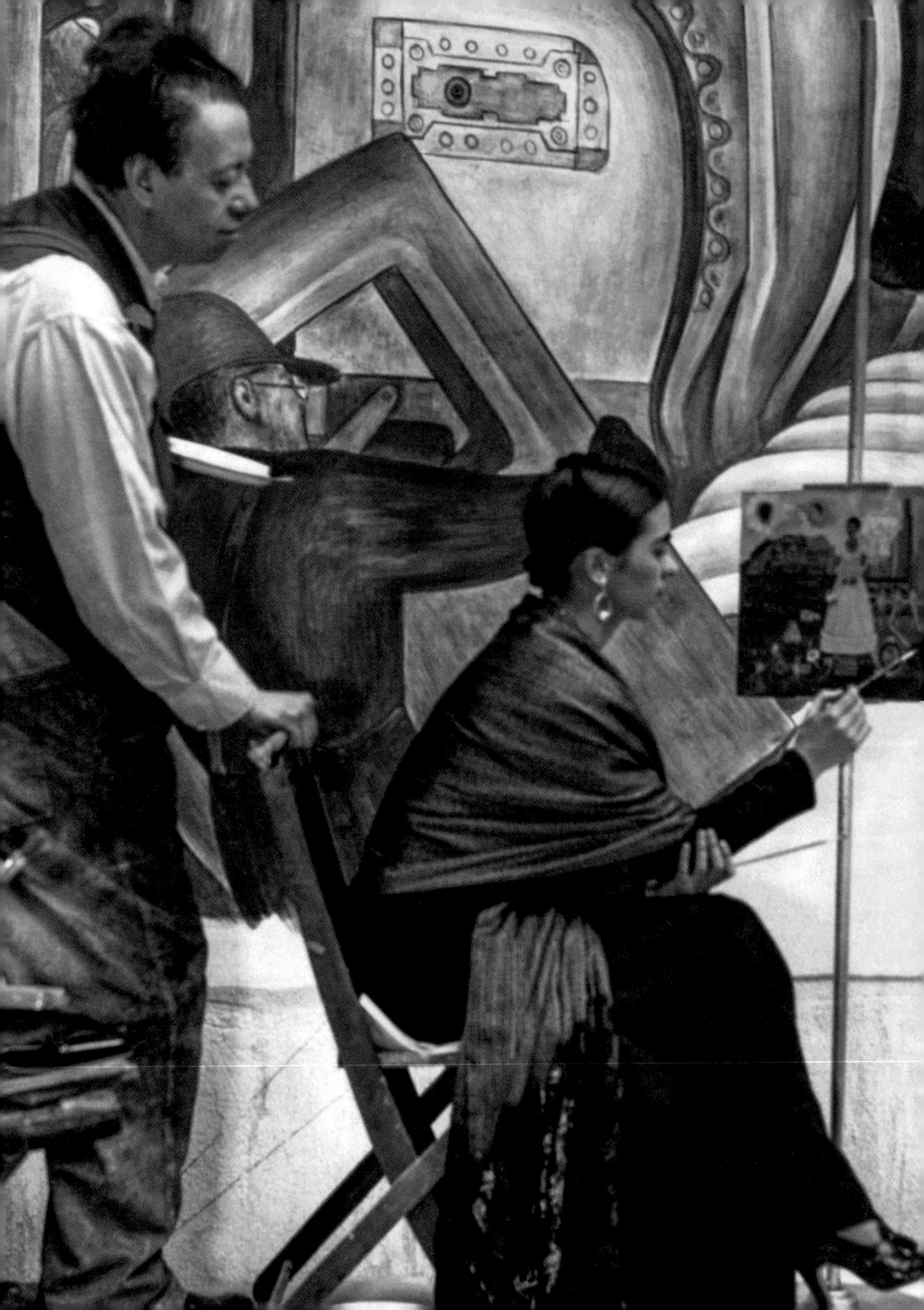

production, that is his work – the house he lives in, the tattered clothes he wears, and the worn-out pickup truck that is as necessary to him as scissors are to a tailor. His treasure consists of a collection of wonderful sculptures, jewels of indigenous art that are the living heart of the real Mexico, which he has managed to accumulate in the course of more than 30 years and with considerable financial sacrifice, in order to place them in a museum he has been building for the last seven years. This he has built through his own creative and financial effort, in other words his marvelous talent and the money he receives for his paintings. He will donate the museum's collection to his country, which will connect the Mexico of today to the most prodigious source of beauty that has ever existed; it will be a gift for the eyes of all Mexicans, to whom it will belong, and a source of incalculable awe for everyone else. Apart from this, he has nothing to speak of financially; he does not own anything other than his ability to work. Last year, after a bout of pneumonia, he did not have enough money to leave the hospital. While he was still recovering he began to paint in order to cover daily living expenses and to pay the wages of the workers who, like guilds in the Renaissance, are laboring with him to accomplish the magnificent project in El Pedregal.

But insults and attacks do not affect Diego. They are simply part of the social phenomena of a decadent world and nothing more. All of life, with its changeable nature, continues to interest and amaze him, and everything surprises him with its beauty, yet nothing actually disappoints or unnerves him because he understands the dialectical mechanisms of phenomena and facts. [...]

There are no words to describe Diego's enormous tenderness for things that are beautiful, his affection for those who are deemed superfluous in today's class society, or his respect for those who are oppressed by it. He has a particular love for our indigenous people, to whom he is connected by blood; he loves them for their elegance and their beauty, and because they are the living products of the cultural tradition of the Americas. He loves children, all animals, especially Mexican hairless dogs, and birds, plants, and rocks. He loves all creatures, and not in a way that is either docile or neutral. He is very loving, but he is never submissive; for this reason, and because he has hardly any time for personal relationships, he is called ungrateful. He is in fact respectful and dignified, and nothing offends him more than abuse or a lack of respect for others. He has no tolerance for tricks or sly deceptions [...] He would rather have intelligent enemies than stupid allies. Most of the time he is cheerful, but he becomes extremely annoyed if people waste his time when

W. J. Stettler, **Diego Rivera watching Frida Kahlo while she paints *Self-portrait***
***(on the Border between Mexico and the United States)* at the Detroit Institute of Arts**, 1932
Gelatin silver print, 21.6 x 18.9 cm (8½ x 7½ in.)
New York, collection of Spencer Throckmorton

he is at work. He finds his entertainment in work itself; he hates social engagements but is thrilled by celebrations that are truly of the people. He is sometimes shy, and while he loves talking and debating with everyone, at other times he takes the greatest pleasure in being completely alone. He is never bored because everything is interesting to him; he studies, analyzes, and explores every aspect of life. He is not sentimental, but is very passionate and emotional. Inertia infuriates him because he is a continuous, powerful, live current. He has exceptionally good taste, and admires and appreciates all forms of beauty, whether its vibration resides within a woman or a mountain. Being perfectly balanced in all his emotions, feelings, and actions, which are motivated by a precise and real materialist dialectic, he never surrenders. Like the cacti of his homeland, he grows strongly and impressively, whether in sand or stones; he blossoms in the brightest red, the most translucent white, and the most solar yellow; cloaked in spines, his tenderness is sheltered within, and with his strong sap he thrives in fierce environments; he projects his own light, like a sun avenging the grayness of stones; his roots continue to live even when they have been torn from the earth, triumphing over the anguish of sorrow and loneliness and all the other weaknesses that crush others. With remarkable vigor he rises up and, like no known plant, puts out flowers and fruit.

Kahlo wrote this text about Rivera around 1949 for his major retrospective exhibition, "Diego Rivera, Cincuenta años de su labor artística," held at the Museo Nacional de Artes Plásticas in the Palacio de Bellas Artes in Mexico City. The catalogue was published jointly in 1951 by the Ministry of Public Education and the Instituto Nacional de Bellas Artes. Kahlo's essay, which was written with the intention of preserving an accurate image of Rivera, is a courageous piece of writing that reveals much about the pact of love and loyalty that bound the two of them together. Theirs was a relationship that did not seek any explanation from outside, and was instead defined on their own terms.

The essay also highlights Kahlo's remarkable ability with the written word, and with her fluid, direct, and sophisticated prose style she shows her understanding of Rivera's place in history, independent of any wishes of her own.

Even so, this excerpt from the full text and the images in the chapter that follow can only scratch the surface of what this unique couple contributed to the history of art and culture in Mexico and the world as a whole.

Frida Kahlo, **Diego and Frida on their fifth anniversary**, New York, 1933
Collage with photograph by Lucienne Bloch mounted on card stock
painted with watercolor, 28.9 x 17.5 cm (11⅜ x 6⅞ in.)
Mexico City, Coyoacán, Museo Frida Kahlo

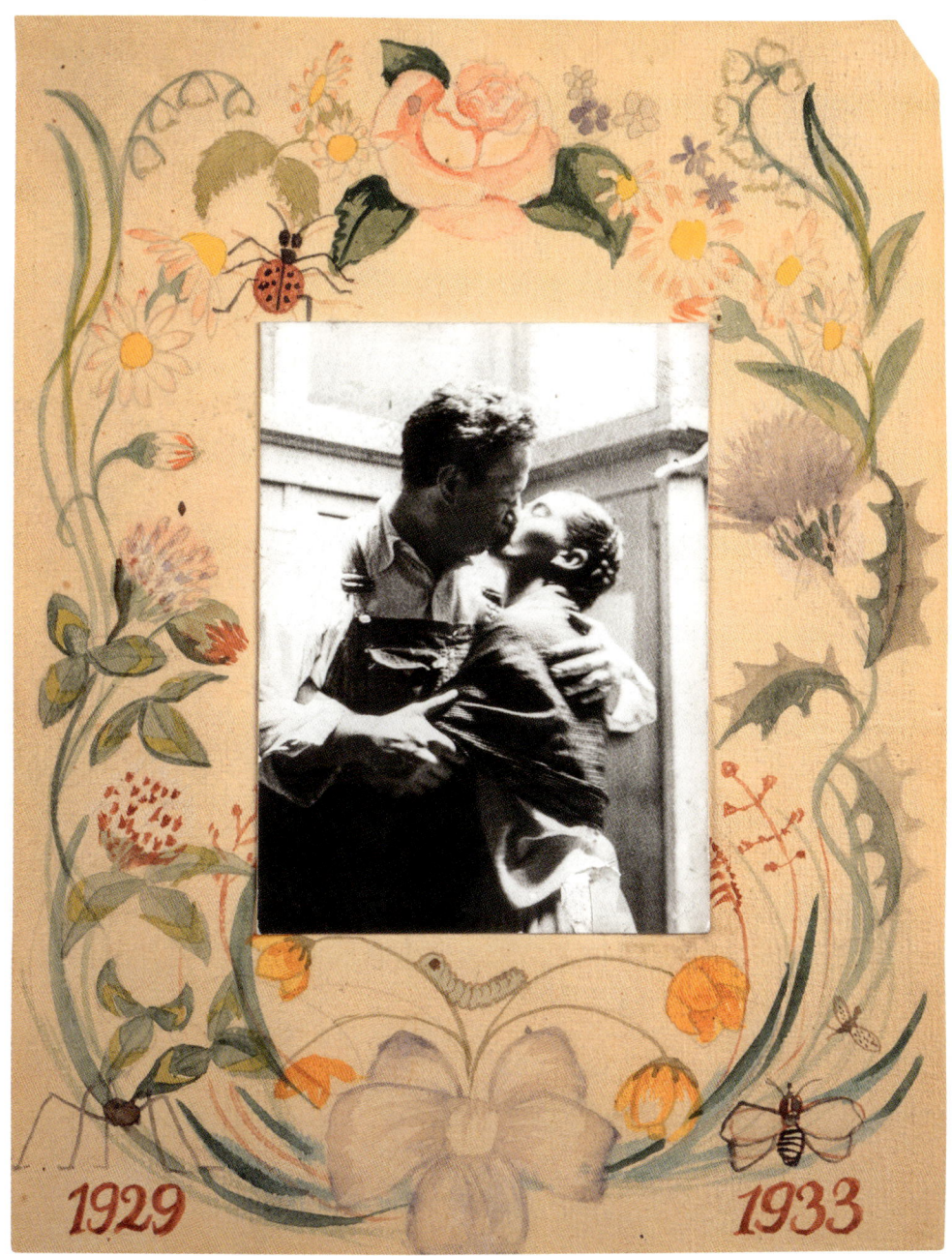

Niño
Te ma...
Dama...
lo de ...
Para ...
papaya...
mermela...
¿Cómo ...
cena? Po...
en México
Te busca...
dicho Ca...
Vino Ch...
que tú me...
do en que...
necesario s...
y cuando a...
chadro, hab...
Habló Suzan...
100 invitacion...
San Angel?...
na en la...
Cuídate muc...
Yo sigo con...
de que lle...
Hidroestrepta...
tengo que aq...
ás piquetes...
rio a David y...
velarte. T...

tienes tiempo de...
Estamos a 27 ya...
rotularlas tú?
Yo te ayudé?
des ocupar al...
las, no crees?
Háblame po...
quiero saber a...
pues aquí estoy tirada...
de a Lucas.
gracias. y m...
de besos de
Frida

llegan a mediados de
Marzo por los artículos
que escribiste sobre Don
Justo Sierra. Urgía
que primara yo, porque
Armán se va mañana pa
pa los E. U. y me dijo
que la tramitación del
cobro, de los 200 pesos se
hará mientras él regresa.
Él te hablará en cuanto llegue.

Niño de mis ojos,
me pareció maravillosa la ofrenda
las demás figuras - Mañana les da
un lugar! Tú y yo - Gracias
mía, por si me encuentras dorm
te dejo millones de besos - Te adora
tu Frisito

23 de Feb. 194...

Habló
dios
una
mañan
una
des tú
Lowe
en
No
p

Niño mío,
Estoy como te digo, un
poco cansada pero bien
en lo demás. Si hoy
viene en la tarde la
muchacha que me va a
ayudar a terminar el
artículo ella me tr
más material para
narlo pronto y entreg
a Carlitos Chávez.
Te extraño mucho t
antigua Ocultadora y
niña Fisita
Millones de...

ANTONI SLONIMSKI
POETA
PEN CLUB
que no se le olvide
la lista que le pro
metiste a la Ministra

...de mi vida,
...carta y por
...he hablado
...a manolo
...está, y
...aquí
...mañana
...Ella
...pasado unos días m...
pero yo creo que com...
pintar me sentiré...
estás tú? y...
bien...
no sirv...
mundo...
en ést...
Te gu...
que se...

descuidar...
Eso es todo...
han que yo...
tranquila.
=No dejes de...
pastillas...
ya te encar...
no sea si...
costura o...
de ellas se...
Si me ne...
quieres forma...
me regreso yo...
Despídeme de...
que le pido, q...
paña mucho...
te dará alegr...
no estés triste...
vive - Yo te...
Toda mi vida...

Certificate of Marriage
8th Day...
TE OF CALIFORNIA
County of San Francis...
Superior Court thereof...
DO HEREBY CERTIF...
in and for said City and Co...
es Martin Monzan...
San Francisco, Cal...
all his official acts as such...
acquainted with the handwrit...
signature to s...
IN TESTIMONY WHER...
ffixed the seal of the said Superior...
Número 168 Derech...
RVICIO CONSULAR MEXICANO...
El suscrito EDMUNDO GONZALEZ...
Cónsul General...de México en San Francis...
fornia, E.U. de N.A....certifica que la firma
es de Martin Monzan, Secretario de la Cd., y Conda...
San Francisco, California, E.U. de N.A....
y la misma que acostumbra usar en todos los documentos que autoriza...
lo cual se le debe dar fe y crédito.
San Francisco, Calif., 11... agosto de 195...

Jueves 29 Mayo / 1946.
Diego mío,
Antes me hicieron la punción para
tratar de sacar el lipiodol pero
no pudieron sacar ni una sola
gota. No sufrí mucho pues aunque
no quisieron darme anestesia general, me aguanté a los macho
tres piquetes con la maldita lata del
lipiodol, pero ya ves tú mi vida,
que suerte tengo, nada salió.
El doctor Wilson no me hizo per-
sonalmente la punción pues me
explicó que el Dr. Straub es el
especialista en estas cuestiones, así
es que no fué porque no estuviera
hecha, sino que desgracia-
damente siempre se puede sa-
Después de la...

dora tu
Frida.

Xolotl te s...
gro, duerm...
a cuerp...

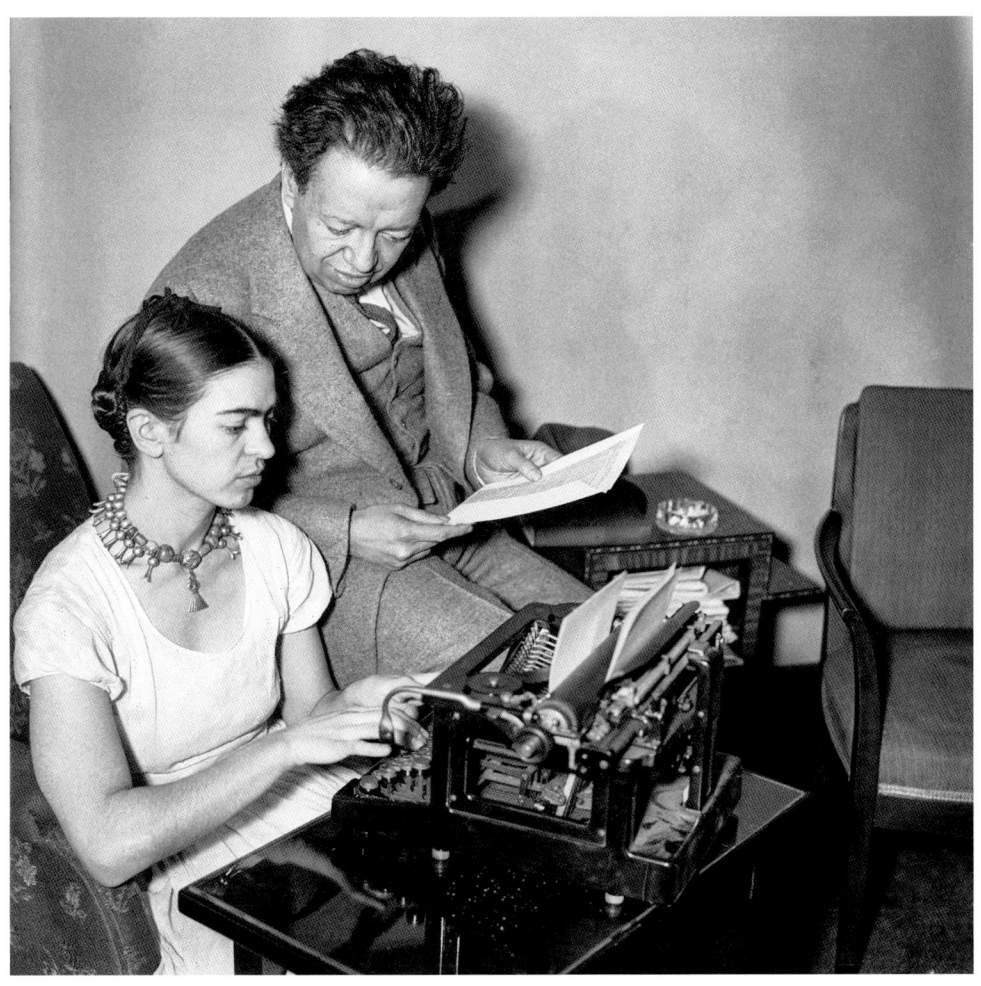

Some of Kahlo's letter's, documents, and photographs, 1932–1953
Courtesy Sotheby's, New York

Kahlo and Rivera, New York, May 11, 1933

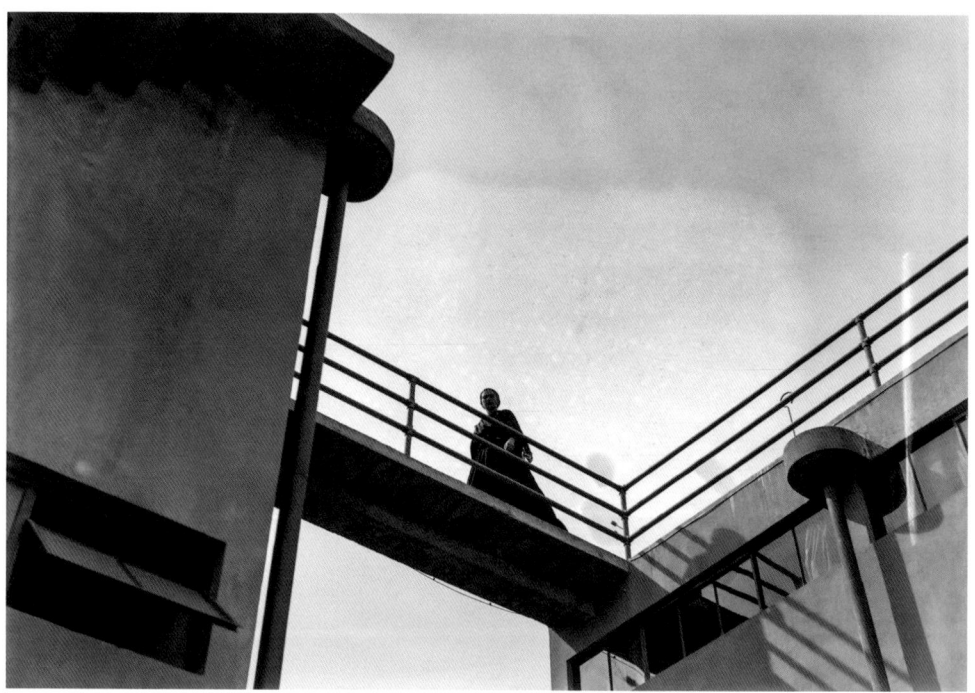

Martin Munkácsi, **Frida Kahlo on the bridge
of the House-Studio**, San Ángel, 1934
Gelatin silver print, 8.9 x 11.9 cm (3½ x 4¾ in.)
New York, International Center of Photography

Martin Munkácsi, **Frida Kahlo in front of the "wall of cacti"
outside the House-Studio** (detail), San Ángel, 1934
Gelatin silver print, 38.1 x 11.9 cm (15 x 4¾ in.)
New York, International Center of Photography

Pages 440/441
The House-Studio of Diego Rivera and Frida Kahlo, San Ángel

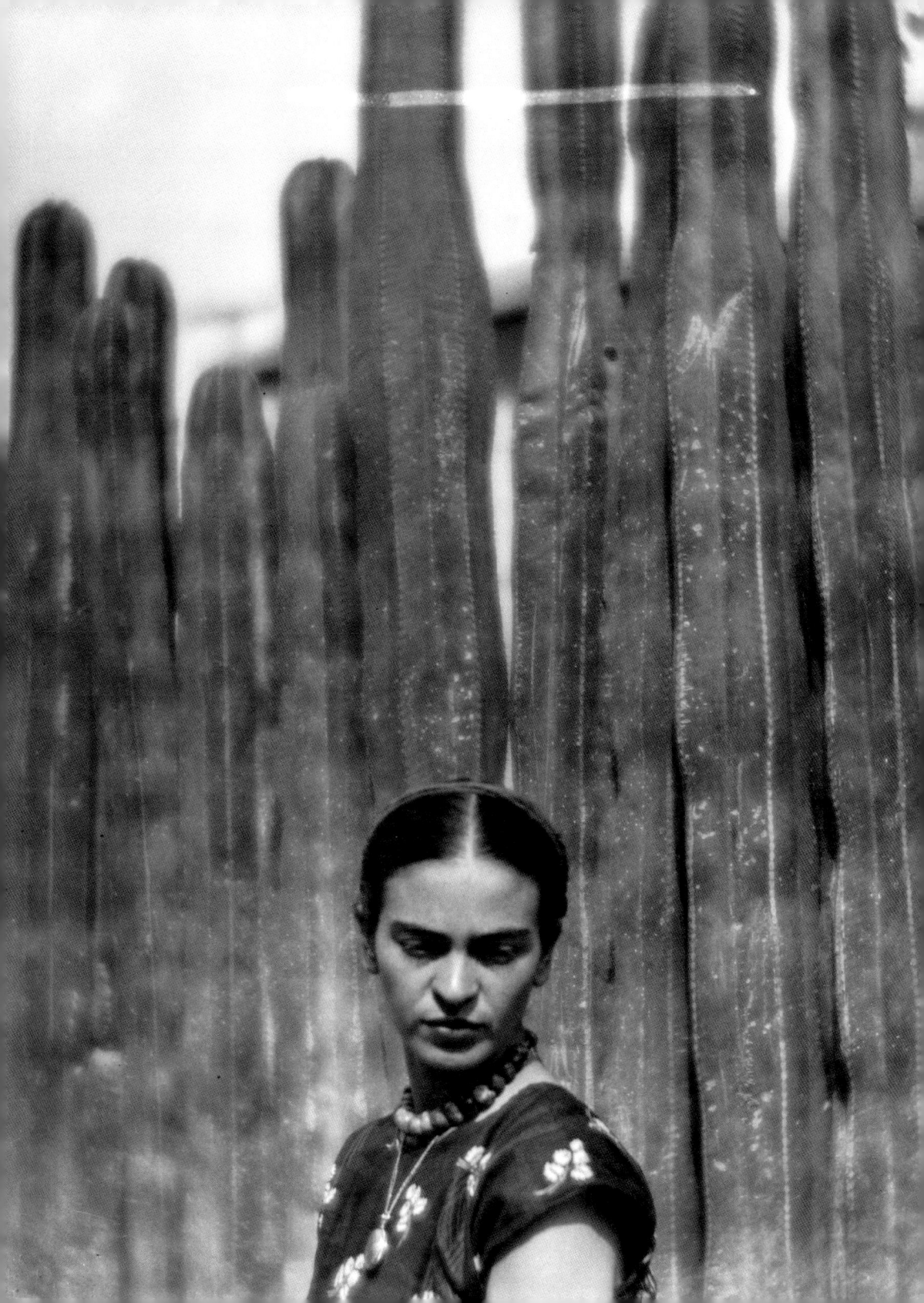

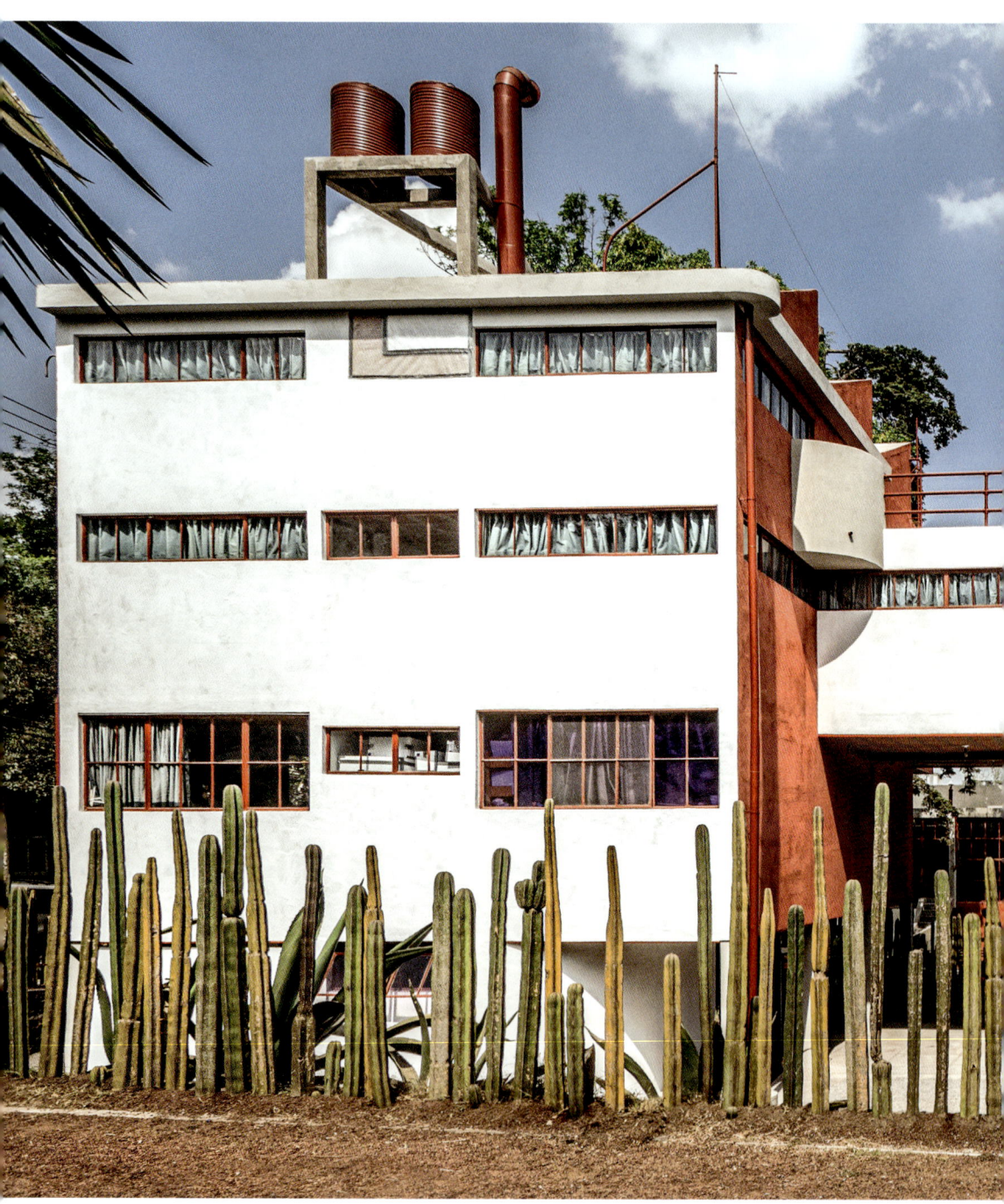

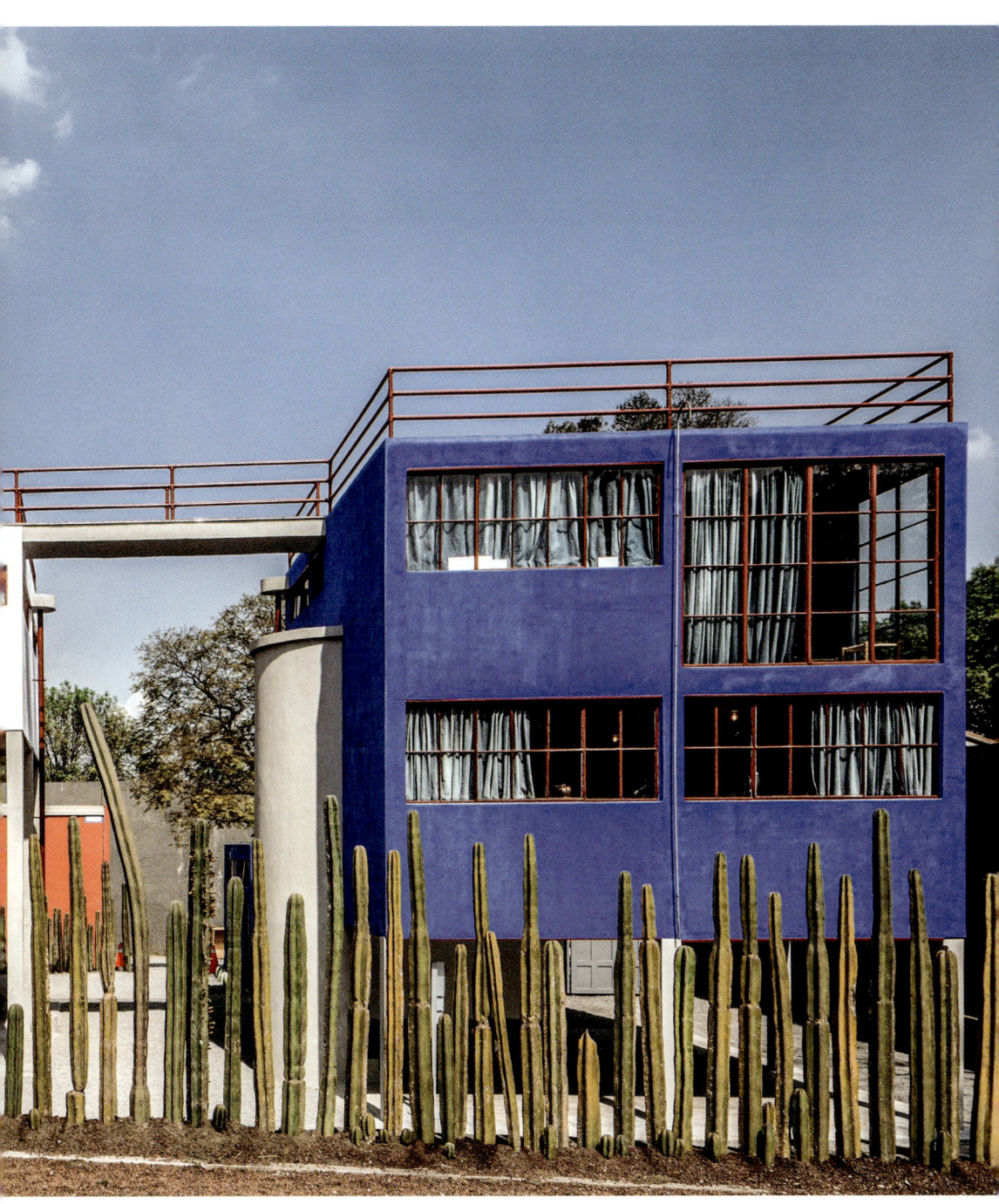

VIII.
The Casa Azul

"*Frida Kahlo is the work, the color, and the
hammer, she is the butterfly that stops still in a
moment and is then multiplied and harmonized
with her own human condition. [...] She is the
events that occur every day amidst birds and
flowers, succulents, calla lilies, and Mexican
marigolds, she is the humidity of a garden and
the smell from a hot griddle.*"

— IGNACIO AGUIRRE, 1986

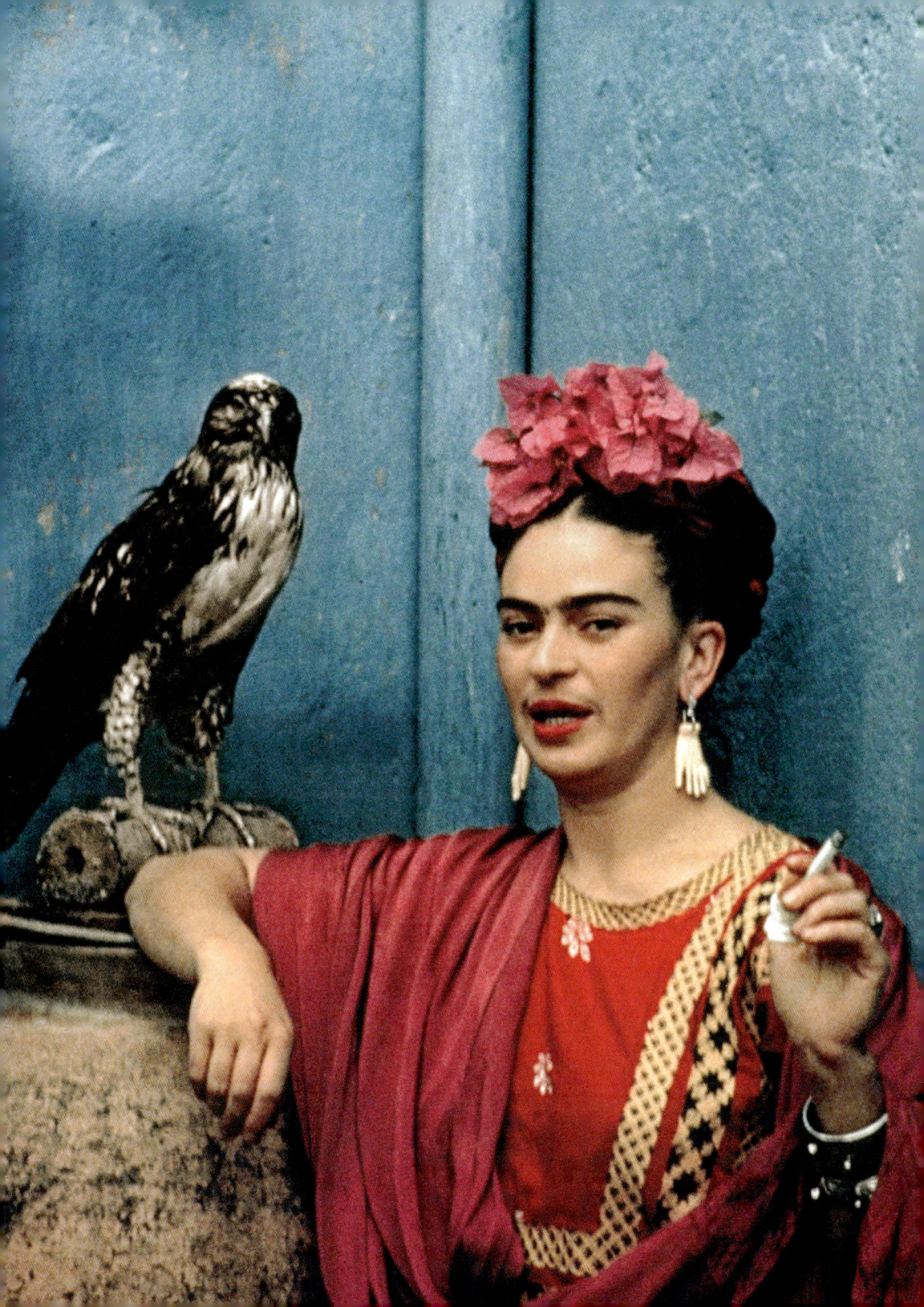

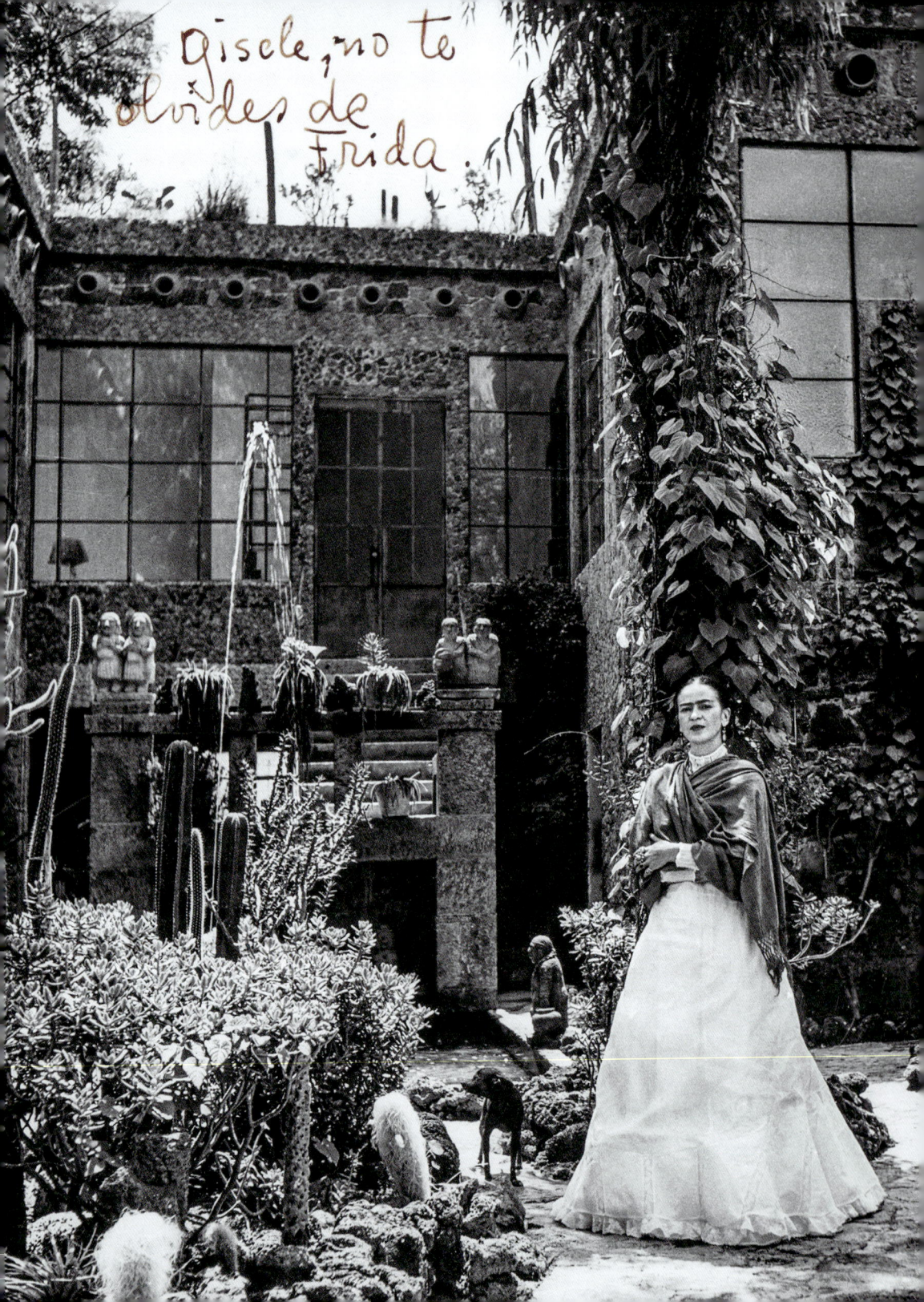

Gisele, no te olvides de Frida.

Kahlo's Casa Azul

The Casa Azul, or Blue House, which today serves as the Museo Frida Kahlo, is located in Coyoacán, formerly a town to the south of Mexico City. It was built in the Del Carmen neighborhood, where Kahlo's father had bought a plot of land on the corner of Londres and Allende streets. The house is a typical example of Mexican vernacular architecture, with high ceilings and a courtyard with an orange tree in the middle, surrounded by flowers to form a small garden; all the doors in the house opened on to this courtyard, filling the rooms with light. Guillermo Kahlo settled here with Matilde Calderón, whom he had married shortly after his previous wife had died. Magdalena Carmen Frieda was born in this house on July 6, 1907, the third of four daughters from this marriage, and the most spirited of the girls.

Kahlo's childhood in Coyoacán was spent amid trees that were more than a hundred years old and which grew alongside the plentiful waters of the Churubusco and Magdalena rivers. In this bucolic setting, filled with flowers and orange, quince, and grapefruit trees, she also lived with various different animals from the surrounding countryside that wandered freely through the quiet streets, far removed from the bustling city life of the capital. She explored the area in the company of her father when the two of them went for walks from Coyoacán to Tlalpan Park.

In 1929, Kahlo and Rivera were married, and for a very brief time they lived in the family home in Coyoacán before moving to a large house in the city center. Even so, photographs taken by Guillermo Kahlo in 1930 show that Rivera still had a studio in the largest room of the Kahlo family home, despite the fact that he and Kahlo had by that time moved to California.

Page 443
Nickolas Muray, **Kahlo with her tame falcon** (detail), Coyoacán, 1939
Chromogenic print, 36 x 24 cm (14⅛ x 9½ in.)
Nickolas Muray Photo Archives

Gisèle Freund, **Frida in the garden of the annex of the Casa Azul**, 1951
With written dedication: Gisele, no te olvides de Frida (Gisele, don't forget Frida)

After they had returned from the United States they moved into one of the new functionalist houses designed by the architect Juan O'Gorman in Altavista, in San Ángel, very near to Coyoacán. In 1935, Kahlo left Rivera when she found out that he had been unfaithful to her with Cristina, her own sister; she then moved into an apartment she bought on Avenida de los Insurgentes, in Mexico City. Once Kahlo had eventually forgiven Rivera she moved back into the house in Altavista, but set up her own studio in the family home in Coyoacán, where she was surrounded by memories of all her loved ones. In 1936, President Cárdenas granted political asylum to Leon Trotsky, and Kahlo and Rivera invited the former revolutionary leader to stay in the house in Coyoacán, making a number of modifications to increase its security. This included Rivera buying the adjoining lot and having a high wall built around the perimeter of the property, together with a guardhouse to control access.

When Rivera later asked for a divorce from Kahlo in 1939, she returned to her parents' house. It had fallen into a state of disrepair after Guillermo had gone to live with his daughter Matilde following the death of Kahlo's mother some years previously. Kahlo lived there during the year of her separation from Rivera, and it was at this time that she began to transform it into the Casa Azul. Color photographs taken by Nickolas Muray show her posing in 1939 in front of vivid indigo walls.

When she and Rivera remarried in 1940, they agreed that they would live in separate houses, and it was then that Kahlo settled permanently into the house in Coyoacán. Over the next 14 years, she devoted herself to converting what had been her parental home into a space that would reflect all her own, personal aspirations, and to make it into a showcase for a fantastical world filled with stories and emotional meaning. Some of Kahlo's most important works were hung on the walls of this house, along with the collection of Mexican painting that she and Rivera had amassed, including 19th-century portraits, ex-votos, religious paintings, and Mexican still lifes. These works shared the space with a carefully chosen collection of traditional Mexican craft items and toys, which Kahlo valued as great treasures and arranged on shelves and in antique display cases. There were also pre-Hispanic objects that Rivera had collected, as well as a dollhouse that Kahlo filled with miniature toy furniture and odd little antiques bought in markets in Mexico and Paris. Kahlo was also fond of the glazed pottery made in Tlaquepaque and Michoacán, as well as ceramics from Tonalá and pressed-glass *pulque* glasses. Judas figures made of papier mâché stood at various points throughout the house, and there were also bits of chinoiserie brought back from San Francisco and New York, as she dreamed of one day

Gisèle Freund, **Fountain and pool in the garden
of the annex of the Casa Azul**, 1951

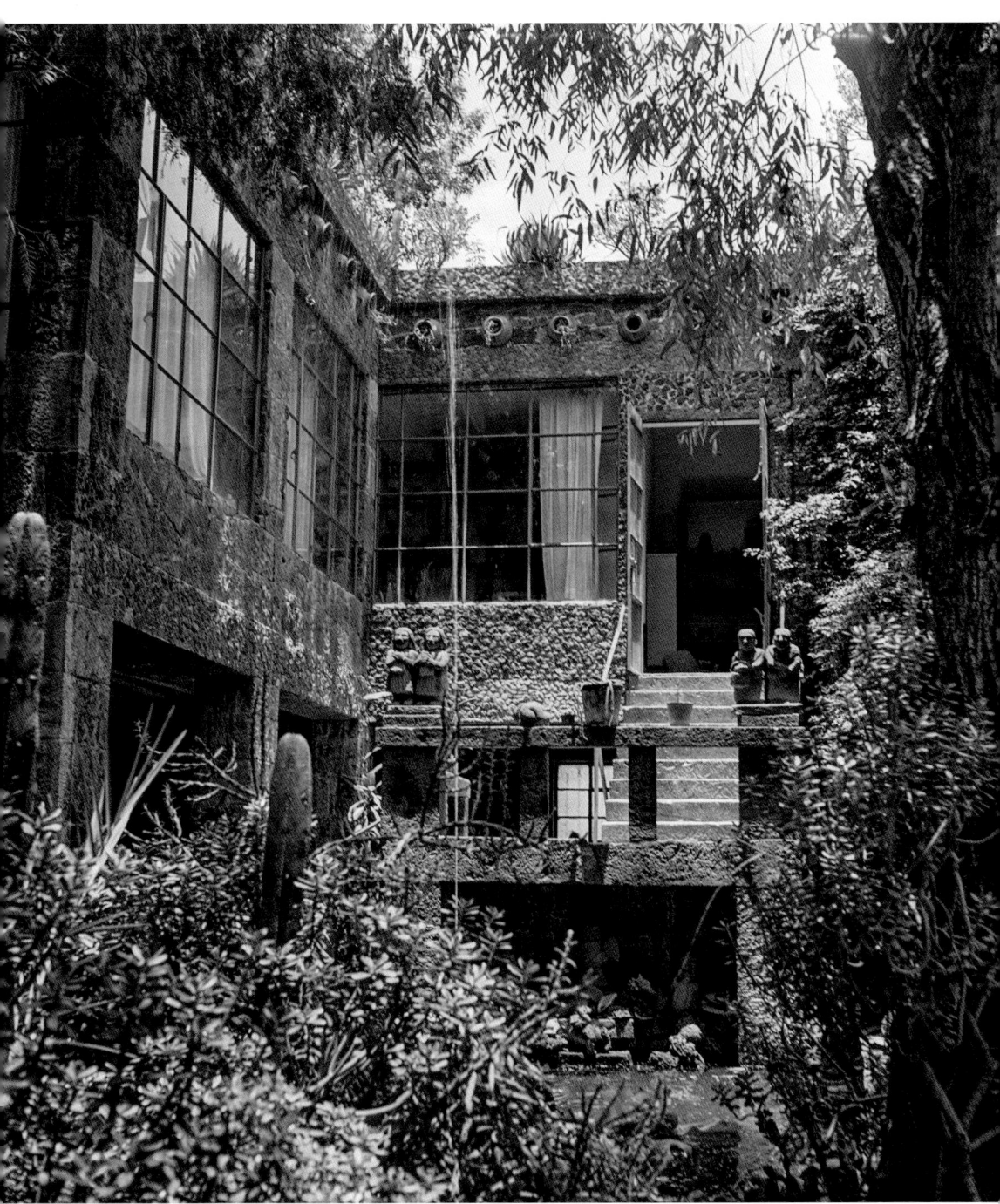

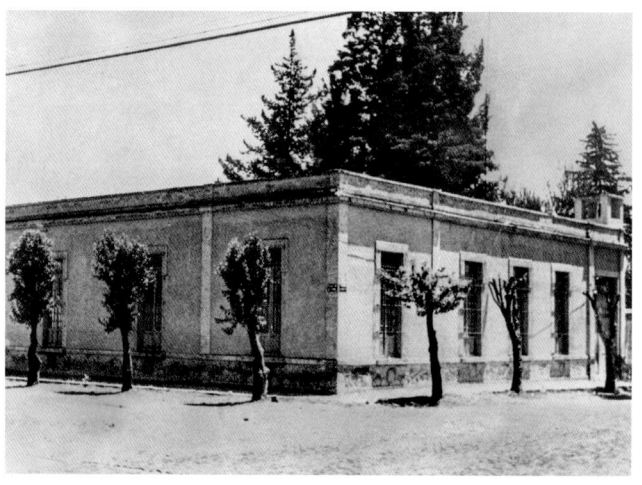

visiting some imaginary, distant, and nameless country in the Far East.

The Casa Azul became a magnet for artists, intellectuals, and famous people, and Kahlo and Rivera welcomed several visitors from abroad who were interested in Mexican art, both wealthy patrons and collectors who included movie stars and film producers. In this way, the Casa Azul became a meeting place for the international jet set of the time. Kahlo's world, however, took in not only the interior of the house but also extended into the garden, where she and Rivera installed several pre-Columbian stone idols and sculptures by Mardonio Magaña. Kahlo loved animals, and kept cats as well as pre-Hispanic xoloitzcuintli dogs, together with parrots, spider monkeys, ducks, chickens, turtles, and even a pond full of fish. She provided food to attract hummingbirds, and kept a fawn called Granizo in her garden, which appeared in more than one of her paintings. Meanwhile, the Casa Azul itself underwent a series of adjustments and modifications. In 1946, Rivera commissioned O'Gorman to design an annex to the building so that Kahlo would have a large and well-lit studio that looked out on to the garden. Its functionalist appearance was covered with pieces of volcanic rock and subtle mosaics of stone surfaces painted by Rivera. In this same year, however, Kahlo had to undergo a difficult operation in New York, and from 1950 her health began to decline, resulting in a prolonged period of further operations and treatments accompanied by extreme physical pain, which in turn affected the splendor and future of the Casa Azul.

When Kahlo died in 1954, Rivera turned to converting the Casa Azul into a museum in her memory, and established a trust with the Banco de México to safeguard the collection and ensure its continued existence. He entrusted the poet Carlos Pellicer with running the museum, and four years later it was opened to the public.

The Kahlo family house, *c.* 1937

Guillermo Zamora, **Diego Rivera and Frida Kahlo in the annex of the Casa Azul**, 1950

Thousands of people from all around the world visit the Casa Azul every year, each of them coming in search of Frida Kahlo. They hope to find some part of her still in the books, photographs, and documents that have been saved, or else in the dresses and jewelry she wore or in the paintings, objects, and furniture that have been preserved. But all of this personal paraphernalia may perhaps be seen in the same way as the remains of a shipwreck, in other words as the absence of a presence that lit up the house in its day. Kahlo would, I am certain, be very pleased to know that her paintings have captured the interest of so many people, but may well have been surprised to see that this extended to the details of her private world. There can be no question, however, that in the Casa Azul, the house that was home to her parents and her family, Frida Kahlo was very happy.

A letter to Frida Kahlo, who lives in the heart of all Mexicans

"So, my child, yesterday I finished fixing up your house, let's see now if you're going to argue with me about everything I've done. In the living room, which you used as a studio all those years ago and where you painted so many wonderful things, I've arranged it with just your own paintings. Do you remember the stack of paintings you sold to

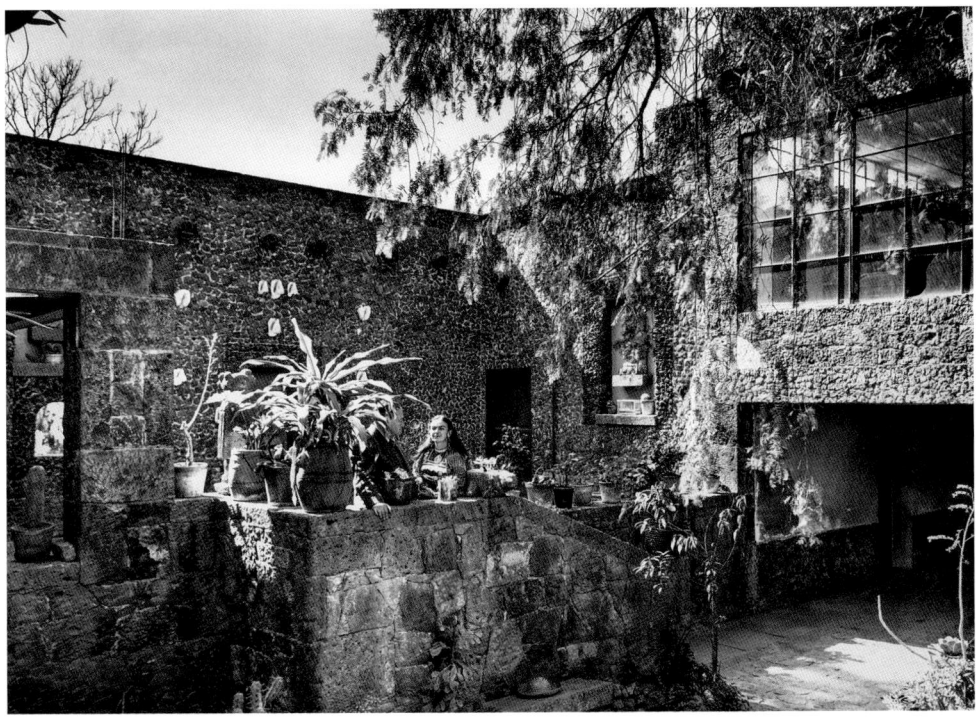

that engineer Morillo Safa? Well, Lolita Olmedo bought them from his widow and then brought them over for me to hang in the living room. How do you like her? What do you think of Lola? She's terrific, isn't she?! I also put up some things from when you were first starting to paint, two portraits, the one of your friend Alicia Galant and the one of that guy who was your boyfriend, both of them absolutely stunning. I really wanted to steal *The Broken Column* for myself, but since everything's been catalogued before it was given to me there was no chance. A kiss for every nail you painted in that picture. Look, there's a whole bunch of them.

But wow, girl, that self-portrait of yours with the monkey and the dog leaves me almost lost for words. What a way to catch the colors! Now that is real painting, that and one or two poems, of course. The portrait of Morillo Safa's mother is one of the most important pieces of Mexican painting. What a painting that is, and what depth it has! Honestly you have a gift to be able to paint things as extraordinary as those!

You'll notice I put your last picture of watermelons next to that poor young woman with all the small nips. That one's a horrible image, you made a real human sacrifice there. The poor watermelons can't stop talking about all the blood.

Now, in the room where you were born I hung the portraits of your family you painted, and I also put out the Tehuana costume you like so much, along with your jewelry and everything. I put your book there too, your wonderful book, although while I was looking through it I did see a sentence you'd written I wish I'd never seen coming from you. It pained my soul. You remember the next three rooms, the ones with the partition and the hideous bathtub, and the other one full of ex-votos? Well, I got rid of the bath and put the ex-votos in the stairwell, I hope you don't mind but they look wonderful there. Then in those three rooms I hung everything there was by the maestro Diego, paintings and drawings from right through his career. Don't you think that's right, if you two spent 25 years here, including the trips abroad? Actually, I was going to give him two rooms, but Lola, who adores your husband, soon persuaded me to add another. Handling Diego's work made me realize once again what a titan he is. There's that drawing for a mural for the Ministry of Education, I almost got it, but guess what? No chance, that one's been catalogued too. Don't tell anyone, but Lola and Teresa Proenza, who have helped me out so much with their smiles and all the rest, have been keeping an eye on these innocent hands of mine. What right do they have? Things disappear, but that doesn't have to mean they've been stolen. It's too bad you can't do the same with people! The ones that make problems,

Guillermo Zamora, **Ceiling with decorative mosaic** (created by Diego Rivera, based on a drawing by Frida Kahlo), in the annex of the Casa Azul, designed by Juan O'Gorman, 1950

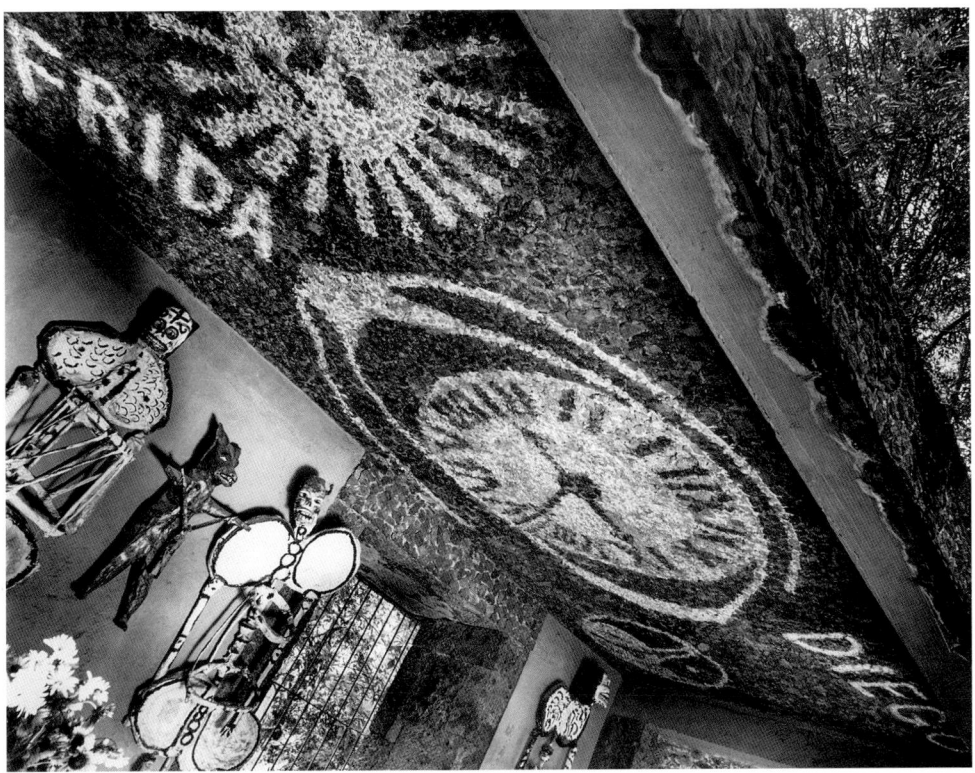

but there's really no way. I wanted to tell you I've put some of the archaeological things in Diego's third room. There's a small display case in there, fixed to the wall, that I filled with some real treasures from Tlatilco and the odd thing from Colima and Chupícuaro. Now, I didn't want to say it, but the truth is it worked out really well. However, I'm still hopeful I can make the display case look even better. I'll tell you how another time. As for your kitchen, it's left exactly as it was. I wonder if you'll get mad because I put a few ex-votos up, but frankly it made me sad to keep them in the house. You've got some marvelous ones, and one day maybe you'll give me some, even if it's only five or six.

The dining room is almost as you left it. All that's changed is there's five of your paintings now, they look great. Lola added some very nice stars from Taxco. Tell Diego I didn't touch his room, and that we laid out his hat, denim overalls, and jacket. Please also tell him, so I don't get into trouble, that I didn't throw out the hideous little pictures he had there. On the table where he did all his writing I left some paper in case he needs it. Will he still be wanting the walking stick from Apizaco? So, we left the floors from the old house the same color as they were before. I hope you won't scold me too much. Oh and I

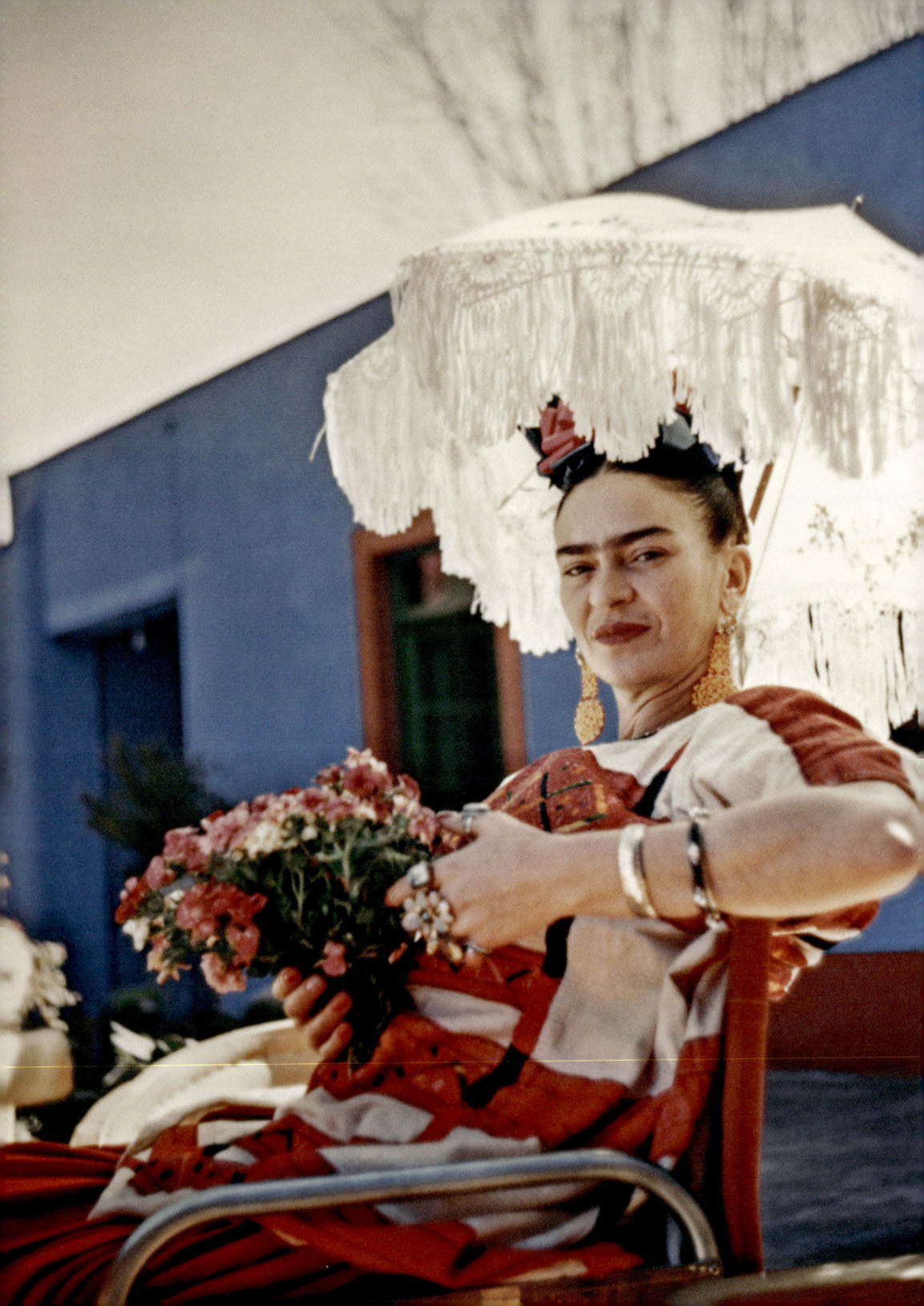

should have said that the best archaeological gifts Diego gave you are in a beautiful glass case the architect Pagelson had specially made. He and Juan O'Gorman have also helped, both of them pointing out the big mistakes I made while arranging your house. You know, when I was putting your archaeological treasures in the case, Lola, Teresa, and Elena Vázquez Gómez didn't leave me on my own for a moment. They even brought in a childhood friend of yours who's now a well-known archaeologist on the pretext of helping me, but he didn't take his eyes off me for a second. The display case looks magnificent. All the same, I'm not kidding when I say people don't understand me. I don't have any friends, and even the directors of the Museo Nacional don't understand my ways. However, one day I'll take you around the museum in Tabasco and then you'll see… why I'm telling you. Well, there's no justification for what they say about me. One incident in Palenque and it all comes back to that. But I can't say any more because there are a lot of people involved and discussion is prohibited. Pita Amor just phoned me to say she'll meet me at your house tonight. You'll be pleased to know I hung your little painting of Dr. Velasco in your studio and also five drawings of that marvelous man, along with some small Clauselles, a print by Orozco dedicated to Diego, and two academic studies by a fellow student of Diego's. I tidied up your bookshelves and put the clothes you're not going to be needing neatly in one corner. Your easel, palette, brushes, and everything are just as you left them. And also your portrait, that beautiful portrait our dearest Roberto Montenegro painted of you and that was sent through me as a present from Dr. Carrillo Gil, such a wonderful artist and his wife is very fond of you. Some of your loveliest pre-Hispanic necklaces I arranged in a little cabinet.

In the hall, where the bed is where you were resting for a few days before you left, everything is as it was. A week before you went, do you remember? I was with you, sitting in a chair beside you, talking and reading you those sonnets I wrote for you, you liked them a lot and I like them for that reason, because you like them so much. The nurse gave you an injection. It was about 10 o'clock. You were just starting to fall asleep when you beckoned me to come closer. I kissed you and then held your right hand. Do you remember? Then I switched off the light. You fell asleep and I stayed there a while, watching you while you were dreaming. Outside, the sky, swept and watered, welcomed me into its mystery, as was natural. You looked exhausted. I shan't deny I cried in the street as I went to find the bus to go home. Now that you have finally found eternal health, I would like to say, or rather say again, say again that… well… you already know. You, like a trampled garden

Florence Arquin, **Portrait of Frida in the courtyard of the Casa Azul**, January 1948
Photographic print, 19 x 14 cm (7½ x 5½ in.). Washington, D.C., Smithsonian Institution,
Archives of American Art, Florence Arquin Papers, 1923–1985

on a night with no sky. You, like a window lashed by the storm; you, like a handkerchief dropped in a pool of blood; you, like a butterfly full of tears; like a day shattered in haste; like a teardrop in a sea of tears; an araucaria singing in its triumph; a ray of light on anyone's path.

Frida, Diego's christening gown is still in your bedroom, in a glass case, and in another one are some of your toys and his from when you were kids. I left the wonderful sleeping dog where you always had it. The men from the Banco de México have been very good. There's also the lawyer Carrillo Flores, someone we hold in the highest regard. And two security guards from the bank, Tomás and Rogerio, have also helped. Chucho, the great Chucho, and Lola have worked with me some nights through until daybreak. Dear Frida, are you going to like what we've done with your house? Well, you dearly beloved thing who are one of a kind, we shall certainly be seeing each other again. Of course, there's still something missing in your house, but it will for ever be in my heart and that thing is you. See you soon, God willing. Oh yes, your little puppet theater, with the Dance of Death, is next to the stairs. Lola and Teresa and Chucho send their love."

Carlos Pellicer, Las Lomas, July 30, 1958

After Kahlo's death, Rivera concentrated on converting the Casa Azul, where Kahlo had been born and had lived with her parents when she was young, into a public museum to keep her artistic legacy alive. He entrusted the responsibility of running the museum to Carlos Pellicer (1897–1977), a noted Mexican poet from the state of Tabasco and a personal friend of Kahlo's. Pellicer organized the museum in such a way that Kahlo's paintings and drawings were integrated with the collection of paintings, pre-Columbian art, and folk art that she and Rivera had collected over the years, together with a significant group of paintings by Rivera that had been part of Kahlo's personal collection. The museum opened in 1958. This letter written by Pellicer in tribute to Kahlo following her death only resurfaced many years later and was published by the Universidad Juárez Autónoma de Tabasco in 1985 in the university's magazine Revista de la Universidad de México.

Mario Monteforte Toledo, **"Tribute to Frida Kahlo"** in the *Mexico in Culture*
supplement of the newspaper *Novedades*, no. 123, June 10, 1951
Photographs by Gisèle Freund

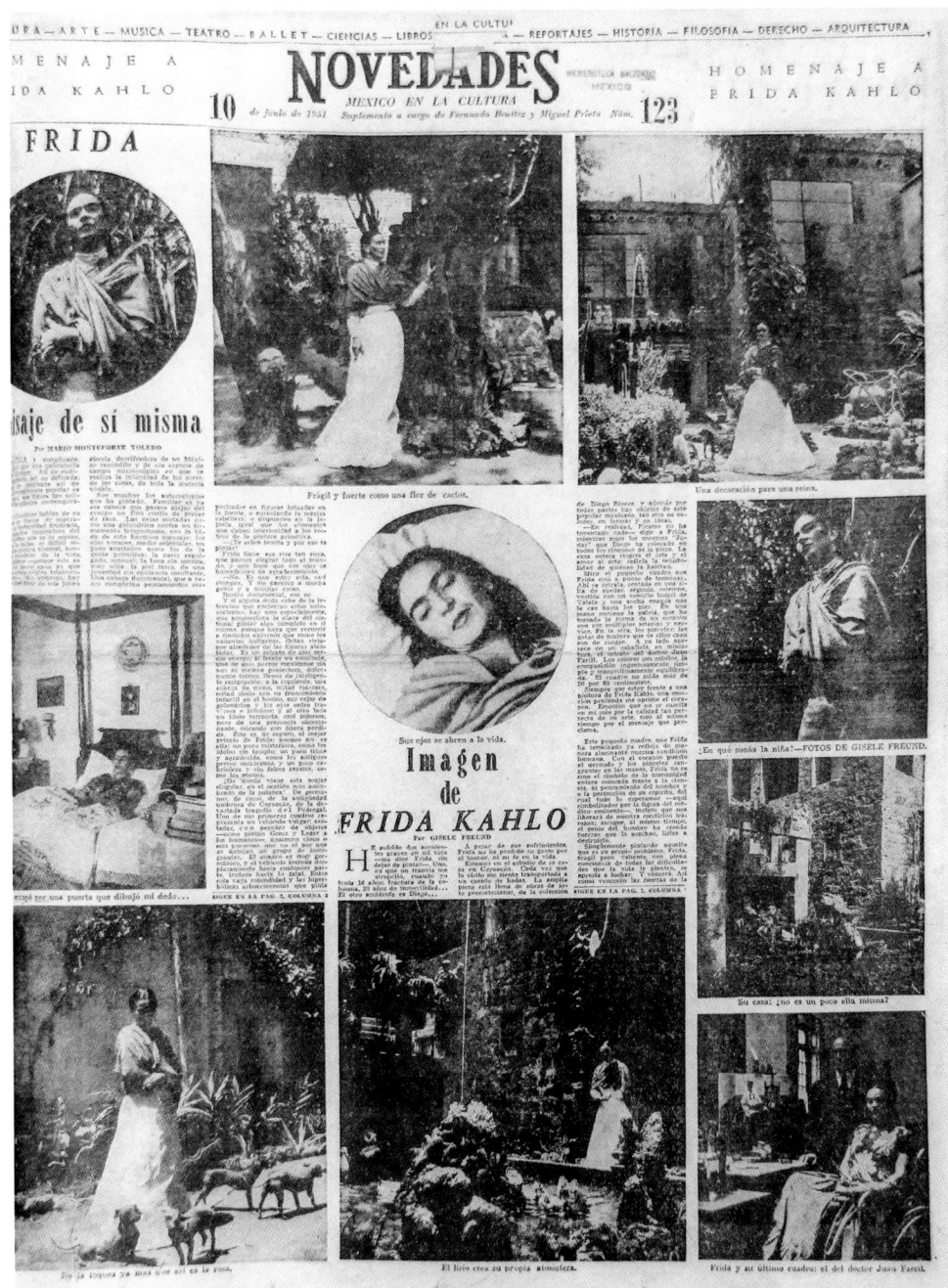

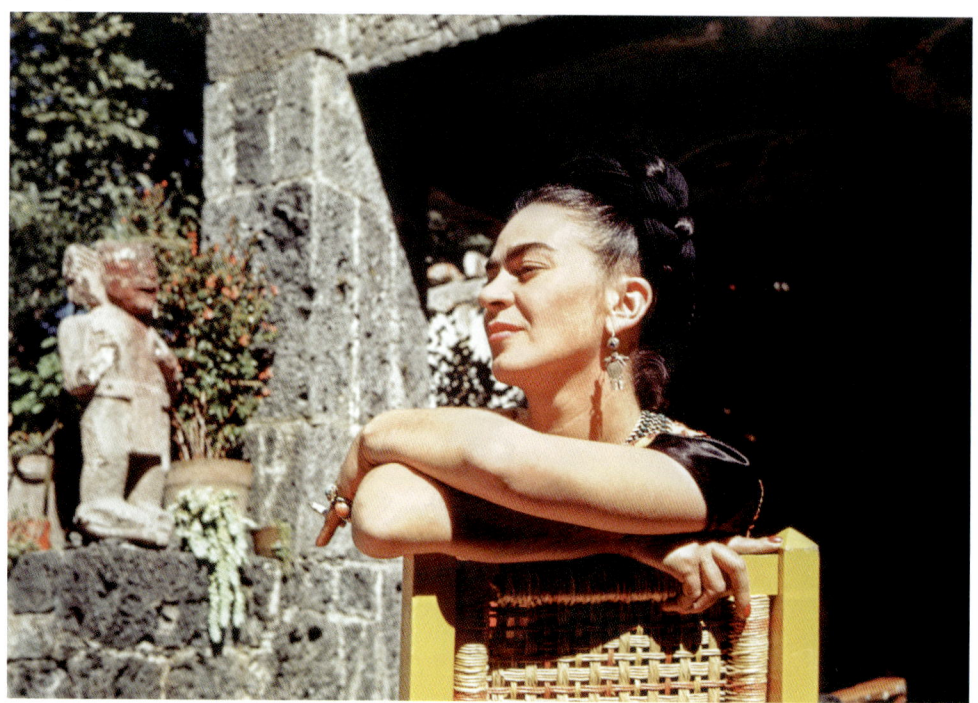

Florence Arquin, **Frida at the annex of the Casa Azul**, January 24, 1948
Cibachrome, 27.9 x 35.5 cm (11 x 14 in.)
New York, collection of Spencer Throckmorton

Gisèle Freund, **Frida beside a Pre-Hispanic sculpture
in the garden of the Casa Azul** (detail), 1951

Pages 458/459
Nickolas Muray, **Frida with Olmec figurine in the garden
of the Casa Azul**, Coyoacán, 1939
Carbon pigment print, 27.3 x 40 cm (10¾ x 15¾ in.)
New York, collection of Spencer Throckmorton/Nickolas Muray Photo Archives

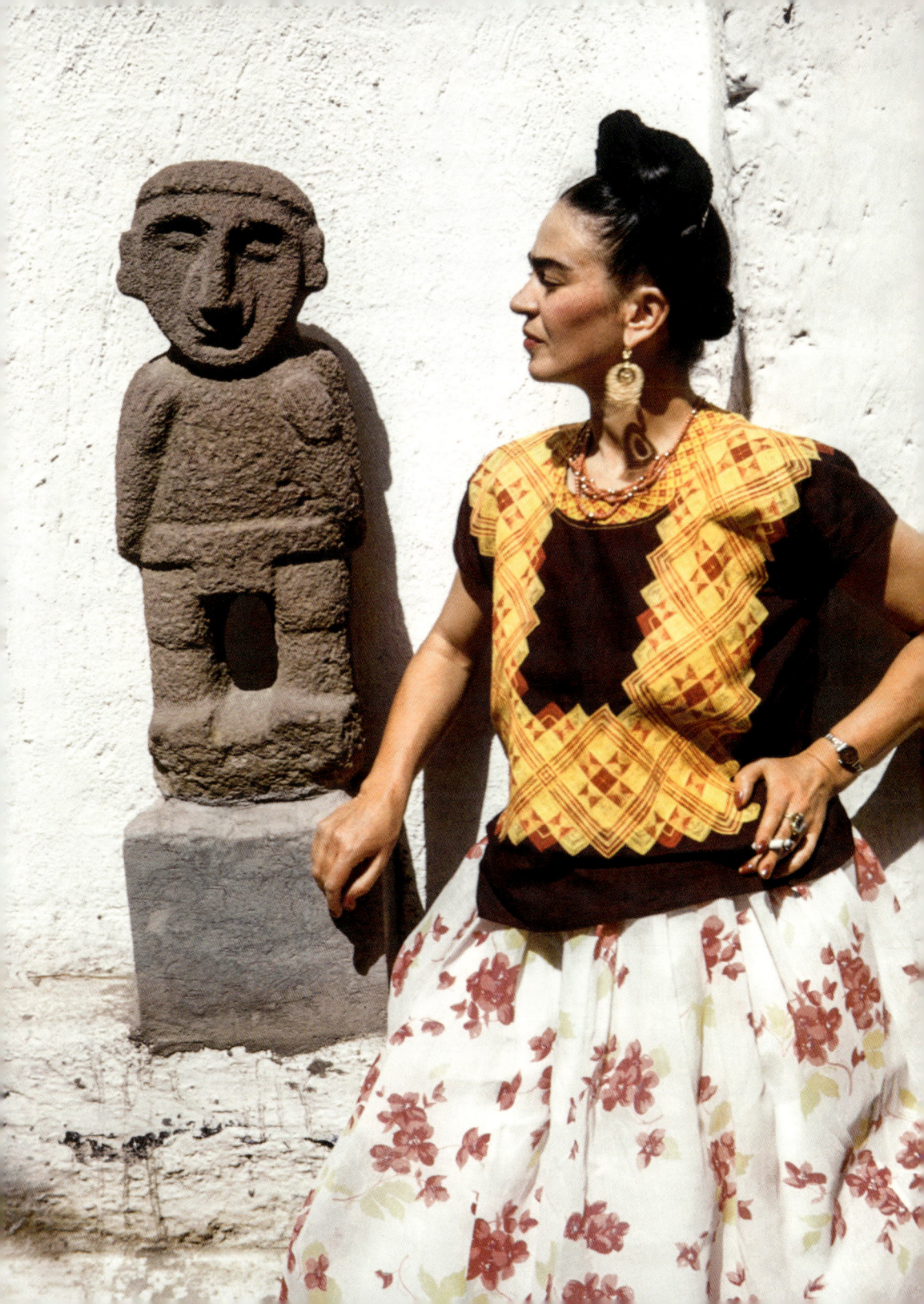

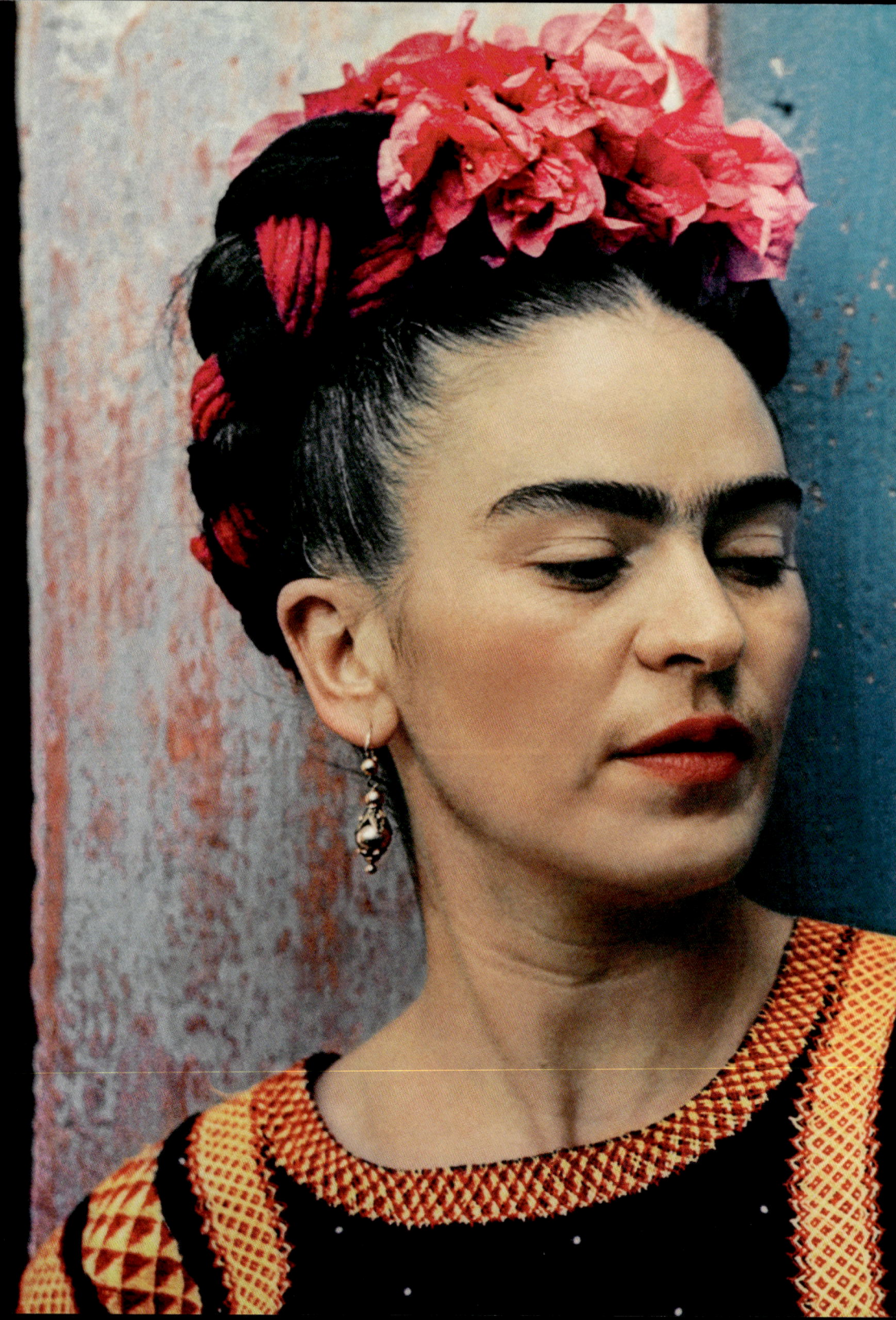

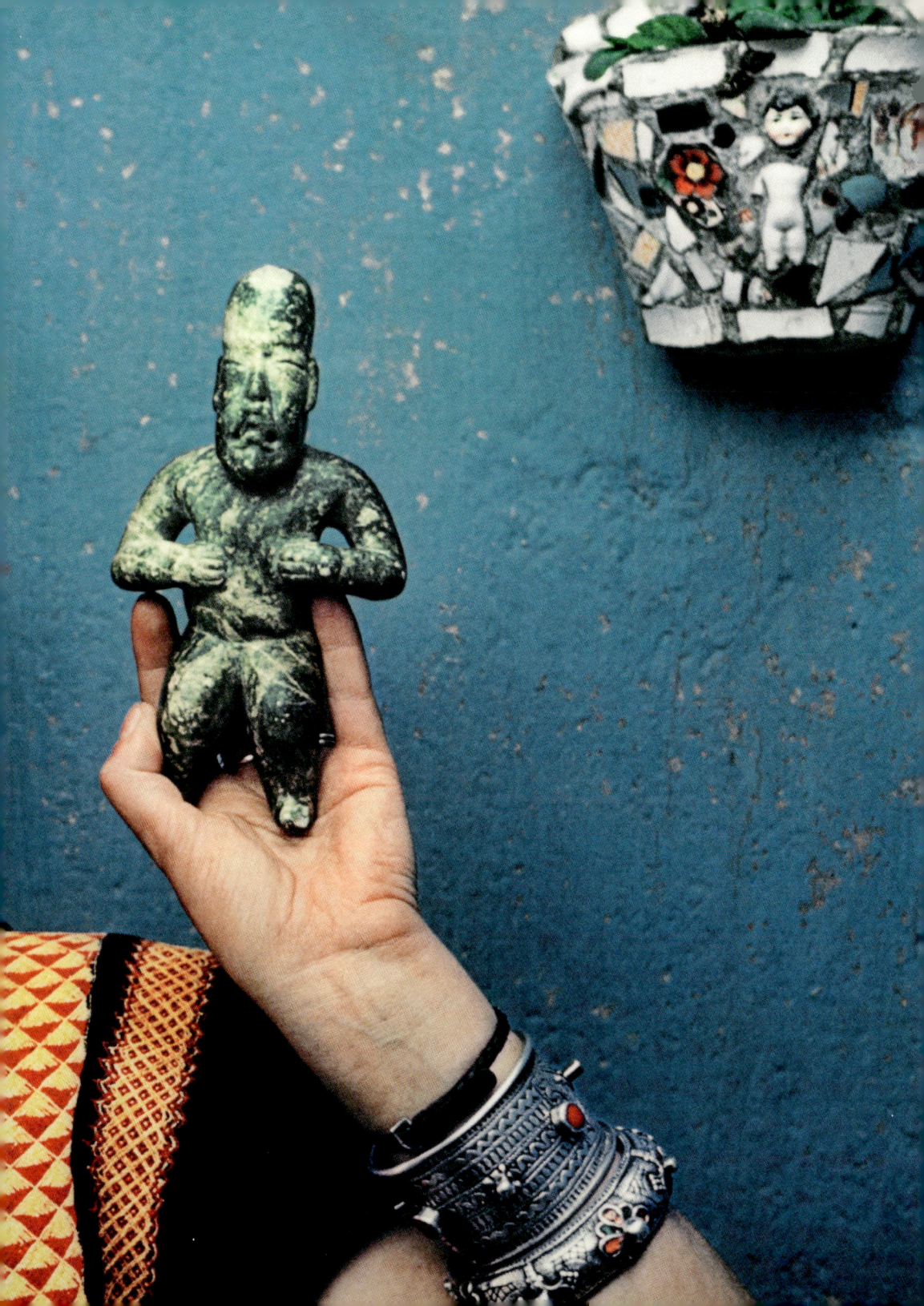

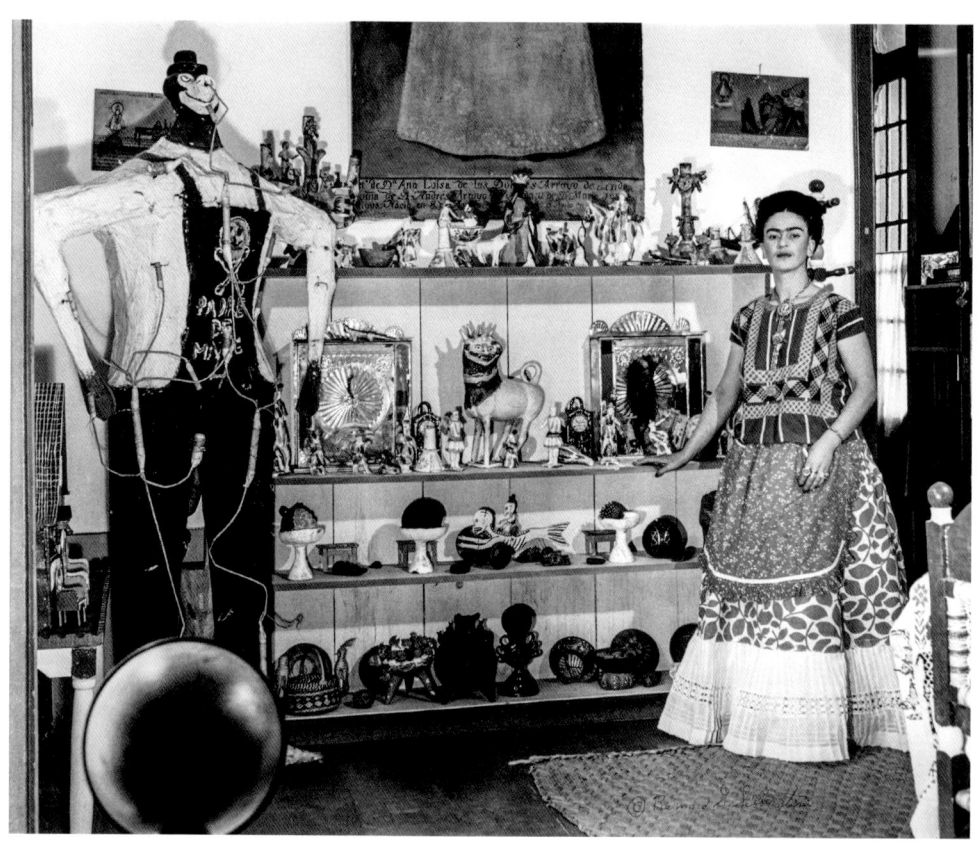

Bernard G. Silberstein, **Frida Kahlo with her collection of Mexican folk art and a large papier-mâché Judas figure in the living room of the Casa Azul**, *c.* 1940
Gelatin silver print, 35.6 x 43.2 cm (14 x 17 in.)
New York, collection of Spencer Throckmorton

Guillermo Kahlo, **Diego and Frida with a large traditional Judas papier mâché figure**, 1931

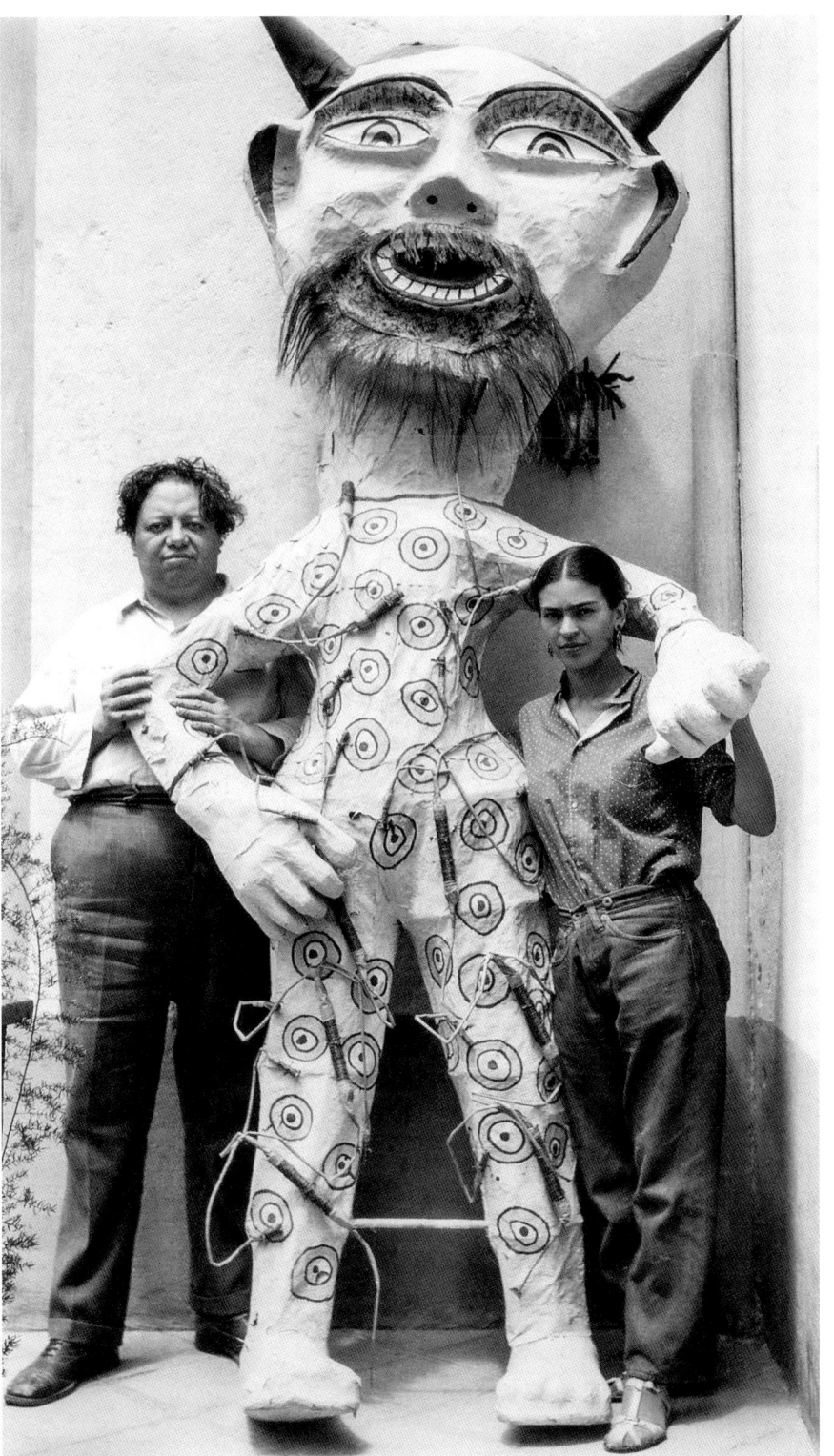

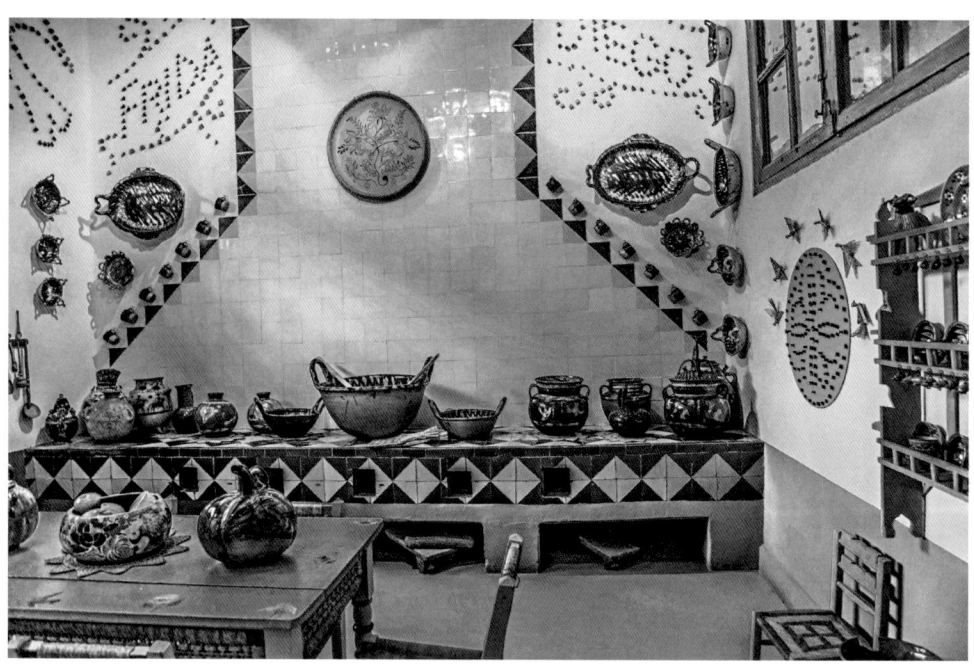

**Re-creation of the kitchen of the Casa Azul within
the present Museo Frida Kahlo**, Coyoacán, 2014

Gisèle Freund, **Frida and Diego's collection
of ex-votos in the Casa Azul**, 1951

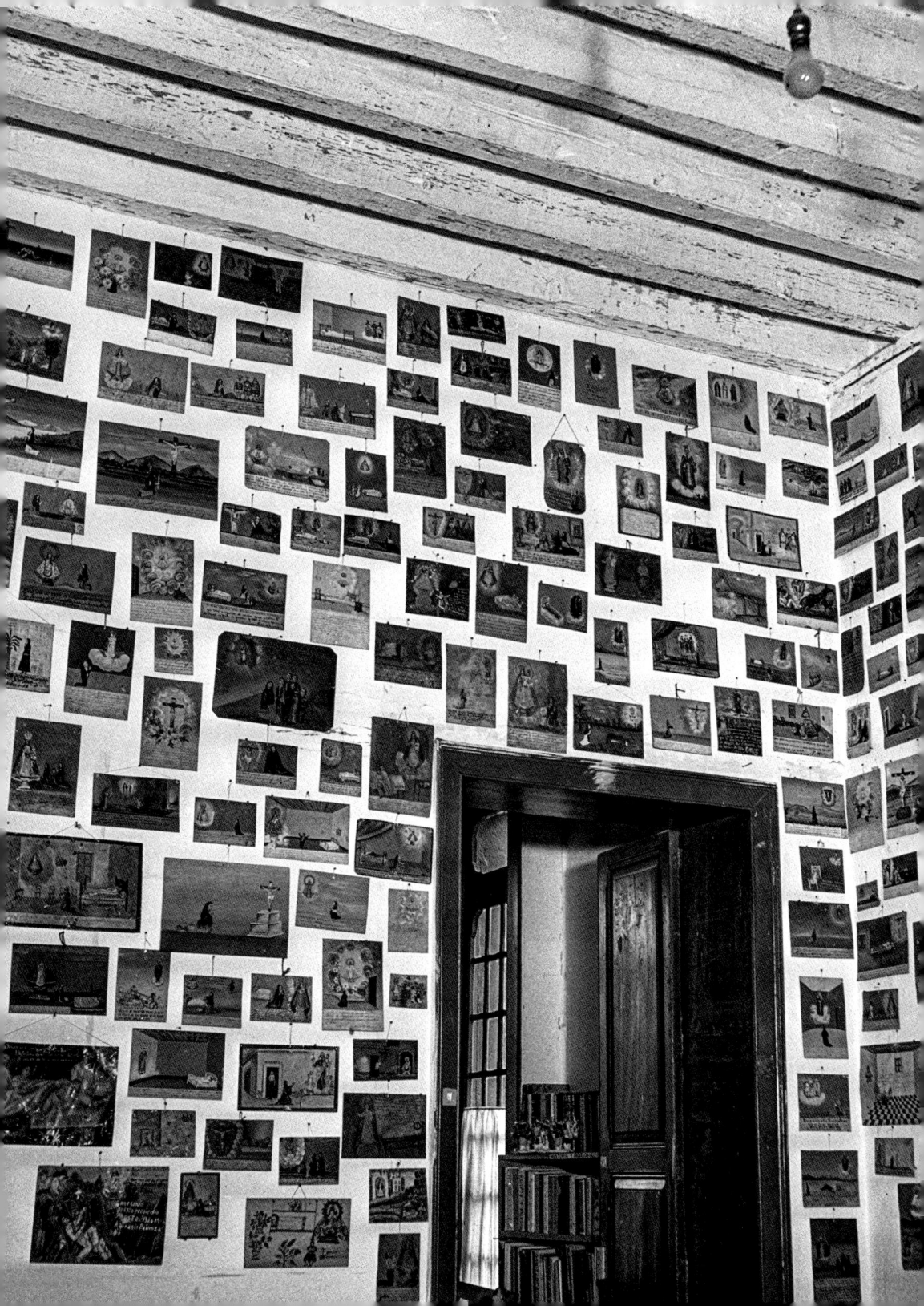

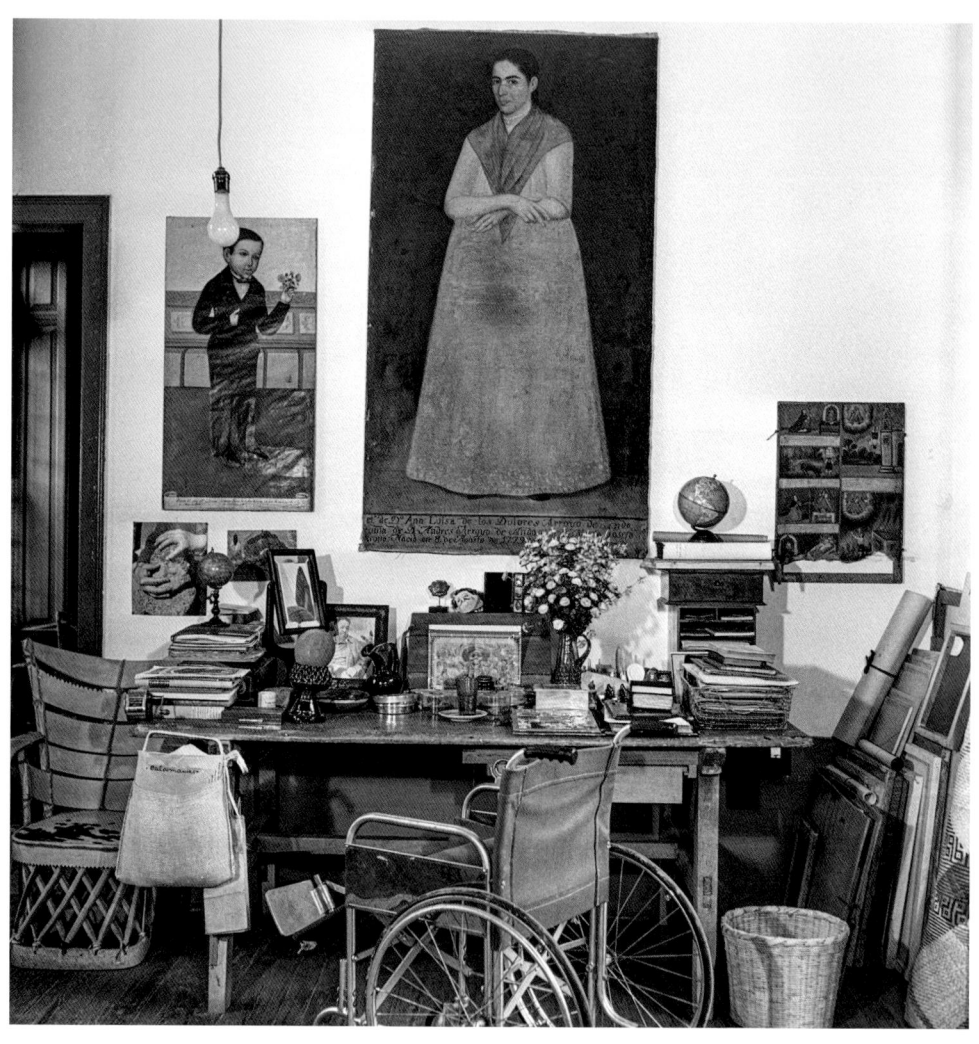

Gisèle Freund, **Frida's desk in the Casa Azul**, 1951

Gisèle Freund, **Frida in her bedroom in the Casa Azul**, 1951

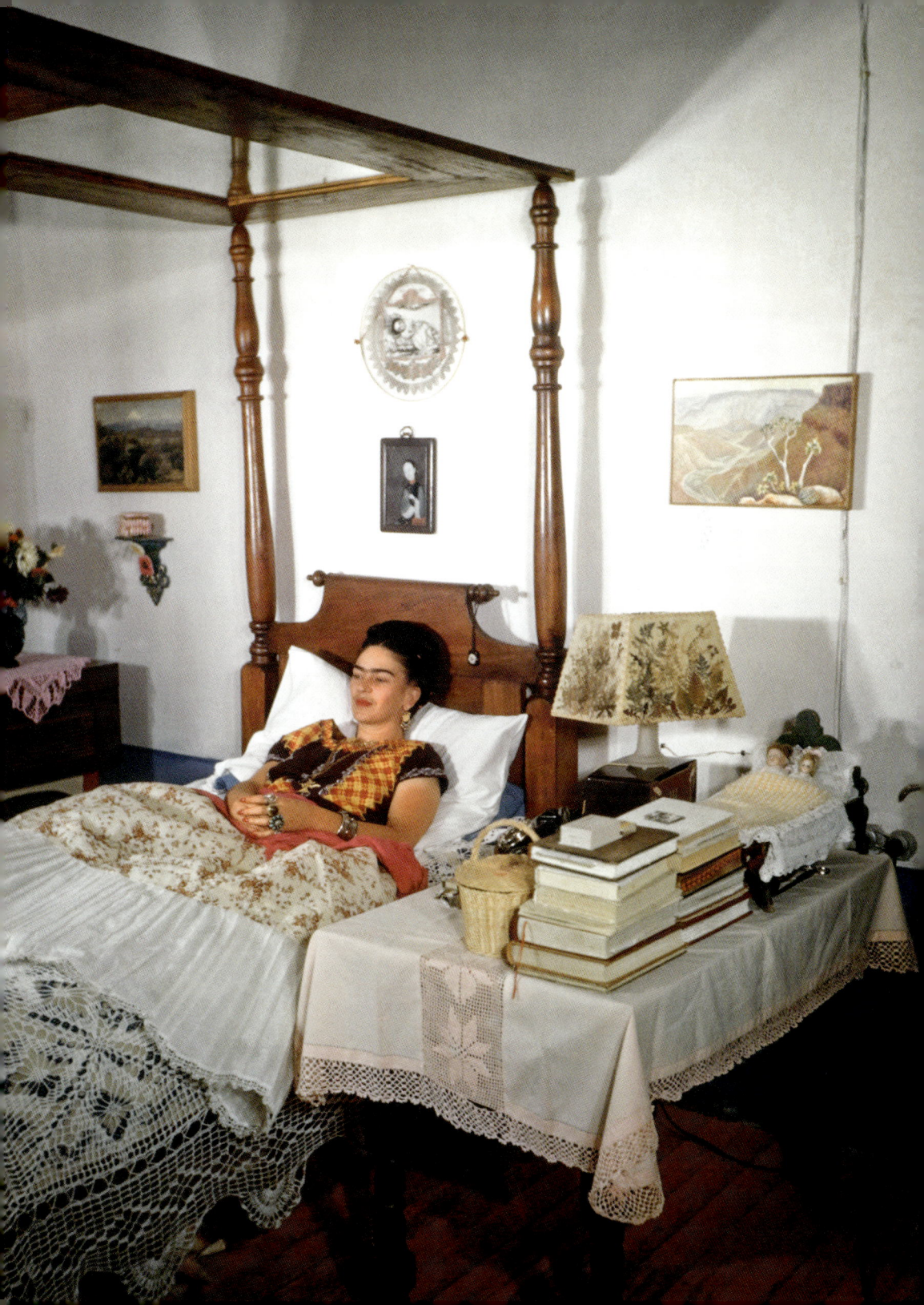

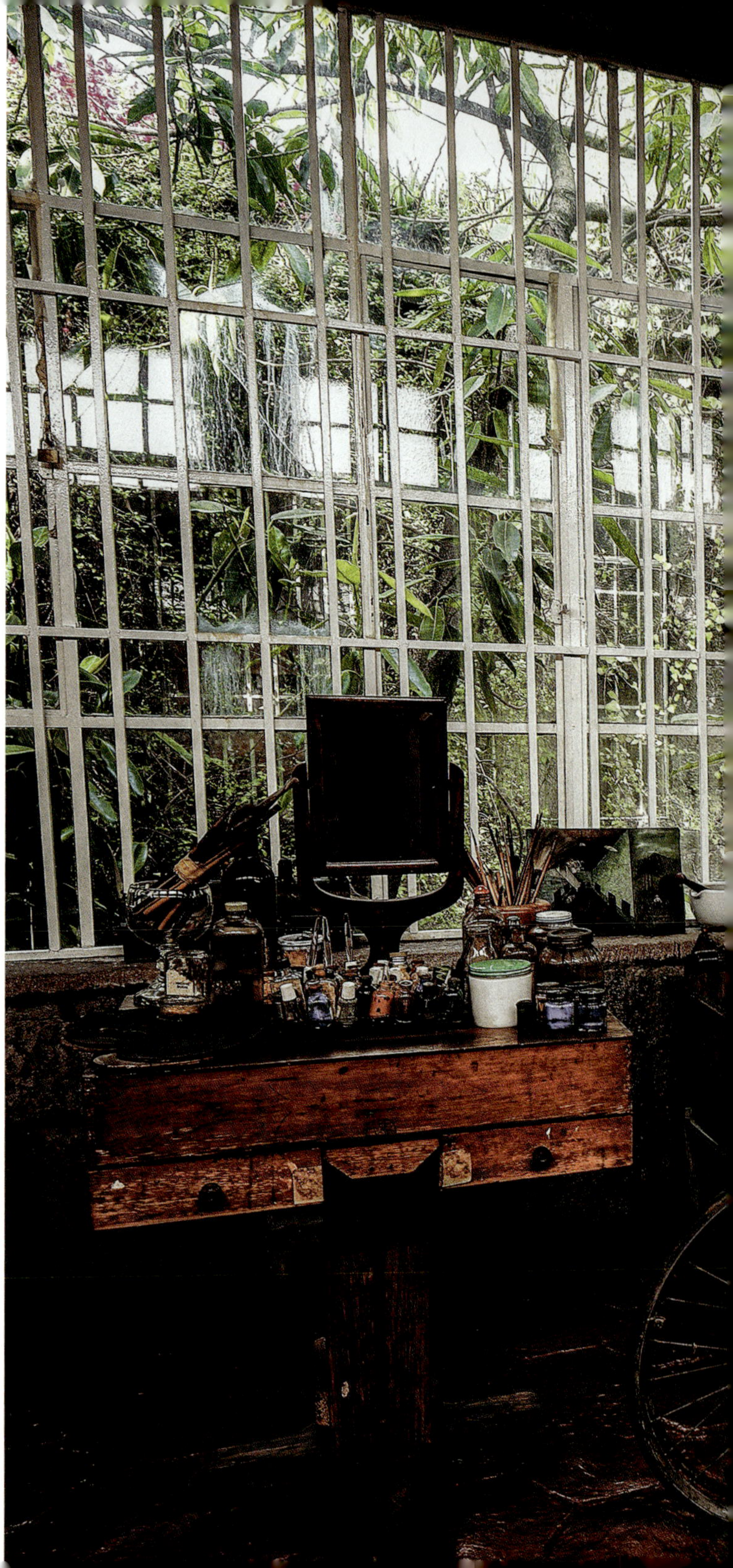

D. Agostini/G. Dagli Orti,
**Frida Kahlo's studio in
the Museo Frida Kahlo**
(detail), Coyoacán, 2016

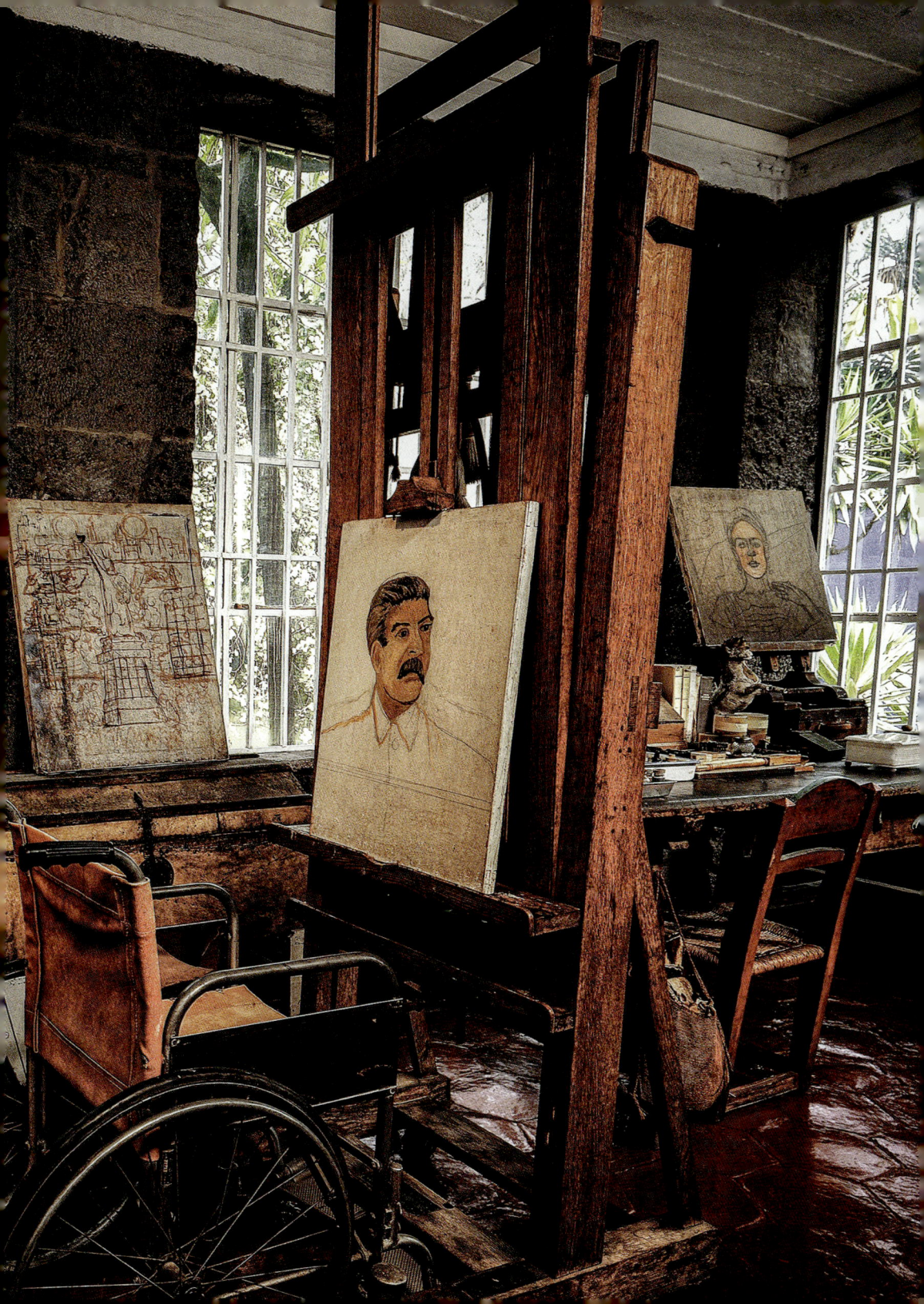

Notes

I. *Why do you study so much? What secrets are you looking for?* The years of learning

1 Mexico City 1992.
2 Prignitz-Poda/Grimberg/ Kettenmann 1988; Herrera 1991.
3 Ipiña 2013.
4 Tibol 2005, p. 13.
5 Tibol 1953.
6 Ipiña 2013.
7 Del Conde 2015, pp. 231–238.
8 Tibol 2007, pp. 25–26.
9 Ipiña 2013.
10 Jaimes 2016.
11 Lozano 2007, pp. 22–23.
12 Casanova 2014, pp. 17–18.
13 Gómez Arias 1977.
14 González Ramírez 1954, p. 14.
15 Frida Kahlo. Sus Fotos 2010, pp. 380–385.
16 Rodríguez 1955.
17 Pinedo Kahlo 2004, p. 127.
18 Cordero 1994, pp. 637–645.
19 Del Conde 2004.
20 Dromundo 1956, p. 187; Gómez Arias 1977.
21 Mexico City 2014, p. 131.
22 Many thanks to Mara Romero and Mara de Anda for showing me these unpublished childhood drawings.
23 Zamora 1987, p. 14. Many thanks also to the art historian Carla Eguiarte for her research which led to Kahlo's educational record being located in the archives of the Universidad Nacional Autónoma de México.
24 Lozano 1998, pp. 163–165; Lozano 2007, pp. 22–24.
25 Lozano 1998, pp. 161–182.
26 Lozano 2000, pp. 18–169.
27 Vázquez Ramos 2016, pp. 80–98.
28 Lozano 1998.
29 Tibol 1977, pp. 28–33.
30 Tibol 1983, p. 48.
31 Zamora 2015, p. 69.
32 A cropped photo bearing a closer resemblance to the painting is in the collection of the Isolda P. Kahlo Archive in Mexico City.
33 Lozano 2000, pp. 32–37.
34 Aguilar Sosa 2017. In 1994, however, another photograph of Ruth Stallsmith de Quintanilla had been published, also attributed to Edward Weston, although no one noticed that it was the source for Kahlo's painting. Cf. Mexico City 1994, pp. 18, 153.
35 Zamora 2015, p. 75.
36 *Ibid.*, p. 73.
37 Dromundo 1956, p. 172.
38 Flores 2004, pp. 208–220.
39 Lozano 2000, pp. 45–52.
40 Tibol 2005, p. 79.
41 Lozano 2000, p. 50; Flores 2013, pp. 200–205.
42 Eberle 2006, pp. 21–38.
43 Valencia/Madrid/Las Palmas 1997/1998.
44 New York 2003.
45 Torriente n. d., Isolda P. Kahlo Archive.
46 Tibol 1954; Tibol 2005, p. 31.
47 Tibol 1977, p. 37.
48 Lozano 2000, pp. 29–30.
49 Maples Arce 1924.
50 Schneider 2013.
51 Mexico City 1991.
52 Mexico City 2014.

II. *My eyes were opened and I saw new things.* The painter broadens her horizons

1 Lee 1999.
2 Herrera 1983, p. 461.
3 *Ibid.*, p. 152.
4 Lozano 2000, p. 71.
5 Herrera 1983, p. 173.
6 Wolfe 1939, p. 347.
7 Hoffmann-Curtius 1993.
8 Herrera 1983, pp. 226, 228, 232, 470.
9 Tibol 1983, p. 12.
10 Lozano 2000, pp. 105–113.
11 Based on Breton's interview with Rafael Heliodoro Valle in the magazine *Revista de la Universidad de México*, June 22, 1938, Heliodoro Valle 1938, pp. 5–8.
12 New York 1938. Text originally in French: "Quels n'ont pas été ma surprise et ma joie à découvrir, seulement comme j'arrivais à Mexico, que son oeuvre, conçue en toute ignorance des raisons qui, mes amis et moi, ont pu nous faire agir, s'épanouissait avec ses dernières toiles en plein surréalisme." André Breton, preface to the catalogue leaflet published to accompany the Kahlo exhibition held at the Julien Levy Gallery in New York, November 1–15, 1938.
13 *Ibid.*
14 Herrera 1983, p. 150.
15 Lozano 1998, pp. 160–182.
16 Herrera 1983, pp. 188–191.
17 Tibol 2001, pp. 167–169.
18 Petitjean 2018.

III. *I will paint pain, love, and affection.* **The lessons of maturity and experience**

1 Tibol 2001, p. 366.
2 This purchase was confirmed by Dr. Marina Vázquez Ramos in the course of her recent research work in Paris.
3 Romano Pace 2010, p. 193.
4 Chadwick 2017, p. 145.
5 Herrera 1983, p. 474.
6 Tibol 2001, pp. 148–152.
7 Petitjean 2018.
8 Herrera 1991, p. 124.
9 Tibol 2001, pp. 88–89.
10 Lozano 2007.
11 Herrera 1993.
12 *The New York Times*, October 22, 1938.
13 Del Conde 2007, pp. 16–23.
14 Colville 1999, p. 174.
15 Lozano 1998, pp. 160–182.
16 Tibol 2005, p. 105.
17 Mexico City 1940.
18 Prignitz-Poda/Lopatkina 2017, pp. 46–56. Many thanks to Mary-Anne Martin for this reference.
19 Lozano 2011, pp. 60–61.
20 Jiménez 2013, pp. 20–22.
21 Tibol 1983, p. 128.
22 Tibol 2001, p. 234.
23 Ross 1942, p. 6.
24 Lozano 1990, pp. 84–85.
25 Kahlo/Eloesser 2007, pp. 199–204.
26 Gómez 2013, p. 276.
27 Lozano 2001, pp. 108, 112, 113.
28 Gómez 2013, pp. 278–279.
29 *Ibid.*
30 Lozano 2000, pp. 122–126.
31 Hurtado 2017, pp. 42–47.
32 Herrera 1983, p. 326.
33 Lozano/Coronel Rivera 2007, pp. 518–519.

34 Tibol 2001, pp. 253–258.
35 Kahlo 1945.
36 Tibol 1984, pp. 208–209.

IV. *I no longer feel the slightest hope. I hope never to return.* **The will to continue painting right up until the end**

1 Tibol 2001, pp. 260–262.
2 Herrera 1983, pp. 351, 485.
3 Lozano 2007, pp. 93–118.
4 Warncke 2004, fol. 15.
5 Tibol 2001, pp. 263–264.
6 Kahlo 1951, p. 38.
7 *Ibid.*
8 Tibol 1983, p. 23.

Exhibitions

List of the 10 most important exhibitions (in chronological order)

1 New York 1938
Julien Levy Gallery: *Frida Kahlo (Frida Rivera)*, November 1–15, 1938.

2 Paris 1939
Galerie Renou & Colle: *Mexique*, foreword and text of the catalogue by André Breton, March 10–25, 1939.

3 Mexico City 1953
Galería Arte Contemporáneo: *Primicias para un Homenaje a Frida Kahlo*, April 13–27, 1953.

4 Mexico City 1977
Palacio de Bellas Artes: *Frida Kahlo – Exposición Nacional de Homenaje*, September–November 13, 1977.

5 Chicago/San Diego/Phoenix/ Austin/Houston/New York 1978/79
Chicago, Museum of Contemporary Art, January 13–March 5, 1978 / San Diego, La Jolla, Mandeville Art Gallery, University of California, April 7–May 17, 1978 / Phoenix Art Museum, June 9–July 23, 1978 / Austin, University Art Museum, The University of Texas, August 13–October 1, 1978 / Houston, The Sarah Campbell Blaffer Gallery, University of Houston, October 14–November 19, 1978 / New York, Neuberger Museum, State University of New York, December 8, 1978–January 14, 1979: *Frida Kahlo (1910–1954)*.

6 Touring exhibition 1982/83 *Frida Kahlo and Tina Modotti*

London/Berlin/Hamburg/ Hanover 1982
London, Whitechapel Art Gallery, March 26–May 2, 1982 / Berlin, Haus am Waldsee, May 14–July 11, 1982 / Hamburg, Kunstverein, July 29–September 12, 1982 / Hannover, Kunstverein, September 26–November 7, 1982: *Frida Kahlo and/und Tina Modotti*

Stockholm 1982/83
Kulturhuset: *Frida Kahlo och Tina Modotti*, November 19, 1982–January 30, 1983.

New York 1983
The Grey Art Gallery and Study Center, New York University: *Frida Kahlo/Tina Modotti*, March 1–April 16, 1983.

Mexico City 1983
Museo Nacional de Arte: *Frida Kahlo – Tina Modotti*, June 4–August 1983.

7 London 2005
Tate Modern: *Frida Kahlo*, June 9–October 9, 2005.

8 Mexico City 2007
Museo del Palacio de Bellas Artes: *Frida Kahlo. Homenaje Nacional 1907-2007*, June 13–August 19, 2007.

9 Minneapolis/Philadelphia/ San Francisco 2007/08
Minneapolis, Walker Art Center, October 27, 2007–January 20, 2008 / Philadelphia Museum of Art, February 20–May 18, 2008 / San Francisco Museum of Modern Art, June 16–September 28, 2008: *Frida Kahlo*.

10 Berlin/Vienna 2010
Berlin, Martin-Gropius-Bau, April 30–August 9, 2010 / Vienna, Bank Austria Kunstforum, September 1–December 5, 2010: *Frida Kahlo. Retrospektive*.

Bibliography

Aguilar Sosa 2017
Aguilar Sosa, Yanet, "Las historias gráficas en El Universal," in: *El Universal*, February 22, 2017.

Ankori 2002
Ankori, Gannit, *Imaging Her Selves: Frida Kahlo's Poetics of Identity and Fragmentation*, Westport/London 2002.

Anonymous 1938
Anonymous, "Dorothy Hale Dies in 16-Story Plunge," in: *The New York Times*, Oct. 22, 1938, p. 34.

Breton 1938
Breton, André, "Preface," in: New York 1938.

Campos/Grimberg 2008
Campos, Olga, "Interview with Frida Kahlo," in: Grimberg 2008a, pp. 55–111 (trans. from original interview in Spanish into English by Salomon Grimberg).

Casanova 2014
Casanova, Rosa, *Guillermo Kahlo. Luz, piedra y rostro*, Bogotá (1st edition 2012) 2nd edition 2014.

Chadwick 2017
Chadwick, Whitney, "I Will Write to You with My Eyes Open," in: *Farewell to the Muse: Love, War and the Women of Surrealism*, London 2017.

Colville 1999
Colville, Georgiana M. M., "Alice Rahon au pays des merveilles," in: *Mélusine. Cahiers du Centre de Recherches sur le Surréalisme 19: Mexique, Miroir magnétique*, ed. Henri Béhar, Lausanne 1999, pp. 174–184.

Cordero 1994
Cordero, Karen, "Deconstruyendo la Escuela Nacional: Diversas formas de abordar el arte popular en el arte mexicano postrevolucionario," in: *Arte e identidad en América, visiones comparativas, Actas del Coloquio Internacional de Historia del Arte 17*, 1993, ed. Gustavo Curiel, Renato González Mello, Juana Gutiérrez Haces, Universidad Nacional Autónoma de México, Instituto de Investigaciones Estética, Mexico City 1994, 3 vols., vol. 1, pp. 637–645.

Del Conde 2004
Del Conde, Teresa, *Frida Kahlo. La pintora y el mito*. Mexico City, 2nd edition 2004.

Del Conde 2007
Del Conde, Teresa, "Frida Kahlo, nuevas lecturas," in: Mexico City 2007, pp. 16–23.

Del Conde 2015
Del Conde, Teresa, "Raquel Tibol," in: *Anales del Instituto de Investigaciones Estéticas 37, 107*, 2015, pp. 233–239.

Detroit 2015
Diego Rivera & Frida Kahlo in Detroit, exh. cat., Detroit Institute of Arts, Detroit, MI, March 15–July 12, 2015, New Haven, CT/London 2015.

Dromundo 1956
Dromundo, Baltasar, *Mi calle de San Ildefonso*, Mexico City 1956.

Eberle 2006
Eberle, Matthias, "Neue Sachlichkeit in Germany: A Brief History," in: New York 2006/07, pp. 21–38.

Emblem Project Utrecht 2006
Emblem Project Utrecht (www. https://emblems.hum.uu.nl; accessed August 2019).

Ferrer 2017
Ferrer, Jaime, *El pincel y la lira. Frida Kahlo y Miguel N. Lira*, n. p., 2017.

Flores 2004
Flores, Tatiana, "Clamoring for Attention in Mexico City: Manuel Maples Arce's Avant-Garde Manifesto Actual No 1," in: *Review: Literature and Arts of the Americas 37 (2)*, 2004, pp. 208–220 (as online resource August 19, 2006; DOI: 10.1080/08905760420002927 81, accessed July 2, 2020).

Frida Kahlo. Sus fotos 2010
Frida Kahlo. Sus fotos, various authors, ed. Pablo Ortíz Monasterio, Barcelona/Mexico City 2010.

Gómez 2013
Gómez, Marte R., *Diego y sus mujeres. Textos inéditos*, Texcoco 2013.

Gómez Arias 1977
Gómez Arias, Alejandro, "Un testimonio sobre Frida Kahlo," in: Mexico City 1977.

González Ramírez 1954
González Ramírez, Manuel, "Frida Kahlo o el imperativo de vivir," in: *Huytlale 2*, 1954, pp. 7–25.

Grimberg 2008
Grimberg, Salomon, *Frida Kahlo. Song of Herself*, London/New York 2008.

Hamburg 2006
Frida Kahlo, exh. cat., Bucerius Kunst Forum, Hamburg, June 15–Sept. 17, 2006, Munich 2006.

Heliodoro Valle 1938
Heliodoro Valle, Rafael, "Diálogo con André Breton," in: *Revista de la Universidad de México*, Mexico City, June 22, 1938, pp. 5–8.

Herrera 1983
Herrera, Hayden, *Frida. A Biography of Frida Kahlo*, New York 1983.

Herrera 1991
Herrera, Hayden, *Frida Kahlo. The Paintings*, New York 1991.

Herrera 1993
Herrera, Hayden, "Beauty to his Beast: Frida Kahlo & Diego Rivera," in: *Significant Others. Creativity & Intimate Partner-*

ship, ed. Whitney Chadwick and Isabelle de Courtivron, London 1993.

Hoffmann-Curtius 1993
Hoffmann-Curtius, Kathrin, *George Grosz: John, der Frauenmörder*, Stuttgart 1993.

Hurtado 2017
Hurtado, Emma, *Mi vida con Diego*, Mexico City 2017.

Ipiña 2013
Ipiña, Alejandro, "De paseo con Raquel Tibol (secretaria de Diego Rivera) por el arte mexicano," in: *Frontera D. Magazine digital*, August 15, 2013 (https://www.fronterad.com/de-paseo-con-raquel-tibol-secretaria-de-diego-rivera-por-el-arte-mexicano/#respond; accessed Sept. 27, 2020).

Jaimes 2016
Jaimes, Héctor, *Tu hija Frida. Cartas a mamá*, Mexico City 2016.

Jiménez 2013
Jiménez, José, "El surrealismo y el sueño," in: *El surrealismo y el sueño*, exh. cat., Museo Thyssen-Bornemisza, Madrid, Oct. 8, 2013–Jan. 12, 2014, Madrid 2013.

Kahlo 1945
Kahlo, Frida, "Hablando de un cuadro mío," in: *Así*, no. 249, 8/18/1945, n. p.

Kahlo 1994
Kahlo, Frida, *Diario. Facsímil y Transcripción*, Mexico City 1994.

Kahlo 2016
Kahlo, Frida, *Tu hija Frida. Cartas a mamá*, compiled, introduced, and annotated by Héctor Jaimes, Mexico City 2016.

Kahlo/Eloesser 2007
Kahlo, Frida/Eloesser, Leo, *Querido doctorcito. Frida Kahlo – Leo Eloesser. Correspondencia/Correspondence*, Mexico City 2007.

Lee 1999
Lee, Anthony W., *Painting on the Left. Diego Rivera, Radical Politics, and San Francisco's Public Murals*, Berkeley/Los Angeles/London 1999.

Lindauer 1999
Lindauer, Margaret A., *Devouring Frida. The Art History and Popular Celebrity of Frida Kahlo*, Hannover, NH, 1999.

London/Berlin/Hamburg/Hanover 1982
Frida Kahlo and/und Tina Modotti, exh. cat., Whitechapel Art Gallery, London, March 26–May 2, 1982; Haus am Waldsee, Berlin, May 14–July 11, 1982; Kunstverein Hamburg, July 29–Sept. 12, 1982; Kunstverein Hannover, Sept. 26–Nov. 7, 1982, London/Frankfurt am Main 1982

Lowe 1991
Lowe, Sarah M., *Universe Series on Women Artists. Frida Kahlo*, New York 1991.

Lozano 1998
Lozano, Luis-Martín, "Frida Kahlo, or the Will to Paint," in: Martigny 1998.

Lozano 2000
Lozano, Luis-Martín (ed.), *Frida Kahlo*, Mexico City 2000 (2nd edition. 2003).

Lozano 2001
Lozano, Luis-Martín, *Frida Kahlo*, Boston/New York/London 2001.

Lozano 2007
Lozano, Luis-Martín, *Frida Kahlo. El círculo de los afectos*, Bogotá 2007.

Lozano 2011
Lozano, Luis-Martín (ed.), *Visiones y revisiones en la colección Pérez Simón*, Mexico City 2011, pp. 60–61, 148.

Lozano 2021
Lozano, Luis-Martín (ed.), *Frida Kahlo. The Complete Paintings*, Cologne 2021.

Lozano/Coronel Rivera 2007
Lozano, Luis-Martín/Coronel Rivera, Juan Rafael, *Diego Rivera. The Complete Murals*, Cologne 2007; *Diego Rivera. Obra mural completa*, Cologne 2007.

Maples Arce 1924
Maples Arce, Manuel, *Urbe. Super poema bolchevique en 5 cantos*, Mexico City 1924.

Martigny 1998
Diego Rivera. Frida Kahlo, exh. cat., Fondation Pierre Gianadda, Martigny, Switzerland, January 24–July 1, 1998, Martigny 1998.

Mayayo 2008
Mayayo, Patricia, *Frida Kahlo contra el mito*, Madrid 2008.

Mexico City 1940
Breton, André/Paalen, Wolfgang/Moro, Cesar, *Exposición internacional del surrealismo*, exh. cat., Galería de Arte Mexicano, Mexico City, January/February 1940, Mexico City 1940.

Mexico City 1977
Frida Kahlo – Exposición Nacional de Homenaje, exh. cat., Palacio de Bellas Artes, Mexico City, Mexico City 1977.

Mexico City 1992
Alfredo Ramos Martínez (1871–1946). Una visión retrospectiva, exh. cat., with texts by Ramón Favela, Karen Cordero et al., Museo Nacional de Arte, Instituto Nacional de Bellas Artes, Mexico City, April–June 1992, Mexico City 1992.

Mexico City 1994
Edward Weston. La mirada de la ruptura, exh. cat., Instituto Nacional de Bellas Artes, Mexico City, Sept.–Nov. 1994, Mexico City 1994.

Mexico City 2007
Tesoros de la Casa Azul. Frida y Diego, exh. cat., Museo Frida Kahlo, Mexico City, 2007, Mexico City 2007.

Mexico City 2014
Escuelas de pintura al aire libre. Episodios dramáticos del arte mexicano, exh. cat., Museo Nacional de Arte, Mexico City, March 2014, Mexico City 2014.

New York 1938
Frida Kahlo (Frida Rivera), exh.

cat., Julien Levy Gallery, New York, Nov. 1–15, 1938, New York 1938.

New York 2003
Christian Schad and the Neue Sachlichkeit, exh. cat., Neue Galerie, Museum for German and Austrian Art, New York, March 14–June 19, 2003, New York et al. 2003.

New York 2006/07
Glitter and Doom. German Portraits from the 1920s, exh. cat., Metropolitan Museum of Art, New York, Nov. 14, 2006–Feb. 16, 2007, New York et al. 2006.

Petitjean 2018
Petitjean, Marc, *Le Cœur, Frida Kahlo à Paris*, Paris 2018.

Pinedo Kahlo 2004
Pinedo Kahlo, Isolda, *Frida íntima*, Bogotá/Buenos Aires 2004.

Prignitz-Poda/Grimberg/Kettenmann 1988
Prignitz-Poda, Helga/Grimberg, Salomon/Kettenmann, Andrea, *Frida Kahlo. Das Gesamtwerk*, Frankfurt am Main 1988.

Prignitz-Poda/Lopatkina 2017
Prignitz-Poda, Helga/Lopatkina, Katarina, "Frida Kahlo's Lost Painting. The Wounded Table – A Mystery," in: *IFAR Journal* 18, 2017, no. 2/3.

Rivera/March 1960
Rivera, Diego, *My Art, My Life. An Autobiography with Gladys March*, New York 1960.

Rodríguez 1955
Rodríguez, Antonio, "Frida Kahlo heroína del dolor," in: *México en la Cultura*, supplement to *Novedades*, no. 330, July 17, 1955.

Rodríguez 1958
Rodríguez, Antonio, "Frida Kahlo: El Homenaje Póstumo de México a la Gran Artista," in: *Impacto* 7, 1958, pp. 49–51.

Romano Pace 2010
Romano Pace, Alba, *Jacqueline Lamba: Peintre rebelle, muse de l'amour fou*, Paris 2010.

Ross 1942
Ross, Betty, "Como pinta Frida Kahlo, esposa de Diego, las emociones íntimas de la mujer" and "Posando para Diego Rivera," in: *Excelsior*, Oct. 21 and 23, 1942.

Schneider 2013
Schneider, Luís Mario, *El estridentismo. La vanguardia literaria en México*, Mexico City 2013.

Tibol 1953
Tibol, Raquel, "Frida Kahlo, artista de genio," in: *La Prensa*, Buenos Aires, July 12, 1953.

Tibol 1954
Tibol, Raquel, "Fragmentos para una vida de Frida Kahlo," in: *México en la Cultura*, supplement to *Novedades*, no. 259, March 7, 1954, pp. 1, 3.

Tibol 1977
Tibol, Raquel, *Frida Kahlo. Crónicas, testimonios y aproximaciones*, Mexico City 1977.

Tibol 1980
Tibol, Raquel, *Frida Kahlo. Über ihr Leben und ihr Werk, nebst Aufzeichnungen und Briefen*, Frankfurt am Main 1980.

Tibol 1983
Tibol, Raquel, *Frida Kahlo. Una vida abierta*, Mexico City 1983.

Tibol 1984
Tibol, Raquel, *José Clemente Orozco: Una vida para el arte. Breve historia documentaral*, Mexico City, 2nd edition 1984.

Tibol 2001
Tibol, Raquel, *Escrituras de Frida Kahlo*, 2nd, corrected, and expanded edition, Mexico City 2001.

Tibol 2005
Tibol, Raquel, *Frida Kahlo en su luz más íntima*, Mexico City 2005.

Tibol 2007
Tibol, Raquel, *Escrituras de Frida Kahlo*, with a foreword by

Antonio Alatorre, Mexico City 2007 (1st edition ed. Lumen).

Torriente n. d.
Torriente, Lolo de la, "Verdad y mentira en la vida de Frida Kahlo y Diego Rivera," Mexico City, undated press clipping.

Valencia/Madrid/Las Palmas 1997/98
Franz Roh y la pintura europea 1917–1936, exh. cat., Instituto Valenciano de Arte Moderno, Valencia, June 19–Aug. 31, 1997; Fundación Caja de Madrid, Sept. 17–Nov. 9, 1997; Centro Atlántico de Arte Moderno, Las Palmas de Gran Canaria, Dec. 2, 1997–Feb. 1, 1998, Valencia et al. 1997.

Vázquez Ramos 2016
Vázquez Ramos, Marina, "El sentimiento mexicano y el hecho anterior de usar siete motivos fundamentales y de no cruzarlos jamás," in: *Adolfo Best Maugard. La espiral del Arte*, Mexico City 2016.

Warncke 2004
Warncke, Carsten-Peter, *Théâtre d'Amour*, Cologne 2004.

Wolfe 1938
Wolfe, Bertram D., "Rise of another Rivera," in: *Vogue*, Nov. 1, 1938, pp. 64, 131.

Wolfe 1939
Wolfe, Bertram D., *Diego Rivera. His Life and Times*, New York/London 1939.

Zamora 1987
Zamora, Martha, *Frida, el pincel de la angustia*, Mexico City 1987.

Zamora 2015
Zamora, Martha, *En busca de Frida*, Mexico City 2015.

Zamora 2018
Zamora, Martha, *Heridas. Amores de Diego Rivera*, Mexico City 2018, p. 267.

Index of Frida Kahlo's Works

Photo Credits

The editor and publisher have made intensive efforts, in accordance with the legal requirements of copyright law, to obtain reproduction rights for the works depicted from the artists, their heirs, agents, or legal successors, and from the creators of the photographs, and pay for those rights. Notwithstanding extensive research, this has not been possible in all cases. Therefore, should claims still exist, we ask the holders of rights or their agents to contact the publisher.

Copyright

For the works of:

Frida Kahlo: © Banco de México Diego Rivera Frida Kahlo Museums Trust / VG Bild-Kunst, Bonn 2024; reproduction authorized by the Instituto Nacional de Bellas Artes y Literatura, 2023; © 2023 La Vaca Independiente.

Diego Rivera: © Banco de México Diego Rivera Frida Kahlo Museums Trust / VG Bild-Kunst, Bonn 2024; reproduction authorized by the Instituto Nacional de Bellas Artes y Literatura, 2023.

Lucienne Bloch: All photographs by Lucienne Bloch (1909–1999) Courtesy Old Stage Studios

Lola Álvarez Bravo: © VG Bild-Kunst, Bonn 2024.

Manuel Álvarez Bravo: © Archivo Manuel Álvarez Bravo, Mexico City.

Paul Delvaux: © VG Bild-Kunst, Bonn 2024.

Otto Dix: © VG Bild-Kunst, Bonn 2024.

Gisèle Freund: bpk / IMEC, Fonds MCC / Gisèle Freund; © IMEC, Fonds MCC, Dist. RMN-Grand Palais / Gisèle Freund.

Fritz Henle: © Fritz Henle Estate.

Hannah Höch: © VG Bild-Kunst, Bonn 2024.

Bernice Kolko: Fundación Zúñiga Laborde A. C., Mexico City.

Leo Matiz: © Fundación Leo Matiz, Mexico City: p. 417.

Martin Munkácsi: © Estate of Martin Munkácsi, Courtesy Howard Greenberg Gallery, New York.

Nickolas Muray: © George Eastman Museum / Nickolas Muray Photo Archives; © Nickolas Muray Photo Archives; © Spencer Throckmorton, New York / Nickolas Muray Photo Archives.

Richard Neutra: © 2023 permissions courtesy of Neutra Institute for Survival Through Design: p. 430.

Juan O'Gorman: © Estate of Juan O'Gorman / VG Bild-Kunst, Bonn 2024.

Carlos Pellicer: © Carlos Pellicer López, pp. 449–454.

Christian Schad: © VG Bild-Kunst, Bonn 2024.

Bernard G. Silberstein: © Edward B. Silberstein: pp. 224–225, 250, 314, 415, 460.

Marcel Sternberger: © 2016 Stephan Loewentheil, New York: p. 298.

Photo credits

Agenzia Fotografica Scala, Antella, Florence: pp. 49, 52; Albright Knox Art Gallery / Art Resource, NY / Scala, Florence: p. 171; Museum Associates / LACMA / Art Resource NY / Scala, Florence: p. 341; The Museum of Modern Art, New York / Scala, Florence: pp. 8–9, 118–119, 169, 231; Photo Schalkwijk / Art Resource / Scala, Florence: pp. 57, 115, 143, 258, 259, 318–319, 322, 351, 352, 355, 356.

akg-images: pp. 21, 45, 54, 58, 59, 61, 62, 69, 73, 99, 103, 105, 107, 109, 112–113, 139, 154 bottom, 155, 156–157, 160, 173, 185, 243, 252, 253, 257, 263, 269, 270, 271, 308–309; akg-images / Erich Lessing: pp. 31, 193, 315; akg-images / Joseph Martin: p. 222.

Alamy: pp. 36, 296, 396; dbimages / Alamy Stock Photo: p. 293; M. Sobreira / Alamy Stock Photo: p. 462; Vintage Space / Alamy Stock Photo: p. 398.

Archive of the publisher, authors, or collectors: pp. 158–159, 196, 210, 214, 221, 223, 423, 425, 426, 429.

Archives of American Art, Smithsonian Institution, Washington, D.C.: p. 414; Florence Arquin Papers, 1923–1985: pp. 316, 452; Emmy Lou Packard Papers, 1900–1990: pp. 81, 370–373.

Archivo Manuel Álvarez Bravo, Mexico City: pp. 104, 411.

Archivo Isolda P. Kahlo, Mexico City: pp. 16, 22, 195, 392, 397, 409.

Association Atelier André Breton, Archigny: pp. 96, 186, 187, 192.

bpk / Ägyptisches Museum und Papyrussammlung, SMB / Margarete Büsing: p. 199; bpk / CNAC-MNAM /

Jean-Claude Planchet: p. 178; bpk / IMEC, Fonds MCC / Gisèle Freund: pp. 290, 447, 457, 463, 464, 465; bpk / The Metropolitan Museum of Art: p. 106; bpk / Nationalgalerie, SMB / Jörg P. Anders: p. 134.

Bridgeman Images: pp. 56, 70–71, 120 left, 220, 232, 254, 466–467; Photo © Fine Art Images / Bridgeman Images: pp. 120–121, 310–311; Photo © Christie's Images / Bridgeman Images: pp. 6–7, 177, 211, 212–213, 216–217, 265, 285, 305; © Photo: Jorge Contreras Chacel / Bridgeman Images: pp. 4–5, 15, 53, 226–227; © Detroit Institute of Arts / Bridgeman Images: pp. 85, 224–225; © Detroit Institute of Arts / Founders Society Purchase, Diego Rivera Exhibition Fund / Bridgeman Images: pp. 124, 405; © Galerie Bilderwelt / Bridgeman Images: pp. 402–403; Granger / Bridgeman Images: pp. 100, 395, 419; © Sotheby's / Bridgeman Images: pp. 246–247; © Tallandier / Bridgeman Images: p. 448.

Andres Cedillo: pp. 440–441.

CEDODAL Collection, Buenos Aires. Diego Rivera Photo Archive: p. 358.

Center for Creative Photography, University of Arizona, Tucson: Lola Álvarez Bravo Archive: p. 172

Christie's, New York: pp. 28, 55, 76, 122, 129, 336–337.

Patty and Jim Cownie: pp. 326, 327, 328, 329, 330.

Courtesy Dallas Museum of Art, Photo: Brad Flowers: p. 204.

Rafael Doniz: pp. 25, 40, 48, 102, 108, 114, 142, 145, 146, 147, 151, 152, 165, 228, 229, 260, 261, 264, 272–273, 275, 277, 279, 281, 283, 320–321, 340, 342–343, 346, 350, 359, 413, 423, 425, 426, 429, 435, 449, 451, 461.

FEMSA, Monterrey: pp. 130–131, 132–133, 135.

Courtesy Fine Arts Museums of San Francisco, Photo: Randy Dodson: Front cover, pp. 1, 2–3, 215, 233.

Fototeca, Hemeroteca y Biblioteca Mario Vázquez Raña, Archivo y Fundación, courtesy Organización Editorial Mexicana (OEM): pp. 41, 88, 154 top.

Fundación Televisa Collection and Archive, Mexico City: p. 295.

Fundación Zúñiga Laborde, Mexico City: p. 301.

Galería Arvil, Mexico City: pp. 140, 332–333, 334–335.

Galerie 1900–2000, Paris: p. 203.

Jacques und Natasha Gelman / The Vergel Foundation, Photo: Gerardo Suter: pp. 123, 126, 128, 136, 137, 141, 148, 149, 236, 238, 251, 267, 317, 324, 325.

George Eastman Museum, Rochester: p. 11.

Getty Images: Bettmann / Kontributor: p. 266; Universal Images / Getty Images: p. 95.

Harry Ransom Center, University of Texas, Austin: pp. 235, 338.

Hemeroteca Nacional, Mexico City: pp. 32, 455.

© Fritz Henle Estate: p. 188.

© IMEC, Fonds MCC, Dist. RMN-Grand Palais / Gisèle Freund: pp. 289, 323.

International Center of Photography, New York: pp. 438, 439.

© Liebieghaus Skulpturensammlung, Frankfurt am Main – ARTOTHEK: p. 201.

LML Archive, Mexico City: pp. 50, 63, 67, 68, 75, 77, 116–117, 153, 181, 214, 218–219, 221, 223, 237, 242, 307, 331, 353; courtesy Agencia El Universal: p. 18; photo courtesy Banco Nacional de México: p. 164; courtesy Fundación JAPS:

Acknowledgments

First and foremost, the publisher would like to thank the authors of the Catalogue of Paintings (Lozano 2021), Andrea Kettenmann and Marina Vázquez Ramos, and also the author and editor of the book, Luis-Martín Lozano, for their contributions and committed teamwork. Luis-Martín Lozano has stood by our side at all times with help and advice, smoothed the way with Mexican institutions, and spared no effort in the difficult and extensive acquisition of images so that many privately owned works could be included.

The publisher would also like to thank the museums, libraries, archives, and institutions named in the captions and photo credits for their friendly support of the publication. Numerous curators and collectors, as well as photographers and photo agencies, have been crucial to the project's success through their personal commitment. We would particularly like to thank: Monique Abadilla, Aurelia Álvarez Urbajtel, Mara de Anda Romeo, Marco Bischof, Jan Böttger, Krista Brugnara, Duani Castelló Serrano, Mark Castro, Patty and Jim Cownie, Lulu Creel, Carolyn Cruthirds, Francisca Cruz, Rafael Doniz, Danelle England, Irina Escartín, Consuelo Fernández Ruiz, Marcel Fleiss, Tod Gangler, Israel Garfias Bernal, Susan Grinols, Leigh Grissom, Marcela Guerrero, Rodrigo Gutiérrez Viñuales, Ella Hall, Barbara Haskell, Tina Henle, Bruce Hucko, Sara Ickow, Paulina Jasso, Achim Kathan, Constance Krebs, Monika Krisch, Gerardo Landa Rojano, Julie Le Men, Lauren Lean, Jamie Lee, Katja Lehmann, Max Loy, Marina Magro Soto Otero, Mimi Muray, Raymond Richard Neutra, Emily Nice, Cortney Norman, Meg Partridge, Ronja Primke, Manuel and María Reyero, Zach Ritter, Norberto Rivera, Deborah Roan, Ana Alicia Rosas Rivera, Peter Schälchli, Piper Wynn Severance, Edward B. Silberstein, Louis Stern, Gerardo Suter, Humberto Tachiquín Benito, Emma Thomas, Spencer Throckmorton, Gilbert Vicario, Andrea Zorrilla, and Ariel Zuñiga. Special thanks go to Mary-Anne Martin, who helped us with great dedication in the acquisition of images and was able to convince private collectors to let us take new photographs of their works for the book. We would like to thank the lithographers Rüdiger and Volker Mayer (Repromayer, Reutlingen) for their outstanding cooperation.

The Author

Luis-Martín Lozano is an art historian specializing in the study of the creative processes of modernist artists in Mexico and Latin America. He is the recipient of a Fulbright scholarship and has conducted extensive research on the work of both Frida Kahlo and Diego Rivera, as well as publishing widely on both artists. Lozano was formerly the director of the Museo de Arte Moderno in Mexico, and has been a guest curator for many art institutions in the United States, Europe, Asia, Latin America, and particularly in Mexico.

In 2021, TASCHEN published *Frida Kahlo – The Complete Paintings* with Luis-Martín Lozano as editor and main author, with a chapter dedicated to Frida Kahlo's Catalogue of Paintings, which is not included in this new edition. We wish to acknowledge that the co-authors of that chapter were Andrea Kettenmann and Marina Vázquez Ramos.

Imprint

EACH AND EVERY TASCHEN BOOK PLANTS A SEED!
TASCHEN is a carbon neutral publisher. Each year, we offset our annual carbon emissions with carbon credits at the Instituto Terra, a reforestation program in Minas Gerais, Brazil, founded by Lélia and Sebastião Salgado. To find out more about this ecological partnership, please check:
www.taschen.com/zerocarbon
Inspiration: unlimited. Carbon footprint: zero.

To stay informed about TASCHEN and our up-coming titles, please subscribe to our free magazine at *www.taschen.com/magazine*, follow us on Instagram and Facebook, or e-mail your questions to *contact@taschen.com*.

© 2024 TASCHEN GmbH
Hohenzollernring 53, D–50672 Köln
www.taschen.com

Original edition: © 2021 TASCHEN GmbH

Project management: Ute Kieseyer and Petra Lamers-Schütze, Cologne
English translation: Joel Schaefer and Kristin Siracusa Fisher for LocTeam, Barcelona
Design: Andy Disl, Los Angeles; Claudia Frey, Cologne

Printed in Bosnia-Herzegovina
ISBN 978-3-8365-9485-1

Front cover
Self-portrait (Dedicated to Doctor Leo Eloesser) (detail), 1940
Oil on masonite, 59.7 x 40 cm (23⅜ x 15¾ in.)
Los Angeles, Lucas Museum of Narrative Art

Back cover and page 11
Nickolas Muray, **Frida with blue satin blouse** (detail), New York, 1939
Carbon print, 22.9 x 17.3 cm (9 x 6¾ in.)
Rochester, New York, courtesy George Eastman Museum/Nickolas Muray Photo Archives

Endpapers
The Two Fridas (detail), 1939
Oil on canvas, 173.5 x 173 cm (68¼ x 68⅛ in.)
Mexico City, Secretaría de Cultura, Instituto Nacional de Bellas Artes y Literatura, Museo de Arte Moderno

Pages 1–3
The Suicide of Dorothy Hale (detail), 1938/39
Oil on masonite with painted wooden frame, 59.7 x 49.5 cm (23½ x 19½ in.)
Arizona, Phoenix Art Museum, anonymous gift, inv. 1960-20

Pages 4/5
My Nurse and I (detail), 1937
Oil on metal, 30.5 x 34.7 cm (12 x 13⅝ in.)
Mexico City, Xochimilco, Museo Dolores Olmedo

Pages 6/7
What Water Gave Me (detail), 1938/39
Oil on canvas, 88 x 69 cm (34⅝ x 27⅛ in.)
Paris, private collection

Pages 8/9
Self-portrait with Cropped Hair (detail), 1940
Oil on canvas, 40 x 27.9 cm (15¾ x 11 in.)
New York, Museum of Modern Art, Gift of Edgar Kaufmann, Jr., inv. 3.1943

Page 12
Nickolas Muray
Frida Kahlo (detail), Coyoacán, 1940
Chromogen, 36 x 24 cm (14⅛ x 9½ in.)
Nickolas Muray Photo Archives